THEATRE

Mayfield Publishing Company

THEATRE

ROBERT COHEN

University of California, Irvine

JOHN VON SZELISKI

Illustrator

Library of Congress Catalog Card Number: 80–84012

International Standard Book Number: 0–87484–459–2

Manufactured in the United States of America

Mayfield Publishing Company

285 Hamilton Avenue, Palo Alto, California 94301

Sponsoring editor: C. Lansing Hays

Special projects editor: Liz Currie

Managing editor: Maggie Cutler

Manuscript editor: Carole H. Norton

Designer: Nancy Sears

Compositor: Dharma Press

Color separator: Solzer & Hail, Inc.

Production manager: Michelle Hogan

Printer and binder: R. R. Donnelley & Sons

Cover designer: Nancy Sears

Text typeface is TxT Zapf International Light and Medium

Text stock is Finch Blue-White Opaque

CREDITS

Page 13 From Styan, *Drama, Stage, and Audience* (Cambridge University Press, 1975).

Page 23 Tennessee Williams, "Afterword" to *Camino Real.* Now published in *Where I Live*, copyright 1953 by Tennessee Williams. Reprinted by permission of New Directions.

Page 31 From the Introduction to *Marat/Sade* by Peter Weiss (Introduction by Peter Brook) by permission of Atheneum Publishers, Inc.

Page 52 From *The Ancient Greek and Roman Theatre* by Peter D. Arnott. Copyright © by Random House, Inc. Reprinted by permission.

Page 58 From *The Acharnians*, translated by Douglass Parker, edited by William Arrowsmith. Copyright © 1961 by William Arrowsmith. Reprinted by arrangement with The New American Library, Inc., New York, New York.

Page 61 Reprinted from Aeschylus *Prometheus Bound*, translated by David Grene by permission of The University of Chicago Press. Copyright © 1956 by The University of Chicago Press.

Page 74 Selections are reprinted from *Oedipus Tyrannus*, Sophocles, translated and edited by Luci Berkowitz and Theodore F. Brunner, A Norton Critical Edition, with the permission of W. W. Norton & Company, Inc. Copyright © 1970 by W. W. Norton & Company, Inc.

Page 82 From "Oedipus: Tragedy of Self-Knowledge" by Laslo Verseny, by permission of *Arion*.

Page 83 Reprinted from *The Trojan Women* by Euripides translated by Richard Lattimore by permission of The University of Chicago Press. Copyright © 1958 by The University of Chicago Press.

Page 86 From *The Frogs* by Aristophanes, translated by Richard Lattimore, edited by William Arrowsmith. Copyright © by William Arrowsmith. Reprinted by arrangement with The New American Library, Inc., New York, New York.

Page 97 From *The Medieval Theatre* by Glynne Wickham. Reprinted by permission of St. Martins Press, Inc., and Wiedenfeld & Nicolson Ltd.

Page 101 From *Theatre & Propaganda* by George H. Szanto, published by the University of Texas Press. Copyright © 1978 by the University of Texas Press.

Page 126 From *Masters of the Drama* by John Gassner (Dover Publications, Inc., 1954).

Pages 148, 317 From *Journey to the Center of the Theatre* by Walter Kerr. Reprinted by permission of the author.

Page 178 From *One-Act Comedies of Molière*, translated by Albert Bermel by permission of Frederick Ungar Publishing Co., Inc. Copyright © 1962, 1963, 1964, 1975 by Albert Bermel.

Pages 227, 325 From *Strasberg at the Actors Studio* by Robert Hethmon. Copyright © 1965.

Page 237 Quotation from Edward Gordon Craig's *On the Art of the Theatre* is used by permission of the publishers, Theatre Arts Books, 153 Waverly Place, New York, N.Y. 10014. Copyright 1956 by Theatre Arts Books.

Page 246 Selection by Jean-Paul Sartre from *Theatre Arts*, July 1946. Reprinted by permission of Mrs. W. A. Bradley.

Page 250 Selections from *Happy Days* by Samuel Beckett. Reprinted by permission of Grove Press, Inc. Copyright © 1961 by Grove Press, Inc.

Page 255 Reprinted from *Commonweal*, October 13, 1961, by permission of Commonweal Publishing Co., Inc.

Page 256 First published in *The Hudson Review*, Vol. XIV, No. 4, (Winter, 1961–62). Reprinted by permission of the author.

Page 264 From *Divine Pastime: Theatre Essays* by Harold Clurman by permission of Macmillan Publishing Co., Inc.

Page 280 "Catastrophe" from *Wings* by Arthur Kopit. Copyright © 1978 by Arthur Kopit. Reprinted by permission of Hill and Wang (a division of Farrar, Straus & Giroux, Inc.).

Page 284 From *Buried Child* by Sam Shepard by permission of Urizen Books, Inc. Copyright © 1979 by Sam Shepard.

Robert Cohen is chairman of the drama department at the University of California, Irvine. He received his doctor of fine arts degree from the Yale University School of Drama. Professor Cohen is the author of *Giraudoux: Three Faces of Destiny*, *Acting Power*, *Acting Professionally*, and (with John Harrop) *Creative Play Direction*. In addition, he has published articles in *Modern Drama*, *Educational Theatre Journal*, *Theatre Survey*, *The Drama Review*, *Contemporary Literature*, and *Education and Innovation*.

John von Szeliski, A.I.A., is chairman of the Theatre Architecture Commission of the U.S. Institute of Theatre Technology. He was formerly chairman of the drama department at Williams College and received his PhD in theatre from the University of Minnesota. Dr. Szeliski is the author of *Tragedy and Fear*.

To Michael Cohen

The following translations and/or adaptations are used in this volume:

Aeschylus, *Agamemnon*. Translation by Richard Lattimore.

Aeschylus, *Prometheus Bound*. Translation by David Grene.

Aristophanes, *The Acharnians*. Translation by Douglass Parker.

Aristophanes, *The Frogs*. Translation by Richmond Lattimore.

Aristotle, *The Poetics*. Translation by S. H. Butcher.

Congreve, *The Way of the World*. Added stage directions by Robert Cohen.

Euripides, *The Trojan Women*. Translation by Richmond Lattimore.

Molière, *The Bourgeois Gentleman*. Translation and added stage directions by Robert Cohen.

Sophocles, *The Bloodhounds*. Translation by Alexander Gross.

Sophocles. *Oedipus Tyrannos*. Translation by Luci Berkowitz and Theodore F. Brunner.

York Cycle Plays. Modern adaptation by Robert Cohen.

Bibliographic information appears elsewhere in this volume.

CONTENTS

II THE PAST 41

III THE PRESENT 205

IV   PHOTO ESSAY: A PLAY IS PUT TOGETHER   291

V   THE PRACTITIONERS   311

Preface

I am sitting in a darkened theatre correcting the galley sheets for the book you are now about to read. A technical rehearsal for a play I am directing is in progress; I am seated at a makeshift desk in the back of the house, my reading illuminated by a tiny covered gooseneck lamp. On stage stand several actors, silent and motionless, as light plays over their faces and bodies. Above me, unseen and unheard, technicians operate, adjust, and record the settings for another of the play's hundred and fifty light cues. To the outside observer, it is the dullest situation imaginable; nothing observable happens for twenty or thirty minutes at a stretch. A pool of light intensifies and then recedes, muffled conversation crackles over headsets, footsteps clang on steel catwalks lacing the ceiling, and a spotlight is carefully repositioned. This has been going on now since eight in the morning, and it is already past dinnertime.

And yet my eye is continually pulled from these pages to the dance of light upon the stage. The violet and amber hues are rich with color, and the sharp shafts of incandescence dazzle with brilliance. I am fascinated by the patient weariness of the actors, alternately glowing in and then shadowed by the lights, endlessly holding their positions which, in performance, they will occupy for only a few transitory seconds. I gaze with admiration at the followspot operator, his hands gloved in asbestos, as he handles his instrument with the precision and sensitivity of a surgeon.

The silence, the stasis, is hypnotic. All is quiet but profound with held-back beats, incipient torrents of passion and exhilaration. The potential is riveting—I am alive with excitement—and I look back to these cold galley sheets with alarm.

How can I have thought to express the thrill of the theatre in these pages? How can I have hoped to make recognizable the joy and awe I feel in theatrical involvement?

The theatre is not merely a collection of crafts, a branch of literature, a collaboration of technique, or even an all-encompassing art form. It is a life. It is people. It is people making art out of themselves. Its full reality transcends by light years anything that could be said or written about it.

What I have tried to do in these pages is not so much to introduce the theatre or to survey it as to *present* the theatre with its liveliness and humanness intact. With its incipient passion and exhilaration always present. With its potential for joy, for awe, for wisdom, and for excitement as clear to the reader as they have been made clear to me.

At the heart of this book lies the presentation—through text samples and correlated visual illustrations—of eight "model plays" drawn from the theatre's history. These eight plays—*Prometheus Bound*, *Oedipus Tyrannos*, *The Trojan Women*, the *York Mystery Cycle*, *Romeo and Juliet*, *The Bourgeois Gentleman*, *The Three Sisters*, and *Happy Days*—are not necessarily the greatest pieces of theatre of the past three thousand years, but in combination they encompass the range and magnitude of the theatrical experience. I do not intend for these presentations to substitute for seeing the plays or for reading them; the presentations merely provide outlines for the reader's understanding and springboards for the reader's imagination. I do hope the outlines will be both stimulating and clarifying. I also hope that the "model play" presentations, together with the broad range of discussions in the book, will provide a foundation upon which the reader can develop an informed and critical enthusiasm for the theatre, an enthusiasm that will ultimately lead to theatrical participation—either as spectator or artist.

ACKNOWLEDGMENTS

I am very grateful to the many persons who contributed their help and concern in the preparation of this volume. Dr. John von Szeliski, in addition to providing the splendid illustrations, offered me invaluable counsel throughout the duration of our labors. Frank Oliva and Andra Weddington graciously aided in the translations of Italian and German source material. Philipa Learned, at the American Conservatory Theatre, was particularly helpful in locating and selecting perfect photographs from the ACT files. My colleagues Olga Maynard, Cameron Harvey, and William Needles also helped me tremendously with my photographic research.

I also am grateful to the many reviewers who made hundreds of suggestions, all of which helped to sharpen my writing and improve my understanding of many fine points: William Brasmer, Denison University; John Ford, Foothill College; Joseph Karioth, Florida State University; Helen Manfull, Pennsylvania State University; Gordon Rogoff, Brooklyn College; Carl White, American River College; Joan-lee Woehler, Santa Rosa Junior College; Stephen Wyman, University of Texas; and James Yeater, Arizona State University. The professionalism of Mayfield Publishing Company again astonished me, and I am particularly thankful for Carole Norton's meticulous editing and Nancy Sears' artful design.

Finally, Lans Hays, the publisher of this volume, served also as its inspiration and guide throughout development, and must rank as a collaborator of the first order. And Lorna Cohen, whose incisive editorial advice solved major structural impasses, and who served as private audience both to my written words and my unwritten thoughts, deserves and has my deep and everlasting gratitude.

Theatre

The Broadway theatre district. This photo taken on 45th Street shows six theatres—the Booth, the Plymouth, the Royale, the Golden, the Imperial, and the Music Box—together with numerous restaurants and cafes.

INTRODUCTION

It is evening in Manhattan. On Broadway and the streets that cross it—44th, 45th, 46th, 47th, 50th, 52nd—marquees light up, "Performance Tonight" signs materialize in front of double doors, and beneath a few box office windows placards announce "This Performance Completely Sold Out." At Grand Central Station three long blocks to the east, and at Pennsylvania Station ten shorter blocks to the south, trains disgorge suburbanites from Greenwich, Larchmont, and Trenton, students from New Haven and Philadelphia, visiting firemen from Boston and Washington. Up from the Seventh and Eighth Avenue subway stations of Times Square troop denizens of the island city and the neighboring boroughs. At the Times Square "TKTS" Booth, hundreds line up in the deepening chill to buy the half-price tickets that go on sale a few hours before curtain time for undersold shows. Now, converging on these few midtown blocks of America's largest city, come limousines, restaurant buses, private cars, and taxis, whose drivers search for a curbside slot to deposit their riders among the thousands of pedestrians who already throng the streets. Financiers and dowagers, bearded intellectuals, bedraggled bohemians, sleek executives, hip Harlemites, arm-in-arm widows, conventioneers, Japanese tourists, honeymooners, out of work actors, celebrities, pushers, the precocious young—all commingle in this bizarre aggregation that is the Broadway audience. It is as bright, bold, and variegated a crowd as is likely to assemble at any one place in America.

It is eight o'clock. In thirty or forty theatres houselights dim, curtains rise, spotlights pick out performers whose lives center on this moment. Here a new musical, there a revival of an American classic, here a British comedy from London's West End, here a re-interpretation of Shakespeare, here a bedroom farce, there a revue transported from Off Broadway, here a ballet, here a touring company from Poland, there a world premiere for a much-touted new playwright. The hours pass.

Eleven o'clock. Pandemonium. All the double doors open as at a signal, and once again the thousands pour out into the night. At nearby restaurants, waiters stand by to receive the after-theatre onslaught. In Sardi's private upstairs room, an opening-night cast party gets under way; downstairs, the patrons rehash the evening's entertainment and sneak covert glances at the celebrities around them and at the actors heading for the upstairs sanctuary to await the reviews that will determine whether they will be employed next week or back on the street.

Now turn back the clock.

It is dawn in Athens, the thirteenth day of the month of Elaphebolion in the year 458 B.C. From thousands of low mud-bricked homes in the city, from the central agora, from temples and agricultural outposts, streams of Athenians and visitors converge upon the south slope of the Acropolis. Bundled against the early damp, carrying with them breakfast figs and flagons of wine, they pay their tokens at the entrance to the great Theatre of Dionysus and take their places in the seating spaces allotted them. Each tribe occupies a separate area. They gather for the Festival of the Great Dionysia, celebrating the greening of the land, the rebirth of vegetation, and the long sunny days that stretch ahead. It is a time for revelry, a time for rejoicing at fertility and its fruits. And it is above all a time for the ultimate form of Dionysian worship: the theatre.

The open stone seats carved into the hillside fill up quickly. The crowd of 17,000 people here today comprises not only the majority of Athenian citizens, but thousands of non-citizens: women, slaves, tradesmen, foreign visitors, and resident aliens. Even the paupers are in attendance, thanks to the 2 obols meted out to each of them from a state fund so they can purchase entry; they sit with the foreigners and latecomers on the extremities of the *theatron*, as this first of theatres is called.

Now as the eastern sky grows pale, a masked and costumed actor appears atop a squat building set in full view of every spectator. A hush falls over the crowd, and the actor, his voice magnified by the wooden mask from which it emanates, booms out this text:

> I ask the gods some respite from the weariness
> of this watchtime measured by years I lie
>   awake . . .

He is the watchman of Clytemnestra, and he waits for news of her husband's return; waits, moreover, for news of the end of the Trojan war—an event imbedded in the personal mythos of every person present in the *theatron* today. The crowd leans forward:

> I wait; to read the meaning in that beacon light,
> a blaze of fire to carry out of Troy the rumor
> and outcry of its capture. . . .

Now suddenly, a torch flares where he is looking; simultaneously (precisely as the astronomers' calculations foretold), the sun breaks over the eastern slope:

> O hail, blaze of the darkness, harbinger of day's
> shining, and of processionals and dance and
>   choirs
> of multitudes in Argos for this day of grace.
> Ahoy!

And the entranced crowd settles back, secure in the knowledge that today they are in good hands. Today they will hear and see a new version of a familiar story—the story of Agamemnon's homecoming and his murder, the revenge of that murder by his son Orestes, and the final disposition of justice in the case of Orestes' act—as told in the three tragedies that constitute *The Oresteia*. This magnificent trilogy will last from dawn to midafternoon, and will be followed by a bawdy, hilarious, and mocking satyr play on the same theme by the same author. It is a story of astounding familiarity, but today it will take on a new complexity owing to the dramatic intrigue, suspense, spectacle, and rhetorical magnificence, and the complicated interpretations of character, motivation, and moral ramifications, supplied by the playwright Aeschylus, the man who has been Athens' leading dramatist for more than forty years. The spectators watch closely, admiring but critical. Tomorrow they or their representatives will have to decide by vote whether the festival prize should go to this group of plays or to one of those shown yesterday or the day before; whether Aeschylus still reigns supreme or the young Sophocles has better sensed the true pulse of the time.

Night falls, the plays are over. Back to the agora, to the baths, to the establishments of the courtesans, and finally to their homes go the Athenians to discuss what they have seen. Even forty years later the comic playwright Aristophanes will be arguing the merits and demerits of this day's work.

It is noon in London, and the first Queen Elizabeth sits on the throne. Flags fly boldly atop three of the taller buildings in Bankside, on the other side of the

Thames, announcing performance day at The Globe, The Rose, and The Swan. Boatmen have already begun ferrying theatre-bound Londoners across the broad river. Meanwhile, north of town, other flocks of Londoners are headed by foot and by carriage up to Finsbury Fields and the theatres of Shoreditch: The Fortune and The Curtain. Public theatres have been banned in the city for some time now by action of the Lords Aldermen; however, an ensemble of trained schoolboys is rehearsing for a private candlelight performance before the Queen.

Now, as the morning sermon concludes at St. Paul's Cathedral, the traffic across the river increases; London Bridge fills with pedestrians hurrying to Bankside, where The Globe players will present a new tragedy by Shakespeare (something called *Hamlet*, supposedly after an old play by Thomas Kyd), and The Rose promises a revival of the late Christopher Marlowe's *Dr. Faustus*. The noisy crowds swarm into the theatres, where the price of admission is a penny; another penny is needed for a pint of beer, and those who wish to go upstairs and take a seat on one of the benches in the gallery—the best place to see the action, both on stage and off—must plunk down yet more pennies.

At the Globe, 2,000 spectators are on hand for the premiere. A trumpet sounds, sounds again, then a sennet of brass. The members of the audience exchange a few last winks with friends old and new, covert and overt invitations to post-performance intimacies of various kinds, and turn their attention to the pillared, trestled, naked stage. Through one giant door Bernardo bursts forth. "Who's there?" he cries. Then through another door, a voice: "Nay, answer me: stand and unfold yourself," and Francisco enters with lighted lantern in hand. In 2,000 imaginations, the bright afternoon turns to midnight, the Bankside gives way to the outskirts of Elsinore. A shiver from the actors on stage sets up an answering chill among the audience as Francisco proclaims, "'Tis bitter cold, and I am sick at heart." The audience strains forward. The tragedy has begun.

It is evening at Versailles, 1664. King Louis XIV nods graciously as the celebrated actor-playwright bows before him. Jean Baptiste Poquelin, known throughout France as Molière, has just presented his *Tartuffe*, with its scathingly witty denunciation of the powerful Church extremists. The courtiers, taking Louis's nod, applaud vigorously; in one corner of the glittering hall, however, a bishop glares coldly at the actor. The Archbishop of Paris will hear of this.

It is 5 A.M. in Moscow, 1898. At a cafe in the shadow of the Kremlin wall, Konstantin Stanislavski and Vladimir Nemirovich-Danchenko hotly discuss the wretched state of the current Russian Theatre. It is too declamatory, they agree; it is also too insensitive, too shallow, too inartistic. Out of this all-night session the Moscow Art Theatre will be formed, bringing to the last days of czarist society the complex, gently ironic masterpieces of Chekhov and an acting style so natural as to astonish the world.

It is midnight in a coffee house in the East Village (or perhaps the locale is Berkeley or Tokyo or Berlin or Rio). Across one end of the room, a curtain has been drawn across a pole suspended by wires. It is near closing time, but one play remains to be seen. A round of espresso, a hum of conversation, isolated laughs, strains from a guitar. Then a ringing of bells, an announcement by a *patron*, an author, an actor, and the curtain opens. Looking on, a confusion of rapt idolators, half-attentive skeptics, and self-immersed nodders and smirkers. And before them, performers, packing crates painted as scenery, a text, and an effort.

There is a common denominator in all these scenes: they are all theatre.

Theatre is the most *ubiquitous* of arts. No culture has ever existed that did not have its theatre in some form. For theatre, quite simply, is the art of people acting out—and giving witness to—their most pressing, most illuminating, and most inspiring concerns. Theatre is at once a showcase and a forum, a medium through which a society's ideas, fashions, moralities, and entertainments can be displayed and its conflicts, dilemmas, and struggles can be debated. Theatre has provided a stage for political revolution, for social propaganda, for civil debate, for artistic expression, for religious proselytization, for mass education, and even for its own self-criticism. It has been a performance ground for shamans and priests, intellectuals, poets, painters, technologists, militarists, philosophers, reformers, evangelists, prime ministers, jugglers, peasants, and kings. It has taken place in caves, in fields and forests, in Chatauqua tents, in inns and in castles, on street corners, and in public buildings grand and squalid all over the world. And it goes on incessantly in the minds of its authors, its actors, its producers, its designers, and its audiences.

For theatre is, above all, a *living* art form; a *process*, an *event* that is fluid in time, feeling, and experience. It is not simply a matter of "plays," but of "playing"; and a play is composed not simply of "acts," but of "acting." As "play" and "act" are both noun and verb, so theatre is both a "thing" and a "happening." It is continually forming, continually present in time. In fact, that very quality of "presentness" (or, in the actor's term, "stage presence") defines great theatrical performance.

Theatre, unlike the more static arts, presents a number of classic paradoxes:

It is unique to the moment, yet it is repeatable.

It is spontaneous, yet it is rehearsed.

It is participatory, yet it is presented.

It is real, yet it is simulated.

It is understandable, yet it is obscure.

The actors are themselves, yet they are characters.

The audience believes, yet it does not believe.

The audience is involved, yet it remains apart.

These paradoxes stem not from any flaw or weakness in the logic of theatrical construction, but from the theatre's essential strength, which resides in its kinship and concern with the ambiguity and irony of human life—our life. It is *we* who are at the same time unique yet conventional, spontaneous yet premeditating, involved yet isolated, candid yet contriving, comprehensible yet fundamentally unknown and unknowable. Theorists of dramatic literature and of dramatic practice commonly ignore these paradoxes in their attempts to "explain" a play or "analyze" the art of the stage; in this they do a grave disservice to art as well as to scholarship, for to "explain" the theatre without reference to its ambiguities is to remove its dynamic tension, in other words, to kill it. And although certainly much valuable information can be got at an autopsy table, it is information pertinent only to the appearance and behavior of a corpse.

In this book we shall not be overly concerned with corpses. Our task will be the harder one—to discover the theatre in being, *alive* and with all its paradoxes and ambiguities intact. From time to time it will be necessary for us to make some separations—between product and process, for example—but we must bear in mind at all times that these separations are conveniences, not representations or fact. In the end we shall be looking at the theatre as part of the human environment, and at the ways in which we fit into that environment—as participants and observers, artists and art critics, role models and role players, actors and persons. So this book about the theatre is also about ourselves.

I

The Theatre:
Its Elements

A cockpit becomes the staging area for this 1977 production of Seneca's Oedipus, *directed by Richard Schechner for New York's Performance Group. Jim Clayburgh designed the environment—a dirt floor, three to four feet deep, surrounded by bleachers—within the converted garage in New York's Soho district that is the Performance Group's home. Drawing after a photograph, with comments by the illustrator.*

WHAT IS THE THEATRE?

W hat *is* the theatre, this art that excites such imagination across so many climes and cultures?

The word derives from *theatron*, the Greek word for "seeing-place," which was coined to describe the semicircular hillside benches that seated the audience during ancient Greek dramatic performances. We still use the word "theatre" to refer to a structure where performances take place, but we also use it to describe the events themselves.

In its various usages "the theatre" today may refer to a culture's entire dramatic literary heritage, or it might encompass only plays, or it might refer as well to mime shows, musical extravaganzas, minstrel entertainments, cabaret revues, acted-out storytellings, even puppet shows. By extension, the word is occasionally broadened to include motion pictures and radio and television productions. Metaphorically, "theatre" has even been applied to political boundaries and military operations (the "Pacific Theatre" and the "European Theatre" of World War II).

For the purposes of this book, we shall consider "the theatre" as simply *that body of artistic work in which actors impersonate characters in a live (that is, not filmed) performance of a scripted play*. This definition is not to be taken as a final pronouncement on the true meaning of the word—should such a thing even be thought possible—but merely as a useful categorization that describes our field of primary interest.

Let us now take a closer look at our definition. It makes six crucial assertions:

1 Theatre is *work*.
2 Theatre is *artistic* work.
3 In theatre, actors *impersonate* characters.
4 Theatre is *performance*.
5 Theatre is *live* performance.
6 Theatre involves a *scripted play*.

What do we mean by these assertions? What do they tell us about the nature of theatre, or, more importantly, the *necessity* of theatre? These are the questions that underlie the opening chapter of our investigation into this complex and rewarding subject.

WORK

The "work" of the theatre is indeed hard work. An original play—as distinct from a revival—usually takes about one year to produce, and often five years or more from conception to actual presentation. Rehearsal alone accounts for a minimum of four weeks, and for most effective productions it goes on a good deal longer. The labors of theatre artists in the final weeks before an opening are legendary: the ninety-hour week becomes a commonplace, expenditures of money and spirit are intense, and even the unions relax their regulations to allow for an almost unbridled invasion of the hours the ordinary world spends sleeping, eating, and unwinding. The theatre enterprise may involve hundreds of people in scores of different efforts—many more backstage than onstage—and the mobilization and coordination of these efforts is in itself a giant task. So when we think of the "work" embodied in the plays of Shakespeare, for example, or of Neil Simon, we must think of work in the sense of physical toil as well as in the loftier sense of *oeuvre*, by which the French designate the sum of an artist's creative endeavor.

The work of the theatre is generally divisible into a number of crafts:

acting, in which actors perform the roles of characters in a play;

designing, in which designers map out the visual and audio elements of a production, including the scenery, properties, costumes and wigs, make-up, lighting, sound concepts, programs, advertising, and general ambience of the premises;

building, in which carpenters, costumers, wig-makers, electricians, make-up artists, recording and sound engineers, painters, and a host of other specially designated craftsmen translate the design into reality by contructing and finishing in detail the "hardware" of a show; and

running, in which technicians execute in proper sequence, and with carefully rehearsed timing, the light and sound cues, the shifting of scenery, the placement and return of properties, and the assignment, laundering, repair, and changes of costumes.

Also involved are a number of managerial functions:

producing, which includes securing all necessary personnel, space, and financing, supervising all production and promotion efforts, fielding all legal matters, and distributing all proceeds derived from receipts;

directing, which includes controlling and developing the artistic product and providing it with a unified vision, coordinating all its components, and supervising all rehearsals;

stage managing, which includes the responsibility for "running" a play production in all its complexity in performance after performance; and

house managing, which includes the responsibility for admitting, seating, and providing for the general comfort of the audience.

And finally, there is *playwriting,* which is in a class by itself. It is the one craft of the theatre that is usually executed away from the theatre building and its associated shops—that may indeed take place continents and centuries away from the production it inspires.

Of course the work of the theatre need not be apportioned precisely as we have indicated above. In any production, some people will perform more than one kind of work; for example, many of the "builders" will also be "runners." Moreover, many a play has been produced with the actors directing themselves, or the director handling production duties, or the dialogue improvised by the actors and director. On occasion most if not all of the craft and managerial functions have been performed by the same person: Aeschylus, for one, not only wrote, directed, and designed his Greek tragedies; he probably also performed the leading parts. But although there is nothing inevitable or necessary about the allocation of craft functions of the theatre's work, the functions themselves have remained fairly constant over the theatre's history. In virtually every era we can look back and see the same sorts of work going on—and the same kinds of efforts being expended—as we see in the work of the theatre today, be it professional or amateur, American or European, commercial or academic. Later on in this book we shall take a closer look at these various craft and managerial functions which go into the creation of a theatrical event.

Theatre is also work in the sense that it is not "play." This is a more subtle distinction than we might at once imagine. First, of course, recall that we ordinarily use the word "play" in describing the main product of theatre work. This is not merely a pecu-

Improvisational theatre is sheer performance—performance without script. Here the Paul Sills company is seen in a presentation of "Story Theatre," which consists of children's stories improvised and acted out by versatile adult performers. Originally produced at the Mark Taper Forum Theatre in Los Angeles, Sills' Story Theatre proved immensely popular and subsequently enjoyed a considerable run on Broadway in 1970.

liarity of the English tongue, for we find that the French *jeu*, the German *Spiel*, and the Latin *ludi* all share the double meaning of the English "play," referring both to plays and playing in the theatrical sense, and to sports activities, or games. This association points to a relationship that is fundamental to the understanding of theatre: theatre *is* a kind of game, and it is useful for us to see how and why this is so.

The theatre and games have a shared history. Both were developed to a high level of sophistication in Greek festivals: the Dionysian festivals for theatre and the Olympian festivals for sport were the two great cultural events of ancient Greece at which the legendary Greek competition for excellence was most profoundly engaged. The Romans merged sports and theatre in their circuses, where the two were performed side by side and in competition with each other. In much the same fashion, the Elizabethan Londoners built playhouses to accommodate both dramatic productions and animal-baiting spectacles somewhat akin to the modern bullfight; the stage that was set up for the plays was simply removed for "play." Today, sports and dramatic quasi-theatre dominate the television fare which absorbs so much leisure time not only in America but in most of the Western world. Moreover, professional athletes and entertainers are among the foremost celebrities of the modern age—and many a retired sports hero has found a second career in acting. Thus it is not extraordinary that sports and the theatre still share in the compound use of the word "play."

For the individual, a link between games and theatre is formed early in life, in "child's play," which usually manifests both game-like and drama-like aspects. The game of hide-and-seek, for example, is a playful competition between children that can be repeated over and over, a harmless but engrossing activity involving counting, hiding, searching, and at last the triumph of finding. It is also an acting out of one of childhood's greatest fears—the fear of separation from the parent, or "separation anxiety," as psychologists term it. Hide-and-seek affords the child a way of dealing with that fear by confronting it over and over "in play" until it loses much of its potency. Play is *often* grounded in serious concerns, and through play the individual gradually develops means of coping with life's challenges and uncertainties.

Drama and sports are different but related adult forms of the same "play." One of the aspects of adult play—in both its forms—is that it attracts a tremendous amateur following; as child's play is engaged in without prompting or reward, so adult sports and theatre commonly yield no remuneration beyond sheer personal satisfaction. Both sports and theatricals offer splendid opportunities for intense physical involvement, competition, self-expression, and emotional engagement—and all within limits set by precise and sensible rules. What is more, both can generate an audience because the energies and passions they project are rarely expressed so openly in daily life beyond the playgrounds of childhood. It is little wonder that persons who spend a lifetime in the theatre or in athletics are often regarded as child-like—or, more pejoratively, as immature and irresponsible—for their "playing" evokes myriad memories of youth.

But the theatre must finally be distinguished from child's play, and from sports as well, because theatre is by its nature a calculated act from beginning to end. Unlike adult games, which are open-ended, every theatre performance has a pre-ordained conclusion. The Yankees may not win the World Series this year, but Hamlet definitely will die in the fifth act. The *work* of the theatre, indeed, consists in keeping Hamlet alive up to that point—brilliantly alive—to make of that foreordained end a profoundly moving, ennobling, even surprising climax to the whole experience.

We might say, finally, that *theatre is the art of making play into work; specifically, into a work of art.* It is exhilarating work, to be sure, and it usually inspires and invigorates the energies and imaginations of all who participate; it transcends more prosaic forms of labor as song transcends grunts and groans. But it is work: that is its challenge, and the great accomplishments of the theatre are always attended by prodigious effort.

The stage is an institution combining amusement with instruction, rest with exertion, where no faculty of the mind is overstrained, no pleasure enjoyed at the cost of the whole. When melancholy gnaws the heart, when trouble poisons our solitude, when we are disgusted with the world and a thousand worries oppress us, or when our energies are destroyed by overexercise, the stage revives us, we dream of another sphere, we recover ourselves, our torpid nature is roused by noble passions, our blood circulates more healthily. The unhappy man forgets his tears in weeping for another. The happy man is calmed, the secure made provident. Effeminate natures are steeled, savages made man, and, as the supreme triumph of nature, men of all ranks, zones, and conditions, emancipated from the chains of conventionality and fashion, fraternize here in a universal sympathy, forget the world, and come nearer to their heavenly destination. The individual shares in the general ecstasy, and his breast has now only space for an emotion: he is a *man*.

Friedrich von Schiller

> Even at the level of clothes and paint and noise, the theatre bombards its audience with a hundred simultaneous capsules of information, anything capable of reaching the mind and imagination through the eye or the ear. The critic, equipped with literary apparatus, the linear logic of cause and effect, cannot cope with such an assault. Yet dramatic simultaneity, the synaesthesia of the senses and perceptions, is the object of study.
>
> J. L. Styan

ART

As we have suggested, the work of the theatre goes beyond the mere perfecting of skills, which is after all a goal of professionals in every field of endeavor. The theatre is *artistic* work. The word "art" brings to mind a host of intangibles: creativity, imagination, elegance, power, aesthetic harmony, and fineness of form; in addition, we expect a work of art to capture something of the human spirit, and to touch upon sensed but intellectually elusive meanings in life. Certainly great theatre never fails to bring together many of these intangibles. In great theatre we glimpse not only the physical and emotional exuberance of play, but the deep yearnings that propel humanity's search for purpose and the life well lived.

The art of the theatre is never "pure" art in the sense that it represents the personal vision of a solitary artist. Indeed, many "pure" artists consider theatrical art a bastard form, combining as it does the several arts of acting, writing, designing, directing, and architecture. It is perhaps significant, however, that such great individual artists as Shelley, Beethoven, Piranesi, Palladio, and Yeats have achieved only moderate success when they turned their efforts to this impure art; the theatre seems to reserve its greatest rewards for those whose artistic lives are first and foremost theatrical. The creative work of the theatre is in its essence collaborative and interdisciplinary, and thus its art can be judged only on its own merits.

IMPERSONATION

The theatrical art involves actors impersonating characters. This feature is unique to the theatre, and separates it quite definitively from other art forms such as poetry, painting, sculpture, music, and the like. Furthermore, impersonation is the single most important aspect of the theatre; it is its very foundation.

Try to imagine what extreme conceptual difficulties the ancient creators of the theatre must have encountered in laying down the ground rules for dramatic impersonation. For how was the audience to distinguish the "real person" from the "character" portrayed, between the actor-as-himself and the actor-as-character? And when the playwright was also an actor, how could onlookers distinguish between the thoughts of playwright-as-himself and those of the playwright-as-character? Questions such as these are often asked by children today as they watch a play, and it is inevitable that when a public press conference is arranged by the producer of a television soap opera, some fans will address the actors by the names of the characters they play and ask them questions pertinent only to their stage lives. Given this confusion in what we like to think of as a sophisticated age, it is easy to see why the ancients had to resolve the problem of actor-character separation before the theatre could become a firmly established institution.

The solution the ancient world found was the mask. We might say that Western theatre had its true beginning that day in ancient Greece when an actor first stepped out of the chorus, placed an unpainted mask over his face, and thereby signaled that the lines he was about to speak were "in character." The Noh Drama in Japan and many of the ritual dance-dramas of Africa, Asia, and native America have used the mask to similar effect. Basically, the mask is the tool of impersonation; at once hiding the face of the performer and projecting that of the "character" de-

NSEMBLU MASK — Bakumu, Zaire

A ritual mask from contemporary Africa. The mask gives the performer a superhuman appearance.

manded by the play. Although today the mask is rarely seen in the dramas of the Western world, it remains the symbol of the theatre—usually in the form of the double masks of Comedy and Tragedy which adorn the prosceniums of numerous playhouses and the letterheads of various theatrical organizations.

The importance of the mask is that it provides a physical as well as a symbolic separation between the impersonator and the impersonated, thus aiding the literal-minded onlooker to suspend awareness of the real world of the former and to accept in its place the stage world of the latter. In a play, it must be the "characters" who have apparent life; the actors themselves are expected to disappear into the shadows, along with their personal preoccupations, anxieties, and career ambitions. This convention gives rise to one of the great paradoxes of the theatre, what the eighteenth-century French encyclopedist Denis Diderot called "the paradox of the actor": when the actor has perfected his art it is the *simulated* character, the mask, which seems to live before our eyes, while the *real* person has no apparent life at all. The strength of such an illusion still echoes in our use of the word "person," which derives from the Latin word for "mask."

But of course we know that the actor does not die behind the mask, and herein lies perhaps an even greater paradox. We believe in the character, but at the end of the play we applaud the actor. Not only that—as we watch good theatre we are always, somewhere in the back of our mind, applauding the actor. Our appreciation of theatre rests largely on our dual awareness of actor and character and our understanding that they live inside the same skin.

The actor, of course, is aware of the same duality. For him, the art of acting is a sublime combination of the freedom that comes with anonymity (since he is hidden in his role) and the ego gratification that comes with exhibitionism. Thus actors commonly report that they both "lose themselves" and "find themselves" in theatrical performances, and indeed that these phenomena sometimes happen simultaneously. The sense of liberation and heightened self-awareness that comes with the fullest pursuit of goals within a standardized, formalized structure is one of the functions of all play, including sport.

BANDA MASK and COSTUME... Guinea.

The African Banda mask and costume incorporates both animal and human features, and is used in a dance-drama that combines magic with myth.

In Jean Genet's The Blacks, *black actors wear white make-up or white masks as shown here in American premiere of the play directed by Gene Frankel in 1961. This bitterly ironic play deals with the social masks an individual wears, and with the way racial accommodation is determined by skin color.*

The act of impersonation, with or without an actual mask, depends on an implicit agreement, or set of agreements, between actor and audience. In essence, the agreement is that the actor will pretend to be a character and the audience will pretend that he is in fact the character he pretends to be. This agreement does not at all mean that the actor must perform his role in a lifelike manner; on the contrary, the agreement concerning mutual pretense makes way for the acceptance on both sides of certain conditions, such as that the character will wear a mask, or speak into a microphone, or perform a dance when he is angered, or any of the scores of other devices and actions that have found acceptance in the theatre over time. In this century, particularly since the rise of motion pictures and television, much attention has been paid to the desirability of the actor's "use of himself" in creating the characters he plays; this emphasis reflects a trend, but not a fundamental shift, in the art of theatrical impersonation. The point to bear in mind is that impersonation itself remains a constant in the theatre despite changing modes and styles of theatrical presentation.

Throughout history actors have often been accused of flirting with a suspect morality in impersonating characters. Audiences too have been castigated for applauding this impiety. The Greek word for actor was *hypokrites*, a term that originally meant "answerer" (the actor "answered" the odes of a chorus), but it came to mean "pretender" as well, and the more negative connotation has come down to us as "one who dissembles." Indeed, the oldest recorded anecdote in theatrical history portrays the ancient lawmaker Solon chiding Thespis, the first actor, for "telling so many lies before such a number of people." When Thespis replies that there is no harm in lying "in play," Solon answers, "Ah, if we honor and commend such 'play' as this, we shall find it some day in our business." At least since Solon's day, actors have had to contend with varying degrees of social skepticism, and the same notoriety that has given them celebrity status has occasioned intense and often disapproving curiosity about their private affairs.

The impersonation that underlies the acting art is not, however, aimed at imposture; its goal is artistic. The actor does not pretend to "be someone else," for a dramatic character is not a person but an abstraction, no more human than paint on a canvas or words on a page. It is true that the dramatic character is represented by a living person who goes through the motions of the character's acts and in many cases experiences them fully as well. It is also true that some characters are drawn from life, and their dialogue may be taken from the actual transcripts of a historical event. Nonetheless, the character is not a "somebody else"; it is an artistic fabrication—a shaped presence—that gains acceptance as a real person only by virtue of the implicit agreement of actors and audience alike. The actor deserves no moral op-

probation for engaging in impersonation, nor should he feel hypocritical about engaging in impersonated acts and feelings, for this is simply part of the artistic work of an old and endlessly creative profession.

Nowadays, as we have seen, the art of impersonation rarely calls for use of a mask that conceals the actor's face; instead, costume, make-up, dialogue, accent, movement, gesture, and a variety of acting methods and techniques support the delineation of character formerly expressed by mask and voice alone. Owing to a twentieth-century emphasis on verisimilitude, most actors in Europe and America today favor, in whole or in part, the concepts of Konstantin Stanislavski, the Russian actor-director and acting teacher, who proclaimed that the actor should "live the life of the character onstage." This view has fostered the development of a number of techniques and training methods to aid the actor not only in performing a character's actions in minute physiological detail, but also in experiencing the character's feelings to such a degree that occasionally even the presence of the audience is forgotten. If this movement of modern times has its fervent supporters, however, it has its equally aroused critics. It is probably fairest to say that the question of the proper relationship between the actor and his role—or of the degree to which the actor ought to "identify with" his part—remains as perplexing today as it was two hundred years ago when Diderot defined the paradox of acting.

PERFORMANCE

Theatre is performance; but what, exactly, does "performance" mean? Simply stated, performance is an action or series of actions taken for the ultimate benefit (attention, entertainment, enlightenment, or involvement) of someone else. We call that someone else the audience.

If two people engage in a strictly private conversation, that is a simple communication between them. If, however, their conversation is undertaken in order to impress or involve a third person who they know is in a position to overhear it, the "communication" becomes a performance and the third person becomes its audience.

Obviously, performance is a part of everyday life; indeed, it has been analyzed as such in a number of recently published psychological and sociological

The medieval trestle stage—a few planks on trestles—was a standard performance space for more than a thousand years. Portable, serviceable, and inexpensive, it could be set up almost anywhere, and could be dismantled in an instant if the actors chanced to be chased out of town—as they often were. Such trestle stages may still be seen at many summertime European festivals.

works. When two teen-age boys wrestle on the schoolground, they may well be "performing" their physical prowess for the benefit of their peers. When a student asks his professor a question in the lecture hall, he is frequently "performing" for his fellow students—and the professor "performs" for the same audience in providing a response. Trial lawyers examining witnesses invariably "perform," often drawing on a considerable repertoire of grunts, snorts, shrugs, raised eyebrows, and disbelieving sighs for the benefit of that ultimate courtroom audience, the jury. Politicians kiss babies for the benefit of mothers (and others) in search of a kindly candidate. Even stony silence can be a performance—if, for example, it is the treatment a woman metes out to an offensive admirer. We are all performers, and the theatre only makes an art out of something we all do every day.

The theatre both reflects man's everyday perfor-

mance and expands that performance into a formal mode of artistic expression.

The theatre makes use of two general modes of performance: direct and indirect. Direct performance is the basic nightclub mode. Nightclub performers continuously acknowledge the presence of the audience: they sing to them, dance for them, joke at them, and respond overtly to their applause, laughter, requests, and heckling. Dramatic forms of all ages have employed these and a variety of other direct presentational methods as well, including asides, soliloquies, direct address, plays-within-plays, and curtain calls.

Indirect performance, however, is probably the more fundamental mode in drama; it is certainly the one that makes drama "dramatic" as opposed to simply "theatrical." For indirect performance is the mode whereby the audience watches interactions that

"KILL THE HOUSE, STRIKE THE DUMMY, FLY THE OFFICE, FIRE UP THE BEDROOM, AND BREAK A LEG!"

It is doubtful if any stage manager has ever barked precisely the instructions cited above, but should he do so his message would be quite clear to his co-workers. Theatre, as a collaborative and quickly paced enterprise, demands precise and unambiguous communications, and over the years a theatrical jargon has developed which is universally understood in the American theatre at all levels. A few terms:

Kill   the stage manager's term for turning anything off. "Kill the sound" means turn off the sound tape; "kill the mikes" means turn off the microphones; "kill the works" means turn off the worklights (backstage lights used for changing scenery only).

House   a multipurpose term, usually referring to the audience portion of a theatre (as in "houselights," meaning the lights that illuminate the audience; "full house," meaning full attendance; "half a house," meaning a half-filled audience area). Sometimes the term refers to the entire theatre from the old term "playhouse." "Kill the house" means turn off the houselights.

Strike   to remove something from the stage. "Strike the set" means remove all the scenery from the stage. "Strike," by itself, means to remove all the scenery from the theatre at the conclusion of a play's "run."

Run   the series of performances given for a play.

Break a leg   the theatrical equivalent of "good luck" (since theatrical superstition has it that it is bad luck to say "good luck"). And please don't whistle in the dressing room.

Fire up   turn on the stage lights.

Stage left   the left side of the stage from the actor's viewpoint; similarly, *stage right* refers to the actor's right.

Downstage   the front part of the stage; that is, the portion of the stage closest to the audience. This term originated in the days of "raked" (sloping) stages, which were angled down toward the audience. *Upstage* is the rear of the stage. Upstage and downstage, as well as stage left and stage right, naturally apply only to theatres in which the audience is located principally on one side of the stage.

Fly   (as a transitive verb) to hoist scenery or actors off the stage. Thus the technician may "fly the wings" by hoisting them out of sight, or "fly Peter Pan" by hoisting him (her) on an "invisible" wire.

Work   to succeed, as of a play or scene. This term implies a theatrical unit is akin to a piece of machinery; actors and directors (and audiences) commonly decide whether a scene "works" or "doesn't work" in the same sort of all-or-nothing fashion that one might judge the mechanical performance of a vacuum cleaner.

---

are staged as if no audience were present at all, and as a result the audience is encouraged to concentrate on the events that are being staged, not on their presentation. In other words, the audience "believes in" the play, and allows itself to forget that the characters are really actors and the apparently spontaneous events that are taking place before their eyes are really a series of scripted scenes. This belief—or, to borrow Coleridge's famous double negative, this "suspension of disbelief"—engenders audience participation via the psychological mechanism of *empathy*; that is, the audience is likely to feel kinship with cer-

tain (or all) of the characters, to identify with their aspirations, sympathize with their plights, exult in their victories, and, in general, to care deeply about what happens to them. When that happens, the audience experiences the "magic" of the theatre. Well-written and well-staged dramas make people *feel*; they draw in the spectator emotionally and leave him in some measure a changed person. This is as much magic as the modern world provides anywhere, and its effect is the same all over the world.

Occasionally either the direct or the indirect mode of performance is taken to an extreme. For examples

Performer-illustrators of Bertolt Brecht's "distanced" theatre combine bold theatricality, songs, and blatant use of stage mechanics to promulgate a social/political aesthetic. This scene is from the recent East Berlin production of Brecht's cabaret opera, The Rise and Fall of The City of Mahagonny.

of the former, one can look at portions of the plays of Bertolt Brecht, the twentieth-century German author who deliberately set out to repudiate the "magic" of the theatre by means of productions replete with direct appeals to the audience on a variety of social and political issues. Brecht's plays featured songs, signs, chalk talks, arguments addressed directly to the house, and slide projections, and he specifically avoided use of concealed stage trickery or "effects." Brecht wanted his audience distanced from the story of the play; he also wanted them to consider his actors as performer-illustrators rather than specific char-

acters with specific involvements, so that the political and social themes of the play would dominate the viewer's awareness.

In this effort, Brecht was specifically attacking the realist movement of the turn of the century, a movement that afforded many cases of the other extreme. It propounded a style of performance in which the actors behaved exactly as they did in life, and in settings made as lifelike as possible (in one notable example, a celebrated New York restaurant was disassembled and reconstructed on stage, complete with its original moldings, wallpaper, furniture, silverware, and linens). At times the indirect mode so dominated in the realist productions that actors spoke with their backs to audiences, directors allowed interminable pauses and inaudible whispers, playwrights culled their dialogue from random fragments of overheard conversations, and house managers timed intermissions to the presumed time elapsing in the play's story. The realistic theatre of that time was sometimes called "the theatre of the fourth wall removed" because its goal typically was to re-create life inside a room, and the sole departure from complete verisimilitude that was allowed was the removal of one wall to let the audience peer in—much as the lab scientist peers at a slide through a microscope.

The two modes of performance, however, can never be entirely separated. The fact is that the Brechtian theatre, despite all the best efforts of Brecht himself and all the resources he had at his disposal, never managed to eliminate audience empathy with the leading characters; and even the most resolutely realistic theatres have never escaped the ultimate audience recognition that the actors are, indeed, performing. As it turns out, theatrical performance is always *both* direct and indirect, and it is always both simultaneously.

What is more, the audience inevitably demands two things of a theatrical performance: it demands characters it can care about and it demands actors it can admire. In other words, the audience wants to see the characters struggle and the actors sweat. In watching a performance, therefore, the members of an audience intuitively look for two things. They look for a well-crafted dramatic story that holds implications for their own lives, and they look for extraordinary individual acting performances. One of these

elements may predominate—as when a cast of brilliant actors submerge themselves in a masterpiece by Chekhov or, conversely, when a relatively trivial script becomes the vehicle for a "star's" bravura performance—but both are always present in a successful production; and when they are, the viewer experiences a complex and deeply satisfying sense of inner expansion.

LIVE PERFORMANCE

Unlike some other theatrical arts, such as television drama and film, the theatre is an arena of living performers interacting with a living audience. This turns out to be an extremely important distinction. Actors who are accomplished in both "live" and filmed performance invariably report a strong preference for the former, despite the usually greater financial rewards of the latter. In explaining this preference, they often make mention of the applause of the crowd, of sensation of "presence" and a special tingle of excitement. Beyond question, some fundamental forces are at work in live theatre.

The first of these forces of course consists in a rapport between actor and audience. Both are breathing, as it were, the same air. Both are involved, at the same time and in the same space, with the stage life depicted by the play, and sometimes their mutual fascination is almost palpable. A collective gasp from the audience at a climactic moment in a play can be the spark that evokes a transcendent performance from an actor. Every actor's performance is affected in some measure, for better or for worse, by the way in which the audience yields up or withholds its responses—

T he theatre is the only place where the tears of the virtuous man and the rogue are mingled. There the mean man regrets the injustices he has committed, feels sorry for the evil he has done, and is indignant toward a man of his own sort. But the impression is made, and it remains in the hearts of each of us, in spite of ourselves. The evil man leaves his seat less disposed to do evil than if he had listened to a severe and pitiless orator.

Denis Diderot

its laughter, its sighs, its applause, its silences. Thus live theatrical performance is always a two-way communication between stage and "house."

A second major element in live theatre has to do with the relationship between the members of the audience who, having arrived at the theatre locked inside their own personalities and predilections, quickly find themselves fused into a common enterprise with total strangers. This particular sort of intra-audience relationship is never developed by television drama, which is directed chiefly to solitary watchers or to small audiences of viewers known to each other—two to four people in each of a million different living rooms. Nor is it likely to happen in motion picture houses, where audiences find themselves in essentially a one-to-one relationship with the screen and rarely break out in any *collective* response. Live play presentations foster the kinds of audience behaviors that are demonstrably *social* in nature: everyone arrives at the theatre at about the same time and all depart together; intermissions allow for an exchange of ideas; theatre programs afford material for conversation. Further, audience responses to the entertainment are social in nature. For example, laughter and applause build upon themselves and gain strength by the audiences' recognition that others are laughing and applauding. The standing ovation—unique to live performance—inevitably involves the audience applauding itself, as well as the performers, for its own understanding and appreciation of theatrical excellence. Plays with social themes can be particularly effective in creating a feeling of audience participation and oneness: in a celebrated example in the 1930s, the American play *Waiting for Lefty* was set up to treat the audience as union members at a meeting, and by the play's end the whole audience was yelling "Strike! Strike!" Obviously, only a live performance could evoke such a response.

Finally, live performance inevitably has the quality of immediacy. The action of the play is taking place *right now* as it is being watched, and anything can happen. Although in most professional productions the changes that occur in performance from one night to another are so subtle that only an expert would notice, the fact is that each night's presentation is unique and everyone present—in the audience, in the cast, and behind the scenes—knows it. This awareness lends an excitement that simply is not present in theatrical events which are wholly "in the can." One reason for the excitement, of course, is that in live performance mistakes can happen; this possibility occasions a certain abiding tension, perhaps even an edge of stage fright, which some people say creates the ultimate thrill of the theatre. But if disaster can come without warning, so can splendor. On any given night, each actor is trying to better his previous performance, and no one knows when this collective effort will coalesce into something sublime. The actors' constant striving toward self-transcendence gives the theatre a vitality that is missing from performance fixed unalterably on tape or celluloid. But perhaps most appropriately, the immediacy of live performance creates a "present-ness" or "presence" that embodies the fundamental uncertainty of life itself. One of the prime functions of theatre is to address the uncertainties of human existence, and the very format of live performance presents a certain moment-to-moment uncertainty right before our eyes. Ultimately this "immediate theatre" helps us to define the questions and confusions of our lives and lets us grapple, in the present, with their implications.

SCRIPTED PLAY

Theatre lives in acted presentations to public audiences; the record it leaves behind after the audience goes home is necessarily a modest one. Generally the most complete record of what was said consists in what is called the playscript. In many minds playscripts are virtually synonymous with "the theatre." That, of course, is a serious misconception. In most cases the playscript bears the same sort of relation to the play itself as a shadow silhouette bears to a human face: it outlines the features but conveys nothing of the spirit, the complexity, the color, or the nuance of the living performance.

Nonetheless, we are indeed fortunate that playscripts have come down to us from every great period of theatre history. At the very least, they provide a historical record of independent interest (many of them make excellent reading), and at best they are a rich source of materials for revivals—new productions which can sometimes be more thrilling than the originals.

Let us now take a closer look at the relations between playscript and play production. First we

A sketch from real life? No, it is a scene from a play by Chekhov (The Three Sisters) *in which a young soldier has just given a spinning top to Irina on her birthday. The semblance of real life is a prime accomplishment of this play—and the actors' individual brilliance must be subordinated to the creation of that lifelike effect.*

should be aware that the finished playscript does not necessarily precede the finished performance. In fact, virtually all important playscripts available to us today were published *following* their initial performance, and the versions we read reflect not only the staging decisions of a director and the portrayal choices of many actors, but the changes in dialogue that took place during the play's rehearsal period and frequently in its performance period as well. While most original play productions are begun with a script in hand (usually it is called the "working script"), that script is rarely treated as a sacred document. The evolution and "doctoring" of new playscripts during rehearsal is a process that took place in past times as well as in the present, as historical accounts amply attest. For revivals, of course, a "fixed" script generally

dictates the dialogue in fairly strict manner, but of course that script was itself fixed by the one or more productions which intervened between the play's first drafting and its eventual publication.

Second, let us bear in mind that even a fixed script is in some ways as notable for what it lacks as for what it contains. Apart from the odd stage set description or acting note (for example, "through her tears," "crossing to the bannister," or "softly"), a written playscript usually tells almost nothing about a play's non-verbal components. For how can it describe the degrees of expression within the range of even the beginning actor? How can it capture the bead of sweat that forms on Hamlet's brow as he stabs Polonius, or Romeo's nervous laugh as he tries to part dueling adversaries? Written stage descriptions (which in any case hardly

A play in a book is only the shadow of a play and not even a clear shadow of it. . . . The printed script of a play is hardly more than an architect's blueprint of a house not yet built or [a house] built and destroyed. The color, the grace and levitation, the structural pattern in motion, the quick interplay of live beings, suspended like fitful lightning in a cloud, these things are the play, not words on paper nor thoughts and ideas of an author.

Tennessee Williams

ever appear in playscripts that antedate the present century) serve mainly to delineate the outer form of a play and do little to convey its inner life. As for the words of dialogue, although they are probably the most important single element of a play they are not in any way the whole experience. Words on a page do not resound in the mind in the same way as words spoken aloud, and even spoken words do not encompass the facial expressions, the color and sweep of costumes, the play of light, the movement of form in space—and the audience response—that conspire to support a living production.

The chief value of playscripts, then, is that they generate theatrical production and they provide an invaluable, albeit imperfect, record of performances past. Two and a half millennia of play productions have left us a repository of thousands upon thousands of scripts, some awful, many ordinary, a few magnificent. This rich store puts us in touch with theatre history in the making and allows us to glimpse the nature of the originals in production. It also suggests ways in which the play of yesterday can serve as blueprints for vital theatre today.

This, then, is the theatre: artistic work, impersonation, live performance, and scripted plays.

It exists *in production* rather than in manuscript, and it consists of actions, sights, sounds, ideas, feelings, and—of course—words.

It consists of playing, and—of course—plays.

What is a play? That question deserves a separate chapter.

CHAPTER 2

WHAT IS A PLAY?

A play is, essentially, a unit of theatre. It is not a "thing" but an event, taking place in real time and occupying real space. It is identified by some sort of title, and it has a recognizable order of presentation which is calculated to engage the attention of an audience. It is through the play that we experience the theatre.

Plays are customarily classified in two ways: by duration and by genre. Although these classifications have been emphasized more in the past than they are today, they still play a part in theatre understanding.

DURATION

A "full-length play" is one that lasts about two to four hours. This duration has been fairly standard since Renaissance times. It is long enough to afford sufficient significance and entertainment value to bring people out of their homes, and short enough to be squeezed into the period between lunch and dinner, or between dinner and bedtime, and still allow time for travel to and from the theatre.

A "short play" lasts about twenty minutes to an hour. Usually it is either combined with one or two others to make a "bill" of sufficient duration to attract a conventional theatre audience, or else it is presented in some other setting, such as a lunch-time theatre, a dramatic festival, a classroom, a street entertainment, or a cabaret.

Occasionally, plays much shorter than twenty minutes' duration or much longer than four hours' are presented with high artistic impact. Samuel Beckett's *Breath*, for example, lasts a minute or so; Robert Wilson's *The Death and Life of Josef Stalin* is performed for eighteen continuous hours. These extremes, however, demand such drastic accommodation on the part of audiences, actors, and behind the scenes personnel that it is highly doubtful they will be commonplace in the future.

GENRE

Genre is a more informative means of classifying plays, even though (or perhaps because) it brings into discussion more subjective criteria. Indeed, dramatic criticism for many centuries seemed to concern itself primarily with defining precise standards for various dramatic genres and then assessing plays in terms of how they measured up to these standards.

The two genres that have dominated dramatic criticism since ancient days are those of *tragedy* and *comedy*, which the Greeks perceived to be so essentially unalike that Aristotle, who is generally recognized as the father of dramatic criticism, concluded the two forms sprang from wholly separate and unrelated sources. It would not be accurate to say that Aristotle arbitrarily divided theatre into the genres of tragedy and comedy; but rather that he found them that way. He thereupon sought to create a poetics (poetic theory) for each, and this effort eventually resulted in a public understanding of their interrelationship as the primary genres of dramatic art.

Today, aestheticians and scholars recognize a number of generic classifications. In addition to the original tragedy and comedy (which are now defined more narrowly than in Aristotle's day), melodrama, farce, tragicomedy, dark comedy, history, epic drama, documentary, and the musical are now seen as major genres into which modern plays (and, retroactively, classical plays) can be classified.

A *tragedy* is a serious play (although not necessarily devoid of humorous episodes) with a topic of universal human import as its theme, in which the central character or characters confront suffering, decline, and often death. Traditionally, tragedy involves the downfall of a character of elevated stature. Tragedy elicits both pity and terror in the audience, and these responses are resolved in what Aristotle described as *catharsis*, or a "purging of the emotions."

A *comedy* is a humorous play with an important theme, in which characters confront themselves and each other with amusing results. Comedy can be intense, passionate, insightful, and moving, but its organization of the dramatic experience avoids sustained pity or terror and elicits more laughter than shock.

A *melodrama* is a serious play with a trivial theme. The protagonists in this popular form are likeable and pleasant rather than heroic, the villains uncompromisingly nasty. Melodrama presents a simple and finite confrontation between good and evil rather than a complex exposition of universal human sufferings and aspirations. Plays in this genre can rarely sustain unpleasant endings, can rarely generate

Melodrama, an exaggerated seriousness, is evident in this moment from American Conservatory Theatre production of The Tavern, *an early twentieth-century theatrical piece by showman George M. Cohan.*

Some of the essence of farce is captured in this production photograph from Georges Feydeau's Hotel Paradiso, *as presented by the American Conservatory Theatre in 1978. Actors' exaggerated expressions and postures, as well as multiple-door setting, are standard features of farcical plays.*

catharsis, and typically end with the intellectually empty but theatrically thrilling victory of the "good guy."

A *farce* is a humorous play—and it had better be *wildly* humorous—on a trivial theme, usually one that is thoroughly familiar to theatregoers. Mistaken identity, illicit romance, elaborate misunderstandings—these are staples of farce. Identical twins, lovers in closets or under tables, full stage chases, switched potions, switched costumes (often involving men in women's costumes or women in men's), mis-heard instructions, and various disrobings, dis-

coveries, and disappearances characterize this age-old and perennially durable form.

Tragicomedy, as the name implies, is a form that attempts to bridge tragedy and comedy. This it does by maintaining a serious theme throughout but varying the approach from serious to humorous, and by concluding without the violent catharsis which its audience is led to expect. It has been called "tragedy that ends happily."

Dark comedy is similar in theme and approach to tragicomedy, but with the obverse outcome: "comedy that ends tragically" is perhaps the most accurate definition of this more modern attempt to combine comedy and tragedy.

The *history* genre was largely set by Shakespeare, although a few plays that would qualify for this category were written before his time. A play of this genre treats historical events in a serious and respectful manner. Shakespeare's history plays are concerned chiefly with English history from roughly 1377 to 1547, and deal specifically with the lives and struggles of the English kings Richard II, Henry IV, Henry V, Henry VI, Richard III, and Henry VIII. These basically serious plays contain many humorous details, but none attains the classical catharsis of tragedy or the overriding humor of comedy.

The *documentary* is a genre of fairly recent development, in which a great deal of authentic evidence is used as a basis for portraying relatively recent his-

torical events. Trial transcripts, news reports and pictures, personal and official records are marshaled as documentation to bring alive a particular issue and point of view. Famous court trials—those of J. Robert Oppenheimer, John C. Scopes, Adolph Eichmann, the "Zoot Suit" gangs, and Leopold and Loeb, for example—have been a prime source of material for documentary dramatizations.

The *musical* genre is defined by its extensive reliance on music, especially on songs. Usually the musical is combined with another genre to create a musical comedy (that is, a comedy with songs, such as *Guys and Dolls*), a musical documentary (such as the World War I–inspired *Oh, What A Lovely War!*), or musical history. A tragedy set to music is called grand opera; musical farce is generally called light opera, or operetta.

Fiddler on the Roof, *an internationally famed American musical by Jerry Bock and Joseph Stein, here seen in East Berlin production (1971) at the Komische Oper (Light Opera) theatre, under direction of Walter Felsenstein. Singing, dancing, acting, spoken dialogue, comedy, sentiment, and a touch of violence are mingled in this composite theatrical form.*

S hakespeare has brightly parodied the division of plays into genres, a practice which in his time was already becoming almost an affectation. In *Hamlet*, he has Polonius describe an acting company as "The best actors in the world, either for tragedy, comedy, history, pastoral, pastoral-comical, historical-pastoral, tragical-historical, tragical-comical-historical-pastoral, scene individable, or poem unlimited."

Potentially, of course, there are as many theatrical genres as the diligent critic wishes to define. No system of classification should obscure the fact that each play is unique, and the grouping of any two or more plays into a common genre is only a convenience for purposes of comparison and analysis. We in the twentieth century have certainly learned that past formulations of tragedy and farce have had little bearing on the long-range assessment of the importance, quality, or worth—on the staying power—of any individual play; and critics who today dwell inordinately on such questions as "Is *Death of A Salesman* a true tragedy?" are doubtless spending too much time deciding what box to put the artistic work in and too little time examining and revealing the work itself.

On the other hand, genre distinctions can be useful if we keep their limitations in mind. They can help us to comprehend the broad spectrum of purposes to which plays may be put and to perceive important similarities and differences. For the theatre artist, an awareness of the possibilities inherent in each genre—together with a knowledge of the achievements that have been made in each—stimulates the imagination and aids in the setting of work standards and ambitions.

STRUCTURE

Plays can be analyzed structurally in two ways: by their components (that is, plot, character, theme, etc.) and by their order of organization (exposition, development, climax, etc.). Both methods are used by most persons who find it worthwhile to analyze dramatic art, and both will be used in this book. However, it must be clear from the outset that a drama which is taken apart in the classroom inevitably loses something. The individual components and the sequential aspects of any given play are never in fact isolated in the theatrical experience, and any truly useful dramatic analysis must end with a resynthesis of the studied portions into a living whole. The complexity of the theatrical experience and its multi-sensual impact decree that we see it always as greater than the sum of its parts.

The Components of a Play

The division of plays into components is an ancient analytical practice. Aristotle in his *Poetics* (425 B.C.) described the components of a tragedy (by which he meant a serious play) as plot, character, theme, diction, music, and spectacle—in that order. Aristotle's list, with some modification and elaboration, still serves as a pretty fair breakdown of what theatre is all about, although the relative importance of each of the components has been a matter of continuing controversy.

Plot

The *plot* of a play is the means by which most people know and describe it; perhaps that is why Aristotle listed it first. Essentially, plot is the mechanics of dramatic storytelling. More than merely conveying a story line, plot determines the structural development of a play's action: entrances, inquiries, recognitions, physical behaviors, and other communications of a kind that can be readily summarized in narrative form. Plot embraces both outer actions (such as Romeo stabbing Tybalt) and inner ones (such as Romeo falling in love with Juliet); the sequence and arrangement of these actions, in a series of scenes and acts punctuated by intermissions, is one of the most difficult and demanding tests of a playwright's skill.

Traditionally, the primary demands of plot are logic and suspense. To satisfy the demand for logic, the actions portrayed must be plausible, and events must follow one upon another in an organic rather than arbitrary fashion. To sustain suspense, the actions portrayed must set up expectations for further actions, drawing the audience along in a story that seems to move inexorably toward an ending that may be sensed but is never wholly predictable. Melodramas and farces tend to rely heavily on intricate and suspenseful plots. The "well-made plays" of the late nineteenth century reflect an attempt to elevate plot construction to the highest level of theatrical art; today, murder mysteries and "whodunits" are likely to be the most plot-intensive works to be seen on the stage.

Characters

The *characters* of a play are the human figures—the impersonated presences—who undertake the actions of the plot. Their potency in the theatre is measured by our interest in them *as people*. The most brilliant plotting in the world cannot redeem a play if the audience remains indifferent to its characters; therefore, the fundamental demand of a play's characters is that they make the audience *care*. To this end, characters cannot be mere stick figures, no matter how elaborately detailed. The great dramatic characters of the past—Hamlet, Masha, Amanda, Iago, Vladimir, Peer Gynt, Phaedra, to name a few—bring to an experienced theatregoer's or playreader's mind personalities as vivid and memorable as those of good friends (and hated enemies); they are whole images, indelibly human, alive with the attributes, feelings, and expectations of real people. We can identify with them; we can sympathize with them.

Character depth is what gives a play its psychological complexity, its sensuality, and its warmth. Without it, we cannot experience love, hate, fear, joy, hope, despair—any of the emotions we expect to derive from theatre; and a theatre devoid of those emotions which stem from the humanness of the characters portrayed would be a theatre without an audience in a matter of days. For this reason many playwrights have scoffed at the notion of primacy of plot, and at the often mechanical contrivances of the well-made play. Indeed, several playwrights have fashioned plays that were quite arbitrarily plotted, with the story line designed simply to show various aspects of a fascinating character.

Theme

Theme is the abstracted intellectual content of a play; it may be described as the play's overall statement: its topic, central idea, or message, as the case may be. Some plays have obvious themes, such as Euripides' *The Trojan Women* (the horrors of war) or Molière's *The Bourgeois Gentleman* (the foolishness of social pretense). Other plays have less clearly defined themes, and the most provocative of these have given rise to much scholarly controversy. *Hamlet, Oedipus Tyrannos*, and *Waiting for Godot* for example, all suggest many themes, and each has spawned a great many debates among adherents arguing fiercely about which theme is central.

Nothing demands that a play have a single theme, of course, or even that it be at all reducible to straightforward intellectual generalization. Indeed, plays that are too obviously theme-intensive are usually considered too propagandistic or too somberly academic for theatrical success: "If you want to send a message," one Broadway saying goes, "go to Western Union." What is more, although the themes of plays address the central questions of society and mankind, their theatrical impact hinges always on audience engagement in the first two play components we have discussed: plot and characterization.

The importance of theme is that a play must have something to say, and that something must seem *pertinent* to the audience. Further, the play must be sufficiently focused and limited to give the audience at least some lucidity on that something within its two- to four-hour framework. Plays that try to say nothing or, conversely, plays that try to say everything, rarely have even a modest impact, no matter how entertaining or well plotted they may be. Thus from the beginning playwrights working in every genre, be it tragedy, comedy, melodrama, or farce, have recognized the merit of narrowing their field of intellectual investigation in crafting a play.

Diction

Diction, which Aristotle listed fourth, relates not only to the pronunciation of spoken dialogue but to the literary character of a play's text, including its tone, imagery, cadence, and articulation, as well as its use of literary forms and figures such as verse, rhyme, metaphor, apostrophe, jest, and epigram.

The theatrical value of poetry has been well established from the beginning; until fairly recent times, as a matter of fact, most serious plays were written largely in verse. Today, comedies as well as more serious plays still make liberal use of carefully crafted dialogue, although the verse form is relatively rare. Many plays succeed on the basis of brilliant repartee, stunning epigrams, poetic language, witty arguments, and dazzling tirades. Other, quite different, sorts of plays feature a poetry of silences and inarticulate mutterings: these, as fashioned by Anton Chekhov or Harold Pinter, for example, can create a diction no less effective than the more ostentatiously crafted verbal pyrotechnics of a Bernard Shaw or a Tom Stoppard (see p. 338).

The diction of a play is by no means the creation of the playwright alone. It is very much the product of the actor as well, and for that reason throughout the history of Western theatre an effective stage voice has been considered the prime asset of the actor. Even today, the study of voice is a primary and continuous obligation at most schools and conservatories of classical acting. The chief aim of these schools is to create an acting voice capable of dealing in quite spectacular fashion with the broad palette of dramatic diction demanded by the works of the world's most noted playwrights.

Music

Any discussion of *music*, Aristotle's fifth component of theatre, forces us to remember that in Aristotle's time plays were sung or chanted, not simply spoken. That mode of presentation has all but disappeared, and yet the musical component remains directly present in most plays performed today, indirectly present in the rest.

Music is directly present in the large number of plays that call for actual music in their presentation. This music takes many forms. Songs are common in the plays of Shakespeare, as well as in the works of contemporary writers, such as Bertolt Brecht, who feature "direct" performance techniques. Many naturalistic writers have found occasion to work familiar songs into their scripts, sometimes by having characters play records on a stage Victrola. Chekhov and Tennessee Williams both make extensive use in their plays of off-stage music—for example, a military marching band can be heard in Chekhov's *The Three Sisters*; and Williams provides for music from a nearby dance hall in *A Streetcar Named Desire*, and from a cantina in *Night of the Iguana*. Directors also frequently add incidental music to play productions—sometimes to set a mood during intermissions or before the play begins, sometimes to underscore the play's action itself. The power of music directly present in the theatre is well known, and its effectiveness in moving an audience to ever deeper feeling is one that few playwrights or directors wish to ignore.

Indirectly, music is present in every play. It is in the rhythm of sounds that, while not specifically tuneful, combine to create a play's "score," its orchestration of sound. Vocal tones, footsteps, sighs, shouts, off-stage railroad whistles, the shrilling of a telephone, muffled drumbeats, gunshots, animal cries, conversations in the next room, and amplified special effects (heartbeats, respiration, other-worldly noises, for instance) are frequently employed by authors and directors to create a symphony of the theatre quite apart from, though supportive of, the plot, characters, dialogue, and theme. Moreover, the spoken word creates, in addition to its semantic impact (that is, its meaning and connotation), an aural impact: it is an integer of pure sound, and it can be appreciated as pure musical vibration. Under the guidance of a skilled director, all of a play's sounds can be orchestrated to produce a performance of such dramatic force that it can thrill even persons wholly unacquainted with the language of the dialogue.

Spectacle

Spectacle, Aristotle's last component, encompasses the visual aspects of production: scenery, costumes, lighting, make-up, properties, and the overall *look* of the theatre and stage. It would be wrong to infer that "spectacle" is synonymous with "spectacular," for some productions are quite restrained in their visual artistry. Rather, it is spectacle in the sense that it is something seen. If this point seems obvious, it is also crucial. Theatre is a visual experience every bit as much as it is an aural, emotional, or intellectual one: the ancient Greeks clearly had this in mind when they chose the name "seeing place" to designate the site of their performances.

Much as the cinema has been called the art of "moving pictures," so the theatre might be called the art of fluid sculpture. This sculpture is fashioned in

W hat's the difference between a poor play and a good one? I think there's a very simple way of comparing them. A play in performance is a series of impressions; little dabs, one after another, fragments of information or feeling in a sequence which stir the audience's perceptions. A good play sends many such messages, often several at a time, often crowding, jostling, overlapping one another. The intelligence, the feelings, the memory, the imagination are all stirred. . . . Shakespeare seems better in performance than anyone else because he gives us more, moment for moment, for our money. This is due to his genius, but also to his technique. The possibilities of free verse on an open stage enabled him to cut the inessential detail and the irrelevant realistic action: in their place he could cram sounds and ideas, thoughts and images which make each instant into a stunning mobile.

Peter Brook

Laura and Jim O'Connor, the "gentleman caller," admire a glass unicorn in one of the central moments of Tennessee Williams' The Glass Menagerie. *Here the stage prop symbolizes the transparency and fragility of the shy young heroine. Arizona Theatre Company. 1977.*

part from the human body in motion, and in part from still or moving scenery and props, natural and manufactured items of both dramatic and decorative importance, all illuminated by natural or artificially modulated light. It is a sculpture that moves in time as well as in space, and although it is generally considered to be primarily a support for the plot, characters, and theme of a play, it has an artistic appeal and an artistic heritage all its own. Certainly some ardent patrons of the theatre pay more attention to settings and costumes than to any other aspect of a play, and in many a successful production dramatic visual effects have virtually carried the play.

Memorable visual elements can be both grand and prosaic, imposing and subtle. Nineteenth-century Romanticism, which survives today primarily in the form of grand opera, tends to favor mammoth stagings featuring processions, crowd scenes, palaces, animals, triumphal arches, and lavish costumes. Twentieth-century movements are more likely to go in for domestic environments and archetypal images: Jimmy and Cliff reading newspapers while Alison irons a shirt in John Osborne's *Look Back In Anger* and Laura playing with her glass animals in Tennessee Williams' *The Glass Menagerie*; or Mother Courage pulling her wagon in Brecht's *Mother Courage* and Nagg and Nell in the ashcans of Samuel Beckett's *Endgame*. In the long run, conceptual richness and precision in a play's visual presentation are far more telling than grandeur for its own sake.

Germaine Montero, as Mother Courage in Brecht's play of that name, pulls her wagon in a celebrated French production at the popular theatre festival in Avignon.

The ashcans of Endgame, by Samuel Beckett, are home for the parents of Hamm (seated). Nagg, Hamm's father, comes up to ask for "more pap," while Clov, standing, mocks his pleas. From original Parisian production, 1957.

Convention

To these six components of every play we should add a seventh which Aristotle apparently never saw reason to consider as a discrete component: theatrical *convention*. The agreement between audience and actor includes a whole set of tacit understandings that form the context of playwatching, conventions such as "when the curtain goes up, the play begins; when the curtain goes down, the play is over." Many of these conditions are so imbedded in the fabric of the theatregoing experience that we tend to forget about them altogether unless something happens that casts them into relief. Our theatre conventions are most visible when we see them from afar—in contrast to the practices of theatres of other cultures. For example, the conventions of the Japanese Noh Drama decree that major characters enter on a gangway, that choruses sing the lines of characters who are dancing, that hand-held fans are used in certain ways to indicate wind, water, rain, or the rising moon. Patrons of the Noh Drama accept these conventions as unquestioningly as we accept the convention that ten actors at a dinner table on stage will all sit on the same side (that is, all facing the audience), or that, when the stage lights dim, we are to ignore the scurrying about of actors and stagehands during a scene change.

Each play sets up its own system of conventions, but in most cases they accord with the traditions of their times and therefore go largely unnoticed (doubtless that is why Aristotle, familiar with no drama other than his own, made no specific mention of them). In modern times, with playwrights and directors becoming increasingly aware of other traditions and possibilities, more and more play productions seek to employ conventions of ancient times or foreign cultures, and even to establish new ones. Peter Shaffer's *Black Comedy*, which supposedly takes place in the dark, utilizes a convention which Shaffer attributes to the Chinese: when the lights are on they are "off," and when they are off they are "on." Eugene O'Neill's *Strange Interlude* gives us to understand that when the actors freeze and speak, we in the audience—but not the other characters in the play—hear their thoughts. Jean Anouilh's *Antigone* uses a variation on the Greek device of the chorus: a single man speaks with the author's voice as the characters on stage freeze in silence. Lanford Wilson, in *The Rimers of Eldritch*, presents a story in more than a hundred tiny scenes that jump back and forth in time, and only at the play's end do we get any real sense of story line. Arthur Miller's *After The Fall* places an imaginary psychiatrist in the midst of the audience, and the play's protagonist repeatedly interrupts the action of the drama to address his analyst in highly theatrical "therapy" sessions. And so it goes. There is no formal requirement for the establishment of theatrical conventions, except that the audience must "agree" (which it does, of course, unconsciously) to accept them.

These seven components of every play—with the seventh more or less framing Aristotle's six—are the raw material of drama. All are important, and certainly the theatre could not afford to dispense with any one. Some plays are intensive in one or more; most great productions show artistry in all. The *balancing* of these components in theatrical presentation is one of the primary challenges facing the director, who on one occasion may be called upon mainly to clarify and elaborate a theme, on another to find the visual mode of presentation that best supports the characters, on another to develop and "flesh out" the characterizations in order to give strength and meaning to the plot, on another to heighten a musical tone in order to enhance sensual effect, on another to develop the precise convention—the relationship between play and audience—that will maximize the play's artistic impact. For as important as each of these components is to the theatrical experience, it is their combination and interaction, not their individual splendor, which is crucial to a production's success.

The Order of a Play

Plays can also be looked at in terms of their temporal (time) structure. Here again, Aristotle affords some help. He tells us that drama has "a beginning, a middle, and an end," and here and there in his *Poetics* he proffers a little detail about the nature of each of these elements. We can expand Aristotle's list somewhat, for by now a number of fairly consistent features can be distinguished in the organization in time of any theatrical experience.

The Gathering of the Audience

Theorists often either ignore the audience in considering the crucial elements of the theatre, or else dismiss it as a "paratheatrical" (para meaning "only somewhat") concern. The gathering of the audience is, however, an extremely important consideration in the presentation of a play, and it entails a process that is not without its artistic and cultural significance. The chief concerns in that process have to do with publicity, admission, and seating. Each of these concerns has given theatre producers much food for thought since ancient times.

For how does the theatre attract its audience in the first place? Theatregoing, after all, is not a need of mankind in the same way that eating is a need; the population of a society does not spend half its waking hours trying to supply itself with theatre in the way it strives to secure food, shelter, and physical security. Rather the theatre, if it is to survive, must go out and recruit attention; in every era, theatre has had the responsibility of gathering its audience.

Therefore, the goal of every theatre producer is to make his theatre accessible, inviting, and favorably known to the widest possible public—and also, in many eras, to the *richest* possible public—and to make theatre as an art form as thrilling and spiritually *necessary* as it can possibly be.

One of the oldest known ways of publicizing the theatre is by means of a procession. The circus parade, which still takes place in some of the smaller towns of Europe and the United States, is a remnant of a once universal form of advertisement for the performing arts that probably began well in advance of recorded history.

The Greeks of ancient Athens opened their great dramatic festivals with a *proagon* (literally, "pre-action") in which both playwrights and actors were introduced at a huge public meeting and given a chance to speak about the plays they were to present on subsequent days. Today, similar conclaves—usually via television talk shows in this global village of ours—are often used to promote theatrical events to the public at large. The Elizabethans flew flags atop their playhouses on performance days, and the flags could

Going to theatre in Shakespeare's London meant, for most patrons, a trip across the Thames to Bankside, for the large public theatres of the day were not permitted inside the city proper. Here, flags atop theatre buildings indicate where performances are scheduled today.

A priest is about to take his designated place in a stone seat in the first row of the ancient theatre of Athens.

be seen across the Thames in "downtown" London and St. Paul's, enticing hundreds away from their commercial and religious activities. The lighted marquees of Broadway theatres around Times Square and of London theatres in the West End are a modern-day equivalent of the flags that waved over those first great English public theatres.

Developments in the printing and broadcast media have spurred the growth of theatre advertising until it is today a major theatrical craft in its own right. Splendid posters, illustrated programs, multi-color subscription brochures, full-page newspaper advertisements, staged media events, articulate press releases, and even the ubiquitous 30-second television commercial have been employed to summon us out of the comfort of our homes and into the theatre. For premieres, or for openings of new playhouses, giant searchlights are often used to beckon the public to the theatrical location. Far from being an inconsequential aspect of theatre, publicity today occupies a place of fundamental importance in the thinking of theatrical producers, and commands a major share of the budget for commercial theatrical ventures.

Procedures for admitting and seating the audience are usually straightforward and conventional; however they can have important—and occasionally decisive—effects on the overall theatrical presentation.

Ordinarily, theatre is supported at least in part by fees charged the audience. These fees make up what is called the "box office revenue." For commercial theatres, box office revenue provides the sole means of meeting production costs and providing a profit to

investors. The admission charge dates from ancient Greek days, and since then only a few amateur or civic productions (such as the religious pageants of medieval England or the free Shakespeare performances in contemporary New York City) have managed to survive without it.

Seating is frequently determined by the price of admission: the best seats cost the most. What determines "best" and "poorest" seating, however, depends on many things. In modern Broadway and West End theatres, the most costly seats are in the orchestra (known in the West End as "the stalls"), which is the ground-level seating area; balcony seats ordinarily cost less, and the higher the balcony, the smaller the price. In the public theatres of Elizabethan London, however, the ground level (which was standing room) provided the cheapest space, and the "gentlemen's rooms" in the balcony—where one could be seen and visited—commanded up to twelve times as much. In the Restoration period, seats on the stage itself brought the highest prices of all, assuring their purchasers the widest possible personal recognition (but affording a ridiculously poor view of the play's action).

Seating is not always scaled according to price, however. In the Greek drama festivals of ancient Athens, the front row seats were reserved for priests, and members of the lay audience sat in sections of the *theatron* reserved for their particular tribe. In many non-commercial theatres today, the best seats go to those patrons willing to wait longest in line to get them. The National Theatre of England has experimented with a seating system designed to reward the most eager of its fans, not the richest; this practice is common in East European countries. In racially divided countries, audiences are segregated according to the color of their skin. This regrettable practice persisted well into the twentieth century in the United States, and indeed in the 1960s was occasionally revived by "Black Theatre" companies. Perhaps the most radical seating experiments occurred in the "New Theatre" movement of the early 1970s, in which audiences were often led one by one to seats determined in an impromptu interview with one or another of the cast members, acting as ushers. What is more, patrons were sometimes ordered to leave their assigned seats in mid-performance to make room for actors!

The Transition

Gathered, admitted, and seated, the audience remains a collection of individuals preoccupied with their daily concerns. Now the theatre must transform them into a community devoted to the concerns of the play and enmeshed in the actions of imaginary characters. The theatre, in other words, must effect in their awareness a transition from real life to stage life, and it must do so in a smooth and agreeable fashion.

The written program is one modern device (modern in the sense that it dates from the eighteenth century) which helps to prepare the audience for the fiction they are about to see. It gives them the locale and time of the action, the names of the characters and of the actors who impersonate them; in these ways it allows the audience to preview the general scope of the play's environment—spatial, temporal, and personal—and to accept the actors as valid impersonators of the play's characters. Having read that Albert Finney is playing Hamlet, for example, we don't spend playwatching time trying to figure who the lead actor is.

Often music is used, in the contemporary theatre, to set the mood or tone of a play, particularly when the action is set in a certain period in the past. For a musical production, an entire orchestral piece—called the overture—usually precedes any action on stage.

Lobby displays are sometimes used to supplement the written programs, featuring either pictures of the actors or other pictures and documents relevant to the play, its period, its author, and its critical reception. Occasionally the seating area is altered to aid in this transition, sometimes by the addition of wall posters, sometimes by other ornamentation. When no curtain is used, the scenery may be "warmed" by "pre-show" lighting that eases the audience into an expectation of the performance to follow—in some productions that "scenery" includes actors sitting, standing, or lying motionless on the set or engaging in quiet, understated movement. Sometimes slide presentations, songs, or improvised activities take place on stage before the play begins, and the patrons may be asked to participate in some way as they find their way to their seats. Many of these methods date from ancient times; all of them have been used to introduce modern plays to an audience and to prepare the audience to enter the world of the stage.

Finally, a swift new transition to stage life occurs: the play begins. Most often this is a shared moment. The houselights dim and a curtain rises or stage lights come up to reveal a scene. Occasionally this transition is more subtle, and each member of the audience glides into the play at his or her own moment of discovery; a "pre-show" improvisation begins to take on a more pronounced, attention-demanding character, or perhaps some small but seemingly significant alteration galvanizes the consciousness to full attention. Either way the transition is complete. The thinking of the audience shifts from workaday concerns to the characters of the play and their story. This, to use a familiar theatrical term, is "magic time."

The Exposition

No important play has ever begun with a character dashing onstage and shouting "The house is on fire!" At best, such a beginning could only confuse the audience, and at worst it could cause them to flee in panic. For at that point they would have no way of knowing what house, or why they should care about it. Most plays, whatever their style or genre, begin with dialogue or action calculated to ease us, not shock us, into the concerns of the characters with whom we are to spend the next two hours or so.

"Exposition" is a word not much in favor now, coming as it does from an age when play structure was considered more scientific than it is today. But it is still a useful term, referring to the background information the audience must have in order to understand "what's going on" in the action of a play.

In the rather mechanical plotting of the "well-made" plays, the exposition is handled with little fanfare, with a few characters, often servants (minor figures in the action to follow), discussing something that is about to happen, and enlightening each other (and of course the audience) about certain details around which the plot will turn. Consider these lines from the opening scene of Henrik Ibsen's 1884 classic, *The Wild Duck*:

PETTERSEN, in livery, and JENSEN, the hired waiter, in black, are putting the study in order. From the dining room, the hum of conversation and laughter is heard.

PETTERSEN: Listen to them, Jensen; the old man's got to his feet—he's giving a toast to Mrs. Sorby.

JENSEN: (*pushing forward an armchair*) Do you think it's true, then, what they've been saying, that there's something going on between them?

PETTERSEN: God knows.

JENSEN: He used to be quite the lady's man, I understand.

PETTERSEN: I suppose.

JENSEN: And he's giving this party in honor of his son, they say.

PETTERSEN: That's right. His son came home yesterday.

JENSEN: I never even knew old Werle had a son.

PETTERSEN: Oh, he has a son all right. But he's completely tied up at the Hoidal works. In all the years I've been here he's never come into town.

A WAITER: (*In the doorway of the other room*) Pettersen, there's an old fellow here . . .

PETTERSEN: (*mutters*) Damn. Who'd show up at this time of night?

After a few more lines, Pettersen, Jensen, and the waiter make their exits and are seen no more. Their function is purely expository—to pave the way for the principal characters. The conversation they are having is a contrivance intended simply to give us a framework for the action—and the information they impart is presented by means of a conversation among servants only because a convention of realism decrees that words spoken in a play be addressed to characters, not to the audience.

The exposition of non-realistic plays can be handled more directly. It was the Greek custom to begin a play with a prologue preceding the entrance of the chorus and the major play episodes; the prologue was sometimes a scene and sometimes a simple speech to the audience. Shakespeare also used prologues in some of his plays. In one particularly interesting example, Shakespeare's *Henry V*, each of the five acts begins with a character called "Chorus" directly addressing the audience and setting the scene for the act:

CHORUS: O for a Muse of fire, that would ascend
  The brightest heaven of invention!
  A kingdom for a stage, princes to act,
  And monarchs to behold the swelling scene!
  Then should the warlike Harry, like himself,
  Assume the port of Mars, and at his heels
  (Leash'd in, like hounds) should famine, sword, and fire
  Crouch for employment. But pardon, gentles all,
  The flat unraised spirits that hath dar'd
  On this unworthy scaffold to bring forth
  So great an object. Can this cockpit hold
  The vasty fields of France? Or may we cram
  Within this wooden O the very casques
  That did affright the air at Agincourt?
  O, pardon! since a crooked figure may
  Attest in little place a million,
  And let us, ciphers to this great accompt,
  On your imaginary forces work.
  Suppose within the girdle of these walls
  Are now confin'd two mighty monarchies,
  Whose high, upreared, and abutting fronts
  The perilous narrow ocean parts asunder.
  Piece out our imperfections with your thoughts;
  Into a thousand parts divide one man,
  And make imaginary puissance;
  Think, when we talk of horses, that you see them
  Printing their proud hoofs i' th' receiving earth;
  For 'tis your thoughts that now must deck our kings,
  Carry them here and there, jumping o'er times,
  Turning th' accomplishment of many years
  Into an hour-glass: for the which supply,
  Admit me Chorus to this history;
  Who, Prologue-like, your humble patience pray,
  Gently to hear, kindly to judge, our play.

This justly famous prologue establishes setting, characters, and audience expectation of plot in an utterly straightforward manner, and begs the audience's indulgence for the theatrical conventions they will be called upon to entertain.

The Conflict

Now is the time for the character to enter shouting "The house is on fire!"

It is a truism that drama requires conflict; in fact the very word "drama," when used in daily life, implies a situation fraught with conflict. No one writes plays about characters who live every day in unimpaired serenity; no one, quite certainly, would ever choose to watch such a play. Conflict and confrontation are the mechanisms by which a situation becomes dramatic.

Why is this so? Why are conflict situations so theatrically interesting? The reasons have to do with plot, theme, and character. Plot can hold suspense only when it involves alternatives and choices: Macbeth has strong reasons to murder King Duncan and strong reasons not to; if he had only the former or only the latter, he would project no real conflict and we should not consider him such an interesting character. We are fascinated by a character's actions largely in light of the actions he rejects and the stresses he has to endure in making his decisions. In other words, plot entails not only the actions of a play but the inactions—the things that are narrowly rejected and do *not* happen. A character's decision must proceed from powerfully conflicting alternatives if we are to watch his behavior with empathy instead of mere curiosity. In watching a character act, the audience must also watch him *think*; a playwright gets him to think by putting him into conflict.

Conflict can be set up between characters as well as within them; it may be reducible to one central situation or it may evolve out of many. Whatever the case, conflict throws characters into relief and permits the audience to see deeply into the human personality. To see a character at war with himself or in confrontation with another, is to see how that character *works*, and this is the key to our caring.

The theme of a play is ordinarily a simple abstraction of its central conflict. In Sophocles' *Antigone*, for example, the theme is the conflict between divine law and civil law; in *Death of a Salesman* it is the conflict between Willy's reality and his dreams. Conflicts are plentiful in farces and comedies as well—the conflicts inherent in the "eternal triangle," for example, have provided comic material for dramatists for the last two millennia. Many of the more abstract philosophical conflicts—independence versus duty, individuality versus conformity, idealism versus pragmatism, integrity versus efficiency, pleasure versus propriety, progress versus tradition, to name a few—suggest inexhaustible thematic conflicts that appear in various guises in both ancient and contemporary plays.

The playwright introduces conflict early in a play, often by means of an "inciting incident" in which one character poses a conflict or confrontation either to another character or to himself. For example:

FIRST WITCH: All hail, Macbeth, hail to thee, Thane of Glamis!
SECOND WITCH: All hail, Macbeth, hail to thee, Thane of Cawdor!
THIRD WITCH: All hail, Macbeth, that shalt be King hereafter!
BANQUO: Good sir, why do you start, and seem to fear Things that do sound so fair?

In this, the inciting incident of Shakespeare's *Macbeth* (which follows two brief expository scenes), a witch confronts Macbeth with the prediction that he will be king, thereby posing an alternative that Macbeth has apparently already considered, judging from the startled response that elicits Banquo's comment.

Once established, conflict is intensified to crisis, usually by a series of incidents, investigations, revelations, and confrontations which the playwright creates. Sometimes even non-events serve to intensify a conflict. Such is certainly the case in the modern classic, *Waiting for Godot*, in which two characters simply wait, through two hour-long acts, for the arrival of a third who never comes. Indeed, with this play, Samuel Beckett virtually rewrote the book on playwriting technique by showing how time alone, when properly managed, can do the job of heightening and developing conflict in a dramatic situation.

The Climax

Conflict cannot be intensified indefinitely. In a play as in life, when conflict becomes insupportable, something has to give. Thus every play, be it comic, tragic, farcical, or melodramatic, culminates in some sort of dramatic explosion.

Aristotle described that dramatic explosion, in tragedy, as a *catharsis*, or purification. Aristotle's conception is susceptible to various interpretations, but it has been widely accepted and broadly influential for centuries. According to Aristotle's system, the catharsis is the crucial axis in the structure of tragedy, evolving out of the tragic hero's recognition (*anagnorisis*) of some fundamental truth, and his consequent reversal (*peripeteia*) of some former ignorance, such as a horrific deed unknowingly performed (*pathos*). The catharsis releases the audience's pity, and thereby permits the fullest experience of tragic pleasure, washing away, as it were, the terror that has been mounting steadily during the play's tragic course. Such catharsis as accompanies Oedipus' gouging out his own eyes as he recognizes his true self illustrates the extreme theatrical explosion of which the classical Greek tragic form is capable.

For any dramatic form, the climax is the conflict of a play taken to its most extreme; it is the moment of maximum tension. At the climax, a continuation of the conflict becomes unbearable, impossible: some sort of change is mandated. Climaxes in modern plays do not as a rule involve death or disfiguration (although there are exceptions: Peter Shaffer's celebrated *Equus* reaches its climax with the blinding of six horses, and Edward Albee's *The Zoo Story* climaxes with one character impaling himself on a knife held by another); however, they inevitably contain elements of recognition and reversal if not of catharsis, and usually the major conflicts of the play are resolved by one or more of these.

The Denouement

The climax is followed, and the play concluded, by an element that is known as the denouement, or resolution, in which a final action or speech, or even a single word or gesture, indicates that the passions aroused by the play's action are now stilled and a new harmony or understanding has been reached.

The tenor of the denouement tends to change with the times. In the American theatre of the 1950s and 1960s, for example, the sentimental and message-laden denouement was the rule: in Robert Anderson's *Tea and Sympathy*, a teacher's wife prepares to prove to a sensitive boy that he is not homosexual; in Dore Schary's *Sunrise at Campobello*, a future American president makes his way on crippled legs to a convention platform. In the current theatre, in this existential age which looks with suspicion on tidy virtues and happy endings, more ironic and ambiguous denouements are to be expected. The current theatre also provides less in the way of purgation than do more classical modes; that is doubtless because the conflicts raised by the best of contemporary drama are not amenable to wholesale relief. But a denouement still must provide at least some lucidity concerning the problems raised by the play, some vision or metaphor of a deeper and more permanent understanding. Perhaps the final lines of *Waiting for Godot* best represent the denouement of the current age:

ESTRAGON: Well, shall we go?
VLADIMIR: Yes, let's go.
They do not move.

The Curtain Call

The last staged element of a theatrical presentation is the curtain call, in which the actors bow and the audience applauds. This convention, which has been customary in the theatre at least since the time of the Romans, plays an important but often overlooked role in the overall scope of theatrical presentation.

The curtain call is *not* simply a time for the actors to receive congratulations from the audience, although many actors today seem to think it is. Historically, it is a time in which the actors show their respect for the audience which patronizes them. And aesthetically, it is a time in which the audience allows itself to see the other side of the "paradox of acting." The curtain call liberates the audience from the world of the play, and when there is no curtain call audiences are palpably distressed and often disgruntled. For it fulfills the last provision, so to speak, in the mutual agreement that characterizes the theatre itself—the agreement by which the audience agrees to view the actors as the characters the actors have agreed to impersonate. It is at the curtain call that actors and audience can acknowledge their mutual belonging in the human society, can look each other in the eye and say, in effect, "We all know what it is to experience these things we've just seen performed, we must all try to understand life a little better, we have enjoyed coming this far together, we are with you, we like you." In the best theatre, this communication is a powerful experience.

The Aftermath: Criticism

What follows the curtain call? The dispersal of the audience, of course, and, most significantly, conversation. Theatre, a public event, lends itself well to public commentary. After the theatre, in restaurants, bars, and coffee houses or simply walking or riding home, theatregoing companions get together and talk. The theatre is intellectually and emotionally stimulating, and good talk is one of the products it stimulates: talk about the play's story, the skills of the performers, the artistry of the direction and design, the significance and validity of the playwright's theme. Persons who see a play together like to compare their reactions to test their observations and weigh their opinions in the give and take of provocative discussion. This, to be sure, is one of the great rewards of theatre attendance.

The formalization of post-play conversation is known as dramatic criticism. Even small towns have their recognized "drama critics," commentators whose reviews of plays focus the main lines of community reaction and provide, it is hoped, an especially well-informed point of view. Their published remarks are likely to carry great weight, not only with those planning to attend productions under review, but with those who, having already attended, wish to compare their own reactions to those of an "expert."

Theatre practitioners have always had an uneasy relationship with professional drama critics. The critics' support is crucial to the welfare of the theatre as a whole, but their selective scorn can spell instant doom for a play or a performer. The reaction of the New York critics, particularly those who write for the prestigious *New York Times*, has been held to be the single most important factor in the success or failure of any Broadway production. Whether this assertion is true or not, there is no question that most New York theatre people get very nervous in the presence of a major critic.

At its highest levels, dramatic criticism is an art form in its own right. The finest critical works tell us a great deal about the nature of theatre itself. Aristotle's *Poetics*, for example, is a masterpiece of analysis that has guided Western theatre for countless generations. Goethe, Coleridge, Shaw, Nietzsche, and Sartre have all made significant contributions when they lent their minds to the writing of dramatic criticism, and many specialists in our own times are justly revered among theatre artists for their insights into this complex human endeavor. Nonetheless, we should be aware that the most sophisticated dramatic criticism has something in common with the post-play conversation of ordinary theatregoers; for everyone who attends the theatre, and then talks about it afterwards, is a participant in the critical process.

THE ANALYSIS OF PLAYS

Our breakdown of plays in two different dimensions—horizontal and vertical slicings, as it were—reveals a remarkable similarity of analytical categories from Aristotle's day to our own. There is obviously some fundamental logic to such categories, and of course they can be of great use when we wish to compare one play with another, or to assess the structure, meaning, or importance of a single theatrical work.

Nonetheless, we must again stress the need for caution in analyzing a play by categories, lest any of its parts—or even the sum of the parts—be mistaken for the whole of drama. Quintessentially, drama is synthesis: it is an art of integration and collaboration. Moreover, drama lives in production rather than on the printed page, for it is an activity of art rather than an object of art.

In the chapters that follow, we shall use the tools of theatre analysis to stimulate understanding, emotional involvement, and appreciation, but analysis should never be seen as a final goal. For theatre is meant to be an immediate experience, accessible primarily to the moment. What is more, the greatest theatre has always been addressed to the general public, not to specialists—and it has always managed to work its magic without the analytic skills or theories of self-proclaimed or world-proclaimed experts. If we do find ourselves doing some surgery on the plays discussed in the following pages, let us continually be reminded that it is only exploratory: the patient must always survive.

II

The Past

WHY include in a study of the theatre an examination of its past?

Because today's theatre rests solidly on that past, which extends back at least five thousand years and is filled with grand experiments, great traditions, and superb achievements.

Because, moreover, the theatre's past still lives. It lives in the revival of great plays that continue to thrill audiences around the world; and it lives in the hearts and minds and everyday experiences of all whose lives are engaged in the production of current, contemporary theatrical art.

The theatre is a conservative art. It hangs on to its past, perennially scavenging for material, for effects, for dramatic structures, for great conflicts, great characters, and great events.

Each new theatre form develops out of the discoveries of its predecessors, and often that development is quite consciously cultivated. A classic comedy by Plautus serves as the basis for a Shakespearean play seventeen hundred years later, which in turn becomes an American musical comedy four hundred years after that. A Roman tragedy becomes a Molière comedy in the seventeenth century and then a French fantasy in the twentieth. Every year, literally hundreds of plays are directly inspired by hundreds of predecessors.

More indirectly, separate moments, patterns, and components of contemporary theatre develop—mostly unconsciously—from past models. The climax of Sophocles's tragedy *Oedipus Tyrannos*, in which the protagonist blinds himself, is echoed in the equally horrific climax of Peter Shaffer's contemporary play *Equus*; the stunning *parabasis* of Greek comedy, in which the chorus suspends the play's action to speak directly to the audience about political matters, becomes an important dramaturgical device in the "alienated" theatre of Bertolt Brecht. More and more, the conventions of the theatre's past are coming forth to freshen and vivify the present; and often those who most avidly look backward for direction are the most avant-garde theatre artists of our time.

Like a tree, the theatre draws much of its nourishment through its roots for all that is manifest above. In studying the past, then, we are not investigating dead things—antiques and oddities and moldering bones—but rather we are seeking to understand the vitality of the theatre in every age.

The theatre had its beginnings well before recorded history. For whole millennia in the ancient world of Egypt and Mesopotamia, Babylonia and Mycenae, however, we have no texts, no pictures, no records other than cryptic references to seasonal rituals carried out by priests in honor of worshipped gods. It is the more "immediate" twenty-five hundred years, the years from the sixth century B.C. to the nineteenth century of our present era, which provide us with the body of known drama and reported theatrical activity that we call the theatre's past. This epoch is detailed in the next four chapters; the theatre of our present century (actually since about 1875) will be dealt with in section III.

It is not our purpose in these four chapters to give a comprehensive survey of the many periods of past theatrical achievement, much less to name the hundreds of authors and thousands of plays known to have contributed to that achievement. Nor shall we undertake to discuss the hundreds of controversies that scholars continue to wage over details of theatrical production in the periods under study.

Our concern here is simply to present a speculative reconstruction of four particularly splendid and interesting times and places from the theatre's past—classical Greece, York of the Middle Ages, England in the Renaissance, and France at the court of Louis XIV—and to make mention of certain other related developments which took place at more or less the same time. "Speculative" is, of course, a necessary qualification, for although some of the playtexts of each of these eras have come down to us reasonably intact, the details of performance were rarely recorded. Hence, any historical reconstruction must rest on fragmentary and often contradictory evidence.

In the coming pages the reader should strive primarily to get a *feeling* of what it meant to produce theatre and to go to the theatre in those times, rather than to discern precisely who did what and when and where and how the curtain fell. We don't quite know the reality and we almost certainly never shall, but we *can* develop a general understanding of the main lines of theatrical effort and the theatrical spirit of those times and places, and we can certainly explore the *possibilities* of theatre as they have variously been attempted throughout the ages. These understandings—of the theatre's aims and its spirit and its possibilities—are the choicest fruits of theatrical research, for they bring us close to the sources of the theatre's enduring vitality.

The Tragic Mask, perhaps the best-known symbol of the Greek theatre. Masks were worn throughout the performance for both comedies and tragedies.

THE GREEKS

T he known history of the Western theatre begins in ancient Greece; that fact alone should suffice to compel our interest. Even more compelling, however, is the fact that the theatre of classical Greece still stands as a monumental artistic achievement—indeed, in many estimations, as an achievement that has never been surpassed.

THE GREEK THEATRE

When theatre historians speak of the "Greek theatre," they are speaking specifically of the theatre of just one locale, Athens, and of just one century, the fifth century B.C. For that span of one hundred years, in a city-state of no more than 150,000 persons, the Athenian population was treated to a theatrical life that was unparalleled in its social importance and aesthetic majesty. Among the contributors to this art form were four of the most brilliant playwrights of all time—Aeschylus, Sophocles, Euripides, and Aristophanes—and the theatre they helped to cre-

ate featured a magnificent and vigorous blend of myth, legend, philosophy, social commentary, poetry, dance, music, public participation, and visual splendor. The heroes of Greek drama have become archetypes in the modern mind, and their actions and examples occupy a major place in our collective cultural endowment. Surviving from the period are forty-three intact plays plus many play fragments and titles of other works, one great piece of criticism (Aristotle's *Poetics*, written in the following century), the archeological remnants of several theatres (also of somewhat later date, but built on the foundations of fifth-century theatres), and numerous anecdotes and commentaries. Taken together, these treasures constitute a record that lets us envision and comprehend the basic experience of the Greek theatre, a theatre at once vastly different from our own and yet seminal to contemporary developments.

In order to best capture the spirit of the Greeks, we must first rid ourselves of a body of misperceptions that have cluttered our knowledge of the Greek theatre at least since the nineteenth century. Victorian revivals of Greek drama suggest a theatre in which white-robed actors strutted ceremonially through white marble buildings uttering sonorous and sententious speeches about morality. This false vision of Greek civilization and art was doubtless inspired in part by the pristine color of Greek ruins, whose original brilliant colors have completely washed away with centuries of weathering. But why several generations of neo-classicists and scholars contributed to the deception is somewhat of a mystery. The theatre of the ancient Greeks was in fact as far from that pallid, stiff Victorian model as could possibly be imagined. It was a spectacle of loud music, vivid colors, and vigorous dancing; it was regularly bawdy, frequently obscene, and often blasphemous, hilarious, scandalous, and carnal; it was always passionate and controversial. Although it is true that in the surviving plays acts of violence always occur off stage, there is reason to believe that this is less a result of rigid convention than a reflection of the sensibilities of later librarians, many of them medieval monks,

who determined which plays would survive and which would not; in any event, both the comic and tragic Greek theatres were firmly rooted in the violence of life, and both persistently and intensely examined the social and ethical aspects of war, murder, lust, and betrayal.

Origins and Evolution

The Greek theatre had its origins in religion, but the Greek religion bore little similarity to the religions of the Western world today. It was a polytheistic religion, and its deities were much more inclined to be belligerent than benevolent. When they were not at war with mankind—which they often were—they were doing battle with one another. Unlike the modern worshipper who looks to a higher power for succor and salvation, the ancient Greek thought of his gods as

The Dithyramb: a conjectural reconstruction. Only a few facts are known about this primitive Greek rite, believed to be a precursor to tragedy; only a few fragments of texts survive. Fifty priest-performers participated in these choric praises of the god Dionysus.

meddlers and disrupters, and the "prayer" of the ancient world was basically an attempt at appeasement rather than a plea for aid. "May the eye inescapable of the mighty gods not look on me" is the great choral cry of Aeschylus' *Prometheus Bound*. It echoes the dread of the gods which underlay all ritual in Greek religion.

The theatre at Athens was dedicated to one god in particular: Dionysus, the god of fertility (hence also the god of wine, agriculture, and sexuality); it was at the annual festival of Dionysus that new dramas were first publicly performed. Apart from drama, the festival of Dionysus featured a week of public wine drinking and phallus worshipping that would today be considered a religious orgy. Something of the sort is actually portrayed in the last known Greek tragedy, Euripides' *The Bacchae*, and it is a terrifying event in which human bodies are torn asunder (a fantasy much in keeping with celebrations of Dionysus, who is himself torn asunder in Greek legend). The early ties

between the theatre and this extraordinary celebration of fertility provide a crucial insight into the basic forces at work in the theatrical experience.

The advance of the Greeks over other known civilizations of that time has been attributed in part to the Greek conception that the gods had human form—that is, they were not giant birds, suns, or turtles (although they apparently could assume such forms at will). As a corollary to this concept, the Greeks, like most of the monotheists who came later, considered themselves to be created in the image of gods. This notion invited human impersonation of the gods, and it was not long before the impersonator came to be seen as a creature halfway between the divine and earthly realms. Anthropologists call one who enjoys that halfway status a *shaman*—which means a religious leader who is accredited with an understanding of the superhuman and has the authority to reveal it to the masses.

Euripides' tragedy The Bacchae *is often seen as a link between ancient dithyramb and tragedy because it harks back in many ways to the origins of tragedy. It is the only surviving tragedy from the Greek classic period in which Dionysus appears as a character, and it ends with a ghastly sequence in which a young man (Pentheus) is torn to pieces by his mother (Agave), who acts under the spell of Dionysus. The tearing apart, or* sparagmos, *recalls the dismemberment of Dionysus in legend. Here, Agave holds head of her murdered son in contemporary production of the play by Théâtre National de l'Odéon in Paris, directed by Michel Cacoyannis (1977).*

THE THYRSUS...

A procession of satyrs and other players. The thyrsus, *a staff twined in ivy and tipped by a pine cone, was carried by the followers of Dionysus.*

What might be called the Greek version of shamanism developed in the prehistory of theatre as the *choric dithyramb*. This was a ritual of rural origin in which fifty priests clad in goatskins danced around a huge phallus erected in the middle of a circle of level earth and chanted odes to the god Dionysus in the presence of an audience of spectators. This ritual apparently occurred all over Greece each spring (at the time of the rebirth of the crops). The circle of earth was probably a threshing circle of the kind still used throughout the Greek peninsula for stamping wheat with the feet to separate the grain from the chaff. The dithyramb was unquestionably a drunken ceremony, for drinking was a part of the religiosity of the celebration; there is also evidence that the celebrants ate hallucinogenic mushrooms. Bulls were torn apart in sacrifice, in commemoration of Dionysus' legendary dismemberment, and the spectators undoubtedly participated in the ritual in some manner.

By the end of the seventh century (that is, by about 600 B.C.) written versions of the dithyrambic text appeared, with authorship occasionally attributed (to, among others, one Archilocus of Paros and one Arion of Corinth); the chant proved to be a dance-rhythm poem in trochaic tetrameter. Competitions between various Dionysian cults were held in regional centers at about this time. By the middle of the sixth century, the ritual had been adopted in Athens as a week-long festival of choric dithyrambs, sacrifices, drinking, and ecstatic revels involving the whole of the flowering Athenian civilization in an outpouring of fervor on behalf of a once obscure god. The persistence of inebriation as a part of the choric dithyramb at this time is made clear by a statement of Archilocus: "I know how to lead the fair song of Dionysus, the dithyramb, only when my wits are fused with wine." Long after the Greek theatre had developed the sophistication which commands our respect today, dithyrambs were

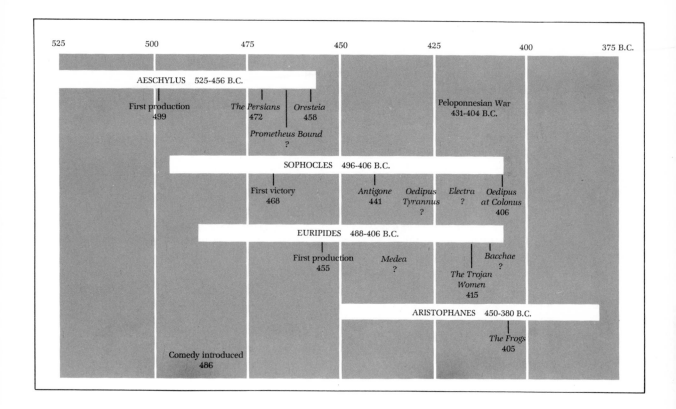

525	500	475	450	425	400	375 B.C.

AESCHYLUS   525-456 B.C.

First production
499

The Persians
472

Oresteia
458

Prometheus Bound
?

Peloponnesian War
431-404 B.C.

SOPHOCLES   496-406 B.C.

First victory
468

Antigone
441

Oedipus
Tyrannus
?

Electra
?

Oedipus
at Colonus
406

EURIPIDES   488-406 B.C.

First production
455

Medea
?

The Trojan
Women
415

Bacchae
?

ARISTOPHANES   450-380 B.C.

The Frogs
405

Comedy introduced
486

still being produced in the theatre at Athens—in fact, they continued up to the very end of the golden age of Athenian civilization.

What did those drunken, improvised, gory chant-dances performed around great phallic monuments by goatskin-clad primitives have to do with the noble verse tragedies of the classic Greek theatre? Aristotle tells us that "tragedy . . . which was at first mere improvisation . . . originating with the dithyramb . . . advanced by slow degrees. Each new element that showed itself was in turn developed. Having passed through many changes, it found its natural form and there it stopped." Aristotle further explains that comedy originated in "phallic songs which are still in use in many of our cities." Aristotle's brevity on the subject of this evolution indicates he knew little about the steps or processes it involved, and indeed many scholars have questioned his entire premise. But the similarities between dithyramb and tragedy (as well as between phallic song, as we can imagine it, and comedy) seem clear enough, and are both suggestive and illuminating.

The Classic Period

By the time the record grows sharper, which is at the beginning of the fifth century B.C., Greek drama consists of two quite dissimilar forms: the ever popular comedy, and the *tetralogy* (four-play sequence), which is now central to the theatrical and spiritual culture. It is this tetralogy which will attract the greatest attention in later times, for it includes the great works of Greek tragedy and best reveals the peculiar genius of the Greek literary mind.

Originally, the tetralogy consisted of three plot-related tragedies—three serious and interrelated plays concerning gods, demigods, and great historical figures—followed by a *satyr play*, which was a grotesque travesty of the three preceding tragedies. This format remains uniquely Greek, for no subsequent theatre artist or movement has ever sought to duplicate or revive it; indeed, it remains essentially *early* Greek, for as the period went on, the outer form was retained but the inner form was abandoned. Unfortunately, no complete early tetralogies have come down to us. By the middle of the fifth century—from which most of the surviving plays date—the tetralogy was usually only a technical arrangement of three tragedies that were either independent of each other in plot and/or theme or only loosely associated, with the satyr play retained as a more or less vestigial remnant of the integrated tetralogy of earlier days.

The satyr play, which in the classic period featured satyrs dressed in goatskins—followers of Dionysus—was perhaps the closest of all the components of the tetralogy to the dithyrambic form of previous centuries. It has been suggested that by the time of Aeschylus and Sophocles the satyr play was retained as a favor (or appeasement) to the sponsor, Dionysus—much as "The Star-Spangled Banner" is played today at sporting events in the United States, or as "God Save the Queen" was played, until recently, prior to theatrical performances in Great Britain. Although Greek tragedy is less obviously related to Dionysian worship, links can be seen today in its name (the Greek work for "tragedy" is *tragōidia*, meaning "goat song"), and its use of singing and dancing choral practices that had counterparts in the performance of the dithyramb.

The greatest difference between the dithyramb and the tragedy/satyr plays was, of course, the appearance in the latter of the actor. This development is attributed to Thespis, an Icarian of whom little is known save that he is said to have been the first to move out of the dithyrambic chorus and assume the role of "answerer," or *hypokrites* (the first word for "actor"). Thespis' bold move introduced into the old singing, dancing, chanting performance the crucial elements of impersonation and enactment. Thespis is also credited with the invention of the mask: this simple device—and the early masks were indeed simple, made plainly of undyed linen—enabled Thespis to portray not one but a number of "characters," in series, engaged in discussions and debates with the chorus. Now a whole story could unfold through the revelation—in action and dialogue instead of in recitation—of numerous points of view. The theatre as we

know it was born. In the year 534 B.C., the ancient chroniclers tell us, it was Thespis who walked off with the first prize in the first tragedy contest in the City Dionysia of Athens.

We have none of the plays of Thespis; in fact, we have precious little writing of any kind from the theatre of the sixth century—only scraps, and most of them of anonymous origin. But we know that except for a few seemingly modest but significant changes, the sixth-century format of the Greek tragedy/satyr tetralogy remained intact. Aeschylus made a significant innovation in the fifth century when he increased the number of actors to two, allowing for dialogue among characters; Sophocles later added a third actor, allowing for "overheard" dialogue situations and more subtle and complex character interactions. By the time of Aeschylus the dithyrambic chorus was reduced to twelve; Sophocles increased it to fifteen. The bawdiness, drunkenness, and scatalogical motifs that pervaded the early rituals probably increased in the satyr plays as they were removed from the tragedies. And of course the internal structure of the tragedies changed enormously during the fifth century as the grand mythic retellings of Aeschylus gave way to the tightly plotted character dramas of Sophocles and the savagely fascinating complexities of Euripides. Still, the tragedy/satyr tetralogy established in the mid-sixth century remained essentially unchanged in form: a limited number of masked characters, a singing and dancing chorus, and a triad of tragedies followed by a satyr piece. Apparently no later "reforms" in the classic period affected these essential elements, and yet the entire format disappeared with the end of the Greek era.

The form of *comedy* that prevailed in the Greek theatre of the fifth century seems to have developed somewhat later than the tragedy/satyr form, and seems to reflect little if any religious origin; moreover, unlike the tragedy/satyr format, the comedy seems amazingly contemporary. Now called Old Comedy to distinguish it from developments of later centuries, it appears to us audacious, sexy, and unabashedly political. It is also astonishingly scatalogical, so much so that until quite recent times few of the surviving plays—all by the author Aristophanes—were considered fit material for translation or publication. The Greek comedy was presented at the City Dionysia from 486 onward, sometimes following the performance of a tetralogy, sometimes on separate days. It was presented at many other festivals as well, including the *Lenaea*, or feast of the wine vats, held in Athens in mid winter during the dormant trade season.

The *Theatron*

The physical features of Athenian theatres of the classic age derived directly from the dithyrambic ceremonies of earlier times. The staging area was essentially a large circle on the ground: the *orchestra* ("dancing-place"), a direct descendant of the rural threshing circle. Although some scholars maintain that the monumental phallus remained in the center of the orchestra, it seems more likely that this was replaced early in the theatre's history by a simple altar, or *thymele*. The audience sat on semicircular tiers of seats dug into a hillside adjoining the orchestra: the hillside seating was called the *theatron*, or "seeing-place." By the beginning of the fifth cen-

Two early phases of Greek theatre development. The orchestra, *a circular playing space, was the major feature of the physical Greek theatre.*

During most of the fifth century, the form of the Greek theatre was an architectural evocation of the function of drama in Greek society. The performance evolved out of society as a manifestation of the public will, a corporate act. The actors were hardly specialist professionals in the modern sense. Although they had mastered a special craft, they were still members of the general public, with wider duties and allegiances. . . . There was as yet no conception of the theatre as an all-absorbing profession, with the participants sharply distinguished from the spectators. This is best signified by the nature of the chorus, for a long time the most important element in the drama, and drawn from the public at large. The average citizen might have been a spectator one year and a participant the next.

Such a theatre produces active spectators. There is one vital difference between the Greek conception of theatre-in-the-round and ours. In the Greek situation, the audience was totally visible. . . . The players could see the audience, and, more important, the audience could see itself. It was conscious of its own presence.

Thus we see operating in the theatre the same factors that governed the conduct of public worship or the workings of Athenian democracy. The Greek concept of worship was not that of an active priest preaching to a passive multitude, nor was democratic government interpreted as meaning the handing down of edicts from the governing body (albeit popularly elected) to the governed. In both activities the entire public was spiritedly involved. Nor did the Greek theatrical concept envisage a passive audience. In all three spheres—less distinct, in any case, than in our world—the public was an active partner, free to comment, assist, and intervene. The very form of the theatre was reminiscent of the places of public assembly and induced the same responses. We observe, in consequence, that many Greek plays are little more than staged debates, with the audience hearing each side in turn as the Athenian audience was accustomed to listen to rival orators on the Pnyx, across the valley from the theatre, where the assembly met.

Peter D. Arnott

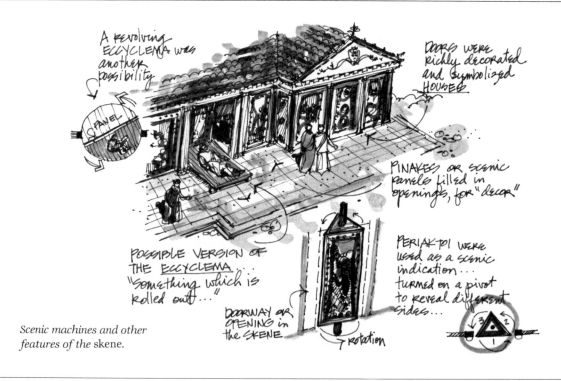

Scenic machines and other features of the skene.

THE EARLY SCENE BUILDING WAS MADE OF WOOD, AND WAS BRIGHTLY PAINTED & DECORATED... PARTLY DUE TO A GREAT INTEREST IN PAINTING OF LANDSCAPE and PERSPECTIVE...

DOORWAYS AT THE REAR ALLOWED ENTRANCES and EXITS AT VARIOUS "HOUSES" OR LOCALES...

OPEN AREAS of the COLONNADE WERE EVENTUALLY FILLED IN IN VARIOUS WAYS TO SUGGEST CERTAIN "SCENIC BACKGROUNDS"

A conjectural reconstruction of the fifth-century skene. *No longer a "hut" but not yet a marble building (that was to come a century later), this structure served as a basic background area for all productions. Later versions of the* skene *were constructed with two levels.*

tury, wooden bleachers made the seating more comfortable; later, stone theatrons were built, some of which survive today in remarkably good condition. A wooden changing room, called a *skene*, was located on the other side of the orchestra, opposite the hillside, and actors (but not the chorus) could enter the orchestra through its door, or perhaps doors. Since the word *skene* originally meant something like "hut" or "tent," we must imagine this structure was originally small and unimposing in appearance; however, it was eventually enlarged sufficiently to permit some scenes to take place on its roof. Many scholars today conjecture that a slightly raised forestage also was added to the front of the skene, together with a few steps leading down to the orchestra below, to enhance the acting area.

And that was it for the theatre "building" of the classic period. The elaborate stone and marble struc-tures that survive at several Mediterranean sites today all date from later periods, and none of our grand reconstructions, such as the Hearst Theatre in Berkeley and the Greek Theatre in Los Angeles, bear significant resemblance to what was seen in Greece in the classic period. There was, of course, no representational scenery, no curtain, no fly gallery, no lighting apparatus. There were some stage "machines," but they were of a rudimentary sort, consisting of rolling platforms that were apparently used to display corpses and immobile tableaux, and cranes to hoist visiting and departing "gods." We know that there were also pivoting prisms, called *periaktoi*, and that Sophocles introduced panels of abstractly painted scenery called *pinakes*, but the precise appearance and function of both of these features is unclear, and their importance to the overall staging is generally assumed to be incidental rather than fundamental.

THE <u>CHITON</u> was the basic dress, worn long by women, short by men...

TIES

extra fold sewn-in

A large patterned cloak: the <u>HIMATION</u> was draped over the shoulder

Most costumes were very colorful, with many decorative patterns...

THE <u>CHLAMYS</u> ... a very short cloak sometimes tied under the arm

Head-dress & hair-style (ONKOS) and footwear (KOTHURNOI) also had theatrical significance

Some representative costumes. Paid for by the choregus, *Greek costumes were lavish, ornate, and colorful.*

The Spectacle

The true spectacle of Greek theatre consisted in what we today would call its costuming, and in acting, dancing, and music. The Greek tragic actors—always male—were costumed in brilliantly colored full-length robes, called *chitons*, which were often supplemented by tunics (either the long *himation* or the shorter *chlamys*) that served primarily for character differentiation. Realism was never the controlling aspect of the Greek tragic costume. Masks, which were of carved wood during the classic era, were full faced, richly painted, and highly stylized, extending up to fanciful wiggings called *onkoi* (singular *onkos*).

Both *onkoi* and the actors' footwear, called *kothurnoi* (singular *kothurnus*), eventually were exaggerated in scale to give the actor the appearance of considerable height. In later ages, the *onkos* and *kothurnus* together became symbols of the tragedian's art.

Comic and satyric costume differed substantially from the tragic dress, being at once more realistic (in comedy) and more obscene (in both). Simulated partial nudity was a notable feature of both comic and satyric costuming—and much of this simulation would be considered shocking to audiences even today. The *phallus* (representing both penis and testicles) was blatantly displayed in costumes for both dramatic forms, and a tail seems to have adorned the goatskin

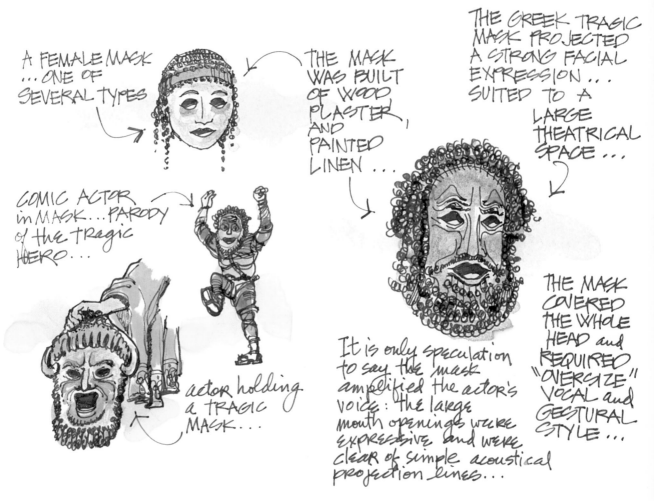

A FEMALE MASK ...ONE OF SEVERAL TYPES

THE MASK WAS BUILT OF WOOD, PLASTER, AND PAINTED LINEN ...

THE GREEK TRAGIC MASK PROJECTED A STRONG FACIAL EXPRESSION... SUITED TO A LARGE THEATRICAL SPACE...

COMIC ACTOR in MASK...PARODY of the TRAGIC HERO...

actor holding a TRAGIC MASK...

It is only speculation to say the mask amplified the actor's voice: the large mouth openings were expressive and were clear of simple acoustical projection lines...

THE MASK COVERED THE WHOLE HEAD and REQUIRED "OVERSIZE" VOCAL and GESTURAL STYLE...

A variety of Greek masks from the fifth century B.C.

THE SATYR PLAY

The satyr play is one of the most puzzling dramatic forms ever to come down to us through history. Its lifetime in the theatre of ancient Greece was as long as that of tragedy, but its origins, aims, and ultimate significance all remain somewhat obscure. Unquestionably comic in tone and entertaining to the audiences of its time, it attracted little attention from manuscript preservers: only one fairly complete satyr play remains—the *Cyclops* of Euripides—together with a long fragment of *The Bloodhounds* by Sophocles. A sample of the dialogue from the latter makes clear the generally ribald, jocular tone of the satyr plays:

FIRST SEMICHORUS:

    1. Hey, satyrs, what can this be?

    2. So big and brown?

    3. It's stinking terribly! You can smell it all around!

SECOND SEMICHORUS:

    1. Here, just take it in your hand!

    2. Do you see what we've got?

    3. Oh, we've really had it. It's cattle turds, that's what!

And then, according to the dialogue, the ordure is thrown about the stage—at the god Apollo, at a nymph named Cyllene, and among the chorus of satyrs themselves. Numerous graphic illustrations of satyr plays, including those found on a magnificent painted vase now in the Naples museum, amply convey the spirit of satyric drama.

FLUTE PLAYER

SATYRS, AS FOLLOWERS OF DIONYSUS, WOULD MOCK OTHER MYTHIC FIGURES

SATYR PERFORMANCE INCLUDED SPECIALIZED COMIC-DEMONIC DANCE FORMS

THYMELE

AN EXPERIMENT with a mask for showing TWO EMOTIONS... according to the side facing the audience...

MASK OF OLD WOMAN...

"SLAVE"

"CITIZEN"

Some masks from the "New Comedy" of later Greek times (fourth century B.C.) New Comedy dealt mainly with domestic subjects, and the masks tended toward social satire and theatrical whimsy.

garb of the satyric actors. The masks for comedy performers, as one might expect, were designed to amuse, often representing absurdly deformed human faces, occasionally representing animals, birds, or insects, and sometimes caricaturing celebrities such as Socrates and Euripides.

The costumes and masks of the classic drama are portrayed in numerous surviving illustrations, mainly from vase paintings made in the fourth century. While these illustrations are not entirely accurate—the vase paintings are themselves stylizations—they give ample evidence of a vigorous aesthetic and a striking theatrical splendor in the staging elements of the fifth-century drama in Athens.

We are on much shakier ground when we try to reconstruct the music, dancing, and acting which were equally crucial to the spectacle, for no records can help us recover the process of an Athenian performance. The music is entirely lost; however, we know the names of its various modes—Dorian, Lydian, Ionian, Aeolian, and Phrygian—and many of the emotional

qualities with which these modes were associated (heroic, lyric, elegiac, and so forth). The dances were equally varied. There were grave dances, exalted ones, ecstatic ones, and hugely comic ones—each separately designated, and each obviously demanding great artistry in execution. Taken all together, the evidence suggests a musical and choreographic sophistication beyond that generally expected today for scripted, text-intensive drama.

The sensual impact of the acting in these spectacular productions, particularly in the tragedies, can only be imagined as a combination of the known elements: flowing robes, singing male voices emanating from mouth-holes in wooden masks, steady dancing movements, and the famed pure light of Greece ever present over all. The resulting theatrical style indeed must have been quite unlike any that has been seen since.

The Greek plays were presented at festivals, most of which lasted several days. The annual week-long City Dionysia at Athens, the grand festival of the era,

A Greek dancer. Dance was an essential element of religious worship as well as of theatrical presentation.

was a competition (virtually everything the Greeks did involved competition), and the main contest in that competition was between the three playwrights who contributed a tragedy/satyr tetralogy apiece. The three tetralogies to be performed each year were chosen in advance by civic authorities (primarily by the *archon*, or mayor), and each playwright whose work was selected was assigned a wealthy producer (the *choregus*) who was required to provide funds for costumes, instruction (rehearsal), and other necessaries of production. Most business came to a halt during the Dionysia to allow virtually every citizen to attend the spectacle. On the first day (the *proagon*, or "before-action," this day was called), introductory ceremonies

AN ARISTOPHANIC PARABASIS

In the parabasis, or author's address to the audience, in his comedy *The Acharnians*, Aristophanes delightfully explains what he believes is his own worth to the state:

CHORUS LEADER: And now, the customary Choral Interlude.
Places, men! It's time for the ANAPESTS.
Off with the cloaks—let's get this atrophied ritual on the road!
Gentlemen, our Playwright is a modest man. Never in his career
has he written his ego into the script, or prostituted his Parabasis
to declare his genius. But now that genius is under attack.
Before the people of Athens (so notorious for their snap decisions),
his enemies charge that he degrades the City and insults the Populace.
And thus our Poet requests this time to defend his Art
before the people of Athens (so illustrious for their reasoned revisions
        of their snap decisions).
                        Our Poet gives his accusers the lie.
He protests that he is a Public Benefactor, instilling in the Body
Politic a healthy resistance to rhetoric. No longer, Gentlemen,
are you ceaselessly victimized by foreign oratory, willingly wallowing,
unthinking and blissful, in flattering unction—wearing a wide-eyed,
slack-jawed gawk as your National Mien. . . .
[T]his is all past, thanks to our Poet—our Public Benefactor.
Consider a second benefit, Gentlemen. Why do you think
that the Allies keep flocking to town to pay the tribute you exact?
Because they love you? Because they hate money? Not in the least.
Because last year, in *The Babylonians*, a Certain Comic Poet*
ripped the lid off the relations between Athens and the rest of the
        Federation,

*Aristophanes, of course; unfortunately, the play does not survive.

were held; at these ceremonies, each playwright introduced his cast and announced the theme of his work. The second day featured processions, sacrifices, and the presentation of ten dithyrambs; on the third day, five comedies were played. On the fourth, fifth, and sixth days the three selected playwrights presented their tetralogies; on the seventh day, judging was conducted (by an intricate tribal voting procedure) and awards were granted to the most popular playwrights and actors. It was a giant outdoor religious and civic celebration, a cultural affair in the fullest sense, at which a society gathered en masse to recall the deeds of its heroes and to engage in the various modes of storytelling—epic, ritual, mocking, and comic—that came to be known as drama. The stories were traditional, contemporary, mythic, domestic, profound, absurd; in short, they spanned virtually the whole range of cultural experience, and religious activities were directly or indirectly present everywhere in the proceedings. Certainly nothing in the theatre that has followed has even begun to approximate this massive open-air intellectual, cultural, and spiritual convocation which allowed a community to celebrate itself for several days each year in words, music, dance, dress, and action. Perhaps the only event in our time that bore a remote resemblance to the spirit of the Greek Dionysia was the famous rock concert at Woodstock, New York, in 1969.

exposing how we democratically democratize our Allies into Complete
    Equality—
with each other, like slaves. So now these Allies are wild to see
this Nonpareil among poets with the Courage to Tell the Truth in Athens.
And they come—and you get the money.
                          This Courage, in fact, is famous
throughout the world, as witness a recent report from Persia:
It seems that the Great King was sounding out a delegation from Sparta,
and asked about the relative strength of their side and ours.
First, of course, he wanted to know which State had the larger
Navy; but *then* he turned to the question of the famous Poet
who criticized his own city without mercy. Which side had *him*?
"The men who have been guided by that adviser," he said,
"are necessarily far superior; their decisive victory in the War
is only a matter of time." And *there* is the reason for the Spartans'
recent suit for Peace . . .
your Fearless, Peerless Poet, ARISTOPHANES. I urge you, Friends,
don't give him up! Don't discard the Voice of Justice!
Hear now the pledge of the Poet as Teacher: his subtle stagecraft
will bear you along to perfect happiness, public and private.
His integrity remains absolute. He will not knuckle, truckle,
hoax, or coax his way into favor. He will not adulterate
the pure matter of his plays with soft soap, bunkum, or grease,
simply to win a prize. His aim is not your applause, or votes,
but your *Edification.* ONWARD AND UPWARD WITH HIS ART!

Translated by Douglass Parker (slightly edited)

TRAGIC MASK
. . . Ostia

*The ancient mask was itself a
subject for veneration. Shown
here, a stone sculpture of a
Greco-Roman mask found atop
a pedestal at the Roman seaport of Ostia.*

THE GREEK PLAYS

Probably thousands of Greek tragedies, comedies, and satyr plays were written and performed in classical times. We know the names of hundreds of these plays, but only 43 playscripts remain in complete form. If this number seems disappointing, we must be aware that it is an incredible fortune that any still exist—considering that they were written two thousand years before the invention of movable type. The surviving plays comprise 31 tragedies, 11 comedies, and 1 satyr play; in addition, we have numerous fragments from other works, mostly culled from later citations. While not all the remaining plays are indisputable masterpieces, they are all from authors who were the most celebrated of their times: Aeschylus, Sophocles, Euripides, and the comic author Aristophanes.

Ever since Aristotle wrote his *Poetics*, theatre critics and historians have labored to deduce common structural characteristics in the dramatic works of the Greek authors. Over the centuries they have come up with these labels for various recurring aspects of dramatic construction: the *prologue* for the opening speech, usually delivered by one or two actors; the *parodos* for the ode subsequently sung by the chorus as it enters the *orkestra*; the *agon* (action) or *episode* (inter-ode) and the *stasimon* (choral ode) for the elements which alternate between actors and chorus as the dramatic story develops; and the *exodos* for the departure ode which concludes the play. Critics have also defined a *parabasis* in Greek comedy, in which, about halfway through the play, the chorus, representing the author, directly addresses the audience in a long speech not necessarily relevant to the immediate action. The existence of such a complete and historically important nomenclature should not, however, lead us to suppose that Greek plays were written with any distinct formula in mind; nor should we conclude from the critics' analyses that any single controlling concept—such as fate, pride, or tragic flaw—necessarily provides the fundamental thematic line for every Greek play. The themes, styles, conclusions, and manners of the four known playwrights are vastly dissimilar, and each of these playwrights exhibits considerable structural and thematic versatility from one play to the next. In looking at the body of Greek drama, then, we must be wary of oversimplifications that tend to amalgamate highly individual works into a "Greek style."

Virtually every one of the extant Greek plays is performed at least occasionally somewhere in the world today; several are perennial staples in European and American theatre repertories. The three plays that we shall examine in some detail below are among those that are currently popular, but they by no means reflect the whole spectrum of Greek dramatic creativity. Rather they are offered as individual achievements which, when viewed in concert, give a sense of the depth of vision of the Greek dramatists and the excellence of their craft.

Prometheus Bound

Aeschylus' *Prometheus Bound* was long thought to be the oldest of the surviving Greek tragedies. In fact that honor probably belongs to Aeschylus' *The Persians*, written in 472, but it is easy to see the reason for the mistake. Compared to the plays of Sophocles and even others by Aeschylus himself, *Prometheus* seems structurally primitive, with its series of two character scenes and its epical narrative speeches; moreover *Prometheus* is a play which looks back to the beginning of time, as though the playwright himself were consciously dwelling on his own culture's recent emergence from barbarism and trying to peer into the shrouded past. As it turns out, *Prometheus* was written late in Aeschylus' long career, but it was deliberately written in an "old-fashioned" style.

The story line of the play is quite simple, as is characteristic of the early plays of Aeschylus. It is a play about gods. Two Olympians, Zeus and Prometheus, have been on the winning side of a war with the Titans, and Zeus, as the leader of the victorious Olympians, has become king of the gods. The two victors have had a falling out, however, after Prometheus gave mankind the gift of fire (and with it, knowledge). Zeus has exiled Prometheus to the outer reaches of the known world, and there has ordered him chained to a cliff. It is at this point that Aeschylus begins his drama, with Might, a demon in service of Zeus, and Hephaestus, Zeus' blacksmith, arguing about the propriety of Pro-

Plays that are analyzed are shown with a vertical rule in the left margin.

metheus' punishment as they seek to execute it:

MIGHT: This is the world's limit that we have come to; this is the Scythian country, an untrodden desolation. Hephaestus, it is you that must heed the commands the Father laid upon you to nail this malefactor to the high craggy rocks in fetters unbreakable of adamantine chain. For it was your flower, the brightness of fire that devises all, that he stole and gave to mortal men; this is the sin for which he must pay the Gods the penalty—that he may learn to endure and like the sovereignty of Zeus and quit his man-loving disposition.

HEPHAESTUS: Might . . . , in you the command of Zeus has its perfect fulfillment: in you there is nothing to stand in its way. But, for myself, I have not the heart to bind violently a God who is my kin here on this wintry cliff. Yet there is constraint upon me to have the heart for just that, for it is a dangerous thing to treat the Father's words lightly.

[TO PROMETHEUS] High-contriving Son of Themis of Straight Counsel: this is not of your will nor of mine. . . . Such is the reward you reap of your man-loving disposition. For you, a God, feared not the anger of the Gods, but gave honors to mortals beyond what was just. . . .

MIGHT: Come, why are you holding back? Why are you pitying in vain? Why is it that you do not hate a God whom the Gods hate most of all? . . .

HEPHAESTUS: You are always pitiless, always full of ruthlessness.

MIGHT: There is no good singing dirges over him. . . . Hurry now. Throw the chain around him that the Father may not look upon your tarrying.

HEPHAESTUS: There are the fetters, there: you can see them.

MIGHT: Put them on his hands: strong, now with the hammer: strike. Nail him to the rock. . . .

HEPHAESTUS: Look now, his arm is fixed immovably!

MIGHT: Nail the other safe, that he may learn, for all his cleverness, that he is duller witted than Zeus.

An actor playing Hephaestus wears mask and on-kos; behind, another actor prepares to don mask. Were real props (the hammer and chains) used? It is quite possible, but we have no firm evidence.

Prometheus is silent during this first scene of the play, but we find out all we need to know not only about the reason for his plight, but about the tone of the argument that surrounds it. For Zeus is portrayed as a monster-god inimical not only to the virtue of Prometheus but also to mankind, for whom Prometheus has made this sacrifice. There is much already in this scene to remind us of two other figures from the Judeo-Christian tradition: the exiled demigod Lucifer (which means "bringer of light") who induced Adam and Eve to eat of the tree of knowledge, and the crucified Jesus Christ who sacrificed his life on behalf of mankind and who, at least for a critical moment, believed himself

given the immobility of the ACTOR, the "OVERSTATEMENT" of the MASK was particularly useful...→

THE CHAINS WOULD PROBABLY HAVE BEEN FAIRLY REALISTIC

REMOVABLE POST

How was Prometheus' bondage originally staged? We have no certain knowledge, but vase paintings suggest that the actor who played Prometheus was chained to a post, which could have been erected either in front of the skene or in the center of the orchestra.

abandoned by God the Father. But if the God of the Bible (or at any rate, the Yahweh of the Old Testament) is a jealous god, the Zeus of the Aeschylean *Prometheus* is a vicious, egotistical, and indecently lustful one: a god who insists on being called "the Father" like some modern-day Mafia warlord, and whose goal is not so much to secure the allegiance of Prometheus as to effect his abject abasement ("that he might learn . . . that he is duller witted than Zeus"). This is a god who hates man, who hates gods who help man, and whose only motivating principle seems to be vanity. This portrayal brilliantly sets up the introduction of Prometheus, Aeschylus' heroic protagonist.

MIGHT: (*to Prometheus*) Now, play the insolent; now, plunder the Gods' privileges and give them to creatures of a day. What drop of your sufferings can mortals spare you? The Gods named you wrongly when they called you Forethought; you yourself *need* Forethought to extricate yourself from this contrivance. (*Prometheus is left alone on the rock.*)

PROMETHEUS: Bright light, swift-winged winds,
      springs of the rivers, numberless
  laughter of the sea's waves, earth, mother of
    all, and the all-seeing
  circle of the sun: I call upon you to see what I,
    a God, suffer
  at the hands of Gods—
  see with what kind of torture
  worn down I shall wrestle ten thousand
    years of time . . .
  You see me a wretched God in chains,
  the enemy of Zeus, hated of all
  the Gods that enter Zeus's palace hall,
  because of my excessive love for Man.

What of course distinguishes Prometheus in his opening speech in the play is that, unlike Might and Hephaestus, Prometheus is revealed as a poet! Here Aeschylus produces a dramaturgical weapon which has since been wielded to great effect by generations of playwrights: the emotional power of poetry. When Might sarcastically tells Prometheus to "play the insolent," he does not know what power he invokes, for he thereby gives Prometheus the opportunity to *perform* in a medium—the theatre—where performance is everything. In the course of *Prometheus Bound*, Prometheus will win by his words what he loses by his chains as he pleads his cause before an audience composed of the very group in whose behalf he is being made to suffer. Obviously, there is no place that Prometheus would rather be, and he loses no time in telling the audience how he is suffering for his love of them.

Now into this setting comes the first of a series of visitors. It is a winged chorus, the daughters of Oceanus, the sea king. This chorus will remain with Prometheus until the very end of the play, sympathizing with him and offering counsel, hearing his woes and serving as a sounding board for his plans. The chorus of the Greek theatre stood both metaphorically and physically between the principal characters and the audience, and for this reason it served a vital function. It allowed playwrights to bridge the narrative and the dramatic forms, permitting the insertion of internal monologues (thinking-out-loud speeches) as well as incendiary public addresses—both used extensively in this play—which would otherwise be difficult to incorporate in the drama.

PROMETHEUS: What is that? The rustle
  of birds' wings near? The air whispers
  with the gentle strokes of wings.
  Everything that comes toward me is occasion
    for fear.
CHORUS: Fear not: this is a company of friends
  That comes to your mountain with swift
  rivalry of wings. . . .
PROMETHEUS: Alas . . . ,
  look, see with what chains
  I am nailed on the craggy heights
  of this gully to keep a watch
  that none would envy me. . . .
CHORUS: I see, Prometheus: and a mist of fear and
    tears
  besets my eyes as I see your form
  wasting away . . .
  Who of the Gods is so hard of heart
  that he finds joy in this?
  Who is that that does not feel
  sorrow answering your pain—
  save only Zeus? For he malignantly,
  always cherishing a mind
  that bends not, has subdued the breed
  of Uranos . . .
PROMETHEUS: . . . there shall come a day for me
  when he shall need me, me that now am
    tortured
  in bonds and fetters—he shall need me then,
  this president of the Blessed. . . .
  Then not with honeyed tongues
  of persuasion shall he enchant me;
  he shall not cow me with his threats
  to tell him what I know,
  until he free me from my cruel chains
  and pay me recompense for what I suffer.
CHORUS: You are stout of heart, unyielding
  to the bitterness of pain.
  You are free of tongue, too free. . . .
PROMETHEUS: I know that he is savage: and his
    justice
  a thing he keeps by his own standard: still
  that will of his shall melt to softness yet . . .

Prometheus uses the chorus as a companion, receiving their sympathy and letting them in on his great secret: that many generations hence, "a man renowned for archery" (Hercules) will free him and force Zeus to take him back into the Olympian fold, a story that Aeschylus was to treat in his next two plays which, unfortunately, do not survive. But Prometheus also rebuffs the chorus for their assessment of him as "too free of tongue." Freedom in all things defines Prometheus' character. While his ultimate strength may be said to come from his knowledge that eventually he will be restored to Zeus' favor, his greater dramatic force proceeds from his absolute refusal to compromise his inner freedom: this stubborn resolve, so distressing to the chorus, is the source of Prometheus' courage and his heroism. The contrast between Prometheus' will to freedom and the chains which pin him to the rock provides the basic dramatic tension of the play, and also its central metaphor: rebellious humanity straining against the shackles of oppressive authority. It is a metaphor applicable throughout civilization wherever freedom of thought is considered to be threatened by intellectual or spiritual restraints. Prometheus is the archetypical rebel, a model for the teenager rebelling against parental control (Zeus, of course is "the Father" in this play), as well as for the romantic spirit struggling to burst free of tradition or the artistic sensibility at war with the bureaucratism, egomania, and arbitrary rule-making of dictatorships the world over.

Apart from the chorus, Prometheus has three single visitors in his rocky exile, all of whom Aeschylus uses to point up the differences between his hero and the common run of humanity. The first, Oceanus, father to the chorus, is brought on primarily so his advice can be rejected:

OCEANUS: . . . My poor friend, give up
    this angry mood of yours and look for means
    of getting yourself free of trouble. Maybe
    what I say seems to you both old and
        commonplace;
    but this is what you pay, Prometheus, for
    that tongue of yours which talked so high and
        haughty:
    you are not yet humble, still you do not yield
    to your misfortunes, and you wish, indeed,

to add some more to them; now, if you follow
    me as a schoolmaster you will not kick
    against the pricks, seeing that he, the King,
    that rules alone, is harsh and sends accounts
    to no one's audit for the deeds he does.
    Now I will go and try if I can free you:
    do you be quiet, do not talk so much. . . .
    [I]t is a profitable thing, if one is wise,
        to seem foolish.

It is interesting to consider Oceanus' advice in "real world" terms, for obviously not one person in a thousand would finally refuse to take it, given the consequences. The facts of human intercourse—which certainly have not changed from Greek times to our own—are that human beings learn to adapt to power struggles by the very tactics Oceanus advises: compromise, tact, realistic appreciation of the strengths of one's adversaries, and prudent silence. The beauty of drama, however, is that it can examine the extreme case, the one in a thousand who chooses to test the universe by confronting its laws directly. Often the playwright has to go into the realm of fantasy or the divine to make a credible illustration of universal principles, but the important thing to realize in this play is that, despite the antiquity of the script or the divinity of the characters, Aeschylus is talking about human courage, human rebellion, and human compromise. The story is applicable in its entire import to the ordinary affairs of humankind.

Prometheus, of course, will have none of Oceanus' suggestions: he rejects them outright and sets himself to wait out his torture defiantly. He challenges the universe, and he is a hero. Even today we use the term "Promethean" to describe a character whose actions, by their extreme courage and recklessness, seem to redefine the human possibility. In drama, particularly in tragedy, some of the great actions are refusals: refusal to compromise, to modify one's demands, to sacrifice one's ideals. *Prometheus Bound* is essentially a play of refusals, with Prometheus receiving a series of offers which he indignantly rejects.

Prometheus' next visitor is Io, a mortal woman who, having unintentionally attracted the lust of Zeus, has been set upon by the jealous Hera and forced to wander eternally through the world pursued by the savage gadfly. Io's transcontinental punishment, so vividly contrasted to Prometheus' immobility, serves both to increase the audience's antipathy toward Zeus and to further ennoble the patiently suffering hero on the rock. It also gives Aeschylus an opportunity to indicate the epic scale of this drama and the international consequences that are focused on the activities here at the world's edge, as he has Prometheus "predict" the travels of Io country by country until he has provided his audience with a breathtaking account of Aegean geography.

And finally to the mountain prison comes Zeus' personal messenger, the "lackey of the gods," Hermes, whose mission is to demand from Prometheus the secret he has earlier hinted to the chorus.

HERMES: [Y]ou thief of fire:
> the Father has commanded you to say
> what marriage of his is this you brag about
> that shall drive him from power. . . .

Prometheus' response is the climax of the play: a rhetorical barrage which mocks the strength of the chains that hold him and the gods who have imprisoned him:

> . . . Do you think I will crouch before your Gods,
> —so new—and tremble? I am far from that. . . .
> There is not
> a torture or an engine wherewithal
> Zeus can induce me to declare these things,
> 'till he has loosed me from these cruel shackles.
> So let him hurl his smoky lightning flame,
> and throw in turmoil all things in the world
> with white-winged snowflakes and deep
>   bellowing
> thunder beneath the earth: me he shall not
> bend by all this to tell him who is fated
> to drive him from his tyranny.

HERMES: Think, here and now, if this seems to your interest.
PROMETHEUS: I have already thought—and laid my plans.
HERMES: Bring your proud heart to know a true discretion—
> O foolish spirit—in the face of ruin.

PROMETHEUS: You vex me by these senseless adjurations,
> senseless as if you were to advise the waves.
> Let it not cross your mind that I will turn
> womanish-minded from my fixed decision
> or that I shall entreat the one I hate
> so greatly, with a woman's upturned hands,
> to loose me from my chains: I am far from that.

HERMES: I have said too much already—so I think—
> and said it to no purpose: you are not softened:
> your purpose is not dented by my prayers.
> You are a colt new broken, with the bit
> clenched in its teeth, fighting against the reins,
> and bolting. . . .
> Think what a storm, a triple wave of ruin
> will rise against you, if you will not hear me,
> and no escape for you. First this rough crag
> with thunder and the lightning bolt the Father
> shall cleave asunder, and shall hide your body
> wrapped in a rocky clasp within its depth; . . .
> Then Zeus's winged hound, the eagle red,
> shall tear great shreds of flesh from you, a
>   feaster
> coming unbidden, every day: your liver
> bloodied to blackness will be his repast. . . .
> This is no feigned boast
> but spoken with too much truth. The mouth of
>   Zeus
> does not know how to lie, but every word
> brings to fulfilment. Look, you, and reflect
> and never think that obstinacy is better
> than prudent counsel.

CHORUS: Hermes seems to us
> to speak not altogether out of season.
> He bids you leave your obstinacy and seek
> a wise good counsel. Hearken to him. Shame
> it were for one so wise to fall in error.

PROMETHEUS: Before he told it me I knew this message:
> but there is no disgrace in suffering
> at an enemy's hand, when you hate mutually.
> So let the curling tendril of the fire
> from the lightning bolt be sent against me: let
> the air be stirred with thunderclaps, the winds
> in savage blasts convulsing all the world.

"The air whispers with the gentle stroke of wings," says Prometheus, as the fifteen-man chorus, playing the daughters of Oceanus, enters the stage from "above"—that is, from behind the slightly elevated skene. The chorus dances and sings to the music of the two-pipe aulos, played by the flautist seated at left. A conjectural reconstruction.

Let earth to her foundations shake, yes to her
    root,
before the quivering storm: let it confuse
the paths of heavenly stars and the sea's waves
in a wild surging torrent: this my body
let Him raise up on high and dash it down
into black Tartarus with rigorous
compulsive eddies: death he cannot give me.

Aeschylus here concludes the play with the same
dramatic ingredient with which he introduced his
hero: poetic magnificence. The heroics of Prometheus are literary in nature; and the theatre, a noble home for the spoken word, now resounds with
his eloquence. Nothing Hermes can threaten, and
nothing the chorus can plead, can match the fire
of Prometheus' language—the fire that was in fact
Aeschylus' gift to mankind.

In the end, the chorus is won over by Prometheus, not he by them. As he refuses to turn
"womanish-minded" from his rebellion, so they
finally become disgusted with the blandishments
of Hermes.

HERMES [*to Chorus*]: [Y]ou, who are so sympathetic
    with his troubles,
  away with you from here, quickly away!
  lest you should find your wits stunned by the
    thunder
  and its hard defending roar.
CHORUS: Say something else
  different from this . . . this word of yours
  for all its instancy is not for us.
  How dare you bid us practice baseness? We
  will bear along with him what we must bear.
  I have learned to hate all traitors: there is no
  disease I spit on more than treachery.

This, the last line spoken by the chorus, expresses
the final *public* judgment of the play—that traitors
must be hated, that treachery must not be borne. In
using the chorus to pronounce this final judgment,
Aeschylus draws the audience further into the
world of his play: it is the *audience*, finally, who will
remain with Prometheus at the play's conclusion,
and who will have made the final moral decision
concerning Prometheus' plight. It is to both chorus
and audience that Hermes speaks at the end of the
play:

HERMES: Remember then my warning before the
    act.
  when you are trapped by ruin don't blame
    fortune:
  don't say that Zeus has brought you to calamity
  that you could not foresee: do not do this:
  but blame yourselves: now you know what
    you're doing. . . .

Hermes brings the chorus—and with them the audience—into the full flush of human responsibility.
It is not Zeus or fate that runs man's life; it is man
himself, his knowledge, his shared sympathy with
the heroic, the persecuted, the noble in spirit. Prometheus who brought knowledge to mankind now
brings to them—to us, actually—the awareness of
our responsibility for that knowledge. We cannot
turn back and pretend ignorance: we are the masters of our fate and we must bear the consequences
of our actions. Aeschylus transforms the audience
into a hero along with Prometheus, making us
reckon with both his suffering and his exaltation.
Therefore, as Prometheus concludes the play with
his last magnificent speech, we shudder with him:

PROMETHEUS: Now it is words no longer: now in
    very truth
  the earth is staggered: in its depths the thunder
  bellows resoundingly, the fiery tendrils
  of the lightning flash light up, and whirling
    clouds
  carry the dust along: all the winds' blasts
  dance in a fury one against the other
  in violent confusion: earth and sea
  are one, confused together: such is the storm
  that comes against me manifestly from Zeus
  to work its terrors. O Holy mother mine,
  O Sky that circling brings the light to all,
  you see me, how I suffer, how unjustly.

No one can tell us precisely how this final scene was
to be played; Greek manuscripts, we must sadly
note, include no stage directions. It almost seems
that Aeschylus himself is rebelling against the restraints of dramaturgy here; Prometheus' declaration that it is "words no longer: now in very truth"
suggest that the author is struggling to transcend
the literary format. But it is with words, of course,
that he paints the cataclysm that is building as this

Might and Violence arrive by motorcycle.

Photographs from the 1978 production of Prometheus *directed by Manfred Karge and Matthias Langhoff at Théâtre de Carouge in Geneva, Switzerland. This extraordinary production was designed by Jean-Claude Maret, with contemporary masks by Werner Strub.*

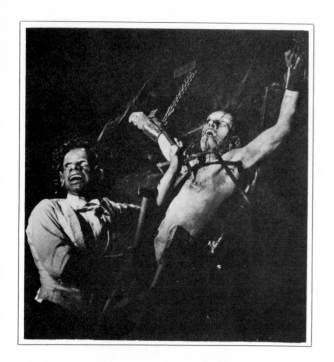

Hephaestus chains Prometheus to his rock.

Alone, Prometheus begins to speak.

Oceanus flies in to visit Prometheus.

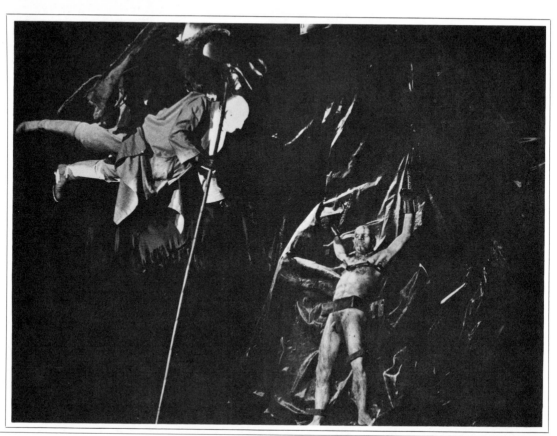

The chorus laments Prometheus' fate.

The arrival of the yoked Io.

Hermes, lackey of the Gods, arrives by jeep.

play ends, words which when they were first sung, danced, and passionately enacted must have provided a supremely thrilling moment in that classical theatre on the hillside at Athens.

Prometheus is a direct play, linear in structure, that probes deeply into a single theme—freedom of thought—and makes use of poetry, staging, and performance to create the Greek tragic hero. The rhetorical heroics of Prometheus are not merely devices to entertain the audience or to display Aeschylus' verbal skills; they are employed to illustrate the transcendent human spirit. The dramaturgy therefore serves the theme of the play; it is the vehicle that delivers the author's points. *Prometheus* is a play that enjoyed great popularity in the romantic era—when Shelley wrote a poetic sequel entitled *Prometheus Unbound*—and not surprisingly, it experienced a new wave of popularity in the socially rebellious 1960s. Indeed, as a clear model of defiance in the face of force, it has few equals in the known literatures of the world.

Oedipus Tyrannos

Oedipus Tyrannos (also known by the Latin title *Oedipus Rex* and the English title *Oedipus the King*) was written in about 425 B.C., a long generation after the first presentation of Aeschylus' *Prometheus Bound*. The author was Sophocles, who succeeded Aeschylus as Athens' leading writer of tragedies. The contrast between the plays, as well as the contrast between the authors of the plays, well illustrates a significant development in the nature of Greek tragedy and in theatre.

Oedipus Tyrannos tells the story of an ancient (and almost certainly legendary) *tyrannos* (abso-

lute ruler) of Thebes who, seeking the murderer of his predecessor, discovers that it is himself; and worse, that his predecessor was in fact his own father and the widow whom he has married is his mother. Utterly appalled at these findings, he goes into his palace and finds that his mother/wife has made the same discovery and has killed herself. He thereupon gouges out his eyes so that he may seek no more. This gory, shocking tale was well known to the audiences of Sophocles' time, but Sophocles' skill in recounting it ensured it a permanent place in Western literature. Even today, his play retains the suspense, majesty, and irony which led Aristotle and two millennia of critics after him to adjudge it the greatest tragedy ever written.

Both *Oedipus* and *Prometheus* are plays which treat the audience to a series of revelations—revelations about the past, which are known dramaturgically as *exposition*, as well as revelations about the future, often called *prophecy*. In one way or another, these sorts of revelations are common to all drama, since they establish the events of the play in a framework of time. What distinguishes the revelations in *Oedipus* from those of the earlier plays, however, is a seemingly simple thing which in fact marks a crucial step in the development of drama. Whereas in *Prometheus* the revelations are made *by* the principal character, in *Oedipus* they are made *to* the principal character, and thus the events of the play are placed beyond the awareness and control of that character. Unlike Prometheus, Oedipus does not know of his own tragic plight as the play's action begins; hence he is powerless in the context of events he himself has unwittingly set in motion. He thus shares one vital characteristic with all mankind: ignorance. He is one of us; and because we know of his ignorance in the face of tragic circumstances, we sympathize.

What Sophocles develops in *Oedipus* is a *human* tragedy; indeed, this concentration on the human individual is a hallmark of his plays. Whereas Aeschylus dealt with abstract themes which he illustrated and embodied by means of articulate spokesmen, Sophocles created finite dilemmas and characters who must struggle to deal with them. Moreover, Sophocles created *personal* drama. For whereas Prometheus' battle must be waged against a force outside himself (Zeus), Oedipus' struggle is self-motivated: he seeks understanding. This dramaturgical development helped to solve one of the great logical problems in creating tragedy— which is, quite simply, how to keep the protago- nist on stage. Given insuperable circumstances, why would not the reasonable protagonist walk away? Aeschylus' solution in *Prometheus* was to chain the protagonist to the stage; Sophocles created circumstances which make Oedipus *want*—despite horrifying revelations—to remain on stage to the play's bitter end, where he will at last discover and confront his allotted fate. This dramaturgical creation, more than any other, brought to the fore the human and sympathetic tragic hero and made him accessible to audiences for all time.

The manner of Sophocles' evocation of the Oedipus story is vastly illuminating. This is a play of questions. Whereas *Prometheus* begins with Hephaestus' declarations, *Oedipus* begins with an investigation: Why is a plague ravaging Thebes? As

A modern production of Oedipus, *mounted by Comédie Française in Paris. Characters wear nearly identical costumes (men and women alike) and, against black background, seem to exemplify the symbolic, mythic realm of the play.*

Oedipus (Douglas Campbell) addresses the chorus in a celebrated production at the Stratford Shakespeare Festival, directed by the late Tyrone Guthrie. The masks, by Tanya Moisewitsch, are contemporary versions of myth-making proportions.

the play opens, Oedipus addresses a gathering of citizens and their priest:

OEDIPUS: What is it, children, sons of the ancient house of Cadmus? Why do you sit as suppliants crowned with laurel branches? What is the meaning of the incense which fills the city? The pleas to end pain?

The cries of sorrow?

How was the first scene of *Oedipus Tyrannos* originally staged? Scholars disagree about many points, particularly about the role and the composition of the citizenry whom Oedipus addresses. Some contend that he addressed the chorus; others say the "citizens" were a group of mute actors (today they would be called "extras"), since the chorus itself would ordinarily have entered later, during its first choral ode (the *parados*). Peter D. Arnott suggests an intriguing possibility: that Oedipus and the priest were the only actors on stage or in the orchestra, and the theatre audience itself represented the citizens. If that was the case, the audience's identification with a stricken multitude must have been particularly poignant, since this play was produced shortly after a plague had ravaged Athens.

Oedipus' investigation is quickly developed as Creon, Oedipus' brother-in-law, returns from the Oracle at Delphi with the revelation that it is the yet unsolved and unavenged murder of Laius, the previous *tyrannos*, which has occasioned this plague. Oedipus, always the conscientious ruler, sees his duty and invokes his curse:

OEDIPUS: I will serve the god and the dead. On the assassin

or assassins, I call down the most vile damnation—

for this vicious act, may the brand of shame be theirs to wear forever. And if I knowingly

harbor their guilt within my own walls, I shall not

exempt myself from the curse that I have called upon them. . . .

I will avenge him [Laius] as I would avenge my own father.

Thus damning himself, although he knows it not, Oedipus embarks on his second and more difficult investigation: Who killed Laius?

In pursuing this second investigation, Oedipus consults with five persons; each gives him (and the audience) a piece of the answer, but until the fifth person speaks, the information is always conveyed in such a way that Oedipus fails to apprehend the whole: he is like a man picking up pieces of a jigsaw puzzle and trying to fit them together without any notion of what the final picture will disclose. For the observer, therefore, the process is as suspenseful as it is pathetic.

The first to give information is Creon. The second, at Creon's suggestion, is the ancient, all-knowing blind seer Teiresias, who reveals information that seems so strange, so incomprehensible, to Oedipus that it only bewilders and enrages him and goads him on in his searching:

OEDIPUS: . . . My lord Teiresias, we turn to you as our only hope. . . . We must find Laius' murderers and deal with them . . . only then will we find release from our suffering.

TEIRESIAS: . . . I should not have come. . . .

OEDIPUS: . . . For God's sake, if you know, don't turn away from us! We are pleading. We are begging you.

TEIRESIAS: Because you are blind! No! I shall not reveal my secrets. I shall not reveal yours.

OEDIPUS: What? You know, and yet you refuse to speak? . . .

TEIRESIAS: . . . Stop asking me to tell; I will tell you nothing.

OEDIPUS: You will not tell? You monster! You could stir the stones of earth to a burning rage! You will never tell? What will it take?

TEIRESIAS: Know yourself, Oedipus. You denounce me, but you do not yet know yourself. . . . I shall say no more. Rage, if you wish.

OEDIPUS: I *am* enraged. And now I will tell you what *I* think. I think this was *your* doing. *You* plotted the crime, *you* saw it carried out. It was *your* doing. All but the actual killing. And had you not been blind, you would have done *that* too!

TEIRESIAS: Do you believe what you have said? Then accept your own decree! From this day on, deny yourself the right to speak to anyone. You, Oedipus, are the desecrator, the polluter of this land. . . . I say that you, Oedipus Tyrannos, are the murderer you seek. . . .

OEDIPUS: You—you cripple! Your ears are deaf, your eyes are blind, your mind—your *mind* is crippled! . . . You live in night, Teiresias, in night that never turns to day. And so you cannot hurt me—or any man who sees the light. . . .

TEIRESIAS: You have eyes, Oedipus, and do not see your own destruction. You have eyes and do not see what lives with you. Do you not know whose son you are?

What is particularly impressive about the exchange between Oedipus and Teiresias is the excessive vigor with which Oedipus errs! That misplaced rage he expresses so vividly becomes especially ironic in light of what happens later—and what the audience knows will happen—and the irony of this and other of Oedipus' proclamations is something for which the play and its author are well known. Indeed, *dramatic irony* is the term given to precisely this sort of theatrical contrivance which allows the audience to see the characters' situation better than the characters do themselves. *Oedipus Tyrannos* is a virtual textbook of dramatic irony. All the accusations Oedipus hurls against Teiresias are to be turned back against himself by the play's end; the audience, knowing this, follows Oedipus' utterances with a dread fascination. Dramatic irony is one of the surest techniques for encouraging the audience to participate emotionally and sympathetically in the action of a play. Sophocles was a master of this technique; in fact, he is often considered to have been its inventor.

Having rejected the report of Teiresias, who in fact knows all, Oedipus struggles doggedly in the ensuing episodes to narrow his investigation through a series of confrontations in which he challenges, taunts, berates, and interrogates other characters until he finally amasses the information that lays bare his own disgrace. But now—and this is the cleverness of Sophocles—all his information comes indirectly and by inference, from the views expressed by persons whose ignorance equals his own. Thus Jocasta, his wife, tries to allay his suspicions and only succeeds in giving him fresh ones:

JOCASTA: In the name of Heaven, my Lord, tell me the reason for your bitterness.

OEDIPUS: I will—because you mean more to me than anyone. The reason is Creon and his plot against my throne.

JOCASTA: But can you *prove* a plot?

OEDIPUS: He says that I—Oedipus—bear the guilt of Laius' death.

JOCASTA: How does he justify this charge?

OEDIPUS: He does not stain his own lips by saying it. No. He uses that false prophet to speak for him.

JOCASTA: Then you can exonerate yourself because no mortal has the power of divination. And I can prove it. An oracle came to Laius once . . . that he would die at the hands of his own child, his child and mine. Yet the story which *we* heard was that robbers murdered Laius in a place where three roads meet. . . .

OEDIPUS: Jocasta—my heart is troubled at your words. . . . Where is this place where three roads meet?

JOCASTA: In the land called Phocis where the roads from Delphi and from Daulia converge.

OEDIPUS: How long a time has passed since then?

JOCASTA: We heard it shortly before you came. . . . What is it, Oedipus? What frightens you?

OEDIPUS: Do not ask me. . . . Just tell me—what was Laius like? . . .

JOCASTA: He was tall and his hair was lightly cast with silver tones, the contour of his body much like yours.

OEDIPUS: O God! Am I cursed and cannot see it?

Here, remembering an incident in which he killed a rude stranger and his entourage at a crossroads, Oedipus begins to suspect that Teiresias has spoken truth because of the very information Jocasta gives to prove Teiresias lied. To find out more, he

Teiresias enters, guided by small boy, in American Conservatory Theatre production of 1970, directed by William Ball. Teiresias' gnarled staff and flowing white beard, and the rough-textured scenery and costumes bespeak a primitive Homeric Greece. Ken Ruta plays Teiresias.

calls for the shepherd who witnessed the incident.

The same pattern is followed in the succeeding episode, in which a messenger from Corinth arrives to announce the natural death of Oedipus' presumed father, Polybus. This news seems at first to disprove the prophecy that Oedipus would kill his father; however, the messenger "dis-disproves"

the prophecy with subsequent information:

OEDIPUS: There was an oracle—a dreadful oracle sent by the gods . . . that I would take my mother for my bride and murder my father with my own hands. That is the reason I left Corinth long ago. . . .

MESSENGER: Is this the fear that drove you away from Corinth? . . . Then you must realize that this fear is groundless.

OEDIPUS: How can that be—if I am their son?

MESSENGER: Because Polybus was no relative of yours.

And the messenger explains that the infant Oedipus had been left to die on the mountainside, his ankles pierced with rivets, when a shepherd found him and gave him to the messenger, who in turn gave him to the *tyrannos* Polybus to raise as a son. Here Sophocles shows well the great possibilities of the three-character scene (it was Sophocles, we remember, who introduced the third actor for just these occasions), for now Jocasta, who remembers the piercing of her infant son's ankles, listens with growing horror to the exchange between Oedipus and the Corinthian—and the audience sees that she now grasps the picture better than either of the men.

MESSENGER: . . [I]t was the swelling in your ankles that caused your name: Oedipus—"Clubfoot."*

OEDIPUS: . . . Who did this to me? . . .

MESSENGER: You will have to ask the man who handed you to me . . . he was of the house of Laius . . . a shepherd. . . .

OEDIPUS: (*addressing the Chorus*) Do any of you know this shepherd? Have you seen him in the fields? Here in Thebes? Tell me now! . . .

CHORUS: I think it is the shepherd you have asked to see before. But the queen will know.

OEDIPUS: Jocasta, is that the man he means? Is it the shepherd we have sent for? Is *he* the one?

JOCASTA: Why? What difference does it make? Don't think about it. . . . It makes no difference.

OEDIPUS: No difference? . . .

JOCASTA: In the name of God, if you care at all for your own life, you must not go on with this. . . .

OEDIPUS: Do not worry, Jocasta. Even if I am a slave—a third-generation slave, it is no stain on your nobility.

JOCASTA: Oedipus! I beg you—don't do this!

*A translator's liberty. Literally, the name means "swollen foot."

OEDIPUS: I can't grant you that. I cannot leave the truth unknown. . . .

JOCASTA: God help you! May you never know what you are!

OEDIPUS: Go, someone, and bring the shepherd to me. Leave the queen to exult in her noble birth.

What we have here is a plot line intricately assembled out of Oedipus' erroneous assumptions, Jocasta's evasive pleadings, and the Messenger's naive partiality. Almost imperceptibly, the investigation begun by Oedipus has shifted to its third and deepest level: from "Who killed Laius?" to "Who am I?" For now the combined prophecies, memories, revelations, and long suppressed fears are beginning to circle closer and closer around one horrible truth. In the narrowing spiral of plot construction—a foreshortening in which the action gets more and more intense as the climax nears—Sophocles makes one character serve the work of two: the shepherd who witnessed the assassination at the crossroads is also the shepherd who had been entrusted with leaving the infant, ankle-pierced son of Laius, on the mountainside to die. And when the shepherd enters, the play's central fact comes to light in perhaps the most gripping scene of ancient drama:

MESSENGER: . . . Do you remember a child you gave me to bring up as my own?

SHEPHERD: What are you saying? Why are you asking me this?

MESSENGER: This, my friend, this—is that child.

SHEPHERD: Damn you! Will you keep your mouth shut!

OEDIPUS: Save your reproaches, old man. . . .

SHEPHERD: . . . He's crazy.

OEDIPUS: If you don't answer of your own accord, we'll make you talk.

SHEPHERD: No! My Lord, please! Don't hurt an old man.

OEDIPUS: (*to the Chorus*) One of you—twist his hands behind his back! . . Did you or did you not give him that child?

SHEPHERD: I did. I gave it to him—and I wish that I had died that day.

OEDIPUS: You tell the truth, or you'll have your wish now.

SHEPHERD: If I tell, it will be worse.

OEDIPUS: Still he puts it off!

SHEPHERD: I said that I gave him the child! . . .

OEDIPUS: Whose? . . . Whose house?

SHEPHERD: O God, master! Don't ask me any more.

OEDIPUS: This is the last time that I ask you.

SHEPHERD: It was a child—of the house of Laius.

OEDIPUS: A slave! Or of his own line?

SHEPHERD: Ah, master, do I *have* to speak?

OEDIPUS: You have to. And I *have* to hear.

SHEPHERD: They said—it was his child. But the queen could tell you best.

OEDIPUS: Why? Did *she* give you the child?

SHEPHERD: Yes, my Lord.

OEDIPUS: Why?

SHEPHERD: To—kill!

OEDIPUS: Her own child!

SHEPHERD: Yes. . . . My Lord, if you are the man he says you are—O God—you were born to suffering!

OEDIPUS: O God! O no! I see it now! All clear! O Light! I will never look on you again! Sin! Sin in my birth! Sin in my marriage! Sin in blood!

And Oedipus goes into the palace, next to emerge with his eyes gouged from his head by his own hand, a stage effect that is enhanced by the audience's foreknowledge—ensured by a palace messenger's report—of what has taken place within. As Oedipus retreats from the scene at the end of the play, victim of his own curse and denied the comfort of his own children, the chorus intones the final words of the tragedy:

> There goes Oedipus . . .
> now he is drowning in waves of dread and
> despair.
> Look at Oedipus—
> proof that none of us mortals
> can truly be thought of as happy
> until he is granted deliverance from life,

Oedipus returns to stage with bloodied eye sockets: a horrific use of make-up replacing more stately masks of ancient tradition. American Conservatory Theatre production of 1970, with Paul Shenar in title role, flanked by Ellis Rabb (Creon) and Ken Ruta (Teiresias).

until he is dead
and must suffer no more.

What was Sophocles' purpose in writing this play? Why, despite its gruesome and bitter conclusion, does it continue to offer some sort of "entertainment" for generations far removed from oracles, seers, mysterious plagues, and ancient tribal superstitions? There are several answers, not mutually exclusive, each illustrating a different attribute of tragedy as well as of *Oedipus*.

The view of Aristotle is that tragedy offers an audience the gift of *catharsis*, a term whose literary meaning, as far as we can tell, Aristotle coined, and one which he used *Oedipus* to exemplify. In the Aristotelian construct, tragedy concerns a great hero who has a flaw, or *hamartia* (the word has also been translated as "error," and "frailty"). The flaw brings him down, so that he experiences a reversal of fortunes (*peripeteia*) and a recognition of higher truth (*anagnorisis*). This process stimulates in the audience feelings of terror and great

John Gielgud as the blinded Oedipus in the Roman version by Seneca (first century A.D.). Actors wore modern dress in this production of the National Theatre (London), directed by Peter Brook. Seneca's nine surviving tragedies, which were probably meant for chamber reading rather than public performance, feature elaborate rhetoric, sententious moralizing, and grisly (although only reported) violence; his works were highly influential in the Renaissance, and served as models for plays such as Thomas Kyd's The Spanish Tragedy *and Shakespeare's* Titus Andronicus.

Oedipus' destiny moves us only because it might have been ours—because the oracle laid the same curse upon us before our birth as upon him. It is the fate of all of us [males], perhaps, to direct our first sexual impulse towards our mother and our first hatred and our first murderous wish against our father. Our dreams convince us that this is so. Oedipus . . . merely shows us the fulfillment of our own childhood wishes. But, more fortunate than he, we have meanwhile succeeded, in so far as we have not become psychoneurotics, in detaching our sexual impulses from our mothers and in forgetting our jealousy of our fathers. Here is one in whom these primeval wishes of our childhood have been fulfilled, and we shrink back from him with the whole force of the repression by which these wishes have since that time been held down within us. While the poet, as he unravels the past, brings to light the guilt of Oedipus, he is at the same time compelling us to recognize our own inner minds, in which those same impulses, though suppressed, are still to be found.

Sigmund Freud

pity for the hero, feelings which mount during the development of the action until they undergo a complete purgation, or *catharsis*, at the climax of the play. In Aristotle's view, Oedipus' tearing out of his eyes—a rending asunder that is akin to the dismemberment of Dionysus in primitive legend—exorcises the audience's anxieties and cleanses their emotions, essentially leaving them with the courage and serenity to face their own mortality. To Aristotle, and to many critics who have followed his formulation, this is the goal of tragedy: to ritualize suffering, and by ritualizing it, to give us perspective on our fears of what lies ahead. Tragedy, in this view, is a sort of sacrifice, in which the hero takes away our own dread by an act of self-immolation. A somewhat similar ritual effect can be seen in the modern-day Spanish bullfight, in which a noble animal with a "tragic flaw" (pride, lack of intelligence), after a series of violent attacks on his tormentors, is finally brought down in the "moment of truth," and then dismembered to the great ovation of the emboldened crowd. The aim of catharsis is well established in primitive rituals of exorcism, and the concept has been used in some contemporary psychotherapies, most notably in "catharsis therapy," in which patients are encour-

aged to act out primal urges and fantasies, and to purge themselves with "primal screams" at the climax of their treatment.

The view of Sigmund Freud, the Viennese psychiatrist who formulated the theory of the "Oedipus complex," is that dramatic tragedy touches upon universal aspects of the human psyche which are repressed in adult life and therefore obstructive to self-realization until they can be liberated from the unconscious. High art affords one means of effecting this liberation. Freud contends that the Oedipus myth springs from the universal desire of the male child to unite sexually with his mother and from his corollary desire, necessary for the fulfillment of the first, to murder his father. According to Freud, these desires are most intense between the ages of three and five years; as the child matures and comes to understand that they cannot be realized and are, moreover, horrifying to contemplate, they are repressed and "go underground" into the unconscious, where they fester and cause anxiety, displaced rage, and neurosis. A performance of *Oedipus* has the effect of freeing us from the control of these unconscious desires, by illuminating and "punishing" them in the central character. To Freud, it is the (male) audience's unconscious rec-

> **O**edipus demonstrates that the urge to know might in itself be an awful thing, a terrible gift of man's which can lead to pain rather than joy. . . . Given man's *daimon* that he must know, and the irrationality that lies at the heart of things, it is not any particular human act but human existence itself that is tragic, and the fault lies not in Oedipus as this particular man but in Oedipus as man living in a world which is ultimately not made for man the knower.
>
> Laszlo Versenyi

ognition of the similarity between Oedipus' plight and their own repressed desires that makes the production moving, thrilling, and profound. Other tragedies, Freud suggests, tap other fundamental aspects of the human psyche and so stir the unconscious to similar response.

Yet a third view advanced to explain the sustained popular success of *Oedipus* on stage is that it echoes man's existential quest for meaning and identity in a universe which confirms neither, and indeed, in the case of Oedipus, repudiates both. *Oedipus* is seen as the archetypical human being striving to contend with blind circumstance, with what one critic calls "the terror of coincidence." By this view, his quest for self-knowledge is as futile as it is heroic. Furthermore, it is dangerous. "I *have* to hear!" he shouts to the terror-stricken shepherd in a rage for self-discovery; and of course what he learns is that *Oedipus tyrannos* and the infant *Clubfoot* are one: as if to find oneself is to destroy oneself—a terrifying but eternally fascinating dramatic theme.

These viewpoints in no way exhaust the interpretations and perspectives that have been put forth concerning this most discussed of all ancient tragedies; they do represent three sorts of approaches—dramaturgical, psychological, philosophical—which can be applied to any fine serious play that deals with the human condition. The play itself is neither summed nor stilled by such analyses. It remains accessible to all who are similarly questing in the struggle for personal, social, and spiritual clarity.

The Trojan Women

Even today, *The Trojan Women* is often regarded as the most powerful antiwar play ever written. Created out of the furious pacifist passion of its author, Euripides, it purportedly deals with ancient history and ancient gods; more accurately, it is about events that had taken place not long before the play's first public performance in 415 B.C.

Euripides differed radically from his two famous predecessors in his dramatic aims as well as his vision of Greece. Aeschylus wrote his epic works in an era of great Athenian military victories over the Persians; the serene, philosophical Sophocles was of the era of Pericles and the golden age of Athenian democracy. Euripides was a firebrand: irreligious, iconoclastic, and enraged at the politics of his times, in which Athens had become an imperialistic and warring nation under the corrupt tyrant Alcibiades. Society was changing, religion was changing, Socrates was soon to be given his hemlock, and Euripides was determined to provide corrective measures. If he lacked the magnificent versifying skills of Aeschylus and the plotting brilliance of Sophocles, he brought to the theatre a combination of acute political insight and psychological awareness that makes him seem the most contemporary of the ancient Greeks. It is significant that more plays of Euripides remain than of Aeschylus and Sophocles combined: this younger tragedian was the one most revered by the generations that undertook to preserve such playscripts as we now have.

The Trojan Women treats that great event of Greek historical mythos, the Trojan War, from an extraordinary perspective: that of the Trojan women who were its survivor-victims. It is rather as if an American playwright were to choose to write about World War II from the point of view of the Empress of Japan, and with a chorus composed of survivors of Hiroshima. For it is Hecuba, Queen of Troy, who is the hero of *The Trojan Women*, and the weeping widows of fallen Troy constitute the chorus. All that is noble and good in this play is Trojan; every utterance that is venal, shallow, and hypocritical is placed in the mouths of Greek despots or Greek gods. There can be little wonder that Euripides failed to win the first prize with this play—what is amazing is that he was allowed to produce it at all.

The dramatic structure of *The Trojan Women* is more like that of *Prometheus* than that of *Oedipus*: a prologue between two gods, an eloquent opening address by the hero, and a series of episodes that is more a sequence of pathetic vignettes than an integrated plot. Like Prometheus, Hecuba is a prisoner (she cannot leave the stage). Unlike the earlier play, however, *The Trojan Women* ends on a note of gloomy defeat rather than heroic defiance, and the overall tone of the two plays could hardly be more different. In fact, the tone of all the works of Euripides is unmistakably modern and pointed. Euripides was not one to extol heroes; quite the contrary, he considered it his job to demythicize the legends of the past—legends he found falsely based. Almost certainly a non-believer for most of his life (he may have undergone a last-minute conversion, judging from his last play, *The Bacchae*), he is known to have been a follower of the pre-Socratic philosophers Anaxagoras and Protagoras, the latter of whom, with his famous phrase "Man is the measure of all things," led an attack on Greek polytheism and the notion of divinity in general. The entire basis of Greek knowledge—in both science and art—was in a process of evolution from *mythos* (myth) to *logos* (logic), and Euripides, in trying to portray the logic of human relationships (what we would today call the sociology and psychology of those relationships), felt it necessary to brush aside the legends and legendary figures of the past quite brutally. Thus in this play the gods

are portrayed as liars, the Homeric heroes as banal egotists, and the Trojan War itself as a sort of fraternity caper that got out of hand.

Euripides opens the play with a shocking prologue—one of his trademarks—in which Athena, goddess of the Achaeans (Athenians), looks over the smoldering ruins of Troy, defeated for her sake, and suddenly decides after all this war and bloodshed to ally herself with her erstwhile enemy, Poseidon, divine patron of the Phrygians (Trojans).

ATHENE: . . . [F]or Troy's sake, on whose ground we stand, I come
    to win the favor of your power, and an ally.

POSEIDON: You hated Troy once; did you throw your hate away
    and change to pity now its walls are black with fire?

ATHENE: Come back to the question. Will you take counsel with me
    and help gladly in all that I would bring to pass?

POSEIDON: I will indeed; but tell me what you wish to do.
    Are you here for the Achaeans' or the Phrygians' sake?

ATHENE: For the Trojans, whom I hated this short time since. . . .

POSEIDON: This is a springing change of sympathy. Why must
    you hate too hard, and love too hard, your loves and hates?

ATHENE: . . . I would do some evil to them [the Achaeans].

POSEIDON: I am ready for anything you ask. What will you do?

ATHENE: Make the home voyage a most unhappy coming home.

And this change of heart, we are led to understand, is what led to the storms and mischances that befell the victors after they departed Troy, the dreadful events recounted in Homer's *Odyssey* and the suffering of the returning Agamemnon. Why does Athene turn her back on her compatriots? Because "they outraged my temple and shamed me," she says, and Poseidon concludes the prologue with its moral:

That mortal who sacks fallen cities is a fool,
who gives the temples and the tombs, the hal-
    lowed places
of the dead to desolation. His own turn must
    come.

What follows is a series of episodes unrivaled for their portrayal of the horrors of war, the meanness of the victors, and the suffering of the vanquished. Hecuba, who has lain crumpled in the orchestra circle as the gods converse in the prologue, now gets slowly to her feet and delivers the play's first human speech in a heroic verse reminiscent of Prometheus:

HECUBA: Rise, striken head, from the dust;
    lift up the throat. This is Troy, but Troy
    and we, Troy's kings, are perished.
    Stoop to the changing fortune.
    Steer for the crossing and the death-god,
    hold not life's prow on the course against
    wave beat and accident.
    Ah me,
    what need I further for tears' occasion,
    state perished, my sons, and my husband?
    O massive pride that my fathers heaped
    to magnificence, you meant nothing.
    Must I be hushed? Were it better thus?
    Should I cry a lament?
    Unhappy, accursed,
    limbs cramped, I lie
    backed on earth's stiff bed.
    O head, O temples
    and sides; sweet, to shift,
    let the tired spine rest
    weight eased by the sides alternate,
    against the strain of the tears' song
    where the stricken people find music yet
    in the song undanced of their wretchedness. . . .
    Come then, sad wives of the Trojans
    whose spears were bronze,
    their daughters, brides of disaster,
    let us mourn the smoke of Ilium.
    And I, as among winged birds
    the mother, lead out
    the clashing cry. . . .

The majesty of this speech is quite extraordinary; in calling herself "Troy's kings," Hecuba brings forth both the royal "we" and the masculine gender, calling into question both the collectivity and masculinity of the Greek victors. She, this "mother" of "winged birds" will "lead out the clashing cry" against the tyranny of the Athenians. And a brutal tyranny it is shown to be. First, Polyxena, Hecuba's youngest daughter, is reported to have been assigned to guard Achilles' tomb—it is later revealed that she is in fact buried in that tomb. Then Hecuba is apportioned off as a slave to Odysseus: of this hero of Homer's great epic she can only say:

HECUBA: Oh no, no!
    Tear the shorn head,
    rip nails through the folded cheeks.
    Must I?
    To be given as slave to serve that vile, that
        slippery man,
    right's enemy, brute, murderous beast,
    that mouth of lies and treachery, that makes
        void
    faith in all things promised
    and that wish was beloved turns to hate. . . .
    I am gone, doomed, undone,
    O wretched, given
    the worst lot of all.

Next, Hecuba's daughter Cassandra enters, carrying a flaming torch and gyrating hysterically in ghastly celebration of her upcoming "marriage" to the tyrant who has claimed her: Agamemnon. Cassandra's description of the Trojan War is a masterpiece of pacifist analysis:

CASSANDRA: The Achaens came . . . and died
    day after day, though none sought to wrench
        their land from them
    nor their own towering cities. Those the War
        God caught
    never saw their sons again, nor were they laid
        to rest
    decently in winding sheets by their wives'
        hands, but lie
    buried in alien ground; while all went wrong
        at home

"Tear the shorn head," cries Hecuba (Eliza Ward), in chains in Royal Shakespeare Company's 1980 version of The Trojan Women, *directed by John Barton.*

as the widows perished, and barren couples
　　raised and nursed
the children of others, no survivor left to tend
the tombs, and what is left there, with blood
　　sacrificed.
For such as this congratulate the Greeks. . . .
The Trojans have that glory which is loveliest:
they died for their own country.

From reported horrors, prophecies, and remembrances, the action moves on to fully dramatized brutalities. In one devastating scene, Euripides portrays the Greek henchman Talthybius taking Andromache's child, Astyanax, from his mother's arms to be thrown from the battlements to his death, for no reason but that he is Hector's child, the son of a Trojan hero. This deeply moving scene is filled with the realistic details for which Euri-

pides was as famous in his own time as in ours:

TALTHYBIUS: O wife of Hector, once the bravest
　　man in Troy
　　do not hate me. . . . I wish I did not have to give
　　this message.
ANDROMACHE: What can this mean, this hint of
　　hateful things to come?
TALTHYBIUS: The council has decreed for your
　　son—how can I say this?
ANDROMACHE: That he shall serve some other master than I serve?
TALTHYBIUS: No man of Achaea shall ever make
　　this boy his slave.
ANDROMACHE: Must he be left behind in Phrygia, all
　　alone?
TALTHYBIUS: Worse; horrible. There is no easy way
　　to tell it.

Image labels: DIONYSUS • EURIPIDES MIGHT HAVE BEEN "ROLLED" OUT ON THE ECCYCLEMA... • AESCHYLUS IN FRONT OF HIS "HOUSE" • LOGEION • SOME OF THE CHORUS IN THE ORCHESTRA

AESCHYLUS VERSUS EURIPIDES: A COMEDIC VIEW

The differences between Aeschylus and Euripides were apparently a particular source of active controversy in ancient Athens. In *The Frogs*, a celebrated comedy written by Aristophanes shortly after Euripides' death, the two tetralogy playwrights engage in a hypothetical debate conducted by Dionysus, who is looking to bring back from the dead whichever of the two is the more clever and can best "help the city survive." The debate is highly amusing, but it also constitutes a veritable seminar in Greek classic dramaturgy.

Some samples:

EURIPIDES: I tell you, I'm a better poet than he is.

DIONYSUS: You heard him, Aeschylus. Don't you have
    anything to say?

EURIPIDES: He's always started with the line of scornful
    silence.

    He used to do it in his plays, to mystify us. . . .
    I know this man. I've studied him for a long time.
    His verse is fiercely made, all full of sound and
        fury,
    language unbridled uncontrolled ungated-in
    untalkable-around, bundles of blast and boast.

AESCHYLUS: Is that so, child of the goddess of the
    cabbage patch?

    You—you jabber-compiler, you dead-beat poet,
    you rag-stitcher-together—you say this to me?
    Say it again. You'll be sorry. . . .

DIONYSUS: Now, gently, gently, Aeschylus:
    criticize, don't yell. It's not becoming for two
        poets

and gentlemen to squabble like two baker's
    wives.

You're crackling like an oak log that's been set
    ablaze.

EURIPIDES: I'm ready for him . . . my rival is a phony.

    His audience was a lot of louts.

    [*To Aeschylus*] When I took over our craft from
        you I instantly became aware

that she was gassy from being stuffed with heavy
    text and noisy air. . . .

I made the drama *democratic.* . . . I taught natural
    conversational dialogue. . . .

I staged the life of every day, the way we live.
    I couldn't deceive

my audience with the sort of stuff they knew as
    much about as I.

They would have spotted me right away.

I played it straight and didn't try

to bind a verbal spell and hypnotize and lead
    them by the nose. . . .

[T]hat's what my plays are about,

and these are my contributions,

and I turn everything inside out

looking for new solutions

to the problems of today,

always critical, giving

suggestions for gracious living,

and they come away from seeing a play

in a questioning mood, with "where are we at?"

and "who's got my this?" and "who took my
    that?" . . .

AESCHYLUS: What if you've broken your trust,

    and corrupted good sound right-thinking people

    and filled them with treacherous lust?

    If poets do that, what reward should they get?

DIONYSUS: The axe. That's what we should do with
    'em.

AESCHYLUS: Then think of the people *I* gave him, and
    think of the people when he got through with
    'em.

I left him a lot of heroic six-footers, a grand
    generation of heroes,

unlike our new crop of street-corner loafers and
    gangsters and decadent queer-o's.

Mine snorted the spirit of spears and splendor, of
    white-plumed helmets and stricken fields,

of warrior heroes in shining armor and greaves
    and sevenfold-oxhide shields. . . .

EURIPIDES: But you, with your massive construction,
    huge words and mountainous phrases—

is that what you call useful instruction?

You ought to make people talk like people.

AESCHYLUS: Your folksy style's for the birds.

    For magnificent thoughts and magnificent
        fancies, we must have magnificent words.

    It's appropriate too for the demigods of heroic
        times to talk bigger

than we. It goes with their representation as
    grander in costume and figure.

I set them a standard of purity. You've corrupted
    it.

EURIPIDES: How did I do it?

AESCHYLUS: By showing a royal man in a costume of
    rags, with his skin showing through it.

    You played on emotions.

The debate, only a small fraction of which is presented here, extends over a wide variety of stylistic, thematic, dramaturgical, and productional elements, including an extended discussion of metrics and a great many references to plays no longer known. It concludes, however, with a debate as to how Athens should be saved, and what should be done about the city-state's ruler, Alcibiades: "a baby who's giving our state delivery pains." That Aristophanes should purport to summon the aid of dead playwrights (one dead more than fifty years) in order to save the civilization is remarkable indeed—as if today we were to call on the spirits of David Belasco and Eugene O'Neill to advise on the impeachment of the current president. It illustrates the centrality of the theatre in Athenian intellectual and social life.

Cassandra (Joyce Ebert) enters with her torch, with the chorus silhouetted behind her, in Michel Cacoyannis' 1964 production of The Trojan Women *at New York City's Circle in the Square theatre, off Broadway in Greenwich Village.*

ANDROMACHE: I thank your courtesy. . . .

TALTHYBIUS: They will kill your son. It is monstrous. Now you know the truth.

ANDROMACHE: Oh, this is worse than anything I heard before.

TALTHYBIUS: Odysseus. He urged it before the Greeks, and got his way.

ANDROMACHE: This is too much grief. . . .

TALTHYBIUS: He said a hero's son could not be allowed to live.

ANDROMACHE: Even thus may his own sons some day find no mercy.

TALTHYBIUS: He must be hurled from the battlements of Troy.

ANDROMACHE: . . . O darling child I loved too well for happiness,

your enemies will kill you and leave your mother forlorn.

Your own father's nobility, where others found protection, means your murder now. . . . I lived never thinking the baby I had was born for butchery

by Greeks, but for lordship over all Asia's pride of earth.

Poor child, are you crying too? Do you know what they

will do to you? Your fingers clutch my dress. What use,

to nestle like a young bird under the mother's wing?

Hector cannot come back, nor burst from underground

to save you, that spear of glory caught in the
    quick hand,
nor Hector's kin, nor any strength of Phrygian
    arms.
Yours the sick leap head downward from the
    height, the fall
where none have pity, and the spirit smashed
    out in death.
O last and loveliest embrace of all, O child's
sweet fragrant body. Vanity in the end.
    I nursed
for nothing the swaddled baby at his mother's
    breast;
in vain the wrack of the labor pains and the
    long sickness.
Now once again, and never after this,
    come close

to your mother, lean against my breast and
    wind your arms
around my neck, and put your lips against my
    lips. . . .
TALTHYBIUS: . . . I am not the man
    to do this. Some other
    without pity, not as I ashamed
    should be herald of messages like this.

By this point in the play, Talthybius is shown to be repulsed at the excesses of his Greek masters; his is the emotional development Euripides wishes to induce in his Greek audience. It is not Greek victory which appalls this author, but Greek immorality and stupidity in the accomplishment of that victory. Menelaus, the only representative of the Greek leadership who appears in this play, enters in the penultimate scene and provides a scathing portrait

Andromache (Carolyn Coates) clings to her son in the Cacoyannis production of 1964, while chorus writhes in anguish behind her. This scene, in which a child is torn from his mother's arms, is one of most horrifying in all dramatic literature.

90

The Trojan Women: *a conjectural reconstruction of the moment when Talthybias takes Astyanax to his death.*

of crassness and imbecility. Fatuously ignorant, he struts into this arena of horrors with a bizarrely out-of-context line:

MENELAUS: O splendor of sunburst breaking forth this day, whereon
    I lay my hands once more on Helen,
        my wife. . . .
    Go to the house, my followers, and take her out;
    no, drag her out. . . . .

And in the semi-tragic, semi-comic scene which follows, it quickly becomes clear that Helen, who ran off with Paris ten years before and thus touched off the whole war, is a simple flirt who will have Menelaus back under her control in a matter of hours, if not minutes. The war, in other words, was a joke: the years of carnage that ended in the physical destruction of one civilization and the moral destruction of another were caused by a trivial domestic infidelity which will assuredly be repeated in short order.

Euripides concludes his play in a fashion which, but for the obvious passion behind every word, could only be described as high melodrama. The broken body of the child Astyanax is brought on stage on Hector's shield, to be prepared for burial. Hecuba, who earlier despaired of calling on the gods ("O gods! What wretched things to call on—gods!—for help.") now gives up on them altogether and tries to lead the chorus into a mass suicide:

HECUBA: O gods! Do I call upon those gods for help?
    I cried to them before now, and they would not hear.
    Come then, hurl ourselves into the pyre.
        Best now
    to die in the flaming ruins of our fathers' house!

But Talthybius prevents her from carrying out her intention, and the women are led off into slavery as the city of Troy is set afire and the Trojan civilization goes into oblivion.

The Trojan Women has frequently been pre-

"Do I call upon those gods for help?" demands Hecuba in the Royal Shakespeare Company's 1980 production.

sented during periods of national guilt—as in America during the Vietnam war. Its immense emotional power, however, was inspired by the author's outrage concerning an event in his own time: the Athenian invasion of Melos in 417–416 B.C. The island of Melos, neutral during the war between Athens and Sparta, had been courted by the Athenians to join their league; the Melians decided to remain neutral, however, inasmuch as they had enjoyed seven hundred years of freedom and harbored hostilities toward no one. The Greeks, incensed at the Melian refusal, surrounded Melos, starved it with a blockade, and eventually, according to the Greek historian Thucydides, "The Melians surrendered to the Athenians, who put to death all the grown men whom they took, and sold the women and children for slaves, and subsequently sent out five hundred colonists and inhabited the place themselves." This high-handed use of force was anathema to all liberal-thinking Athenians, and certainly to Euripides: it is unquestionable that *The Trojan Women* is much more

about Melos than about Troy, and the audience was obviously aware of that. Thus in 415 B.C., when Poseidon closed the prologue with the words "That mortal who sacks fallen cities is a fool. . . . His own turn must come," there could have been few in the audience who failed to reflect upon the import of the Melian massacre that had taken place the previous year. The statement proved awesomely prophetic: the Peloponnesian War ended in 405 with a Spartan victory; the Athenians, dispirited at the end, caved in more as a result of internal dissension and confusion than from military enfeeblement. The grand age of Athenian civilization was dead, and with it, the grand age of tragedy.

Since Euripides' time playwrights have frequently drawn upon ancient history and legend to cast light on current policies and used the theatre as a forum for political statements which might otherwise be suppressed. Thus in 1943, during the German occupation of Paris, French author Jean Anouilh wrote and produced his classic drama of confrontation between the free spirit and the ef-

Masks are used in Royal Shakespeare Company's 1980 production of The Trojan Women *to symbolize the faceless world of (male) bureaucratic/military violence.*

ficient but arbitrary totalitarian bureaucracy—all couched in the legend of *Antigone*. Nazi officials saw nothing offensive about this "Greek play" until it began attracting record audiences every night, whereupon they decided it should be closed on general principles. Across town, however, another theatre continued its presentation of Jean-Paul Sartre's *The Flies*—seemingly just a retelling of the Electra myth, but in fact an incisive commentary on contemporary moral responsibility and commitment. In both of these Occupation dramas, as in *The Trojan Women*, the playwright has universalized the experience of the immediate situation by placing it in the context of history and myth to create an enduring artistic masterpiece rather than a limited polemic. Universality is a fundamental attribute of the artistic transformation: the true artist always perceives in the immediate condition implications that are unbounded in space and time. Therefore, while we may well lament the destruction of Melos some 2500 years ago, we cannot be altogether rueful that it inspired the creation of *The Trojan Women*.

The tragedies of Euripides became the pri-mary models for the Roman authors who followed, and through them, for the authors of the Renaissance and neo-classic eras. The penetrating psychological realism of these tragedies, as well as their frank bitterness and their final skepticism toward gods, prophets, and heroes, found great appeal in later ages. What is more, the domestic affairs with which Euripides' characters often wrestled supplied stimulation for the tragicomedy of the future. As Euripides struggled against the restraints of the dramatic form handed him, his choruses become less and less crucial to the play's development. In addition, the actions required of his characters increasingly worked toward the abandonment of old acting styles and conventions—for example, we can imagine that scenes like that in which Andromache kisses her child Astyanax must have strained to the breaking point the conventional use of the actor's mask. Insofar as Euripides was the model for the drama that followed the Greeks, the old format had to be changed and broken in order for theatre to survive. And broken it was—but not before leaving the theatre a priceless heritage.

CHAPTER 4

THE MIDDLE AGES

The "Middle Ages" is the label historians have given to those years of European history between the fall of Rome (476 A.D.) and the coming of the Renaissance; it is a curiously colorless designation for one of the most diversely creative periods in the annals of Western civilization. It embraces a thousand years that were dominated by a feudal political and economic system of bishoprics and dukedoms, a chivalric order of knights, and a sharp differentiation between nobility and peasants. This was a cultural empire without an emperor, and it was held together by a common language, Latin, and a common piety, Christianity.

We tend to think of the Middle Ages as a transitional time, and also as a primitive one. It is certainly true that the civilization of the period was essentially rural, that the literature was mostly doctrinaire, and that the physical and social technology—roads, sewers, and political institutions—lacked the sophistication of either the preceding epoch or the succeeding one. It is also true that the first five centuries of the Middle Ages—the centuries known to historians as the "Dark Ages"—are mostly lost to history, and few of the hu-

man accomplishments of those years survived the deaths of their effectors. Yet none of this should obscure the fact that the years we do know well—the so-called High Middle Ages from the tenth and eleventh centuries on—were as active and productive of lasting accomplishment as any comparable time span in recorded civilization. If we think of the great cathedrals of Chartres and Salisbury and the magnificent abbeys of Cluny and St. Denis, if we reflect upon the incalculable social energy that produced crusades, kingdoms, religious revolutions, and the bursting forth of modern languages and literatures, we recognize a medieval civilization of sublime creativity and daring, wholly in command of its own intellectual, artistic, and material resources. The Middle Ages were neither transitional nor primitive, and in truth some of the achievements of that day, including the theatrical ones, have never been surpassed in magnitude or in popular appeal.

The great theatre of the Middle Ages was a religious one—a profoundly religious one. Upon examination, it reveals many important parallels with the Greek theatre. Like the Greek theatre, the medieval theatre began as a springtime religious observance ritualizing the resurrection of a divine figure—in this case, Jesus Christ—and, by analogous extension, the rebirth of vegetation in the fields. Also like the Greek theatre, the medieval one was intensely public and communal, attracting a mass audience for the celebration and illustration of a common mythos (the Old and New Testaments of the Christian Bible). Finally, once again like the Greek theatre, the medieval theatre became a function of the evolving civic government; that is, a part of the political and social life of the community as well as a vehicle for its religious expression.

It is true that the drama of the Middle Ages never produced a body of work demonstrating great individual literary genius—no Sophocles speaks to us from the 1400s—and even the best poetry of the period strikes our ears as charmingly naive. Nonetheless, if we expand our criteria for measuring dramatic effectiveness to include sheer scale and public response, we must appreciate and wonder at this theatre which unquestionably served as the ancestor of much of what has followed it in time.

THE *QUEM QUERITIS:* FROM TROPE TO DRAMA

The medieval theatre was born in the liturgy of the Christian Church of the early tenth century, when a series of liturgical elaborations, known as *tropes* (from the Latin *tropus*, meaning "added melody"), expanded the offices (services) of the Mass. The most significant of these tropes, the *Quem Queritis*, appeared in the Easter Mass. It celebrates, in responsive chanting, the visit of the three Marys to the tomb of the crucified Christ: they are met by an angel who tells them that Christ has risen, and their grief turns to joy. The text comes straight from the New Testament:

ANGEL: *Quem queritis in sepulchro, O Christicole?*
(Whom seek ye in the sepulchre, O Christian women?)
MARYS: *Jesum Nazerenum crucifixum, O caelicolae.*
(Jesus of Nazareth, the crucified, O heavenly one.)
ANGEL: *Non est hic, surrexit sicut praedixerat.*
Ite, nuntiate quia surrexit de sepulchro.
(He is not here; He is risen, as He foretold.
Go, announce that he has risen from the sepulchre!)

This was not yet drama—there was no impersonation

attempted—but it was dialogue, and it apparently proved a popular and meaningful addition to the Easter Mass. A similar trope was added to the Christmas Mass; it concerns shepherds seeking the infant Jesus.

The step from trope to full-fledged drama occurred late in the century, and by a rare stroke of fortune one of the earliest manuscripts for this drama, complete with full stage directions, exists today as part of a major medieval document, the *Concordia Regularis*, prepared in about 980 by St. Ethelwold, Bishop of Winchester (and therefore of England). In the *Concordia*, which governed all English church procedures for centuries to follow, were the following instructions for the enactment of the *Quem Queritis* in English Easter masses:

While the third lesson is being chanted, let four brethren vest themselves. Let one of these, vested in an alb, enter as though to take part in the service, and let him approach the sepulchre without attracting attention and sit there quietly with a palm in his hand. While the third respond is chanted, let the remaining three follow, and let them all, vested in copes, bearing in their hands thuribles with incense, and stepping delicately as those who seek something, approach the sepulchre. These things are done in imitation of the angel sitting in the monument, and the women with spices coming to anoint the body of Jesus. When therefore he who sits there beholds the three approach him like folk lost and seeking something, let him begin in a dulcet voice of medium pitch to sing *Quem queritis?* And when he has sung it to the end, let the three reply in unison *Jesum Nazarenum.* So he, *Non est hic, surrexit sicut praedixerat. Ite, nuntiate quia surrexit a mortuis.* At the word of his bidding let those three turn to the choir and say *Alleluia! Resurrexit Dominus!* [Hallelujah! The Lord is risen!] This said, let the one, still sitting there and as if recalling them, say the anthem *Venite et videte locum* [Come and see the place]. And saying this, let him rise, and lift the veil, and show them the place bare of the cross, but only the cloths laid there in which the cross was wrapped. And when they have seen this, let them set down the thuribles which they bore in that same sepulchre, and take the cloth, and hold it up in the face of the clergy, and as if to demonstrate that the Lord has risen and is no longer wrapped therein, let them sing the anthem *Surrexit Dominus de sepulchro* [The Lord is risen from the sepulchre], and lay the cloth upon the altar. When the anthem is done, let the prior, sharing in their gladness at the triumph of our King, in that, having vanquished death, He rose again, begin the hymn *Te Deum laudamus* [We praise Thee, O God]. And this begun, all the bells chime out together.

The *completeness* of this wholly satisfying liturgical mini-opera is apparent. Structurally, it contains all the classical requirements of serious drama, including exposition, conflict, recognition, reversal, and even a mini-catharsis attendant on the singing of the *Alleluia*. Theatrically, it presents its viewers with dramatic demonstration (the showing of the empty cloth), ritualization (the laying of the cloth on the altar), and celebration (the singing of the *Te Deum*). It is moreover a drama wholly impersonated, for although the priest-performers are not to be thought of as naturalistic actors, they seek to embody the characters they perform through costume (copes for the Marys and an alb for the angel), vocal modulation ("a dulcet voice of medium pitch"), carefully staged movements ("stepping delicately"), and, in general, what we call "acting" ("like folk lost and seeking something"). The staging of this drama includes furniture (something on which the angel sits), a set piece of some sort (the sepulchre), props (the palm, the thuribles, the cloth), pantomime (showing the cloth and making clear what is *not* there), singing, and a concluding orchestral effect ("the bells chime out together"); there is even a suggestion of stage trickery in the pre-play entrance of the priest who plays the angel and who, lacking scenery or a proscenium to lurk behind, must enter the staging area "as though to take part in the service . . . without attracting attention [and] sit there quietly." It is as if the whole of theatrical possibility—the sacred and the sham—were compressed into this tiny, seminal playlet from the first millennium A.D.

What is further significant about this playlet is its centrality to the Christian religion: it concerns the single most crucial episode of the Christian mythos—Christ's resurrection, which both "proved" His divinity and signified, by analogy, the redemptive power of God. Thus drama in its use as a part of the Easter Mass was not relegated to a decorative or subsidiary function, but rather was accorded the highest function of the liturgical office: to ritualize and bring life to this most important moment in the

The importance of these instructions [in the *Concordia Regularis*] can scarcely be exaggerated: not only do they inform us that the Easter Introit (the *Quem Queritis*) was conceived of in the tenth century as *officium*, not *ludus*, liturgical office, *not* play or game, but they give us a vivid picture of the style of acting and the means adopted to identify character and locality in this 'imitation of the angel sitting in the monument, and the women with spices coming to anoint the body of Jesus.' It was clearly intended that the congregation should be confronted with a double image. The Maries are men, not women. They wear copes, not fashionable female attire or historical 'period' dress. The dialogue is in Latin, not English; chanted, not spoken; and punctuated with hymns and anthems. The climax is the Te Deum, the most famous and familiar Christian hymn of praise and thanksgiving in which actors and audience participate together. Thus the event of Christ's resurrection is commemorated by re-enactment in the most artificial and formal manner imaginable: yet what is patently a highly ornate ritual from one standpoint is just as patently a dramatic representation of a turning point in Christian history when viewed from another. This dichotomy of visual image exactly parallels the dichotomy that was present in the fusion of historical time with actual time to form ritual time, and resulted in a form of dramatic representation that existed simultaneously as liturgical ritual and mimetic re-enactment. The result is liturgical music-drama for which the theatre is the basilica itself, the occasion a festival of rejoicing. The style is recognizably Romanesque.

Once a ceremony of this kind has been standardized . . . three developments are likely to follow: the original ceremony may be embellished and expanded, similar ceremonies modelled on it may legitimately figure in the liturgies for other festivals, and the individuals responsible for creating them may develop a technical awareness of what they are actually doing. The imitative aspect of the ceremony may thus come to possess an importance of its own, artistic rather than strictly religious. Proof exists that all three of these developments overtook liturgical music drama in the course of the eleventh century.

Glynne Wickham

The Quem Queritis *trope, staged near church altar.*

story of Christ. Obviously, any expansion of dramatization beyond the *Quem Queritis* episode would of necessity be in the direction of the "less-holy."

And indeed that is the direction which Christian drama took. The *Quem Queritis* grew longer as additional dialogue and then story lines were added to the central episode. Soon there were additional playlets showing the events leading up to the Resurrection and following it. More and more the dialogue departed from holy writ and was developed simply by surmise, and increasingly with an eye to theatricality. The language was "vulgarized," both in the literal sense—that is, it was translated from Latin into the "vulgar" or "common" languages of English, French, Flemish, German, and so forth—and in the figurative sense. It became, in short, grander, funnier, and more theatrical. By the middle of the twelfth century, it was a full-fledged "liturgical drama" consisting of playlets tracing man's history from the Creation to Judgment Day. Moreover, it was now staged not only at the cathedral altar but in the apse and transepts, and it was attracting not only the faithful parishioners but hundreds of curious strangers. As time passed, its dazzling display of costumes, set pieces, and "acting" performances was less and less tied to the sacred office of the Mass which had given it birth, more and more aimed at art and entertainment. The next step was perhaps inevitable: the medieval liturgical theatre outgrew the Mass, outgrew the liturgy, outgrew the production capabilities of the clergy, outgrew the cathedral itself—and burst forth upon the medieval marketplace.

THE LAICIZATION OF DRAMA

Drama left the Church during the thirteenth century. It left in part because, as we have seen, it had grown too large for presentation in the cathedrals and the time needed for its preparation and production exceeded the reasonable limits the clergy could allow. But there were other reasons as well. Eventually, the Church officers felt constrained to rebel at lending their blessing to a theatrical style whose characters and language had so little to do with the Bible; there is also indication that the clergy began to grow alarmed at the sheer popularity of the dramatic format and to fear it might supplant the more traditional means of religious worship and devotion. It was for some of these reasons that Pope Innocent II, in 1240, actually issued a decree that ordered drama from the Church and forbade clerical participation in dramatic activities.

Thus far we have examined the more negative reasons why drama left the Church. On the positive side, what happened was that the theatre's function had increased beyond the sacred ritualizing of ancient mythos. From beginning to end, the medieval theatre was devotedly and devoutly religious—but in the thirteenth century it became many things else besides. It became social and aesthetic. It became commercial. It became entertaining. And it needed a forum more appropriate to these added functions and opportunities.

The city fathers saw that need and responded.

They had not failed to notice that the larger liturgical dramas—particularly those performed in the springtime—drew hundreds of farmers and citizens from neighboring towns into the cathedrals; by the middle of the thirteenth century it had become evident to them that civic pride and commercial interest stood to benefit from such gatherings. And so it was that the civic community took over the production of the expanded devotional plays. It was a community that included guilds, brotherhoods, municipal governments, and religious associations, all of them united in a concept of congruity between faith and commerce, ritual and entertainment, devotion and artistry, salvation and society. As a result of this mingling of interests and opportunities, an immense flowering of the medieval theatre occurred all over Europe from about 1250 until well into the sixteenth century. This theatre, conceived on a scale which we can hardly even imagine today, was devoted above all to the dramatic glorification of Christ; in pursuit of that aim, it proved a powerful force for the moral instruction of an illiterate but ethically receptive populace, the ritualization of the two Testaments of Biblical mythos, the urbanization of a rural society—and the festive amusement and entertainment of the European community after a long winter locked in against the cold.

What was this flowering medieval theatre like? We can cite no single "typical" example, because it evolved over the course of more than two hundred years of annual productions performed in hundreds of towns in more than a dozen different languages and cultures. The plays have been given numerous names (mystery plays, passion plays, cycle plays, pageant plays, miracle plays, Corpus Christi plays); but basically, their pattern was always the same: a series of playlets inspired by stories in the Bible, written in a common language of the populace, presented in sequence, performed in, on, and/or around a stage or series of stages. Some stages were rolled about from one location to another; others were stationary. The total production told the story of mankind as it was understood in the Christian thought of the day.

Scale and duration were two of the most imposing features of medieval plays. Virtually all of them lasted a number of days. One passion play lasted forty days, and had three hundred actors playing five hundred roles. Playlets were performed on elaborately crafted temporary stages (sometimes called *mansions* in France) which were set up in public squares and moved about from day to day (or, in some cases, from playlet to playlet). Convenience rather than aesthetic convention governed the methods of production: medieval directors produced their works wherever it seemed most practical—in earthen amphitheatres of contemporary construction, in the ruins of Roman arenas, in marketplaces and public squares, and in processions through village streets. The two-day festival at Lucerne, Switzerland, took place in the Wine Market Square, which survives today much in its original form; the stage plans and directions for the 1583 production at Lucerne reveal that the performance utilized, in addition to *mansion* stages erected in the square, the doors, windows, facades, and balconies of fronting buildings. The 1509 perfor-

mance at Romans, France, took place in the garden of a monastery, where temporary bleachers were set up for audience seating and scaffolding was erected for the staging area and *mansions*.

The English plays of the Middle Ages hold particular interest for the English-speaking reader and theatre-goer, not only because they are among the first literary works written in the English language, but also because they utilized one of the most astonishing staging practices of all time, the rolling procession. At least 125 English towns produced passion plays, which in England were generally called "cycle plays" because of their peculiar staging format, or "Corpus Christi plays" because they were commonly performed at the time of the church festival of Corpus

The "stations" of a Passion Play, set up in a public square very much as was originally staged inside the church. The action of the play flowed from one area to the next.

Christi (literally, "body of Christ"). This festival occurred in spring some time between late May and late June (on the Thursday following Trinity Sunday) and, as the name implies, it celebrated the mystery of divinity in the body of Jesus Christ: it was therefore seen as an appropriate holy day for the reaffirmation of the spiritual aspects of human existence by means of humanly enacted drama. Of the surviving English medieval plays, most come from Corpus Christi dramas that were performed at Chester, Wakefield, and York; it is to the York festival which we now turn for specific illumination and a reconstruction of the excitement of medieval theatre.

THE CORPUS CHRISTI PLAYS AT YORK

Corpus Christi plays are known to have been produced at York, in northeast England, from at least the year 1378; they were probably going on long before that. Historical records tell us that King Richard II attended the York festival in 1397, and actual playtexts survive from the early fifteenth century. These, along with court records, other documents, and information from other festivals, permit a fairly clear reconstruction of the content and staging of the plays and convey a vivid sense of the dramatic vitality of the times.

In York, as in most of England, the town corporation, or governing body, was charged with the overall coordination of Corpus Christi plays. The individual playlets (at York there were forty-eight of these) were allocated by the corporation to various craft guilds, which were somewhat akin to modern-day craft unions, and each guild assumed responsibility for casting, funding, rehearsing, and producing its assigned playlet. This association of government, guild, and theatre could only have come about with the universal rise in the late Middle Ages, of a civic and commercial bourgeoisie—a middle class which, while properly obedient to Church and King, depended on neither clergy nor royalty for lifeblood support; indeed, it was a time when urban and commercial interests were growing at the expense of the landed aristocracy. The theatre of the High Middle Ages was resolutely middle class. It was also "professional," not in the sense that we speak of professional theatre today, but in the sense that it was created and supported by highly motivated professional craftsmen and artisans who employed their skills to the fullest in the service of their dramatic assignments. Perhaps a comparison to a later age can be made with respect to El Teatro Campesino in California, which allied with the Farm Workers Union in the 1970s to produce a series of plays that did much to dignify not only the union's cause but also the social aspirations of migrant farm workers and Mexican-Americans in the Western United States.

All the surviving English plays are of unknown

authorship, although various "hands" have been identified in their writing—the "York realist" and the "Wakefield master," for example. Creative anonymity was characteristic of the medieval age, which was in general devoted more to piety than to self-celebration; even the great Gothic cathedrals of the period were "unsigned." Many hands aided in the writing of the York plays, most of which underwent numerous revisions as they were handed down from generation to generation (and perhaps from guild to guild as well); and the complete collection of forty-eight playlets which was kept in a "register" by the York corporation shows a great diversity of writing styles from playlet to playlet. The forty-eight cycles of the York plays and the guilds which presented them were as follows:

1 The Creation and the Fall of Lucifer—Barkers
2 From the Creation to the Fifth Day—Plasterers
3 God Creates Adam and Eve—Cardmakers
4 Adam and Eve in the Garden of Eden—Fullers
5 Man's Disobedience and Fall—Coopers
6 Adam and Eve Driven from Eden—Armorers
7 Sacrifice of Cain and Abel—Glovers
8 Building of the Ark—Shipwrights
9 Noah and the Flood—Fishers and Mariners
10 Abraham's Sacrifice—Parchmenters and Bookbinders
11 The Israelites in Egypt, the Ten Plagues, and Passage of the Red Sea—Hosiers
12 Annunciation and Visitation—Spicers
13 Joseph's Trouble about Mary—Pewterers and Founders
14 Journey to Bethlehem, Birth of Jesus—Tile Thatchers
15 The Angels and the Shepherds—Candlemakers
16 Coming of the Three Kings to Herod—Masons
17 Coming of the Three Kings, the Adoration—Goldsmiths
18 Flight into Egypt—Marshals (i.e., horse grooms)
19 Massacre of the Innocents—Girdlers and Nailers
20 Christ with the Doctors in the Temple—Spurmakers and Bitmakers
21 Baptism of Jesus—Barbers
22 Temptation of Jesus—Blacksmiths

23 The Transfiguration—Curriers
24 Women Taken in Adultery, Raising of Lazarus—Capmakers
25 Christ's Entry into Jerusalem—Skinners
26 Conspiracy to Take Jesus—Cutlers
27 The Last Supper—Bakers
28 The Agony and Betrayal—Cordwainers
29 Peter Denies Jesus, Jesus Examined by Caiaphas—Bowyers and Fletchers (i.e., bow and arrow makers)
30 Dream of Pilate's Wife, Jesus before Pilate—Tapiters and Couchers (i.e., makers of tapestry and carpets)
31 Trial Before Herod—Litsters (i.e., dyers)
32 Second Accusation Before Pilate, Remorse of Judas, Purchase of Field of Blood—Cooks and Water-leaders
33 Second Trial Continued, Judgment on Jesus—Tilemakers
34 Christ Led Up to Calvary—Shearmen
35 The Crucifixion—Pinners and Painters
36 Mortification of Christ—Butchers
37 The Harrowing of Hell—Saddlers
38 The Resurrection, Fright of the Jews—Carpenters
39 Christ's Appearance to Mary Magdalen—Winedrawers
40 Travelers to Emmaus—Sledmen
41 Purification of Mary; Simeon and Anna Prophesy—Hatmakers, Masons, and Laborers
42 Incredulity of Thomas—Scriveners
43 Ascension—Tailors
44 Descent of the Holy Spirit—Potters
45 The Death of Mary—Drapers
46 Appearance of Our Lady to Thomas—Weavers
47 Assumption and Coronation of the Virgin—Ostlers (i.e., stablemen)
48 Judgment Day—Mercers (i.e., dealers in cloth)

The numerological features of this forty-eight play sequence would certainly have attracted the medieval mind, addicted as it was to discerning patterns in the universe. The number of plays is not only twice the number of hours in the day (the Chester cycle, more perfectly, contained twenty-four plays), but also effects what was taken to be a sacred geometric balance: the annunciation of Christ's coming occurs one-quarter of the way through the overall drama, and the Crucifixion—Resurrection (covered in four plays) falls at the three-quarter point, giving the whole a mathematical order that achieved, in the view of its spectators, an echo of divine organization.

The means of presentation at York, as in other parts of England, was truly astonishing, even for medieval times. It was a procession through town in which each of the entire series of playlets was "toured" on its own rolling stage (known as a "pageant" or "pageant wagon") to ten, twelve, sometimes even sixteen different locales ("stations") throughout the city for as many separate performances as there were stations. This resulted in a daylong procession, beginning at four-thirty in the morning and apparently lasting until very late at night, until each of the forty-eight playlets had been performed at every station! In trying to imagine the sheer magnitude of this enterprise, some modern-day theatre historians have come to suspect that we may have erred in our interpretation of the records (see bibliographical note, p. 434); however, it would seem entirely possible that a society possessed of the energy and exuberance to build grandiose cathedrals and to pursue ambitious and costly crusades would not shrink from the hard work and spiritual dedication implicit in the York cycle processional.

What the rolling pageant wagon looked like we cannot say for certain. A reference from the early seventeenth century describes it as a four- or six-wheeled two-story cart with a curtained dressing room below and an acting area above. It is clear that all wagons had at least two vertical levels, possibly more, and that all afforded some means of access to the street. It has been suggested that scaffolding might have been erected at each station to afford additional acting space, or that more than one wagon might have been used for playlets requiring more staging facilities than a single wagon could accommodate. Some such arrangement would seem necessary, for example, for the staging of the last of the York sequence, the Judgment Day.

We know beyond question that the wagons were elaborate and expensive structures: guilds which did not own them had to rent them for the enormous sum of five shillings (about $1,000 today), and guilds which did own them had to rent buildings to store them from one Corpus Christi day to the next. The skills of the guild members were frequently employed in the building of the wagons and their attendant scenic elements—it was, of course, no coincidence that the Shipwrights were allocated the "Noah" pageant and the Goldsmiths the "Adoration"—and if we can believe that the York craftsmen lent anything like as much artistry to the making of pageant wagons as they did to the construction of York Minster, their magnificent cathedral, we must imagine that those wagons were splendid structures indeed.

The great majority of actors in the York plays were local guild members and their friends. Literally hundreds of actors were required, and for most the play was doubtless viewed primarily as a major annual social activity. However, performers received some wages, and premium wages were paid to those with special abilities. Although the secular theatre had died with the fall of Rome, its tradition of miming, juggling, "mumming," and minstreling had never been wholly extinguished during the Dark Ages, and in the pageant plays of the High Middle Ages the inheritors of this performing tradition found an opportunity to combine their skills with dramatic performance. Some roles—chiefly those of the grand villains of the Bible (Herod, Pilate, Satan) and the most eloquent deities (God and Jesus)—demanded considerable acting skill to fulfill the expectations of the medieval audience. Other roles, more playful and rustic, became vehicles for greatly entertaining comedic performances. The rehearsal of these plays, for which only a few days were usually allotted, is amusingly (if perhaps unfairly) satirized by Shakespeare in A Midsummer Night's Dream (see p. 121) in a manner which gives a sense of both the vitality and the struggle that marked this early stage in the development of English acting art.

To envision something of the ultimate effect of the York processional drama, we might do well to compare it to the Rose Bowl Parade that is currently held each New Year's Day in Pasadena. This annual outdoor holiday procession (staged in the eternal springtime of Southern California) features a number of floats, each sponsored, funded, and prepared by a civic or community group, each dedicated to an overall theme chosen by the parade's governing body, and each stopping by a reviewing stand for some sort of "living tableau" with amateur "performers" waving, smiling, and conveying some sort of idea or topic.

Some wagons may have had a third level... and stage machinery...

A SCAFFOLD MAY HAVE BEEN SET UP, WITH SEATING and an ADDITIONAL PLAYING AREA

AN ACTOR "IN the LOWER ROOM"

Some playlets required three distinct acting "levels," as for Heaven, Earth, and Hell; others required large acting areas. These illustrations suggest possible ways of adapting wagons to meet these requirements effectively.

Just as the floats of Pasadena are advertisements for their sponsors, so the pageant wagons at York attested to the professional and commercial merits of the guilds that built them; and as the Pasadena floats have grown in technological sophistication over the years, so we might expect that the medieval wagons became increasingly splendid and elaborate over the course of their more than two hundred–year history. The cycle plays outdid the Pasadena parades, of course, by being dramatic as well as theatrical and processional, and by stopping at numerous stations instead of a single reviewing stand; nonetheless, the parallel may bring into focus the extraordinary public spectacle of York theatre five and six centuries ago.

*Pageant wagons in
a town square;
a conjectural
reconstruction.*

SECTION TWO: THE PAST

The York Cycle

Of the forty-eight playlets that constituted the York sequence, we shall look at four, none of which consumed more than fifteen or twenty minutes in playing time. In combination—which is the only way that we can fairly look at them—they give a general picture of the main themes and theatrical practices of the entire cycle.

The Creation and *The Fall of Lucifer*

The first playlet in the York sequence was, naturally, the Creation. It is one of the shorter texts—only 166 lines—and, when delivered with a great deal of action, could be expected to provide a snappy opening for the entire forty-eight–cycle marathon. It is staged alternately in Heaven and Hell, and therefore requires (as do most of the playlets) at least two acting areas, probably at different vertical levels.

The action begins in Heaven. God appears, announcing himself to a host of angels and, by extension, to the audience gathering in the early morning streets of York.

GOD: I am Alpha and Omega, the Life, the Way, the
    Truth,
    the First and the Last.
I am gracious and great, God without
    beginning;
I am maker unmade, all might is in me;
I am life and way unto wealth-winning;
I am foremost and first; as I bid shall it be.
On blessing my blee shall be blending,
And hielding from harm to be hiding,
My body in bliss ay abiding,
Unending without any ending.*

Here we can see at a glance the distance between medieval verse and our own, and the remarkable directness and simplicity of the dramaturgy. The

exposition is absolutely straightforward, as of course it must be in this short dramatic form. The writer cannot waste time on subtle or clever story development, and he has no need to introduce characters as familiar as God (and, later, Adam, Eve, Jesus, and Pilate). As for the language, not only is it remote in time, but it is written in a verse form that is often (incorrectly) called doggerel, a form somewhat irregular in meter and rhyme and alliterative to an extraordinary degree ("foremost and first," "hielding from harm," "gracious and great," "on blessing my blee shall be blending"). Indeed, Shakespeare also satirized this form of versifying in *A Midsummer Night's Dream* (see p. 121), and today we have to look into it quite closely to discern the source of its impact in its own time. The verse of the medieval theatre was aimed first and foremost at conveying a sense of spiritual majesty comparable to that attained by the use of Latin in the earlier liturgical plays: the play was to be perceived as a message of divine origin, of scriptural import. The use of verses which fit into subtle mathematical metric and rhyme schemes —as many of the verses in these plays do—was intended to elevate the medieval drama beyond the ordinary and into the mystical, and to give a sense that their anonymous authors were not ordinary mortals at all, but scribes of the divine. Thus, fundamentally, the verse of the medieval theatre was created for purposes of religious instruction, not for aesthetic reasons; its whole justification was to support the notion of divine intent behind the play's messages and themes. To the medieval mind, then, the stylization of the verse was not perceived as a literary decoration, but as a proper means of communicating spiritual *truth*; thus it affords a rare but revealing case whereby a stylization of language leads to the creation of greater sense of "reality" than could possibly be achieved in the ordinary language of the day.

Let us now return to our playlet. God, having announced himself, then creates the world:

GOD: Here underneath me an island I neven
    [name],
    Which island shall be Earth. Now there be
Earth, wholly, and Hell; this—highest Heaven,
And all that wealth wields, here give I to ye.
This grant I you, ministers mine,

---

*The spelling in this speech has been modernized, but the passage is otherwise unedited to show the characteristics of Middle English verse. Passages that appear later have been lightly edited for this text. "Blee" is a meaningless word, utilized solely for its poetic sound. "Heilding" means hiding; the verse features abundant repetition.

Lucifer tempts Eve in the York Cycle, as staged in York, England, before the ruined Abbey in 1980.

As long as y'are stable in thought.
As far as those that are nought—
They in my prison shall pine.

Then, turning to his archangel Lucifer, God appoints him second in command, and introduces the playlet's central conflict and the great division of the universe into two worlds: good and evil.

GOD: Of all the mights I have made most next after
    me,
I make thee as master and mirror of my
    might;
I bield [protect] thee here bainly [now], in bliss
    for to be,
And I name thee Lucifer—bearer of light.

Next the angels sing a hymn, "Holy, Holy, Holy, Lord God of Hosts," and praise this act of God:

ANGELS: Ah, merciful Maker, full mickle [powerful] is thy might,
That all this work at a word worthily has
    wrought.
Ay, praised be that lovely Lord of his light,
That us mighty has made, that before were but
    nought.

The scene bears some uncanny resemblances to the Greek *Prometheus*. Like Prometheus, Lucifer is a close ally of God (Zeus) and is the bearer (and namesake) of light, the beloved benefactor of lesser demigods and, as it turns out, one who will eventually be spurned by God for too great a prideful exploitation of his gifts. But despite the parallels, what a world of difference! For this light-bearer occasions no sympathy in the audience. Whatever majesty the medieval author had to command was expended on the higher character, the one who began the play with the splendid, metaphorical "I am the Alpha and Omega, the Life. . . ." This was no struggle between co-equals in the divine realm, but a simple confrontation between right and wrong in the moral arena.

God leaves the stage, and Lucifer rants. Ranting was apparently considered a particularly effective means of character portrayal by medieval authors and directors; it allowed villainous characters to strut and storm about on the stage and in the audience in colorful exhibitions of bragging, posturing, and rage—doubtless to the delight of all concerned. (Later, Shakespeare was to refer to one of the great villains of medieval plays when he had Hamlet warn his actors not to "tear a passion to tatters . . . it out-herods Herod!") A sample of Lucifer's boasting illustrates how the medieval villain was portrayed:

LUCIFER: All the mirth that is made is marked in
    me!
The beams of my brightness are burning so
    bright,
And so seemly in sight myself now I see,
For like a lord I am left to live in this light
More fairer by far than my feers [friends],
In me is no point to impair,
I feel me so famous and fair,
My power is passing my peers!

Certainly Prometheus also had a high opinion of himself, but the unabashed rantings of Lucifer are comic in their exaggeration; they are neither terrifying nor touching. Nonetheless Lucifer continues, until he takes the insupportable step of likening himself to God. Again, however, his challenge is foolish rather than frightening:

LUCIFER: In glorious glamour my glittering gleams!
I shall bide in bliss through my brightness of
    beams!
In Heaven I'll set myself, full seemly to sight,
To receive all reverence, through my right of
    renown.
I shall be like unto him that is highest on hight,
Oh! How I am deft—Oh!!! Deuce!!! All goes
    down!!
My might and my main have stopped calling!
Help, Fellows! In faith, I am FAALLLLINGGG!

And with that, Lucifer, with his angel admirers, falls into the lower staging area—into "Hell."

The staging of Hell was one of the medieval masterpieces. In continental Europe, where stationary *mansions* were commonly used, the "Hellmouth" was a vividly horrifying stage piece designed to swallow "sinners." The presence of Hell in the cycle—it is portrayed in both the first and the last playlets—reflects its pervasive influence in medieval life. Hell was the supreme terror which both religion and drama sought to explain and to exorcise. It seems unlikely that there would be anything truly frightening about this Yorkish Hellmouth which was carted through the village streets on a wagon, but it must have generated the kind of visceral excitement that was needed to get the attention of an early-rising audience and to put them in an active mood of participation on a springtime morning.

As Lucifer and his cohorts land in Hell, the angels (now devils) fight with each other in a roust-about scene of frenzied denunciation:

LUCIFER: Out! Out! Torment! Helpless! HOT it is here!

This is a dungeon of dole into which I am dight [put]!
I, Lucifer, once so comely and clear,
Now am I loathest that ever was light!
My brightness is black and blue now!

A DEVIL: Out! Out! I wail in woe! My wit is all went now!
Our food is but filth we find us beforn [before]!
We that were bathed in bliss, in bogs are we burnt now,
Out on thee, Lucifer! Lummox! Our light thou has lorn [stolen]!

LUCIFER: Out! Away! Woe is me now—it is worse than it was!
Don't bother to chide me, I said but a thought.

One version of a medieval "Hellmouth," as used in a stationary staging on the European continent.

another variation of the Devil costume... the Devil was a warning, but was also *entertaining*.

the role required a sword →

devil mask

MEDIEVAL ACTOR in DEVIL Costume...

Variations on satan's costume. Satan was a significant character in many medieval dramas, and the actor cast in the part was a particularly skilled performer.

DEVIL: Out, Lummox! Thou lost us!

LUCIFER: You lie! Out! Alas!

I wished not this woe should be wrought.

Out on you, lummoxes! You smother me in smoke.

DEVIL: This woe you have wrought us!

LUCIFER: You lie! You lie!

DEVIL: YOU lie, and now you will cry.

Out, lummox! Have at you! Come devils, let's poke!

A general battle ensues in the street, much, one must presume, to the merriment of enchanted spectators.

The play concludes with a final scene in Heaven, where God, reappearing, draws the moral in typically unequivocal fashion:

GOD: Those fools from their fairness into fantasy fell,

And made moan of might that marked them and made them.

So passing of power they thought them,

They would not me worship that wrought them.

Therefore my wrath shall over go with them.

And then God proceeds with creation, deciding first to create man ("Mankind of mould [earth] will I make") and then to create night for the devils ("In Hell shall never murkiness be missing,/The murkiness which I name the night") and daylight for mankind:

The day, that call I this light,

My afterworks shall they be guiding.

And now in my blessing I divide them in two,

The night from the day, so that they shall meet never.

But rather to separate gates go they to,

Both night-time and day, different duties forever.

[*to the audience*] To you I'll give guidance unceasing.

This day's work is done—ring the bell,

For all this work likes me right well,

And now I give it my blessing.

With that, the wagon rolls off to the next station, leaving God's benediction behind.

It was a brilliant stroke to end this playlet with the creation of daylight, for as timed by the play's producers, that action occurred simultaneously with the first slanting of the sun's rays over the Yorkshire dales. The goal of the medieval theatre was to show the harmony between Heaven and nature as revealed in the cycles of history, the cycles of life, and the cycles of the day. The play was timed to set all three in motion simultaneously.

In comparing this simple, short playlet with the thematically similar *Prometheus*, we can see both shared characteristics and important differences. On the one hand, we feel compelled to ask how it was that two wholly different cultures, utterly unknown to each other and separated in time by two thousand years and in space by two thousand miles, each came to create a drama of a light-god second in command to a more omnipotent deity, and to show in these dramas how the presumption of the light-god caused his fall into a sort of eternal imprisonment whence he battled on against his antagonist. Moreover, we must wonder what caused both cultures to feature this drama at an outdoor springtime festival associated with religious worship and celebration. The answers perhaps lie in the need for both cultures, coming out of their separate dark ages of primitivism and religious monasticism, to come to grips with growing pressures toward individuality and general enlightenment. Both dramas imply an awareness of man's potential to defy the laws laid down by religious revelation, and to seek out answers to life's perplexities through personal investigation and imagination. Both deal with the struggle of one character to break free from the restraints imposed by a higher authority, and both examine the possibilities of an individual's failure to conform in an otherwise spiritually rigid community. The sin of Lucifer is essentially that of Prometheus: the Greeks called it *hubris*, which means wanton arrogance or outrageous presumption. What is more, the medieval author, in using a demigod for his challenger, capitalized on the very same structure used by Aeschylus to make the challenge to the high god seem possible and credible.

On the other hand, of course, the differences between these plays are amply apparent even on the superficial level. The story told in the York playlet is a simple one based on an uncomplicated theme. It features a good god rather than a rapacious one and a foolish challenger rather than a magnificent one; its climaxes come in simple fights and benedictions rather than in philosophically complex and poetically powerful odes; and its staging is always more entertaining than awesome, more comic than piteous, and more spontaneous than stylistically formalized. The medieval theatre was not yet ready to deal with outsized heroics; this was still an age of the deepest popular piety, and indeed probably more than one would-be rebel decided to toe the mark after seeing the fate of Lucifer and others like him. The emergence and acclaim of individual genius was to come with the Renaissance.

The Fall of Man

The playlet concerning the Fall of Man, the fifth in the York cycle, expands upon this special topic of ancient drama—man's knowledge and the balance of despair and pride which that knowledge demands—in a manner touchingly realistic and rural for such a profound theological issue. Its action is set in Hell, Earth, and Heaven, and portrays Satan donning the disguise of a serpent (or a "wicked worm," in the alliterative language of the play) and seducing Eve, who then persuades Adam to eat of the forbidden fruit from the tree of knowledge. The temptation is intellectual, not sensual:

SATAN: Eve . . . thou wilt see
    Who eats the fruit of good and ill
    Shall have knowing as well as He.
EVE: Why, what kind of thing art thou
    That tells this tale to me?
SATAN: A worm, that knowest how
    That ye may worshipped be.
EVE: What worship should we win thereby?
    To eat thereof we needeth nought.
    We have lordship to make mastery
    Of all things that on earth are wrought.
SATAN: Woman, do way! (*giving her the fruit*)
    To greater state may ye be brought!
EVE: To do that would make us loath
    That should our God mispay.
SATAN: It surely is no wothe [harm];
    Eat it safely, ye may.
    For peril right none therein lies,
    But worship, and great winning.
    For just as God shall ye be wise,
    Equal to him in everything.
    Ay, gods shall ye be,
    Of ill and good to have knowing,
    And you will be as wise as He.
EVE: Is this sooth that thou says?
SATAN: Yea, why trust you not me?
    I would by no ways
    Tell but truth to thee.

Here we see that *knowledge* is the fruit forbidden to man, particularly the knowledge of "good and ill," which up to that time, according to the

A modern production of The Mystery Cycle, *directed by Nagle Jackson at American Conservatory Theatre, 1972. Three actors play tree with forbidden fruit, R. Aaron Brown plays Satan, and Deborah May plays Eve in this highly stylized adaptation.*

The Fall of Man. A conjectural reconstruction showing Adam and Eve on the wagon platform, with God above and Satan (as the Serpent) in the street.

myth, had been the sole prerogative of God. The Bible suggests that the reason for God's subsequent harsh punishment of Adam and Eve was that He regarded them as potential rivals. Surely priests and others charged with transmitting and interpreting the divine intent have always shared this concern with respect to human knowledge. And just as surely, their concern has been justified. As the Greek *mythos* had once struggled with (and lost out to) the *logos* of Greek scientific reasoning, so now the medieval authors perceived in man's quest for individual knowledge a threat to religious and revealed truth. Indeed, this quest would become one of the main themes of medieval drama, and the reason is twofold: first, the society was emerging from medieval absolutism and moving toward the spirit of questioning that was soon to inspire the

Renaissance and the Reformation; and second, the theatre itself was (and is) particularly well designed to portray such a quest and to celebrate the seeker. We get little of the Reformationist or Renaissance questioning here, of course, and none of the heroics of the free thinker; the medieval theatre was doggedly conservative—even anti-intellectual—and it unfailingly reflected a bias in favor of unthinking obedience. But we do get the topic, and with it a hint of the longing for intellectual independence which was latent in late medieval culture and literature.

God's visit to Adam after the eating of the fruit is as artless an interrogation scene as the drama provides. It conjures a vision of two Yorkishmen meeting in a field to talk over a problem of poaching. However, the penalty is appropriately Biblical:

GOD: Adam! Adam!

ADAM: Lord?

GOD: Where art thou? Yare!
     [Speak up!]

ADAM: I hear thee, Lord, and see thee nought.

GOD: Say, whereon is it long? [What's going on
     here?]
     This work—why has thou wrought?

ADAM: Lord, Eve made me do wrong.
     And to that breach me brought.

GOD: Say, Eve, why hast thou caused thy mate
     Eat fruit I told thee should hang there still,
     And commanded none of it to take?

EVE: A worm, Lord, enticed me theretill.
     Alas, that ever I did that deed so dill.

And God commands that the snake shall henceforth glide on its "womb," and that Adam and Eve shall henceforth "sweat and swink and travail" (sweat and toil and labor) for their food. Adam and Eve depart from Paradise, wringing their hands ("our hands may we wring"), as the wagon rolls away.

The Fall of Man playlet requires three areas of action, presumably on three different levels—one where Satan dresses himself in a worm costume below Paradise; one where God enters; and finally, one to show a middle ground where God orders his angels to drive Adam and Eve after the Fall. There is also a tree in Paradise, from which Eve plucks the fruit. All this indicates a staging of some complexity, if not grandeur. In no way should the visual effect of this staging be thought of as realistic, however. The visual elements of the medieval stage were highly symbolic—or "iconographic," as historians would say—and they were standardized both in meaning and appearance, with an economy of detail. The tree of knowledge, for example, was seen as a precursor of the cross on which Christ died, and the symbolic parallel was carried through in the staging as well as in the conceptualization of these plays. The importance of the cycle was in its totality and in the harmony of its elements, which focused always on the conclusion to which the cycle led—the passion of Christ, the harrowing of Hell, and the final judgment. The independent playlets were considered important only as they fit into the grand design of the total production and, implicitly,

as they fit into the Grand Design of the Divine Source Himself.

In addition to its use of familiar symbols in the props and scenery, the medieval theatre clothed its actors in familiar dress (those playing Adam and Eve in The Fall playlet wore "naked suits" of flesh-colored, stocking-like material; later, in the Cain and Abel playlet, Adam and Eve were dressed in ordinary Yorkish peasant garb), and the lines were spoken in the rural dialect that was the common vernacular of the audience. These features served to bring the world of the Bible into the here and now of medieval life. It was the *message* of the play that was important, not the artistry or historical accuracy of its presentation; thus, while elegance may have been desirable insofar as it represented hard work dedicated to God, it was never aimed at verisimilitude. The Fall of Man playlet was not meant to create a remote or exotic mood; indeed, had it done so its content might have been overwhelmed. Rather, it was constructed to communicate a message, and whatever other information it conveyed was distinctly subordinate to that message.

The Crucifixion

The Crucifixion playlet was the pivotal one in all the cycle plays because it portrayed the central visual image of Christianity—Christ on the cross, as He appeared above the altar in every medieval church and cathedral in Europe—and at the same time dealt with the physical agony of Christ—the "Passion"—which bespoke the extent of His sacrifice for mankind. So central was this episode, in fact, that the name "passion plays" became a popular designation for the entire medieval religious theatre. The Crucifixion scene is the most intense moment of the one surviving passion play (inspired by the medieval cycle plays, but of later vintage), which is performed every ten years at Oberammergau in southern Germany; and indeed, many isolated crucifixion plays are still performed at Eastertime in various parts of the world, including the United States. (These performances are usually illegal, owing to the tendency of the actors to pursue undue realism, occasionally with calamitous results.)

The York Crucifixion playlet, thirty-fifth in the cycle, was performed in late afternoon and was staged on a wagon representing Calvary. It showed the torture of Christ by four soldiers, who both tied and nailed Him to the Cross, then lifted it into an erect position. The tying of the actor to the Cross was, of course, a sheer practical necessity, but the medieval author ingeniously made it part of the torture—in fact, the worst part:

FIRST SOLDIER: Put on that cord,
      And tug him to, by top and tail. . . .
      These cords have evil increased his pains. . . .
SECOND SOLDIER: Yea, asunder are both sinews and
          veins. . . .

This scene once again calls to mind the opening scene of *Prometheus*, in which the divine hero is chained to his place of torture by baser, more dull-witted attendants; and as in *Prometheus*, the majesty of Christ is conveyed primarily by His si-lence in the face of these terrible abuses. Only twice does Jesus speak: in two short, lovely, eloquent prayers which soar above the brutish exchange of the torturers to plead for all mankind. The dramatic achievement of this playlet is that it communicates the transcendence which is the essence of religious experience; Jesus, in less than twenty-five lines out of the playlet's 300, convincingly rises above evil, pain, intolerance, and the sheer wickedness of intentional indifference:

JESUS: Almighty God, my Father free,
      Let these matters be marked in mind;
      Thou bade that I should ready be
      For Adam's fall to be thus pined [tortured].
      Here to death I offer me,
      From Adam's sin to save mankind,
      And, my God, beseech I thee

The Crucifixion scene in the 1980 York city production of the York Cycle.

That man for me may favor find.
God, from the fiend mankind defend,
And give them wealth without an end,
For I have naught else to crave.

In this, Jesus' first speech, He harks back to the tale of Adam and reveals that his own death will atone for the sins of this (Biblical and dramaturgical) predecessor. Also, like Aeschylus' Prometheus, He makes clear that He is the friend of man, the patron of the audience, for whose sake He suffers. It is a spiritual appeal that gains in eloquence by its simplicity and by its contrast to the bickering and fierce selfishness of the four tormentors.

SECOND SOLDIER: Give me this wedge; I shall it in drive.

FOURTH SOLDIER: Here is another yet on hand.

THIRD SOLDIER: Give it to me—look alive!

FIRST SOLDIER: Lay on then fast!

THIRD SOLDIER: Yes, I warrant
There, now I'll thrive
Now will this cross full stably stand
And if he rave—it will not rive [tear apart].

FIRST SOLDIER (*to Christ*): Say, sir, how likes you now
This work that we have wrought?

FOURTH SOLDIER: We pray you tell us how
You feel, if you faint not!

JESUS: All men that walk by way or street,
Look well you see this body mine
Behold my head, my hands, my feet,
And fully feel now, while you're still fine,
If any mourning may be meet,
Or any misery marked as mine.
My Father, that all bales may beet [ills may cure],
Forgive these men that do me pine.
What they work, know they nought.
Therefore, my Father, I crave,
Let not their sins be sought,
But see their souls to save.

FIRST SOLDIER: Well! Hark! He jangles like a jay!

SECOND SOLDIER: Methink he patters like a pie [magpie]!

THIRD SOLDIER: He has been doing so all day,
And made great moving of mercy.

FOURTH SOLDIER: Is this the same that did us say
That he was God's Son almighty?·

Then, wrangling over the disposition of Jesus' garments, the soldiers speak of moving off as the pageant wagon rolls away.

The centrality of this playlet is temporal as well as spiritual. Temporally, it links the sin of presumption which is brought out in earlier playlets —in the Fall of Lucifer story and the story of Adam and Eve—with the salvation offered by Christ. And spiritually, it personifies forgiveness and redemption in the suffering Christ—that is, in the actual body of Christ, or Corpus Christi, as portrayed by a medieval performer assuming a priestlike function. Moreover, if the playlets that precede the Crucifixion are overwhelmingly cautionary in their moral messages, those that follow the Crucifixion resoundingly repudiate despair, thus setting the positive theme that the complete cycle is intended to convey. For the medieval pageant was, above all else, a joyous celebration of faith and salvation, and of the wholeness and purposefulness of temporal and spiritual life.

The personage of Christ in the medieval playlet is structurally similar to the Prometheus in Aeschylus' play, but emotionally and spiritually the two are poles apart. Whereas Prometheus' heroism is expressed in pride, recklessness, and defiance, Jesus is portrayed by his medieval authors as a wholly gentle, beatific, and accessible individual. What is more, whereas the Greek Prometheus suffers for a principle, the medieval Jesus suffers out of the purest *love*. One could hardly expect the anonymous and untrained authors of the medieval world to rival the verbal magnificence of Aeschylus; nonetheless, the simple, kind, and exquisitely human words they gave to Jesus in the York cycle leave a powerful impression even on modern audiences, and when coupled with the staggering imagery and physicality of the Crucifixion's staging they must have created a theatrical experience that the medieval visitor to York would remember for a lifetime.

The Judgment

The last playlet in the York cycle portrayed Judgment Day, and almost certainly it was always performed very late in the day. One scholar has

The Crucifixion scene from the York Cycle, as produced at Britain's National Theatre in 1978. Environmental staging in the small Cottesloe Theatre (part of the National Theatre complex in London) permits spectators to sit right at the foot of the play's action, just as in medieval times. Photo by Michael Mayhew.

concluded that it could not possibly have begun earlier than 2:30 A.M.; if that is the case some sort of artificial lighting must have been used. One can imagine how a pious audience must have looked forward to the final "deliverance" promised by this playlet after the long series of moral messages that led up to it.

As befits the conclusion of a Christian drama, it is Jesus who plays the central role in this playlet. After a long prologue in which God reviews the major events in the history of the universe (as illustrated by the preceding forty-seven playlets), Christ returns to earth in bodily form (again the Corpus Christi) to "deem dooms," that is, to pronounce judgments:

JESUS: This woeful world is brought to an end.
My Father of Heaven, He wills it be.
Therefore to earth now will I wend
Myself to sit in majesty.
To deem my dooms I will descend.
This body will I bear with me.
How it was tortured, man's Fall to mend,
All mankind there shall it see.

Christ's vow that "all mankind" shall see his wounds in this final action of the play serves notice that what is to follow is a message intended for every member of the audience, an affirmation for the faithful and a warning for any souls who lurk about unconverted, or who are dallying with impious ideas. It was no coincidence that the last station of the York procession, where this last of the hundreds of performances in the complete cycle took place, was situated on York's own judgment square, a public area known as "the Pavement," where York's real villains and criminals were publicly tried, sentenced, and hanged for their transgressions. Here the staged suffering of Christ, the "Passion" of God's only begotten Son, was to be held up for final evaluation by man—and for man's ultimate acknowledgment and support.

JESUS: Here may ye see my wounds wide,
The which I suffered for your misdeed,
Through heart and head, foot, hand, and hide,
Not for my guilt, but for your need.
Behold both body, back, and side,

How dear I bought your brotherhead
    [brotherhood]!
These bitter pains did I abide
To buy you bliss, thus did I bleed.
My body was scourged without any skill.
As a thief cruelly did they me treat.
On a cross they hanged me on a hill,
Bloody and red, so I was beat
With a crown of thorns, and thrust full ill
This spear into my side was set;
My heart's blood spared they not to spill.
Man, for thy love would I not let [stop them].
Man, sure ought thee to quake,
This dreadful day this sight to see.
All this I suffered for thy sake:
Say, man, what suffered thou for me?

Here the action turns outward from the stage and onto the audience. "Man," as here addressed, is not a character in the play but the spectator who watches the production. The audience is asked to examine its own behavior and to measure its own actions against those of the "good souls" and the "bad souls" who appear in this staged judgment. Moreover, the audience is now asked to reckon its own standing in terms of the lessons conveyed in all the preceding playlets of the cycle.

Jesus offers salvation to the good souls, praising them with the words "when I was hungry, ye me fed," and explaining that any good deed done anywhere, to "any that need," is in fact a tribute to God and a token of the doer's salvation. Similarly, he attacks the bad souls:

JESUS: When I was sick and sorryest,
Ye visited me not, for I was poor;
When I in prison hard was stressed,
None of you looked how I did fare.
When I knew never where to rest,
With darts you drove me from your door.
But ever proudful then you pressed;
My flesh, my blood, ye oft forswore.
Clotheless when I was oft, and cold,
In need of you, went I full naked.
Nor house nor harbor, help nor hold
Had I from you, although I quaked.

My misery saw ye manifold;
And none of you my sorrow slaked,
But ever forsook me, young and old.
Therefore shall ye now be forsaked.

When the bad souls argue that they did no such things, that they never saw Jesus naked or harborless, Jesus responds substantially as he did to the good souls:

JESUS: Caitiffs, as oft as it betid [happened]
That needy folks asked in my name,
You heard them not, your ears ye hid,
Your help to them was not at home.
To me was that unkindness kid [shown].
Therefore ye bear this bitter blame;
To least or most, when it ye did
To me ye did the self and same.

MEDIEVAL THEATRE: A SATIRICAL VIEW

The conventions and verse forms of medieval theatre lend themselves readily to satire, as Shakespeare made clear in a clever parody woven into his *A Midsummer Night's Dream* (*c.* 1594). There a group of village craftsmen produce the "play" of "Pyramus and Thisbe," and we are privileged, in the course of *Dream*, to watch the casting, rehearsing, and finally the presentation of this play within a play.

"Pyramus" is described as a "most lamentable comedy," and lamentable indeed is its production by these well-meaning amateurs. Afraid that the "audience" will mistake a character's stage death for a real murder, the actors demand a prologue that will explain "that I Pyramus am not Pyramus, but Bottom the Weaver: this will put them out of fear." Lest the ladies in the audience be terrified of the lion, the actor who plays "Lion" insists that half his face "must be seen through the lion's neck," and that he must say, during the course of the play, "Fair ladies . . . I would entreat you not to fear, not to tremble. . . . If you think I come hither as a lion, it were pity of my life: no, I am no such thing; I am a man as other men are . . . Snug the Joiner." Since the story of the "play" calls for Pyramus and Thisbe to meet by moonlight, one actor is required to play the moon—that is, to hold a lantern above him and to "disfigure, or to present, the person of moonshine." Because the "play" calls for a wall, and a crack within it, another actor "must present wall: and let him have some plaster, or some loam, or some roughcast about him, to signify wall; and let him hold his fingers thus, and through that cranny shall Pyramus and Thisbe whisper."

The versification of "Pyramus" is reminiscent of medieval stanzas—over-alliterative, short-footed, and tortured into rhymes:

PYRAMUS: Sweet moon, I thank thee for thy
sunny beams;
I thank thee, moon, for shining now so bright;
For, by thy gracious, golden, glittering gleams,
I trust to take of truest Thisbe sight.
But stay, O spite!
But mark, poor knight,
What dreadful dole is here!
Eyes, do you see?
How can it be?
O dainty duck! O dear!
Thy mantle good,
What, stain'd with blood!
Approach, ye Furies fell!
O fates, come, come,
Cut thread and thrum,
Quail, crush, conclude, and quell!

Shakespeare encases this parody within one of his most lyrical and elegant comedies; indeed, the juxtaposition of crude verse and elementary stage devices with the complexity of Shakespeare's poetic dramaturgy emphasizes both the professional sophistication of the later writer and the experimental amateurism of the medieval stage. In laughing at the "rude mechanicals" who present this playlet, the characters in Shakespeare's larger drama share with the audience an indulgent superiority over preceding generations and, by implication, exult in the presumed progress of civilization since the days of such rudimentary theatricals.

MORRIS DANCER: mocking pantomime

Side by side with the religious drama of the Middle Ages existed a secular theatre which had its roots in the Dark Ages and the mimes of ancient Rome. This was a theatre of rural dancing, pagan ritual, primitive magic, and farcical tomfoolery. Singers, dancers, jongleurs, and other entertainers of many sorts are known to have performed throughout the medieval period, often working in an "underground theatre" that enabled them to escape official prohibition and punishment.

MASKS, MAGIC, and MIME... Elementary mime performances carried on a mime/theatre tradition through the DARK AGES...

NARR: A GERMAN FOOL... strangles his goslings to save them from drowning

FARCE and basic MYTHICAL material were emphasized...

BUFFOON in traditional JESTER costume

Therefore, according to this conclusion at York, Christ is everywhere in human life, and goodness to man is rewarded by divine salvation. The forty-eight pageants have added up to medieval life's great moral lesson, and as the final wagon departs and we hear and see (according to a final stage direction) "the melody of angels crossing from place to place," we are left with an indelible instruction concerning the realities of eternal life and the ordering of the human and divine cosmos of the Middle Ages.

The York cycle plays are not generally counted among the masterpieces of medieval dramatic literature—the *Second Shepherd's Play*, which was performed at Wakefield, and the morality play *Everyman* are usually considered more prominently in English literary surveys. Nevertheless, in their total theatrical impact the cycle plays well represent the most astonishing aspects of the medieval contribution to theatrical history. The integration of forty-eight separate plays (produced by at least as many separate guilds) into a harmonious whole was in itself a vast achievement. Even more impressive is the fact that the story line, albeit traditional, was highly selective toward achieving a sharp focus on a central, pivotal plot event, and the entire production was contrived to deliver a final, over-arching ethical message. The sensational mode of production, with its combination of rolling carts, ambulatory casts of actors, multi-level staging effects, and extremely close audience-actor interplay, has never been duplicated to any significant degree in modern times—nor has the production organization, which drew upon every element of the social and theological order.

Something of the sheer joy of the enterprise reaches down to us across the centuries as we read the rustic texts and imagine the crowds and the bright wagons rolling through the springtime streets. For the medieval participants, this annual retelling of mythic history which so imaginatively combined literature and entertainment and religion and art must have been a transcendent experience.

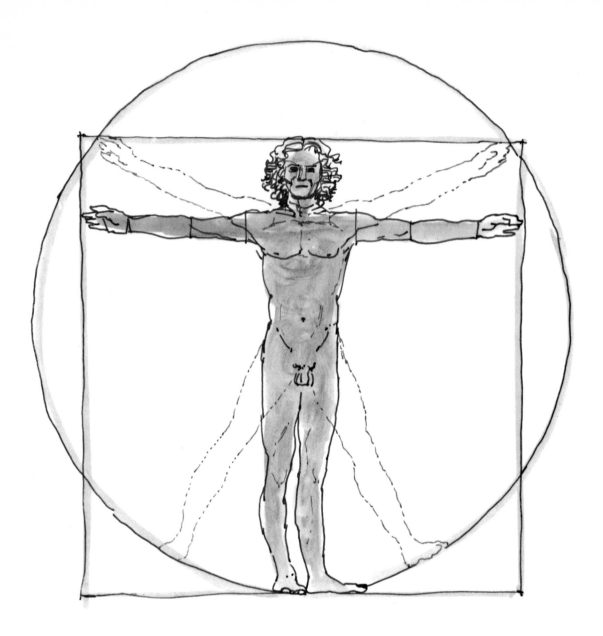

Man as "the center" of geometrical perfection, from the famous sketch by Leonardo. Humanist art of the Renaissance—and certainly that of Elizabethan drama—was powered by a spirit of possibility through the exercise of man's will, gifts, and desires.

SECTION TWO: THE PAST

CHAPTER 5

THE SHAKESPEAREAN ERA

THE RENAISSANCE

What exactly was the Renaissance? Literally, the word means "rebirth" and, strictly speaking, it refers to the renewed interest in classical (Greek and Roman) civilization which burgeoned throughout Western Europe in the fifteenth and sixteenth centuries. That definition, however, is too technical. More to the point, the Renaissance was a grand revolution in thinking, a new kind of awareness of the potential of man as a reasoning, creative, and possibly heroic being. It was also a process of mind expansion which grew out of medieval times and has continued right up to the present day. The Renaissance is part of our lives—in many ways, still coloring our behavior and our judgments.

The emergence of a Renaissance was first celebrated in southern Europe, most notably in Italy, during the 1400s. At its center was humanism, which is the belief that was first expressed by the Greek philosopher Protagoras when he said, "Man is the measure of all things." *Man*, not God.

The Renaissance was not at all an atheistic era; in fact it gave birth to some of the most wonderfully successful religious art and philosophy the Western World has ever seen. But it was a time that brought an end to capitulation to dogma and to humility concerning man's stature in the universe. Perhaps the most apt visual symbol for the Renaissance is the drawing by Leonardo da Vinci that shows man's body as the basis for geometry: man was the ultimate embodiment of reason, order, and form; man, in short, was the modern Apollo.

In Italy the Renaissance was marked by the greatest development in painting and sculpture the world had yet known; in Spain the Renaissance was a time of exploration and conquest; in France the Renaissance brought unparalleled developments in social organization and philosophy; in England the Renaissance gave us, above all, the theatre of William Shakespeare.

SHAKESPEARE

Shakespeare. The name all but leaps up off the page. He is almost universally acclaimed as the greatest writer in the English language, the most famous Englishman who ever lived, and the greatest playwright, sonnetteer, and dramatic poet in the separate histories of all those literary forms. He is now virtually deified in England, where his birthplace is a national shrine; his life has inspired innumerable biographies, novels, and plays, and his works constitute the basic repertoire of literally dozens of full-time professional theatres. He is the most frequently produced playwright in the world today, not only in England and America but in Germany, the Soviet Union, and many other countries in which his works are known only in translation. Actor, producer, director, commentator, and author—his consummate achievement as "man of the theatre" has set the standard for every dramatic artist since his time.

And yet, although Shakespeare towers above his age, the fifty-odd years of English Drama which his lifetime encompassed would have been a celebrated theatrical era even had he never existed. One playwright, Christopher Marlowe, born the same year as Shakespeare (1564), was equally as accomplished as the Bard of Avon at the moment of his tragic and untimely death in 1593. Ben Jonson, John Webster, and John Ford, all playwrights more or less contemporary with Shakespeare, were also complementary to him, and their works are still presented with considerable regularity. But the list does not end there. Thomas Kyd, John Lyly, Robert Greene, George Chapman, John Marston, Thomas Dekker, Thomas Middleton, Cyril Tourneur, Francis Beaumont, John Fletcher, Philip Massinger, James Shirley—every one of these dramatists contributed works of lasting significance and enhanced the glory of that startlingly productive time in theatre history.

Sometimes it is called the Elizabethan Age, that period of drama in which Shakespeare played the central role. However, that term is a bit misleading, since technically it refers only to the reign of Elizabeth I (1558–1603), whereas Shakespeare and his contemporaries flourished equally under the subsequent rule of King James I, in the so-called Jacobean Era (1603–1625). Indeed, their heyday did not end until the Puritan revolution of 1642, when the theatres they built were burned to the ground and the theatrical tradition they had fostered was abruptly terminated. It seems most appropriate for our purposes, therefore, to forget about the names of the regal tenants and call this age for Shakespeare himself—for it is certain that "the Shakespearean era" betokens something of far more lasting significance than the skirmishes of princes, kings, armies, and religious despots.

The key to life is for Shakespeare, as it is for his age, the assertion of individuality. He creates highly individualized characters more abundantly than any other dramatist, and the conflicts in his plays are invariably produced by the exertions of the human will. Man struggles against man, and not against Fate, god, heredity, or glands. Shakespearean drama is drama of the individual will....

The zest for life so abundantly felt in a dynamic age pulsates in every page of his work. Laughter and tears, concentrated ambition and wasted motion, serious employment and the blithe pursuit of pleasure, jostle each other in the same work. Intensity is all! His characters are nearly all active personalities, from the heroes who win crowns or glory to the vagrants who cut purses or revel in the stews, from passionate queens to promiscuous 'queans' and nubile girls who dress in boys' clothes to follow the men of their desire.

John Gassner

The Theatres

In Shakespeare's time there were almost a dozen London playhouses, most of them presenting plays regularly to large paying audiences, and at the same time providing a livelihood for literally dozens of professional acting companies and dramatic poets. It was a level of theatrical activity that was not to be duplicated in scope for more than two hundred years anywhere, and then only after London and the other capitals of Europe had increased their population by tenfold and more. The London playhouses of the sixteenth and seventeenth centuries were of two major types: outdoor "public" theatres and more intimate, indoor, "private" ones. Less is known about either type than we would wish, but enough documents have survived from those centuries to provide us with a general idea of how these theatres were constructed and a fairly good idea of what kind of experience awaited the Londoner who set out to attend a Shakespearean play in the early 1600s.

The big public theatres were unquestionably among the greatest attractions of Elizabethan London. There were nine of them: Shakespeare's Globe, plus The Swan, The Rose, The Theater, The Fortune, The Curtain, and The Hope. All were located outside the city limits, for the Puritan city officials forbade the public presentation within the city of "unchaste fables, lascivious devices, shifts of cozenage & matters of like sort" which allegedly served as meeting places for "horse stealers, whoremongers, cozeners, conny-catching persons, practicers of treason & such." These theatre buildings were impressive wooden structures that towered over the residences in London's northern and southern suburbs and displayed a brilliance of theatrical architecture that has never been surpassed. Each was built on three levels, enclosed on all sides but only partially roofed to leave a large central expanse open to the sky. The walls surrounded a "yard," at one end of which the players performed on a raised stage. The stage was for the most part backed by a *tiring house* (literally, "attiring house," or dressing room), which provided actors a variety of entries to the stage: windows, balconies, and two or more large doors. Below the stage was a "cellarage," with access via a 4 × 4-foot trap door; above was the gilded "heavens" —a projected semi-canopy from which, occasionally, actors descended via pulleys. Virtually all areas not occupied by the stage and tiring house were used to accommodate spectators, as many as three thousand

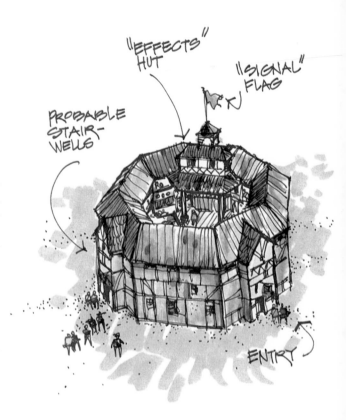

The first Globe Theatre. This conjectural view assumes The Globe to have been an octagonal structure. Inside, a corridor allowed access to various sections of the galleries.

of them, according to one account. They sat in the galleries, stood in the yard, sometimes even perched on the stage itself.

There has been a great deal of conjecture as to the exact size, appearance, and use of these public playhouses; hence, any reconstruction—including that presented here—must be regarded as hypothetical. The documentary evidence is distressingly skimpy: a single contemporary drawing—indeed, a foreigner's *re*drawing of a friend's lost illustration—of The Swan Theatre, and two surviving building contracts, one for The Fortune and one for The Hope. The Fortune contract is particularly frustrating in that it refers to an "attached diagram" which has never been found, and it further informs the builder that the stage proportions should be "contrived and fashioned like unto the Stage of the playhouse called the Globe." Of the construction of the Globe, unfortunately, we know virtually nothing except that it was built at least in part from the timbers of the dismantled Theater.

We can presume, however, that the public playhouse capitalized on three pre-existing architectural or staging elements: the medieval innyard, the trestle stage, and the pageant wagon. Inns were a common sight all over medieval England, both on the rural roadways and in the towns and villages; even London had its inns which, in addition to providing wayfarers with food and lodging, were local gathering places and centers of public activity and entertainment. The typical English inn was U-shaped, and stood two or three stories high; the semi-enclosed yard was a perfect place for traveling players to set up their stage and perform, and the balconies that extended from the upper stories afforded a perfect vantage from which to view their performance.

Putting on a play in an innyard meant little more than arriving and setting up a stage, which itself

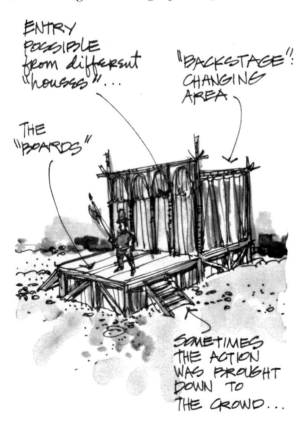

ENTRY POSSIBLE from different "houses"...

"BACKSTAGE": CHANGING AREA

THE "BOARDS"

SOMETIMES THE ACTION WAS BROUGHT DOWN TO THE CROWD...

A portable trestle stage of the kind that might be set up in an Elizabethan innyard.

would consist of little more than a series of boards mounted and secured upon trestles, or sawhorses ("the boards," of course, has since become a metaphor for the theatre itself). The inn doors probably served as stage entrances, the inn windows as stage balconies. The combination of three-storied inn, yard, and platform stage was doubtless carried forth in the permanent public theatre (in fact, we know that at least two public theatres had removable trestle stages instead of permanent ones, to allow bear-baiting entertainments to alternate with play productions on a daily basis). Also carried over from the earlier time was the general procedure for audience accommodation, with some patrons free to wander in the yard during the performance and others taking more privileged (and higher priced) gallery seats above.

However, the simple trestle stage clearly would have been insufficient for the staging of Shakespeare's plays and for those of many of his contemporaries. Thus the public playhouse was developed beyond the innyard staging. One addition, we know, was the tiring house; another was apparently some sort of balconied and draped architectural unit that has long baffled (but not silenced!) the historians as to its placement and function. Most of the evidence available to us today leads to the supposition that it was a structure—usually called a pavilion—which stood at the rear of the Shakespearean platform, butting against the facade of the tiring house and permitting entrances through curtains or other openings located in it. This pavilion seems to have been modeled on the pageant wagon, and apparently it served much the same purpose: it created upper-level acting areas and gave the director the option of closing off interior spaces by drapery, allowing sudden and dramatic "reveals" when a curtain was drawn open before a tableau of actors.

To these three medieval influences that can be seen in the Elizabethan public playhouse—the innyard, the trestle stage, and the wheel-less pageant wagon, or pavilion—we should perhaps add one more architectural carryover: the Roman amphitheatre. At least that is how The Swan was described by the Dutchman whose illustration of that theatre survives. This Dutchman, Johannes de Witt by name, explained that The Swan's columns were "painted in such excellent imitation of marble that it is able to deceive even the most cunning," and he went on to say that in form, scale, and splendor the theatre resembled a

THE INNS' UPPER FLOORS ARE SIMILAR TO THE LATER "GALLERIES"

TRESTLE STAGE SET UP AGAINST THE FOURTH WALL OF THE INNYARD...

THE INTERIOR YARD WAS A NATURAL FOCAL POINT

An Elizabethan innyard theatre, as seen from behind the stage.

"Roman work," an "amphitheatre of notable beauty . . . magnificent." This disclosure is not so surprising when we recall that this, of course, was the time of the Renaissance, when it was not thought sufficient merely to develop and exceed the standards of the Middle Ages—it was necessary to reach back to antiquity and outshine the Caesars themselves.

That we know more of the spirit than of the precise details of these public theatres is not by any means a catastrophe, for it is the spirit rather than the theatre measurements which most clearly distinguishes the dramatic art of Shakespeare and his contemporaries. The fact is that in the Shakespearean era there was no formal aesthetic which demanded that plays be written or staged in a certain way, and Shakespeare's own plays were performed in many types of theatres, often in quite rapid rotation. In addition to using the three public theatres operated at

various times by his company—The Theater, The Curtain, and The Globe—Shakespeare produced his works at "private theatres" and at court. The so-called private theatres, like the public theatres, were open to the general public; however, because they charged a considerably higher admission price, they attracted a more elite audience. Also, they were indoor theatres, rectangular and candlelit, quite different from the round, octagonal, or square public theatres open to the sky. The court theatre, of course, was truly private. Shakespeare was often called upon to provide entertainment to Queen Elizabeth (*A Midsummer Night's Dream* is thought to have been written upon her commission), and his plays were frequently remounted on the shortest of notice in royal palaces, particularly at Whitehall for the annual Twelfth Night Revels. A Queen's officer, the Master of Revels, was charged specifically with overseeing these royal en-

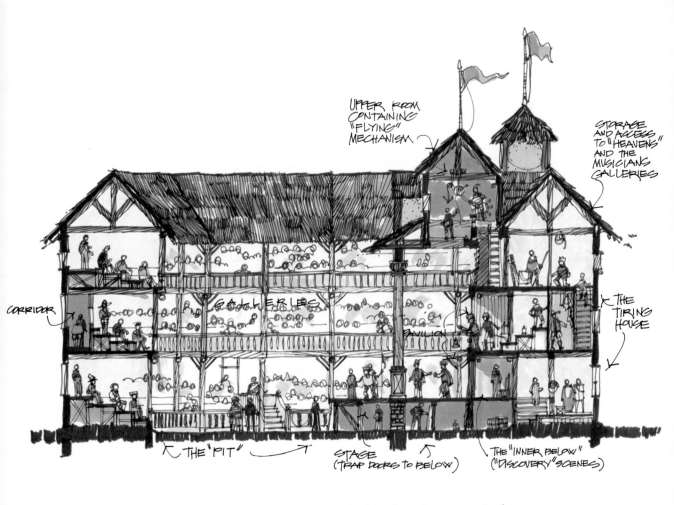

UPPER ROOM
CONTAINING
"FLYING"
MECHANISM

STORAGE
AND ACCESS
TO "HEAVENS"
AND THE
MUSICIANS
GALLERIES

CORRIDOR

GALLERIES

PAVILION

THE
TIRING
HOUSE

THE "PIT"

STAGE
(TRAP DOORS TO BELOW)

THE "INNER BELOW"
("DISCOVERY" SCENES)

A cutaway view of the original Globe Theatre. This hypothetical reconstruction (no original plan exists) shows the basic relationships among the main parts of the theatre interior. Note the "hut" on the third level above the stage: it is possible that scenic units or actors were sometimes raised and lowered through the ceiling over the stage.

tertainments, to which all theatrical companies in London sought invitation.

Finally, Shakespeare's theatre was also a touring company, and few seasons passed without travels to entertain at the Inns of Court, at college halls at Oxford and Cambridge, and at various castles, manor houses, and palaces in the country. During times of plague, the entire theatrical season was "on the road," for public gatherings in or about the city were forbidden by law. For these reasons, Shakespearean stagecraft is marked by flexibility rather than rigidity; plays were written to be staged and restaged in a variety of lo-

cales and settings, and no particular stage architecture or staging practice could be considered fixed in the drama of the times, except insofar as it promoted a bold, fluid, vigorous theatre centering on the actor and the spoken text.

The Players

Traveling players were commonly seen throughout Europe as the religious drama of the Middle Ages gave way to the dramatic entertainments of the Renaissance. These were the players (actors) who performed

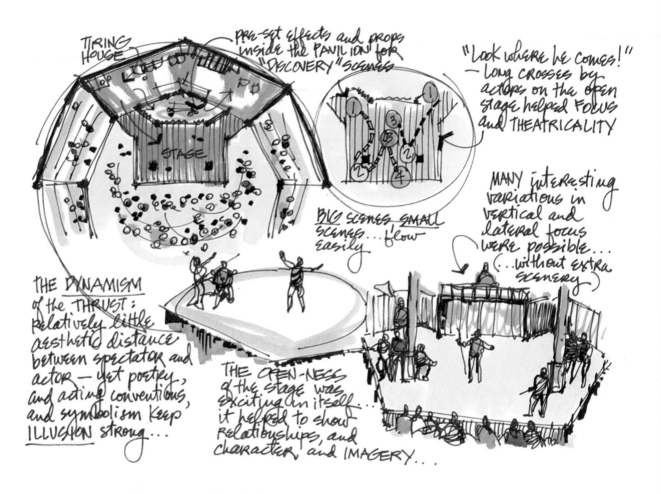

TIRING HOUSE

pre-set effects and props inside the PAVILION for "DISCOVERY" scenes

STAGE

"Look where he comes!" — long crosses by actors on the open stage helped FOCUS and THEATRICALITY

MANY interesting variations in vertical and lateral focus were possible... (...without extra scenery)

BIG scenes, SMALL scenes... flow easily

THE DYNAMISM of the THRUST: Relatively little aesthetic distance between spectator and actor — yet poetry, and acting conventions, and symbolism keep ILLUSION strong...

THE OPEN-NESS of the stage was exciting in itself... it helped to show relationships, and character, and IMAGERY...

The open stage of the Elizabethan theatre offered many possibilities for dynamic staging. An "Elizabethan revival" movement in our own century has brought this form of staging into common use once again.

on hastily erected trestle stages in the medieval inn-yards, in the public streets and squares, and in the castles and country manors of the nobility. Their performances were made exceptionally hasty when local authorities from time to time outlawed dramatic exhibitions, whether religious or secular. Often, to protect themselves against the whims of provincial aldermen and to guarantee winter employment, these troupes sought and received patronage from celebrated nobles of the realm. By 1486 the Earls of Essex had become patrons to such a company, known as Essex's Men, and not long thereafter the King himself,

Henry VII, extended his sovereignty over a troupe of four players who were specifically commissioned to provide the royal entertainment.

The troupes of players that came together in England during the sixteenth century were talented and skilled performers, fully as adept as their more famous Italian counterparts, the performers of the *commedia dell'arte* (see p. 140), at singing, dancing, juggling, acrobatics, poetic recitation, and grand rhetorical set speeches. They carried their plays with them in their heads, owning them as magicians own their rabbits. The "players" portrayed in *Hamlet*—that

is, the characters within that play who come to perform at the Danish court—aptly represent the English
traveling actors of that time: men able to spin out
speeches from a number of plays, to present any given
play at a moment's notice, and even to alter plays to
suit a patron's desire (as when Hamlet asks the
players to revise "The Murder of Gonzago" for his
own purposes). Royal entertaining, of course, was the
highest goal and the most lucrative possibility for a
traveling troupe, and a summons to participate in the
royal performances on and around Twelfth Night (the
twelve days of Christmas), which were commissioned
and supervised by the Master of the Revels, represented the epitome of acting attainment. Shakespeare,
needless to say, was well represented at Twelfth Night
festivities in his time.

The troupes were all male. Women never appeared on the English stage during Shakespeare's
lifetime nor, indeed, for some fifty years thereafter.
The female parts were played by boys who were ap-
prenticed to the troupe. The whole group traveled
as a family, rarely staying long in any one location,
but shifting between court and city and country as
economic, social, and legal conditions dictated. For although they could hole up for a time in a London inn,
such as the Boar's Head in Cheapside (Falstaff's famous tavern), sooner or later the plague or the city aldermen or declining audiences would drive them
out. Eventually these troupes became known all over
England and even on the Continent. Certainly many
troupes visited Shakespeare's birthplace, Stratford on
Avon, which is about 100 miles northwest of London;
and tradition has it that some time in the late 1580s
the young Will Shakespeare simply followed one of
them out.

There were two particularly celebrated troupes of
players in Shakespeare's own time. The first was the

A modern version of Shakespeare's "wooden O"
theatre, at Cedar City, Utah, seen here during the
1980 Utah Shakespeare Festival production of
Macbeth. Not an exact replica, the Utah theatre
nonetheless captures the open-air surround of the
Shakespearean public theatre, supplemented by
electric lighting and made comfortable with
conventional modern seating.

A NOBLEWOMAN

"BOY ONE"

"BOY TWO"

JULIET

Boys played all the female roles in the Elizabethan acting companies; most companies had boys of two "types"—one a blond, fair-skinned boy who played serious roles, the other a shorter and darker lad who appeared in comedies. Shakespeare's comedies, which often involve a young woman dressing in male disguise, played tricks with this convention: a boy (actor) was required to play a girl (character) pretending to be a boy (character).

of *Henry the Fourth*) fell into the hands of the greatly ambitious Henslowe.

The second troupe, to which Shakespeare belonged for all but the earliest portion of his professional career, was unique in Shakespeare's time and has never really been duplicated since: it not only owned its own theatre; its overall acting skills made it the most accomplished company in the land and, of course, Shakespeare's plays gave it a superior original repertoire. Known as the Chamberlain's Men under the rule of Queen Elizabeth, this troupe came under the personal patronage of King James I upon his succession in 1603, and was known thereafter as the King's Men. Shakespeare was a member of this company from at least 1594 onwards, as actor, playwright, and investor. He consistently gave the group one or two plays a year to produce as the core of its repertoire. Moreover, he was a part owner of the troupe itself and of its real estate holdings; his total share in the enterprise varied over the years but was always substantial. The Chamberlain's Men had no need to arrange playing space with an outside producer like Henslowe, for they owned their own space: the first theatre they had was The Theater, built in 1576; subsequently, they owned the famous Globe, which was built in 1599. Furthermore, after The Globe was destroyed by fire in 1613 the company was rich enough to rebuild it entirely, in a form grander than any private building then in London. And finally, in 1623, this company crowned its achievements with the posthumous publication of the collected plays of Shakespeare. It was a signally productive union of performing and literary artistry and economic self-ownership.

Lord Admiral's Men, a group that included an enterprising (if somewhat unscrupulous) manager/producer named Philip Henslowe, a celebrated tragic actor named Edward Alleyn, and the great playwright Christopher Marlowe. The Admirals' Men were generally in residence at one of the theatres managed by Henslowe, principally The Rose and The Fortune. At one time or another virtually every promising English dramatist of the time either wrote for The Admirals' Men or collaborated in a play that was produced by them. Shakespeare was no exception: two of his early plays (*Titus Andronicus* and one part

THE BOY COMPANIES

An oddity of the Shakespearean era—odd because it seems to have had no counterpart in any other period—was the presence on the London theatrical scene of several acting companies composed entirely of young boys. These companies began as outgrowths of school programs, but by the 1580s many of them had become partly or wholly professional, and at one point they seemed to pose a serious threat to the adult companies—as Shakespeare himself makes clear in an extended comment in *Hamlet*:

HAMLET: Do [the players] hold the same estimation they did when I was in the city? Are they so follow'd?

ROSENCRANTZ: No indeed are they not.

HAMLET: How comes it? do they grow rusty?

ROSENCRANTZ: Nay, their endeavor keeps in the wonted pace; but there is, sir, an aery [bird's nest] of children, little eyases [nestlings], that cry out on the top of question, and are most tyrannically clapp'd for 't. These are now the fashion, and so berattle the common stages—so they call them—that many wearing rapiers are afraid of goose-quills and dare scarce come thither.

One of these companies operated out of the Chapel Royal (the "Chapel Boys"), another out of St. Paul's ("Paul's Boys"); these and other boy companies performed adult dramas—some of which were written expressly for them—in a variety of indoor theatres, including the Blackfriars before it was taken over by Shakespeare's company in 1608. They were often in trouble with the local authorities and encountered much hostility from adult theatre companies and from rival boy companies; moreover, they were faced with the inevitable problem of their participants' growing up. After 1610 one finds no mention of them; the best of their artists had simply been absorbed into the adult theatre, and their stages were taken over by the new "private" theatre movement which came into prominence at about that time.

The Plays

And what plays these players of the Shakespearean era carried about with them! Gone, almost without a trace, were the religious playlets of the Middle Ages, for in fact the cycle plays had been legally forbidden by Queen Elizabeth in 1559, and thereafter only one Elizabethan play of any note, George Peele's *The Love of King David and Fair Bethsabe* (1599), was to treat a Biblical theme. Gone too were the rural settings, the irregular rhyming verse, and the domestic environments of the medieval shepherd's plays and moral allegories. In their stead, playwrights wrote of exotic locales all over the world, of settings and times befitting the imagination of the new and intellectually emerging Londoner, and of tales calculated to thrill him with discovery, perspective, and awe. Much as the early film directors exploited history and geography in the first cinema epics of the present century, so the Renaissance playwright of sixteenth-century England roamed far and wide in his search for subject matter. The great plays of the years immediately preceding Shakespeare's meteoric rise were set in distant parts of Europe and Asia—*The Spanish Tragedy* by Kyd; Marlowe's two-part epic concerning a Scythian hero, *Tamburlaine the Great*; Thomas Preston's antique tragedy (perhaps England's first), *The Life of Cambises, King of Persia*. And Shakespeare's plays, when he came to write them, also were set in distant times and places—either well back in history, like his magnificent eight-part chronicle of the wars of York and Lancaster, or well beyond England's shores in locales such as Verona, Venice, Cyprus, Rome, Denmark, Navarre, Athens, Egypt, Padua, Sicily, and Bohemia. The Renaissance was not the age to revere the commonplace or the close-to-home; it was the time of Drake and Magellan, of the first explorations and settlements of America, and of Copernicus and Galileo—a time of courage, curiosity, adventure, and discovery.

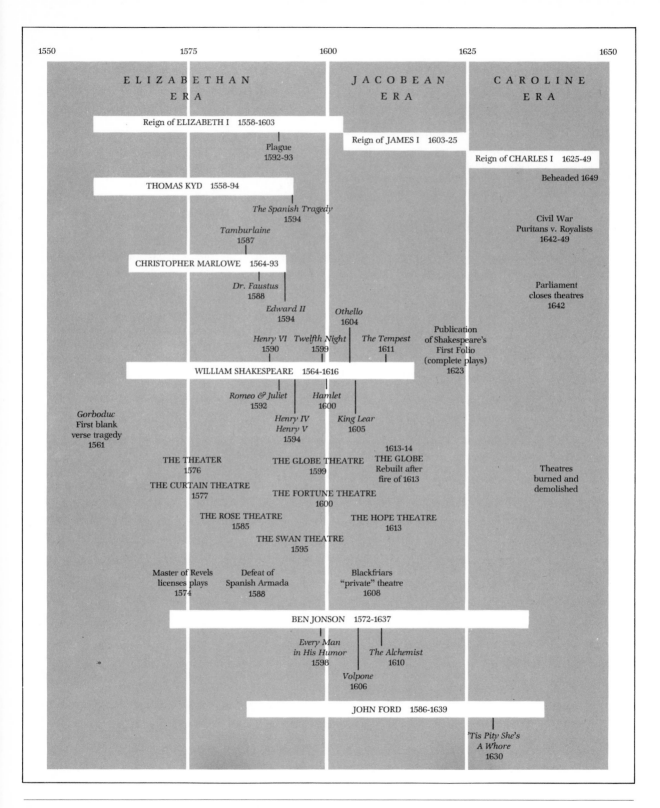

| 1550 | 1575 | 1600 | 1625 | 1650 |

**ELIZABETHAN
ERA**

**JACOBEAN
ERA**

**CAROLINE
ERA**

Reign of ELIZABETH I   1558-1603

Reign of JAMES I   1603-25

Plague
1592-93

Reign of CHARLES I   1625-49

Beheaded 1649

THOMAS KYD   1558-94

The Spanish Tragedy
1594

Civil War
Puritans v. Royalists
1642-49

Tamburlaine
1587

CHRISTOPHER MARLOWE   1564-93

Parliament
closes theatres
1642

Dr. Faustus
1588

Edward II
1594

Othello
1604

Henry VI   *Twelfth Night*   *The Tempest*
1590   1599   1611

Publication
of Shakespeare's
First Folio
(complete plays)
1623

WILLIAM SHAKESPEARE   1564-1616

Romeo & Juliet
1592

Hamlet
1600

Henry IV   *King Lear*
Henry V   1605
1594

Gorboduc
First blank
verse tragedy
1561

THE THEATER
1576

THE GLOBE THEATRE
1599

1613-14
THE GLOBE
Rebuilt after
fire of 1613

THE CURTAIN THEATRE
1577

THE FORTUNE THEATRE
1600

Theatres
burned and
demolished

THE ROSE THEATRE
1585

THE HOPE THEATRE
1613

THE SWAN THEATRE
1595

Master of Revels
licenses plays
1574

Defeat of
Spanish Armada
1588

Blackfriars
"private" theatre
1608

BEN JONSON   1572-1637

*Every Man
in His Humor*
1598

The Alchemist
1610

Volpone
1606

JOHN FORD   1586-1639

*'Tis Pity She's
A Whore*
1630

The Elizabethan reign was a time of international awareness. Nationalism was still freshly minted from the scrap of the Holy Roman Empire, and cultural, political, and economic ties between the European nations were tightly secured and enmeshed. Literature in particular showed a penchant for moving across boundaries; some plays and novellas were translated into foreign languages almost as soon as they were produced. Not only did Shakespeare (and his fellow playwrights) take most of his plots from foreign sources; he frequently peppered his dialogue with foreign phrases, which his audience was expected at least partially to comprehend. Indeed, the fact that Shakespeare's *Henry The Fifth* remains today the only significant English play to have an entire scene written in a foreign language (French), bespeaks the tremendously cosmopolitan flavor of the theatre of the age.

Literally thousands of English plays were written and performed between the first production of Preston's *Cambises* in 1561 and the legally mandated closing of the theatres at the onset of civil war in 1642. Philip Henslowe's Admiral's Men produced twenty-one new plays in a single year—and his was but one of many troupes. Henslowe, a man of great pragmatic and commercial sense, if not of demonstrable aesthetic sensitivity, maintained a stable of authors not unlike that of the mid twentieth-century Hollywood film studio. Most of these men were continually mortgaged to Henslowe's operation by the threat of debtor's prison, and they therefore had strong reasons to make themselves productive. They commonly worked in collaboration—sometimes as many as five to a play—and virtually all the dramatists of the time took part at least occasionally in such joint ventures.

Of those thousands of plays, hundreds survive. History has not always selected with care, of course, and many of the survivors are quite wretched. The best, however, are among the world's masterpieces of dramatic literature. Taken as a whole, the best and the worst, the drama of the Shakespearean era forms a vast pattern of documentation for a period in history that never ceases to amaze us with its vigor, its openness, its lyricism and love of beauty, its intellectual complexity and, at the best junctures, its profundity. To the Elizabethans, drama became the crucible of culture: of art, literature, politics, science, love, fashion, friendship, intrigue, heroics, dance, music, adventure, entertainment, and discovery. It was the major force for opinion making and acculturation in the life of the city, and, on tours, in country life as well. At once the child of the Crown itself—or at least its stepchild—and the refuge of "horse stealers, whoremongers, cozeners," and the like, it was the universal and all but ubiquitous cultural medium of the age.

The original published versions of the plays which survive bear little resemblance to the carefully edited and annotated versions which we commonly see today. Dramatic publication in the Shakespearean era tended to be a rather shabby venture, often bordering on the illegal. Since plays were owned by the companies which commissioned them (or purchased them), and since there was no copyright law to protect the interests of the author, neither author nor producing company stood to gain anything by publication; therefore it was usually only "stolen and surreptitious" copies of the major plays, including many by Shakespeare, which turned up in single-play "quarto" editions. Some of these copies are believed to have been pure piracies, consisting mainly of remembered and transcribed dialogue gleaned from the recollections of former actors. Others were probably printed from pilfered manuscripts. Not until the time of Shakespeare's death, in 1616, did an author undertake to supervise a publication of his own collected "Works": this was Ben Jonson, the Bard's somewhat younger contemporary. Shakespeare's own "Folio" of collected plays, as edited by two shareholders and fellow actors in his company, followed in 1623.

The plays of the era were of many kinds: tragedies, comedies, tragicomedies, chronicle or "history" plays, city plays, domestic dramas, and elegant court masques. The predominant language structure was verse, most notably the so-called blank verse which is written in unrhymed iambic pentameter (a ten-syllable line with stress on the second, fourth, sixth, eighth, and tenth syllables); however, some works were written exclusively in prose, and in general there was a movement during the era away from verse and toward prose. Also present in many plays were songs, sonnets, and rhymed couplets. Some writers, including Shakespeare, even made use of the alliterative "doggerel" style of the Middle Ages, particularly in plays written in the Elizabethan era. Throughout the times, dramatic authors were known as "poets," a perhaps significant usage.

The plays were staged boldly and rapidly on the

SHAKESPEARE AND MARLOWE

Christopher Marlowe, born in the same year as Shakespeare (1564), was actually the more successful of the two rival playwrights at the time of his death in 1593. His mastery of the blank verse form—which Ben Jonson termed "Marlowe's mighty line"—paved the way for the grandeur of Shakespearean dramatic poetry. Marlowe received a clerical and classical education at Canterbury, where he was born, and at Cambridge University, before he moved on to stun London with his powerful two-part verse tragedy, *Tamburlaine The Great*, in 1587–88. The exotic theatricality which Marlowe imparted to this tale of a barbaric Scythian warlord made it an epic adventure for the stage, especially as enacted by the thunderous tragedian Edward Alleyn. *The Tragedy of Dr. Faustus*, Marlowe's masterpiece, followed in 1588, again with Alleyn in the title role, and soon became one of the most performed plays of the era. Faustus' closing speech, as he yields his soul to the devil Mephistopheles, is one of the supreme creations of English dramatic verse:

(*The clock strikes eleven.*)

FAUSTUS: Ah, Faustus,
   Now hast thou but one bare hour to live,
   And then thou must be damned perpetually!
   Stand still, you ever-moving spheres of heaven,

That time may cease, and midnight never come;
Fair Nature's eye, rise, rise again and make
Perpetual day; or let this hour be but
A year, a month, a week, a natural day,
That Faustus may repent and save his soul!
O lente, lente, currite noctis equi!
The stars move still, time runs, the clock will
  strike,
The Devil will come, and Faustus must be
  damned.
Oh, I'll leap up to my God! Who pulls me down?
See, see where Christ's blood streams in the
  firmament!
One drop would save my soul—half a drop: ah,
  my Christ!
Ah, rend not my heart for naming of my Christ!
Yet will I call on him: O, spare me, Lucifer!—
Where is it now? 'tis gone; and see where God
Stretcheth out his arm, and bends his ireful
  brows!
Mountain and hills come, come and fall on me,
And hide me from the heavy wrath of God!
No! no!
Then will I headlong run into the earth;
Earth gape! O, no, it will not harbor me!
You stars that reigned at my nativity,
Whose influence hath allotted death and hell,

stages of the public theatres (and presumably on indoor stages as well), and except in court masques, there was little scenery as we know it today. Instead, the permanent architectural features of the stages were worked into the action. There was much coming and going—through the tiring-house doors; in, out, around, and above the pavilion; through the trap door on the stage; and, via pulleys, to and from the "heavens" above. Stage properties, however, were apparently in common use. A surviving inventory that was maintained by Philip Henslowe lists the following properties and set pieces: trees, rocks, mossy banks, steeples, stairs, and "the city of Rome" (presumably this last was a painted cloth, but possibly it was a sign or a stage piece). Costuming reflected little concern for historical realism; however, it was apparently splendid. Numerous foreign visitors commented admiringly on the opulence of the English costumes, and it is believed that many of the clothes were donated from the wardrobes of noble patrons and supporters. The performers were thoroughgoing professionals—full-time practicers of their art—and many of them developed brilliant rhetorical skills to match the verbal sophistication of the plays.

It is extremely doubtful that the audiences in Shakespeare's time expected much in the way of long,

Now draw up Faustus like a foggy mist
Into the entrails of yon laboring clouds,
That when you vomit forth into the air,
My limbs may issue from their smoky mouths,
So that my soul may but ascend to heaven,
                (The clock strikes the half hour.)
Ah, half the hour is past! 'twill all be past anon!
O God!
If thou wilt not have mercy on my soul,
Yet for Christ's sake whose blood hath ransomed
    me,
Impose some end to my incessant pain;
Let Faustus live in hell a thousand years—
A hundred thousand, and at last be saved!
O, no end is limited to damnèd souls!
Why wert thou not a creature wanting soul?
Or why is this immortal that thou hast?
Ah, Pythagoras' *metempsychosis*! were that true,
This soul should fly from me, and I be changed
Unto some brutish beast! all beasts are happy,
For, when they die,
Their souls are soon dissolved in elements;
But mine must live, still to be plagued in hell.
Curst be the parents that engendered me!
No, Faustus: curse thyself; curse Lucifer
That deprived thee of the joys of heaven.
                        (The clock strikes twelve.)

O, it strikes, it strikes! Now, body, turn to air,
Or Lucifer will bear thee quick to hell.
                  (Thunder and lightning.)
O soul, be changed into little water-drops,
And fall into the ocean—ne'er be found.
My God! my God! look not so fierce on me!

          Enter DEVILS.

Adders and serpents, let me breathe awhile!
Ugly hell, gape not! come not, Lucifer!
I'll burn my books!—Ah Mephistopheles!
                          Exeunt

Marlowe was active in political life (he apparently engaged in official espionage for Queen Elizabeth), and when he was killed in a tavern brawl there was some suspicion that he had been assassinated. He was twenty-nine years old at the time, the most celebrated writer in London and a highly controversial figure in town. The strange circumstances of his life and death continue to engage researchers today; it has even been suggested, although on only the flimsiest of evidence, that Marlowe's death was fabricated, and that he continued to live and write underground, issuing his plays under the name of an otherwise undistinguished actor named William Shakespeare. This speculation, it should be made clear, has been rejected by virtually all serious scholars.

pregnant pauses or studiously projected "moments of truth." Two of the most notable characteristics of the drama of Shakespeare's time—and of the theatre which presented it—were action and boldness: robust activity and vigorous lyricism. The swordplay scene was as common on the English stage as the shoot-out scene is in action films of today; *wordplay* was pervasive. The soliloquy, a speech addressed directly to the audience, was generally an occasion for self-debate or self-prodding rather than for meditation on a theme. Generally speaking, there was precious little introspection in Elizabethan drama, and it is partly for that reason that when it did appear (as in Macbeth's "To-morrow and to-morrow and to-morrow" soliloquy and in several other plays written by Shakespeare—see p. 142), it tended to gain a lot of attention for its author. Even melancholy—a favorite Elizabethan theme—was usually pursued with great vigor, as when the lovesick (and melancholic) Duke Orsino begins Shakespeare's *Twelfth Night* with the cry "If music be the food of love, play on. Give me excess of it." Jokes, puns, taunts, challenges, curses, vows, crudities, and ringing declarations fill the Elizabethan drama with a liveliness and an energy of language that knows no equivalent in any other period of English writing.

Piccolo Teatro, the celebrated commedia *troupe of Milan, Italy, in a dance between Columbina and Arlecchino.*

THE *COMMEDIA DELL'ARTE*

Although Shakespeare's theatre in England was certainly the high-water mark of Renaissance drama, it was by no means the only theatrical activity of the age. Public theatre in Germany was stimulated by traveling English players; and a Spanish public theatre that was somewhat comparable to the Elizabethan flourished under the genius of playwrights Miguel de Cervantes and Lope de Vega. But unquestionably the theatre of greatest and most lasting importance apart from Shakespeare's was the *commedia dell'arte.* This theatre began in Italy and toured throughout Europe, mainly on medieval-type platform stagings in marketplaces, during the sixteenth and seventeenth centuries and beyond.

The Renaissance *commedia* has left us no scripts, for it was a theatre largely improvised on the spot by troupes of masked actors independently responding to audiences in towns all over the continent. Most of the performances were built around a *scenario*—or rudimentary plot—and made use of set speeches, stock characters, and set physical business, usually (but not always) of a comedic, even farcical nature. But the most outstanding characteristic of the *commedia* was its magnificent energy: the vivacity of its characters, the extraordinary whimsicality of its masks and costumes, and the audacity of its improvisation generated terrific excitement wherever it moved, through towns and countries and across centuries.

Commedia actors were complete professionals,

skilled in all the performing arts. Each performer tended to play the same character for many years, sometimes for a lifetime. There were young lovers, *innamorato* and *innamorata* (male and female, for females performed in the *commedia*), the foolishly bragging soldier Capitano, the too-shrewd Venetian merchant Pantalone, the absurdly pompous Bolognese academician Dottore, and the wily Bergamese servant Arlecchino (Harlequin). Each character had his or her standard costume and standard mask

striking Pantalone's bottom—was a traditional device that was to lend its name to the whole genre of physical farce.

The *commedia* was and remains a somewhat enigmatic phenomenon. Its origins are unknown, and its history mysterious; it seems to have flourished from about the middle of the sixteenth century, but its roots may go back centuries before that. Its impact on the theatre since Renaissance times has been incalculable. Molière was greatly influenced by the *comme-*

A commedia dell'arte *performance as it may have occurred in Italy, or elsewhere in Europe, during the sixteenth and seventeenth centuries.*

(except for the lovers, who were barefaced); each had a standard dialogue or style of speaking. *Commedia* plots revolved around commonplace predicaments: young love thwarted, marital fidelity compromised, social climbing unrewarded, and the presumptions of the rich vis-à-vis the righteous poor. Pantalone, Dottore, and Capitano always came out the losers in this highly pro-plebeian drama of the European Renaissance.

The action of the *commedia* was broadly physical. Plot development, such as it was, often was suspended for long periods while comic characters performed stock bits of clownish business, called *lazzi.* Arlecchino's "slapstick"—a wooden sword with a hinged flap that made an exaggerated clap when

dia actors with whom he shared stage space for much of his early career, and the Punch and Judy of English puppet theatre are direct descendants of the *commedia*'s Pulcinello and his fellows. Many companies today seek to carry on the *commedia* tradition, and several are wholly dedicated to this purpose; current street theatre in Europe and America is rarely without its pretenders to the *commedia* heritage; and *commedia* masks are now standard equipment for actor-training in both scripted and improvisational exercises. Thanks to its prototypical conflicts and characters, its costumes, and its eternal laugh-provoking potential, the *commedia dell'arte* has strong universal appeal and is still very much a vital force in theatre today.

THE PLAYS OF SHAKESPEARE

Shakespeare himself was the author of some thirty-seven plays, by general count, although some of these may in fact have been collaborations (particularly those written at the very beginning and the end of his career). At the time of the first publication of his collected dramatic works, these plays were divided into three categories: tragedies, comedies, and histories; it now seems obvious that this division served primarily as an editorial convenience that need not be perpetuated. Shakespeare was born, raised, and married in Stratford on Avon, in Warwickshire, and is believed to have gone to London in the late

---

SHAKESPEARE'S SOLILOQUIES

Although the dramatic soliloquy is not unique to Shakespeare, or even to the Shakespearean era, it is universally associated with Shakespeare's great tragic heroes; it is one of the principal means by which he created a direct relationship between his characters and his audience, and some of the most famous lines in the English language are contained in these character-to-audience communications.

Typically, Shakespeare's soliloquies deal with major decisions and challenges faced by a character in a time of crisis and change:

HAMLET: To be, or not to be, that is the question:
Whether 'tis nobler in the mind to suffer
The slings and arrows of outrageous fortune,
Or to take arms against a sea of troubles,
And by opposing, end them. . . .

This, the most quoted of all soliloquies, is an open debate on the issue of how one ought to respond to dangerous occasions; it epitomizes the challenge of maturity and, in Hamlet's case, manliness.

King Lear's decision to relinquish the prerogatives of power is also eloquently expressed in soliloquy as he looks back with remorse on his long life and vows to seek a greater understanding of his fellow beings:

KING LEAR: Poor naked wretches, wheresoe'er you are,
That bide the pelting of this pitiless storm,
How shall your houseless heads and unfed sides,
Your loop'd and window'd raggedness, defend
     you
From seasons such as these? O, I have ta'en
Too little care of this! Take physic, pomp,
Expose thyself to feel what wretches feel,

That thou mayst shake the superflux to them,
And show the heavens more just.

And Lear follows his self-directed advice by ripping off his garments, determined to share the suffering of the common poor whom he has carelessly ruled.

Macbeth, at the end of the play in which he is the title character, confronts the meaning of life and death. Told by a messenger of the demise of his wife, his partner in murder, Macbeth turns away to share his bitter grief with us:

MACBETH: She should have died hereafter;
There would have been a time for such a word.
To-morrow, and to-morrow, and to-morrow,
Creeps in this petty pace from day to day,
To the last syllable of recorded time;
And all our yesterdays have lighted fools
The way to dusty death. Out, out, brief candle!
Life's but a walking shadow, a poor player,
That struts and frets his hour upon the stage,.
And then is heard no more. It is a tale
Told by an idiot, full of sound and fury,
Signifying nothing.

This is no mere cry of self-pity; it is a poetic commentary on human mortality—a reality that concerns not merely Macbeth and his wife, but Shakespeare and ourselves. Through the convention of the soliloquy, Shakespeare steps across four centuries to strike chords in our contemporary consciousness. And inasmuch as a "poor player" is both Shakespeare's metaphor for life and his instrument for delivering that metaphor, this particular soliloquy engages us on several levels simultaneously, thrusting us deeply into infinite regressions in both time and human perception.

1580s, as an actor. He is first cited as a playwright in a deprecatory reference from 1592; by 1598 he was being hailed as a poet comparable to Ovid, as the "most excellent" writer of comedy and tragedy in England, as one in whose "fine-filed phrase" the Muses themselves would speak if the Muses were to speak English: the "mellifluous & hony-tongued Shakespeare." In 1610, or thereabouts, he returned to Stratford, and to his wife and two surviving children, leaving his great repertoire of *Hamlet, King Lear, Richard III, As You Like It, Othello, Julius Caesar, Much Ado About Nothing,* and the rest, as the mainstay of his company in London. In all, it had taken him about twenty years to create the whole body of works that were to constitute his priceless literary legacy to the world.

Romeo and Juliet

Romeo and Juliet well exemplifies the special qualities of the English Renaissance drama, and of Shakespearean tragedy during the Elizabethan era. It is certainly one of Shakespeare's most famous plays; it seems the world in general agrees with the Prince's conclusion in its closing lines:

> For never was a story of more woe
> Than this of Juliet and her Romeo.

It is indeed woeful, this tragic tale of love which has become virtually a metaphor for adolescent romance and youthful passion; it is also lyrical, bustling, active, and intense. It is one of Shakespeare's early plays, quite possibly his first tragedy (with the exception, perhaps, of the horrific *Titus Andronicus*). It is based on an original novella (short story) by the Italian writer Matteo Bandello; Shakespeare probably read the novella in an English verse translation by Arthur Brooke, which was itself based on an intermediate French version by Pierre Boaistuau; dozens of other versions, including at least one dramatic one, circulated in England and on the Continent for at least thirty years before Shakespeare got around to writing his play in the early 1590s. The play was first published in 1597, in an inaccurate pirated edition, and thereafter it cropped up in a number of versions. It has long been a staple of Shakespearean repertory groups throughout the world, and it has served as the basis for numerous operas, ballets, and films. Indeed,

there can be few persons of moderate education in the Western world who have not at least heard of *Romeo and Juliet* and, in one way or another, measured their own passions against those of these fictional Veronese teenagers.

Let us try to reconstruct, in some detail, the actual staging of this play as it might have looked and sounded and felt in its first performances. Any reconstruction, of course, must rely primarily on informed conjecture, for there is virtually nothing of the staging about which we can be absolutely certain. There are, however, a few stage directions in the first editions of the play; these and many other specific pieces of evidence, and general understandings derived from them, can guide us in our task.

Imagine, then, a theatre like the one depicted on page 146. A sizable standing audience crowds about a thrusting platform stage that stands shoulder high and measures about forty feet wide by thirty feet deep. Three tiers of packed galleries line each wall that looks onto the stage. Behind the stage is a tiring house, with two doors slanted toward the center on either side, and a pavilion that is curtained below and balconied above. A flag flies over the playhouse; in the yard and galleries below, patrons gather to drink ale, meet friends, discuss yesterday's sermon at St. Paul's, and gossip about the Queen.

A trumpet sounds. The crowd quiets down, and those in the yard jostle to secure good positions—the lucky ones will reach the stage rail, and can lean on it for support as the afternoon wears on. Others perch on rain barrels or lean back against the gallery supports. Suddenly, atop the pavilion roof, a black-clad figure appears, bearing a laurel wreath. This is the "Chorus" to the play: a single actor, otherwise uninvolved in the action, who speaks in introduction of the play.

His speech is a sonnet, of the Italianate form at which Shakespeare excels, and its words transform the naked architecture of the theatre into both locale for the play and metaphor for its strife-torn action.

> "Two households . . . " (and he points to the two tiring-house doors from which the warring families will shortly and separately emerge)

"both alike in dignity . . . " (and his gesture emphasizes that the doors are identical and dignified, as are the positions of their respective families)

"In fair Verona, where we lay our scene . . . " (and he firmly establishes the locale of the play and the self-awareness of the players as they embark on its presentation).

The Chorus' sonnet now expands the metaphor of the theatre doors: from households, they become the inhabitants of the households, then the children of those households:

From forth the fatal loins of these two foes
A pair of star-cross'd lovers take their life;

implying, in alliterative tones, an astrological fatality which is a hallmark of this play, even here at its prologue:

The fearful passage of their death-mark'd love,
And the continuance of their parents' rage,
Which, but their children's end, nought could remove,
Is now the two hours' traffic of our stage.

In 1979 American Conservatory Theatre production of Romeo and Juliet, *opening sonnet was sung by a troubador, who was surrounded by a "chorus" garbed as monks; this chorus witnessed the entire action of the play, and occasionally moved scenery and properties as well.*

We are being set up: we will be here for two hours; we will see two young and star-crossed lovers emerge from these families, these households, these doors, and we will see them die, ending at last their parents' enmity. It is going to be a tragedy of the old kind—of *Prometheus* and *The Trojan Women*—for we know the end before we begin, and we can only watch in dread and pity as the terrible events overtake these splendid young people. And we know we will be home in time for dinner, too; for the youthful Shakespeare was perhaps a shade diffident in his belief that he could not hold his audience much longer. The line reminds us of the tale teller who keeps promising to "make a long story short."

That very diffidence may have stimulated the first scene, which now ensues; it is an extraordinarily exciting play beginning, almost overwrought in its energy. First, out of one door, come two servants of the Capulets, speaking generally of the animosity they bear for the Montagues, and speaking specifically in the language of puns:

SAMPSON: Gregory, on my word, we'll not carry coals [bear insults].
GREGORY: No, for then we should be colliers [coal dealers].
SAMPSON: I mean, an we be in choler, we'll draw [I mean, if we are made angry, we'll have to fight].
GREGORY: Ay, while you live, draw your neck out of collar. [try to avoid hanging].

Virtually incomprehensible to audiences today, this witty banter between the two servants greatly amused the Elizabethan audience, who were well attuned to verbal hijinks. Quickly now, the puns turn sexual, increasing the delight of the bawdry-loving Londoners:

SAMPSON: . . . when I have fought with the men, I will be civil with the maids; I will cut off their heads.
GREGORY: The heads of the maids?
SAMPSON: Ay, the heads of the maids, or their maidenheads, take it in what sense thou wilt.
GREGORY: They must take it in sense that feel it.
SAMPSON: Me they shall feel while I am able to

stand [i.e., able to maintain an erection]; and 'tis known I am a pretty piece of flesh.
GREGORY: 'Tis well thou art not fish. . . . Draw thy tool, here comes two of the house of Montagues.

And out the other door come two servants of Montague, symmetrically balancing the Capulets who have preceded them. A spirited exchange of insults ensues, with Sampson biting his thumb—the classic Italian gesture of obscene ridicule. Swords are drawn and the four men duel. Next Benvolio, a friend of Romeo, appears at center, from under the pavilion. Stepping forward, he draws his sword and cries:

BENVOLIO: Part, fools!
Put up your swords, you know not what you do.

His intervention, however, is misinterpreted by the arch-enemy of all Montagues, Tybalt, who appears at the top of the pavilion and behind the peace-loving Benvolio:

TYBALT: What, art thou drawn among these heartless hinds?
Turn thee, Benvolio, look upon thy death.

Benvolio slowly turns around and looks up. He pleads:

BENVOLIO: I do but keep the peace. Put up thy sword,
Or manage it to part these men with me.

But Tybalt will have none of this:

TYBALT: What, drawn and talk of peace? I hate the word
As I hate hell, all Montagues, and thee.
Have at thee, coward!

With that, he leaps from the pavilion, this swashbuckling and ill-tempered versifier, and lands on the stage platform to engage Benvolio. Now from both doors pour out the citizens and servants of both sides, armed with clubs and "partisans" (spear-swords). The old patriarchs, Capulet and Montague, follow from their respective doors as their wives and women servants appear above them in balcony "windows" that surmount each door. Scarcely three minutes into the play and the

Romeo and Juliet. The opening scene, as it might have looked in the first production at Burbage's The Curtain, c. 1594 or 1595. From the upper level of the pavillion Prince Escalus stops the fighting between members of the households of Montague and Capulet.

stage is filled with flashing swords, leaping duelists, servants grappling hand to hand, tottering old men and screaming women—all this right in the midst of two thousand or more spectators, many of them standing mere feet and inches away.

Then, suddenly, Prince Escalus, the ruler of Verona, enters with his train of attendants on the top level of the pavilion. With a tone of immense authority, he freezes the action:

PRINCE: Rebellious subjects, enemies to peace,
    Profaners of this neighbor-stained steel—

Capulet and Montague pause briefly, then move as if to resume their futile struggle.

PRINCE: Will they not hear?—What ho, you men, you
    beasts!
  That quench the fire of your pernicious rage
  With purple fountains issuing from your
    veins—
  On pain of torture, from those bloody hands
  Throw your mistempered weapons to the
    ground,
  And hear the sentence of your moved prince.

And, with a clatter of steel, twelve swords are dropped on the stage platform and the men who held them drop to their knees in a display of submission and supplication.

In but a few minutes of stage time, we have moved from a scene-setting (and metaphor-establishing) sonnet to servant-class punning to Italianate insults to a street brawl to the regal rhetoric of a prince. We have also met several characters who interest us: the gentle Benvolio, the fiery Tybalt, the Prince, and the patriarchs. And we have come to understand fully the world of the play, with its hot-tempered families, its propensity for violence, its love of language, its youth and exuberance. What we have *not* seen is what we came to see—we have not yet seen or even heard of the Montagues' Romeo or the Capulets' Juliet, and we won't for yet a bit longer. It was Shakespeare's general technique to develop the world of his play first, and only then to introduce his principal characters. This allowed him to detail characters of stature with great individuality, by showing how they differed from the more ordinary or stereotyped characters who appeared in the opening scene or scenes.

There is something most peculiar about Shakespeare's methods of characterization, something unique about the *manner* in which his fretting shadows acquire life. His characters aren't stylized, as Molière's are. His characters aren't archetypal, as Sophocles' are. Neither are they psychological in the Euripidean sense, with rather schematized idiosyncrasies still not entirely free of the guiding hands of the gods. Shakespeare's men and women *are* free. They are almost free of him. More than any playwright who ever lived, I think, Shakespeare gave his imagined figures his blessing and their liberty, allowing them an individuality that need not be categorized and cannot be readily explained because it is *theirs*: willful, perverse, self-contradictory, electric, mercurial, evanescent, ineffable, inevitable, *there*. Could you prick them, they would bleed. But you cannot prick them any more than you can seize lightning bolts; once you've seen the flash, it's too late. They're alive not as analyzable brain waves, emotions erupted from such depths that their sources can never be charted. In the very same moment they are present and have passed. Untrappable, unchallengeable.

Walter Kerr

When Romeo first appears, later in the scene, all have departed save Benvolio; now Romeo reveals to his friend (and, through his friend, to us) that he is in love—with a chaste maid called Rosaline! "The all-seeing sun/Ne'er saw her match since first the world begun," he claims:

ROMEO: . . . she hath Dian's wit;
> And in strong proof of chastity well arm'd,
> From Love's weak childish bow she lives
>> unharm'd.
> She will not stay the siege of loving terms,
> Nor bide th'encounter of assailing eyes,
> Nor ope her lap to saint-seducing gold.
> O, she is rich in beauty, only poor
> That when she dies, with beauty dies her store.

BENVOLIO: Then she hath sworn that she will still
> live chaste?

ROMEO: She hath, and in that sparing makes huge
> waste;
> For beauty starv'd with her severity
> Cuts beauty off from all posterity.
> She is too fair, too wise, wisely too fair,
> To merit bliss by making me despair.
> She hath forsworn to love, and in that vow
> Do I live dead that live to tell it now.

BENVOLIO: Be rul'd by me, forget to think of her.

ROMEO: O, teach me how I should forget to think.

This is love poetry, of course; blank verse amended with many rhyming end-syllables ("poor . . . store," "chaste . . . waste"), parallel phrasings ("not stay . . . nor bide . . . nor ope . . . "), antipodal constructions ("rich in beauty, only poor that . . . "), oxymorons ("Do I live dead . . . "), alliterations ("stay the siege," "saint-seducing") and almost too-clever verbal compilations ("too fair, too wise, wisely too fair") that are the hallmarks of romantic lyricism, particularly in the early Elizabethan and Shakespearean drama.

Romeo and Benvolio exit through the Montague door, whereupon old Capulet, a servant, and the County (Count) Paris enter through the door opposite; this denotes a change of scene (but not scenery) and/or the passage of time. The drama of Shakespeare's age was typically divided into scenes of this sort, with perhaps only the most momentary pauses between scenes; each such division, however, could indicate a new locale and/or an advance in the clock or calendar. Shakespeare was particularly adept at "speeding up" the action of his plays: the story of Romeo and Juliet takes place in less than a week's time in this play, but it spanned nine months in the original novel. This time reduction is an aspect of dramatic economy, or tightening, which gives the action a greater sense of urgency and immediacy. Such time lapses and place changes as were required by any story in Shakespeare's time were indicated simply by this convention of emptying the stage. Then, immediately, new characters entered and perhaps a word or two of dialogue was inserted to clarify what changes were to be considered to have taken place.

Capulet and the Count now discuss a young Capulet daughter, yet unnamed, who "hath not seen the change of fourteen years," but whom Paris is suing to marry. A party is announced, and a servant is left behind to invite guests from a list given by old Capulet. The servant is called "clown" in the original stage direction, and this role is known to have been played by the great comedian Will Kempe. Left alone on stage, the clown reveals to the audience that he cannot read—hence he cannot decipher the names on the list. We cannot tell exactly how Kempe played the scene, but when in the later *Hamlet* the prince instructs the players: "Let those that play your clowns speak no more than is set down for them," we get the idea that Kempe was not above embroidering his part, not only with antic behavior but with words of his own devising. What Shakespeare wrote for him to say is this:

SERVANT: Find them out whose names are written
> here! It is written that the shoemaker should
> meddle with his yard and the tailor with his
> last, the fisher with his pencil and the painter
> with his nets; but I am sent to find those per-
> sons whose names are here writ, and can never
> find what names the writing person hath here
> writ. I must to the learned.

Perhaps if we imagine these lines as said by one of our contemporary old-style gross comics—by Buddy Hackett, or Red Skelton, or Marty Feldman, or Jerry Lewis, for example—we shall get the feeling of the

Will Kemp takes the stage alone. "Find out whose names are written here!"—he addresses the audience with theatrical mischief in his eye. Kemp, the great clown of Shakespeare's company, would have made the most of this solo turn. Part of the painted "heavens" above the stage can be seen here.

delivery better than by trying to imagine a "Shakespearean actor."

Benvolio and Romeo return now via their door. The clown asks them to read the list, and Romeo, agreeing, comes across Rosaline's name. They decide to crash the party. Where is it? they ask. "Up," says the clown: "My master is the great rich Capu-

let, and if you be not of the house of Montagues, I pray come and crush a cup of wine." Then the two men retreat to the Montague door resolving to go anyway, and the scene changes again.

This time the curtains are quickly drawn (by servants) around the pavilion posts. Out the Capulet door come Capulet's wife (Lady Capulet) and a nurse; but now the setting, for the first time, is indoors—as the placement of the curtains makes clear.

WIFE: Nurse, where's my daughter? Call her forth
      to me.
NURSE: Now by my maidenhead at twelve year old,
    I bade her come. What, lamb! What, ladybird!
    God forbid! Where's this girl? What, Juliet!

And the nurse draws the curtains aside to reveal Juliet within the pavilion, seated on the edge of her bed.

JULIET: How now, who calls?
NURSE: Your mother.

Juliet crosses out of the pavilion and descends to her mother. They talk, and the nurse talks—and talks! Three different times we are told that Juliet is thirteen years old, as if Shakespeare feared his audience might fail to take in this bit of information, and both mother and nurse try to persuade Juliet to accept Count Paris' offer of marriage:

WIFE: Well, think of marriage now; younger than
      you,
    Here in Verona, ladies of esteem,
    Are made already mothers. By my count,
    I was your mother much upon these years
    That you are now a maid. Thus then in brief:
    The valiant Paris seeks you for his love.

The Nurse and Juliet, in the American Conservatory Theatre production of 1979.

NURSE: A man, young lady! Lady, such a man
 As all the world—why, he's a man of wax!
WIFE: Verona's summer hath not such a flower.
NURSE: Nay, he's a flower, in faith, a very flower.
WIFE: What say you? Can you love the gentleman?

What is remarkable in this dialogue is its simplicity, its earthiness, its genuinely human sense of humor. Neither grand nor pedestrian, the language bespeaks three characters of remarkable individuality: three great roles for actors and three splendidly lifelike personages.

 This scene between the three women (all played by boys, of course) was played in and around the pavilion, making use of the bed inside for sitting, rocking, and listening. At the end, Juliet agrees to wait and see: "I'll look to like, if looking liking move"; and she, her mother, and the nurse are summoned out by the antic clown:

SERVANT: Madam, the guests are come, supper
 serv'd up, you call'd, my young lady ask'd for,
 the nurse curs'd in the pantry, and every thing
 in extremity. I must hence to wait; I beseech
 you follow straight.

They do, with the laughter of the audience trailing after them, and the curtains of the pavilion are pulled fully back and out of view: we are going outside again. From the Montague door come Romeo and Benvolio, masked for the Capulet party and accompanied by six or seven other maskers, including one of Shakespeare's most vitally memorable characters, the rakish Mercutio. They are accompanied by torchbearers, Shakespeare's indication that it is now nighttime in Verona and also his symbol for the purity of love:

ROMEO: Give me a torch, I am not for this ambling;
 Being but heavy, I will bear the light.
MERCUTIO: Nay, gentle Romeo, we must have you
 dance.
ROMEO: Not I, believe me. You have dancing shoes
 With nimble soles, I have a soul of lead
 So stakes me to the ground I cannot move.
MERCUTIO: You are a lover, borrow Cupid's wings,
 And soar with them above a common bound.
ROMEO: I am too sore enpierced with his shaft

To soar with his light feathers, and so bound
I cannot bound a pitch above dull woe;
Under love's heavy burthen do I sink. . . .
A torch for me. Let wantons light of heart
Tickle the senseless rushes with their heels.
For I am proverb'd with a grandsire phrase,
I'll be a candle-holder and look on:
The game was ne'er so fair, and I am done.
MERCUTIO: Tut, . . . we'll draw thee from the mire
 Of this sir-reverence love, wherein thou
  stickest
 Up to the ears. Come, we burn daylight, ho!
ROMEO: Nay, that's not so.
MERCUTIO: I mean, sir, in delay
 We waste our lights in vain, like lights by day!

Typically, Shakespeare mixes imagery with specifics; he will, in this play, relentlessly pursue the symbol of light (representing purity, love, and life itself) as the antagonist of black (representing night, evil, and death): this imaginative use of that symbol has antecedents that go back at least as far as Prometheus (the giver of light) and may even be considered one of the archetypal images of theatre itself.

 Mercutio now regales Romeo with an extraordinary tale of Queen Mab, "the fairies' midwife," as the men hasten to dinner at the Capulets. There is an interesting original stage direction here: "They march about the stage, and Servingmen come forth with napkins." Presumably Romeo, Benvolio, Mercutio, and their train of followers simply parade about the platform while the servingmen appear at the top of the pavilion: the clown, of course, has already established that the Capulet house, where the party will take place, is "up," and in Shakespeare's day the marching about was all that was required to indicate another change of scene—or, in this case, an overlapping of scenes. After the servants engage in a bit of tomfoolery concerning the party preparations, while other servants, below, dress the pavilion curtains in a festive manner, Capulet and his family and guests appear through the central door and come to the pavilion's center:

CAPULET: Welcome, gentlemen! Ladies that have
 their toes

"A torch for me," says Romeo (Christopher Walken) in the Stratford Shakespeare Festival production of 1968, as Mercutio entertains the masquers who will accompany them to the Capulets' house.

Unplagu'd with corns will walk about with you.
Ah, my mistresses, which of you all
Will now deny to dance? She that makes dainty,
She I'll swear hath corns. Am I come near ye
    now?
Welcome, gentlemen! I have seen the day
That I have worn a visor and could tell
A whispering tale in a fair lady's ear,
Such as would please; 'tis gone, 'tis gone, 'tis
    gone.
You are welcome, gentlemen! Come, musi-
    cians, play.

And musicians, seated in a small room in the very top gallery of the theatre itself, play as the masked ladies and gentlemen dance. Capulet and his aged cousin retreat backstage and reappear at the top of the pavilion, where servants have placed benches, there to sit and watch the proceedings.

CAPULET: Nay, sit, nay, sit, good cousin Capulet,
    For you and I are past our dancing days.

It is at this point that Romeo sees Juliet for the first time; clearly it is a moment for which the audience, primed with their great familiarity with this tale, has anxiously waited.

The maskers' dance, as seen from an upper gallery.

ROMEO: (*to a servant*) What lady's that . . . ?

SERVANT: I know not, sir.

ROMEO: O she doth teach the torches to burn bright!
It seems she hangs upon the cheek of night
As a rich jewel in an Ethiop's ear—
Beauty too rich for use, for earth too dear!
So shows a snowy dove trooping with crows,
As yonder lady o'er her fellows shows. . . .
Did my heart love till now? Forswear it, sight!
For I ne'er saw true beauty till this night.

Note the lavish use of light imagery in this passage. Juliet is brighter than fire itself, shining brilliantly as a diamond on a black earlobe, against "the cheek of night"; she is above all other women as a snowy dove is whiter than the crows: this imagery vis-à-vis Juliet will remain consistent throughout the rest of the play. Rosaline is forgotten (although presumably she is present at the party, she is not mentioned in the play text; directors usually make an effort to identify her by some action at the beginning of the scene). Thus, out of the background of dueling and antagonism with which the play begins, true love and its celebration emerge to engage the play's development.

Now Tybalt comes on the scene—hate and the threat of death are never long absent from the stage in this play. He enters above with his servant, at the top of the pavilion to the side of Capulet, and he overhears Romeo's words.

TYBALT: This, by his voice, should be a Montague.
　　　Fetch me my rapier, boy. What, dares the slave
　　　Come hither . . . ?

But old Capulet stops him: they argue, the old man protecting his well-ordered party and also standing up for common decency and hospitality, and Tybalt raging but finally relenting. Why is this scene played above? Because below, at the stage level, Romeo is approaching Juliet, and Juliet Romeo; as the menacing exchange occurs up on the pavilion, romance is engendered below, a perfect use of the multi-leveled stage space. By the time Romeo and Juliet first exchange words, they already have made substantial communication with their eyes:

ROMEO: If I profane with my unworthiest hand
　　　This holy shrine, the gentle sin is this;
　　　My lips, two blushing pilgrims, ready stand
　　　To smooth that rough touch with a tender kiss.
JULIET: Good pilgrim, you do wrong your hand too
　　　much,
　　　Which mannerly devotion shows in this;
　　　For saints have hands that pilgrims' hands do
　　　touch,
　　　And palm to palm is holy palmer's kiss.
ROMEO: Have not saints lips, and holy palmers too?
JULIET: Ay, pilgrim, lips that they must use in
　　　pray'r.
ROMEO: O then, dear saint, let lips do what hands
　　　do. . . .

They kiss. And only then, following that first kiss, do they find out:

ROMEO: Is she a Capulet?
　　　O dear account! my life is my foe's debt!

And

A DEMOCRATIC AUDIENCE

Despite the richness of its language and the sumptuousness of its costumes, the English theatre of the Shakespearean era charged a remarkably low admission price: it cost a mere penny, which was no more than the price of a quart of beer or an Elizabethan newspaper. The cheapest London dinner cost three times as much, and a quart of Falstaffian sack (sherry) eight times; thus the cost of attending a Shakespearean premiere—and standing up in the pit, to be sure—was roughly the same as the cost of going to a university "workshop" production in America today, or seeing an afternoon movie at a second-run house offering early-bird discounts. This brought theatregoing well within the range of virtually all Londoners, with the result that the typical audience was an amazingly diverse collection encompassing every social stratum,

as John Davies noted in an epigram in 1595:

For, as we see at all the playhouse doors,
When ended is the play, the dance, and song,
A thousand townsmen, gentlemen, and whores,
Porters and serving-men together throng.

Much of the breadth and vigor of Shakespeare's art can be accounted for by the nature of the audience he had to please, which included laborers and intelligentsia, merchants and courtiers, farmers' sons and earls. To succeed in the public theatre of Shakespeare's day, every play had to have at least something for the "groundlings" (the standing audience in the pit) as well as something for the "gentlemen's rooms" (the privileged and higher-priced segregated seating in the gallery).

NURSE: His name is Romeo, and a Montague,
  The only son of your great enemy.
JULIET: My only love spring from my only hate!
  Too early seen unknown, and known too late!

The party ends, and the tragedy is on. The stage is empty; at this point it is convenient to think that "Act I" is over—for so it is indicated in most modern editions of the play—but there were no intermissions in the theatre of this time, and the re-entrance of the chorus at this point is not so much a signal for "Act II" as a recognition that the tragedy now moves to its next level.

  The chorus, from his high pavilion position as before, again delivers a scene-setting sonnet to the audience, this time commenting on the end of Romeo's infatuation with Rosaline and the difficulties the lovers face in the new alliance; meanwhile, below, stagehands perhaps erect a simulated stone wall behind the closed curtains of the pavilion frame. At the chorus' departure, the curtains part to reveal Romeo:

ROMEO: Can I go forward when my heart is here?
  Turn back, dull earth, and find thy centre out.

Upon hearing the shouts of Benvolio ("Romeo! My cousin Romeo! Romeo!"), Romeo hurdles the wall and hides at its base. Benvolio and Mercutio come

Romeo crouches beside the wall as Benvolio and Mercutio search for him with torch and lantern. The wall is a conjecture of the author and illustrator, but such stage properties are known to have been used from time to time where appropriate and helpful to the staging. The wall could have been pre-set behind the drawn curtain.

up behind the wall and, peering beyond, search for
their friend:

MERCUTIO: He is wise,
    And, on my life, hath stol'n him home to bed.
BENVOLIO: He ran this way and leapt this orchard
        wall.
    Call, good Mercutio.
MERCUTIO: Nay, I'll conjure, too.
    Romeo! humors! madman! passion! lover! . . .
    I conjure thee by Rosaline's bright eyes,
    By her high forehead and her scarlet lip,
    By her fine foot, straight leg, and quivering
        thigh,
    And the demesnes that there adjacent lie,
    That in thy likeness thou appear to us! . . .
BENVOLIO: Come, he hath hid himself among these
        trees
    To be consorted with the humorous night.
    Blind is his love and best befits the dark.
MERCUTIO: If love be blind, love cannot hit
        the mark. . . .
    Romeo, good night. I'll to my truckle-bed,
    This field-bed is too cold for me to sleep.
    Come, shall we go?

They leave, but much has been established in this
little scene: the orchard setting, the darkness and
cold of night, Romeo's furtiveness now that he is
genuinely in love, the evocation (conjuring) of sexual desire, and, imagistically, the premonition of
darkness and blindness that will attend this particular love.

    His friends gone, Romeo stands and comes
forward, saying of Mercutio:

    He jests at scars that never felt a wound.

It is the beginning of the most famous scene in the
play, surely one of the most celebrated love scenes
in all literature. Juliet appears on the pavilion roof,
and, characteristically, Romeo sees her as light
itself:

ROMEO: But soft, what light through yonder
        window breaks?
    It is the east, and Juliet is the sun.
    Arise, fair sun, and kill the envious moon. . . .

Is Juliet aware of his presence? To herself (presumably) she speaks:

JULIET: O Romeo, Romeo, wherefore art thou
        Romeo?
    Deny thy father and refuse thy name;
    Or, if thou wilt not, be but sworn my
        love,
    And I'll no longer be a Capulet.
ROMEO (aside): Shall I hear more, or shall I speak at
        this?
JULIET: 'Tis but thy name that is my enemy;
    Thou art thyself, though not a Montague.
    What's Montague? It is nor hand nor foot,
    Nor arm nor face, nor any other part
    Belonging to a man. O be some other name!
    What's in a name? That which we call a rose
    By any other word would smell as sweet;
    So Romeo would, were he not Romeo call'd,
    Retain that dear perfection which he owes
    Without that title. Romeo, doff thy name,
    And for thy name, which is no part of thee,
    Take all myself.

And Romeo, needing no more than this, declares
himself:

ROMEO: I take thee at thy word.
    Call me but love, and I'll be new baptiz'd;
    Henceforth I never will be Romeo.

But is there more to this exchange than meets the
eye? It is, of course, one of the conventions of
Shakespearean drama that characters can address
the audience (as if speaking to themselves) without
being overheard by others on stage; this can be
even more easily conveyed if, as in the present case,
the characters are standing on different levels. Still,
there is the suggestion that Juliet would at least like
to be overheard by her new-found idol, to whom
her words are addressed apostrophically. One of
the more subtle variations on this convention—and
one at which Shakespeare was particularly adept
—is to turn the characters into an audience for each
other; that is, to let them overhear each other's
thoughts.

    And what are we to make of these two young
people who express themselves so eloquently? Modern audiences sometimes have difficulty accept-

ing the notion that such brilliantly turned verses could issue from the mouths of a thirteen-year-old girl and her adolescent swain. But this, too, reflects a convention of the theatre, and should not be analyzed too critically. It is, after all, no more absurd to find Romeo and Juliet speaking in the fine phrases of Shakespearean poetry than to find them speaking in English (for they are Italians), or, for that matter, to find them on a London stage. The theatre is always only a metaphor for life, and the love language of Romeo and Juliet expresses the free flight of the author's imagination as he seeks to exact from his characters an image of star-crossed passion that will register indelibly in the audience's mind. Realism is not the goal, although the play deals with real human emotions. To that end, the language is art, it is expression, and in its own way it is truth.

JULIET: My ears have not yet drunk a hundred words
Of thy tongue's uttering, yet I know the sound.
Art thou not Romeo, and a Montague?
ROMEO: Neither, fair maid, if either thee dislike.
JULIET: How camest thou hither, tell me, and wherefore?
The orchard walls are high and hard to climb,
And the place death, considering who thou art,
If any of my kinsmen find thee here.
ROMEO: With love's light wings did I o'erperch these walls,
For stony limits cannot hold love out,
And what love can do, that dares love attempt;
Therefore thy kinsmen are no stop to me.
JULIET: If they do see thee, they will murther thee.
ROMEO: Alack, there lies more peril in thine eye
Than twenty of their swords! Look thou but sweet,
And I am proof against their enmity.
JULIET: I would not for the world they saw thee here.
ROMEO: I have night's cloak to hide me from their eyes,
And but thou love me [if you do not love me], let them find me here;
My life were better ended by their hate,
Than death prorogued [postponed], wanting of thy love.

Juliet is called away; she comes back. They agree to marry. She is again called away; again she comes back.

JULIET: 'Tis almost morning, I would have thee gone—
And yet no farther than a wanton's bird,
That lets it hop a little from his hand. . . .
ROMEO: I would I were thy bird.
JULIET: Sweet, so would I.
Yet I should kill thee with much cherishing.
Good night, good night! Parting is such sweet sorrow,
That I shall say good night till it be morrow.
ROMEO: Sleep dwell upon thine eyes, peace in thy breast!
Would I were sleep and peace, so sweet to rest!
Hence will I to my ghostly father's cell,
His help to crave, and my dear hap to tell.

And Romeo leaves to visit his "ghostly sire," Friar Lawrence, to ask that he perform the wedding ceremony the next day.

Although the foregoing is a love scene, it is filled with the imagery of death: the swords of the Capulet kinsmen ("My life were better ended with their hate"), the bird that would be killed with too much cherishing, and the "ghostly" confessor, whose well-intentioned intervention will ultimately cause the double suicide with which the play will end. This imagery sustains the undertone of pathos, established at the very outset of the play, that is the foundation for tragedy in this celebration of light and love.

The play starts to pick up momentum at this point, with a series of short scenes in different locales accelerating the action. Romeo leaves by one tiring-house door and Friar Lawrence, basket in hand, enters from the other. The position of the curtains tells us that we are still outdoors. It is the following morning; the words set the scene:

FRIAR: The grey-ey'd morn smiles on the frowning night,
Check'ring the eastern clouds with streaks of light. . . .

and Romeo enters and tries to persuade the Friar to marry him to Juliet.

FRIAR: Holy Saint Francis, what a change is here!
    Is Rosaline, that thou did'st love so dear,
    So soon forsaken? Young men's love then lies
    Not truly in their hearts, but in their eyes.
    Jesu Maria! . . .

But he is persuaded, and together they enter through the curtains into Friar Lawrence's "cell," as Romeo has called it, which is represented by a curtained area of the lower pavilion. Benvolio and Mercutio enter the stage from the Montague door:

MERCUTIO: Where the dev'l should this Romeo be?
    Came he not home to-night?
BENVOLIO: Not to his father's. I spoke with his man.
MERCUTIO: Why, that same pale hard-hearted
    wench, that Rosaline,
    Torments him so, that he will sure run mad.
BENVOLIO: Tybalt, the kinsman to old Capulet,
    Hath sent a letter to his father's house.
MERCUTIO: A challenge, on my life.
BENVOLIO: Romeo will answer it.
MERCUTIO: Any man that can write may answer a
    letter.
BENVOLIO: Nay, he will answer the letter's master,
    how he dares, being dar'd.
MERCUTIO: Alas, poor Romeo, he is already dead. . .

And the plot relentlessly advances. Think what we have to contend with at this point, only a third of the way into the play: five young men (Romeo, Ben-volio, Tybalt, Mercutio, Paris), two young women (Juliet and the unseen Rosaline), and various assorted elders—a prince, a friar, a nurse, a clown, and four parents—all drawn with a good deal of attention to their individuality, all blended skillfully in a plot of considerable complexity. In addition, we have already seen a full-stage street brawl, an elegant party with music and dancing, an unforgettable love scene, and a sampling of comedy that ranges from the broad tomfoolery of the servant-clown to the sparkling eloquence of Mercutio. And now we are headed into a marriage on the one hand, and a duel on the other: love and death, the two most profound themes of art in any age.

Romeo has summoned Juliet to Friar Lawrence's cell: this Juliet learns in a message from the nurse, delivered on the highest pavilion level after a long and anxious wait that is amusingly described to us in Juliet's soliloquy:

JULIET: The clock struck nine when I did send the
    nurse;
    In half an hour she promised to return.
    Perchance she cannot meet him—that's not so.
    O, she is lame! . . .
    Now is the sun upon the highmost hill
    Of this day's journey, and from nine till twelve
    Is three long hours, yet she is not come. . . .
    But old folks—many feign as they were dead,
    Unwieldy, slow, heavy, and pale as lead.
    O God, she comes! . . .

Shakespeare's characters, like those in real life, are very commonly misunderstood, and almost always understood by different persons in different ways. The causes are the same in either case. If you take only what the friends of the character say, you may be deceived, and still more so, if that which his enemies say; nay, even the character himself sees himself through the medium of his character, and not exactly as he is. Take all together, not omitting a shrewd hint from the clown or the fool, and perhaps your impression will be right; and you may know whether you have in fact discovered the poet's own idea, by all the speeches receiving light from it, and attesting its reality by reflecting it.

Samuel Taylor Coleridge

And, having at last extracted the good news from the older woman, she leaves her platform as the curtains open below to reveal Romeo and the friar. Shortly, Juliet joins them, "somewhat fast and embraceth Romeo" according to an original stage direction, and the curtain is drawn again around them as they are wedded by Friar Lawrence within the "cell."

Now a variation of the first scene takes place.

Benvolio, Mercutio, and several followers come out the Montague door, soon to be met by Tybalt and others from the Capulet door opposite. They meet center; angry words are exchanged. Benvolio, consistent with his character, tries to make peace, but the antagonism escalates between the proud, hot-tempered Tybalt and Mercutio. Romeo, hearing the dispute, enters from the cell, center, and tries to explain to Tybalt; this only inflames Tybalt

"Come, sir, your passado." Tybalt and Mercutio begin their fight, as Romeo and Benvolio stand to one side.

SECTION TWO: THE PAST

the more, and scandalizes Mercutio. Tybalt and Mercutio fight; Romeo tries to intervene; Mercutio is mortally wounded:

MERCUTIO: I am hurt.
    A plague a' both houses! I am sped.
    Is he gone and hath nothing?
BENVOLIO: What, art thou hurt?
MERCUTIO: Ay, ay, a scratch, a scratch, marry, 'tis
    enough.
    Where is my page? Go, villain, fetch a surgeon.
ROMEO: Courage, man. The hurt cannot be much.
MERCUTIO: No, 'tis not so deep as a well, nor so wide
    as a church-door, but 'tis enough, 'twill serve.
    Ask for me to-morrow, and you shall find me a
    grave man. . . . Why the dev'l came you be-
    tween us? I was hurt under your arm.
ROMEO: I thought all for the best.
MERCUTIO: Help me into some house, Benvolio,
    Or I shall faint. A plague a' both your houses!
    They have made worms' meat of me. I have it,
    And soundly too. Your houses!

And Benvolio helps Mercutio out through the center pavilion curtains, now no longer Friar Lawrence's cell, but a neutral "house" between the two other "houses" left and right—the same two "households" pointed out by the chorus in the first line of the play; upon them both Mercutio hurls his dying curse, his wit dissolving in desperation in this deepening moment of the tragic pattern. Thus does this play move from violence to love and back again in an alternating fashion, each time getting closer to the core, in an inward-spiraling, self-accelerating course.

Romeo, at the nadir of his life (his "I thought all for the best" is one of the most pathetic lines in all drama), reflects on the ambiguity of manliness:

O sweet Juliet,
Thy beauty hath made me effeminate,
And in my temper soft'ned valor's steel.

Upon seeing the re-entering Tybalt, Romeo challenges and kills him in impetuous rage. The stage is filled with people; chaos is come:

Romeo and Juliet in balcony scene from American Conservatory Theatre production of 1979, directed by Allen Fletcher. Julia Fletcher and Thomas Nahrwold play the young lovers; here Romeo is about to descend the "corded ladder" for his escape to Nantua.

BENVOLIO: Romeo, away, be gone!
　　　The citizens are up, and Tybalt slain.
　　　Stand not amazed, the prince will doom thee
　　　　　death
　　　If thou art taken. Hence be gone, away!
ROMEO: O, I am fortune's fool!

As Romeo flees, the Prince again appears at the top level of the pavilion to restore order and send down his punishment: Romeo is banished and the families are fined.

Romeo and Juliet have a final love scene, "aloft" as the stage directions say, at the top pavilion level. They have made love (in the fine film adaptation by Franco Zeffirelli, this scene is played in the nude, a possibility that Shakespeare could not even contemplate, given his boy Juliet) and, as in the balcony scene, daylight threatens.

JULIET: Wilt thou be gone? It is not yet near day.
　　　It was the nightingale, and not the lark,
　　　That pierc'd the fearful hollow of thine ear;
　　　Nightly she sings on yond pomegranate tree.
　　　Believe me, love, it was the nightingale.
ROMEO: It was the lark, the herald of the morn,
　　　No nightingale. Look, love, what envious
　　　　　streaks
　　　Do lace the severing clouds in yonder east.
　　　Night's candles are burnt out, and jocund day
　　　Stands tiptoe on the misty mountain tops.
　　　I must be gone and live, or stay and die.
JULIET: Yond light is not day-light, I know it, I;
　　　It is some meteor. . . .
　　　O now be gone, more light and light it grows.
ROMEO: More light and light, more dark and dark
　　　　　our woes.

The alternation of imagery between light and dark begins to accelerate; day and night come faster on each others' heels as the plot moves inexorably toward its fatal conclusion. Romeo descends from the pavilion with his rope ladder; Juliet's mother then appears and tells Juliet she is to marry Paris. The curtains below open to reveal Paris in the midst of a discussion with Friar Lawrence about the wedding date:

FRIAR: On Thursday, sir? The time is very short.

And the time has been made to appear shorter by Shakespeare's dramaturgy, which begins the scene with the friar's response, making us deduce what Paris' question had been by inference.

The climax of the play is developed around the friar's plan: alone with Juliet, he gives her a vial containing a "distilling liquor" which will make her appear dead; later, and in secret, he will come with Romeo to take her, freshly revived, from her open tomb, thereby saving her from an unwanted second marriage. Back in her "room" under the pavilion, Juliet draws the vial from her bosom:

JULIET: Farewell! God knows when we shall meet
　　　again.
　　　I have a faint cold fear thrills through my veins,
　　　That almost freezes up the heat of life.
　　　I'll call them back again to comfort me.
　　　Nurse!—What should she do here?
　　　My dismal scene I needs must act alone.
　　　Come, vial.

Shakespeare is the most stage-conscious, and in a sense the most self-conscious, of dramatists; an actor himself, he explicitly uses the stage as a metaphor for life: Juliet, in this scene, sees herself as an actress "acting" a "scene." It is not entirely unlike her apostrophe to Romeo from the balcony: she is aware of her words—they are not mere fragmentary mutterings—and she speaks aloud as if to test her own sincerity and motivation.

Juliet swallows the potion, and, in an original stage direction, "falls upon the bed within the curtains," which are drawn around her. Now much bustle takes place on the platform in front of her. Lord and Lady Capulet enter and command their servants to action: spices are sent for, meats are ordered baked, a cock crows, a curfew bell rings, servants come in bearing logs and are ordered to get drier ones. Carnality is in the air—a marriage is to be held today, music is heard from the Count's commissioned performers, and Lady Capulet accuses her husband of flirting with the help. Paris has arrived. The Nurse goes to the curtains to waken Juliet:

NURSE: Mistress, what, Mistress! Juliet!—Fast, I
　　　warrant her, she.—
　　　Why lamb! why lady! fie, you slug-a-bed!
　　　Why, love, I say! madam! sweet heart! why,
　　　bride!

What, not a word? You take your pennyworths
    now;
Sleep for a week, for the next night, I warrant,
The County Paris hath set up his rest
That you shall rest but little. God forgive me!

She draws aside the curtains. Juliet is dead, apparently. What follows is a scene that is peculiarly Elizabethan, and virtually impossible to perform today—a scene of lamentation:

NURSE: O woe! O woeful, woeful, woeful day!
    Most lamentable day, most woeful day
    That ever, ever, I did yet behold!
    O day, O day, O day! O hateful day!
    Never was seen so black a day as this.
    O woeful day, O woeful day!
PARIS: Beguil'd, divorced, wronged, spited, slain!
    Most detestable Death, by thee beguil'd,
    By cruel cruel thee quite overthrown!
    O love, O life! not life, but love in death!
CAPULET: Despis'd, distressed, hated, martyr'd,
    kill'd! . . .
    (etc.)

The later Shakespeare would probably have considered this scene an embarrassment—he was to satirize just this sort of writing just a year or two later in *A Midsummer Night's Dream*—still, it exemplifies the Elizabethan notion that the use of language had no limits, and that every feeling, idea, and emotion could be transcribed into blank verse. The later Shakespeare would write these words for a father looking upon his dead daughter:

KING LEAR: And my poor fool is hang'd! No, no, no
    life!
    Why should a dog, a horse, a rat, have life,
    And thou no breath at all? Thou'lt come no
    more,
    Never, never, never, never, never.
    Pray you undo this button. Thank you, sir.
    Do you see this? Look on her! Look her lips,
    Look there, look there!

By the time Shakespeare wrote those lines, his own father and son were dead; in *Romeo and Juliet*, he was still speculating on grief, not reporting it.

The final scene of *Romeo and Juliet* takes place in the "monument" where Juliet lies "buried." Romeo, it turns out, has not received word from Friar Lawrence explaining the use of the potion—the messenger was deterred by a quarantine—and instead he learns (falsely) that Juliet is dead. He thereupon buys a poison from an apothecary (possibly played by Shakespeare) and hastens back to Verona. He enters the stage by a tiring-house door and confronts the pavilion once more; it now houses the tombs of Juliet and Tybalt. The curtains are closed. His servant, Balthazar, holds a lantern (once more it is night); Romeo wrests it from him:

ROMEO: Give me the light. Upon thy life I charge
    thee,
    What e'er thou hearest or seest, stand all aloof,
    And do not interrupt me in my course. . . .
    The time and my intents are savage-wild,
    More fierce and more inexorable far
    Than empty tigers or the roaring sea.

Balthazar leaves. With a crowbar, Romeo attacks the pavilion curtains:

ROMEO: Thou detestable maw, thou womb of
    death,
    Gorg'd with the dearest morsel of the earth,
    Thus I enforce thy rotten jaws to open,
    And in despite I'll cram thee with more food.

The curtains part; the tombs (biers—such are listed in Henslowe's list of properties for The Rose) are revealed. Paris, who had entered previously and hidden to watch this scene, reappears and challenges Romeo. They duel, Paris is slain, and Romeo drags the body into the tomb, as Paris has requested with his dying breath. Now the alternations between love and violence, savagery and affection, light and darkness, follow upon each other as fast as heartbeats.

ROMEO: I'll bury thee in a triumphant grave.
    A grave? O, no, a lanthorn, slaughter'd youth;
    For here lies Juliet, and her beauty makes
    This vault a feasting presence full of light.
    Death, lie thou there, by a dead man interr'd.
        (*Laying Paris in the tomb.*)
    How oft when men are at the point of death
    Have they been merry, which their keepers call

A lightning before death! O how may I
Call this a lightning? O my love, my wife,
Death, that hath suck'd the honey of thy
    breath,
Hath had no power yet upon thy beauty:
Thou are not conquer'd, beauty's ensign yet
Is crimson in thy lips and in thy cheeks,
And death's pale flag is not advanced there.
Tybalt, liest thou there in thy bloody sheet?
O, what more favor can I do to thee,
Than with that hand that cut thy youth in twain
To sunder his that was thine enemy?
Forgive me, cousin! Ah, dear Juliet,
Why art thou yet so fair? Shall I believe
That unsubstantial Death is amorous,
And that the lean abhorred monster keeps
Thee here in dark to be his paramour?
For fear of that, I still will stay with thee,
And never from this palace of dim night
Depart again. Here, here will I remain
With worms that are thy chambermaids; O
    here
Will I set up my everlasting rest,
And shake the yoke of inauspicious stars
From this world-wearied flesh. . . .

With a last embrace, a swallow of poison, and a final kiss, Romeo falls: "Thus with a kiss I die." Consider the superb ironies of this scene. In seeing that Juliet looks as if alive, Romeo fails to realize that she *is* alive. In thinking to shake off the "yoke" of his "inauspicious stars" he is only fulfilling the astrological prediction made at the play's beginning— this love is indeed star-crossed, and therefore what the stars foretold is true. In his fear that Death will become Juliet's "paramour," he kills himself to guard her from that fate—and in so doing yields her up to Death. Dramatic irony, which is the device of letting the audience in on information unknown to the characters, has rarely been more skillfully exploited than in this scene; the audience, despite their prior knowledge of the denouement, all but stand in their chairs to shout Romeo from his fatal course.

Friar Lawrence enters the tomb, takes in the ghastly scene, and realizes his mistake; no sooner has he done so than Juliet revives. From that mo-

ment, neither he nor anyone else can forestall the play's conclusion.

JULIET: O comfortable friar! where is my lord?
    I do remember well where I should be,
    And there I am. Where is my Romeo?
FRIAR: I hear some noise, lady. Come from that nest
    Of death, contagion, and unnatural sleep.
    A greater power than we can contradict
    Hath thwarted our intents. Come, come away.
    Thy husband in thy bosom there lies dead;
    And Paris too. Come I'll dispose of thee
    Among a sisterhood of holy nuns.
    Stay not to question, for the watch is coming.
    Come, go, good Juliet. I dare no longer stay (*he
        leaves*).
JULIET: Go get thee hence, for I will not away.
    What's here? A cup clos'd in my true love's
        hand?
    Poison, I see, hath been his timeless end.
    O churl, drunk all, and left no friendly drop
    To help me after? I will kiss thy lips,
    Haply some poison yet doth hang on them,
    To make me die with a restorative (*kisses him*).
    Thy lips are warm.

There is noise: a watchman cries.

JULIET: Yea, noise? Then I'll be brief. O happy
        dagger (*seizes Romeo's dagger*),
    This is thy sheath (*stabs herself*); there rust,
        and let me die.

And she dies. Finally love and death are fully unified: she dies, as he did, with a kiss, and the final (and somewhat gratuitous) death blow is made with Romeo's dagger, for which she becomes a sheath: a sexual image of mortal intercourse that unites the passions of violence and love that have pursued each other throughout the play.

The play has climaxed, and the climax is towering. It is a development of flowing plot and action, of leaps over walls and from platforms and marches about the stage, of rope ladders, musicians and torchbearers, a ghostly father in his cell, a blabbering nurse, an officious father, a savagely funny friend who almost (but not quite) manages to die laughing. It is empty as narrative alone: when the friar, in the play's final moments of resolution, makes an effort to explain all that has gone on, he can only say

> I will be brief, for my short date of breath
> Is not so long as is a tedious tale.

But the two hours' traffic on the stage has been anything but tedious. What would be little more than sentimental versification in a narrative poem has been made thrillingly dynamic through its embodiment in passionate performance and flowing, immensely varied theatrical staging. The sheer theatrics of Shakespeare's craftsmanship—the rapid and important alternation of daytime and night, indoors and out, lovemaking and street brawling, poetry and prose, humor and pathos, dancing and killing, ecstasy and lamentation, thundering sonority and silken eloquence—has created a richly patterned tale that delivers to its audience a riveting and memorable experience. We pity Prince Escalus at having to hear Friar Lawrence's necessarily lame narration of this tale, for we have seen it all. We have shared in its feelings and we know, *really* know, its people: we see, in them, ourselves.

One can only speculate as to the conversations that took place among Elizabethan theatregoers after their first exposure to Shakespeare's *Romeo and Juliet*. One imagines certain reconsiderations: of the role of parents in the arrangement of marriages, of the age at which infatuation becomes overwhelming, of the function of romantic love in family affairs, of the applicability of Italian passions to English morals. It is inescapable that some lives were changed and some long-held prejudices weakened. Can we also sense a great satisfaction, a profound sympathy, a quiet but irresistible awe?

Romeo and Juliet is not, perhaps, a play of great intellect or majesty. The same author's *Hamlet* and *King Lear* are surely more complex, his *Othello* and *Macbeth* more intense, his *Twelfth Night* and *As You Like It* more wittily brilliant, *The Winter's Tale* and *The Tempest* more hauntingly beautiful. But those are all later plays, written in the fullest vision of Shakespeare's maturity. What *Romeo and Juliet* provides its audience is a bold portrayal of the passions and playfulness of youth as seen by an author who was himself barely out of his twenties. With its masterful depiction of first love, *Romeo and Juliet* has leaped the centuries; it is one of those theatrical experiences that liberate us from our own time and free us to share in the sensibility of the ages as we relive this timeless human experience.

CHAPTER 6

THE ROYAL THEATRE

The Renaissance exploded upon the world in a tumult of upheaval and exaltation, carrying with it an extravagance of feeling and a burst of creative energy. It was to be followed by a period of consolidation, refinement, and the imposition of rational sensibility and order.

Historians today call this maturation period the Enlightenment, this time in the eighteenth century when the fires of the Renaissance were banked and channeled into a general social and philosophical illumination. The Enlightenment became an age of intellectual classifications and structures: it brought forth the physical laws of Issac Newton, the political and social analysis of the Baron de Montesquieu, the rational philosophies of René Descartes, John Locke, Immanuel Kant, and David Hume, and the comprehensive encyclopedias of Denis Diderot. It was an age that saw the establishment of great scientific and literary academies that worked to regularize wisdom and codify knowledge; it was also an age of politesse and social decorum, of powdered wigs, gilded snuffboxes, fine laces, and carved walking sticks. Elegance was the order of the day in that era governed by aristocratic tastes and the complex niceties of an emerging code of precisely modulated social behavior.

It was not the first time such a consolidation had occurred, nor would it be the last. There seems to be a pattern in the history of civilizations whereby great bursts of creative energy—Dionysian, religious, omni-sensual, and rhapsodic—are followed by intellectual structurings and forms—Apollonian, rational, synthesizing, and constrained. Great theatre art, that is, art that encompasses what is widely perceived as truth and beauty, tends to appear between the peaks in this pattern, at those transitional moments in history when *mythos* is turning into *logos* and the raw creative forces brought forth into a culture are just on the verge of coming into rational focus. Pure rawness, as of the Greek dithyramb, creates a theatre that is ultimately anarchic and publicly uncommunicative; pure form and focus, on the other hand, create a theatre that is stultified by its own discipline. And so it was that right between the Renaissance and the Enlightenment—in a brilliantly creative half-century after the one era and before the other—that the theatre experienced another of its great periods: the "Royal

Theatre" of the European Court. The time was the last half of the seventeenth century; the locale was London, Madrid, and, particularly, Paris.

A THEATRE FOR COURTS AND KINGS

We choose to call this theatre the Royal Theatre owing to its fundamental association with the courts of kings. In Spain, at the court of King Philip IV, the plays of Pedro Calderón de la Barca provided light entertainment and philosophical food for thought for audiences at the palace and at the royal hunting lodge, La Zarzuela. In England, under charter from the restored Merry Monarch, Charles II, the acidulous comedies of William Wycherley and William Congreve, and the neo-classic verse tragedies of John Dryden, were featured at the Theatre Royal in Drury Lane and at another royally chartered stage at Lincoln's Inn Fields. And in France, under the spectacular reign of the Sun King, Louis XIV, the stirring tragedies of Pierre Corneille and Jean Racine and the scintillating, pointed comedies of Molière flourished at a variety of theatres in and out of Paris and at the country residences of king and court. The major kings of Europe were the prime patrons of these theatres, and the theatres—both the public ones in the cities and the private stagings in the palaces and chateaux—occupied a central

EARLY COURT THEATRICALS: MASQUES AND REVELS

The Royal Theatre of the courts of Charles II and Louis XIV did not simply materialize out of thin air, for the performance of plays and entertainments at court was customary from the fifteenth century onward. Classical Roman comedies were performed in the Italian court as early as 1485, and both Henry VII and Henry VIII in England maintained acting troupes for holiday theatricals in the sixteenth century. With the accession of Elizabeth to the English throne in 1558, court theatre became a major enterprise under the direct administration of a court officer known as the Master of Revels. It was his duty not only to supervise court productions but also to license plays and players for public theatre appearances.

The early European presentations at court included neo-classic comedies modeled on the works of Roman authors, and "interludes," which were short comic pieces that carried a moral message. Re-stagings of public theatre plays were also presented, particularly during the Shakespearean era: at Christmas time in 1612, Shakespeare's *Henry the Fourth Part One, Julius Caesar, Much Ado about Nothing, Othello, The Winter's Tale,* and *The Tempest* were presented at the court of James I, along with Beaumont & Fletcher's *Philaster, The Maid's Tragedy,* and *A King and No King,* Ben Jonson's *The Alchemist,* and sixteen other plays.

But the most notable form of court presentation of the sixteenth and early seventeenth century was the *masque,* which originated in Italy and became a great favorite first of Henry VIII in England, and then of James I. The masque was a musical dance-drama, performed by a mix of professional actors (who did the singing and speaking) and talented courtiers (who danced). The masque also featured extravagant scenery and staging which served as inspiration for much of the set design of succeeding centuries. Inigo Jones, an Italian-schooled Londoner who was court architect to James I, became England's foremost scene designer on the basis of his magnificent settings for the masques performed for the Stuart court and for the court of Charles I; the elaborate and costly settings which Jones created within the masque form from about 1605 to 1640 were to have a profound impact on English design for several generations.

For all its scenic splendor, the masque was undistinguished as literature. The texts were limited by a simplistic allegorical structure which allowed for only the most superficial treatment even when written by as skilled a dramatist as Ben Jonson, who wrote several. Shakespeare never attempted a masque, and Jonson abandoned the form after a humiliating dispute with Inigo Jones. The theatrical importance of the court masque was always acknowledged to be scenic rather than literary. This curiosity of the late Renaissance, however, was a significant precursor to the truly brilliant Royal Theatre of the late seventeenth Century.

position not only in royal society but also in the affairs of state.

Never in history has a body of theatre been so directly and so deliberately associated with national rule. Whether performances were public or private—and at different times they were both—the voice of the court and the voice of the king ultimately decreed what should happen in the theatre and what should not. "The great test of all your plays," said Molière, "is the judgment of the Court: it is the Court's taste which you must study if you want to find the secret of success."

What was the court? It was an aristocracy, in each country numbering in the thousands, a landed nobility drawn into the social circle of the King and sometimes into the King's very household. Manners and decorum became paramount political tools; splendid appearance, verbal dexterity, intellectual dispassion, social grace, and an abiding sense of whimsy and irony became the most prized of personal gifts in the royal court of the seventeenth century. The King's authority, which was absolute, extended well beyond politics to encompass art, religion, literature, dress, deportment, and morality. The King's every activity became national gossip, the King's every expressed opinion had the effect of a verdict. When, in the theatre, the King applauded, a general ovation surrounded him; when he was silent, the courtiers rolled their eyes heavenward and reached for their fans and snuffboxes with an ostentatious show of despairing condescension.

All the European courts had much in common. France's Louis XIV was, after all, the son-in-law of Spain's Philip IV, and England's Charles II had spent his enforced exile in Paris, learning kingship at the French court while he waited out the time until the Restoration would call him home to rule. The theatres of these European courts, naturally, had much in common as well. They were fundamentally elitist theatres, playing to highly restricted audiences. They were often housed in royal palaces and chateaux—and when they went into public buildings, these were intimate, indoor, candlelit spaces that accommodated mere hundreds, not thousands, of spectators.

The Audiences

The courtly audience was a fraternal one: a wealthy and urbane intelligentsia consisting for the most part of titled and untitled courtiers, members of the emerging professional class of civil servants and lawyers, and a few representatives of the upper crust of the emerging bourgeoisie; needless to say, every audience also included a complement of social pretenders of every variety.

The theatre served as a veritable clubhouse for its audience. Seated in their boxes, gathering in the loges, milling about in the aisles and even perching upon the skirts of the stage, the courtly audience came to the theatre to see one another and to be seen, to make contacts and conduct business, to dally and contrive assignations. It was an audience always at least as interested in itself as in any goings-on on stage; it was an audience dressed to kill, anxious to be noticed, and quite blatantly on the prowl. The diaries of the English government official Samual Pepys give us a delightful description of such an audience: in one account of a visit to the theatre Pepys reported that he saw nothing of the play, so diverted was he by the ladies of the gallery. When the King was present, the audience's attention was particularly susceptible to distraction; hence dramatic authors and actors alike were sorely challenged in the Royal Theatre era to find effective means of capturing and keeping the audiences' attention.

The Dramaturgy

The dramas of the Royal Theatre were governed by critical standards that began to develop during the Renaissance and had since been expanded and refined by classical scholars and aestheticians who professed to take their lead from Aristotle: thus the term *neo-classicism* ("new classicism") is used to describe the accepted dramaturgy of the Royal era. Primary among the critical foundations of dramatic neo-classicism was the avoidance of stage violence and vigorous physical action: the ideal play was one in which the characters spent most of their time simply posing, gesturing, and talking. The brawling, swashbuckling, rough action of the Elizabethans was altogether banished; even Shakespeare was considered somewhat primitive in the late seventeenth century: his plays were "purified" by courtly writers of the day to make them more acceptable to the new sensibilities.

Central to the dramatic standards of the era were the "Rules" of playwriting. These consisted of a set of ideas, purportedly derived from Aristotle, which had been codified into principles to be applied in writing

the room itself as scenery...

STEEP HORSESHOE SEATING surrounding the main space

THE MAIN PORTION of the AUDITORIUM was a COURTLY ARENA...

The "picture frame" theatre of the Royal Theatre era gave physical form to the sense of theatre as a decorative diversion, an elegant and courtly meeting place. The proscenium divided audience and stage, elaborately framing the action of the play for those who wanted to look at it. Painted scenery, often in the form of receding "wings" delineated in strict perspective, was a notable feature of Royal Era staging.

plays. They covered everything from dividing a play into acts and scenes to structuring the plot and applying the proper metrics to the verse. The most famous section of the Rules dealt with the so-called Unities: the unities of place, time, and action (see p. 172), and the unity of tone, which dictated that no tragedy was to contain comic relief, no comedy was to harbor sustained moments of pathos, and a verse pattern could not be altered in the course of a play; tonal "irregularities" were deemed offensive to the sensibility of the Court. So fiercely were the "Rules" propounded that they became virtually mandatory; playwrights

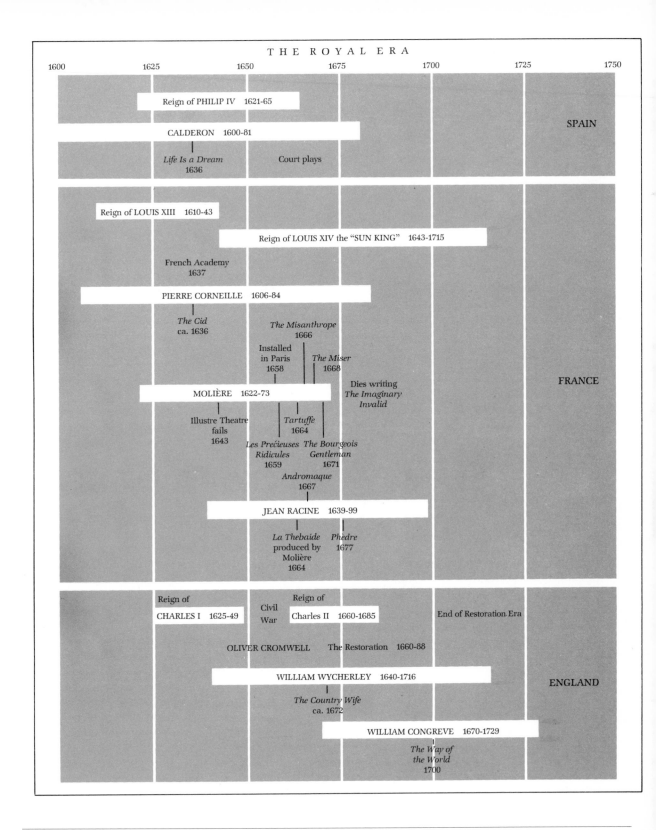

THE ROYAL ERA

1600   1625   1650   1675   1700   1725   1750

Reign of PHILIP IV   1621-65

CALDERON   1600-81

Life Is a Dream   Court plays
1636

SPAIN

Reign of LOUIS XIII   1610-43

Reign of LOUIS XIV the "SUN KING"   1643-1715

French Academy
1637

PIERRE CORNEILLE   1606-84

The Cid   *The Misanthrope*
ca. 1636   1666

Installed   *The Miser*
in Paris   1668
1658

Dies writing
*The Imaginary
Invalid*

MOLIÈRE   1622-73

Illustre Theatre   *Tartuffe*
fails   1664
1643

*Les Précieuses   The Bourgeois
Ridicules   Gentleman*
1659   1671

Andromaque
1667

JEAN RACINE   1639-99

La Thebaide   Phèdre
produced by   1677
Molière
1664

FRANCE

Reign of   Reign of
CHARLES I   1625-49   Civil   Charles II   1660-1685   End of Restoration Era
War

OLIVER CROMWELL   The Restoration   1660-88

WILLIAM WYCHERLEY   1640-1716

The Country Wife
ca. 1672

WILLIAM CONGREVE   1670-1729

*The Way of
the World*
1700

ENGLAND

THE RULES

Nothing is more perplexing about French neo-classic drama than the "Rules" formulated by critics of the time to define the requirements of play construction. For tragedy in particular, the formal structure dictated by the Rules was imposed almost as if by civil law. The observance of certain "Unities" was deemed to be essential. Among other things, a play was required to concern a single action, which must be conceived to take place in a single locale and within a single day's time. As a result of these restrictions, quite sprawling stories were sometimes muscled into strangling time confines: Corneille's great classic *The Cid*, for example, packs two duels, a proposal of marriage, a war, and dozens of crisis points into one day's action.

The Rules also dictated an avoidance of onstage violence, a five-act structure—with the stage clear at the end of each act—and, for poetic dramas, the most elaborate verse form known to the theatre: a fixed quatrain of six-foot iambic lines, each couplet rhyming in an alternating pattern of masculine and feminine (stressed and extended stress) endings, each line having a momentary break (*caesura*) after the sixth syllable. In effect, every play was also a word puzzle.

Not surprisingly, few dramatists succeeded in satisfying all the requirements. It is arguable, however, that when the Rules were addressed by a playwright of the genius of Racine or Molière, they fostered such a compression and focus of creative talent that the result shone incandescently from the friction of tight form and imaginative impulse.

---

who were said to have violated them often spent the bulk of their time thereafter defending themselves, and many finally gave up writing altogether.

The Royal Theatre was one in which its principals consciously wrote for posterity as well as for the moment; as a result, our records of the period are replete with documents: hundreds of plays with prefaces and whole volumes of contemporary criticism, theatre anecdotes, and descriptions of performances. It was in this period that dramatic criticism first truly came into its own and came to exercise a significant influence over its subject. It was said that a critic who had the King's ear could singlehandedly "reform" the stage, and many set out to do just that. Some of the most fascinating works of the times are plays that criticize other plays; their mere existence attests to the potential dramatic impact of criticism and the extent to which the "shop talk" of dramatists could engage contemporary audiences.

Staging Practices

The staging practices of the Royal Theatre derived from practices that had been in use in Italy since the Renaissance. Italian Renaissance theatres were the first to make use of the proscenium and, with that, to establish a clear frontal relationship of audience to actors. The original proscenium was an arch that divided the theatre in half, sharply defining the house and stage areas: this design was adopted by theatres of the Royal era. It made way for a liberal use of painted, illusionistic scenery and, in some cases, the use of hoisting machinery. Later, in the Baroque period, designers would use the proscenium itself to create spectacular effects, but the major plays of the Royal Theatre were staged fairly simply, with the scenery placed well back of the actors. There was little movement on stage—no dueling, of course—and courtiers who wanted to receive special attention from the audience could feel quite safe in purchasing seating on the stage itself.

The most important theatrical development of the Royal Theatre era, however, occurred not in the area of dramatic structure or scenery and staging, but in the expanded admission of women into the acting profession. This development had begun in Italy more than a century before, during the 1540s, and had spread to Spain and France before being decreed by Royal Charter in England in 1660. The widespread introduction of actresses brought a fundamental and irreversible change in the level of abstraction that had characterized Western theatre since its inception more than 2000 years previously. The appearance of real women on the European stage—particularly of women clad in the revealing decolletage of the times —introduced a sensual realism which invigorated even the most turgid productions. No longer were romance, marital infidelity, sexual lust, and sexual jealousy portrayed in the abstract by men and boys "in drag"; the chemistry of heterosexual attraction could be created live, on stage, simultaneously with the play—by the simple expedient of having men play male roles and women play female roles. The impact of this development on theatrical life—both onstage and off—has been overwhelming.

THE FRENCH THEATRE

Royal Court and Tennis Court

Unquestionably the most spendid theatre of the Royal era was the French theatre of the 1660s and 1670s. This was the theatre that brought together the brilliantly humane comedies of Molière, the exquisite verse tragedies of Racine, and the incomparably talented court of King Louis XIV. In turning to this apex of monarchial civilization, we are immediately struck by the dual location of dramatic presentation: at palaces and at playgrounds.

WOMEN ON STAGE IN THE RESTORATION

In the same Royal Charter by which he established the first two theatres in England after his accession to the throne, King Charles II ordered an end to the practice of having women's roles acted by men. In that document, dated August 21, 1660, the King proclaimed:

And for as much as many playes formerly acted doe conteine severall prophane, obscene and scurrilous passages, and the women's part therein have byn acted by men in the habit of women, at which some have taken offence, for the preventing of these abuses for the future, wee doe hereby strictly commande and enjoyne, that from henceforth noe new play shall be acted by either of the said companies conteyning anie passages offensive to pietie or good manners, nor any old or revived play conteyning any such offensive passages as aforesaid, untill the same shall be corrected and purged by the said masters or governors of the said respective companies from all such offensive and scandalous passages as foresaid: And wee doe likewise permit and give leave that all the woemen's part to be acted in either of the said two companies for the time to come may be performed by woemen soe long as their recreacones, which by reason of the abuse aforesaid were scandalous and offensive, may by such reformation be esteemed not onely harmless delight, but useful and instructive representations of humane life, to such of our good subjects as shall resort to the same. . . .

Although with this action England merely went the way of France and Italy, there were those who sought to claim the practice as a British innovation, as these lines from the prologue to one Restoration play* imply:

Did not the Boys Act Women's Parts last Age?
Till we in pitty to the Barren Stage
Came to Reform your Eyes that went astray,
And taught you Passion the true English Way.

*From Elkanah Settle, *The Conquest of China*, 1675

It is not surprising, of course, that the King should choose to make his palaces places of entertainment for his court; that practice had been common in royal circles for centuries. During the reign of Louis XIV the Louvre, Versailles, the Tuileries, the Palais Royale, Fontainbleau, St. Germaine-en-Laye, and the hunting chateau of Chambord were première sites for the plays of Molière and many another *grand siècle* playwright.

But the association of the French public theatre with a once popular tennis game is perhaps more surprising; certainly it is intriguing. We have noted earlier, in Chapter 1, how sports and the theatre have been intertwined since ancient times: how the Romans staged plays in the intervals between gladiatorial contests, the Shakespearean theatre was at times

A jeu de paume court with game in progress.

A jeu de paume court after conversion to theatre. The conversion consisted mainly in the addition of a simple stage at one end of the building and the creation of spaces where actors could enter and leave the stage.

alternated with bear-baiting bouts, and the overall functions and development of theatre and sports display some significant parallels. Now that theme surfaces anew. The Royal Theatre in France, however, was associated with tennis, not bear-baiting, and indeed this association points up some of the fundamental cultural dissimilarities between Elizabethan England and the France of Louis XIV.

The public theatre building in seventeenth-century France was for the most part an adaptation—and a rather modest adaptation at that—of a type of structure that was first built to accommodate a game called *jeu de paume*, a forerunner of modern-day tennis. *Jeu de paume*, or "palm game," was originally a simple handball sport which, with the addition of racquets much like contemporary ones, became the favorite game of the French King Henry IV (r. 1589–1610): it is estimated that by the end of the sixteenth century there were a thousand or more *jeu de paume* courts in

Paris alone, with many more in the countryside.

The *jeu de paume* (the name refers to the building as well as the sport) was a rectangular structure with spectator galleries on the two long sides and an open or windowed area running around the building below the roof. Because they were free of partitions and provided for both daylight (the windows) and the seating of spectators (the galleries), the *jeux de paume* lent themselves well to theatrical conversion—particularly to the frontal, proscenium type theatre which became the order of the day. It was only natural, as the tennis game waned in popularity and the theatre grew, that this conversion would take place. Even the theatres that were not converted tennis courts—and the most famous one, the Hotel de Bourgogne, was not—were designed almost as if in imitation of them, for the rectangular, galleried shape became the dominant form of theatre architecture for the entire period.

A conjectural reconstruction of the Hotel de Bourgogne, a leading Parisian public theatre from 1548 until 1783. The Hotel de Bourgogne was originally a fairly rudimentary theatre and did not have a proscenium until its renovation in 1647.

The public theatre that developed from this *jeu de paume* configuration also bore a certain resemblance to the public theatre of Shakespeare's London in that it featured a large standing-room area (the *parterre*, or pit) and surrounding, costlier *loges*, or galleries. Builders' records for many of these theatres remain, most significantly for the Théâtre du Marais, reconstructed in 1644 on the site of its predecessor of the same name which had burned to the ground after a fire started during a performance. The reconstructed Marais was indeed like a tennis court, with the standard 3:1 length-to-width ratio that characterizes such structures: the theatre building was approximately 105 feet by 35. Two rows of galleries rose on each long side, and each row was divided into nine loges, or thirty-six in all; each loge held several people in its 4 × 6–foot configuration. At the rear of the building were four more boxes, bringing the total to forty, and behind these was an amphitheatre, steeply raked backwards to afford seating on long benches. More benches above the side loges provided further seating. In the midst of all this, at ground level, was the parterre and, opposite the amphitheatre, the stage.

The Marais stage was not an elaborate affair: it was small, and with provision for audience seating on its sides it became even smaller. Essentially, it was a raked platform about 39 feet across and 32 feet deep, raised to about head level of the patrons standing in the parterre. The Marais also featured a balconied pavilion akin to that of the Elizabethan model, which extended the full width of the stage: it was 13 feet high and 6 feet deep, with a protective rail at its front and well holes at the back; it could easily have been used for balcony scenes, as well as for stage machinery and special effects. Behind this multiple-level stage were ten dressing rooms, five on the lower stage level and five on the upper. Oddly enough, we can only presume that a proscenium existed at the Marais. We know that prosceniums already existed at other Parisian theatres of the time—at the Palais Cardinal and the Petit Bourbon, for example—but the records of the Marais do not specify an arch.

The Public Theatre Audience

It was a varied audience which attended the Parisian public theatres of the seventeenth century, a mixture of old nobility and newer bourgeoisie. The Parisian audience has never been shy or aloof, but this audience was particularly notable for its audacious appearance and its vociferous voicing of opinion. The seventeenth-century parterre was a veritable bazaar of ideas, fashions, philosophies, and political intrigues. Many of the spectators were already on hand when the theatre doors opened at one o'clock, a full two hours before the performance was to begin. They crowded inside and filled the intervening time with activity: political and romantic assignations; brawls at the door as flippant cavaliers tried to enter without paying and ran up against stalwart doorkeepers; and the continual hawking and peddling of "refreshing drinkables: lemonades, lemon sherbert, strawberry, currant, and cherry waters, dried confitures, lemons, Chinese oranges, and, in winter, drinks which warm the stomach, such as rose liquors and Spanish wines." Unlike the pit of the Elizabethan theatre, which was sought out mainly by reason of its low price, the Parisian parterre was regarded as a splendid place to be noticed, second only to the more costly stage seating as a place to display one's fine dress and deportment. Gossip, gawking, and gallivanting—not to mention the possibility of actually rubbing elbows with the King—were fully as much motivation for this Parisian theatrical crowd as the prospect of seeing a play.

MOLIÈRE

No one, certainly, better typifies the Royal Theatre age than Molière.

Born Jean Baptiste Poquelin (it is hazarded that he changed his name to protect his family from being dunned for his early debts), Molière was to become the most produced French playwright of all time. He personifies the wit, the charm, the ebullience, and above all the genius of his era; he was, as well, one of its most fascinating and complex individuals. An actor, producer, critic, and comic playwright, he was what the French call *un homme du théâtre*, a complete "man of the theatre," whose gifts and achievements radiated into every aspect of theatrical culture. He is today the best loved foreign-language playwright on the English-speaking stage. In France he is a national hero comparable to Shakespeare in England, and his theatre company still remains the core and the source of France's great national theatre, the *Comédie Française*, which has now performed continuously for more than three hundred years following its creation seven years after his death.

You are most amusing with your rules of Art, with which you embarrass the ignorant, and deafen us perpetually. To hear you talk, one would suppose that those rules of Art were the greatest mysteries in the world; and yet they are but a few simple observations which good sense has made, the same good sense which in former days made observations every day without resorting to Horace and Aristotle. I should like to know whether the great rule of all rules is not to please, and whether a play which attains this has not followed a good method? Can the public be mistaken in these matters, and cannot every one judge what pleases him? Let us laugh at the sophistry with which the critics would trammel public taste, and let us judge a play only by the effect which it produces upon ourselves. Let us give ourselves up honestly to whatever stirs us deeply, and never hunt for arguments to mar our pleasure.

Molière

Molière is known primarily as an author of comic plays: his *Tartuffe, The Misanthrope, The Miser,* and *The Doctor in Spite of Himself,* for example, have found such favor with audiences around the world that they are now essential pieces of repertoire in many companies. He was also, however, a theatrical manager of singular capability: he was not only the leader of his own celebrated troupe but also the producer of dozens of plays by other writers, including Pierre Corneille, with whom he once collaborated, and France's premiere tragedian, Jean Racine, whom Molière actually discovered and first produced. In addition, he was a fine actor who played the leading roles in most of his productions—to the great delight of his audiences and patrons. And he was a critic— for although he often railed against excessive critical strictures, his works themselves embody some of the most incisive dramatic criticism of his time.

Nor was France the only country on which Molière's genius had impact in his own time: English Restoration drama owes an incalculable debt to Molière. William Wycherley's *The Plain Dealer,* one of the outstanding Restoration comedies, is in part an adaptation of Molière's *The Misanthrope,* and the general influence of Molière's style and structure can be felt throughout the English comedy of the era.

Molière's theatrical career spanned the gamut from abject failure to dizzying success. He was born in Paris, the son of the Royal Upholsterer to King Louis XIII; thanks to his father's position, he gained an early exposure to the court. After receiving a superior classical education at the College of Clermont and a degree in Law at Orléans, Molière renounced both his academic training and his father's business in order to enter the theatre, shortly before his twenty-first birthday, in 1643.

His first enterprise—the Illustre Théâtre in Paris —failed within two years, and he was imprisoned for the theatre's debts. Following his release, Molière and his troupe headed south, where for the next twelve years they entertained public and gentry alike in the street theatres and private homes of the French provinces. During this time Molière became the principal director of his troupe and, for the first time, an author of comedies in the troupe's repertoire; when finally the company was invited to Paris to play before the King—now Louis XIV—it was one of Molière's own plays, an afterpiece to the main work of the evening, that secured the royal favor and led to Molière's installation, at the King's direction, at the Théâtre du Petit Bourbon in the French capital. An odd arrangement faced Molière at that theatre—at first his company could perform only on the "off" days; a popular *commedia dell'arte* troupe had all the most prestigious afternoons already booked. But as Molière's brilliant plays began drawing ever greater attention, his company moved to the "on" days—and soon to the more elegant Palais Royale, where they received from Louis the official name of "King's Comedians." Thus, Molière's return to Paris had become a triumph, and for the rest of his life he was one of the most celebrated and controversial figures in the French court and in Parisian literary life.

It was a glittering life. At the theatre, Molière continued to share a bohemian and rather notorious existence with his intimate company family. In the days of his Illustre Théâtre he had acquired as his mistress the actress Madeleine Bejart, with whom he had lived throughout the twelve years of provincial touring. He now married Madeleine's sister Armande —or, as many believed at the time, Madeleine's daughter and possibly even Molière's own daughter. What is more, both Bejarts continued to perform with his company through several years of communal living sparked with allegations of gross (and painful) infidelities which provided endless fodder for the popular press. In the literary world, Molière was active in a circle of writers who gathered regularly at the Mouton Blanc, a Parisian cafe; included in that group were the tragedian Jean Racine, the critic Nicolas Boileau, and the fabulist Jean de La Fontaine.

But perhaps the most remarkable aspect of Molière's life was his relationship with the Sun King himself, the *Grand Roi* of that *grand siècle*. Louis XIV provided Molière with his theatre and his title. He granted Molière an annual pension and was godfather to his first child. In finally permitting the public presentation of Molière's controversial *Tartuffe*, King Louis overrode the violent objections not only of the Archbishop of Paris and the established deaconry of France, but also of his own mother, Queen Anne of Austria. Louis further commissioned plays from Molière annually, and bade Molière to premiere virtually all his other plays at court before their public debuts; he even *performed* in two Molière comedies at their court presentations. Finally, toward the close of his life and with Molière long dead, King Louis paid final tribute to his erstwhile protégé by staging private productions of several of Molière's comedies for his own personal enjoyment.

The Court was not the sole audience to Molière's theatre, of course, nor was it his sole source of inspiration. The influence of the boisterous *commedia* is as evident in his plays as is the neo-classic style which he fashioned after Terence (whose works Molière knew by heart in the original Latin). Indeed, the fact that Molière's theatre still gloriously survives two hundred years after the French monarchy was toppled by revolution, indicates how well his vision transcended courtly preciosity. Molière bespoke the best impulses of his age. His works glorify sensibility, rational temperament, personal freedom, and common justice. They deplore pompousness, greed, artifice, and humbuggery. In so artfully exposing the foibles of his own time, Molière hit at man's timeless ingenuity at contriving disguises for ambition, exploitation, and lust. A complex man himself—and his life seems to have been riddled with conflict and despair, even in his most successful years—he well understood the difficulty of arriving at sensible, simple solutions to many

There is in Molière's writing a colloquial, rough quality and there is also an elegance: on the one side humor, which shows the characters as unintentionally funny; on the other side wit, by means of which the characters are deliberately funny. . . . The sources of the dualism are not difficult to determine. The colloquial elements, especially the naturalness of his language, whether in prose or verse, were shaped by his experience as a traveling performer and fortified by his knack for clothing dramatic ideas in what look suspiciously like everyday sentences. The elegance comes partly from the strained, even stilted, literary mannerisms of his time, partly from the nature of the Court audiences to whom he played in the later years of his career, partly from his striving for a new and elevated style in the writing of comedy.

Albert Bermel

of life's problems. His comedies repeatedly explore irreconcilable human conflicts: common sense versus implacable desire, hard reality versus galloping irrationality, personal integrity versus political and social ambition. Certainly an element of self-therapy is suggested in Molière's best work—particularly when we consider that his plays were written to be performed by him, his often estranged wife, his best friends, and his past and present mistresses. Indeed, it seems likely that Molière drew heavily upon his own predicaments to help his audiences laugh at the human comedy. At all events, it is certain that he knew whereof he wrote. For that reason, his plays constitute a "humane comedy" of universal applicability.

The Bourgeois Gentleman

The Bourgeois Gentleman is characteristic of most of Molière's work in two respects: it is a social satire, and it pleased court and public alike with its rare combination of wit, romance, sharp-edged social commentary, and farcical hijinks. A comedy-ballet in five acts (the ballet, with music by Jean Baptiste Lully, separates the acts and also works into the main action), it is structured as a typical royal *divertissement*: a frothy entertainment of simple format designed solely for the diversion of the court, to be savored with relish and quickly forgotten. Owing to Molière's comic genius, however, this play escaped the fate of most of its kind and became one of the best loved and most admired comedies of all time. Commissioned by Louis XIV for a 1670 premiere at the Royal Chateau of Chambord (a palatial hunting lodge in the Valley of the Sologne, about one hundred miles south of Paris), *The Bourgeois Gentleman* achieved great initial acclaim, and after several repeat performances it was brought north to Paris, first to play at the suburban Palace of Saint-Germain-en-Laye, then in the public theatre of the Palais Royale; ever since that time it has continued to attract public favor. It is today a staple of the Comédie Française, and it is regularly translated, produced, and enjoyed around the world.

The Bourgeois Gentleman is a comedy of character, and it deals with a phenomenon as familiar in our day as it was in the seventeenth century: social climbing. Its central character, one Monsieur Jourdain, is a merchant of the bourgeois (middle) class who aspires to gentility and the status of nobility; his attempts to improve his standing are at first amusing, finally ridiculous and hilarious as he sacrifices family obligations, common sense, and his own welfare in pursuit of his goal. It is not merely ambition that Molière satirizes here, but foolish perceptions: what Jourdain takes for "gentle" elegance is mere foppery, what he takes for "gentle" admiration is mere flattery. Molière himself was no stranger to ambition—he the upholsterer's son turned court favorite—and he knew well the tortuous path of social ascent. As both author of the play and original performer of the role of Monsieur Jourdain, Molière had his subject well in hand.

Our imaginary reconstruction of the Palais Royale production of *The Bourgeois Gentleman* is based on incomplete evidence, but from the time of Molière onward we do begin to have a fair body of written and pictorial documentation of theatrical production.

The theatre of the Palais Royale, which was Molière's public home for most of his career, was the most elegant theatre in Paris at that time. It had originally been built in 1641 for Cardinal Richelieu in the Cardinal's own palace (the Palais Cardinal) directly across from the Louvre. The Palais Cardinal was renamed the Palais Royale after Richelieu's death. The theatre was a tennis-court sized structure that measured about 108 × 36 feet and was equipped with a handsome proscenium arch. It was a lavish work of theatre architecture that showed strong signs of Italian influence. Although its galleries were set up in the fashion of the *jeu de paume*, it differed from other Parisian theatres in that it originally contained a curious "amphitheatre" arrangement of stone steps which rose in the parterre across from the stage and supported twenty-seven rows of wooden bleachers. This arrangement ultimately proved unsuccessful. The bleachers were uncomfortable and somewhat treacherous—Queen Anne of Austria, the stern mother of Louis XIV, is said to have toppled backward on one of the rows while watching a play, exposing her undergarments for several hilarious minutes as she tried to right herself—and someone, probably Molière, had the seats removed, returning the parterre to its more familiar function

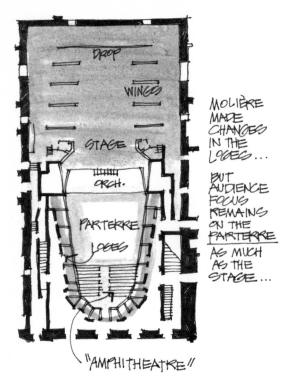

MOLIÈRE
MADE
CHANGES
IN THE
LOGES ...

BUT
AUDIENCE
FOCUS
REMAINS
ON THE
PARTERRE
AS MUCH
AS THE
STAGE ...

The Palais Royale, as remodeled by Molière.
Molière removed the stone benches of the amphi-
theatre, leaving in their place a few rows of seats
and a traditional parterre; *he also divided the gal-*
leries into separate loges, *or boxes.*

as a standing and ambling space. Situated conveniently close to court, splendidly equipped with machinery, ornate in its interior design and fittings, the Palais Royale theatre held many attractions for distinguished audiences. And beyond question it presented magnificent plays, performed by one of the greatest acting troupes ever.

The Bourgeois Gentleman is set in the home of Monsieur Jourdain; in Molière's day the interior setting was created by two angle wings, representing interior sidewalls, and by a shuttered backdrop called a *ferme.* The angle wings were quite realistically painted, and in perspective; seemingly three-dimensional bays were skillfully painted onto the flat surface, and the realistic appearance was heightened by the addition of actual moldings and sconces. A ceiling cloth enhanced the general illusion. Yet there was no effort at realism in the con-

temporary sense at all. For example, no actual doorways were provided: the angle wings did not connect with the painted *ferme* at the rear, and performers simply made their entrances and exits in the space between these two elements or else downstage of the entire setting.

How was Monsieur Jourdain's house decorated? We have a rare glimpse of it in a frontispiece to the published edition: this shows, in addition to tapestries, a set of wall sconces that take the excruciating form of a cherub's severed arm, mounted somewhat like stags' heads on the angle wings. It is an element of decor meant to represent Jourdain's lack of taste, one of the first known examples of background scenery used for a specific satiric effect.

The Bourgeois Gentleman opens with a musical overture, played by a "great assemblage of instruments" located in front of the stage. This overture, composed by Jean Baptiste Lully—the "other Jean Baptiste" who was later to become Molière's rival for the King's attentions—foretokens the *divertissement* format which this play follows: a theatrical combination of scenes, songs, and dances. This is the precursor of the musical comedy mode of modern times.

As the overture proceeds, the candles of the onstage candelabra are lit and slowly hoisted to positions above and to the sides of the action. The costs of tallow were not insignificant, and producers always waited until the last moment to light the stage, letting the afternoon sunshine from the upper windows provide illumination insofar as possible.

A chair and table are seen at the middle of the stage; on the chair sits a "music student," at work composing a song which will figure into the ensuing dialogue. It would be a simple matter for the furniture to be pre-set and the actor likewise, but it is also possible that chair, table, and "music student" rose mechanically through the floor; machinery for that very purpose existed in the Palais Royale at the time, and the effect would have bridged overture and story in a fine bit of musical stagecraft.

The overture ends. From rear wings on either side come two groups—a music master and his musicians, and a dancing master and his dancers. After the music master checks his "student's"

SECTION TWO: THE PAST

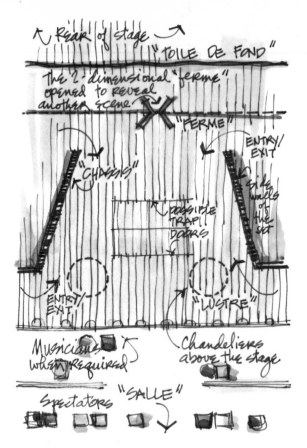

A plan of the set of The Bourgeois Gentleman, *as it may have been realized on the Palais Royale stage. Note that the angle wings do not touch the* ferme, *and that actors' entrances are made through the open spaces between scenery pieces. The* toile de fond, *or backdrop, is seen only in the last act of the play, when the* ferme *parts to reveal it.*

composition, the two masters are left on stage to discuss the absent hero:

MUSIC MASTER: (*grinning broadly*) We have found here just the man we need: our "ticket to ride," this (*sniffs loudly*) Monsieur Jourdain—with his visions of gallantry and *noblesse oblige* flitting about his head (*chortles pompously*). A true "pay-trone of the ahts," this "Mon-sewer"—I only wish there were more where he came from!

DANCING MASTER: (*mincing, with a flourish of his*

walking stick) Well, I suppose, but I certainly wish he knew something about the arts he patronizes!

MUSIC MASTER: He knows nothing, doesn't he? (*they both laugh*) But he pays through the nose, and that's what counts: that's what the arts need these days, my dancing friend, money!

DANCING MASTER: But to PLAY for these fools! (*he crosses down toward the audience, studying them while talking to the Music Master*) For me, I confess I hunger more for the applause of those who can tell good work from bad, who can sense the refinements and delicacies of art, who know beauty when they see it (*he poses prettily, clasping his hands upon his stick*)—and who can reward an artist with the honor of their favor and praise (*he smiles*).

MUSIC MASTER: (*following him: enthusiastically*) Of course, of course; nothing is better than that—but we also must live! Praise must be mixed with something solid if we are to pay our rent: tell your people of refinement to put their money where their mouth is! (*they face each other*) This Jourdain, it's true, is somewhat unenlightened (*the Dancing Master snorts agreement*)—he speaks backwards and forwards at the same time (*the Dancing Master chuckles approvingly*)—and he applauds only when he's not supposed to (*the Dancing Master breaks out in a burst of laughter*)—but his money makes up for everything: he has great wisdom in his purse, and his praise comes in the coinage of the realm. (*the Music Master ambles away, jingling his purse full of coins*)

DANCING MASTER: (*scowling*) Well, you're right, as usual, but I don't like it; you're just too money-minded, my friend.

MUSIC MASTER: And you? You take what he gives out, just as I do!

DANCING MASTER: (*self-righteously*) Yes, but it hurts me to do so! (*the Music Master clutches his heart in mock pain*) I only can wish for a more tasteful benefactor!

MUSIC MASTER: (*realistically*) Well, of course, so would we all—but that's life, my friend. In any event, Monsieur Jourdain is giving us the chance to make names for ourselves at Court —and if you will take my advice, you'll let him pay us what the Court won't, and let the Court praise us as this imbecile can't!

DANCING MASTER: (*quickly*) Shhhhh! Here he comes.

Like Hephaestus and Might in the opening scene of *Prometheus*, these masters argue in order to give us a foretaste of the central character and his basic predicament; here, however, the set-up of the hero is clearly comic and devoid of awe. Molière, of course, must tread a fine line in his satire in this scene, for he cannot afford to alienate true patrons of the arts: his own fortunes rest on the sustained approval of often less than tasteful followers.

Monsieur Jourdain's "prepared" entrance follows Molière's own direction, as explained by him in his "rehearsal play," *The Versailles Rehearsal*, as that of the "ridiculous marquis" always "guaranteed to get laughs":

MOLIÈRE: Now remember to come in as I've instructed you, with that put-on pomposity that is called grandness, combing your wig, and humming a little tune between your teeth, like this: la la la la la la la.

Jourdain is a sight to behold. He is followed by two lackeys, and at his entrance the singers and dancers, who had earlier retired from the scene, again emerge from the wings. He is a model of outrageous foppery:

M. JOURDAIN: (*crossing to the two masters and nodding grandly*) Well, gentlemen? And what do we have here? You have made for me, I presume, some little drollery for the afternoon?

DANCING MASTER: (*confused*) Drollery?

M. JOURDAIN: (*delighted*) Ah, yes! (*then, fearful he has said something wrong*) Ah, no! (*desperate*) But how do you call it? (*to each of them, in turn*) Your prologue? Your, um, dialogue? Your singing and dancing?

DANCING MASTER: (*relieved*) Ah, yes!

MUSIC MASTER: (*overly hearty*) At your service!

M. JOURDAIN: (*thrilled*) I know I've made you wait a bit, but it is only because I have decided today to dress in the fashion of quality folk, and my tailor has sent me (*he raises the hem of his gown*) these stockings—(*confidentially*) silk, of course—which (*angrily, to his lackeys*) take forever to get on! (*he hastily lowers his gown*)

MUSIC MASTER: (*embarrassed*) We are here to attend your convenience.

M. JOURDAIN: (*hastily*) Well, then, you mustn't go —they are bringing my new suit, and you must see me in it!

DANCING MASTER: (*obsequiously*) Whatever pleases you.

M. JOURDAIN: (*proudly*) Then you will see me in the height of fashion—from toe to head!

MUSIC MASTER: (*trying not to laugh*) We don't doubt it.

M. JOURDAIN: (*turning about*) My dressing gown *à la indienne*; do you like it?

DANCING MASTER: (*smiling, through gritted teeth*) *Très, très chic!*

M. JOURDAIN: (*gesturing grandly with the folds of the garment*) My tailor tells me it's the morning fashion of quality folk!

MUSIC MASTER: (*with an ironic wink to the Dancing Master*) Suits you perfectly!

M. JOURDAIN: (*suddenly and imperiously*) Lackeys! I say, LACKEYS!

THE LACKEYS: (*springing forward in terror*) Yes, Monsieur?

M. JOURDAIN: (*turning to look at them*) Oh, nothing, nothing. (*as though it were obvious*) Just checking! (*The lackeys return to their position, puzzled. Jourdain admires them and turns, beaming, to the masters.*) How do you like their liveries?

DANCING MASTER: Magnificent.

M. JOURDAIN: (*as one bestowing a precious gift, opens his gown, revealing red velvet tights and a hideous green velvet jacket*) My little underdress outfit for the morning exercises!

MUSIC MASTER: (*grinning through his revulsion*) Oh, *très gallant, très gallant* indeed.

This scene is classic comic fun in the spirit of a theatrical tradition that goes back as far as Aristophanes: funny clothes, funny manners, and funny speeches. With that combination, common social pretensions can be taken to outlandish extremes. Here, the foppery and foibles of Jourdain are wonderfully satirized by his absurd dress and behavior and the slickly comic repartee.

The first two acts of *The Bourgeois Gentleman* provide a series of variations on this opening scene. Successively, a fencing master, a philosophy master, and finally a tailor visit Jourdain, each offering advice and instruction on the art of being a gentleman.

The scene with the fencing master is pure physical farce which owes its effect to a great deal of inventive stage business interspersed with brisk commands:

FENCING MASTER: (*giving Jourdain a sword*) Come, sir, your bow! (*Jourdain bows deeply and stiffens; his back has gone out*) Up! (*Fencing Master playfully points his sword at Jourdain's belly: Jourdain quickly straightens up*) Body erect! More to your left! Not so far apart, those legs! Square your feet! Your wrist opposite your hip! (*Jourdain grows confused as the Fencing Master barks his orders faster and faster*) The tip of your sword across from your shoulder. Relax your arm! Your left hand at eye level! Your left shoulder—square it! Head up! (*Jourdain is now twisted like a pretzel*) Look fierce! (*Jourdain makes a ludicrous attempt to look warlike*) Advance! (*Jourdain advances and stumbles.*) Body firm! (*Jourdain sighs; Fencing master slashes at Jourdain's sword; Jourdain*

Monsieur Jourdain's fencing lesson. The inelegant buffoonery is greatly enjoyed by the gallants in the parterre, *as well as by one patron (at left) seated on the stage. The tallow candles used as footlights supplement light from unseen chandeliers above.*

screams as his sword vibrates out of control) *Touché!* One, two, retreat! (*Jourdain retreats, still trying to gain control of his vibrating sword*) Again: stand firm! (*Jourdain tries to resume his warlike mien*) Jump back! (*Jourdain does so*) The sword forward and the body back. One! Two! (*Fencing Master hits Jourdain's sword again, Jourdain yelps*) *Touché!* Keep coming! Advance! (*Jourdain begins to whimper*) Body firm! Advance! (*Jourdain is crying*) From there! One! Two! Retreat! (*Jourdain starts to run away; Fencing Master "spanks" him with his sword*) Again! Jump back! *En garde*, sir, *en garde!*

M. JOURDAIN (*in a paroxysm of terror, contorted, but still trying to look his best*) Owwwwww!

MUSIC MASTER: (*grinning*) You're doing fine!

FENCING MASTER: (*didactically, illustrating each point with a flourish of his foil*) It is as I said before, the whole secret of fencing lies simply in hitting (*swats Jourdain*) and not being hit. Do you understand? It is more blessed to give blows (*swats again*) than to receive them—did I not explain that sufficiently the other day? All you need concentrate on is that little outward movement of the wrist—(*stops for a moment, afraid of having contradicted himself*) or is it a little inward movement . . .

M. JOURDAIN: (*overjoyed*) You mean if I could learn that, I could be certain of killing my opponent—without myself being killed?

FENCING MASTER: (*fiercely*) Of course! Isn't that what I just showed you?

M. JOURDAIN: (*trying to put the best face on it*) Oh! Yes, of course.

The fencing scene is a classic rendition of the comic tradition of poking fun at physical braggadocio; this tradition can be traced through a long line of comic swordsmen in theatrical history, including Aristophanes' Lamachos, Plautus' Miles Gloriosus, and Shakespeare's Falstaff. The satire of the braggart soldier derives from a fundamental human fear—the fear of armed physical assault—and gains in hilarity precisely as it touches unconscious terrors.

The next scene portrays yet another familiar predicament—intellectual intimidation—and another character—the pedant—that has theatrical antecedents dating back to the time when Aristophanes caricatured Socrates on the Athenian stage.

MASTER OF PHILOSOPHY: (*with grave sonority*) There are five vowels, A, E, I, O, and U!

M. JOURDAIN: (*nodding sagely*) Yes, I know.

MASTER OF PHILOSOPHY: (*studiously*) The sound "A" is formed by opening the mouth wide. (*he does so, saying*) "A."

M. JOURDAIN: (*imitating*) "A" . . . "A" (*smiling*) Yes!

MASTER OF PHILOSOPHY: The sound "E" is made by closing the jaws. (*opening his mouth*) "A" (*closing it*) "E."

M. JOURDAIN: (*opens and closes his mouth, mechanically*) "A"–"E" "A"–"E." (*beams*) My god! You're right! How wonderful learning is!

MASTER OF PHILOSOPHY: (*grimly*) And to make an "I" you close your jaws even further, and spread your cheeks to your ears: "A"–"E"–"I."

M. JOURDAIN: (*with exaggerated movement*) "A"–"E"–"I." "I." (*spreads his cheeks as wide as he can with his fingers*) "I!" "I!" It's true! Magnificent! Long live science!

MASTER OF PHILOSOPHY: (*stalwartly*) Now, to make an "O" you must open your jaw and bring together the corners of your lips: "O."

M. JOURDAIN: (*does as told*) "O." "O." Nothing could be more wonderful than this! (*moving his face in absurdly exaggerated configurations*) "A"–"E"–"I"–"O." "I"–"O"! Splendid! "I"–"O"! "I–O"!

MASTER OF PHILOSOPHY: (*as to a four-year-old, making a circle with his finger*) The shape of your mouth, you see, is a little round "o."

M. JOURDAIN: (*astounded, making the same circle with his finger and then tracing his lips in an "o"*) "O"–"O"–"O"—you're soooooooo right. Oooooooooo. Ah, what a beautiful thing to knoooooooow something (*beams at his own cleverness*).

MASTER OF PHILOSOPHY: (*relentlessly continuing*) The sound "U" is made by bringing the teeth together, by spreading the lips, and then making them come together without quite touching: "U."

M. JOURDAIN: "U." "U"—nothing could be truer: "U"!

MASTER OF PHILOSOPHY: (*suddenly making a grotesque face at Jourdain, who recoils in shocked surprise*) It's like making a face at someone: if you want to make fun of somebody, just say "U" at them.

M. JOURDAIN: "U"–"U"! Oh, its truuuuuuuue! Oh, why didn't I take up education earlier, I would have known all this!

Jourdain then asks the Master of Philosophy for a great favor:

M. JOURDAIN: (*crossing to him and looking about before he speaks*) Now I must be very confidential with you. I am in love with a grand lady of quality, and I want you to help me write a little love note (*he giggles*) that I can drop at her feet (*giggles again*).

MASTER OF PHILOSOPHY: (*trying to hide his disdain*) Very well.

M. JOURDAIN: (*with a comradely wink*) Something *très gallant*, yes?

MASTER OF PHILOSOPHY: (*grimacing*) Of course. Some verses?

M. JOURDAIN: (*horrified*) No, no. No verses.

MASTER OF PHILOSOPHY: (*relieved*) Ahah! Entirely in prose, then.

M. JOURDAIN: (*equally horrified*) No, no, no—no prose either.

MASTER OF PHILOSOPHY: (*beginning to weary, despite himself*) Well, it must be one or the other.

M. JOURDAIN: (*suddenly confused*) Why?

MASTER OF PHILOSOPHY: (*as if to a child*) Because, Monsieur, there are only the two: prose—and verse.

M. JOURDAIN: (*bewildered*) There is only prose—and verse?

MASTER OF PHILOSOPHY: Only. Whatever is not prose—is verse; and whatever is not verse—is prose.

M. JOURDAIN: (*beginning to understand*) And talking, what is that?

MASTER OF PHILOSOPHY: (*with great patience*) That is prose.

M. JOURDAIN: (*on the verge of a great discovery, his eyes widening all the time*) It is? When I say, "Nicole, bring me my slippers and my nightcap," that's—(*almost unwilling to believe it*) prose?!

MASTER OF PHILOSOPHY: (*as in benediction*) That's prose.

M. JOURDAIN: My God! (*starts dancing about*) For forty years I've been speaking PROSE without knowing it! Oh, thank you, THANK YOU, thank you, thank you.

Finally, the scene with the tailor completes Jourdain's lessons in social deportment, bringing the world of costume fashion into the theatre in both hilarious and provocative ways. The tailor arrives with garments and assistants, and in short order the scene becomes a comic ballet of movement and language:

MASTER TAILOR: (*entering, trailed by assistants, and carrying an elaborate gown*) Here—this is the most beautiful new suit ever fashioned for the Court, serious but colorful, a masterpiece no one in Paris could even touch. (*With a flourish, he and his assistants hold the gown up for general examination. Jourdain gasps.*)

M. JOURDAIN: (*unbelieving*) But—my good man—the flowers are upside down!

MASTER TAILOR: (*stunned, looks at his mistake, but immediately recovers and takes the offensive*) Well—you never told me you wanted them rightside up!

M. JOURDAIN: (*dismayed*) You mean I'm supposed to tell you?

MASTER TAILOR: (*vastly relieved, he boldly continues*) Of course! Persons of quality like them like this!

M. JOURDAIN: (*utterly perplexed*) Persons of quality like their flowers upside down?

MASTER TAILOR: Yes, of course.

M. JOURDAIN: (*making the best of it*) Oh. Well, it's all right then.

MASTER TAILOR: (*pressing advantage*) If you wish, I'll redo them.

The tailor presents gown to startled Monsieur Jourdain (Charles Hallahan) in the 1976 production of The Bourgeois Gentleman, *produced by the American Conservatory Theatre. Notice upside-down flowers and profusion of contrasting fabrics and patterns in gown.*

M. JOURDAIN: (*frightened*) Oh, no, no.

MASTER TAILOR: (*wickedly*) Just say the word—

M. JOURDAIN: (*urgently*) No, no, I tell you, they're PER-FECT . . . Here, give it to me, I'll put it on.

MASTER TAILOR: Wait, wait. That's just not DONE, Monsieur. I've brought my people to dress you properly—(*his eyes lofting heavenward*) in RHYTHM! (*reverentially*) Clothing like this must be put on with ceremony—BOYS!

(*the orchestra strikes up a minuet: four tailoring assistants dance forward and Jourdain whirls around*)

Dress Monsieur as a Man of Quality!

A ballet ensues, with the assistants undressing Jourdain and redressing him in his new suit, to the light strains of Lully's orchestral rendition. Jourdain parades around in his new garments as the dancers pretend to admire him.

MASTER TAILOR: (*as the dance concludes, to Jourdain,*

gracefully) My dear gentleman, you may now give my boys their gratuity. •

M. JOURDAIN: What did you call me?

MASTER TAILOR: (*a little frightened*) My dear gentleman?

M. JOURDAIN: (*overjoyed*) Gentleman! That's what happens when you dress in quality, they call you gentleman! No one calls you that if you dress like a petty bourgeois! Here (*giving money to the tailor*) this is from your "dear gentleman"!

MASTER TAILOR: (*pleased with himself*) My lord, we are all obliged to you.

M. JOURDAIN: (*stunned*) My lord! Oh! Oh! My lord! Wait, HEY! wait, my friend, "My Lord" means something more. "My Lord," why that's not just a little thing: here, here's what "My Lord" will give you. (*he gives more money to the tailor*)

MASTER TAILOR: Well, well, we drink the health of Your Excellency, don't we, boys?

M. JOURDAIN: Your Excellency! Oh, oh oh! Wait, wait! Me, Your Excellency! (*turns away from them, to the audience*) My god, if he goes up to "your Highness," my purse is his. (*turns back to the tailor*) Here, here's from "Your Excellency." (*gives yet more money*)

MASTER TAILOR: (*who now would rather leave than milk Jourdain further*) My lord, we thank you humbly. (*he bows and turns away*)

M. JOURDAIN: (*turning again to the audience, confidentially*) Thank God. I was just about to give him all I had!

With this, the second act ends. Another ballet follows, danced by the tailor's assistants, and costumed attendants come onto the stage and into the auditorium, trimming the wicks of the candles which by now have begun to sputter and smoke.

The first two acts are virtually plotless: a series of "lessons" around a theme, their frivolous tomfoolery contrived of verbal wit, visual gags, costume and prop humor, traditional and novel whimsicality. Jourdain, the focal point for all this comedic revelry, is seen to be foolish but not malicious; as will be true in the rest of the play as well, he is continually delighted throughout his dupedom, and his gaiety is as infectious as his taste is deplorable:

his last line in Act II ("Thank God. I was just about to give him all I had!") even suggests that he may not be wholly without perspective, and that he may indeed share a certain amusement at his comic condition.

Act III introduces a whole new set of characters around Jourdain: his wife, his intended mistress (Dorimène, the intended recipient of the love note he discusses with the philosophy master), her lover (Dorante), Jourdain's daughter (Lucile), her suitor (Cléonte), Jourdain's valet (Covielle), and a housemaid to the Jourdains (Nicole). The masters and tailors of the first two acts will not return to the play—their function, to establish the character of the *bourgeois* who would be a *gentilhomme*, is completed. The intrigue of Act III is traditional: Jourdain seeks to woo Dorimène, to marry Lucile to a marquis, and to deceive his wife; he is instead duped by Dorante and evaded by Lucile, and the tough and commonsensical Madame Jourdain sees through him completely, as does the saucy Nicole:

M. JOURDAIN: (*summoning the maid imperiously*) Nicole!

NICOLE: (*rushes in and, seeing Jourdain's costume with its upside-down flowers, curtseys in an effort to keep from laughing out loud*) Yes?

M. JOURDAIN: Listen to me!

NICOLE: (*bursting into giggles*) Hee hee hee hee hee hee hee hee!

M. JOURDAIN: (*infuriated*) What are you laughing at?

NICOLE: (*swallows her laughter, then breaks out again, even louder*) Hee hee hee hee hee hee hee hee hee!

M. JOURDAIN: (*exasperated*) What's that supposed to mean?

NICOLE: (*trying to get it out*) Hee hee hee. The way you're dressed. Hee hee hee.

M. JOURDAIN: Dressed? How am I dressed?

NICOLE: Ahh, well, My God! Hee hee hee hee hee!

The bourgeois emperor's new clothes have failed their very first test; not even his housemaid finds them impressive. Jourdain's efforts to justify his dress only mire him deeper in mortification as his wife enters the scene:

M. JOURDAIN: (*turning away in fury*) Nicole, you jabber pretty well for a peasant.

MME. JOURDAIN: (*patting Nicole on the back as the housemaid struggles to recover her composure*) Nicole's right, and she has better sense than you do. (*crossing over to her husband and shaking her finger at him*) What are you doing with a dancing master at your age, I'd like to know?

NICOLE: (*stifling more giggles*) And a foot-clomping swordsman who's going to tear the house apart with his "lessons"?

M. JOURDAIN: (*rising to his full height—or as high as his high heels can bring him*) Shut up, both of you . . . You are both stupid and I am ashamed of your ignorance. (*wickedly*) Do either of you know, for example, what it is you are talking right now?

MME. JOURDAIN: (*in no-nonsense tone*) Talking? I'm talking good common sense, and you better think about reforming your behavior pretty fast.

M. JOURDAIN: (*in pursuit*) That's not what I'm asking—I'm asking you what are these WORDS you're speaking?

MME. JOURDAIN: Sensible ones, unlike yours!

M. JOURDAIN: I'm not speaking of that! I'm asking you (*fumbling about to express himself*) what we're saying, what we have been speaking, what is it?

MME. JOURDAIN: (*humoring him*) Drivel?

M. JOURDAIN: (*thundering*) No! (*triumphant*) It's prose, you imbecile!

MME. JOURDAIN: (*amused*) Prose?

M. JOURDAIN: (*as if announcing a new religion*) Yes, prose! (*sonorously*) Everything that is not verse is prose! Everything that is not prose is verse! And that's education for you! (*turns away*) How infuriating it is to deal with ignorant women!

Jourdain thereupon decides to teach Nicole how to fence, and she ends up beating the daylights out of him.

Jourdain's education in manners has taught him nothing about economics, and in subsequent developments Jourdain lends the rakish Count Dorante a large sum of money—with no assurance or collateral beyond Dorante's all too obvious flattery and lies.

DORANTE: (*pretending to admire Jourdain's costume*) Why, Monsieur Jourdain, how magnificent you look!

M. JOURDAIN: (*pleased*) Ah, you like it?

DORANTE: The suit is—well it's—(*he searches for the right description*) it gives you a splendid appearance—(*and, finding the perfect ambiguous compliment*) none of the young men at court could possibly come up with anything like it!

M. JOURDAIN: (*ecstatic*) Ay yi! Ay yi!

MME. JOURDAIN: (*to the audience*) It's you scratch my back, and I'll . . .

DORANTE: (*interrupting her, afraid that Jourdain will overhear*) Turn around . . . (*Jourdain does so*) Ah, how gallant, how . . .

MME. JOURDAIN: (*still to the audience*) It's as stupid in the be-hind as in the front . . .

DORANTE: (*hurrying to interrupt*) In faith, Monsieur Jourdain (*walking Jourdain away from his wife, his hand on Jourdain's back*) I could hardly wait to get here this morning, for I esteem you far above all other men. Why this very morning I—(*whispers confidentially in Jourdain's ear*) I found myself speaking of you, once again, right in the King's Chamber!

M. JOURDAIN: (*stunned, suddenly doffs his hat and bows clumsily, obsequiously to Dorante; with true humility*) You do me too much honor, Monsieur! (*crosses to his wife*) Did you hear that? In the King's Chamber!

DORANTE: (*crossing to him*) Ah, Monsieur, please, put on your . . .

M. JOURDAIN: (*turns to Dorante, still clutching his hat in his hand*) I am overcome with respect, Monsieur.

DORANTE: (*with ingratiating sincerity*) My God, please, put on your hat, I beg you, there must be no artificial ceremony between us.

Nicole stifles her giggles at idiocy of M. Jourdain's pretensions in the ACT production.

M. JOURDAIN: (*utterly overawed at Dorante's kindness*) Monsieur!

DORANTE: (*with oily charm, taking off his own hat*) Put it back on, I tell you, you are my FRIEND.

M. JOURDAIN: (*almost falling to his knees, his legs trembling*) Monsieur, I am your servant.

DORANTE: (*with sudden mock anger*) I will not put on my hat unless you do!

M. JOURDAIN: (*quickly, with mustered dignity, puts on his hat*) If you insist. (*his hand trembles with anxiety as he lets go of the brim; Dorante puts his hat back on also*)

DORANTE: (*coming to his true subject, now that Jourdain has been primed*) I am your debtor, as you know.

MME. JOURDAIN: (*throwing up her hands and walking away, to the audience again*) Oh yes, we know all right!

And Dorante begins to total up his 18,000-franc debt—and then to borrow 200 pistoles more.

Many of Molière's plays involve issues of money; one of his greatest plays, *The Miser*, centers on the subject. Money, in the developing commercial world of the seventeenth century, is pure existential reality; when weighed against words and postures and posings, it highlights the difference between feigned values and intrinsic ones, between hollow presumption and solid worth. Flattery, Molière implies, is cheap; words are freely used and equally freely abused, and only coin has lasting

More somber tones for The Bourgeois Gentleman *were brought out in Jean Louis Barrault's production at the Comédie Française in 1973, an interpretation emphasizing the darker sides of this comedy-ballet. Contemporary music by Michel Colombier was featured in this production, which dispensed with the music of Lully and much of the frilly paraphernalia of the Royal Theatre age.*

value: on a coin, it matters not if the crowned head smiles or frowns. Years of dealing in the provinces with the promises and flattery of noble patrons had doubtless taught Molière a great deal about the difference between verbal and fiscal support, and about the final impoverishment of those who seek to dine on eloquence. As a fashioner of words himself, and as the manager of a thriving enterprise, it is equally probable that Molière was not above a few Dorante-like capers of his own. There is, in any event, nothing remote in this comedy, nothing more than a mask's breadth from human experience.

The third act culminates in a giant dinner party which Dorante has persuaded Jourdain to give on behalf of Dorimène, Dorante's own intended, who remains delightfully ignorant of Jourdain's pursuit of her. The occasion allows Molière some fun on a classic comedy subject, and one often treated by him: the foolish older man pursuing a younger woman. This topic has a certain piquancy here, since Molière himself had married a woman half his age (Armande Molière played the daughter, Lucile, in the original production of *The Bourgeois Gentleman*), and was generally known as a much-cuckolded husband. Certainly there could be no better model for the futile lover than Jourdain:

M. JOURDAIN: (*with increasing desperation*) Madame, it is a great honor for me to see myself so blessed as to be able to be so happy as to have the great and good fortune of having your good will to grant me the grace of doing you the

The dinner party in The Bourgeois Gentleman, *as staged in a Parisian theatre in the 1950s. Simple, symmetrical staging is characteristic of French* mise en scène.

honor of honoring me with the favor of your presence—and if I also could have the merit of meriting a merit such as you provide, and that heaven . . . envious of my great fortune . . . has granted me . . . (*breaking into a nervous sweat*) the advantage of making me worthy . . . of . . .

DORANTE: (*enjoying this spectacle, but finally cutting it short*) That's quite all right, Monsieur Jourdain. She doesn't like compliments, actually, and she knows a man of spirit when she sees one. (to Dorimène) Ridiculous, isn't he?

DORIMÈNE: (*to Dorante, with great sarcasm*) How clever of you to say so.

Having given Dorante a diamond to pass on to Dorimène (which of course Dorante has presented as his own gift), Jourdain is now informed by the count: "To be a true gallant, you must act as though it wasn't you who gave it to her!" And so Jourdain does as he is advised:

M. JOURDAIN: (*taking her hands*) Ah, what beautiful hands you have!

DORIMÈNE: (*radiantly*) My hands are only hands, Monsieur Jourdain; perhaps you are speaking of this beautiful diamond?

M. JOURDAIN: (*despairingly*) I, Madam? God forbid I should speak of it; no gallant man would call attention to that trifle.

DORIMÈNE: (*greatly amused*) How weird.

M. JOURDAIN: (*relieved*) Ah, you are too kind, Madame, too kind.

Madame Jourdain, tipped off by Nicole, bursts in upon the dinner scene to foil her husband's plans vis-à-vis Dorimène, which would have come to naught in any case. This intervention hardly matters to the plot, however, because by then, true to the fashion of the *divertissement*, Molière has jumped adroitly into other topics. We are now concerned, in the last two acts of the play, with Jourdain's plan to marry off his daughter to a marquis, and the honest Cléonte's attempt to win her hand: this situation also is a typical Molière theme, one which he pursued on a far more serious level in the dark comedy of *Tartuffe*. Here, however, there is just foolery: it transpires that Jourdain has no specific marquis in mind for his daughter;

hence there is no one to contest the action to follow when Jourdain's hopes are thwarted by the traditional "wily servant," in this instance Covielle, a direct descendant of the *commedia* character of Arlecchino. It is Covielle's plan that Cléonte will disguise himself and participate in a little comedy masquerade designed to induce Jourdain to yield his daughter. Thus the last two acts of *The Bourgeois Gentleman* turn on that hoary metatheatrical device, the play within the play:

COVIELLE: (*sprightly*) All this seems a little like a comedy, but with Jourdain there's no reason to be subtle; he's the kind of man who will play his role to the hilt . . . I'll get the actors and the costumes, leave it to me.

Covielle's play within the play is the final gulling of Jourdain, who is led on by nothing but his own fantastical desires:

COVIELLE: (*disguised, to M. Jourdain*) Do you know that the son of the Grand Turk is in town?

M. JOURDAIN: (*confused*) Me? No.

COVIELLE: (*his hand on Jourdain's shoulder, confidentially*) Really? He has a most magnificent retinue—the whole town has come to see him; he's being received as a *grand seigneur*.

M. JOURDAIN: (*amazed*) My word. I had no idea.

COVIELLE: (*conspiratorially*) And what's more, he's in love with your daughter.

M. JOURDAIN: (*astonished*) The son of the Grand Turk?

COVIELLE: (*triumphantly*) Yes indeed, he wants to be your son.

M. JOURDAIN: (*overwhelmed*) My Son? The son of the Grand Turk?

COVIELLE: (*grandly*) The son of the Grand Turk! Your son-in-law! Indeed, he was just telling me that. We had hardly begun our conversation when he said to me, (*in heroic mock-Turkish*) "*Acciam croc coler ouch alla moustaph gidelum amanahem varahini oussere carbulath.*" That is, "Do you know the pretty young girl who's the daughter of Monsieur Jourdain, the Parisian gentleman?"

M. JOURDAIN: (*utterly intrigued*) The son of the

Grand Turk said that of me? A Parisian gentleman?

COVIELLE: (*pouring it on*) Yes, he did. And I told him I knew you well, and that I knew Lucile. "Ah," he said to me, *"Marababa sahem."* "How I love her."

M. JOURDAIN: (*figuring it out*) *Marababa sahem* means "how I love her?"

COVIELLE: Yes.

M. JOURDAIN: Lordy, thanks for telling me. I never would have thought *marababa sahem* meant "how I love her." (*exalted*) What a magnificent language, Turkish!

Covielle further announces that it is the desire of the Grand Turk's son to make Jourdain a *Mamamouchi:* "there are no persons in the world more noble than the *Mamamouchi*—you will be the equal of the greatest *seigneurs* on earth!" Now Cléonte, disguised as the Grand Turk's son himself, enters to complete the masquerade:

CLÉONTE: (*grandly*) *Ambousahim oqui boraf, Iordina salamalequi.*

COVIELLE: (*translating*) That means: "Monsieur Jourdain, may your heart flourish like a year-round rose." (*whispers*) They go in big for compliments in Turkey.

M. JOURDAIN: (*responding through Covielle, with a bow*) I am the very humble servant of his Turkish Highness.

COVIELLE: *Carigar camboto outsin moraf.*

CLÉONTE: *Outsin yoc catamelequi basum base alla moran.*

COVIELLE: He says, "Let heaven give you the strength of the lion and the wisdom of the serpent."

M. JOURDAIN: His Turkish Highness honors me too much, and I wish him all sorts of prosperity.

COVIELLE: *Ossa binamen sadoc babally oracaf ouram.*

CLÉONTE: *Bel men.*

COVIELLE: (*excitedly*) He says you must go right away with him and prepare yourself for the ceremony, and bring your daughter so that he and she can get married.

M. JOURDAIN: (*puzzled*) All that in two words?

COVIELLE: (*reassuring*) O yes, Turkish is like that: few words suffice. Go quickly!

And Jourdain goes off as Covielle remarks, "He couldn't have played his role better if he had learned it by heart." The little metatheatrical joke here cannot fail to be subtly amusing, for Molière, as the original Jourdain, had not only learned the role by heart, he had written it—and Covielle's role too! This kind of playing with playing, of theatre about "acting," is as typical of Molière as it is of Shakespeare; both of these actor-playwrights took much inspiration from, and provided much illumination on, the complex relationship between the drama and the "great stage of fools" called life.

The *Mamamouchi* ceremony, in which Jourdain is vested in the gown and turban of a Turkish prince, is the true highlight of this comedy-ballet. With music by Lully, who also choreographed and played the role of the Mufti (high priest), the ceremony is the ballet that divides Act IV from Act V; indeed, it is apparently the scene that inspired the play's entire commission, for it is recorded that King Louis had requested a play on a Turkish theme owing to the excitement occasioned at Court that winter by a visit from the Sultan's ambassador.

A Turkish ceremony he got. Majestically, the *ferme* at the rear of the stage parts: behind it is a grand arch—and behind that, a splendid Oriental vista. We are suddenly plunged into a fantastical extravaganza, for the house of Jourdain simply disappears into the larger setting of Jourdain's imagination. The audience is not fooled—the domestic angle wings, with their bizarre sconces, remain to show where we "really" are—but Covielle's play within the play calls forth a stage setting within a stage setting: a metatheatrical vision for which Jourdain's house has become the proscenium.

The stage has been enlarged at least by half to accommodate this vision, and we are thrust into the world of grand comic ballet. Jourdain is brought in in a Turkish gown, his head completely shaven, and guided to a position on his hands and knees; his back, bedecked by a dusty copy of the Koran, becomes the pulpit for the Mufti, whose turban is illuminated by four or five concentric rings of lighted candles. Around and about dance dervishes

Backed by an oriental vista, the Mufti and his dervishes, rings of lighted candles on their heads, dance around the gullible Monsieur Jourdain.

Turkish scimitars, turbans, exotic banners—and ever-present French chandelier—dress the stage for the mamamouchi ceremony in William Ball's 1976 ACT production.

and Turkish lords, chanting in a mixture of Molière's French, Lully's Italian, and pseudo-Turkish mumbo-jumbo:

TURKS: (*singing and dancing*) Hi valla. Hi valla.

THE MUFTI: (*chanting grotesquely*) Ha la ba, ba la chou, ba la ba, ba la da.

THE TURKS: Ha la ba, ba la chou, ba la ba, ba la da.

M. JOURDAIN: (*cringing, as the Turks beat upon the Koran placed on his back*) Ouf!

THE MUFTI: (*invoking unseen gods*) Ti non star furba?

THE TURKS: (*in mock horror*) No, no, no.

THE MUFTI: Non star forfanta?

THE TURKS: No, no, no.

THE MUFTI: (*furiously—the start of an incantation*) Donar turbanta!

And the Turks dance about Monsieur Jourdain, dressing him in the grand turban of the *Mama-*

MOLIÈRE'S STAGING

It is likely that formal staging for most of Molière's works—except for the ballets—was kept to a minimum by Molière the director. This conclusion is suggested by several bits of evidence. First, we know that the stage of his theatre was relatively small and apparently did not have the pavilion-type upper level described for the Marais, that courtier-spectators were often seated on the periphery of the stage itself, and that Molière was regularly called upon to re-stage works at court. Add to that the highly verbal nature of the plays themselves and his troupe's twelve years of ensemble touring with its *commedia* associations. All of these factors indicate a staging pattern that could be improvised by the actors on the spot. Molière portrays precisely that sort of situation in his play *The Versailles Rehearsals*, in which he has the director saying to some actors "You there—arrange yourselves about, these aren't the sort of people who crowd each other," and telling two others to jump up and sit down as they wish, according to their "natural anxiety" in the scene.

mouchi and beating him soundly with their Turkish swords.

After this grand musical masterpiece, the fifth act of the play is mere wrap-up and resolution. Dorante will marry Dorimène, Cléonte will marry Lucile, and even Covielle will marry, with the servant Nicole. As for Jourdain, he will return to his practical Mme. Jourdain, being none the wiser for his follies and delighted, as ever, to watch—along with the real audience—the ballet with which the play concludes.

For that, indeed, is *The Bourgeois Gentleman* from beginning to end: *a divertissement* for audience and actors alike, for the King and for Molière's own company. Everything in it is calculated to entertain: the music, the dancing, the characters, the human foibles, the dialogue, the costumes, the scenery, and the delightfully bogus *Mamamouchi* ceremony contrived to enchant a court faddishly fascinated with the Orient. The play radiates good fun and good humor, and despite some potentially weighty themes (the aristocrat's fleecing of the bourgeois, the bourgeois's willingness to sacrifice his daughter's future to his own social pretensions), Molière's manner is to skirt the real issues by trivializing their consequences—and by giving way to song and dance at the least provocation.

The Bourgeois Gentleman was Molière's last great success. Louis told Molière at the time it premiered that he had never done better, yet in just a couple of years the King was to give over Molière's monopoly on the Palais Royale to Lully, who had successfully maneuvered himself above Molière in the royal favor. Thus it seems the scene in which Lully, as the Mufti, preached over Molière's (Jourdain's) back during the Turkish ballet sequence was remarkably prophetic and indeed, quite probably, not wholly accidental.

In 1673 Molière produced his last work, *The Imaginary Invalid*; it was his first play in more than a decade not to premiere at court. In its fourth public performance, Molière, who was by that time something of a true invalid, not an imaginary one, had a convulsion while performing the title role; he finished the performance, but within a few hours he was dead. He had remarked earlier the same day that it was about time for him to "*quitter la partie*"; with his death, and that of Racine six years later, the party itself came to an end. The great age of French neo-classic drama was over.

Although Molière's troupe persisted and soon amalgamated with the rival Marais and Hotel de Bourgogne companies to form the royally chartered Comédie Française, the King thereafter was drawn

MACHINE PLAYS

Stage machinery was unnecessary in most neo-classic drama, but was nonetheless developed to an extraordinary degree for the staging of opera, ballets, and so-called machine plays in the Royal era. Giacomo Torelli, an Italian stage designer, brought Italian skills and technologies to Paris in 1645, converting the Petit Bourbon and the Palais Royale to mechanically sophisticated theatres suitable for hugely elaborate stagings, which proved quite popular. Fifteen years later another Italian designer, Gaspare Vigarani, came to Paris at the request of Cardinal Mazarin, and there created his *Salle des Machines*, a theatre specifically intended for spectacular stage effects, in the Tuileries Palace; this "Machine Hall" opened in 1662. Both Torelli's and Vigarani's theatres featured ornate prosceniums, deep stages (the *Salle des Machines* had a stage depth of 140 feet—vis-à-vis an auditorium depth of only 92 feet), wing and drop scenery elaborately painted in careful perspective, and impressive flying and hoisting machinery. Some of Molière's later plays, including *Amphitryon* and *Psyché*, were "machine plays" that Molière had written so that they could be staged in such theatres.

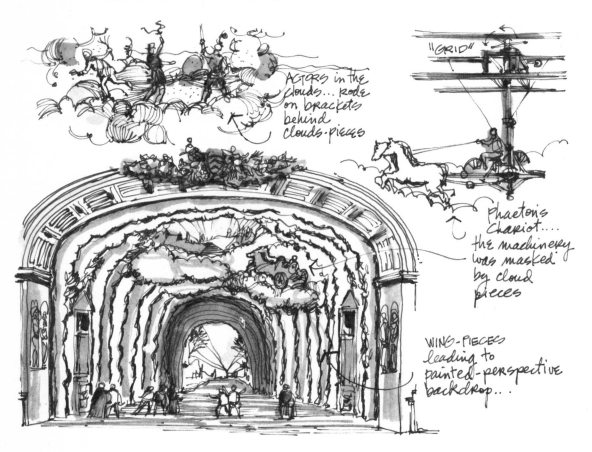

ACTORS in the clouds... rode on brackets behind clouds-pieces

"GRID"

Phaeton's Chariot.... the machinery was masked by cloud pieces

WING-PIECES leading to painted-perspective backdrop...

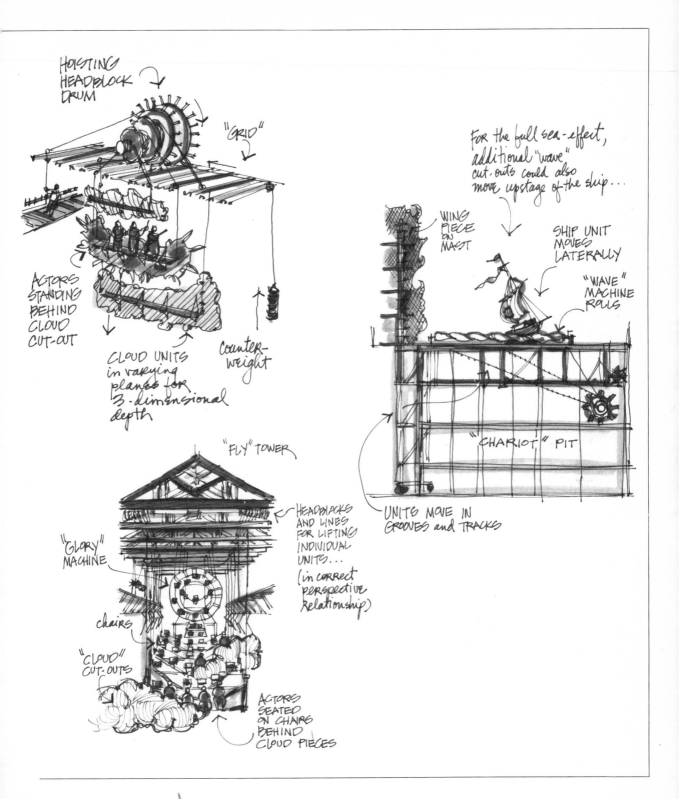

HOISTING HEADBLOCK DRUM

"GRID"

For the full sea-effect, additional "wave" cut-outs could also move upstage of the ship...

WING PIECE ON MAST

SHIP UNIT MOVES LATERALLY

"WAVE" MACHINE ROLLS

ACTORS STANDING BEHIND CLOUD CUT-OUT

CLOUD UNITS in varying planes for 3-dimensional depth

Counter-weight

"CHARIOT" PIT

UNITS MOVE IN GROOVES and TRACKS

"FLY" TOWER

HEADBLOCKS AND LINES FOR LIFTING INDIVIDUAL UNITS... (in correct perspective relationship)

"GLORY" MACHINE

chairs

"CLOUD" CUT-OUTS

ACTORS SEATED ON CHAIRS BEHIND CLOUD PIECES

Curtain call for ACT production of The Bourgeois Gentleman *illustrates level of high-energy comedy of this royal divertissement, adapted to the tastes of American audiences of the twentieth century.*

increasingly into international politics and spent less and less time with theatricals and literary entertainments. So it was that the glittering theatre world that begot *The Bourgeois Gentleman* dissolved into a harsher reality; the play was one of the last efflorescences of a brief but brilliant age.

ENGLAND: THE RESTORATION THEATRE

The theatre of England during the reign of King Charles II (1660–1685) and for about fifteen years thereafter was the Royal Theatre of our own English language. Today it is known as the Restoration Theatre because it came into being with the restoration of the English monarchy, in 1660, following a period of revolution and Puritan domination. The Restoration Theatre never achieved quite the breadth or brilliance of its French model and counterpart, but it is every bit as fascinating historically, and it produced the finest English comedy since the time of Shakespeare and Ben Jonson.

The Restoration Theatre was by no means a continuation of the Elizabethan and Jacobean theatres that preceded it. Civil War broke out in England in 1642, leading to the trial and beheading of King Charles I in 1649, and the succession of republican rule which in 1652 became the Protectorate headed by the Puritan Oliver Cromwell. Theatres were outlawed at the very beginning of this period; actors were jailed as rogues, and the playhouses themselves were burned to the ground.

Most of the English courtiers who survived the upheaval escaped to France, where they were royally received by Louis XIV. When the English monarchy was restored in 1660 and Charles II ascended the throne, the theatre he commissioned into existence owed far more to the French neo-classicists, especially to Molière, than it did to Shakespeare and the theatre managers of the time of Queen Elizabeth.

The English Restoration playhouses had little in common with the "wooden O's" of Shakespeare's day; rather they followed the French fashion wholly and unequivocally: the first two theatres chartered by Charles II were converted tennis courts. One was under the directorship of the King's friend Thomas

WING SCENERY

PROSC. DOORS

CHANDELIERS ABOVE

A Restoration theatre, with two proscenium doors on each side of the stage.
Some theatres had just one door on each side.

Killigrew; the other was managed by a long-time London producer named William Davenant. Both of these men first converted tennis courts into temporary stages and then modeled new theatre buildings—Killigrew's Theatre Royal in Drury Lane, designed by Christopher Wren, and Davenant's Lincoln's Inn Fields Theatre—after the *jeu de paume* style.

The Restoration theatres each featured a rectangular hall divided in two by a proscenium arch, with a pit surrounded by two or (usually) three galleries. There were a few clear improvements over the French model, however. The Restoration pit was raked to slope toward the stage, and lined with rows of backless benches; standing room thereby became a thing of the past, and sight lines were much improved. The stage also was raked, enhancing the perspective of flat "wing and border" scenery which moved in and out on grooves, and the French *ferme* was replaced with a shutter at the rear of the stage. A peculiar innovation of the Restoration stage was a large "apron" built to project into the audience, and a set of doors in the proscenium itself that opened onto that apron, or forestage, providing entrances and exits for the actors well in front of the scenery. These "proscenium doors," which were surmounted by windows, recall the tiring-house doors of Shakespeare's day, and may indeed represent a vestigial carryover from that time.

The acting apron, the small, raked auditorium, the elegant decor, and the official patronage of King and Court created in the Restoration theatre much the same atmosphere of intimacy and sophistication as that which prevailed in the Royal Theatre in France. Also as in France, the English Restoration audience was largely a self-selected club of self-celebrating luminaries. Afternoon performances began at three o'clock, but, again as in Paris, the doors opened well before then to allow the patrons a few hours of pre-performance frivolity and social intercourse. The performers' splendid satin and silk costumes, high heels (for both men and women), towering "perukes" (wigs), handkerchiefs that draped almost to the floor, and elocutionary acting styles created a spectacle well suited to the tastes of a court conspicuously preoccupied with sexual assignation and dalliance. Indeed, the whole mood of the Restoration Theatre was one of blatant sexual provocation. Samuel Pepys' candid diaries make clear that the addition of women to the acting companies had given rise to a backstage social scene quite as lively as that on stage, and he tells us that during and after performances the King's voice was frequently heard in the actresses' dressing rooms. Nell Gwynne, a celebrated Restoration actress, was even more celebrated for her offstage role as mistress of Charles II; and for the benefit of those young "sparks" (gallants) not so favored by theatre personalities, elegant prostitutes wearing *vizard* (face) masks were always in bold attendance in the audience, competing with the play for general attention. One such charmer is described by dramatic poet John Dryden in these lines:

But stay: methinks some vizard masque I see,
Cast out her lure from the mid gallery:
About her all the flutt'ring sparks are rang'd;
The noise continues though the scene is changed.

The adoption of the mask by select members of the audience must have added a piquant note of audience participation to the Restoration stagings, for of course the mask was the very symbol of the actor. And in truth these were performances in which actors and audience alike played parts, and a good deal of the "acting" took place backstage and "in the house."

The dramas of the Restoration included heroic and neo-classic tragedies, tragicomedies, and a range of musical entertainments, but certainly the greatest glory of the era was achieved in the exquisite comedies of William Wycherley (*The Country Wife*), Sir George Etherege (*The Man of Mode*), and William Congreve (*The Way of the World*). The scintillating wit, ribaldry, topicality, and invective which these writers brought to the stage faithfully mirrored the age and its dominant values. Their plays portray in detail the snuff-snorting pomposity of the men, the wily coquetry of the women, and the aristocratic snobbery of a court intoxicated with its new-found power. Many of the scenes are set right in London—sometimes just streets away from the theatres where the comedies first played—and many of the characters are drawn quite literally from the sparks, the fops, the rakes, the lords and the ladies who sat in the audience.

The Puritans, of course, despised such plays. According to Anglican clergyman Jeremy Collier, they were "faulty to a scandalous degree of nauseousness and aggravation ·. . . viz. their smuttiness of expression; their swearing, profaneness, and lewd application of Scripture; their abuse of the clergy; their making their top characters libertines, and giving them success in their debauchery." But, as a character in a Wycherley play would reply, "'Tis a pleasant, well-bred, complaisant, free, frolic, good-natured, pretty age; and if you do not like it, leave it to us that do."

The Way of the World

Perhaps the greatest masterpiece of Restoration comedy is Congreve's *The Way of the World*, which premiered near the end of the era, in 1700. Although the plot is rather typical for the time, revolving as it does about love and money, sexual freedom and security, marriage and social standing, *The Way of the World* transcends its genre by virtue of its perfectly honed dialogue, its brilliant epithets and ripostes, and its incisive portrayal of the manners and values of the Restoration aristocracy.

The wooing scene between the two chief char-

Michael Pennington as Mirabell and Judi Dench as Millamant, in the 1978 Royal Shakespeare Company production of The Way of the World. *Beryl Reid as Lady Wishfort looks on, her beauty spot a characteristic adornment of the period.*

acters, the rakish bachelor Mirabell and the capricious and captivating Mistress Millamant, illustrates Congreve's genius at balancing playful banter with penetrating wit; one must imagine the characters elegantly dressed, artfully posed, and flawlessly articulate:

MIRABELL: (*unlocking the door and surprising her in the salon*) Do you lock yourself up from me to make my search more curious? Or is this pretty artifice contrived to signify that here the chase must end and my pursuit be crowned, for you can fly no further?

MISTRESS MILLAMANT: (*points at him with her closed fan*) Vanity! (*pirouettes playfully and turns from him, opening her fan to shield her face*) No, I'll fly and be followed to the last moment. Though I am upon the very verge of matrimony, I expect you should solicit me as much as if I were wavering at the gate of a monastery, with one foot over the threshold. I'll be solicited to the very last, nay, and afterwards!

MIRABELL: (*raising his eyebrows*) What, after the last?

MISTRESS MILLAMANT: (*assuredly*) Oh, I should think I was poor and had nothing to bestow if I were reduced to an inglorious ease and freed from the agreeable fatigues of solicitation. (*walks away from him*)

MIRABELL: (*following*) But do not you know that when favors are conferred upon instant and tedious solicitation, they diminish in their value, and that both the giver loses the grace, and the receiver lessens his pleasure . . . ?

MISTRESS MILLAMANT: (*stopping his question with her*

upraised hand) It may be in things of common application; but never sure in love. (*with one hand at her breast, staring at him directly and advancing on him*) Oh, I HATE a lover that can dare to think he draws a moment's air independent of the bounty of his mistress. There is not so impudent a thing in nature as the saucy look of an assured man, confident of success. The pedantic arrogance of a husband has not so pragmatical an air. (*turning, coquettishly, to the audience*) Ah! I'll never marry, unless I am first made sure of my will and pleasure.

MIRABELL: (*slyly seizing upon her last word*) Would you have them BOTH before marriage? Or will you be contented with the first now, and stay for the other till after grace?

MISTRESS MILLAMANT: Ah! Don't be impertinent! (*holds her fan across her breast, in mock heroic apostrophe to her soon-to-be former freedom*) My dear liberty, shall I leave thee? My faithful solitude, my darling contemplation, must I bid you then adieu? Ah, adieu, my morning thoughts, agreeable wakings, indolent slumbers, all ye *douceurs*, ye *sommeils du matin* [i.e., sweetnesses and morning naps]! (*with renewed insistence, firmly*) I can't do't, 'tis more than impossible. Positively, Mirabell, I'll lie abed in a morning as long as I please. (*turns and walks away, snapping her fan closed*)

MIRABELL: (*brightly*) Then I'll get up in a morning as early as I please.

MISTRESS MILLAMANT: Ah! Idle creature, get up when you will. (*turns back on him, pointing her fan wickedly*) And, d'ye hear, I won't be called names after I'm married; positively I won't be called NAMES.

MIRABELL: Names?

MISTRESS MILLAMANT: (*choosing her words with delicious disdain*): Aye, as Wife, Spouse, My Dear, Joy, Jewel, Love, SWEETHEART, and the rest of that nauseous cant, in which men and their wives are so fulsomely familiar; I shall never bear that. Good Mirabell, don't let us become familiar or fond, nor kiss before folks, like my Lady Fadler and Sir Francis; nor go to Hyde Park together the first Sunday in a new chariot, to provoke eyes and whispers and then never be seen there again, as if we were proud of one another the first week, and ashamed of one another ever after. Let us NEVER visit together, nor go to a play together. But let us be very strange and well-bred; let us be as strange as if we had been married a great while, and as well-bred as if were not married at all!

MIRABELL: (*benificently*) Have you any more conditions to offer? Hitherto your demands are pretty reasonable.

MISTRESS MILLAMANT: (*triumphant in her victory, walking confidently in circles about him and gesturing as she speaks*) Trifles!—As liberty to pay and receive visits to and from whom I please; to write and receive letters without interrogatories or wry faces on your part; to wear what I please, and choose conversation with regard only to my own taste; to have no obligation upon me to converse with wits that I don't like because they are your acquaintance, or to be intimate with fools because they may be your relations! Come to dinner when I please; dine in my dressing room when I'm out of humor, without giving a reason. To have my closet inviolate; to be sole empress of my tea-table, which you must never presume to approach without first asking leave. And lastly, wherever I am, you shall always knock at the door before you come in. (*coming to a stop beside him, grandly*) These articles subscribed, if I continue to endure you a little longer, I may by degrees dwindle into a wife.

Surely the Women's Movement of the nineteenth and twentieth centuries has never framed an appeal for female freedom in marriage with such articulate bravado. Congreve's verbal mastery spans the centuries with its lively engagement of fundamental marital issues and consequences. It is to just this kind of approach that the best of Restoration drama owes its continuing appeal.

III

The Present

THE HERITAGE of the theatre—a past stretching back more than two millennia—is luminous with masterworks that will serve as inspiration to theatrical creativity for uncountable generations to come.

But the past, of course, is not the whole of theatre. What we see in the theatre today is the visible edge of an age every bit as exciting as any in the past: the age of modern theatre. No period of theatrical activity has been more varied, more rich in experimentation, more controversial or more socially influential than this modern age.

It is not always easy for us to recognize the great achievements of our own era. Our admiration for old masters often blinds us to the splendors of the present, and nostalgia for the past often dims our appreciation of the here and now. Thus "They don't make them like they used to" is an oft-heard cry. The same cry was heard in the times of Molière, Shakespeare, and Euripides, and no doubt in the time of Aeschylus himself. But now as always, it is an irrelevant observation.

They certainly *don't* make them like they used to, and the reason they don't is that the theatre is a living art. As such, it is continually engaged in a process of evolution. A vital theatre cannot be content simply to reproduce masterpieces; the accomplishments of the past may provide lessons, but they cannot establish doctrines or formulas. Stimulation and discovery are two proper goals of any art, and the modern theatre, while perhaps not yet aged enough to claim the laurels of the classic and neo-classic theatres, has already proved itself every bit as stimulating and adventurous as any of its predecessors.

The modern theatre can be said to date from about 1875; thus it is now well into its second century. Its recognizable origins, however, lie deep in the social and political upheavals that developed out of the Enlightenment and dominated European and American culture in the nineteenth century.

Revolution characterizes those times. Political revolution in the United States (1776) and France (1789) irrevocably changed the political structure of the Western world, and industrial/technological revolution cataclysmically overhauled the economic and social systems of most of the world. In the wake of these developments came an explosion of public communication and transportation, a tremendous expansion of literacy, democracy, and public and private wealth, and a universal demographic shift from country to town. These forces combined to create in Europe and the United States mass urban populations hungering for social communion and stimulation: a fertile ground for the citified and civilized theatre of our times.

Simultaneously, intellectual revolution—in philosophy, in science, in social understanding, and in religion—was altering human consciousness in ways far transcending the effects of revolutionary muskets and industrial consolidation. The intellectual certainty of a Louis XIV, ruling by divine right, appeared ludicrous in an age of Enlightenment governed by secular scientific investigation; the clear-sightedness of Molière seemed simplistic in an age of existentialism signalled by the soul-searching, self-doubting analyses of Sören Kierkegaard.

The intellectual revolution was an exceedingly complex phenomenon which occurred in many spheres of thought and was to gain momentum with each passing decade. It continues to this day.

The Copernican theory had already made clear that man does not stand at the geographic center of the universe, but rather that our world, indeed our universe, is swept up in a multiplicity of interstellar movements. Now scientists would press much farther than that, until presently the revelations of Einstein, Heisenberg, and others would remove all our "hitching posts in space" and establish man as little more than a transformation of kinetic energy, wobbling shiftily in a multi-gravitational atomic field marked by galaxies and black holes, neutrinos and quarks, matter and anti-matter, all in a vast dance of inexplicable origin and doubtful destiny.

Darwinian theory would demonstrate that man is not an animal wholly distinct from other breeds, but rather a creature that has much in common with all other organisms and is moreover a close relative of the orangutan. The work of Freud would disclose the existence of the Unconscious: a dark and lurking inner self aswarm with infantile urges, primordial fantasies, and suppressed fears and rages. The writings of Karl Marx would contend that all social behavior has its basis in economic greed, class struggle, and primal amorality. "Everlasting uncertainty and agitation" is the nature of human intercourse, according to Marx, and society comprises "two great hostile camps" continually engaged in civil war.

These and scores of other serious challenges to previous thinking were accompanied everywhere by public debate and dispute. By the turn of the present century, an investigative ferment had seized European and American civilization: data were being collected on every conceivable topic, and scientific questioning and testing replaced intuition and dogma as the accepted avenue to truth. Experimentation, exploration, documentation, and challenge became the marching orders of artist and intellectual alike.

The modern theatre has its roots in these political, social, and intellectual revolutions. Ever since its outset it has been a theatre of challenge, a theatre of experimentation. It has never been a theatre of rules or simple messages, nor has it been a theatre of demigods or of absolute heroes and villains. It has reflected, to a certain degree, the confusions of its times, but it has also struggled to clarify and to illuminate, and to document and explore man's destiny in a complex and uneasy universe.

A scene from Maxim Gorky's The Lower Depths *(1902), one of the most celebrated naturalistic plays produced by Konstantin Stanislavski at the Moscow Art Theatre. The play describes characters at "the lower depths" of Russian society before the Revolution: Stanislavski had his actors visit flophouses like the one in which the play is set, in order to develop the realism of their character portrayals. The play was so truthfully performed that spectators actually expressed fears of being infected by vermin during performances.*

CHAPTER 7

THE REALISTIC THEATRE

The movement toward a realistic theatre began as a revolt against the intentional artifice of neo-classic form. Theatre ought to hold up a mirror to nature, the anti-neo-classicists asserted, and why must the five-act structure and the Alexandrine couplet intervene to distort the image? Rebellion against contrived manners and elitist snobbery also fueled the attack—and thus the European theatre that followed the seventeenth century was to develop a distinctly democratic, anti-Royalist air.

The first efforts in these directions took the form of sentimental comedies and pathetic tragedies featuring admirable characters and noble (if prosaic) sentiments. Richard Steele's *The Conscious Lovers* (1722) and Joseph Addison's *Cato* (1713) still stand as landmarks of this minor period of the theatre's history in England; the eighteenth-century plays and essays of Voltaire (François Marie Arouet) and Denis Diderot exemplify the same trends in France.

The first truly significant result of this artistic rebellion, however, was *Romanticism*, a movement that spread through Europe in the very late eighteenth century and gained widespread acceptance in all the arts in the first half of the nineteenth century. Romanticism in the theatre took the form of a florid attempt to re-activate passion, which the Romanticists contended had been dormant since the time of Shakespeare. Works inspired by the Romantic movement include Johann Wolfgang von Goethe's *Faust* (Part I, 1808; Part II, 1832), Victor Hugo's *Hernani* (1830), and Alexandre Dumas's dramatization of his novel *The Three Musketeers*. With its emphasis on free-form, picaresque stories, exotic locales, grotesque heroes, and sprawling dramatic structure, Romanticism gave rise to a liberated and awesome theatricality which survives today primarily in the form of grand opera and Grand Guignol. "Grand" is indeed the proper appellation for Romantic theatre, for it strove mightily—and self-consciously—to free dramaturgy from the strictures of neo-classic formulas by means of flamboyant verse, boisterous action, epic adventure, passionate feeling, and majestic style. Unappalled by sentiment and unafraid of crackling rhetoric, the romantic authors explored deeply into the theatre's possibilities for moving, dazzling, and enthralling an audience, and many of the discoveries they made are subtly reflected in the drama of present times.

It is to the Romantic period that we owe the virtually universal adoption, in Europe and America, of the proscenium theatre building, which remains today the most common form of indoor theatre architecture in the Western world. Built to accommodate rapid changes of painted scenery—most notably the intricately realized scenic flats and backdrops greatly favored by Romantic authors—the proscenium theatre of the nineteenth century featured an immense stage, of which only a relatively small fraction was used for playing; the rest served solely for the display or storage of illusionistic scenery. Only in the past two decades has this design been seriously challenged in the construction of new theatrical facilities, for the bulk of existing theatres today either date from the Romantic era or were constructed in at least partial imitation of the theatres of that time.

With respect to dramatic achievement, however, the aims of Romanticism proved more influential than lasting. The Romanticists succeeded in laying bare the possibilities of theatre in an age of rapid change. They also succeeded in wooing a democratic audience into the theatres, and they removed from the drama an edge of academic pretension which in the neo-classic era had threatened to destroy the theatrical experience by inhibiting its liveliness. By appealing to the emotions as well as to the mind, the credos and works of Romanticism also stimulated a popular taste for rapture, adventure, and discovery in the theatre, and for rebelliousness in both politics and art.

REALISM

Thus far, the movement that has had the most pervasive and long-lived effect on modern theatre is, beyond question, realism.

Realism has sought to create a drama without conventions or abstractions, in simple consonance with life itself. *Likeness to life* is realism's goal, and in pursuit of that goal it has renounced, among other things, idealized or prettified settings, versifications, contrived endings, and stylized costumes and performances.

Realism is a beguiling aesthetic philosophy, since the theatre has *always* taken "real life" as its fundamental subject, and realism seems at first glance to be an appropriate style with which to approach the reality of existence. Instead of having actors represent characters, the realists would say, let us have the actors *be* those characters; instead of having dialogue stand for conversation, let us have dialogue which *is* conversation; instead of scenery and costumes that convey a sense of time and place and atmosphere, let us have scenery that is genuinely inhabitable, and costumes that are real clothes.

It is perhaps unnecessary to point out that realism has its limits—that any dramatic piece must inevitably involve a certain shaping and stylization, no matter how lifelike its effect; the advocates of theatrical realism are well aware of this inevitability. Nevertheless, the ideology of realism was tested, during the last years of the nineteenth century and the first years of the present one, in every aspect of theatre—acting, directing, design, and playwriting—and the results of those tests form a body of theatre that is both valid and meaningful, and a style which remains enormously significant.

In essence, the realistic theatre is conceived to be a laboratory in which the nature of relationships, or the ills of society, or the symptoms of a dysfunctional family are "objectively" set down for the final judgment of an audience of impartial observers. Every aspect of realistic theatre should strictly adhere to the "scientific method" of the laboratory; nothing must ring false. The setting is to resemble the prescribed locale of the play as closely as possible; indeed it is not unusual for much of the scenery to be acquired from a real-life environment and transported to the theatre (in one famous instance, American producer David Belasco went so far as to purchase a New York restaurant, dismantle it, and rebuild it within the confines of his Broadway stage). Costumes worn by characters in the realistic theatre follow the actual dress of "real" persons of similar societal status; dialogue is prized as it re-creates the cadences and expressions of daily life.

Early on in the realist movement the proscenium stage of the Romantic era was modified to accommodate scenery that was constructed in box sets, with the walls given full dimension and with real bookcases, windows, fireplaces, swinging doors, and so forth, built into the walls just as they are in a house interior. In the same vein, the acting of the realists was judged effective insofar as it was drawn from the behavior of life, and insofar as the actors seemed to be

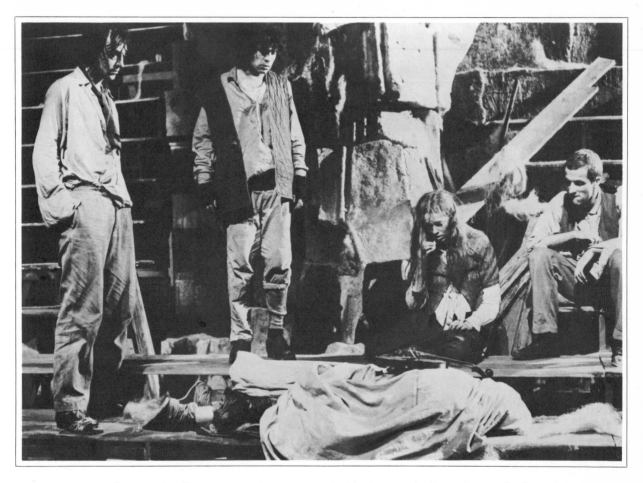

Elements of realism are everywhere apparent in this photograph of a modern production of Victor Hugo's romantic verse trilogy The Burgraves *(1843). Scenery, costume, make-up, and acting in this 1978 production—by the Théâtre de Gennevilliers in France—are realistically detailed, but the plot and language are from the Romantic tradition.*

genuinely speaking to each other instead of playing to the audience. A new aesthetic principle was spawned: "the theatre of the fourth wall," in which the life on stage was conceived to be the same as life in a real-world setting, except that in the case of the stage one wall—the proscenium opening—had been removed. Thus the "fourth wall" theatre was like a laboratory telescope and the stage like a microbiologist's slide: a living environment set up for judicious inspection by neutral observers.

Thus realism presents its audience with an abundance of seemingly real-life "evidence" and permits each spectator to arrive at his or her own conclusions.

There is some shaping of this evidence by author and performer alike, to be sure, but much of the excitement of the realistic theatre is occasioned by the genuine interpretive freedom it allows the audience, and by the accessibility of its characters, whose behaviors are familiar enough to the average spectator that they may be easily assimilated and identified.

Moreover, in presenting its evidence from the surface of life, realism encourages us to delve into the mystery that lies beneath—for the exploration of life's mystery is the true if unspoken purpose of every realistic play. Realism's characters, like people in life, are defined by detail rather than by symbol or abstract idealization: like persons we know, they are ultimately unpredictable, humanly complex rather than ideologically absolute.

The success of realism is well established; indeed, realism remains one of the dominant modes of drama to this day. At its most profound, when crafted and performed by consummately skilled artists, the realistic theatre can generate extremely powerful audience empathy by virtue of the insight and clarity it brings to real-world moments. In giving us characters, the realist playwright gives us *friends*; fellow travelers on the voyage of human discovery with whom we can compare thoughts and feelings. In the uncertainties and trepidations, the wistfulness, the halting eloquence and conversational syntax of these characters we recognize ourselves, and in that recognition we gain an understanding of our own struggles and a compassion for all human endeavors.

Pioneers of Realism

The realistic theatre had its beginnings in the four-year period which saw the premieres of *A Doll's House* (1879), *Ghosts* (1881), and *An Enemy of the People* (1882), three plays by the Norwegian author Henrik Ibsen. Earlier in his career, Ibsen had been a stage director and dramatic poet, and his previous works for the theatre included the magnificent Romantic/epic poem-play *Peer Gynt* (1867). With these three plays, which dealt, respectively, with the issues of womens' roles in society, hereditary disease and mercy killing, and political hypocrisy, he turned to the realistic mode. Ordinary people populate Ibsen's realistic world, and the issues addressed in these dramas affect ordinary husband-wife, mother-son, and brother-brother relationships, played out in the interiors of ordinary homes. These plays, controversial beyond measure in their own time, retain their edge of pertinence even today and still have the power to inform, to move, and even to shock. The reason for their lasting impact lies in Ibsen's choice of issues and his skill at showing both sides through brilliantly captured psychological detail.

The realistic theatre spread rapidly throughout Europe as the controversy surrounding Ibsen's plays and themes stimulated other writers to follow suit. The result was a proliferation of "problem plays," as they were sometimes called, which focused genuine social concern through realistic dramatic portrayal. In Germany, Gerhart Hauptmann explored the plight of the middle and proletarian classes in several works, most notably in his masterpiece *The Weavers* (1892). In England, Irish-born George Bernard Shaw created a comedic realism through which he addressed such issues as slum landlordism (in *Widower's Houses*, 1892), prostitution (in *Mrs. Warren's Profession*, 1902), and urban poverty (in *Major Barbara*, 1905). In France, under the encouragement of innovative director André Antoine, Eugène Brieux wrote a series of realistic problem plays that included *Damaged Goods* (1902), which deals with syphilis, and *Maternity* (1903), which deals with birth control. By the turn of the century realism was virtually the standard dramatic form in Europe.

Naturalism

Naturalism, a movement whose development paralleled that of realism but was essentially independent of it, represents an even more extreme attempt to dramatize man's reality without the appearance of dramaturgical shaping. The naturalists, who flourished primarily in France during the late nineteenth century (Emile Zola was their chief theoretician), based their aesthetics on nature, and particularly on man's place in the natural (Darwinian) environment. To the naturalist, man was merely a biological phenomenon whose behavior was determined entirely by genetic and social circumstances. To portray a character as a hero, or even as a credible force for change in society, was anathema to the naturalist, who similarly eschewed dramatic conclusions or climaxes. Whereas realist plays at that time tended to deal with well-defined social issues—women's rights, inheritance laws, worker's pensions, and the like—naturalist plays offered nothing more than a "slice of life" in which the characters of the play were the play's entire subject, and any topical issues that were brought in served merely to facilitate the interplay of personalities and highlight their situations, frustrations, and hopes.

The naturalists sought to eliminate every vestige of dramatic convention: "All the great successes of the stage are triumphs over convention," declared Zola. Their efforts in this direction are exemplified by August Strindberg's elimination of the time-passing intermission in *Miss Julie* (instead, a group of peasants, otherwise irrelevant to the plot, enter the kitchen setting between acts and dance to fill the time Miss Julie is spending in Jean's offstage bedroom), and Arthur Schnitzler's elimination of conventional scene beginnings, endings, and climaxes in the interlocking series of cyclical love affairs which constitute the action of *La Ronde*.

Inasmuch as sheer verisimilitude, presented as "artlessly" as humanly possible, is the primary goal of the naturalist, the term "naturalism" is often applied to those realistic plays which seem most effectively lifelike. This is not a particularly felicitous use of the term, however, because it ignores the fundamental precept of naturalism—that man is a mere figure in the natural environment. Naturalism is not merely a matter of style; it is a philosophical concept concerning the nature of the human animal. And naturalist theatre represents a purposeful attempt to explore that concept, using extreme realism as its basic dramaturgy.

CHEKHOV

If the realistic theatre came to prominence with the plays of Henrik Ibsen, it attained its stylistic apogee in the major works of Anton Chekhov. Chekhov was a doctor by training and a writer of fiction by vocation; toward the end of his career, in association with realist director Konstantin Stanislavski and the Moscow Art Theatre, he also achieved success as a playwright through a set of plays that portray the end of the Czarist era in Russia with astonishing force and subtlety: *The Sea Gull* (1896), *Uncle Vanya* (1899), *The Three Sisters* (1901), and *The Cherry Orchard* (1904). The intricate craftsmanship of these plays has never been surpassed; even the minor characters seem to breathe the same air that we do.

Chekhov's technique is to create deeply complex relationships among his characters, and to develop his plots and themes more or less between the lines. Every Chekhovian character is filled with secrets, none of which are ever fully revealed by the dialogue.

In the Soviet Union today, Chekhov is revered as a literary hero, and his plays are continually revived with all details of their original production by the Moscow Art Theatre intact. Audiences return again and again to see them, as if to visit dear friends and to understand them better.

The Three Sisters

Chekhov's *The Three Sisters* epitomizes the realistic theatre; in addition to being one of the finest plays of the genre, it is perhaps the most widely known of all Russian plays. Written for Stanislavski's company in 1901, *The Three Sisters* is a play immensely rich in characterization. It is also immensely rich in its potential for profoundly moving performances; hence it is a favorite of actors wherever the world's great repertory is performed.

There are ten major characters in *The Three Sisters* and, true to the realistic format, no one of them can be regarded as the principal character or protagonist. The play focuses primarily on the network of relations among these characters—and, to a lesser extent, on their interactions with the four minor characters.

Three of the characters do stand apart from the rest, however, as the title indicates. These are three young women, sisters, in whose family home the action takes place. As the play begins, Olga, the elder sister, is a provincial schoolteacher; Masha, the middle sister, is the wife of a provincial schoolteacher; and Irina, the youngest, is vocationally and maritally uncommitted. They are all in their twenties (Act I takes place on Irina's twentieth birthday), they are orphans, and they have but one dream: to leave their remote village and move to Moscow. It is a dream which both haunts and inspires them, and it provides the inner motive force for the play.

Provincial dreamers the sisters may be, but they do not lack family or friends or admirers—and each of the play's four acts, which all together span about three and a half years, is built around some kind of occasion for which virtually the entire cast gathers. A brother to the three sisters, Andrei, and his fiancée, Natasha (later his wife), are permanent members of the household. Kulygin, Masha's husband, is a constant visitor. And a nearby military base—the focal point of the town's social life—provides the sisters with admirers and suitors: the elderly Doctor Tchebutykin, who is billeted in the sisters' house, and the youngish officers Vershinin, Baron Tusenbach, and Solyony. These ten characters, plus two younger officers (Fedotik and Roday) and two aged servants (Anfisa and Ferapont), interweave their lives and fortunes for the four acts

STANISLAVSKI AND CHEKHOV

Stanislavski and Chekhov were the two towering figures of Russian realism, the first as actor-director and the second as playwright. Their collaboration in the Moscow Art Theatre productions of *The Sea Gull* (1898), *Uncle Vanya* (1899), *The Three Sisters* (1901), and *The Cherry Orchard* (1904) still rank among the most magnificent achievements of the realist stage. "It was Chekhov who suggested to me the line of intuition and feeling," said Stanislavski; and Chekhov, for his part, had to admit that his first great success in the theatre was achieved only after he put *The Sea Gull* into Stanislavski's hands—the play had excited little enthusiasm in an earlier production in St. Petersburg.

Relations between these two titans were never placid, however. Chekhov often contended that Stanislavski ignored the poetry of his dramaturgy and did not fully understand the complexity of his characters. At one point Chekhov threatened to withdraw *The Sea Gull* from the Moscow Art Theatre unless one important role was recast; Stanislavski refused to recast the role.

But there can be little doubt that Stanislavski recognized the difficulty in creating a Chekhovian theatrical style. In the following passages from his autobiography, *My Life In Art* (Moscow, 1925), Stanislavski looks back on the exhausting rehearsals for *The Three Sisters* and recalls how one apparent impasse was resolved.

> The actors worked with spirit. We rehearsed the play, everything was clear, understandable, true, but the play was not lively, it was hollow, it seemed tiresome and long. There was *something* missing. How torturing it is to seek this *something* without knowing what it is. All was ready, it was necessary to advertise the production, but if it were to be staged in the form we had achieved, we were faced with certain failure. Yet, we felt that there were elements that augured great success, that everything with the exception of that magic *something* was there. We met daily, we rehearsed to a point of despair, we parted company, and next day we would meet again and reach despair once more. . . .
>
> One evening at one of our agonizing rehearsals, the actors stopped in the middle of the play, ceased to act, seeing no sense in their work. They no longer had any trust in the stage director or in each other. Such a breakdown usually leads to demoralization. Two or three electric lights were burning dimly. We sat in the corners, crestfallen. We felt anxious and helpless. Someone was nervously scratching the bench. The sound was like that of a mouse. It reminded me of home: I felt warm inside, I saw the truth, life, and my intuition set to work. Or, maybe, the sound of the scratching mouse and the darkness and helplessness had some meaning for me in life, a meaning I myself do not understand. Who can trace the path of creative superconsciousness?
>
> I came to life and knew what it was I had to show the actors. It became cosy on the stage. Chekhov's men revived. They do not bathe in their own sorrow. On the contrary, they seek joy, laughter and cheerfulness. They want to live and not vegetate. I felt the truth in Chekhov's heroes, this encouraged me and I guessed what had to be done.

of the play, until by the final curtain every life has been touched by every other.

The play begins in the drawing room of the sisters' fine old house. A table is being set in the room beyond: the occasion is an open house for Irina's birthday, and the whole town is expected. The sun streams in through the windows; the sisters await their guests. Each is individualized: Olga is correcting lessons, Masha is reading a book of poetry, Irina, in a white dress, stands lost in thought, planning her future.

OLGA: Father died just a year ago, on this very day—the fifth of May, your birthday, Irina. It was very cold, snow was falling. I felt as though I should not live through it; you lay fainting as though you were dead. But now a year has passed and we can think of it calmly; you are

The cast of The Three Sisters *in the 1976 production by the Mark Taper Forum of Los Angeles, directed by Edward Parone. This posed photograph shows the sisters and their friends and courtiers: the "family" of the play, in which each character is consummately drawn.*

already in a white dress, your face is radiant. . . . It is warm today, we can have the windows open, but the birches are not in leaf yet. Father was given his brigade and came here with us from Moscow eleven years ago and I remember distinctly that in Moscow at this time, at the beginning of May, everything was already in flower; it was warm, and everything was bathed in sunshine. It's eleven years ago, and yet I remember it as though we had left it yesterday. Oh, dear! I woke up this morning, I saw a blaze of sunshine. I saw the spring and joy stirred in my heart. I had a passionate longing to be back at home again! . . . Being all day

in school and then at my lessons till the evening gives me a perpetual headache and thoughts as gloomy as though I were old. And really, these four years that I have been at the high school I have felt my strength and my youth oozing away from me every day. And only one yearning grows stronger and stronger—

IRINA: To go back to Moscow. To sell the house, to make an end of everything here, and off to Moscow—

OLGA: Yes! To Moscow, and quickly!

Olga, an unwilling spinster by accident of fate, is the leader of the sisters; she is the family histo-

The three sisters and their nurse, at the beginning of the play in the Stratford Festival production (Ontario, Canada) directed by Robin Phillips in 1976. Maggie Smith, in black, plays Masha; Marti Maraden, in white, is Irina, and Martha Henry is Olga. Amelia Hall plays the nurse, Anfisa.

rian, the repository of confidences, the strong hand that holds the household on an even keel. Irina represents the future and the hope of the family. The doctor enters, and Irina addresses him

IRINA: Tell me, why is it I am so happy today? As though I were sailing with the great blue sky above me and big white birds flying over it. Why is it? Why? . . . When I woke up this morning, got up and washed, it suddenly seemed to me as though everything in the world was clear to me and that I knew how one ought to live. Dear doctor, I know all about it. A man ought to work, to toil in the sweat of his brow, however he may be, and all the purpose and meaning of his life, his happiness, his ecstasies lie in that alone. How delightful to be a workman who gets up before dawn and breaks stones on the road, or a shepherd, or a schoolmaster teaching children or an engine driver —oh dear! to say nothing of human beings, it would be better to be an ox, better to be a humble horse and work than a young woman who wakes at twelve o'clock, then has coffee in bed, then spends two hours dressing—Oh, how awful that is! Just as one has a craving for water in hot weather I have a craving for work. And if I don't get up early and work, give me up as a friend, dear doctor!

TCHEBUTYKIN: (*tenderly*) I'll give you up, I'll give you up—

Chekhov's way is gentle irony; it suffuses the dialogue until almost every word expressed seems to contradict the underlying sentiment of the speaker. Olga speaks of radiance and warmth and flowers and sunshine and joy, but her tones are of unmistakable melancholy, heartache, longing, and despair. Irina's inexperience and her idealism are betrayed a thousand times in her artless "Why is it am I so happy today?" speech as she expounds upon her discovery of the verities of life. Does she really believe it would be "delightful to be a workman who gets up before dawn and breaks stones on the road"? That is the life of a convict in Siberia! Irina's enthusiasm is fervid enough to be engaging, but too shallow to be inspiring; neither pathetic nor

Promethean, it is typically human and typically Chekhovian.

When Masha, the third sister, speaks, we find she is given not to prolonged discourses but to apparently idle quotations and cryptic comments.

MASHA: (*quoting from a poem by Pushkin*) "By the sea-strand an oak-tree green—upon that oak a chain of gold—upon that oak a chain of gold—" (*gets up, humming softly*)

OLGA: You are not very cheerful today, Masha. (*Masha, humming, puts on her hat.*)

OLGA: Where are you going?

MASHA: Home.

IRINA: How queer!—

OLGA: To go away from a birthday party!

MASHA: Never mind—I'll come in the evening. Goodbye, my darling—(*kisses Irina*) Once again I wish you, be well and happy. In the old days, when father was alive, we always had thirty or forty officers here on birthdays; it was noisy, but today there is only a man and a half, and it is as still as the desert.—I'll go—I am in the blues today, I am feeling glum, so don't you mind what I say (*laughing through her tears*). We'll talk some other time, and so for now goodbye, darling, I am going—

IRINA: (*discontentedly*) Oh, how tiresome you are—

OLGA: (*with tears*) I understand you, Masha.

The pauses (indicated in this playtext by dashes), the repetitions, and the vagueness are typical of realistic writing, and are aimed at demonstrating the rhythms and muddled inanities of natural speech more than the focus of theatrical phrasing. The impact is gradual and imprecise. Masha twice says goodbye, twice says she's going, makes every gesture of departure, but in fact does not go. She twice cautions her sisters not to mind what she says—but she goes on saying it. She laughs but she cries; indeed, "laughing through tears," which is virtually a Chekhovian trademark, epitomizes the emotional complexity conveyed through realism: the happiest memories are seen to evoke the most painful realizations, and feelings are shown to be most confused when they are most sharply encountered.

"Oh, how tiresome you are," Irina says to Masha, reading her book, in the Parone production of The Three Sisters. *Barra Grant and Laurie Kennedy are the actresses in this Los Angeles production of 1976.*

A series of brief exchanges during this birthday celebration establishes the expository mode of this play; they are encounters that seem obvious in their lifelike simplicity, and yet their ultimate "meaning" is obscure. Inappropriateness is characteristic of all of them: inappropriate words, dress, actions, or conclusions.

For example, Tchebutykin, the doctor, presents a birthday gift to Irina—a silver samovar:

OLGA: (*putting her hands over her face*) A samovar! How awful! (*goes out to the table in the dining room*)

IRINA: My dear doctor, what are you thinking about!

TUSENBACH: (*laughs*) I warned you!

MASHA: Doctor, you really have no conscience!

TCHEBUTYKIN: My dear girls, my darlings, you are all that I have, you are the most precious treasures I have on earth. I shall soon be sixty, I am an old man, alone in the world, a useless old man.—There is nothing good in me except my love for you, and if it were not for you, I should have been dead long ago—(*to Irina*) My dear, my little girl, I've known you from a baby—I've carried you in my arms—I loved your dear mother—

IRINA: But why such expensive presents?

TCHEBUTYKIN: (*angry and tearful*) Expensive presents.—Get along with you! (*to the orderly*) Take the samovar in there—(*mimicking*) Expensive presents—

But it is not just that the gift is unwarrantedly expensive; it is also a social gaffe: as every member of a Russian audience would know, a silver samovar was a traditional silver anniversary present, an utterly inappropriate gift for a young lady's twentieth birthday. The confusion of emotion is wonderfully theatrical on stage, what with Olga's embarrassment and anger, tinged with spinsterish envy, and her abrupt departure; Irina's charmed consternation; and, most particularly, the doctor's fussy, semi-coherent explanations and deprecations, all centering about a splendidly silvered prop samovar glittering in the midst of these ill-at-ease adults: a classic moment of pure realist theatre. What we do not know yet—and indeed will never be sure of—is Tchebutykin's entire motivation in giving this gift; for what indeed was his relation with Irina's mother, the only woman he ever loved? As the play goes on, the suspicion grows on us (although not on Irina) that quite possibly the doctor is Irina's real father; however, true to realistic playwriting, this suspicion is never confirmed or denied by the author or his characters. Thus the samovar might or might not be as inappropriate as Olga and we at first suppose. This ambiguity is but one of many which the audience will be challenged to explore as the play's actions unfold.

Now the handsome, married, middle-aged Colonel Alexander Vershinin arrives on the scene.

Kitty Winn, as Irina, places silver samovar on dining table in American Conservatory Theatre production of The Three Sisters, *directed by William Ball. Notice realism of costumes, furniture, and properties in this production (including real flowers and real candles in the chandelier), and the contrasting stylization of background.*

Keith Baxter, as Vershinin, reaches for the hand of Maggie Smith, playing Masha, in the Stratford Festival 1976 production of The Three Sisters. *The contrast between the two actors' facial expressions reveals the cross purposes of the play's character interactions.*

He announces that he dimly remembers the sisters from many years past, in Moscow:

VERSHININ: I have the honor to introduce myself, my name is Vershinin. I am very, very glad to be in your house at last. How you have grown up! Aie-aie!

IRINA: Please sit down. We are delighted to see you.

VERSHININ: (*with animation*) How glad I am, how glad I am! But there are three of you sisters. I remember—three little girls. I don't remember your faces, but that your father, Colonel Prozorov, had three little girls I remember perfectly. How time passes! Hey-ho, how it passes!

TUSENBACH: Alexander Vershinin has come from Moscow.

IRINA: From Moscow? You have come from Moscow?

VERSHININ: Yes. Your father was in command of a battery there, and I was an officer in the same brigade. (*to Masha*) Your face, now, I seem to remember.

MASHA: I don't remember you.

VERSHININ: So you are Olga, the eldest—and you are Masha—and you are Irina, the youngest—

OLGA: You come from Moscow?

VERSHININ: Yes. I studied in Moscow. . . . I used to visit you in Moscow.

Masha and Vershinin are destined to become lovers; their deepening, largely unspoken com-

Ken Ruta and Miss Michael Learned, as Vershinin and Masha, from the American Conservatory Theatre production. The lovers betray themselves by their proximity.

munion will provide one of the most haunting strains in the play. And how lifelike is the awkwardness of their first encounter! Vershinin's enthusiastic clichés ("how time passes") and interjections ("Aie-aie!") are the stuff of everyday discourse, and the news that he comes from Moscow is repeated to the extent that it becomes amusing rather than informative, a revelation of character rather than of plot.

Masha's first exchange with Vershinin gives no direct indication of the future of their relationship; it is a crossed communication in which one character refuses to share in the other's memory. Is this a personal repudiation or is it a teasing provocation? The acting, not simply the text, must establish their developing rapport. The love between Vershinin and Masha will tax to the maximum the capabilities of the actors who play their parts to express deep feeling through subtle nuance, through the gestures, the glances, the tones of voice, and the shared understandings and sympathetic rhythms that distinguish lovers everywhere: it is a theme that strongly affects the mood of the play but is rarely explicit in the dialogue.

Inasmuch as both Masha and Vershinin are married to others, their relationship is necessarily furtive; this circumstance contributes to a general obliqueness in the play's dialogue, as is evident even in the early exchanges between Masha and her husband, Kulygin:

KULYGIN: (*to the assembled guests, his hand around Masha's waist, laughing*) Masha loves me. My wife loves me.—These window curtains should be put away with the carpets—Today I feel cheerful and in the best of spirits. Masha, at four o'clock this afternoon we have to be at the headmaster's. An excursion has been arranged for the teachers and their families.

MASHA: I am not going.

KULYGIN: Dear Masha, why not?

MASHA: We'll talk about it afterwards. (*Angrily*) Very well, I will go, only let me alone please— (*walks away*)

KULYGIN: And then we shall spend the evening at the headmaster's. In spite of the delicate state of his health, that man tries before all things to be sociable. He is an excellent, noble personality. A splendid man. Yesterday, after the meeting, he said to me: "I am tired, Fyodor Ilyitch, I am tired." (*Looks at the clock, then at his watch*) Your clock is seven minutes fast. "Yes," he said, "I am tired."

Social awkwardness can be a source of daily anxiety for many an ordinary man; certainly the bumbling good will of Kulygin echoes a good many of our own mundane disasters. Intended pleasantries that strike unexpected notes of discord, anecdotes that disintegrate in the retelling, idle observations that impart an excruciating dullness to spoken discourse: these conversational features are by no means indigenous only to Russia at the turn of the century, and Chekhov inserts them into this play with characteristic accuracy and wit. Neither wicked enough to merit our scorn nor ridiculous enough to generate our laughter, they serve rather to stimulate our understanding and our compassion for a wholly recognizable character whose ineptness is not unlike our own.

Two more feasible love affairs are broached in the first act—more feasible in the sense that they involve unmarried young adults. The first involves Tusenbach, an idealistic "Baron" of German descent, and the youngest sister, Irina. Tusenbach expresses his adoration for her; she, however, shows no inclination to reciprocate:

TUSENBACH: What are you thinking of? (*pause*) You are twenty, I am not yet thirty. How many years have we got before us, a long, long, chain of days full of my love for you—

IRINA: Nikolai Lvovich, don't talk to me of love.

TUSENBACH: (*not listening*) I have a passionate craving for life, for struggle, for work, and that craving is mingled in my soul with my love for you, Irina, and just because you are beautiful it seems to me that life too is beautiful! What are you thinking of?

IRINA: You say life is beautiful—Yes, but what if it only seems so! Life for us three sisters has not been beautiful yet, we have been stifled by it as plants are choked by weeds. I am shedding tears—I mustn't do that (*wipes her eyes and*

Kitty Winn and Paul Shenar, as Irina and Tusenbach, in the American Conservatory Theatre production. "For five years now I have loved you," Tusenbach says to his adored Irina, who looks balefully down and away from her unwanted pursuer.

smiles). I must work, I must work. The reason we are depressed and take such a gloomy view of life is that we know nothing of work.

Irina and Tusenbach are perfectly suited to each other—but she does not love him! No amount of rational rapport can outweigh that consideration. Irina will barely listen to Tusenbach's declarations, and Tusenbach, for his part, refuses to acknowledge Irina's dissatisfactions. This one-sided love will provide another line of tension in the play, jangling gently until the baron's suicidal duel at the play's conclusion.

And at the very end of Act I, Andrei, brother to the three sisters, is seen to fall in love with the peasant girl Natasha. Unlike the other relationships in the play, that of Andrei and Natasha will result in marriage—but it will be a union that undermines the family rather than enhances it. Shy, ridiculed at her first entrance for gauchely wearing a green sash with a pink dress, Natasha seduces Andrei from the family gathering and wrings from him a promise of marriage as the Act I curtain falls. Her motives are obscure, but Andrei's fumbling vulnerability foretells the direction of their lives:

(*Natasha runs from the dining room, followed by Andrei*)

ANDREI: Stop, I entreat you—

NATASHA: I am ashamed—I don't know what's the matter with me and they make fun of me. I know it's improper for me to leave the table like this, but I can't help it—I can't (*covers her face with her hands*).

ANDREI: My dear girl, I entreat you, I implore you, don't be upset. I assure you they are only joking, they do it in all kindness. My dear, my sweet, they are all kind, warm-hearted people and they are fond of me and of you. Come here to the window so they can't see us—(*looks around*)

NATASHA: I am so unaccustomed to society!—

ANDREI: Oh youth, lovely, marvelous youth! My dear, my sweet, don't be so distressed! Believe me, believe me—I feel so happy, my soul is full of love and rapture— Oh, they can't see us, they can't see us! Why, why, I love you, when I first loved you—oh, I don't know. My dear, my sweet, pure one, be my wife! I love you, I love you—as I have never loved anyone—(*a kiss*)
(*Two officers come in and, seeing the pair kissing, stop in amazement.*)

Curtain

This is a scene of physical seduction. Natasha plays first upon Andrei's pity and then upon his lust; hence her tears and her use of her hands are more crucial to this scene than any words can be. Andrei's confusion and desire make him a poor match for Natasha's manipulations, and we watch with a mixture of amusement and chagrin as he ineloquently stammers out his infatuation. As we find so often in this play, Andrei's protestations of happiness, love, and rapture are undermined by his obvious sense of personal inadequacy; his failure to avoid public scrutiny (he indeed pulls Nata-

sha right into the path of the amazed officers) is but a symbol of the greater failures which will mark the course of this ill-founded union.

Acts II and III, which are set approximately one and two years after the first, introduce no new characters and no new plot lines; rather these acts serve to show the developing relationships between the various characters, the subtle changes that mark the passage of time and the shifting of interpersonal dominances. Both acts, like the first, are social gatherings of sorts: Act II, occurring in the same drawing room as Act I, is an evening tea party preparatory to a carnival dance; Act III takes place in the bedroom of Olga and Irina, where, at three o'clock in the morning, the family and friends organize emergency relief efforts for victims of a neighborhood fire. One must look and listen closely to grasp what is happening and what has happened. Natasha has given birth: to son Bobik by Act II, to daughter Sophie by Act III; the children's presence by turns silences the revelry of the carnival dancers and drives the adults out of the main portion of the house (thus forcing Olga and Irina to share a bedroom in Act III). Servants are dismissed, illicit affairs are somewhat meanly pursued, the unwed sisters become more noticeably unwed, and everyone quite subtly grows older. The doctor becomes more drunkenly morose, the baron becomes more ardent in his hapless romancing, Andrei becomes wearier and more helpless, and Kulygin becomes even more of a bore. The love between Vershinin and Masha deepens and thus becomes more poignant in its futility. Natasha takes a lover, one Protopopov, whose spiritual presence, like that of her children (the latter of whom is probably his), becomes more and more oppressive in the play.

And yet none of this is explicitly stated. Unlike the television soap opera—which is a realistic form superficially Chekhovian in structure—this play presents growth and change and even the definition of relationships in an infinitely complex and humanly obscure manner: nothing is analyzed and nothing is resolved. To discuss the plot of *The Three Sisters* is to *interpret* the play, for Chekhov has simply drawn the action and left it to the audience to draw the consequences. Masha and Vershinin do not exchange a single word in Act III, but when they hum a song together and laugh we know all—or at least all that we will know. Olga rages at the doctor for his drunkenness, but we know that Natasha is the real cause for her anger; she simply does not have the courage to confront her sister-in-law face to face. Kulygin never directly addresses his wife's infidelity, but when he says to her "I am content, I am content, I am content," we feel she gets the message—as do we.

The fourth and final act, in which the story lines are concluded if not resolved, remains subtle, oblique, and suffused with ironic indirection.

It is noon on a summer day; for the first time we are outdoors, on the verandah of the family house. The familiar world of the sisters has come to a sudden end; the military garrison is being evacuated to Poland, far away; the soldiers are preparing to depart. Only Baron Tusenbach will remain behind, for he has resigned his commission to marry Irina, who has finally relented to his pursuit. The rest will embark that day, and a farewell champagne party, given by the saddened sisters, has just concluded; it is now time for leave-taking. Whereas most playwrights reserve the final act for tying up loose ends, Chekhov in *The Three Sisters* instead portrays an unraveling of such slight fabric as has been woven in the first three acts.

Tusenbach and Irina's marriage is not to be. We learn, although Irina does not, that Tusenbach has a rival: the foolish Solyony contests his right to marry Irina, and has challenged him to a duel; before the act is over Tusenbach will be dead. Therefore, ironically, it is Tusenbach's which will be the truest leave-taking in the play.

IRINA: Our town will be empty now.

TUSENBACH: Dear, I'll be back directly.

IRINA: Where are you going?

TUSENBACH: I must go into the town, and then—to see my comrades off.

IRINA: That's not true—Nikolai, why are you so absent-minded today? (*a pause*) What happened yesterday near the theatre?

TUSENBACH: (*impatiently*) I'll be here in an hour and with you again (*kisses her hands*). My beautiful one—(*looks into her face*) For five years now I have loved you and still I can't get used to it, and you seem to me more and more lovely. What wonderful, exquisite hair! What eyes! I shall carry you off tomorrow, we will

work, we will be rich, my dreams will come true. You shall be happy. There is only one thing, one thing: you don't love me!

IRINA: That's not in my power! I'll be your wife and be faithful and obedient, but there is no love, I can't help it. (*weeps*) I've never been in love in my life! Oh, I have so dreamed of love, I've been dreaming of it for years, day and night, but my soul is like a wonderful piano of which the key has been lost. (*a pause*) You look uneasy.

TUSENBACH: I have not slept all night. There has never been anything in my life so dreadful that it could frighten me, and only that lost key frets at my heart and won't let me sleep—Say something to me—(*a pause*) Say something to me—

IRINA: What ? What am I to say to you? What??

TUSENBACH: Anything.

IRINA: There, there! (*a pause*)

TUSENBACH: What trifles, what little things suddenly *a propos* of nothing acquire importance in life! One laughs at them as before, thinks them as nonsense, but still one goes on and feels that one has not the power to stop. Don't let us talk about it! I am happy. I feel as though I were seeing these pines, these maples, these birch trees for the first time in my life, and they all seem to be looking at me with curiosity and waiting. What beautiful trees, and, really, how beautiful life ought to be under them! (*a shout offstage of "Halloo!" calling him to the forest and his duel*) I must be off; it's time—See, that tree is dead, but it waves in the wind with the others. And so it seems to me that if I die I shall still have part in life, one way or another. Goodbye my darling—(*kisses her hands*) Those papers of yours you gave me are lying under the calendar on my table.

IRINA: I am coming with you.

TUSENBACH: (*in alarm*) No, no! (*goes off quickly, stops*) Irina!

IRINA: What is it?

TUSENBACH: (*not knowing what to say*) I didn't have any coffee this morning. Ask them to make me some (*goes out quickly*).

This, one of the saddest scenes imaginable, achieves its almost monumental pathos by what is *not* said rather than by what is. Tusenbach's groping for direction, for confirmation, for love and meaning in his life, is epitomized by his desperate stammer "Say something to me—Say something to me—" and by Irina's agonized inability to respond except in kind. Unable to achieve the rapport he so desires, he speaks of trees, of papers, and finally of morning coffee. The life-and-death confrontation that looms but minutes away remains an unspoken terror, against which Tusenbach can only utter his mirthless, absurdly noble cry of "I am happy!"

Eloquence, which is a characteristic of rhetorical playwrights since Aeschylus, is equally characteristic of the best work of the realists. However, the eloquence of realism, as Chekhov magnificently demonstrates, consists in details of dialogue and action rather than in cogent declamation. Tusenbach's "I didn't have any coffee this morning" stands as one of the great exit lines in theatre, but the key to its greatness lies in its profound understatement. It is a line out of context, out of the morning office break; juxtaposed against the passion of the dramatized moment, however, it reveals a depth of feeling and layers of character quite beyond the reach of direct verbalization.

Chekhov's poetry is of actions as well as words, and its rhythm is fashioned out of the silences, self-deceptions, petty boasts, unguarded responses, and empty promises of his characters. Even their attempts at lyricism—as when Tusenbach tries to liken himself to a dead tree—are touching more for their clumsiness than for their majesty. It is human fallibility—in expression as well as in act—that is the basic stuff of realism.

The farewell between Masha and Vershinin is the centerpiece of the final act, and it affords us the only fully explicit information we are to have concerning the depth of passion to which this relationship has led. But this too is to be a scene without rhetoric, for the pair are vouchsafed neither the time nor the privacy to voice their feelings. Vershinin's speeches are mere time-filling commonplaces addressed to Olga while he waits for Masha to arrive, and Masha's words, when they finally come out, are a mad reiteration of the Pushkin poem she recited in the play's beginning, chanted to ward off the sympathy of her sister and hus-band—the latter of whom absurdly tries to distract her from her misery by donning false whiskers. All Masha and Vershinin can exchange is a kiss, but that kiss outweighs volumes of poetry and rational explanation. Here is the scene:

VERSHININ: (*to Olga*) Everything comes to an end. Here we are parting (*looks at his watch*). . . . Well—Thank you for everything—Forgive me if anything was amiss—I have talked a great deal: forgive me for that too—don't remember evil against me.

OLGA: (*wipes her eyes*) Why doesn't Masha come?

VERSHININ: What else am I to say to you at parting? What am I to theorize about—(*laughs*) Life is hard. It seems to many of us blank and hopeless; but yet we must admit that it goes on getting clearer and easier, and it looks as though the time were not far off when it will be full of happiness. (*looks at his watch*) It's time for me to go! In old days men were absorbed in wars, filling all their existence with marches, raids, victories, but now all that is a thing of the past, leaving behind it a great void which there is so far nothing to fill: humanity is searching for it passionately, and of course will find it. Ah, if only it could be quickly! (*pause*) If, don't you know, industry were united with culture and culture with industry—(*looks at his watch*) But, I say, it's time for me to go—

OLGA: Here she comes!

(*Masha comes in*)

VERSHININ: I have come to say goodbye—

MASHA: (*looking into his face*) Goodbye—(*a prolonged kiss*)

OLGA: (*who has moved away to leave them free*) Come, come—

(*Masha sobs violently*)

VERSHININ: Write to me—Don't forget me! Let me go!—Time is up! Olga, take her, I must—go—I am late. (*Much moved, he kisses Olga's hands, then again embraces Masha and quickly goes off*)

OLGA: Come, Masha! Leave off, darling—

(*Enter Kulygin, Masha's husband*)

KULYGIN: (*embarrassed*) Never mind, let her cry—

let her— My good Masha, My dear Masha!— You are my wife, and I am happy, anyway—I don't complain; I don't say a word of blame— Here, Olga is my witness—we'll begin the old life again, and I won't say one word, not a hint—

MASHA: (*restraining her sobs*) By the sea-strand, an oak-tree green—Upon that oak a chain of gold— Upon that oak a chain of gold—I am going mad—By the sea strand—an oak tree green—

OLGA: Calm yourself, Masha—Calm yourself— Give her some water.

MASHA: I am not crying now—

KULYGIN: She is not crying now—she is good— (*the dim sound of a faraway shot*)

MASHA: By the sea strand an oak tree green, upon that oak a chain of gold—the cat is green—the oak is green—I am mixing it up now—(*drinks water*) My life is a failure. I want nothing now. —I shall be calm directly— It doesn't matter— what does "strand" mean? Why do these words haunt me? My thoughts are in a tangle. (*enter Irina*)

OLGA: Calm yourself, Masha. Come, that's a good girl. Let us go indoors.

MASHA: (*angrily*) I am not going in. Let me alone! (*sobs, but at once checks herself*) I don't go into that house now and I won't.

IRINA: Let us sit together, even if we don't say anything. I am going away tomorrow, you know— (*a pause*)

KULYGIN: I took a false beard and moustache from a boy in the third grade yesterday, just look. (*puts on the beard and moustache*) I look like the German teacher. (*laughs*) Don't I? Funny creatures, those boys.

MASHA: You really do look like the German teacher.

OLGA: (*laughs*) Yes!

(*Masha weeps*)

As elsewhere in this playscript—and in realistic playscripts in general—this scene comes fully alive only insofar as the reader can imagine it being acted. The verbal simplicity of Vershinin and Masha's goodbyes, the inanity of Vershinin's theorizing while looking at his watch, the pathetic attempts of Kulygin to soothe his wife, and Masha's whirlwind of anger and tears: these are the bare outlines of complex reactions that can be captured only through the artistry of actors who are conversant with the psychological intricacies of behavior and are moreover sufficiently liberated to delve into those intricacies on a stage. In the hands of a superb acting ensemble—which is, of course, what Stanislavski created for the production of Chekhov's plays—the pattern of details and behaviors in *The Three Sisters* becomes resoundingly meaningful; the inappropriateness of individual words and acts are seen to be integral to a larger and more harmonious vision, in which the portrayal of human fallibility is balanced by a portrayal of human compassion, strength, and endurance.

Masha will not enter the house because Natasha has taken it over; Natasha has also installed her lover, Protopopov, in the residence, and driven even Andrei out of doors, where he walks her latest child (almost certainly not his) in a perambulator. And the distant shot indicated in the script—a shot

I remember when Stanislavski as Vershinin came to say goodbye to Masha in *The Three Sisters*. They had tried not to show their love for each other, but the band was playing, and they looked at each other, and then they grabbed each other. I'll never forget that grabbing. I remember literally holding onto the seat. The simple reality of that goodbye, of the two people holding on as if they wouldn't let go, of both literally clinging to each other, will stay with me always.

Lee Strasberg

which is unacknowledged on stage and perhaps not even noticed by the audience—will deprive Irina of her fiance and her only apparent hope for a worthwhile and independent future. As the fourth act draws to a close, a military band is playing in the distance: the garrison is marching away. The doctor, who will leave tomorrow, has returned to bring the news of Tusenbach's demise. He now sits on a garden bench singing "Ta ra ra boom de-ay." And the sisters, arms around each other, speak their final thoughts:

MASHA: Oh, listen to that band! They are going away from us; one has gone altogether, gone forever. We are left alone to begin our life over again— We've got to live—we've got to live—

IRINA: A time will come when everyone will know what all this is for, why there is this misery; there will be no mysteries and, meanwhile, we have got to live—we have got to work, only to work! Tomorrow I shall go alone; I shall teach in the school, and I will give all my life to those to whom it may be of use. Now it's autumn; soon winter will come and cover us with snow, and I will work, I will work.

OLGA: (*embraces both of her sisters*) The music is so gay, so confident, and one longs for life! Oh my god! Time will pass, and we shall go away forever, and we shall be forgotten, our faces will be forgotten, our voices, and how many there were of us; but our sufferings will pass into joy for those who live after us, happiness and peace will be established upon earth, and they will remember kindly and bless those who have lived before. Oh, dear sisters, our life is not ended yet. We shall live! The music is so gay, so joyful, and it seems as though a little more and we shall know what we are living for, why we are suffering— If we only knew—if we only knew!

DOCTOR: (*humming softly*) Tarara-boom-de-ay. (*reads his paper*) It doesn't matter, it doesn't matter.

OLGA: If we only knew, if we only knew!

Curtain

Here, in the last moments of the play, we find a lyricism of longings that epitomizes Chekhovian theatrical poetry. Counterpointed by the music of the departing regiment and the humming of the doctor as he turns the pages of his newspaper, the sisters' plaints echo their opening monologues in the first act. Thus the dramatist completes a frame around the action of the play that focuses the blended stories and characters and at the same time provides a memorable testament of human courage in adversity.

We have seen how the realists tend to write of man's ignorance and failure, and of human confusion in a complicated world and human isolation in an uncaring cosmos. But that perspective would be theatrically unsatisfying were it not for the complementary realist vision of man as a creature possessed of a giant will for struggle, survival, and even triumph. The sisters may not get to Moscow, may never love the men they marry or marry the men they love, but one feels certain that they will persist and endure—that they will continue to knock at the door of their desired destiny even if they never get in. Chekhov provides his characters with opportunities; these may be squandered or exploited, but they will never be taken away absolutely. This approach, too, is fundamental to realism, for what could be more true to life than a portrayal of the continual, unending, passionately pursued human quest for a better love and a better world?

The characters of the realists, like people in real life, are neither performers nor object lessons. Kulygin is perhaps as ridiculous in his false moustache and beard as Monsieur Jourdain, in *The Bourgeois Gentleman*, is in his Turkish gown and turban, but Kulygin is one of us in a way that Jourdain never could be, and in the end we cannot but be moved by the kind intentions beneath his clumsy ministrations. The sisters, by turns foolish and noble, innocent and worldly-wise, shallow and profound, leave us with an admixture of feelings; like members of our own families they are continually shifting figures in our consciousness, impossible to categorize, easy to scorn, easier to forgive. The love-making in *The Three Sisters* is as awkward as our own and the speech-making as inarticulate, but that never prevents our appreciation of the

The three sisters, alone at the end, hold onto each other as they listen to the sounds of the departing army. Angela Paton (Olga), Kitty Winn, and Miss Michael Learned in the American Conservatory Theatre production.

> In his plays, Chekhov is master of both outer and inner truth. There is no one who can use lifeless properties, scenery and lighting effects like he does—to make them live. He has shown us the life of things and sounds and lighting which, in the theatre as in life, exert a profound influence on the human soul. Twilight, sunrise and sunset, thunderstorm and rain, the songs of awakening birds, the clatter of horses' hoofs and the rumble of a carriage, the striking of a clock, the stridulation of a cricket, the pealing of bells—Chekhov uses all these not for stage effect, but for the purpose of showing us man's soul. Where is the line dividing us and our feelings from the world of light, sound and things which surround us and on which human psychology so depends?
>
> Konstantin Stanislavski

characters; rather it provokes our shared sympathy. If Tusenbach, in asking for coffee as he goes off to his death, is less self-possessed than Mercutio crying "Ask for me tomorrow and you shall find me a grave man," we understand him better and, through him, we understand the forces that underlie human reticence immeasurably better.

Realistic acting is the medium of realist drama, and it took the staging breakthroughs achieved by Stanislavski and his fellows to accommodate the action of realistic plays such as *The Three Sisters*. The "prolonged kiss" between Masha and Vershinin is representative of a revolution in theatrical performance as great as almost any in the theatre's history, for a kiss is a *biological* act that implies emotional consequences unrealizable through words alone. A prolonged kiss would have been impossible in the Greek or Elizabethan theatre, since it would only call attention to the theatrical conventions separating the play from normal life (that is, the Greek masks, and the Elizabethan boy actors in the female roles), and in the Royal Theatre such a kiss, like any other robust physical action, was deemed too rude for the stage. Even in the Romantic period kissing was idealized: one showed one's affection in that era by reciting great torrents of verse while displaying physical self-denial. But because the realistic theatre demands the actions of life, lovers in realistic theatre must be seen to kiss —and, in many later works, to do much more than that. Moreover, the sheer physiological reality of Masha's and Vershinin's kiss—meaning, of course, the physiological reality of the actors' kiss—is integral to the play's climax in a way that becomes clear when one sees the play performed.

Scenery, costumes, and particularly props and music also figure prominently in the theatrical texture of Chekhovian realism. Vershinin looks at his watch three times during his final conversation with Olga; could we even imagine Prometheus looking at his watch (assuming the Greeks had such a thing as a watch), or Romeo? The doctor's newspaper, the silver samovar, the faded window curtains Kulygin complains about, Irina's white dress, Masha's hat and her book of poetry, Natasha's green sash, a broken clock, a child's top, a marching band, the offstage sound of masquers playing: these are the mundane elements, artfully selected, from which Chekhov has fashioned a symphony of meaning.

Participation in the realistic theatre is akin to participation in life itself; the realistic theatre makes inroads into our biological and psychological cognition and leaves us *personally* moved and shaken. The characters' situations resonate with the strains of our own; Irina's wistfulness, Masha's desolation, Olga's determination, Tusenbach's compulsiveness, Kulygin's jovial desperation: these are ours too, and their staged re-enactments affect us in ways we find difficult to express. We leave the theatre after *The Three Sisters* as we would leave a party given by the sisters themselves—

filled with the contradictory and ambivalent feelings of warmth and sadness, criticism and kindly thoughts, annoyances and admirations, understandings and a wealth of further questions.

The purest form of realism allows no firm conclusions. *The Three Sisters* has given rise to a whole spectrum of evaluations and interpretations, from outright condemnation of the sisters and their social milieu to high praise for their fortitude and gentility. Certainly if they were *our* sisters, there is much we would find to criticize in them, much to admire. The genius of the play resides in the complexity and individuality of the characters and the intricacy of the pattern which links them in a social network. The playwright has given us as much detail as we are likely to observe in reality itself. He has also given us *people*: to laugh at, to gossip about, to analyze, and to sympathize with. He has presented us with all this evidence and encouraged us to draw our own conclusions. And when it all comes together on a stage, theatrical magic as potent as any in the past can work its spell.

A scene from Samuel Beckett's Endgame (1957), *in which Nagg and Nell, an aged couple, presumably live in ashcans. These characters became instant symbols of the Theatre of the Absurd and well illustrate post–World War II attempts to create a stylized, non-realistic theatre.*

THE STYLIZED THEATRE

Realism was the first new movement to make itself strongly felt in the modern theatre, but it was not the only one. Indeed, a counterforce, equally powerful, was to follow almost on its heels.

This counterforce was first manifest in the movement known as Symbolism. From that beginning it evolved and expanded into what we shall call "Stylized Theatre," which swept across Europe and quickly began contesting the advances of realism virtually step by step.

THE SYMBOLIST REBELLION

The Symbolist movement began in Paris during the 1880s as a joint venture of artists, playwrights, essayists, critics, sculptors, and poets. Symbolism had one goal: to crush what its adherents deemed to be a spiritually bankrupt realism, and to replace it with traditional aesthetic values: poetry, imagery, novelty, fantasy, extravagance, profundity, audacity, charm, and superhuman magnitude. United in their hatred for literal detail and for all that they considered mun-

dane or ordinary, the Symbolists demanded abstraction, enlargement, and innovation; the Symbolist spirit soared in poetic encapsulations, outsized dramatic presences, fantastical visual effects, shocking structural departures, and grandiloquent speech. Purity of vision, rather than accuracy of observation, was the Symbolists' aim, and self-conscious creative innovation was to be their primary accomplishment.

The first Symbolist theatre, founded in 1890 by Parisian poet Paul Fort, was intended as a direct attack on the naturalistic Théâtre Libre of André Antoine, founded three years earlier. Fort's theatre, the Théâtre d'Art, was proposed as "a theatre for Symbolist poets only, where every production would cause a battle." In some ways Antoine's and Fort's theatres had much in common: both were amateur, both gained considerable notoriety, each served as a center for a "school" of artistic ideology that attracted as much attention and controversy as any of its theatrical offerings.

But the two theatres were openly, deliberately, at war. While Antoine was presenting premieres of naturalistic and realistic dramas by Strindberg, Zola, and Ibsen, Fort presented the staged poems of Rimbaud, Verlaine, Shelley, Milton, Marlowe, Maeterlinck,

At the first performance of [Ibsen's realistic play] *Ghosts* I could not escape from an illusion unaccountable to me at the time. All the characters seemed to be less than life-size; the stage, though it was but the little Royalty stage, seemed larger than I had ever seen it. Little whimpering puppets moved here and there in the middle of that great abyss. Why did they not speak out with louder voices or move with freer gestures? What was it that weighed upon their souls perpetually? Certainly they were all in prison, and yet there was no prison. In India there are villages so obedient that all the jailer has to do is draw a circle upon the ground with his staff, and to tell his thief to stand there so many hours; but what law had these people broken that they had to wander round that narrow circle all their lives? . . .

What is there left for us . . . but . . . to rediscover an art of the theatre that shall be joyful, fantastic, extravagant, whimsical, beautiful, resonant, and altogether reckless?

William Butler Yeats

and Edgar Allen Poe. Whereas Antoine would go to great lengths to create realistic scenery for his plays (for example, he procured sides of real beef and hung them on real meathooks for his presentation of *The Butchers*), Fort would prevail upon leading impressionist easel painters, including Pierre Bonnard, Maurice Denis, and Odilon Redon, to dress his stylized stage. Silver angels, translucent veils, and sheets of crumpled wrapping paper were among the decors that backed the Symbolist works at the Théâtre d'Art.

Fort's theatre created an immediate sensation in Paris. With the stunning success, in 1890, of *The Intruder*, a mysterious and poetic fantasy by the Belgian Symbolist Maurice Maeterlinck, the anti-realist movement was fully engaged and, as Fort recalled in his memoirs, "the cries and applause of the students, poets, and artists overwhelmed the huge disapproval of the bourgeoisie."

The movement spread quickly as authors and designers alike awakened to the possibilities of a theatre wholly freed from the constraints of verisimilitude. Realism, more and more people concluded, would never raise the commonplace to the level of art; it would only drag art down into the muck of the mundane. It ran counter to all that the theatre had stood for in the past; it throttled the potential of artistic creativity. Soon such naturalistic and realistic

authors as Ibsen, Strindberg, Hauptmann, and Shaw came under the Symbolist influence and abandoned their social preoccupations and environmental exactitude to seek new languages and more universal themes. As an added element, at about this time the researches of Sigmund Freud were becoming generally known, and his theories concerning dream images and the worlds of the Unconscious provided new source material for the stage.

By the turn of the century, the counterforce of theatrical stylization set in motion by the Symbolists was established on all fronts; indeed, the half-decade on either side of 1900 represents one of the richest periods of experimentation in the history of dramatic writing. Out of that decade came Gerhart Hauptmann's archetypal fairy tale *The Sunken Bell* (Germany, 1896), Alfred Jarry's outrageously cartoonish and scatalogical *Ubu Roi* (France, 1898), Henrik Ibsen's haunting ode to individualism *When We Dead Awaken* (Norway, 1899), August Strindberg's metaphoric and imagistic *The Dream Play* (Sweden, 1902), William Butler Yeats' evocative poetic fable *Cathleen ni Houlihan* (Ireland, 1903), George Bernard Shaw's philosophical allegory *Man and Superman* (England, 1903), and James Barrie's whimsical, buoyant fantasy *Peter Pan* (England, 1904). Almost every dramatic innovation that has followed since that time was at least

Barrie's Peter Pan *features the famous flying young man, Peter, who symbolizes eternal youth. The role is always played by a female actress. The play is most widely known today through a musical adaptation, here staged on Broadway in a 1979 revival starring Sandy Duncan as Peter.*

in part prefigured by one or more of these seminal works for the non-realist theatre.

The realist-vs.-Symbolist confrontation affected every aspect of theatre production. Symbolist-inspired directors and designers, side by side with the playwrights, were drastically altering the arts of staging and decor to accommodate the new dramaturgies that surged into the theatre. Realist directors like Antoine and Stanislavski suddenly found themselves challenged by scores of adversaries and renegades: a school of Symbolist and poetic directors rose in France, and a former disciple of Stanislavski, the

Shaw's Man and Superman *includes a dream sequence in which all the "modern" characters play out their inner lives in a dream-like fantasy set in Renaissance Spain. The dream sequence is often performed by itself, as a one-act play entitled "Don Juan in Hell." Here it is part of the full production as staged by the American Conservatory Theatre in 1976.*

"Constructivist" Vlesevod Meyerhold, broke with the Russian master to create a non-realist "bio-mechanical" style of acting and directing in sharp contrast to that established at the Moscow Art Theatre. With the advent of electrical stage lighting, opportunities for stylizing were vastly expanded: the new technology enabled the modern director to create vivid stage effects, starkly unrealistic in appearance, through the judicious use of spotlighting, shadowing, and shading. Technology, plus trends in post-Impressionist art that were well established in Europe by 1900, led to scenery and costume designs that departed radically from realism. Exoticism, fantasy, sheer sensual delight, symbolic meaning, and aesthetic purity became the prime objectives of designers who joined the anti-realist rebellion.

> **R**ealism is a vulgar means of expression bestowed upon the blind. Thus we have the clear-sighted singing: 'Beauty is Truth, Truth Beauty—that is all ye know on earth, and all ye need to know.' The blind are heard croaking: 'Beauty is Realism, Realism Beauty—that is all I know on earth, and all I care to know—don't 'ya know!' The difference is all a matter of love. He who loves the earth sees beauty everywhere: he is a god transforming by knowledge the incomplete into the complete. He can heal the lame and the sick, can blow courage into the weary, and he can even learn how to make the blind see. The power has always been possessed by the artist, who, in my opinion, rules the earth. . . .
>
> The limited section of playgoers who love beauty and detest Realism is a small minority of about six million souls. They are scattered here and there over the earth. They seldom, if ever, go to the modern theatre. That is why I love them, and intend to unite them.
>
> Gordon Craig

In some respects the Symbolist aim succeeded perhaps beyond the dreams of its originators. Paul Fort's art theatre, although it lasted but a year, now has spiritual descendants in every city in the Western world where theatre is performed.

THE ERA OF "ISMS"

But the Symbolist movement itself was short-lived. It was, after all, essentially a *negative* movement: its adherents were united chiefly by what they opposed. In art and aesthetics, negative movements cannot last long, for art is, finally, a constructive process, not a destructive one. Within months of the Symbolist advances, therefore, Symbolism *as a movement* was deserted by founders and followers alike. Where did they go? Off to found newer movements: Futurism, Dadaism, Idealism, Aestheticism, Impressionism, Expressionism, Constructivism, Esotericism, Surrealism, Formalism, Theatricalism; and perhaps a hundred other isms now lost to time.

The first third of this century, indeed, was an era of theatrical isms, an era rich with continued experimentation by movements self-consciously seeking to redefine theatrical art. "Ism" theatres sprang up like mushrooms, each with its own fully articulated credo and manifesto, each promising a better art—if not, indeed, a better world. It was a vibrant era for the theatre, for out of this welter of isms the aesthetics of dramatic art took on a new social and political significance in the cultural capitals of Europe and America: a successful play was not merely a play, it signified a *cause*; and behind that cause was a body of zealous supporters and adherents who shared a deep aesthetic commitment.

Nothing quite like that ism spirit exists today, for we have lost the social involvement that can turn an aesthetic movement into a profound collective belief. But the experiments and discoveries of those early days of this century, and the non-realist spirit of Symbolism itself, survive and flourish under a variety of formats: Ritual Theatre, Poetic Theatre, Holy Theatre, Theatre of Cruelty, Existentialist Theatre, Art Theatre, Avant-garde Theatre, Theatre of the Absurd, and Theatre of Alienation. These present-day groupings, unlike the isms, are critic-defined rather than artist-defined; indeed, most theatre artists today reject any "grouping" nomenclature whatever. However, the formats these groupings pursue can be shown to reflect the general approach to structure, style, and experimentation that began with the Symbolists in the late nineteenth century.

MODERN STYLIZED THEATRE

We have chosen the rather loose term "Stylized Theatre" to embrace the entire spectrum of non-realistic modern theatre, which, although disparate in its individual manifestations, exhibits a universal insistence on *consciously stylizing reality* into larger-than-life theatrical experience. Any theatre mode in any era, of course, has its distinctive style, but in past eras that style was always largely *imposed* by current convention and technological necessity. The modern dramatist, by contrast, has consciously *selected and created* styles to satisfy his aesthetic theories, his social principles, or simply his desire for novelty and innovation.

Modern Stylized Theatre attempts to create new theatrical formats, not merely to enhance the portrayal of human existence but also to disclose fundamental patterns underlying that existence: patterns of perception, patterns of association, patterns of personal and environmental interaction.

The styles employed by this modern theatre come from anywhere and everywhere: from the past, from exotic cultures, and from present and futuristic technologies. The modern theatre artist has an unprecedented reservoir of sources to draw upon, and he is generally unconstrained in their application by political edict, religious prohibition, or mandated artistic tradition. The modern Stylized Theatre is undoubtedly the freest in history: neither the dramatist, the director, the actor, nor the designer is limited in his efforts save by the universal factors of physical resources and his own imagination. Virtually anything may be put upon a stage, and in the twentieth century it seems that virtually everything has been.

The Stylized Theatre does not altogether dispense with reality, but it wields it in often unexpected ways and freely enhances it with symbol and metaphor, striving to elucidate by parable and allegory, to deconstruct and reconstruct by language and scenery and lighting. Further, it makes explicit use of the theatre's very theatricality, frequently reminding its audience, directly or indirectly, that they are watching a performance, not an episode in somebody's daily life. Stylization inevitably reaches for universality. It tends to treat problems of psychology as problems of philosophy, and problems in human relations as problems of the human condition. Stylization reaches for patterns, not particulars; it explores abstractions and aims for sharp thematic focus and bold intellectual impact.

In the Stylized Theatre, characters usually represent more than individual persons or personality types. Like the medieval allegories, modern stylized

---

If we remember that the movement of the actor, and the graduation and the color of the lighting, are the two elements that distinguish the stage picture from an easel painting, we may not find it difficult to create an art of the stage ranking as a true fine art. Mr. Gordon Craig has done wonderful things with the lighting, but he is not greatly interested in the actor, and his streams of colored direct light, beautiful as they are, will always seem, apart from certain exceptional moments, a new externality. We should rather desire, for all but exceptional moments, an even, shadowless light, like that of noon, and it may be that a light reflected out of mirrors will give us what we need.

M. Appia and M. Fortuny are making experiments in the staging of Wagner for a private theatre in Paris, but I cannot understand what M. Appia is doing, from the little I have seen of his writing, excepting that the floor of the stage will be uneven like the ground, and that at moments the lights and shadows of green boughs will fall over the player that the stage may show a man wandering through a wood, and not a wood with a man in the middle of it. One agrees with all the destructive part of his criticism, but it looks as if he himself is seeking, not convention, but a more perfect realism. I cannot persuade myself that the movement of life is flowing that way, for life moves by a throbbing as of a pulse, by reaction and action. The hour of convention and decoration and ceremony is coming again.

William Butler Yeats

plays often involve characters who represent forces of nature, moral positions, human instincts, and the like—entities such as death, fate, idealism, the life force, the earth mother, the tyrant father, and the prodigal son. And the conflicts associated with these forces, unlike the conflicts of realism, are not responsive to any human agency: they are, more often than not, represented as permanent discords inherent in the human condition. The Stylized Theatre resonates with tension and human frustration in the face of irreconcilable demands.

But that is not to say that the Stylized Theatre is necessarily grim: quite to the contrary, it often uses whimsy and mordant wit as its dominant mode. Although the themes of the Stylized Theatre are anxious ones—for example, the alienation of man, the futility of communication, the loss of innocence, the intransigence of despair—it is not on the whole a theatre of pessimism or of nihilistic outrage. Indeed, the glory of the Stylized Theatre is that, at its best, it refuses to be swamped by its themes; it transcends frustration; it is the victory of poetry over alienation, comedy over non-communication, and artistry over despair. The Stylized Theatre aims at lifting its audience, not saddling them; and if it proffers no solutions to life's inevitable discords, it can provide considerable lucidity concerning the totality of the human adventure.

EARLY STYLIZATIONS

The diversity of stylized theatrical works precludes further generalization about their shared characteristics, but three brief examples from plays written before the close of World War II will serve to establish the main lines of the earlier modern stylized plays.

The Hairy Ape

Of all the isms, Expressionism is the one that has given rise to the most significant body of modern theatre, probably because of its broad definition and its seeming alliance with Expressionism in the visual arts. The theatrical Expressionism which was much in vogue in Germany during the first decades of the century (particularly in the 1920s) featured shocking and gutty dialogue, boldly exaggerated scenery, piercing sounds, bright lights, an abundance of primary colors, a not very subtle use of symbols, and a structure of short, stark, jabbing scenes that built to a powerful (and usually deafening) climax.

America's first major playwright, Eugene O'Neill, came under the influence of the Expressionists after earlier ventures into naturalism, and in the 1920s O'Neill wrote a series of explosive plays concerning human nature in an industrial landscape. *The Hairy Ape*, produced in 1921, is almost a textbook case of Expressionist writing. Although this play seems clumsy, transparent, and naively ineffective today, it well illustrates the extreme stylization popular with "ism" writers. It is a one-act play featuring eight scenes. Its workingman–hero Yank meets and is rebuffed by the genteel daughter of a captain of industry. Enraged, Yank becomes violent and eventually crazed; he dies at play's end in the monkey cage of a zoo. Scene Three illustrates the tenor of the writing:

> *The stokehole. In the rear, the dimly outlined bulks of the furnaces and boilers. High overhead one hanging electric bulb sheds just enough light through the murky air laden with coal dust to pile up masses of shadows everywhere. A line of men, stripped to the waist, is before the furnace doors. They bend over, looking neither to right nor left, handling their shovels as if they were part of their bodies, with a strange, awkward, swinging rhythm. They use the shovels to throw open the furnace doors. Then from these fiery round holes in the black a flood of terrific light and heat pours full upon the men who are outlined in silhouette in the crouching, inhuman attitudes of chained gorillas. The men shovel with a rhythmic motion, swinging as on a pivot from the coal which lies in heaps on the floor behind to hurl it into the flaming mouths before them. There is a tumult of noise—the brazen clang of the furnace doors as they are flung open or slammed shut, the grating, teeth-gritting grind of steel against steel, of crunching coal. This clash of sounds stuns one's ears with its rending dissonance. But there is order in it, rhythm, a mechanical regulated recurrence, a tempo. And rising above all, making the air hum with the quiver of liberated energy, the roar of leaping flames in the furnaces, the monotonous throbbing beat of the engines.*
>
> *As the curtain rises, the furnace doors are*

Eugene O'Neill's The Hairy Ape *in its original New York production by the Provincetown Playhouse. The setting is of the opening of Scene Three.*

shut. *The men are taking a breathing spell. One or two are arranging the coal behind them, pulling it into more accessible heaps. The others can be dimly made out leaning on their shovels in relaxed attitudes of exhaustion.*

PADDY: (*from somewhere in the line—plaintively*) Yerra, will this divil's own watch nivir end? Me back is broke. I'm destroyed entirely.

YANK: (*from the center of the line—with exuberant scorn*) Aw, yuh make me sick! Lie down and croak, why don't yuh? Always beefin', dat's you! Say, dis is a cinch! Dis was made for me! It's my meat, get me! (*A whistle is blown—a thin, shrill note from somewhere overhead in the darkness.* YANK *curses without resentment.*) Dere's de damn engineer crackin' de whip. He tinks we're loafin'.

PADDY: (*vindictively*) God stiffen him!

YANK: (*in an exultant tone of command*) Come on, youse guys! Git into de game! She's gettin' hungry! Pile some grub in her. Trow it into her belly! Come on now, all of youse! Open her up! (*At this last all the men, who have followed his movements of getting into position, throw open their furnace doors with a deafening clang. The fiery light floods over their shoulders as they bend round for the coal. Rivulets of sooty sweat have traced maps on their backs. The enlarged muscles form bunches of high light and shadow.*)

YANK: (*chanting a count as he shovels without seeming effort*) One—two—tree— (*His voice rising exultantly in the joy of battle*) Dat's de stuff! Let her have it! All togedder now! Sling it into her! Let her ride! Shoot de piece now! Call de toin on her! Drive her into it! Feel her move. Watch her smoke! Speed, dat's her middle name! Give her coal, youse guys! Coal, dat's her booze! Drink it up, baby! Let's see yuh sprint! Dig in and gain a lap! Dere she go-o-es.

In the scene [in *The Hairy Ape*] where the bell rings for the stokers to go on duty, you remember that they all stand up, come to attention, then go out in a lockstep file. Some people think even that is an actual custom aboard ship! But it is only symbolic of the regimentation of men who are the slaves of machinery. In a larger sense, it applies to all of us, because we all are more or less the slaves of convention, or of discipline, or of a rigid formula of some sort.

The whole play is expressionistic. The coal shoveling in the furnace room, for instance. Stokers do not really shovel coal that way. But it is done in the play in order to contribute to the rhythm. For rhythm is a powerful factor in making anything expressive. You can actually produce and control emotions by that means alone.

Eugene O'Neill

(*This last in the chanting formula of the galley gods at the six-day bike race. He slams his furnace door shut. The others do likewise with as much unison as their wearied bodies will permit. The effect is of one fiery eye after another being blotted out with a series of accompanying bangs*).

PADDY: (*groaning*) Me back is broke. I'm bate out— bate—(*There is a pause. Then the inexorable whistle sounds again from the dim regions above the electric light. There is a growl of cursing rage from all sides*).

YANK: (*shaking his fist upward—contemptuously*) Take it easy dere, you! Who d'yuh tink's runnin' dis game, me or you? When I git ready, we move. Not before! When I git ready, get me!

VOICES: (*approvingly*) That's the stuff!
Yank tal him, py golly!
Yank ain't affeerd.
Goot poy, Yank!
Give him hell!
Tell 'im 'e's a bloody swine!
Bloody slave-driver!

YANK: (*contemptuously*) He ain't got no noive. He's yellow, get me? All de engineers is yellow. Dey got streaks a mile wide. Aw, to hell wit him! Let's move, youse guys. We had a rest. Come on, she needs it! Give her pep! It ain't for him. Him and his whistle, dey don't belong. But we belong, see!

We gotter feed de baby! Come on! (*He turns and flings his furnace door open. They all follow his lead. At this instant the* SECOND *and* FOURTH ENGINEERS *enter from the darkness on the left with* MILDRED *between them. She starts, turns paler, her pose is crumbling, she shivers with fright in spite of the blazing heat, but forces herself to leave the* ENGINEERS *and take a few steps nearer the men. She is right behind* YANK. *All this happens quickly while the men have their backs turned*).

YANK: Come on, youse guys! (*He is turning to get coal when the whistle sounds again in a peremptory, irritating note. This drives* YANK *into a sudden fury. While the other men have turned full around and stopped dumfounded by the spectacle of* MILDRED *standing there in her white dress,* YANK *does not turn far enough to see her. Besides, his head is thrown back, he blinks upward through the murk trying to find the owner of the whistle, he brandishes his shovel murderously over his head in one hand, pounding on his chest, gorilla-like, with the other, shouting*) Toin off dat whistle! Come down outa dere, yuh yellow, brass-buttoned, Belfast bum, yuh! Come down and I'll knock yer brains out! Yuh lousy, stinkin', yellow mut of a Catholic-moiderin' bastard! Come down and I'll moider yuh! Pullin' dat whistle on me, huh? I'll show yuh! I'll crash yer skull in! I'll drive yer teet' down yer troat! I'll slam yer nose trou de back of yer head! I'll cut yer guts out for a nickel, yuh lousy boob, yuh dirty, crummy, muck-eatin' son of a—(*Suddenly he becomes conscious of all the other men staring at something directly behind his back. He whirls defensively with a snarling, murderous growl, crouching to spring, his lips drawn back over his teeth, his small eyes gleaming ferociously. He sees* MILDRED, *like a white apparition in the full light from the open furnace doors. He glares into her eyes, turned to stone. As for her, during his speech she has listened, paralyzed with horror, terror, her whole personality crushed, beaten in, collapsed, by the terrific impact of this unknown, abysmal brutality, naked and shameless. As she looks at his gorilla face, as his eyes bore into hers, she utters a low, choking cry and shrinks away from him, putting both hands up before her eyes to shut out the sight of his face, to protect her own. This startles* YANK *to a reaction. His mouth falls open, his eyes grow bewildered*).

MILDRED: (*about to faint—to the* ENGINEERS, *who now have her one by each arm—whimperingly*) Take me away! Oh, the filthy beast! (*She faints. They carry her quickly back, disappearing in the darkness at the left, rear. An iron door clangs shut. Rage and bewildered fury rush back on* YANK. *He feels himself insulted in some unknown fashion in the very heart of his pride. He roars*) God damn yuh! (*And hurls his shovel after them at the door which has just closed.*

It hits the steel bulkhead with a clang and falls clattering on the steel floor. From overhead the whistle sounds again in a long, angry, insistent command).

Curtain

O'Neill's forceful combination of visual and auditory effects lends this Expressionistic play a crude, almost superhuman power. The use of silhouette in the staging and lighting, the "masses of shadows everywhere," the "tumult of noise," the "monotonous throbbing heat of the engines," the "fiery light," the "rivulets of sooty sweat," the massed chanting and the movements in unison, the "peremptory, irritating note" of the "inexorable whistle," the shouting of curses and bold ejaculations, the animal imagery, and the "horror, terror . . . of . . . unknown, abysmal brutality, naked and shameless," are all typical of the extreme stylization of early twentieth-century Expressionism. The scene also demonstrates how O'Neill and his fellows in the American theatre spurned realism and Romanticism in their effort to arrive at a direct presentation of social ideology and cultural criticism.

Six Characters in Search of an Author

Six Characters in Search of an Author, first produced in 1921, expresses from its famous title onward a "Theatricalist" motif in which the theatre itself becomes part of the content of play production, not merely the vehicle. "All the world's a stage," said Shakespeare; but in this play Luigi Pirandello explores how the stage is also a world—and how the stage and the world, illusion and reality, relate to each other. In this still stunning play, a family of dramatic "characters"—a father, his stepdaughter, a mother, her children—appear as if by magic on the stage of a provincial theatre where a new play by Pirandello is being rehearsed: the "characters," claiming they have an unfinished play in them, beg the director to stage their lives in order that they may bring a satisfactory climax to their "drama." This fantasy treats the audience to continuingly shifting perceptions, for clearly a "play within the play" is involved, but which is the real play and which the real life? There are actors playing actors, actors playing "characters," and actors playing actors-playing-"characters"; there are also scenes when the actors-playing-"characters" are making fun of the actors playing actors-playing-"characters." It is no wonder that most audiences give up trying to untangle the planes of reality Pirandello proposes in this play; they are simply too difficult to comprehend except as a dazzle of suggestive theatricality.

Pirandello contrasts the passionate story of the "characters"—whose "drama" concerns a broken family, adultery, and a suggestion of incest—with the artifice of the stage and its simulations; in the course of this exposition Pirandello's performers discuss the theatricality of life, the life of theatricality, and the eternal confusions between appearance and reality:

THE FATHER: What I'm inviting you to do is to quit this foolish playing at art—this acting and pretending

The six characters from Liugi Pirandello's Six Characters in Search of an Author, *in William Ball's 1970 production at American Conservatory Theatre. The six characters come from a world of fantasy, but as this production photograph well illustrates, their dramatic intensity gives them the appearance of a superior reality.*

—and seriously answer my question: WHO ARE YOU?

THE DIRECTOR: (*amazed but irritated, to his actors*) What extraordinary impudence! This so-called character wants to know who I am?

THE FATHER: (*with calm dignity*) Signore, a character may always ask a "man" who he is. For a character has a true life, defined by his characteristics—he is always, at the least, a "somebody." But a man —now, don't take this personally— A man is generalized beyond identity—he's a nobody!

THE DIRECTOR: Ah, but me, me—I am the Director! The

Producer! You understand?

THE FATHER: Signore— Think of how you used to feel about yourself, long ago, all the illusions you used to have about the world, and about your place in it: those illusions were real for you then, they were *quite* real—But now, with hindsight, they prove to be nothing, they are nothing to you now but an embarrassment. Well, signore, that is what your present reality is today—just a set of illusions that you will discard tomorrow. Can't you feel it? I'm not speaking of the planks of this stage we stand on, I'm speaking of the very earth under our feet. It's sinking under you—by tomorrow, today's entire reality will have become just one more illusion. You see?

THE DIRECTOR: (*confused but amazed*) Well? So what? What does all that prove?

THE FATHER: Ah, nothing, signore. Only to show that if, beyond our illusions (*indicating the other characters*), we have no ultimate reality, so your reality as well—your reality that touches and feels and breathes today—will be unmasked tomorrow as nothing but yesterday's illusion!

These lines illustrate Pirandello's use of paradox, irony, and the theatre as metaphor to create a whimsical drama about human identity and human destiny. By contrasting the passion of his "characters" and the frequent frivolity of his "actors," Pirandello establishes a provocative juxtaposition of human behavior and its theatricalization—and the whole fantastical style is nothing but an exploitation of the theatrical format itself.

No Exit

No Exit is one of the most compelling short plays ever written. In this one-act fantasy written in 1944, Jean-Paul Sartre, the well-known French Existentialist philosopher, establishes a unique "Hell" which is a room without windows or mirrors. Into it come three persons, lately deceased, all condemned to this nether world because of their earthly sins. The three are brilliantly ill matched: Garcin, the sole man, tends toward homosexuality; so does Inez, one of the two women. Estelle, the final occupant of this bizarre inferno, tends toward heterosexual nymphomania: she pursues Garcin, Garcin pursues his fellow spirit Inez, and Inez pursues the beautiful Estelle in a triangle of misdirected affection which, one presumes, will continue maddeningly through all eternity. The infinite bleakness of this play's fantastical situation and the numbing futility of each character's aspirations provoke Garcin to beg for some good old-fashioned torture—but nothing quite so simple is forthcoming. Instead, he is forced to conclude: "Hell is other people." And the play ends with a curtain line that is characteristic of the modern stylized theatre:

GARCIN: Well, well, let's get on with it.

This line suggests that although the play concludes, the situation continues, eternally, behind the drawn curtain.

 No Exit is a classic dramatic statement of Existentialism, of which Sartre was this century's leading exponent. Remove the fantastical elements —that this is Hell and the characters are ghosts— and we have Sartre's vision of human interaction: every individual forever seeks affirmation and self-realization in the eyes of the Other. Each character in the play carries with him or her a baggage of guilt and expectation, each seeks from another some certification of final personal worth, and each is endlessly thwarted in this quest. We are all condemned to revolve around each other in frustratingly incomplete accord, suggests Sartre; we are all forced to reckon with the impossibility of finding meaning out of the unrelated events that constitute life.

 One can accept or reject Sartre's view—which is perhaps more than usually pessimistic for having been written during the Nazi Occupation of Sartre's Paris—but there can be little dispute for the assertion that his technique for dramatically stylizing it is quite brilliant. The fantastical Hell, an amusing "valet" who brings each character onto the stage, and the highly contrived assemblage of mismatched characters all serve to focus the intellectual argument precisely. Sartre's characters are philosophically representative rather than psychologically whole; there is no intention on Sartre's part to portray individual people with interesting idiosyncracies, and there is no feeling on our part that the characters have a personal life beyond what we see in the play. Biographical character analysis would be useless for an actor assigned to play one of these roles, and the interlock of psychological motivation, even in this sexually charged atmosphere, is deliberately ignored by the author. What Sartre presents instead is a general understanding of human affairs: a philosophy of interpersonal relations.

Although these three plays do not begin to demonstrate all the ways in which the theatre was explored stylistically in the first half of the twentieth century, they suggest, in combination, the broad range of newer stylization techniques that were developed, and they give a clue to the capacity of the theatre to express, through bold and direct means, ideas, images, conflicts, and philosophies germane to the times. Each of these plays is independently significant as dramatic literature; taken together, they show a theatre active in redefining itself and its collective possibilities.

POSTWAR STYLIZATIONS

There have been many attempts at theatrical stylization since the end of World War II, including Theatre of Cruelty, Theatre of Fact, and Theatre of Protest. But two approaches have dominated the postwar era: Theatre of the Absurd and Theatre of Alienation. Neither represents a certain school of thought or constitutes a movement in the ordinary sense; rather each label signifies a line of development adduced by critical observers to distinguish a major grouping of dramatic works. We shall examine these two forms in some detail.

EXISTENTIALISM, ABSURDISM, AND WORLD WAR II

Both Sartre's Existentialism and Camus's Philosophy of the Absurd were forged largely in the outrages of World War II, when both men were leading figures in the French Resistance movement. A hellish world that affords "no exit," and in which human activity is as meaningless as Sisyphus' torment, seems perfectly credible during such desperate times, times of national occupation and genocidal slaughter. After the war Jean-Paul Sartre, who was France's foremost exponent of Existentialism and one of that country's leading dramatists in the 1940s and 1950s, spoke eloquently of his first experience as playwright and director, which occurred when he was a prisoner of war:

> My first experience in the theatre was especially fortunate. When I was a prisoner in Germany in 1940, I wrote, staged and acted in a Christmas play which, while pulling the wool over the eyes of the German censor by means of simple symbols, was addressed to my fellow prisoners. This drama, biblical in appearance only, was written and put on by a prisoner, was acted by prisoners in scenery painted by prisoners; it was aimed exclusively at prisoners (so much so that I have

never since then permitted it to be staged or even printed) and it addressed them on the subject of their concerns as prisoners. No doubt it was neither a good play nor well acted: the work of an amateur, the critics would say, a product of special circumstances. Nevertheless, on this occasion, as I addressed my comrades across the footlights, speaking to them of their state as prisoners, when I suddenly saw them so remarkably silent and attentive, I realized what theatre ought to be—a great collective, religious phenomenon.

> To be sure, I was, in this case, favored by special circumstances; it does not happen every day that your public is drawn together by one great common interest, a great loss or a great hope. As a rule, an audience is made up of the most diverse elements: a big business man sits beside a traveling salesman or a professor, a man next to a woman, and each is subject to his own particular preoccupations. Yet this situation is a challenge to the playwright: he must create his public, he must fuse all the disparate elements in the auditorium into a single unity by awakening in the recesses of their spirits the things which all men of a given epoch and community care about.

Quoted in *Theatre Arts*

Theatre of the Absurd

The name Theatre of the Absurd applies to a grouping of plays that can be shown to share certain common structures and styles and to be tied together by a common philosophical thread: the theory of the absurd as formulated by French essayist and playwright Albert Camus. Camus likened man's condition to that of the mythological Corinthian king Sisyphus, who because of his cruelty was condemned forever to roll a stone up a hill in Hades only to have it roll down again upon nearing the top. Camus saw modern man as similarly engaged in an eternally futile task, the absurd task of searching for some meaning or purpose or order in human life. To Camus, the immutable irrationality of the universe is what makes this task absurd. On the one hand, human beings yearn for a

"lost" unity and lasting Truth; on the other hand, the world can only be seen as irrecoverably fragmented—chaotic, unsummable, permanently unorganized and permanently unorganizable.

The plays that constitute the Theatre of the Absurd are obsessed with the futility of all action and the pointlessness of all direction. These themes are developed theatrically through a deliberate and self-conscious flaunting of the "absurd"—in the sense of the ridiculous. Going beyond the use of symbols and the fantasy and poetry of other non-realists, the absurdists have distinguished themselves by creating clocks that clang incessantly, characters that eat pap in ashcans, corpses that grow by the minute, and personal interactions that are belligerently non-credible.

The Theatre of the Absurd can be said to include mid twentieth-century works by Jean Genet (French),

The Old Man addresses an imaginary audience sitting in real chairs—in The Chairs *by Eugène Ionesco, a classic short play of the absurdist theatre. From the Théâtre Gramont production, Paris.*

Eugene Ionesco (Rumanian), Friedrich Duerrenmatt (Swiss), Arthur Adamov (Russian), Slawomir Mrozek (Polish), Harold Pinter (English), Edward Albee (American), and Fernando Arrabal (Spanish); however, the unquestioned leader of the absurdist writers is Samuel Beckett (Irish). And although Paris is the center of this theatre—so much so that Ionesco, Adamov, Arrabal, and Beckett all write in French rather than in their native tongues—its influence is felt worldwide.

As I get it, The Theatre of the Absurd is an absorption-in-art of certain existentialist and post-existentialist philosophical concepts having to do, in the main, with man's attempts to make sense for himself out of his senseless position in a world which makes no sense—which makes no sense because the moral, religious, political, and social structures man has erected to 'illusion' himself have collapsed.

Edward Albee

Samuel Beckett

Samuel Beckett, poet, playwright, and novelist, is perhaps the foremost explorer of human futility in Western literature. Beckett eschews realism, romanticism, and rationalism to create works that are relentlessly unenlightening, that are indeed committed to a final obscurity. "Art has nothing to do with clarity, does not dabble in the clear, and does not make clear," argues Beckett in one of his earliest works, and his theatre is based on the thesis that man is and will remain ignorant regarding all matters of importance.

Born in Dublin in 1906, Beckett emigrated in 1928 to Paris, where he joined a literary circle centered about another Irish emigré, James Joyce. Beckett's life before World War II was an artistic vagabondage, during which he wrote several poems, short stories, and a novel; following the war and his seclusion in the south of France during the Occupation, he produced the masterworks for which he is justly famous: the novels *Molloy*, *Moran Dies*, and *The Unnamable*, and the plays *Waiting for Godot* and *Endgame*. It was *Godot* which first brought Beckett to worldwide attention: the play's premiere in Paris in 1953 occasioned a great stir among French authors and critics, and its subsequent openings in London and New York had the same effect there.

Waiting for Godot

Waiting for Godot is a parable without message. On a small mound at the base of a tree, beside a country road, two elderly men in bowler hats wait for a "Mr. Godot" with whom they have presumably made an appointment. They believe that when Godot comes they will be "saved"; however, they are not at all certain that Godot has agreed to meet with them, or if this is the right place or the right day, or whether they

Endgame, *by Beckett, is perhaps the bleakest play in the modern stylized theatre repertoire. It features two characters who live in ashcans, a blind and paralyzed man (Hamm) who sits in a chair, and a demented servant, Clov, who attends them in their grim post-holocaust isolation. Here, in original Parisian production of 1958, Clov tortures Hamm with an alarm clock.*

A photograph of the original production of Waiting for Godot *at the Théâtre Babylone in Paris, 1953. In front of neutral backdrop and barren tree, Estragon (barefooted) and Vladimir doff their hats to listen for ticking of Pozzo's pocket watch—but all they hear is Pozzo's heartbeat.*

will even recognize him if he comes. During each of the two acts, which seem to be set in late afternoon on two successive days (although nobody can be sure of that), the men are visited by passersby—first by two men calling themselves Pozzo and Lucky, subsequently by a young boy who tells them that Mr. Godot "cannot come today but surely tomorrow." The two old men continue to wait as the curtain falls. Although there is substantial reference in the play to Christian symbols and beliefs, it is not clear whether these imply positive or negative associations. The only development in the play is that the characters seem to undergo a certain loss of adeptness while the setting blossoms in rebirth (the tree sprouts leaves between the acts).

What Beckett has drawn here is clearly a paradigm of the human condition: an ongoing life cycle of vegetation serving as background to human decay, hope, and ignorance. Beckett's tone is whimsical: the characters play enchanting word games with each other, they amuse each other with songs, accounts of dreams, exercises, and vaudevillian antics, and in general they make the best of a basically hopeless situation. Beckett's paradigm affords a field day for critical investigators. *Waiting for Godot* has already generated a veritable library of brilliantly evocative discussions, and few plays from any era have been so variously analyzed, interpreted, and explored for symbolic meaning and content. Owing largely to the international critical acceptance of this play and its eventual public success, not only absurdist drama but the whole of Stylized Theatre was able to move out of the esoteric "art theatre" of the world capitals and onto the stages of popular theatres everywhere.

Beckett repeatedly conjures up what appear to be terminal situations, and phenomena come into focus in his plays only to reveal their ambiguity. *Endgame*, Beckett's second major play, involves four characters who are seeming survivor-victims of some nuclear holocaust. They live out their last days (two—who reside in the famous ashcans—seemingly die during the play's action, although one cannot be quite sure of this) in a surrealistic landscape where there is no more painkiller to assuage their physical and mental agony. *Krapp's Last Tape* portrays a solitary man with his tape recorder, dictating what will be—judging from the play's title—the last of his annual birthday memoirs.

And *Happy Days* displays a woman partially buried alive (?) in a mound of earth.

Happy Days

Happy Days, which was first produced in America (1961), is an appropriate model of absurdist drama and of the Stylized Theatre in general. It is extreme in its use of symbols, comedic in its tone, devastating in its implications. Because it is also an easy play to visualize, it serves admirably to demonstrate to the reader the impact and tone of a theatre dedicated to delving into the irrationalities of human existence.

The setting for both acts of this two-act play is a small mound, covered with "scorched grass" and bathed in "blazing light." Behind the mound is "unbroken plain and sky receding to meet in far distance," a setting the author describes as having "maximum of simplicity and symmetry."

In the exact center of the mound, embedded up to above her waist, is Winnie, the central character of the play. She is "about fifty, well preserved, blond for preference, plump, arms and shoulders bare, low bodice, big bosom, pearl necklet." Beside her are her props: a big shopping bag, a collapsible parasol. Willie, her husband and the play's only other character, is as yet unseen.

As the play begins, Winnie is discovered sleeping, her head resting on her arms. There is a long pause; Winnie sleeps on. A bell "rings piercingly" for about ten seconds; still she does not move. The bell rings again; Winnie opens her eyes and the bell stops. Winnie looks forward; there is another long pause, then, slowly, Winnie raises her torso erect. Laying her hands on the ground, Winnie throws her head backward and stares above her. Finally:

WINNIE: (*gazing at zenith*) Another heavenly day.

What's going on here? First-time audiences to Theatre of the Absurd presentations often react with annoyance or hostility to the sheer peculiarity of the depicted situation. They may even demand realistic explanations; for example, Where are we? Who is she? Why is she buried like that?

The answer is that there are no answers—not even at the end of the play. The situation Beckett creates is insinuative, not realistic: it evokes feelings, intuitions, and flashes of understanding rather than everyday acts with logical consequences. All of Stylized Theatre is perplexing at its outset; it makes demands on its audience from the rise of the curtain onwards. Fortunately, though, when a play is as masterfully constructed as *Happy Days*, audience annoyance and hostility soon gives way to rapt involvement.

Happy Days is particularly rich in suggested associations. The mound of scorched earth, bathed in blazing light, may provoke thoughts of nuclear blasts, of holocaust and miraculous survival. Or, as in *Waiting for Godot*, it may stimulate the notion of Calvary, with Winnie, gazing heavenward and speaking of a "heavenly day," perhaps recalling the moment of Christ's presumed forsakenness. The half-burial surely reminds us of human mortality: Winnie—a member of our tribe—appears halfway in (halfway out of?) a metaphoric grave, and we too are locked in the cycle of life, springing from the earth to which we are fated to return. The shopping bag and parasol, rather neat symbols of man's worldly preoccupations (a bag to collect material acquisitions, a parasol to protect against the elements), are dwarfed by the desolate surroundings and mocked by the surreal atmosphere: of what use is either shopping bag or parasol in the vast, empty, indifferent universe?

Madelaine Renaud as Winnie, in famous French production of Happy Days *directed by her husband, Jean-Louis Barrault (Barrault also played Willie). Winnie holds parasol aloft to shield her from the elements; futility of her gesture is emphasized by shadow on backdrop.*

Structurally, *Happy Days* has much in common with *Prometheus Bound*, for in both works the dramatic hero is imprisoned, center stage, for the play's duration; in both, too, the hero uses verbal rhetoric in an effort to surmount the physical oppression of the setting and situation. Both Winnie and Prometheus surge with unflagging positivism and self-theatricalizing bravado which stand in sharp contrast to the bleakness of their stylized environments. Both characters repudiate despair with an astonishing energy which at once inspires and verges on the ridiculous.

But unlike the Aeschylean work, *Happy Days* attempts no explanations: the cause of Winnie's particular entrapment is nowhere even hinted at, much less explained and analyzed. Her situation must simply be viewed as an inexplicable phenomenon in an absurd world, although we may be sure that it is an *analogy* of man's permanent condition. Further, unlike her Aeschylean prototype, Winnie's actions betray no heroic revolt, and her rhetoric never achieves the heights of godlike denunciation; rather, her actions consist of mundane behaviors borrowed from the realistic stage—rummaging in her bag, brushing her teeth, polishing her spectacles—and her speech is largely inconsequential small talk directed either to herself or to Willie, who sleeps behind the mound out of sight of the audience. Thus the play opens:

WINNIE: (*gazing at zenith*) Another heavenly day. (*Pause. Head back level, eyes front, pause. She clasps hands to breast, closes eyes. Lips move in inaudible prayer, say ten seconds. Lips still. Hands remain clasped. Low.*) For Jesus Christ sake Amen. (*Eyes open, hands unclasp, return to mound. Pause. She clasps hands to breast again, closes eyes, lips move again in inaudible addendum, say five seconds. Low.*) World without end Amen. (*Eyes open, hands unclasp, return to mound. Pause.*) Begin, Winnie. (*Pause.*) Begin your day, Winnie. (*Pause. She turns to bag, rummages in it without moving it from its place, brings out toothbrush, rummages again, brings out flat tube of toothpaste, turns back front, unscrews cap of tube, lays cap on ground, squeezes with difficulty small blob of paste on brush, holds tube in one hand and brushes teeth*

with other. She turns modestly aside and back to her right to spit out behind mound. In this position her eyes rest on WILLIE. She spits out. She cranes a little further back and down. Loud.*) Hoo-oo! (*Pause. Louder.*) Hoo-oo! (*Pause. Tender smile as she turns back front, lays down brush.*) Poor Willie—(*examines tube, smile off*)—running out—(*looks for cap*)—ah well—(*finds cap*)—can't be helped—(*screws on cap*)—just one of those old things—(*lays down tube*)—another of those old things—(*turns towards bag*)—just can't be cured—(*rummages in bag*)—cannot be cured—(*brings out small mirror, turns back front*)—ah yes—(*inspects teeth in mirror*)—poor dear Willie—(*testing upper front teeth with thumb, indistinctly*)—good Lord!—(*pulling back upper lip to inspect gums, do.* *)—good God!—(*pulling back corner of mouth, mouth open, do.*)—ah well—(*other corner, do.*)—no worse—(*abandons inspection, normal speech*)—no better, no worse—(*lays down mirror*)—no change—(*wipes fingers on grass*)—no pain—(*looks for toothbrush*)—hardly any—(*takes up toothbrush*)—great thing that—(*examines handle of brush*)—nothing like it—(*examines handle, reads*)—pure . . . what?—(*pause*)—what?—(*lays down brush*)—ah yes—(*turns towards bag*)—poor Willie—(*rummages in bag*)—no zest—(*rummages*)—for anything—(*brings out spectacles in case*)—no interest—(*turns back front*)—in life—(*takes spectacles from case*)—poor dear Willie—(*lays down case*)—sleep for ever—(*opens spectacles*)—marvellous gift—(*puts on spectacles*)—nothing to touch it—(*looks for toothbrush*)—in my opinion—(*takes up toothbrush*)—always said so—(*examines handle of brush*)—wish I had it—(*examines handle, reads*)—genuine . . . pure . . . what?—(*lays down brush*)—blind next (*takes off spectacles*)—ah well—(*lays down spectacles*)—seen enough—(*feels in bodice for handkerchief*)—I suppose—(*takes out folded handkerchief*)—by now—(*shakes out handkerchief*)—what are

*EDITOR'S NOTE: The direction *do.*, which appears in several places in this playscript, stands for "ditto," or "repeat the action."

Peggy Ashcroft as Winnie and Harry Lomax as Willie in British National Theatre production of Happy Days, *directed by Peter Hall in 1975. What is going on here?*

those wonderful lines—(*wipes one eye*)—woe woe is me—(*wipes the other*)—to see what I see—(*looks for spectacles*)—ah yes—(*takes up spectacles*)—wouldn't miss it—(*starts polishing spectacles, breathing on lenses*)—or would I?—(*polishes*)—holy light—(*polishes*)—bob up out of dark—(*polishes*)—blaze of hellish light. (*Stops polishing, raises face to sky, pause, head back level, resumes polishing, stops polishing, cranes back to her right and down.*) Hoo-oo! (*Pause. Tender smile as she turns back front and resumes polishing. Smile off.*) Marvellous gift—(*stops polishing, lays down spectacles*)—wish I had it—(*folds handkerchief*)—ah well—(*puts handkerchief back in bodice*)—can't complain—(*looks for spectacles*)—no no—(*takes up spectacles*)—mustn't complain—(*holds up spectacles, looks through lens*)—so much to be thankful for —(*looks through other lens*)—no pain—(*puts on spectacles*)—hardly any—(*looks for toothbrush*) —wonderful thing that—(*takes up toothbrush*) —nothing like it—(*examines handle of brush*) —slight headache sometimes—(*examines handle, reads*)—guaranteed . . . genuine . . . pure . . .

what?—(*looks closer*)—genuine pure . . .—(*takes handkerchief from bodice*)—ah yes—(*shakes out handkerchief*)—occasional mild migraine—(*starts wiping handle of brush*)—it comes—(*wipes*)—then goes—(*wiping mechanically*)—ah yes—(*wiping*)—many mercies—(*wiping*)—great mercies—(*stops wiping, fixed lost gaze, brokenly*)—prayers perhaps not for naught—(*pause, do.*)—first thing—(*pause, do.*)—last thing—(*head down, resumes wiping, stops wiping, head up, calmed, wipes eyes, folds handkerchief, puts it back in bodice, examines handle of brush, reads*)—fully guaranteed . . . genuine pure . . .—(*looks closer*)—genuine pure . . . (*Takes off spectacles, lays them and brush down, gazes before her.*) Old things. (*Pause.*) Old eyes. (*Long pause.*) On, Winnie.

This opening speech by Winnie is fairly typical of the play's entire action, which consists in the main of Winnie talking to no one in particular or to a rarely responding, rarely visible Willie. Although the play is thus virtually a monologue—and for that reason a *tour de force* for the actress who attempts it—the monologue is unusually dynamic in that Winnie addresses multiple audiences: for in addition to Willie, Winnie also speaks to us, to her god, and to the universe at large: to whoever it is that rings the piercing bell that wakes her up every day, and who is "looking at me still. (*Pause*) Caring for me still." Although Beckett has provided his actress with a forlorn setting, he has given her a great variety of voices with which to address her thoughts and concerns about it.

The opening speech sets forth Winnie's major quests for the course of the play. She tries to better her appearance, tries to read what is written on the handle of her toothbrush, tries to clean her glasses, tries to make the best of her physical encumbrance, tries to reach out to Willie through her "Hoo-oo"-ing, and tries to reach her god through prayer. She more or less fails at all tasks: the meaning of the words on the toothbrush handle remains obscure, Willie remains almost totally unresponsive to her comments, prayers are "perhaps not for naught" but certainly remain unanswered in our presence, and both her spectacles and her eyes are "old things" that fail her when she needs them.

Would she "bob up out of dark?" she asks? And, if so, would she see a "holy light" or a "hellish light?" She doesn't know and never finds out.

And thus she is reduced to giving herself survival commands, pep talks: "Begin, Winnie. Begin your day." And, speaking to herself as if she were one of Santa's reindeer, "On, Winnie."

Winnie seeks the rhetoric of old: "What are those wonderful lines?" It is a theme that runs throughout the play, as Winnie yearns and pleads "To speak in the old style. The sweet old style. . . . " "What is that wonderful line . . . ?" "The old style!" In this theme Beckett is not ridiculing the plays and languages of the past; he is merely saying that we can no longer encapsulate our plight in balanced phrases, no longer appeal to our gods in confident, ringing tones. Instead, we must fall back on a determined cheerfulness, a compulsive buoyancy that surmounts resignation and defeatism. "On, Winnie!" she cries.

At last the idle Willie stirs himself. From behind the mound, we see the yellow page tops of his newspaper and hear his occasional mutter of a sentence from that paper, such as "Opening for smart youth." Meanwhile, Winnie busies herself, talking all the while. Out of her bag come medicine, lipstick, a magnifying glass, a hat, a mirror, and a revolver. The business of the day begins:

WINNIE: . . . My hair! (*Pause.*) Did I brush and comb my hair? (*Pause.*) I may have done. (*Pause.*) Normally I do. (*Pause.*) There is so little one *can* do. (*Pause.*) One does it all. (*Pause.*) All one can. (*Pause.*) Tis only human (*Pause.*) Human nature. (*She begins to inspect mound, looks up.*) Human weakness. (*She resumes inspection of mound, looks up.*) Natural weakness. (*She resumes inspection of mound.*) I see no comb. (*Inspects.*) Nor any hairbrush. (*Looks up. Puzzled expression. She turns to bag, rummages in it.*) The comb is here. (*Back front. Puzzled expression. Back to bag. Rummages.*) The brush is here. (*Back front. Puzzled expression.*) Perhaps I put them back, after

Beckett puts the conventions he utilizes into the service of an unheard-of-dramaturgy. It is a dramaturgy which appears to be a repudiation of the ordinary purposes of the theater but is actually a miraculous resuscitation of those purposes through a process of purification, deepening and a change of ground.

The miracle lies in the fact that here every element that has been thought to be necessary to the theatre's conquest of life—plot, character, movement, linear revelation, the resolution of struggle—has dwindled to a set of notations and gestures, if anything at all remains; and yet life continues to rise from Beckett's stage as it does from few others.

Happy Days is Beckett's furthest move so far in the direction of absolute stillness, of a kind of motionless dance in which the internal agitation and its shaping control are described through language primarily and through the spaces between words ... (one of Beckett's chief supports, as well as one of his main themes, is the tension produced by the struggle between speech and silence and by the double thrust of words towards truth and lies). . . . From it arises a sense of life apprehended in its utmost degree of non-contingency and existential self-containment, with all its cross-purposes, vagaries, agonies and waste, its oscillation between hope and despair, affirmation and denial—a new enunciation of Beckett's special vision.

Richard Gilman

---

use. (*Pause. Do.*) But normally I do not put things back, after use, no, I leave them lying about and put them back all together, at the end of the day. (*Smile.*) To speak in the old style. (*Pause.*) The sweet old style. (*Smile off.*) And yet . . . I seem . . . to remember . . . (*Suddenly careless.*) Oh well, what does it matter, that is what I always say, I shall simply brush and comb them later on, purely and simply, I have the whole—(*Pause. Puzzled.*) Them? (*Pause.*) Or it? (*Pause.*) Brush and comb it? (*Pause.*) Sounds improper somehow. (*Pause. Turning a little towards* WILLIE.) What would you say, Willie? (*Pause. Turning a little further.*) What would you say, Willie, speaking of your hair, them or it? (*Pause.*) The hair on your head, I mean. (*Pause. Turning a little further.*) The hair on your head, Willie, what would you say speaking of the hair on your head, them or it?

Long pause.

WILLIE: It.

WINNIE: (*turning back front, joyful*) Oh you are going to talk to me today, this is going to be a happy day! (*Pause. Joy off.*) Another happy day.

Circular and monotonous, the day's events are so confounded that we can have little recollection of them: Winnie's perplexity extends to whether she did or didn't comb her hair, whether she should or shouldn't comb it, and whether "hair" is a singular or plural noun. On one level, her chatter is simply a satire on domestic conversation. On another level, it is a commentary on the persistence—and futility—of human attempts to communicate. Beckett's dialogue, punctuated by the famous "pauses" which have virtually become his dramatic signature, continually reminds us of the silence which we attempt to surmount by conversation, but which ultimately must prevail over the dialogue of all living things: each of Winnie's statements, feeble in content as it may be, is a little victory over nothingness. But words are not always enough:

WINNIE: . . . Words fail, there are times when even they fail. (*Pause.*) Is that not so, Willie? (*Pause.*) Is not that so, Willie, that even words fail, at times? (*Pause.*) What is one to do then, until they come again? Brush and comb the hair, if it has not been done, or if there is some doubt, trim the nails if they are in need of trimming, these things tide one over.

If words fail, one is left with physical actions,

and in Beckett's theatre the options in that regard also are notably restricted. What kind of actions can be sustained by one character buried bosom-deep and another hidden behind a mound? The physical action of *Happy Days* is confined but subtle; Beckett's dramaturgy compels the audience to pay close attention to physical nuance and demands superior acting performance. In addition, *Happy Days*, like all of Beckett's plays, is written for presentation in a relatively small theatre; it probably could not be performed successfully in a giant auditorium, since its full impact can be achieved only if the audience can clearly perceive the performers' every action and facial expression. Such action as Winnie's opening her parasol, for example, conveys meaning and importance by a poetry of pauses, turns, gazes, and shifts of hand positions:

WINNIE: (. . . *Looks at parasol.*) I suppose I might— (*takes up parasol*)—yes, I suppose I might . . . hoist this thing now. (*Begins to unfurl it. Following punctuated by mechanical difficulties overcome.*) One keeps putting off—putting up —for fear of putting up—too soon—and the day goes by—quite by—without one's having put up—at all. (*Parasol now fully open. Turned to her right she twirls it idly this way and that.*)

Ah yes, so little to say, so little to do, and the fear so great, certain days, of finding oneself . . . left, with hours still to run, before the bell for sleep, and nothing more to say, nothing more to do, that the days go by, certain days go by, quite by, the bell goes, and little or nothing said, little or nothing done. (*Raising parasol.*) That is the danger. (*Turning front.*) To be guarded against. (*She gazes front, holding up parasol with right hand. Maximum pause.*) I used to perspire freely. (*Pause.*) Now hardly at all. (*Pause.*) The heat is much greater. (*Pause.*) The perspiration much less. (*Pause.*) That is what I find so wonderful. (*Pause.*) The way man adapts himself. (*Pause.*) To changing conditions. (*She transfers parasol to left hand. Long pause.*) Wearies the arm. . . .

Happy Days is built of such business as this: of words that circle their subjects without coming to grips with them, and physical actions that prove pointless and wearying. Before the end of the first act, Willie recommences his newspaper, Winnie plays a waltz from *The Merry Widow* on her mu-

---

Beckett, the old fox, is becoming more and more acrobatic—or is it Aeschylean? He is steadfastly exploring how much the theatre can do without and still be theatre. He has already written a near-monodrama for actor and tape recorder, as well as a brief act without words; in *Happy Days*, as in Aeschylus's *Suppliants*, we are reduced once again to two characters, one of whom does almost all the speaking. And this protagonist is, like Aeschylus's Prometheus, immobilized. For Beckett's unfortunate heroine who stands for the human condition, stands for it buried up to her waist during act one; in act two, life has inhumed her up to her chin, and only her head is still distinguishable from the landscape. The image is striking, both visually and symbolically, but it does rather cramp one's dramatic style. Of course, it is very much part of Beckett's scheme to inhibit dramatic, i.e., human action, but the maneuver is extremely dangerous. Beckett the acrobat has hung on to his dramatic thread first by his feet, then by one hand, next by his teeth, and now he proceeds to take out his dentures in mid-air. Needless to say, he is performing without a net. And there are moments, indeed minutes, when the play lapses into *longueurs*, when the existential *ennui* becomes plain old-fashioned boredom. All the same, the play is full of that Beckettian strategy which presents the most innocuous trifles of human existence dripping with blood and bile, and the most unspeakable horrors rakishly attired and merrily winking. The heroine who keeps blithering about the great mercies of existence as she is pressed deeper and deeper into the sod is an egregiously valid theatrical metaphor. . . ."
John Simon

sic box, and the parasol inexplicably bursts into flames. Then, with the act nearing its conclusion, Winnie exclaims: "Oh this *is* a happy day! This will have been another happy day!" She pauses, then adds: "After all. (*Pause*). So far."

The second act conveys the impression of a subsequent day in the existence of these same characters: again the bell rings and Winnie opens her eyes, again Willie is invisible behind the mound. However, in Act II Winnie is embedded all the way up to her neck; her head is rigidly immobilized in the mound of scorched earth, and will remain so throughout the balance of the play. Here the dramaturgical challenge Beckett poses for himself—to create dramatic conflict with almost no possibility of physical movement, business, or visible interaction—is extraordinary.

> *Bell rings loudly.* [WINNIE] *opens eyes at once. Bell stops. She gazes front. Long pause.*
>
> WINNIE: Hail, holy light. (*Long pause. She closes her eyes. Bell rings loudly. She opens eyes at once. Bell stops. She gazes front. Long smile. Smile off. Long pause.*) Someone is looking at me still. (*Pause.*) Caring for me still. (*Pause.*) That is what I find so wonderful. (*Pause.*) Eyes on my eyes. (*Pause.*) What is that unforgettable line? (*Pause. Eyes right.*) Willie. (*Pause. Louder.*) Willie. (*Pause. Eyes front.*) May one still speak of time? (*Pause.*) Say it is a long time now, Willie, since I saw you. (*Pause.*) Since I heard you. (*Pause.*) May one? (*Pause.*) One does. (*Smile.*) The old style! (*Smile off.*) There is so little one can speak of. (*Pause.*) One speaks of it all. (*Pause.*) All one can. (*Pause.*) I used to think . . . (*pause*) . . . I say I used to think that I would learn to talk alone. (*Pause.*) By that I mean to myself, the wilderness. (*Smile.*) But no. (*Smile broader.*) No no. (*Smile off.*) Ergo you are there. (*Pause.*) Oh no doubt you are dead, like the others, no doubt you have died, or gone away and left me, like the others, it doesn't matter, you are there. (*Pause. Eyes left.*) The bag too is there, the same as ever, I can see it. (*Pause. Eyes right. Louder.*) The bag is there, Willie, as good as ever, the one you gave me that day . . . to go to market. (*Pause. Eyes front.*) That day.

(*Pause.*) What day? (*Pause.*) I used to pray. (*Pause.*) I say I used to pray. (*Pause.*) Yes I must confess I did. (*Smile.*) Not now. (*Smile broader.*) No no. (*Smile off. Pause.*) . . .

Two themes that were broached in the first act combine to form the action and conclusion of the second: these are the themes of Winnie's song, and "Brownie," the couple's revolver.

Winnie's song is something which, we are led to understand, she ritually sings at the end of her day: "To sing too soon is a great mistake, I find," says Winnie in Act I, adding, "One cannot sing just to please someone, however much one loves them, no, song must come from the heart, that is what I always say, pour out from the inmost, like a thrush." In Act II the urge to sing one's song—and the timing of the singing—becomes a matter of great importance:

> WINNIE: . . . The day is now well advanced. (*Smile. Smile off.*) And yet it is perhaps a little soon for my song. (*Pause.*) To sing too soon is fatal, I always find. (*Pause.*) On the other hand it is possible to leave it too late. (*Pause.*) The bell goes for sleep and one has not sung. (*Pause.*) The whole day has flown—(*smile, smile off*)—flown by, quite by, and no song of any class, kind or description. (*Pause.*) There is a problem here. (*Pause.*) One cannot sing . . . just like that, no. (*Pause.*) It bubbles up, for some unknown reason, the time is ill chosen, one chokes it back. (*Pause.*) One says, Now is the time, it is now or never, and one cannot. (*Pause.*) Simply cannot sing. (*Pause.*) Not a note. (*Pause.*) . . .

Winnie's song, we feel, represents her most exuberant expression: song is surely what passes, in the world of *Happy Days*, as a symbol of the human life force at its fullest flower. Song, of course, is the first medium of the Western theatre, evolving out of the dithyramb to the choral ode of Aeschylus, and the plaintive tune Winnie sings at the end of this play stands in almost grotesque contrast with the harmonies of the classic tragedies of the past.

"Brownie" (for Browning) symbolizes the opposite of song in *Happy Days*; the revolver which Winnie pulls from her bag in the early moments

Willie appears in tuxedo in the 1976 British National Theatre presentation. "Well, this is an unexpected pleasure!" cries Winnie. Note that revolver points directly at Winnie: what will it be used for?

of the play remains to the end as a mark of past contemplations and present potential.

WINNIE: (*. . . plunges hand in bag and brings out revolver. Disgusted.*) You again! (*She . . . brings revolver front and contemplates it. She weighs it in her palm.*) You'd think the weight of this thing would bring it down among the . . . last rounds. But no. It doesn't. Ever uppermost, like Browning. (*Pause.*) Brownie . . . (*Turning a little towards* WILLIE.) Remember Brownie, Willie? (*Pause.*) Remember how you used to keep on at me to take it away from you? Take it away, Winnie, take it away, before I put myself out of my misery. (*Back front. Derisive.*) *Your* misery! (*To revolver.*) Oh I suppose it's a comfort to know you're there, but I'm tired of you. (*Pause.*) I'll leave you out, that's what I'll do. (*She lays revolver on ground to her right.*) There, that's your home from this day out. . . .

And from then until the end of the play, fully visible and, in the author's stage direction, "conspicuous" at the opening of Act II, the revolver remains to do quickly what the rising earth and blazing sun do slowly: to extinguish Winnie's life. But in Act II Winnie cannot reach it; her hands are in the earth:

WINNIE: (. . . *Eyes open. Pause. Eyes right.*) Brownie of course. (*Pause.*) You remember Brownie, Willie, I can see him. (*Pause.*) Brownie is there, Willie, beside me. (*Pause. Loud.*) Brownie is there, Willie. (*Pause. Eyes front.*) That is all. . . .

Brownie, of course, symbolizes death—and perhaps the brown earth, the earthball, in which Winnie is surely being swallowed up. Perhaps too, we have a parody of those classic lines from Robert Browning, "Grow old along with me!/The best is yet to be," lines which seem almost idiotic in the face of Beckett's austere vision of the realities of aging.

The counterpoint of these two themes, interwoven and contradictory, constitutes the inner action of *Happy Days*: an interplay between the celebration of life and the lure of instant death, played out amidst an encroaching disablement in a landscape blazing with light yet resistant to understanding. Beckett's play ends in a striking *coup de théâtre*, an event unpredicted by anything in the play up to this point, yet wholly consistent with all that has gone before.

WINNIE: . . . I can do no more. (*Pause.*) Say no more. (*Pause.*) But I must say more. (*Pause.*) Problem here. (*Pause.*) No, something must move, in the world, I can't any more. (*Pause.*) A zephyr. (*Pause.*) A breath. (*Pause.*) What are those immortal lines? (*Pause.*) It might be the eternal dark. (*Pause.*) Black night without end. . . . (*Long pause.*) I hear cries. (*Pause.*) Sing. (*Pause.*) Sing your old song, Winnie.

But she does not yet sing her song. Instead, around the mound, comes Willie for the first time. Astonishingly, he is "dressed to kill," in top hat, morning coat, and striped trousers. He sports a "very long bushy white Battle of Britain moustache." And he is crawling on all fours.

WINNIE: Well this is an unexpected pleasure!

The two look at each other, Willie dropping his hat to do so, and moving within Winnie's field of vision. It is a ghastly effect: the woman in earth to her chin, staring obliquely; the man in formal attire, on his hands and knees, staring up at her; and, of course, conspicuously between them, Brownie the revolver. Willie collapses, his head falling to the ground.

WINNIE: . . . Where were you all this time? (*Pause.*) What were you doing all this time? (*Pause.*) Changing? (*Pause.*) Did you not hear me screaming for you? (*Pause.*) Did you get stuck in your hole? (*Pause. He looks up.*) That's right, Willie, look at me. (*Pause.*) Feast your old eyes, Willie. (*Pause.*) Does anything remain? (*Pause.*) Any remains? (*Pause.*) No? (*Pause.*) I haven't been able to look after it, you know. (*He sinks his head.*) You are still recognizable, in a way. (*Pause.*) Are you thinking of coming to live this side now . . . for a bit maybe? (*Pause.*) No? (*Pause.*) Just a brief call? (*Pause.*) Have you gone deaf, Willie? (*Pause.*) Dumb? (*Pause.*) Oh I know you were never one to talk, I worship you Winnie be mine and then nothing from that day forth only titbits from Reynolds' News. (*Eyes front. Pause.*) Ah well, what matter, that's what I always say, it will have been a happy day, after all, another happy day. (*Pause.*) Not long now, Winnie. (*Pause.*) I hear cries. (*Pause.*) Do you ever hear cries, Willie? (*Pause.*) No? (*Eyes back on WIL-LIE.*) Willie. (*Pause.*) Look at me again, Willie. (*Pause.*) Once more, Willie. (*He looks up. Happily.*) Ah! (*Pause. Shocked.*) What ails you, Willie, I never saw such an expression! (*Pause.*) Put on your hat, dear, it's the sun, don't stand on ceremony, I won't mind. (*He drops hat and gloves and starts to crawl up mound towards her. Gleeful.*) Oh I say, this is terrific! (*He halts, clinging to mound with one hand, reaching up with the other.*) Come on, dear, put a bit of jizz into it, I'll cheer you on. (*Pause.*) Is it me you're after, Willie . . . or is it something else? (*Pause.*) Do you want to touch my face . . . again? (*Pause.*) Is it a kiss you're after, Willie . . . or is it something else? (*Pause.*) There was a time when I could have given you a hand. (*Pause.*) And then a time before that again when I did give you a hand. (*Pause.*) You were always in dire need of a hand, Willie. (*He slithers back to foot of mound and lies with face to ground.*) Brum! (*Pause. He rises to hands and knees, raises his face towards her.*)

Have another go, Willie, I'll cheer you on. (*Pause.*) Don't look at me like that! (*Pause. Vehement.*) Don't look at me like that! (*Pause. Low.*) Have you gone off your head, Willie? (*Pause. Do.*) Out of your poor old wits, Willie? *Pause.*

WILLIE: (*just audible*) Win.

Pause. WINNIE's *eyes front. Happy expression appears, grows.*

WINNIE: Win! (*Pause.*) Oh this *is* a happy day, this will have been another happy day! (*Pause.*) After all. (*Pause.*) So far.

Now Winnie begins her song. It is to the tune of her music box:

Though I say not
What I may not
Let you hear,
Yet the swaying
Dance is saying,
Love me dear!
Every touch of fingers
Tells me what I know,
Says for you,
It's true, it's true,
You love me so!

The bell rings. Winnie smiles. Willie is still on his hands and knees, looking at her. The smile disappears. "They look at each other. Long pause. CURTAIN." And the play is over.

Why was Willie climbing the mound? "Is it me you're after, Willie," asks Winnie, "or is it something else?" If it is the revolver, we ask, does he want to kill her, or to kill himself, or to kill them both? Is his "just audible" cry of "Win" simply her nickname, or is the author invoking an association of winning, of victory? And under these circumstances, what are we to make of Winnie's song, with its depiction of a declaration dance of love?

Beckett provides no answers to these questions, and neither should critical analysis. In the Theatre of the Absurd, and in Stylized Theatre in general, the elucidation of meaningful questions is what marks an author's genius and accomplishment, not the discovery of practical solutions. The

problems addressed in *Happy Days*—the inevitability of aging and death, the inscrutability of human affection, the obscurity of human motives, and the necessity for arbitrary commitment and action in a universe without final meaning—are inherent conditions of life: they can be diagnosed and epitomized with symbols, but they cannot be remedied. Beckett posits lucid metaphors, intriguing patterns, and evocative images; he does not proffer moral codes or even helpful advice. *Happy Days* stimulates but does not explain; it fascinates but does not presume to lead us out of the dark.

For Beckett and the rest of the absurdists are intent upon portraying mankind as eternally and feebly groping in a darkness which can never be penetrated by the superficial light of human understanding. Reversing the symbolism of Prometheus—who in bringing light brought the hope of knowledge, understanding, joy, and victory over life's mysteries—Beckett suggests that light makes only the inconsequential luminous, thus trivializing the human experience and making man oblivious to the greatest grace: total obscurity. Rather in line with the medieval association of light with Lucifer, not enlightenment, Beckett makes the "blazing light" of *Happy Days* a malign symbol of final ignorance, a light that reveals nothing beyond the absurdity of man's efforts to "see." Indeed, in the first act, while she can still use her hands, Winnie makes all too clear what the truly "happy day" will be when she finally manages to make out the words on the toothbrush handle:

WINNIE: [*reading*] Fully guaranteed . . . genuine pure . . . hog's . . . setae. (*Pause.*) Hog's setae. (*Pause.*) That is what I find so wonderful, that not a day goes by—(*smile*)—to speak in the old style—(*smile off*)—hardly a day, without some addition to one's knowledge however trifling, the addition I mean, provided one takes the pains. . . . And if for some strange reason no further pains are possible, why then just close the eyes—(*she does so*)—and wait for the day to come—(*opens eyes*)—the happy day to come when flesh melts at so many degrees and the night of the moon has so many hundred hours. (*Pause.*) That is what I find so comforting when I lose heart and envy the brute beast.

Thus the happy day is to come at the end of these "Happy Days," when the eyes can close, when one takes no further pains to add to one's store of "knowledge," when the blazing light will incinerate Winnie's flesh as it incinerates her parasol, when she can acquire a deeper knowledge illuminated only by the "night of the moon."

Beckett's vision is unique, and the body of theatre he has created is only one small part of the modern drama; other writers associated with the absurd often hold visions less relentlessly severe. Because the extreme situations he creates are unrelieved by sentiment, his work is often called "uncompromising." Yet his plays are undeniably comedies, for they always explore the human condition with irony and a bizarre humor. If the condition of man is terminal, its staged incarnation is hilariously sprightly. Winnie's enthusiasm, although "absurd" in the ordinary sense as well as in the philosophical sense, is infectious: we share in her small triumphs of self-deception and cheer her on in singing against her suspicions and confronting her plight with such unbridled whimsy. Whatever its provocation, whistling in the dark can be agreeable music, and it is this upbeat tone which suffuses Beckett's plays.

Thus, perhaps surprisingly, there is nothing depressing about *Happy Days*, for its uncompromising vision is presented with an always compassionate irony. Nothing is more evident in the works of Samuel Beckett than the author's kindly attitude toward his characters, an attitude which, we feel, also extends across the footlights to us. Beckett is not a prophet of despair; he is simply a reporter of the ineffable and inexplicable: he may not lead us out of the dark, but he *will* hold our hands while we stumble about. Thus if there is no message in his plays, there is amusement and there is comfort. In the lostness of our times, that is about all any artist or friend can presume to deliver.

Theatre of Alienation

The Theatre of the Absurd is one of the two main lines of the contemporary Stylized Theatre; the Theatre of Alienation, or of *distancing* (the German word is *Verfremdung*) is the other. In contrast to the hermetic, self-contained absurdist plays with their message concerning the essential futility of human endeavors, the sprawling, socially engaged "epic" theatre of Bertolt Brecht and like-minded theatre artists concentrates on man's potential for growth and his capacity to effect social change.

Bertolt Brecht

The guiding genius of the Theatre of Alienation is Bertolt Brecht, theorist, dramatist, and director. No single individual has had a greater impact on postwar theatre than Brecht. This impact has been felt in two ways. First, Brecht has introduced theatre practices which are, at least on the surface, utterly at variance with those in use since the time of Aristotle; second, his accomplishments have invigorated the theatre with an abrasive humanism that has reawakened its sense of social responsibility and its awareness of the capacity of theatre to mold public issues and events.

Brecht was born in Germany in 1898 and emerged from World War I a dedicated Marxist and pacifist. Using poems, songs, and eventually the theatre to promote his ideals following the German defeat, Brecht vividly portrayed his country during the Weimar Republic as caught in the grips of four giant vises: the military, capitalism, industrialization, and imperialism. His *Rise and Fall of the City of Mahagonny*, for example, an "epic opera" of 1930, proved an immensely popular blending of satire and propaganda, music and expressionist theatricality, social idealism and lyric poetry; it was produced all over Germany and throughout most of Europe in the early 1930s as a depiction of a rapacious international capitalism evolving toward fascism.

Brecht was forced to flee his country upon Hitler's accession to the chancellorship. Thereafter he moved about Europe for a time and then, for much of the 1940s, settled in America. Following World War II he returned in triumph to Berlin, where the East German government established for him the Berliner Ensemble Theatre; there Brecht was allowed to consolidate his theories in a body of productions developed out of his earlier plays and the pieces he had written while in exile.

Brecht's theatre draws upon a potpourri of theatrical conventions, some derived from the ancients, some from Eastern drama, and some from the German Expressionist movement in which Brecht himself played a part in his early years. Masks, songs, verse,

Brecht's Rise and Fall of the City of Mahagonny *in contemporary production of the (East) German Light Opera (Komische Oper). The play satirizes American society and world capitalism, represented here by giant bottles of American bourbon and Italian vermouth in a fanciful, theatrical, pseudo-Alaskan setting.*

exotic settings, satire, and direct rhetorical address are fundamental conventions which Brecht adopted from other theatre forms. In addition, he developed many conventions of his own: lantern-slide projections with printed "captions," asides and invocations directed to the audience to encourage them to develop an objective point of view, and a variety of procedures aimed at de-mystifying theatrical techniques (for example, lowering the lights so that the pipes and wires would be displayed) became the characteristics of Brecht's theatre.

He eschewed the use of sentimentality and the notion of audience empathy for characters, and attempted instead to create a performance style which was openly "didactic": the actor was asked to alienate himself, or distance himself, from the character he played—to "demonstrate" his character rather than to embody that character in a realistic manner. In Brecht's view the ideal actor was one who could establish a *critical objectivity* toward his character which would make clear the character's social function and political commitment. In attempting to repudiate the "magic" of the theatre, he demanded that it be made to seem nothing more than a place for

Another photograph of Brecht's Mahagonny *in its contemporary realization, showing use of bold "ringside" lighting (much of play is set in a prizefight arena) and deliberate use of stage machinery (overhead battens and wires).*

workers to present a meaningful "parable" of life, and he in no way wished to disguise the fact that the stage personnel—actors and stagehands—were merely workers who were engaged in doing a job of work. In every way possible, Brecht attempted to prevent the audience from becoming swept up in an emotional, sentimental bath of feelings: his goal was to keep the audience "alienated" or "distanced" from the literal events depicted by the play so they would be free to concentrate on the larger social and political issues which the play generated and reflected. Brecht considered this theatre to be an "epic" one because it

attempted, around the framework of a parable or archetypal event, to create a whole new perspective on human history, and to indicate the direction which political dialogue should take to foster social betterment.

Brecht's theories were to have a staggering impact on the modern theatre. In his wholesale renunciation of Aristotelian catharsis, which depends on audience empathy with a noble character, and his denial of Stanislavski's basic principles concerning the aims of acting, Brecht provided a new dramaturgy that encouraged playwrights, directors, and designers to

> The first thing we recognize in the Brecht productions is their *reality*: an utterly engrossing reality. We feel we are looking directly at the core and substance of what the plays are about. We do not sense any element of staginess, arty ornament or eye-deceiving illusion. At the same time, we are not only at ease—the ordinary naturalistic production always seems a little strenuous by comparison—but thoroughly absorbed. We are at once in the theatre—with all its sense of festival and fun—and soberly in the midst of life. We do not sweat with anxiety or often split our sides with laughter; yet we are stirred by what is serious and refreshed by what is humorous.
>
> Harold Clurman

tackle social issues directly rather than simply by means of implication through contrived dramatic situations. Combining the technologies and aesthetics of other media—the lecture hall, the slide show, the public meeting, the cinema, the cabaret, the rehearsal—Brecht fashioned a vastly expanded arena for his *dialectics*: his social arguments that sought to engender truth through the confrontation of conflicting interests. These ideas were played out, in Brecht's own works and in countless other works inspired by him, with a bold theatricality, an open-handed dealing with the audience, a proletarian vigor, and a stridently entertaining, intelligently satirical, and charmingly bawdy theatre. This theatre has proven even more popular in the 1970s and 1980s than it was in Brecht's day, because since then the world seems to have grown even more fragmented, more individualistic, and more suspicious of collective emotions and sentimentality.

The Good Woman of Sezuan

No play better illustrates Brecht's dramatic theory and method than his *The Good Woman of Sezuan* (1943). This play, set in western China (of which Brecht knew virtually nothing —thus adding to the "distancing" of the story), tells the story of a kind-hearted prostitute, Shen Te, who is astounded to receive a gift of money from three itinerant gods. Elated by her good fortune, Shen Te uses the money to start a tobacco business. She is, however, quickly beset by petty officials seek-

ing to impose local regulations, self-proclaimed creditors demanding payment, and a host of hangers-on who simply prey upon her good nature. At the point of financial ruin, Shen Te leaves her tobacco shop to enlist the aid of her male cousin Shui Ta, who strides imperiously into the tobacco shop and routs the predators, making it safe for Shen Te to return. But the predators come back, and Shen Te again has to call on the tyrannical Shui Ta to save her. A simple story—but Brecht's stroke of genius is to make Shui Ta and Shen Te the same character: Shui Ta is simply Shen Te in disguise! The aim of the play is not to show that there are kind-hearted people and tyrannical people, but that people can choose to be one or the other. What kind of society is it, Brecht asks, that forces us to make this sort of choice?

Brecht is no mere propagandist, and his epic theatre is not one of simple messages or easy conclusions. At the end of *The Good Woman of Sezuan*, Shen Te asks the gods for help, but they simply float off into the air reciting inane platitudes as the curtain falls. The gods do not have the answer—so the audience must provide it. In the play's epilogue, a character comes forward and addresses us:

> Hey, honorable folks, don't be dismayed
> That we can't seem to end this play! You've stayed
> To see our shining, all-concluding moral,
> And what we've given you has been this bitter
> quarrel.

We know, we know—we're angry too,
To see the curtain down and everything askew.
We'd love to see you stand and cheer—and say
How wonderful you find our charming play!
But we won't put our heads into the sand.
We know your wish is ever our command,
We know you ask for *more*: a firm conclusion
To this alarming more-than-mass confusion.
But what is it? Who knows? Not all your cash
Could buy your way—or ours—from this mish-
    mash.
Do we need heroes? Dreams? New Gods? Or
    None?
Well, tell us—else we're hopelessly undone.
The only thing that we can think to say
Is simply that it's *you* must end this play.
Tell us how our own good woman of Sezuan
Can come to a good ending—if she can!
Honorable folks: you search, and we will trust
That you will find the way. You must, must, must!

Brecht's parables epitomize the conflicts between social classes; they do not presume to solve these conflicts. Indeed, the social problems he addresses are not
to be solved on the stage but in the world itself: the
audience must find the appropriate balance between
morality and greed, between individualism and social
responsibility. Brecht's plays re-enact the basic intellectual dichotomy posed by Marx's dialectical ma-
terialism; thus they are, in a sense, Marxist plays
but they certainly are not Leninist, much less Stalinist.
They radiate a faith in the human potential. Yet while
they are both socially engaged and theatrically eclec-
tic—qualities not particularly noticeable in the Theatre
of the Absurd—they still resound with the fundamental human uncertainty that pervades all of Stylized
Theatre.

FUTURE DIRECTIONS IN STYLIZED THEATRE

Beckett and Brecht represent what are generally considered the two main directions of contemporary
non-realistic theatre, directions which Peter Brook, in
an influential essay, called the "holy" and "rough"
theatres. Beckett's work, the "holy" theatre, ritualizes
man's permanent condition, whereas Brecht's work
undertakes the "rough" approach of grappling with
society and changing social situations. Holy and
rough, absurd and epic, impressionist and expressionist—these are terms that today occasion much
critical contention and many hours of analysis. But it
is well to remember that history probably will not
accord much notice to the critical lines we now seek
so diligently to draw. If the past is any guide to the
future, individual genius and individual artistry will
determine who will be the lasting voices of our age.

Contemporary non-realist drama appears to have
achieved at least coequal status with realism as an
accepted format of modern theatre; indeed, in the
reckoning of serious twentieth-century drama—as
distinct from strictly commercial dramatic entertainment—the stylized play now enjoys a superior prestige. In an age when reality tends to disappoint, we are
looking for more than reality in the theatre. We are
looking for radiations of truth rather than observations of detail. We are looking for syntheses and listening for harmonies. In an age when the temporary
and the transitional seem everywhere obvious, with
human relationships becoming increasingly diver-
sified and short-lived, we are looking for enduring
symbols, patterns, and motions, for the subatomic
structures of our lives. In an age flooded with propaganda and bewildering masses of data, we are looking
for simple elegance, for art.

The modern theatre doubtless will take new turns
in the coming decades. We may come to consider
distinctions such as realist and non-realist, epic and
absurd, mere vestigial remains of irrelevant perspectives. The theatre of the future may spurn the acknowledged masters of our immediate past and turn
in directions still unforeseeable. But what is certain
is that it will reflect the needs and respond to the
spiritual inquiries of its time.

Stylized Theatre came about not simply because
some few persons created it; it derives fundamentally
from human needs. No less than the dithyramb of
ancient Greece, the Stylized Theatre of today addresses a mystery and seeks to fill a hollowness in our
understanding. Its goal is not merely to add to man's
pleasure, but to add to *man*: to complete the human
consciousness. It gives every indication of pursuing
those goals with some success for many years to come.

THE CURRENT THEATRE

Theatre current theatre exists on stage, not on the pages of this or any other book.

The current theatre is being performed this very night, in the multi-million-dollar theatres of the great cities of the world as well as on the simpler stages of schools and communities, dinner theatres and nightclubs, roadhouses and experimental theatre clubs everywhere.

The current theatre is all around us, simply waiting to be discovered, seen, heard, felt, and experienced. The easiest and best way to apprehend its fundamental impulse is to go out and see for oneself.

We cannot evaluate our current theatre with the same objectivity as we do that of the past—even the recent past. Theatre is a business as well as an art, and the flurry of promotion, publicity, and puffery that surrounds each current theatrical success makes a cool perspective difficult. While poets and painters are often ignored in their own time, the opposite is more often true of theatre artists: they are frequently lionized in their own time, only to be forgotten just a few years later. A permanent place in the repertory of

world theatre is the achievement of very few indeed. Among the playwrights once deemed equal to Shakespeare or better are such now dimly remembered figures as John Fletcher, Joseph Addison, Edward George Bulwer-Lytton, August Friedrich Ferdinand von Kotzebue, Eugene Brieux, and Maxwell Anderson. Which of our present-day writers and actors and other theatre artists will achieve more than ephemeral glory? Which, if any, will leave a mark on future generations? No one can answer either question for sure. But there are some directions in the current theatre that show signs of becoming established, and these are worthy of examination.

The current theatre signifies the start of a new phase of the modern theatre, a phase that succeeds one hundred years of "modernism," as we have discussed it in the previous two chapters, following an anomalous and chaotic interruption.

The first phase—from about 1875 to about 1975—witnessed the development of two great rival strains of theatrical ideology: realism and stylization. Each of these two strains first promulgated a purity of form, and each subsequently gave rise to a theatre of great diversity and virtuousity.

Nothing so characterized that one hundred years as artistic freedom. What is more, it was a freedom that was successively enhanced by each new generation. Ibsen's austere and unflinching portrayals of Victorian oppression, Chekhov's complex, gentle dramas of human weakness and courage—these works were strange fare indeed for audiences accustomed to "storm and stress" romanticism and sensationalism. However, they rang of truth in their times, and thus they brought change to the theatre. They also broke political and aesthetic constraints under which playwrights had labored for centuries. In their wake came the growing public acceptance of Shaw's neo-Marxist sermonizing, of Pirandello's paradoxical metatheatrics, of O'Neill's overpowering gutter-speak and then his brooding introspection, of Sartre's grim existential pessimism, and of Beckett's wryly obscure absurdism, each one successively broadening the palette of the theatre artist to previously unthinkable dimensions in what seems now to have been a steady evolutionary process.

But all that changed in the violent decade from the late 1960s through the early 1970s. In that decade political and racial riots erupted in America and abroad; the superpowers came into growing confrontation in the Third World, in Vietnam and Africa; a series of political crises in the United States culminated in the Watergate debacle; and cultural upheaval rumbled throughout the world. The theatre responded to these forces with an artistic freedom that was truly frightening in its extremity. As play-licensing laws fell in England and as legal censorship became locally unenforceable in America, bold profanity, total nudity, and direct political accusation—all unknown in the serious theatre since ancient times—became almost commonplace. Plays popular in America included one accusing the sitting President of murder, one accusing the past Pope of complicity in genocide, one featuring the copulation of a farm boy and his pig, one exhibiting genitalia and mass masturbation, and one concluding with a semi-nude march out of the theatre and into the streets in public protest. Audiences were physically assaulted (in some productions theatregoers were moved about, often by surly command; in one outlandish production they were even urinated on), actors engaged in onstage sexual activity, sexual activity occurred between actors and audience—these and other extreme behaviors became part of the license claimed by a theatre

purportedly trying to make itself heard above the societal din of war and corruption. Or were its adherents only clamoring for personal attention? In any event, it was a decade of violence in the theatre.

By 1975, this mood of violence was largely spent. From what we can see now, the current theatre seems destined to mark the start of a new era, not a continuation or conclusion of its immediate predecessor.

The current theatre has withdrawn, first of all, from the self-conscious extremism of the 1960s. While nudity, profanity, and sexual topics are very much a part of the current theatre, they have lost their edge of political stridency; no longer dramatically novel, they can no longer be effectively exploited for their own sake or used to shame the bourgeoisie or the military-industrial complex. Formalistic experimentation, once considered artistically rebellious, is now the artistic norm, so much so that a play that begins at the chronological end and ends at the chronological beginning, such as Harold Pinter's *Betrayal*, can be considered "conventional," and non-linear, multi-scened, cinemagraphically structured plays can be considered almost tediously "well made."

The worldwide information explosion has also had its impact on the structure of the current theatre, which is the best reported and most widely known in history. The theatre's alliance with films and television, the enormous interest the mass audience has taken in the intricacies of acting and the lives of actors, the national and international communication networks that bring yesterday's London dramatic hit to Los Angeles tomorrow, have all decreased the impact of theatrical surprise and, at the same time, increased the potential for theatrical quality. The current theatre has witnessed a tremendous increase in revivals—of Shakespeare and Shaw, for example, as well as of American musicals such as *Oklahoma!* and *Peter Pan*—and also a great many new plays of artistic merit that explore serious themes. Sheer novelty has become less important to the theatre than it was, as traditional entertainment values and thought-provoking intellectual adventures have reasserted their stageworthiness and their dramatic importance.

These seem to be serious times, and the problems that threaten the world today seem to be particularly tangible ones: resource depletion, mass starvation, nuclear confrontation. It is not a time for the theatre to make frivolous accusations or to sensationalize

Ubu Roi (King Ubu) *shocked Paris from its opening word ("Merdre!"—a French euphemism best translated as "Shittle!") to its closing curtain when it premiered in 1898. This play by Alfred Jarry is a satiric and often juvenile comedy—a farce of the ridiculous. Its theatricality, however, seems eternal, and the play is frequently revived, as here in the Yale Repertory Theatre's production of 1980.*

unimportant aberrations. The underlying themes in the current theatre tend once again to be timeless: death and dying, old age, the preservation of political liberty, social justice, and a secure future world. Formalistic innovation is rarely praised for its own sake, but must be judged against its objectives: does it enhance the dramatist's point, does it make us think, does it make us feel, does it make us care? Less and less, in the current theatre, do audiences tolerate

empty excitement; more and more they demand direction, sensitivity, intelligence, and passionate conviction.

The modern theatre might be entering its greatest phase in this second century. Certainly there is more theatre now than at any time in the past, and there is more interest in theatre. It is odd to think it was only a few decades ago, when developments in cinema and television were much before the public eye, that it became fashionable to consider the theatre a dying art form, a "fabulous invalid" doomed by technological backwardness and the yoke of tradition. Theatre has not just survived; it has thrived. Virtually every U.S. city of any size now has its professional theatres, and most well-populated regions have several college and community theatres as well. The number of professional plays mounted in the United States every year is vastly greater than the number of professional films made for cinema and television combined, and the number of amateur theatricals staged each year boggles the imagination. In Europe the story is perhaps even more impressive: national theatres exist in every country, and in every major city municipal theatres play in permanent repertory with both classics and modern plays while first-rate commercial theatres, particularly in France and England, vie with them for popularity and artistic recognition. The theatre has more than challenged the great boom of the electronic media; it has triumphed. And its triumphs are there to be experienced on any given evening of the theatrical season.

WHERE IT'S HAPPENING

The current theatre happens all over the world: in rural villages, summer resorts, exurban dinner theatres, festival towns, classrooms, prisons, and civic auditoriums, atop mobile street trestles, within ancient palaces, aboard ocean liners—even, in the case of one recent Russian production, inside an interurban railway car.

But mostly the current theatre is "celebrated" in the cities—in the traditionally great theatrical capitals such as New York, Moscow, London, Paris, Vienna, Tokyo, and Berlin, as well as in cities of more modest theatrical repute, such as Kyoto, Zurich, Hamburg, Cracow, Chicago, San Francisco, Seattle, Minneapolis, New Haven, Louisville, Los Angeles, Hartford, Boston, and Washington, D.C.

In America, New York City is without question the center of the nation's theatrical activity. Every year it is the site of more performances, more openings, more revivals, more tours, and more dramatic criticism than any half-dozen other American cities put together. Theatrically, it is the showcase of the nation. In the minds of audiences, the "Big Apple" is *the* place to experience theatre; thus the New York theatre is a

prime tourist attraction and a major factor in the city's economy. In the minds of theatre artists—actors, directors, playwrights, and designers—New York is the town where the standards are the highest, the challenge is the greatest, and the rewards are the most magnificent. "Will it play in Peoria?" may be the big question in the minds of film and television producers, but "Will it make it in New York?" remains the cardinal issue in the rarefied world of American professional theatre. Thus the reality of New York is surrounded by a fantasy of New York, and in a "business" as laced with fantasy as is the theatre, New York commands a strategic importance of incomprehensible value in the theatrical world.

Broadway

Broadway is the longest street on Manhattan, slicing diagonally down the entire length of the island. What gives Broadway its distinction, however, is not its length but the thirty to forty theatres that cluster about its midpoint—in the block or two left and right between 44th Street and 52nd Street. This is the legendary "Great White Way": a concentration of professional theatres of astounding diversity, exuberance, and extravagance.

It is not a fashionable part of town, nor even a comfortable one. Hot dog stands, souvenir shops, tourist emporiums, pinball parlors, multiple-X "adult" film houses, and other even more sleazy enterprises line the main streets of Broadway and Eighth Avenue, while on the side streets the theatres are surrounded by grim looking offices, windowless walls, and delivery elevators. One gazing upon this scene in the harsh light of day might be tempted to suspect that the London aldermen of Shakespeare's time did right when they banished the theatres across the Thames.

But come evenings—Sundays excepted—it suddenly becomes clear why the word "Broadway" is synonymous with "excitement" in the minds of so many theatre lovers.

Marquees are lit everywhere; on some streets you can see five or six glittering facades at a single glance. Each bank of lights proclaims a play title and the names of principal actors; those actors whose names are "above the title" are the town's top attractions of the moment, the "stars" who will appear "live, on stage" eight times a week for the gawking approval of tourists, students, conventioneers, honeymooners, celebrities, and unemployed actors alike.

Bright, colorful show posters adorn walls and windows, particularly on block-long "Shubert Alley" connecting two playhouses owned by the family of that name. Huge blown-up photographs of favorable reviews, and of scenes from plays, compete for the attention of the crowds milling about in search of tickets, canceled reservations at SRO (standing room only) attractions, and autographs from their favorite stars. Lines of people stretch into the street, where police mounted on horses ride patrol and taxicabs inch in to disgorge their passengers. The romance and sheer theatrical excitement of the scene is apparent to first-timer and playgoing veteran alike; it is a romance floated on memories of Bernhardt and Barrymore, of Streisand and George M. Cohan, of Burton and Olivier, and on performances long since completed on the boards but perennially lingering in the atmosphere of 46th Street.

Over the years, the Broadway theatre has acquired a reputation for being glittery but conventional, expensive but neither innovative nor adventurous. This is somewhat misleading. It is true that the Broadway theatre has become, by and large, a showcase for plays originated elsewhere; the Broadway production format is simply too cumbersome and too expensive for experimental try-outs of serious plays, most of which begin their production history in regional theatres, off-Broadway theatres, or in the subsidized theatres of Europe. It is also true that the Broadway playhouses tend to be poorly equipped and architecturally old-fashioned; most of them have had little revamping since they were built around the turn of the century, most have rigid proscenium formats, outmoded equipment, and drafty dressing rooms. And finally, it is true that Broadway has proven itself so successful as a home for American musical theatre that to many minds Broadway simply *means* musical theatre. Still, notwithstanding

Waiting for standing room tickets to a hit Broadway musical, crowds line up in fabled Shubert Alley and gaze at theatre posters adorning wall.

all this, the Broadway stage remains the place in America where theatrical works find their greatest and most lasting impact. For in the end, Broadway is where the audience is, and actors, authors, and directors find that fact difficult if not impossible to resist.

Off Broadway and Off-Off Broadway

Not all of New York theatre is performed within the geographical and commercial confines of the Broadway district: distinctly non-Broadway theatres have operated in the nation's largest city for many decades. The symbolic centrality of Broadway, however, is so strong that these theatres are named not for what they are, but for what they are not: they are the "*off-Broadway*" theatres. "Off Broadway" is a term that came into theatrical parlance during the 1950s. It refers to professional theatres operating on significantly reduced budgets. They are to be found primar-ily in Greenwich Village, in the area south of Houston Street ("SoHo"), and on the upper East and West sides of Manhattan. A few houses in the Broadway geographical area itself fall into this category, but only because they operate under off-Broadway financing structures. Yet another category of theatre is known as "*off-off Broadway*," a term dating from the 1960s. This category consists of semi-professional or wholly amateur theatres which are located throughout the metropolitan area, often in church basements, YMCAs, coffee houses, and converted studios or garages.

The off-Broadway and off-off Broadway theatres generate a great deal of fertile and vigorous activity; leaner and less costly than the Broadway stage, they attract specialized cadres of devotees, some of whom would never allow themselves to be seen in a Broadway house. Much of the original creative work in the American theatre since World War II has been done in these theatres, and their generally low ticket prices

The "TKTS" booth on New York's Duffy Square (Broadway at 46th Street) sells half-price tickets for Broadway and off Broadway shows on day of performance only. Here, New York patrons brave rain to purchase seats at one of more than three dozen shows performing that evening.

SWEENEY TODD

Sweeney Todd is one of those works which must be classed as an American Broadway musical, for it boasts a theatrical format that is quintessentially American: bold, lavish, and spectacular. At the same time, it differs radically from most American musical theatre of the past in that it incorporates strains from both the epic theatre of Bertolt Brecht and the early Expressionist theatre of Eugene O'Neill.

Musical plays are customarily "authored" by a triumvirate, with one person writing the spoken dialogue, or book, a second person writing the lyrics, a third writing the music. Two writers collaborated in the creation of Sweeney Todd: Hugh Wheeler wrote the book, and Stephen Sondheim wrote the music and lyrics. Sondheim, clearly the leading figure in this collaboration (which also included director Harold Prince), has played a major role in the creation of an impressive number of American musicals of the 1950s, 1960s, and 1970s, including West Side Story, Gypsy, Follies, Company, and A Little Night Music.

Sweeney Todd is based on a contemporary British version, by author Christopher Bond, of a nineteenth-century English melodrama. It tells the story of the "Demon Barber of Fleet Street," who decides to wreak revenge upon a corrupt English judiciary by butchering his customers and, with the help of his landlady, Mrs. Lovett, grinding their corpses to make salable meat pies. That this grisly tale should serve as the basis of an American musical is in itself a startling idea, but the concoction of songs and staging effects created by Sondheim, Wheeler, and Prince have added to the sensation by virtually redefining the musical form.

The staging of Sweeney Todd is something only the Broadway theatre could finance or accommodate. Onto the stage of the cavernous Uris Theatre, designer Eugene Lee brought a gigantic, real nineteenth-century factory which had been found abandoned in Rhode Island. This structure was painstakingly disassembled at its original site and just as painstakingly reassembled in the theatre. The desired effect was not realism, for Sweeney Todd is not set in a factory; instead, the old building, complete with its steel girders,

Angela Lansbury and Len Cariou sing a duet in Broadway production of Sweeney Todd, *directed by Hal Prince in 1978–79. The original Broadway stage setting for* Sweeney Todd, *designed by Eugene Lee, featured an entirely reconstructed factory, within which a cube represented Mrs. Lovett's meat shop, and Sweeney's barber shop above. In background is painted drop of the London harbor used in play's opening scenes; pulleys and catwalks abound as industrial set dressing. Len Cariou is barber in this photograph of Broadway production.*

ancient windows and skylights, catwalks and pulleys, and broken-down machinery, served as a surround for the action, a symbol indicative of a certain social atmosphere: the oppression of industrial London and the grimy sordidness which is the economic and moral background for the play's action. The action itself takes place, for the most part, in a setting which represents Todd's and his landlady's London quarters. Expressionist effects, such as a cruelly piercing factory whistle that sounds at the play's moments of crisis, punctuate the action; and the songs, often as not, are addressed directly to the audience in pure Brechtian fashion.

It is clear that *Sweeney Todd* has opened up the possibility of a reinvigoration of the American Broadway musical, partly by infusing that form with current intellectual and aesthetic developments in the theatre, partly by reasserting traditional elements of melodrama, grand opera, and Grand Guignol from the nineteenth-century theatre, and partly by dint of sheer genius and creative extravagance on the part of its creators.

have lured successive generations of theatre audiences their way to see original works before they are showcased to the Broadway masses, works still raw with creative energy and radiating the excitement of their ongoing origination.

In composite, Broadway and non-Broadway theatres provide almost every conceivable opportunity for theatrical exploration and achievement, making New York one of the greatest theatre cities—if not *the* greatest—in the world. Neither Broadway nor its once- and twice-removed competitors should be seen in isolation or in simple opposition, for they stimulate each other and are extraordinary primarily in combination. Between them, they present in season about fifty professional and one hundred amateur productions *each night*; they also mount close to a thousand new productions each year. Their offerings are a great conglomeration of original scripts, classical revivals, opulent musicals, provocative imports, and a basic collection of workman-like thrillers, reviews, comedies, and holdover dramas. What is more, thanks to extensive press coverage in the national media— weekly news magazines, monthly journals of opinion, television talk shows and specials, and the annual televising of the "Tony" awards ceremonies—the New York theatrical season does not long remain a strictly local phenomenon: it becomes a centerpiece of American cultural activity, and before long the world is privy to its innovations, its successes, its radical ideas, its catastrophes, and its gossip.

The American Road and the Regions

For more than a hundred years preceding the last decade, the popular American theatre was effectively divided between Broadway and "the road," the latter being a quaint descriptive term first applied to the half-dozen theatre stages in major cities across the land where Broadway successes would play once their New York runs terminated. Sometimes these "national tours" were first-class productions throughout, complete with original casts and in all important ways indistinguishable from the original overall design. Often, however, they involved second-string companies playing short engagements while the original cast continued to play in New York—and the posters that proclaimed "Direct from New York!" in front of the theatre in Wilkes-Barre referred only to the play,

not to the cast or the scenery or anything else. "The road" was a colorful era in the American theatre—an era that gave us the memorable phrase "one-night stand"—and indeed national tours still play a role in the overall theatrical scene of many U.S. cities.

But the regional theatre, or the resident theatre as it is often called, is a far more vital force in American theatre today. It consists of non-commercial professional theatres, loosely associated in a league (the League of Resident Theatres, or LORT), which are independent producing groups now found in close to a hundred cities, each presenting a season of plays with a semi-permanent resident group of artists. Some of these theatres operate two or more facilities simultaneously and present audiences with a substantially varied repertory of plays. Several such theatres have produced important world premieres. Ordinarily the resident theatres are not expected to show a profit; they therefore tend to use their relative security to produce a mix of classical revivals and experimental contemporary plays. Some of the best of these groups tour nationally and internationally, and a few, such as the American Conservatory Theatre (San Francisco), the Actor's Theatre of Louisville, the Long Wharf Theatre (New Haven), the Arena Stage (Washington, D.C.), the Tyrone Guthrie Theatre (Minneapolis), the Trinity Square Repertory Company (Providence), and the Center Theatre Group (Los Angeles), are widely known for their excellence and/or their innovation.

Regional theatres enjoy a relationship with New York theatres that is much like that which exists between Broadway and non-Broadway: the two are inextricably linked—and although much is made of their relative gains and losses, a healthy competition and sharing of resources prevails between them. Plays that are favorably received in the regional theatres often make their way to New York, and vice versa, and the same sort of exchange goes on with respect to actors, directors, and designers. The communications headquarters for the regional theatres, an organization known as the Theatre Communications Group, is located in New York for the good and sufficient reason that important regional developments usually receive widespread attention only when they are "noticed" by the national news media—which are also headquartered in New York.

The growth of regional theatre has certainly been one of the most exciting developments in American theatre in the past thirty years. Aided by the first significant government grants to the arts in our national history (beginning in the 1960s), regional theatre has become a major institution for the creation of original, non-imitative works addressed to an ever-growing dramatic audience. In responding to the tastes and interests of local audiences as well as to more strictly aesthetic challenges, regional theatres have explored political, social, and historical issues that heretofore could never have been aired on Broadway—and, in the process, they have greatly expanded our entire concept of the function of theatre. Above all, the growth of regional theatre has led to a healthy diversification in the theatre profession itself: an actor or designer or director may now aim at making a reasonable living in the theatre in virtually any major city in the country—a possibility that, quite shockingly, was utterly unheard-of only a few decades ago.

Theatre Abroad

European theatre is highly institutionalized, with state-supported and city-supported theatres the norm rather than the exception in all but a few localities. West Germany, for example, prides itself on its 137 governmentally funded theatres; East Germany has 113. In those and other European countries, theatres are as routinely financed by public monies as are libraries and museums in America. State support has its drawbacks, of course, including the intransigent threat of bureaucratic meddling and the occasional imposition—or threat of imposition—of political control over the artistic product. However, the generously funded public theatres of Europe are spared a great many financial worries and can undertake the production of a wide variety of classics and experimental plays without fear of sudden collapse at the box office.

England

England is likely to be the first and most rewarding stop for American students on a European theatre tour, first because the language is familiar, and second because the English theatre is currently one of the most vigorous in the world. Two subsidized companies provide the focus of English theatrical activity: the National Theatre, operating three stages in a fabulous complex overlooking the River Thames on Shakespeare's Bankside; and the Royal Shakespeare Company, which operates theatres both in London (the Aldwych) and in Shakespeare's natal town of Stratford on Avon. Each of these companies has several plays in repertory at any given time, and in a week's visit, split between London and Stratford, it would be possible with adroit scheduling to view nearly a dozen different productions.

Commercial theatres in London also are active year round (although as in New York, the most active period is the "season" stretching from October through May), and many fine plays and productions may be seen at the theatres which line Shaftesbury Avenue in the West End, a district comparable to Broadway, and at "fringe" theatres, located elsewhere in the city, which correspond to our off-Broadway and off-off Broadway ventures. Regional theatre, or "provincial theatre" as it is called in England, is as active there as in the United States, with publicly supported theatres in every major town performing plays in repertory or stock during the seasonal period. Indeed, the "provincial rep" of English towns is the traditional training ground for English actors, who are considered by many to be the most polished and versatile actors in the world.

So esteemed is England in the world of theatre—owing to the past contributions of Shakespeare, Marlowe, Garrick, and Shaw, as well as the splendid contemporary achievements of playwrights such as Tom Stoppard, Edward Bond, Harold Pinter, Simon Gray, Alan Ayckbourne, David Storey, Trevor Griffiths, and Peter Shaffer—that several American colleges have set up summer drama programs to allow their students to experience the riches of English theatre and scholarship at first hand. Flocks of Americans, students and tourists alike, descend every year upon the meccas of London and Stratford and on the summer festivals of Chichester and Edinburgh.

France and Germany

France and Germany, which spawned the Theatre of the Absurd and the Theatre of Alienation, respectively—as well as the earlier Symbolist and Expressionist dramatic movements—remain active theatre centers today. Both countries provide a mix of traditional and strikingly original theatre.

French theatre, headquartered as always in Paris, maintains the traditional Royal Theatre style in the Comédie Française, which continues to operate in the French capital much as it has since 1680. But newer nationalized theatres, including the touring Théâtre

National Populaire and the provincial Théâtre National de Strasbourg, have specialized in experimental and aesthetically revolutionary works, and they now dominate the French theatrical scene. Comedies of the Broadway type (but entirely Gallic in flavor) are the basic fare at the commercial theatres along the boulevards; indeed, the term "boulevard theatre" in France signifies a light, diverting piece, invariably having to do with marital infidelity. More experimental works can be seen throughout the city and in the suburbs, where beaches, parks, and abandoned factories are more likely to serve as dramatic venues than traditional theatres. An annual summer theatre festival at the ancient city of Avignon, in the south of France, brings together the most significant of the avant-garde and popular productions of the preceding year and presents them in the spectacular setting of the former Papal Palace, offering visitors a unique opportunity to sample the entire range of contemporary French dramatic endeavor.

In contrast to France, Germany has no theatre capital; rather, it boasts a myriad of civic theatres —and every year one or more of them does something that causes a national sensation. In recent years, Hamburg, West Berlin, Munich, Frankfurt, Cologne, Bochum, and Bremen have all been sites of exciting theatrical activity in West Germany, and on the other side of the Iron Curtain, East Berlin and Rostock have

The Comédie Française, founded in 1680, presents classic French plays in the traditional manner, but also experiments with contemporary stagings. Here, in a recent production of Molière's Don Juan, *the traditional chandeliers are used in a novel fashion to enhance a sense of decadence.*

A Comédie Française production of Racine's Britannicus, *staged in modern dress, 1978. The Comédie remains the repository of French neo-classical tradition, but is free to experiment with contemporary staging practices.*

had notable successes. German theatre, adhering to none of the traditions of its past, is perhaps the most radically innovative in the Western world, particularly in the areas of directing and design; thus a visit to German theatre, particularly in a broad sampling, can be of inestimable value even to the theatre student who has no knowledge of the German language. Richly imaginative and frequently visually aston-

ishing, the German theatre offers a wealth of fresh insights into the possibilities of theatrical aesthetics.

In combination, America, England, France, and Germany provide a dazzling spectrum of contemporary theatre; a survey of all four, either through personal observation or through the vast literature of the theatre, would be an immensely rewarding undertaking for anyone interested in the stage, in contem-

The annual Avignon Festival, in France, features dozens of experimental productions gathered from all over the nation and from abroad. Shown are the municipal theatre of Angers (France) presentations of Aventures et Aventures Nouvelles (TOP), *and* Calques (BOTTOM), *two avant-garde works.*

The outdoor stage of the Papal Palace, where principal productions are staged, here being readied for a musical performance.

porary art and aesthetics, in worldwide intellectual movements and developments, and in social art and culture. But these theatres hardly exhaust the activity in theatre today.

Other Countries

The Russian theatre, perhaps the most impressive in the world in terms of sheer magnitude, is one of the glories of the Soviet Union, where it enjoys a centrality in the life of the people that is unknown in most of the Western democracies. The theatres of Eastern Europe, particularly in Poland and Czechoslovakia, are now famous for their innovative direction, design, and architecture; indeed, it may be said that America is a theatrical backwater when compared to Eastern Europe in certain areas of technological development. Contemporary Japanese theatre, offering both traditional Noh and Kabuki forms and new forms portraying extreme eroticism and sado-masochistic violence, has created a blend of theatrical fares that rivals any in its provocative creativity. And a single playwright from South Africa, Athol Fugard, has done more than any other native son to bring international attention to the political suppression that obtains in that land of racial *apartheid*.

Only our own cultural insularity keeps us imagining ourselves at the center of the universe, the true and legitimate heirs of those who invented theatre; the truth is that theatre is happening throughout the known world, and in forms so diverse as to defy accounting or assimilation. Every component of theatre—from architecture to acting, from dramaturgy to directing—is in the process of change, of learning, of rebelling from convention, of building anew. The theatre's diversity is its very life, and change is the foremost of its vital signs. We must not think to pin it down, but rather to seek it out, to produce it ourselves, and to participate in its growth.

THREE PLAYS OF THE CURRENT THEATRE

The plays of the current theatre exhibit an enormous range of structures, themes, and styles; the traditional genre designations seem singularly inappropriate to describe most serious current works, and even the newer categorizations are usually ill suited to the most recent works. Moreover, contemporary playwrights seem particularly loath to see their art labeled, and virtually all of them eschew "schools" or aesthetic causes. Aside from those brief generalities tentatively broached at the beginning of this chapter, the current theatre seems defined mainly by its diversity, and this diversity can be best illustrated by a few examples.

The following three plays differ widely in tone and treatment. All three have achieved considerable popular success in their American stagings of the late 1970s and early 1980s; however, none has established itself as a classic—not even as a modern classic. They simply indicate some of the directions the modern theatre is taking as it enters its second century.

Wings

Wings, by American author Arthur Kopit (previously known for his intriguingly titled *Oh Dad, Poor Dad, Mama's Hung You in the Closet and I'm Feeling So Sad*), was originally written as a play for radio. It was subsequently revised for the stage, and was presented first at the Yale Repertory Theatre in New Haven, Connecticut, whence it eventually moved to Broadway.

The play is one of a growing number of dramatic works that present "case studies" of individuals in medical distress: other recent plays with similar themes include Bernard Pomerance's *The Elephant Man* (American, 1979), dealing with extreme disfigurement; Albert Innaurato's *The Transfiguration of Benno Blimpie* (American, 1978), dealing with obesity; Peter Shaffer's *Equus* (British, 1973), dealing with schizophrenic behavior; and Brian Clark's *Whose Life Is It Anyway* (British, 1978), dealing with total paralysis. Medical issues are not the dominant concern of these plays, of course, but in each case a medical problem furnishes a perspective for the playwright's philosophical investigations.

Wings takes place in a setting that is nothing but "a system of black scrim panels that can move silently and easily, creating the impression of featureless, labyrinthine corridors." The setting, therefore, represents both a hospital and the inside of a patient's mind—the patient being a Mrs. Stilson, former aviatrix, now a victim of brain stroke. Mrs. Stilson sits in a chair downstage of the panels, and what we in the audience see and hear is a confusion of images, sounds, words, and illusions which represent Mrs. Stilson's "inner self," where "time and space are without definition," and "information is coming in too scrambled and too fast to be properly decoded." "Were her head a pinball game," Kopit says, "It would register TILT."

Kopit achieves this "scrambled" effect through a brilliant dramaturgical design whereby the information conveyed on stage assumes the form it would take in the perceptions of the stroke victim herself: in other words, by his fashioning of the dramatic dialogue and imagery, Kopit gives his audience the opportunity not merely to observe stroke, but to experience it. The first scene, entitled "Catastrophe," illustrates his technique:

IMAGES	SOUNDS OUTSIDE HERSELF	MRS. STILSON'S VOICE
	(SOUNDS live or on tape, altered or unadorned)	(VOICE live or on tape, altered or unadorned)
	Of wind.	
Mostly, it is whiteness. *Dazzling, blinding.*	Of someone breathing with effort, unevenly.	*Oh my God oh my god oh my God—*
	Of something ripping, like a sheet.	*—trees clouds houses mostly planes flashing past, images without words, utter disarray disbelief, never seen this kind of thing before!*
Occasionally, there are brief rhombs of color, explosions of color, the color red being dominant.	Of something flapping, the sound suggestive of an old screen door perhaps, or a sheet or sail in the wind. It is a rapid fibrillation. And it is used mostly to mark transitions. It can seem ominous or not.	*Where am I? How'd I get here?*
The mirrors, of course, reflect infinitely. Sense of endless space, endless corridors.	Of a woman's scream (though this sound should be altered by filters so it resembles other things, such as sirens).	*My leg (What's my leg?) feels wet arms . . . wet too, belly same chin nose everything (Where are they taking me?) something sticky (What has happened to my plane?) feel something sticky.*
	Of random noises recorded in a busy city hospital, then altered so as to be only minimally recognizable.	*Doors! Too many doors!*
Nothing seen that is not a fragment. Every aspect of her world has been shattered.	Of a car's engine at full speed.	*Must have . . . fallen cannot . . . move at all sky . . . (Gliding!) dark cannot . . . talk (Feel as if I'm gliding!).*
	Of a siren (altered to resemble a woman screaming).	
Utter isolation.	Of an airplane coming closer, thundering overhead, then zooming off into silence.	*Yes, feels cool, nice . . . Yes, this is the life all right!*
In this vast whiteness, like apparitions, partial glimpses of doctors and nurses can be seen. They appear and disappear like a pulse. They are never in one place for long. The mirrors multiply their incomprehensibility.	Of random crowd noises, the crowd greatly agitated. In the crowd, people can be heard calling for help, a doctor, an ambulance. But all the sounds are garbled.	*My plane! What has happened to my plane!* *Help . . .*
	Of people whispering.	

IMAGES	SOUNDS OUTSIDE HERSELF	MRS. STILSON'S VOICE

—all around faces of which nothing
known no sense ever all wiped out
blank like ice I think saw it once
flying over something some place all
was white sky and sea clouds ice
almost crashed couldn't tell where I
was heading right side up topsy-
turvy under over I was flying actually if I can I do yes do recall was
upside down can you believe it almost scraped my head on the ice
caps couldn't tell which way was up
wasn't even dizzy strange things
happen to me that they do!

Of many people asking questions
simultaneously, no question
comprehensible.

*Sometimes the dark panels are
opaque, sometimes transparent. Always, they convey a sense of layers,
multiplicity, separation. Sense constantly of doors opening, closing,
opening, closing.*

Of doors opening, closing, opening,
closing.

Of someone breathing oxygen
through a mask.

VOICES: (garbled) Just relax. / No
one's going to hurt you. / Can you
hear us? / Be careful! / You're
hurting her! / No, we're not.
/ Don't lift her, leave her where she
is! / Someone call an ambulance!
/ I don't think she can hear.

*Fragments of hospital equipment
appear out of nowhere and disappear just as suddenly. Glimpse always too brief to enable us to
identify what this equipment is, or
what its purpose.*

MALE VOICE: Have you any idea—

*What's my name? I don't know my
name!*

OTHER VOICES: (garbled) Do you
know your name? / Do you know
where you are? / What year is this?
/ If I say the tiger has been killed by
the lion, which animal is dead?

*Where's my arm? I don't have an
arm!*

*Mrs. Stilson's movements seem ran-
dom. She is a person wandering
through space, lost.*

A hospital paging system heard.

What's an arm?

*Finally, Mrs. Stilson is led by atten-
dants downstage, to a chair. Then
left alone.*

Equipment being moved through
stone corridors, vast vaulting space.
Endless echoing.

*AB-ABC-ABC123DE451212 what?
123—12345678972357 better yes no
problem I'm okay soon be out soon
be over storm . . . will pass I'm sure.
Always has.*

SECTION THREE: THE PRESENT

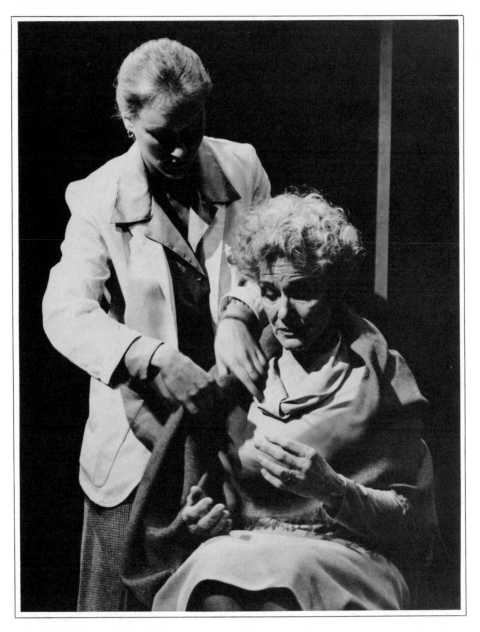

Constance Cummings as Mrs. Stilson, in original production of Wings *by the Yale Repertory Theatre, directed by John Madden. Cummings is attended by Marianne Owen as Amy.*

By an ingenious combination of voices, non-verbal sounds, colors, and movements with an intricate interplay of actors, hospital equipment, and panels, Kopit captures the intellectual dislocation caused by brain trauma and compels his audience to partake of the victim's fear, bewilderment, and sense of helplessness. *Wings* is a disturbing play, but it is also extremely thought-provoking. Beyond the purely medical issues, it explores a whole range of philosophical and epistemological questions: What is communication? What is emotional support? What is learning? What are words and what are they worth? Finally, the play is inspiring as a portrait of a human being whose struggle to control her inner world has intense meaning for every sensitive person.

Buried Child

Buried Child, a play by American actor-author Sam Shepard, was originally produced at the Magic Theatre of San Francisco in 1978, and moved to New York's off Broadway stage the following year. Shepard established himself as an American avant-garde playwright in the 1960s and 1970s with such works as *The Tooth of Crime, Operation Sidewinder, Angel City*, and *Curse of the Starving Class*. All of his plays have the characteristic of "supra-realism"; that is, they are ostensibly realistic but actually suffused with patterns of menacing obscurity and mythic symbolism.

Buried Child is set in a decaying farmhouse in the American Middle West; the degenerate condition of the house is echoed by that of the family who inhabit it. The setting is realized in wholly realistic detail, down to the "pale, frayed carpet," the "upright lamp with a faded yellow shade," and the "large, old-fashioned brown TV" which is left on during much of the play. The dialogue too is of the everyday variety, but the incidents, the interactions, and the involvements of the play are just enough removed from the familiar to create an atmosphere of mystery, menace, and doom.

This scene, which comes near the beginning of the play, conveys something of the overriding spirit of *Buried Child*. In it, the aged, irascible Dodge—who sits on a sofa watching the TV—calls in his middle-aged son, Tilden, over shouted objections of his offstage wife, Halie. Inexplicably, Tilden enters with an armload of freshly picked, unshucked corn:

DODGE: (*yelling off left*) Tilden!

HALIE'S VOICE: Dodge, what are you trying to do?

DODGE: (*yelling off left*) Tilden, get in here!

HALIE'S VOICE: Why do you enjoy stirring things up?

DODGE: I don't enjoy anything!

HALIE'S VOICE: That's a terrible thing to say.

DODGE: Tilden!

HALIE'S VOICE: That's the kind of statement that leads people right to the end of their rope.

DODGE: Tilden!

HALIE'S VOICE: It's no wonder people turn to Christ!

DODGE: TILDEN!!

HALIE'S VOICE: It's no wonder the messengers of God's word are shouted down in public places!

DODGE: TILDEN!!!!

DODGE *goes into a violent, spasmodic coughing attack as* TILDEN *enters from stage left, his arms loaded with fresh ears of corn.* TILDEN *is* DODGE'S *oldest son, late forties, wears heavy construction boots, covered with mud, dark green work pants, a plaid shirt and a faded brown windbreaker. He has a butch haircut, wet from the rain. Something about him is profoundly burned out and displaced. He stops center stage with the ears of corn in his arms and just stares at* DODGE *until he slowly finishes his coughing attack.* DODGE *looks up at him slowly. He stares at the corn. Long pause as they watch each other.*

HALIE'S VOICE: Dodge, if you don't take that pill nobody's going to force you.

The two men ignore the voice.

DODGE: (*to* TILDEN) Where'd you get that?

TILDEN: Picked it.

DODGE: You picked all that?

TILDEN *nods.*

DODGE: You expecting company?

TILDEN: No.

DODGE: Where'd you pick it from?

TILDEN: Right out back.

DODGE: Out back where!

TILDEN: Right out in back.

DODGE: There's nothing out there!

TILDEN: There's corn.

DODGE: There hasn't been corn out there since about nineteen thirty-five! That's the last time I planted corn out there!

TILDEN: It's out there now.

DODGE: (*yelling at stairs*) Halie!

HALIE'S VOICE: Yes dear!

DODGE: Tilden's brought a whole bunch of corn in here! There's no corn out in back is there?

TILDEN: (*to himself*) There's tons of corn.

HALIE'S VOICE: Not that I know of!

DODGE: That's what I thought.

HALIE'S VOICE: Not since about nineteen thirty five!

DODGE: (*to* TILDEN) That's right. Nineteen thirty five.

TILDEN: It's out there now.

DODGE: You go and take that corn back to wherever you got it from!

TILDEN: (*After pause, staring at* DODGE) It's picked. I picked it all in the rain. Once it's picked you can't put it back.

DODGE: I haven't had trouble with neighbors here for fifty-seven years. I don't even know who the neighbors are! And I don't wanna know! Now go put that corn back where it came from!

TILDEN *stares at* DODGE *then walks slowly over to him and dumps all the corn on* DODGE'S *lap and steps back.* DODGE *stares at the corn then back to* TILDEN. *Long pause.*

DODGE: Are you having trouble here, Tilden? Are you in some kind of trouble?

TILDEN: I'm not in any trouble.

DODGE: You can tell me if you are. I'm still your father.

TILDEN: I know you're still my father.

DODGE: I know you had a little trouble back in New Mexico. That's why you came out here.

TILDEN: I never had any trouble.

A confrontation in Buried Child, *centering on Bradley's artificial leg and a bouquet of flowers. From 1979 American Conservatory Theatre production, directed by Edward Hastings.*

DODGE: Tilden, your mother told me all about it.

TILDEN: What'd she tell you?

> TILDEN *pulls some chewing tobacco out of his jacket and bites off a plug.*

DODGE: I don't have to repeat what she told me! She told me all about it!

TILDEN: Can I bring my chair in from the kitchen?

DODGE: What?

TILDEN: Can I bring in my chair from the kitchen?

DODGE: Sure. Bring your chair in.

> TILDEN *exits left.* DODGE *pushes all the corn off his lap onto the floor. . . .*

Where did the corn come from? Why does Tilden bring it in? Why does he drop it on Dodge's lap? What was the "trouble" in New Mexico? We will never receive overt answers to these questions. *Buried Child* is a play that radiates implication and never becomes explicit. It creates the impression of a theme not by rational plot development or logical moral positioning, but by a pattern of seeming non sequiturs, abrupt transitions, and bizarre, enigmatic actions.

There was, we find out, a baby that was killed many years ago and buried by Dodge out in back; this is the "buried child" of the title, a metaphorical fertilizer for Tilden's corn and a symbolic seminalization for mid America, which the play gives us to understand was established by acts of murder and built by successive cover-ups. A series of demented children—there is also a crazed amputee, Bradley, and Tilden's shell-shocked and psychotic son, Vince —uncover the family's horrific past in the play's ambiguous (but curiously cathartic) conclusion.

Shepard plays upon our natural fascination with —and fear of —the unexpected and the unusual. The contrast between Dodge's violent spasm of coughing and Tilden's silent, corn-laden entrance exemplifies the theatricality of Shepard's technique: it is a wholly unforgettable—if inexplicable—moment of theatre. So also is Tilden's act of throwing the corn on Dodge's lap. The repetition of lines

TILDEN: Can I bring my chair in from the kitchen?

DODGE: What?

TILDEN: Can I bring my chair in from the kitchen?

seems at first a simple mimicry of humdrum conver-

sation; as part of an overall pattern of dialogue, however, it enhances rhythms of uncertainty and confusion: unanswered questions about the possibilities of communication between these characters in their insistent attempts to get through to . . . something.

Shepard's supra-realism, with its highly theatrical use of rhythms and juxtapositions, creates an electrified surface intensity around an obscure center. Similar techniques are discernible in the recent plays of British authors Harold Pinter (*The Caretaker, The Homecoming, Betrayal*), David Storey (*The Contractor, The Changing Room, Home*), and Simon Gray (*Butley, Otherwise Engaged, Close of Play*), as well as in the plays of American authors Edward Albee (*Who's Afraid of Virginia Woolf?, Tiny Alice, The Lady from Dubuque*) and David Mamet (*Sexual Perversity in Chicago, American Buffalo, A Life in the Theatre*). Finally, supra-realism is a device that seeks patterns beneath the surface of everyday reality, and meanings in the silences that punctuate everyday speech.

Bedroom Farce

Bedroom Farce is one of a series of contemporary English comedies written by British dramatist Alan Ayckbourn (others include *Absurd Person Singular, The Norman Conquests,* and *Absent Friends*). *Bedroom Farce* was first produced in 1975 by the Library Theatre in Scarborough, England, with which Ayckbourn is associated; the play was subsequently produced by the National Theatre in London in 1977 and came to Broadway and various other American cities shortly thereafter.

Like all of Ayckbourn's works, *Bedroom Farce* is an ingenious comedy of current manners, novel in its dramatic structure and reasonably true to life in its concerns. The setting for *Bedroom Farce* is three bedrooms, all in view simultaneously; the characters consist of four couples who, for reasons cleverly worked out in the plot, find themselves in one bedroom after another by turns. While the innuendos of this play are highly sexual, the action consists primarily of animated verbal exchanges and comic business and pratfalls; thus does the play live up to the farcical structure promised by its title.

The opening scene of *Bedroom Farce*, an exchange of dialogue between Ernest and Delia, the oldest couple in the play, typifies the witty and very British repartee mastered by Ayckbourn. The scene takes place in that bedroom which is described as a "large Victorian" room "in need of redecoration":

> . . . DELIA *sits in her bedroom at her dressing table mirror. She is going out. She is in her slip and finishing her make-up. An elaborate operation.* ERNEST *wanders in. Birdlike, bumbling, nearly sixty. He is in evening dress. He stares at* DELIA. *They are obviously going to be late but* ERNEST *has learnt that impatience gets him nowhere.*

ERNEST: Have you got much further to go?

DELIA: (*without turning*) Not long now.

ERNEST: Good. Good show. (*he walks out humming restlessly*) No, that is definitely a damp patch, you know.

DELIA: Mmm?

ERNEST: A damp patch. Definitely. It's getting in from somewhere. I've just been standing on the spare bed in there feeling the ceiling. The verdict is, very very damp.

DELIA: Oh dear.

ERNEST: Yes. Which only goes to confirm my suspicion that those chaps we had crawling about the roof for six months didn't know their job. (*he leans out of the window backwards*)

DELIA: What are you doing?

ERNEST: I'm trying to catch a glimpse of the re-pointing. It's seeping in from somewhere.

DELIA: You'll fall out in a minute.

ERNEST: No. You can't see a thing. That gutterwork's obscuring the whole. . . Good lord. That needs a spot of attention. It's hanging off at one end. Good lord.

DELIA: Darling, you're in my light.

ERNEST: There's a whole chunk of guttering here hanging on by a screw. (*he comes in*) Hadn't noticed that before.

DELIA: Oh, did I tell you. Susannah phoned this afternoon.

ERNEST: (*thoughtful*) Did he? Did he indeed.

DELIA: No, not he. Susannah.

ERNEST: Who?

DELIA: Susannah.

ERNEST: Oh, Susannah. Jolly good. Very worrying that guttering, you know. One light to medium monsoon, we'll have a water-fall in the dining room.

DELIA: She sounded very agitated.

ERNEST: Oh yes.

DELIA: Things are not good between her and Trevor.

ERNEST: Ah. It's twenty past, you know.

DELIA: All right, all right.

ERNEST: We're booked for eight o'clock.

DELIA: They'll hold the table.

ERNEST: They might not.

DELIA: Of course they will.

ERNEST: You never know. Not these days.

DELIA: They'll hold the table for us. We're regulars. We go there every year.

ERNEST: Oh, well, It's your anniversary.

DELIA: And yours.

ERNEST: True, true. I think I should have given these shoes another polish.

DELIA: Well, go and do it.

ERNEST: No, it doesn't matter. Nobody'll notice.

DELIA: It would appear that things between Susannah and Trevor are coming to a head.

ERNEST: Ah.

DELIA: He was always a difficult boy. I sometimes think if you hadn't ignored him quite as much—

ERNEST: I did?

DELIA: Of course you did. You hardly said a word to him all the time he was growing up.

ERNEST: I seem to remember chatting away to him for hours.

DELIA: Well. Chatting. I meant conversation. Conversation about important things. A father should converse with his son. About things that matter deeply.

ERNEST: Doesn't really leave them much to talk about then, does it?

DELIA: And that if I may say so is typical. No. Let's admit it. We weren't good parents. You did nothing and I tried to make up for it, and that's why he's like he is today. I mean if he'd had a stable childhood, he'd never have completely lost his sense of proportion and married Susannah. I mean, I sometimes feel on the rare occasions one does see them together that she's not really— awful thing to say but—not really resilient enough for Trevor. He wants somebody more phlegmatic. That Jan girl for instance would have been ideal. Do you remember her?

ERNEST: Jan? Jan? Jan?

DELIA: Nice little thing. Beautifully normal. She came to tea, do you remember? You got on very well with her.

ERNEST: Oh yes. She was jolly, wasn't she? She was very interested in my stamps. What happened to her?

DELIA: Oh, she married—someone else, I think. She still writes occasionally.

ERNEST: I must say I preferred her to Susannah. Never really hit it off with her, I'm afraid.

DELIA: Well, she's a very complex sort of girl, isn't she? Hasn't really made up her mind. About herself. I mean, I think a woman sooner or later has simply got to make up her mind about herself. I mean, even if she's someone like Carolyn—you know, Mrs. Brightman's Carolyn—who looks at herself and says, right, I'm a lump I'm going to be a lump but then at least everyone can accept her as a lump. So much simpler.

ERNEST: I think he should have married this other one.

DELIA: Jan? I don't think she was that keen.

ERNEST: She was altogether much jollier.

DELIA: Well, we're saddled with Susannah as a daughter-in-law—at least temporarily. We'd better make the best of it—I think I've put these eyes on crooked—we'd better make the best of it.

ERNEST: It's their bed. They can lie on it.

DELIA: Yes. I think that's one of the problems.

ERNEST: Eh?

DELIA: B — E — D.

ERNEST: B — E — D? Bed?

DELIA: Enough said.

ERNEST: Good lord. How do you know?

DELIA: One reads between the lines, darling. I've had a little look around their house. You can tell a great deal from people's bedrooms.

ERNEST: Can you? Good heavens. (*he looks about*)

DELIA: If you know what to look for. Now then. Do I wear what I wore when I went to the Reynolds or shall I wear the stripy thing that you loathe.

ERNEST: I'd wear the Reynolds thing.

DELIA: Or there's the little grey.

ERNEST: Oh.

DELIA: Or the blue.

ERNEST: Ah.

DELIA: No, that isn't pressed. You decide, darling. Stripy or the other one.

ERNEST: Er . . .

DELIA: Or the grey.

ERNEST: Er . . .

DELIA: Right I've decided, it's the other one. Good. Now, in the spare wardrobe in Trevor's old room on the top shelf, there's a little black handbag. Could you fetch me that? . . .

(DELIA *goes into the bathroom*)

ERNEST: Little black handbag, right. (*looking round*) I don't think you can tell very much from this bedroom. Except the roof's leaking from somewhere.

There is nothing obscure or difficult in *Bedroom Farce*, which stands out in the contemporary theatre mainly for its capacity to entertain, to titillate, and to dazzle with cleverness. Indeed, Ayckbourn makes clear his purely comedic intentions in the selection of his title, which suggests an even more frivolous diversion than Ayckbourn actually provides. For what the author has created in *Bedroom Farce* is, ultimately, something more than just another series of hijinks and dramatic clichés: it is a wry combination of social satire, middle-class insights, and boisterous good fun. The intricacy of his plot design, which is echoed if not exceeded in his other plays (*Absurd Person Singular* takes place, successively, in the kitchens of three married couples; *The Norman Conquests* consists of three interlocking plays, occurring simultaneously, involving the same cast of characters in three parts of the same house), reflects a skill at construction that borders on pure genius. This kind of craftsmanship alone would suffice to elevate any comedy far beyond the usual level of television skit or sitcom: in Ayckbourn's case, it enables his stage works to reach the heights of inspired farce.

Although comedy remains a staple of the theatre,

The opening scene from Alan Ayckbourn's Bedroom Farce, *The National Theatre, London, 1977.*

particularly in England, France, and America, amazingly few writers are consistently successful in the genre. Only Ayckbourn in England and Neil Simon in America have accounted for any real body of comic works for the contemporary stage; others may succeed here and there with a single comic play, but the comic form today seems particularly resistant to mastery.

CONCLUSIONS ON THE CURRENT THEATRE?

Can there be any conclusions concerning the current theatre? No, there cannot—simply because what is current is never concluded. The current theatre is in process; it is like a book we are just beginning. The plays and playwrights discussed in this chapter may not, in the end, be accorded very significant positions in our era of theatre; even the movements they now seem to represent may prove distinctly minor and transitory. We are not in a position even to hazard guesses at this point: we can only indicate certain directions in which to look for clues as to where the future will lead us.

Meanwhile the evidence, it should be clear, plays nightly on the stages of the theatre world. It is there to apprehend, there to enjoy, there to appreciate, and there, finally, to be refined by opinion and encapsulated into critical theory and aesthetic categorization—if that is our wish.

More than being a play, or a series of plays, or a spectrum of performances, the current theatre is a worldwide event, a *communication* between people and peoples that raises the level of human discourse and artistic appreciation wherever it takes place. The current theatre responds to the impulses of creativity and expression, and to the demands of human contact and understanding. It synthesizes the impulses of authors and artists, actors and audiences to foster a medium of focused interaction that incorporates the human experience and embodies each culture's aspirations and values. No final chapter can be written on this medium, no last analysis or concluding categorization. All that is certain is that the art, and the feeling, of theatrical life will endure.

IV

Photo Essay: A Play Is Put Together

DOZENS OF PEOPLE are routinely involved in the full production of even a simply mounted play. The photographs that follow illustrate various aspects of planning, staging, and performance for a production of *Equus*, a play by Peter Shaffer, which was staged by the University of California, Irvine, in the winter of 1980. The production was directed by Robert Cohen, and featured William Needles as "Dr. Dysart"; both Cohen and Needles were members of the UC Irvine faculty. The scenery, costumes, and masks for the production were designed by Barney Johnson, and the lighting by Arpad Petrass; Johnson and Petrass were graduate students at the University.

Planning meeting. In a faculty office, director (left) meets with scene designer (center) and lighting designer to discuss goals of production and visual development of director's concept. Ideas are noted, some rough sketches exchanged.

Production conference. In design studio scene, designer Johnson presents a scale model of the basic set for the approval of the director, as supervising faculty members Triplett and Howell (center and right) offer suggestions. At this meeting, final decisions are reached concerning construction scheduling and the handling of specific technical problems. The model will serve the shop as a construction guide, and as an aid to the director in planning the blocking.

Auditions. The director holds individual preliminary auditions by appointment, with actors presenting prepared monologues of their choice as well as readings from Equus *script. A stage manager, the only other participant at preliminary auditions, reads with the actors in* Equus *scenes. "Callbacks" will bring back the most suitable actors for a second round of readings, and for grouped readings; sometimes several callback sessions are needed —for* Equus *there were two.*

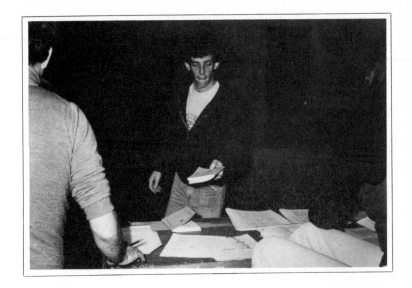

The cast meets. The selected cast gathers for the first time. There is a general round of introductions, scripts are distributed, the director states the chief aim of the production, the stage manager announces rehearsal schedules, telephone numbers are exchanged, and, after a coffee break, the text is read aloud.

Rehearsing. Scripts in hand but with lines learned, actors who will play "Alan" and "Jill" get into their roles by the basic expedients of eye contact and gesture.

Blocking. The director stages a scene between "Dr. Dysart" and "Mrs. Strang," as actors write blocking notes on their scripts. The "set" is represented by makeshift pieces, which were quickly assembled to allow actors to adjust to required props before the set is constructed.

Excitement. The director communicates script's energy and enthusiasm to the actors; his gesture is not an illustration of stage business, but a general encouragement for actors to let loose.

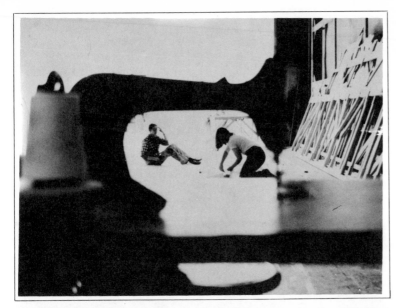

Building. Shop carpenters assemble wooden frames in the scene shop; these will shortly become platforms for stage bleachers.

Assembly and painting. The set is built in the scene shop for later transportation to theatre, eventually for transportation to San Diego, where the production will be remounted on tour. A shop technician paints the underside of the bleacher seats to prevent reflection; two others erect back panels of set.

Mask construction. For this production, horse masks required by the play will be built from clear plastic tubing; this construction makes use of relatively new scene technology in lucite welding. A polyurethane horse head is the model, and tubing is heated by an acetylene torch; technicians wear asbestos gloves.

Mask fitting. A mask is fitted to its designer in a test of its balance and its movement capability.

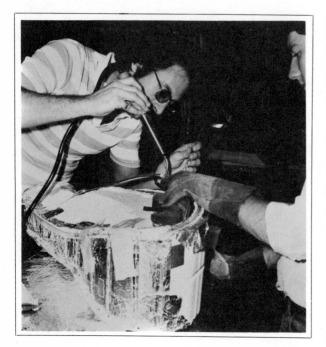

Mask try-out. An actress dons her horse mask and walks about set, now erected in the theatre. Observers note effects on the mask of stage light and actress' movements.

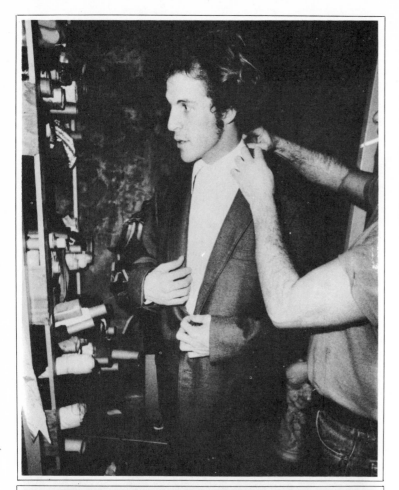

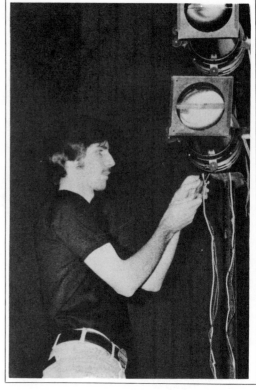

Costume fitting. All costumes, apart from horse costumes, are to be contemporary and realistic; most will be "pulled" from University costume storage, taken from the actors' personal wardrobes, or purchased from retail stores. Here "Mr. Strang" is fitted into a jacket in the costume room—note rolls of fabric at left. Dozens of jackets were tried with no success; eventually the actor wore suit of clothes owned by director.

Sound. The sound designer, who is also sound operator, sets intensities of his musical cues with a series of potentiometers on sound control board above stage. Tape decks are behind him. Equus utilized a musical score compiled from several sources; score also included a recorded speech by "Dr. Dysart" and various special effects: heartbeats, ocean waves, screams, and ticking of metronome.

Lighting. Hundreds of lights are to be used for Equus, *including fifty lights hung on two rings of pipe directly above the stage—as called for by play's author. Here, side lights are hung on a light pole and focused by a lighting technician under guidance of lighting designer,* left.

Putting it together. At table erected in middle of the house, lighting designer and stage manager (with official production script in front of her) call cues at one of several technical rehearsals—day-long affairs in which light cues, sound cues, scene-shifting cues, and quick-change costume cues are all run until perfect, then re-run in coordination with running of entire show. Process of technical refinement continues through dress rehearsals, when, however, stage manager's table disappears and show is "called" from backstage or from overhead. In Equus, *show was called from theatre's large light booth above and behind audience.*

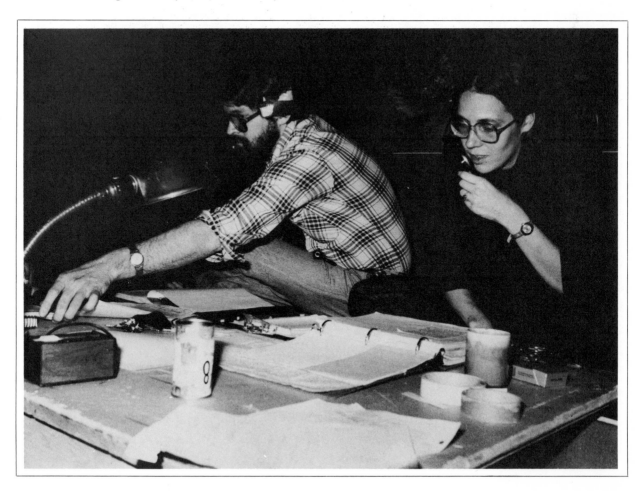

Technical rehearsal. Here, timing and intensities of lighting, volume of sound, and movements of set and props are adjusted; although the actors as yet wear no costumes or make-up, play begins to look "theatrical."

Equus. Completed, the play is staged for a one-week run, fairly typical for a University production. The show is a success: it receives glowing reviews, draws full houses and standing ovations each night. Eveyone has done his or her work well. It is not always like this; the actors, designers, and director relish their compliments, knowing the next such response may be several years coming. They also try to remain critical about their work, in continual quest for self-improvement. The show tours for a weekend, then closes. It is over—only photographs and memories remain.

NURSE: *I hope you're not going to make a nuisance of yourself. You'll have a much better time of it here, you know, if you behave yourself.*

DYSART: *Now tell me. Why is Equus in chains?*
ALAN: *For the sins of the world.*
DYSART: *What does he say to you?*
ALAN: *"I see you. I will save you."*

DALTON: *You clean it out with this. What we call a
    hoof-pick. Mind how you go with it. It's very
    sharp.*

ALAN: Equus, I love you! *Now!—Bear me away! Make us One Person!*

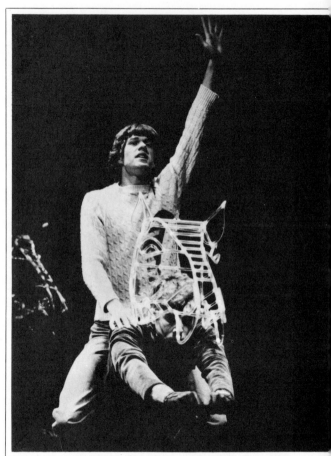

ALAN: *WEE! WAA! WONDERFUL! I'm stiff! Stiff in the wind! My mane, stiff in the wind! My flanks! My hooves! Mane on my legs, on my flanks, like whips! Raw! Raw!* I'm raw! Raw!

ALAN: *Amen!*

DORA: *All right—laugh! Laugh, as usual!*

DYSART: *Alan—look. Everything I say has a trick or a catch. Everything I do is a trick or a catch. That's all I know to do. But they work—and you know that. Trust me.*

DYSART: *Tell me about Jill.*

ALAN: *She put her mouth in mine. It was lovely!* Oh, it was lovely!

DYSART: *Let me tell you exactly what I'm going to do to him! I'll heal the rash on his body.*
I'll erase the welts cut into his mind by flying manes.

DYSART: *I need—more desperately than my children need me—a way of seeing in the dark. What way is this?* . . . What dark is this?

V

The Practitioners

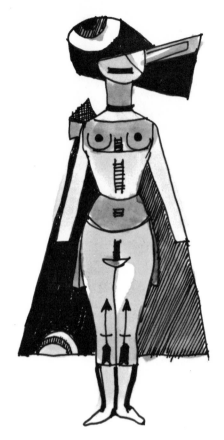

The actor as an ideological symbol, in an Expressionist design by George Grosz for the 1924 Berlin production of Ivan Goll's Methusalem. *Most theories of acting admit of more human personality and expressiveness than this design allows.*

THE ACTOR

He stands alone in the darkness, waiting in the wings, listening with one ear to the insistent rhythms of the dialogue played out upon the stage immediately beyond. His heart races, and he bounces lightly on the balls of his feet, fighting the welling tension, exhilarated by the sense of something rushing toward him, about to engulf him.

The stage ahead of him is ablaze with light; dazzling colors pour on from all possible directions. The energy on stage is almost tangible: it is there in the eyes of the actors, the pace of the dialogue, the smell of the make-up, the sparkle of sweat and saliva glittering in the lights, the bursts of audience laughter and applause, the sudden silence punctuated by a wild cry or a thundering retort.

He glances backward impatiently. Other actors, costumed like himself, wait in the backstage gloom. Some perform kneebends and roll their necks against the tension. Some gaze thoughtfully at the action of the play; some stare at the walls. In one corner a stage manager, his head encased in electronic paraphernalia, his body hunched over a dimly lighted copy of the script, whispers commands into an intercom. The backstage shadows pulse with anticipation.

Suddenly the on-stage pace quickens: the lines, all at once, take on a greater urgency and familiarity. It is the cue . . . if only there were time to go to the bathroom . . . it is the cue . . . he takes a deep breath, a deeper breath, a gasp . . . it is *the cue* and he bounds from the dimness into the dazzle: he is on stage, he is an actor!

It is perhaps the world's most bewildering profession.

At the top, it can be extraordinarily rewarding. The thrill of delivering a great performance, the roar of validation from an enraptured audience, the glory of getting inside the skin of the likes of Hamlet, Harpagon, and Hecuba: these are excitements and satisfactions few careers can match. Nor are the rewards purely artistic and intellectual ones: audience appreciation, and the producer's eye for profit, can catapult some actors to the highest income levels in the world, with salaries in the millions of dollars for actors achieving "star" status in films. And the celebrity that can follow is legendary: the private lives of the most universally admired actors become public property, their innermost thoughts the daily fare of television talk shows and fan magazines.

And yet, for all the splendor and glamour, the actor's life is more often than not depressingly anxious, beset by demands for sacrifice from every direction: psychological, financial, and even moral. Stage fright —the actor's great nemesis—is an ever-present nightmare that often increases with experience and renown. Fear of failure, fear of competition, fear of forgetting lines, fear of losing emotional control, fear of losing one's looks, fear of losing one's audience —this combination is endemic to acting as to no other profession.

Nor are the economic rewards in general particularly enticing: the six- and seven-figure salaries of the stars bear little relation to the scale pay for which most actors work: theirs is the lowest union-negotiated wage in the capitalist economy, and actors as a rule realize less income than the janitors who clean the theatres or the assistant stage managers who bring them coffee. Neither are the working conditions of the average actor much to envy: frightfully long hours, drafty and unpainted dressing rooms, tawdry and unheated rehearsal halls, long stretches of idleness, and weeks and months of grueling travel "on the road." And although the stars billed "above the title" may be treated like celebrities or royalty, the common run of actors are freely bullied by directors, bossed about by stage managers, capriciously hired and fired by producers, dangled and deceived by agents, squeezed and corseted by costumers, pinched by wig dressers, poked and powdered by make-up men, and traduced by press agents. Certainly no profession in the world entails more numbing uncertainties than acting, none demands more sacrifices, and none measures its rewards in such extreme and contradictory dimensions.

WHAT IS ACTING?

What is acting, after all?

It is as old as the theatre, for it is the first art of the theatre: the first to be created and the first to be perceived by the spectator.

It began when Thespis, or his spiritual ancestor, stepped out of the chorus, masked himself "in character," and declaimed something such as "I am Odysseus," or "I am the sun!" It began, in other words, with impersonation, which preceded playwriting or direction or design.

It is also the first craft of the theatre that we see: the "out front" activity of drama which is exposed, quite nakedly, to public examination. Even today the public knows the theatre primarily by its actors. The man on the street can name more actors than he can playwrights, directors, and designers put together— what is more, he feels confident in evaluating their art even though he has no special training to do so. Chances are he even entertains thoughts of acting himself. Acting is an obvious art—but it is also one shrouded in mystery.

Four aspects of acting, of staged impersonation, have been considered important throughout the centuries: character simulation, character embodiment, performing virtuosity, and "magic." Not everyone would use precisely these terms of course—even the man on the street feels free to set up his own categories—but by one name or another, these four elements have been present in all great performances from Greek times to the present day.

Character Simulation

The simulation of a character is the most obvious task of the actor—so much so that many persons (including many beginning actors) assume that simulation is all there is to acting. That assumption is incorrect; nevertheless, simulation is indeed a crucial element of the actor's performance.

Simulation of a character simply requires that the actor live up to the audience's minimal preconceptions of that character so that they can believe the actor is the character he plays. It is not enough, for example, for an actor to say "I am Odysseus"; he must also *resemble* Odysseus, if not in clinical, realistic detail, then in some abstract, associative way. Audience preconceptions are fluid; they precede the play when the character is known to history (or to stage history), and they grow during the play from what the character says and does and from what is said and done about him. If the character is old but is acted as young, if he is fat but is acted as thin, if he is powerful but is acted as feeble, the actor has failed to satisfy the demand of rudimentary simulation and the performance quite obviously rings false. Sometimes audience preconceptions can be vigorously shaken and changed, and sometimes superficial non-simulation can be overridden by deeper points of consonance, but an acting performance that provides the audience with no easy identification between actor and character is certain to radiate a fundamental lack of conviction and a fatal dissonance between actor and role.

Therefore it has always been one of the actor's tasks to achieve the skills of simulation: to be able to walk like a king when called upon to do so, to talk like a whore, to dissemble like a knave, to fence like a prince, and to banter like a diplomat. The mask, make-up, and costume—which until the present century were generally created by the actors who used them—are further tools for the actor's simulative tasks: a slender, blond young patrician can be as fat as Falstaff, as black as Othello, as ugly as Pantalone, and as ancient as Lear through the artful use of draped fabric, molded papier-maché, and burnt cork. But there are also internal tools for use in this art of simulation, characterizations which reach into the subtleties of psychology and deportment—attitudes, quirks, stares, gazes, trembles, halts, and tones of voice. Indeed, modern depictions of character tend to rely far more on intellectual and philosophical identifications than on fixed outward shows; the art of character simulation has become incredibly complex and individualistic as audiences have proven their willingness to break free of stereotypes and to accept highly abstracted simulations.

Character Embodiment

Embodiment is the obverse of simulation, the supportive counterpart to the actor's resemblance of the role. By embodying a role, the actor puts his own *body*

into it, and in the process fills the simulated character with his own respiration, his own blood, his own hormones, and, to a certain unavoidable extent, his own emotions. To that extent, therefore, the actor is always playing himself as well as his character, as Diderot perceived when he wrote of the paradox of acting. That great encyclopedist of the eighteenth century considered that all great actors had a "double personality," and the actor who could "convey the sublimity of nature" was the one "who can feel it with his passion and his genius, and reproduce it with complete self-possession." But what of that "feeling"? How much does the actor "feel" that he actually "is" the character he plays? How much does he (or should he) feel what the character supposedly feels? How much does his personal feeling add to his performance—or subtract from it? These have been controversial questions for centuries; Diderot was not the first to try to answer them.

All we can say for sure is that the actor's embodiment of a role is pervasive. It involves his entire physiological functioning and carries with it, of necessity, a certain psychophysiological complexity as well. The actor is a living person; he sees, hears, smells, feels, and experiences on stage as well as off. To the degree to which he is involved on stage, he is a full participant, a spontaneous embodiment of a living character. Indeed, it is embodiment more than any other element that brings life into the theatre.

The actor may work on his feelings actively, and some even develop ruses to stimulate them. For example, in the late days of the Greek theatre one celebrated tragic actor, Polus of Aegina, took the ashes of his dead son from their resting place and placed them

> One time I had this scene where I was to walk into this actress' dressing room and say something like 'I love you; will you marry me?' We managed to make it better by having the girl go into her bathroom and close the door and I had to say those lines to a closed door. I learned to work with counterpoint. To make the material more interesting I would find ways to create obstacles for the character—frustrate him in what he wants to accomplish. That makes the character more sympathetic, because everybody understands frustration.
>
> Jack Lemmon

in the vase which, in the play *Electra*, held the presumed ashes of Orestes. Then, playing the role of Electra mourning Orestes, Polus clasped the urn containing his own son's ashes and, according to an ancient writer, "embraced them as if they were those of Orestes, and filled the whole place not with the appearance and imitation of sorrow, but with genuine grief and unfeigned lamentation. While it seemed that a play was being acted, it was in fact real grief that was enacted." Polus' case is just one in a long history of actors' attempts to make their onstage feelings real and personal by interjecting associations with their off-stage life. Some actors today carry favored personal belongings with them on stage; others stimulate themselves with memories of real-life parents, lovers, enemies, and challengers, in order to provoke a heightened and honest stage emotion.

The demand for simulation, then, requires that the actor resemble the character; the demand for embodiment requires that the character resemble the actor. Needless to say, a certain subjectivity governs the weighing of these two demands and the determination of their relative importance in achieving an effective performance. There is no question, however, that some combination of the two is needed for a performance high in credibility, conviction, and liveliness, a performance that defines a role acceptably and makes it breathe with theatrical vitality. The two are necessary components because sheer simulation without embodiment rings hollow, and sheer embodiment—"being oneself"—lacks dramatic definition; most acting approaches aim at blending the two in theatrically effective ways.

The other two aspects of acting, while equally fundamental to the process, are rarely achieved except by the greatest of actors.

Virtuosity

Greatness in acting, like greatness in almost any endeavor, demands a superb set of skills.

The characters of drama are rarely mundane; they are exemplary, and so must be the actors who portray them. Merely to impersonate—to simulate and embody—the genius of Hamlet, for example, one must deliver that genius oneself. Similar personal resources are needed to project the depth of Lear, the lyricism of Juliet, the fervor of St. Joan, the proud passion of Prometheus, the bravura of Mercutio, or the heroics of Hecuba. Outsized characters demand outsized abilities and the capacity to project them.

Moreover, it is ultimately insufficient for an actor merely to fulfill the audience's preconceptions of his character; finally it is necessary that the actor strive to transcend those preconceptions and to create the character afresh, transporting the audience to an understanding of—and a compassion for—the character that they would never have achieved on their own.

Both of these demands require of the actor a considerable virtuosity of dramatic technique.

Traditionally, the training of actors has concentrated on dramatic technique. Since Roman times (and probably before then), actors have spent most of their lifetime perfecting such performing skills as juggling, dancing, singing, versifying, declaiming, clowning, miming, stage fighting, acrobatics, and sleight of hand. Certainly no actor before the present century had any chance of success without several of these skills, and few actors today reach the top of their profession without fully mastering at least a few of them.

Whatever the individual skills required of an actor over time, the sought-after dramatic technique that is common to history and to our own times can be summed up in just two features: a splendidly supple body and a magnificently expressive voice. These are the tools every actor strives to attain, and when brilliantly honed they are valuable beyond measure.

The actor's voice has received the greatest attention through history; Greek tragic actors were awarded prizes for their vocal abilities alone, and many modern actors, such as Richard Burton, Katharine Hepburn, Glenda Jackson, and Marlon Brando, are celebrated for their distinctive use of the voice. The potential of the acting voice as an instrument of great theatre is immense: the voice can be thrilling, resonant, mellow, sharp, musical, stinging, poetic, seductive, compelling, lulling, dominating—and an actor capable of drawing on many such "voices" clearly can command a spectrum of acting roles and lend them a splendor that the less gifted actor or the untrained amateur could scarcely imagine. A voice that can articulate, that can explain, that can rivet attention, that can convey the subtlest nuance, that can exult, dazzle, thunder with rage and flow with compassion: this, when used in the service of dramatic impersonation, can hold an audience utterly spellbound for as long as its owner cares to recite.

> M r. [Richard] Burton happens to possess a vocal instrument that . . . is exactly what we expect to hear, and almost never do hear, on going to the theatre. The sounds produced in the living theatre are not meant to be the sounds produced in day-to-day life, though that is what actors have been giving us for years on end. We look for a "liveness" that has been intensified, as it is so often intensified in the control rooms of recording studios. Mr. Burton was his own control room, sending out sounds that swept the walls of the theatre clean with an apparently effortless power, magnifying the "natural" until we were caught up in its gale, left stunned and breathless. And yes, we said to ourselves, this is precisely the penetrating resonance all actors should possess, if the tonalities of the stage are to be differentiated from those of film. Not everyone, to be sure, can be born in Wales. But the sound, with all of its nuances and its pressures, can be acquired, as Irene Worth has acquired it. It is thrilling when heard, and the thrill is what playhouses are for.
>
> Walter Kerr

The actor's use of his body—his capacity for movement—is the other element of his fundamental technique, the second basis for his dramatic virtuosity. Most of the best actors are strong and supple; all are capable of great physical self-mastery and are artists of body language. The effects that can be achieved through stage movement are as numerous as those which can be achieved through voice. Subtly expressive movement in particular is the mark of the gifted actor, who can accomplish miracles of communication with an arched eyebrow, a toss of the head, a flick of the wrist, a whirl of the hem, or a shuffle of the feet. But bold movements, too, can produce indelible moments in the theatre: Helene Weigel's powerful chest-pounding when, as Mother Courage, she loses her son, Laurence Olivier's breath-taking fall from the tower, as Coriolanus—these are sublime theatricalizations accomplished through the actors' sheer physical skill and strength.

Virtuosity for its own sake can be appealing in the cabaret or lecture hall as well as in the theatre, but when coupled with the impersonation of character it can create dramatic performances of consummate depth, complexity, and theatrical power. We are always impressed by skill—it is fascinating, for instance, to watch a skilled cobbler at his bench—but great skill in the service of dramatic action can be abso-

lutely transporting. Of course virtuosity is not easy to acquire, and indeed it will always remain beyond the reach of many people. Each of us possesses natural gifts, but not all are gifted to the same degree; some measure of dramatic talent must assuredly be inborn, or at least early learned. But the training beyond one's gifts, the shaping of talent into craft, is an unending process. "You never stop learning it," said actor James Stewart after nearly fifty years of stage and film successes, and virtually all actors would agree with him.

Traditional notions of virtuosity in acting went into a temporary eclipse in the middle of this century, owing mainly to the rise of realism, which required that acting conform to the behaviors of ordinary people leading ordinary lives. The *cinéma vérité* of the post-World War II era in particular fostered an "artless" acting style, to which virtuosity seemed intrusive rather than supportive. It is certainly true that the virtuosity of one age can seem mere affectation in the next and that modern times require modern skills, a contemporary virtuosity that accords with contemporary dramatic material. Yet even the traditional skills of the theatre have made a great comeback in recent decades: circus techniques, dance, and songs are now a part of many of the most experimental of modern stagings, and multi-skilled, multi-talented performers are in demand as never before. The performer rich in talent and performing skills, capable not merely of depicting everyday life but of fashioning an artful and exciting theatrical expression of it, once again commands the central position in contemporary drama.

Magic

Beyond impersonation and virtuosity, though incorporating them, remains a final acting ingredient which has been called "presence," "magnetism," "charisma," and many other terms. We shall call it "magic."

It is a quality that is difficult to define but universally felt, a quality we cannot explain except to say we know it when we are under its spell.

We must always remember that the actor began not as a technician of the theatre, but as a priest—and that he embodied not ordinary men, but gods. We may witness this function directly today in certain tribal dramas, in which a shaman or witch doctor is accepted by his co-celebrants as the possessor of divine attributes—or as one possessed by them.

The modern secular actor also conveys at least a hint of this transcendent divinity. Elevated upon a stage and bathed in light for all to see, charged with creating an intensity of feeling, a vivid characterization, and a well-articulated eloquence of verbal and physical mastery, the actor at his finest becomes an almost extra-terrestrial being, a "star," or, in the French expression, a "sacred monster."

The actor's presence, his ability to project an aura of magic—this does not come about as a direct result of his skills at impersonation or his technical virtuosity. It does, however, depend on the actor's inner confidence, which in turn can be bred from a mastery of his craft. Therefore, while "magic" cannot be directly acquired or produced, it can be approached, and its fundamental requisites can be established. For gifted individuals it might come quite quickly; for others, despite abundant skills and devoted training, it comes late or not at all and they can never rise above pedestrian performances. It is perhaps frustrating to find that acting greatness depends so heavily on this elusive and inexplicable goal of "magic," but it is also true that every art incorporates elements that must remain as mysteries. The best acting, like any art, ultimately transcends the reach of pure descriptive an-

alysis; it cannot be acquired mechanically. The best acting strikes chords in the non-reasoning parts of our being; it rings with a resonance we do not fully understand, and it evokes a reality we no longer fully remember. We should extol, not lament, this fact.

BECOMING AN ACTOR

How does one become an actor? Many thousands ask this question every year; many thousands, indeed, *act* in one or more theatrical productions every year. The training of actors is now a major activity in hundreds of colleges, universities, conservatories, and private and commercial schools in the United States, and theories of actor-training constitute a major branch of artistic pedagogy.

Essentially, actor-training entails two distinct phases: development of the actor's instrument, and development of the actor's method of approaching a role. There is no general agreement on the order in which these phases should occur, but there is a widespread understanding that both are necessary and the two are interrelated.

The Actor's Instrument

The actor is his own instrument; his mind and mettle and metabolism are the materials of his own performance. An actor's voice is his Stradivarius; his body is his sculpting clay. An actor is a portrait artist who works from inside himself, creating characters with his own organs and his own physiological systems. It is obvious that a great artist requires first-rate equipment: for the actor this means a responsive *self*, disciplined yet uninhibited, capable of rising to the challenges of great roles.

The training of the actor's instrument is both physiological and psychological; for that reason it must be accomplished under the personal supervision of qualified instructors. In the past, acting instructors were invariably master actors who took on younger apprentices; even today, students of classical French and Japanese acting styles learn their art by relentless imitation of the actors they hope to succeed. In America, however, acting instruction has expanded to include a great many educational specialists who may or may not have had extensive professional acting experience themselves; indeed, some of the most celebrated and effective acting teachers today are play directors, theatrical innovators, and academicians.

No one, however, has yet discovered the art of training an actor's instrument simply by reading books or thinking about problems of craft. This point should be borne in mind in reading the rest of this chapter.

Voice and speech, quite naturally, are the first elements of the actor's physiological instrument to be considered: "Voice, voice, and more voice" was the answer Tommaso Salvini, the famed nineteenth-century Italian tragedian, gave to the question: "What are the three most important attributes of acting?" We have already discussed the importance of vocal skills in the acting profession: voice and speech training programs are aimed at acquainting the actor with a variety of means to achieve and enhance these skills.

The basic elements of voice (breathing, phonation, resonance) and of speech (articulation, pronunciation, phrasing)—as well as their final combination (projection)—are all separate areas of the integrated instruction a good vocal training program will provide. Such a program ordinarily takes three years or longer, and many actors continue working on their voice and speech all their lives.

As devoted as teachers and scientists have been to the problems of perfecting voice and speech, however, a certain mystery still surrounds much of their work. Even the fundamental question of how the voice actually works is still a subject of fierce dispute among specialists in anatomy and physiology. Moreover, the processes involved in breathing and speaking have acquired a certain mystique—for example, the dual meaning of "inspiration" as both "inhalation" and "spirit stimulus" has given rise to a number of exotic theoretical dictums that border on religiosity. Some of the fundamental practices of vocal and speech instruction, however, are generalized on the following page (see box).

Movement is the other main factor to be considered in training the actor's physiological instrument, and this factor is developed primarily through exercises and instruction designed to create physical relaxation, muscular control, economy of action, and expressive rhythms and movement patterns. Dance, mime, fencing, and acrobatics are traditional training courses for actors; in addition, circus techniques and masked pantomime have become common courses in recent years.

Sheer physical strength is stressed by some actors: Laurence Olivier, for example, accords it the absolutely highest importance because, he contends, it gives the actor the stamina he needs to "hold stage" for several hours of performance, and the basic resilience to accomplish the physical and psychological work of acting without strain or fatigue.

The actor's control of his body permits him to stand, sit, and move on stage with alertness, energy, and seeming ease. Standing tall, walking boldly, turning on a dime at precisely the right moment, extending the limbs joyously, sobbing violently, springing about uproariously, and occupying a major share of stage space are among the capacities of the actor who has mastered body control, and they can be developed through training and confidence. In the late days of the Greek theatre, known as the Hellenistic period, actors used elevated footwear, giant headdresses, and sweeping robes to take on a larger-than-life appearance; the modern actor has discovered that the same effect can be achieved simply by tapping the residual expansiveness of his own body.

Economy of movement, which is taught primarily through the selectivity of mime, permits the conveyance of subtle detail by seemingly inconspicuous movement. The waggle of a finger, the flare of a nostril, the quiver of a lip can communicate volumes in a performance of controlled movement. Whereas the beginner is often recognized by his fidgeting, shuffling, aimless pacing, and fiddling with his fingers—behaviors which he hopes will make him inconspicuous but which actually draw unwanted audience attention—the professional understands the value of physical self-control, and the explosive potential of a simple movement that follows a carefully prepared stillness. *Surprise*, which is one of the actor's greatest weapons, can be achieved only through the actor's mastery of his body.

Imagination, and the willingness and ability to use it in the service of art, is the major *psychological* component of the actor's instrument. At the first level, the actor must use his imagination to make the artifice of the theatre *real enough to himself* to convey that sense of reality to the audience: painted canvas flats must be imagined as brick walls, an off-stage jangle must be imagined as a ringing onstage telephone, and an actress no older than the actor himself must be imagined as his mother or grandmother.

THE COMPONENTS OF VOICE AND SPEECH

Breathing pumps air through the vocal tract, providing a carrier for the voice; "breath support," through expansion of the rib cage and lowering and controlling the diaphragm, is a primary goal, as is natural, deep, free breathing that is sufficient to produce and sustain tone, but not so forced as to create tension or artificial huffing and puffing.

Phonation is the process whereby vocal cord oscillations produce sound, a process which remains something of an anatomical and physiological mystery even today. Vocal warm-ups are essential for the actor to keep his vocal cords and other laryngeal (voice box) tissues supple and healthy, and to prevent not only strain and the growth of "nodes" which may cause raspiness and pain but also phonic failure (laryngitis).

Resonance is the sympathetic vibration, or "resounding" of the voice as it is amplified in the throat, chest, and head. Resonance gives phonation its *timbre* or tonal quality, its particular balance of "bass" and "treble" sounds. Open-throatedness—the actual lowering of the larynx within the neck, as by a yawn—increases the resonance in the pharynx (throat) and is a major goal in voice work. Keeping the mouth open while speaking and raising the soft palate also increase resonance and add to vocal quality.

Articulation is the shaping of vocal sound into recognizable *phonemes*, or language sounds—40 of which are easily distinguishable in the English language; programs of speech training aim at improving the actor's capacity to articulate these sounds distinctly, naturally, and unaffectedly; that is, without slurring, ambiguous noise, or self-conscious maneuvering of the lip and tongue. A lazy tongue and slovenly speaking habits inhibit articulation, and must be overcome with persistent drill and disciplined attention.

Pronunciation makes words both comprehensible and appropriate to the character and style of the play; clear standard pronunciation, unaffected by regional dialect, is a crucial part of the actor's instrument, as is the ability to learn regional dialects and foreign accents when required. Occasionally an actor achieves prominence with the aid of a seemingly permanent dialect—Andy Griffith and Sissy Spacek are two examples—but such actors are likely to find their casting opportunities quite limited unless they can expand their speaking range.

Phrasing makes words meaningful and gives them sound patterns that are both rhythmic and logical. The great classical actors are masters of nuance in phrasing, capable of subtly varying their pitch, intensity, and rate of speech seemingly without effort from one syllable to the next. They rarely phrase consciously; rather they apparently develop their phrasing through years of experience with classical works and a sustained awareness of the value of spontaneity, naturalness, and a commitment to the dramatized situation. Training programs in speech phrasing aim at enabling an actor to expand the pitch range of his normal speech from the normal half-octave to two octaves or three, to double his clear-speaking capacity from 200 words a minute to 400, and to develop his ability to orchestrate prose and verse into effective and persuasive crescendos, diminuendoes, sostenutos, and adagios just as if he were responding to a musical score.

Projection, which is the final element in the delivery of voice and speech to the audience, is what ultimately creates dramatic communication; it governs the force with which the character's mind is heard through the character's voice, and it determines the impact of all other components of the actor's voice on the audience. Anxiety and physical tension are the great enemies of projection because they cause shallow breathing, shrill resonance, and timid phrasing; therefore, relaxation and the development of self-confidence become crucial at this final stage of voice and speech development.

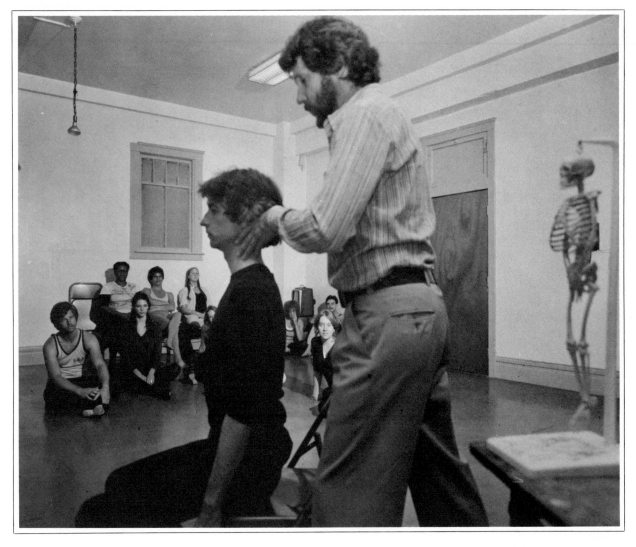

The Alexander technique, stressing spinal alignment and relaxed diaphragmatic breathing, is a widely used actor-training method. Developed by F. Matthias Alexander in the last century, it is now taught in many schools and conservatories, including the American Conservatory Theatre in San Francisco, pictured above.

At the second, far more important level, the actor must *imagine himself in an interpersonal situation created by the play*: in love with Juliet, in awe of Zeus, in despair of his life. This imagination must be broad and all-encompassing; the successful actor is able to imagine himself performing and relishing the often unspeakable acts of his characters, who may be murderers, despots, or monsters; insane or incestuous lovers; racial bigots, atheists, devils, perverts, or prudes. To the actor, nothing must be unimaginable; the actor's imagination must be a playground for expressive fantasy and darkly compelling motivations.

At the third, deepest level, the actor's imagination must become more active; it must go beyond the mere accommodation of an accepted role pattern to become a *creative* force that makes characterization a high art.

For each actor creates his role uniquely—each Romeo and Juliet are like no others before them, and each role can be uniquely fashioned with the aid of the actor's imaginative power. The final goal of creating a character is to create it freshly, filling it with the pulse of real blood and the animation of real on-the-spot thinking and doing. The actor's imagination, liberated from stage fright and mechanical worries, is the crucial ingredient in allowing the actor to transcend the pedestrian and soar toward the genuinely original.

The liberation of imagination is a continuing process in actor-training; exercises and "theatre games" designed for that purpose are part of most beginning classes in acting, and many directors use the same exercises and games at the beginning of play rehearsal periods. Because the human imagination tends to rigidify in the course of maturation—the child's imagination is usually much richer than that of the adult—veteran professional actors often profit from periodic returns to "mind-expanding" or imagination-freeing exercises and games.

Discipline is the fourth and final aspect of an actor's instrument, and to a certain extent it is the one that rules them all.

The imagination of the actor is by no means unlimited, nor should it be. It is restricted by the requirements of the play, by the director's staging and interpretation, and by certain established working conditions of the theatre. The actor's artistic discipline keeps him within these bounds and at the same time ensures his artistic agility.

The actor is not an independent artist, like a writer or painter. The actor works in an ensemble of his fellows; he is but one employee (paid or unpaid) in a large enterprise that can succeed only as a collaboration. Therefore, although actors are sometimes thought to be universally temperamental and professionally difficult, the truth is exactly the opposite: actors are among the most disciplined of artists, and the more professional they are, the more disciplined they are.

The actor, after all, leads a vigorous and demanding life. Make-up calls at 5:30 in the morning for film actors, and nightly and back-to-back weekend live performances for stage actors, make for schedules that are difficult to maintain on a regular basis. Furthermore, the physical and emotional demands of the acting process, the need for extreme concentration in rehearsal and performance, the need for physical health and psychological composure, the need for the actor to be both the instrument and the initiator of his performance, and the special demands of interacting with fellow performers at a deep level of mutual involvement—these aspects of the actor's life do not permit casual or capricious behavior among the members of a cast or company.

The truly professional actor practices the most rigorous discipline over his work habits. He makes all "calls" (for rehearsal, costume fitting, photographs, make-up, audition, and performance) at the stated times, properly warmed up beforehand; he learns lines at or before stipulated deadlines, he memorizes stage movements as he is directed, he collaborates with the other actors and theatre artists toward a successful and growing performance, and he continually studies his craft. If he does not do these things, he simply ceases to be an actor. Professional theatre producers have very little sympathy or forgiveness for undisciplined performers, and this professional attitude now prevails in virtually all community and university theatres as well.

Being a disciplined actor does not mean being a slave, nor does it mean foregone capitulation to the director or the management. The disciplined actor is simply one who works rigorously to develop his physiological and psychological instrument, who meets all of his technical obligations unerringly and without reminder, and who does his utmost to ensure the success of the entire production and the fruitful association of the whole acting ensemble. The disciplined actor asks questions, offers suggestions, invents stage business, and creates his characterization in harmony with the directorial pattern and the acting ensemble. When there is a serious disagreement between actor and director (a not uncommon occurrence), the disciplined actor seeks to work it out through discussion and compromise, and will finally yield if the director cannot be persuaded otherwise. Persistent, willful disobedience has no place in the serious theatre, and is not tolerated by it.

The Actor's Approach: Two Traditional Methods

How does an actor approach a role? How does he prepare himself to simulate a character? to embody a character? to create stage magic in a performance?

These questions have been answered in many ways, and they are still shrouded in subjectivity and controversy.

Historically, the answers have generally gravitated toward one or the other of two basic methods the one often called "external" or "technical," and the other often called "internal" or "truthful." These terms are inexact and even somewhat misleading; nevertheless, their historical importance and wide dissemination demand that we pay them some attention at the outset of this discussion.

The "external"–"internal" dichotomy refers back to the basic paradox of the theatre itself, and to the fact that the actor both simulates and embodies his role. The "external" methods of approaching a role have concentrated on the actor's acquisition of technique, on his development of virtuoso abilities, and on his facility at simulating emotions and behaviors without regard to his personal feelings. Diderot himself, who first articulated the paradox, was an extremist in this position, contending that the best acting was done with cool dispassion, and that "the great actor watches appearances . . . he has rehearsed to himself every particle of his despair. He knows exactly when he must . . . shed tears; and you will see him weep at the word, at the syllable, he has chosen, not a second sooner or later. . . . At the very moment when he touches your heart he is listening to his own voice." Believers in such an external approach treat the actor's performance as an analogue of reality rather than a direct embodiment of it, a calculated *presentation* of a character's life rather than its living representation on stage.

Contrarily, "internal" methods have focused on the actor's personal assumption of his character, his "use of himself" in the portrayal of his role and his actual "experiencing" of the events which he goes through as he embodies his role. These methods tend to expand the psychological dimensions of a performance, and to aid the actor in assimilating the physiological reality of his character—down to the heartbeats and flushes and hormonal activities the character would undergo if the dramatized situation were real. Internal methods profess to reach the actor's rationally uncontrollable states, and to awaken in him feelings and reflexes that are beyond sheer technical manipulation. Konstantin Stanislavski, the founder of the Moscow Art Theatre (1898) and one of the all-time great teachers of acting, is most close-

ly associated with the "internal" method; so famous has his approach become in America that it is now widely known simply as "The Method," with no other name or adjective attached. Stanislavski's maxim was "You must live the life of your character on stage." In order to achieve this end, he developed research into the subconscious, vigorously studied the intricacies of the lives of characters he was to play, and demanded that his actors be "in character" not only during intermissions and while waiting for cues in the wings, but for the entire day of the performance. It is the actor's "sense of truth which supervises all of his inner and physical activity," said Stanislavski. "It is only when his sense of truth is developed that he will . . . express the state of the person he is portraying and . . . not merely serve the purposes of external beauty, as all sorts of conventional gestures and poses do."

The follower of the "internal" approach is likely to judge the "external" performance to be "hollow," "shallow," "merely technical," "empty," "unfeeling," or "cold." "I didn't believe it," is the frequent complaint of the Stanislavski adherent. The "externalist's" criticisms, by contrast, are usually couched in terms such as "unclear," "muddy," "self-indulgent," "overemotional," "melodramatic," "sentimental," "unfocused," and "confused." Partisans for one or the other position are often more distinguishable by their criticisms of other performances than by significant accomplishments of their own.

Integrated Methods

The two traditional methods have had an extraordinary impact on the theatre of the present century. European acting has been responsive to many of the presentational techniques suggested by Diderot, whereas American acting has been particularly influenced by the teaching of Stanislavski—and by the acting of several of Stanislavski's followers who studied at Lee Strasberg's celebrated Actor's Studio in the 1950s and 1960s, most notably Marlon Brando, James Dean, Paul Newman, and Julie Harris. The division of acting into two easily defined, easily opposed "schools" has proven convenient for purposes of discussion, and has encouraged countless debates in theatre green rooms and academic classrooms around the world.

But in the current theatre, the division seems

curiously obsolete. Much of what now passes for Stanislavski-inspired "Method" acting is little more than intentional shuffling, stumbling, and slurring calculated to convince an audience that the actor is "real." Much of what is called "technical" acting involves no technique at all beyond the ability to mouth schoolboy rhetoric and look handsome.

The contemporary theatre has come to realize that acting involves *both* simulation and embodiment, *both* impersonation and virtuosity, and that, therefore, *both* external and internal processes are involved; the debate between them is irrelevant. Acting approaches of the present day thus tend to integrate the best of the traditional methods, and to combine these with new approaches suggested by recent discoveries in psychology and communications, stressing all the while a contemporary awareness of human identity and of the function of the actor in creating and theatricalizing that identity.

The integrated methods of approach favored by most teachers of acting today encourage the student to study the *situational intentions* of the character, the *variety of tactics* the character can employ in the fulfillment of those intentions, and the specific *mode of performance* demanded by the playwright and/or the director.

By "situational intentions" we mean the goals or desires the character hopes to achieve: the victories he has set ahead for himself. Romeo's intention, for example, is first to win the love of Juliet, then to marry her—and then to join her in Heaven. Hecuba's intention is to shame the Athenians; Monsieur Jourdain's intention is to awe his family and friends. If the actor concentrates as fully as possible on such intentions, they focus his energy, drive out his stage fright, and set up the foundation for the fullest use of his instrument.

By "tactics" we refer to those actions by which the character moves through the play, as propelled by his intentions. Romeo woos Juliet through his expressive use of language, his kisses, and his ardent behavior. Hecuba shames the Athenians by taunting them for their weakness and by defeating their rhetoric with her own more noble recitations. Jourdain awes his family—or tries mightily to do so—by parading in what he considers to be fashionable garments. The point is not that the characters must succeed with their tactics, or even that they must fulfill their intentions—for those matters are finally determined by the play-

wright, not the actor—but that the actor must be fully engaged in the pursuit of his character's intentions, and quite imaginative in his employment of tactics to get what he wants. An actor who is fully and powerfully engaged, who commands the language of the play and the action of the dramatized situation, can create a character who is magnificent even in defeat: he can thus transport the audience and deliver a fully theatrical performance.

By "mode of performance" we mean the intended relationship between the play's characters and its audience. For example, the actor must know whether the audience is expected to empathize with the characters, to analyze them, to be socially instructed by them, or merely to be entertained by them. The contemporary theatre has utilized many different performance modes, some entirely realistic, others radically anti-realist in tone and structure. We have seen how the theatre of Bertolt Brecht, for example, theoretically eschews "theatre magic" altogether, and demands that the actors simulate their characters without fully embodying them. Other performance modes which have adopted and created distinctive theatrical conventions include improvisational theatre, street theatre, music theatre, and the "holy theatre" of Jerzy Grotowski. All of these impose, for the actor, performance requirements quite beyond the impersonation of character through intentions and tactics.

It is at the junction of tactics, intentions, and performance modes that simulation, embodiment, and virtuosity come together. For they all stand upon the same foundation: the actor's assumption of his character's intentions, and his committed pursuit of his character's goals. Forceful tactics derived from that pursuit, such as power and precision in speaking, articulate wit, authoritative bearing, and the implicit threat of pent-up passions, give an acting performance its strength; seductive tactics derived from the same pursuit, such as poetic sensitivity, disarming agreeability, sexual enticement, and evocative nuance, create the magnetism of stage performance.

The aspects of acting, separate in this analysis, come together again in both the actor's mind and in that of the audience. Even Brecht found, despite his theories, that performances under his direction created the very magic he decried and occasioned incontrovertible examples of character embodiment. Great stylized performances are both "felt" by the

THE ACTORS STUDIO

The most influential school of acting in the United States has been New York's Actors Studio, which was founded by director Elia Kazan and others in 1947, and achieved prominence following the appointment of Lee Strasberg (1901–) as artistic director in 1951. Strasberg, an Austrian by birth and a New Yorker by upbringing, proved a magnetic teacher and acting theorist, and his classes revolutionized American acting, producing such notable performers as Marlon Brando, James Dean, Julie Harris, Paul Newman, Geraldine Page, Shelley Winters, Al Pacino, Ellen Burstyn, and Marilyn Monroe.

The Studio is not actually a school, but an association of professional actors who gather at weekly sessions to work on acting problems. The methodology of the Studio derives in part from Stanislavski, and in part from the working methods of the Group Theatre—a pre-World War II acting ensemble that included Kazan and Strasberg, and playwright Clifford Odets. But Strasberg himself has proven the key inspiration of Studio teaching, and of the American love affair with "method acting" attributed to the Studio work.

Strasberg's work is not reducible to simple formulas, for the Studio is a working laboratory, and the Studio work is personal rather than theoretical; direct rather than general. Much of the mythology that has arisen about the Studio—that actors are encouraged to mumble their lines and scratch their jaws in the service of naturalness—is quite fallacious: Strasberg is a fierce exponent of firm performance discipline and well-studied acting technique; insofar as the Studio developed a reputation for producing actors that mumbled and fidgeted, this seems to have been only a response to the personal idiosyncracies of Marlon Brando, the Studio's first celebrated "graduate."

Strasberg does demand great depths of character relationships from his actors, and he will go to almost any length to get them. Explanation is only one of his tools, but it is the only one that can be made available to readers. The following quotes are from Strasberg himself:*

The human being who acts is the human being who lives. That is a terrifying circumstance. Essentially the actor acts a fiction, a dream; in life the stimuli to which we respond are always real. The actor must constantly respond to stimuli that are imaginary. And yet this must happen not only just as it happens in life, but actually more fully and more expressively. Although the actor can do things in life quite easily, when he has to do the same thing on the stage under fictitious conditions he has difficulty because he is not equipped as a human being merely to play-act at imitating life. He must somehow believe. He must somehow be able to convince himself of the rightness of what he is doing in order to do things fully on the stage.

When the actor explores fully the reality of any given object, he comes up with greater dramatic possibilities. These are so inherent in reality that we have a common phrase to describe them. We say, "Only in life could such things happen." We mean that those things are so genuinely dramatic that they could never be just made up. . . .

The true meaning of "natural" or "nature" refers to a thing so fully lived and so fully experienced that only rarely does an actor permit himself that kind of experience on the stage. Only great actors do it on the stage, whereas in life every human being to some extent does it. On the stage it takes the peculiar mentality of the actor to give himself to imaginary things with the same kind of fullness that we ordinarily evince only in giving ourselves to real things. The actor has to evoke that reality on the stage in order to live fully in it and with it.

*Quotations from Robert Hethmon, *Strasberg at the Actors Studio* (New York, 1965), pp. 78, 197–98.

actors and "believed" by audiences; technical virtuosity, the actor's ability to shift easily and uninhibitedly among a great variety of tactics and to commit fully to a compelling set of character intentions, underlies great acting in any style and any performance motif.

Finally, every actor finds his own method of approaching a role. Moreover, every actor learns eventually that the process is an ever-changing one: every role is different, every role makes different demands on the actor's instrument, and every role strikes different chords within the actor's own psychological experience and understanding. An accomplished actor's method will change with each role, with each director, and to a certain extent with each rehearsal and each performance. The more flexible the actor's approach, the more versatile he can be and the more capable he is of meeting the multiple demands of his art. The more encompassing his method, the more unblinking his self-analysis and the more sophisticated his technique, the more he will be able to apply himself rigorously and creatively, which will lead him further and further into the depth and breadth of his art.

THE ACTOR'S ROUTINE

In essence, the actor's professional routine consists of three stages: auditioning, rehearsing, and performing. The first is the way the actor gets his role, the second is the way he learns it, and the last is the way he produces it, either night after night on a stage or one time for film or taping. Each of these stages merits independent consideration, for each imposes certain special demands on the actor's instrument and on his approach.

Auditioning

For all but the most established professionals, auditioning is the primary process by which acting roles are rewarded. A young actor may audition literally hundreds of times a year. In the film world, celebrated performers may be required to audition only if their careers are perceived to be declining: two of the more famous (and successful) auditions in American film history were undertaken by Frank Sinatra for *From*

Here to Eternity, and by Marlon Brando for *The Godfather*. Stage actors are customarily asked to audition no matter how experienced or famous they are.

The actor's audition affords him an opportunity to demonstrate to the director (or producer, or casting director) how well he can fulfill the role he seeks; in order to show this, the actor presents either a prepared reading (which may be taken from any play) or a "cold reading" from the script whose production is planned.

Every actor who is seriously planning for a career in the theatre will prepare several audition pieces to have at the ready in case an audition opportunity presents itself. For the most part these pieces will be one- or two-minute monologues from plays, although sometimes short narrative cuttings from novels, stories, and poems are used. Each audition piece must be carefully edited for timing and content (some alteration of the text, so as to make a continuous speech out of two or three shorter speeches, is generally permissible); the piece is then memorized and simply staged. The staging requirements should be flexible to permit adjustments to the size of the audition place (which might be a stage but could just as well be an agent's office), and should not rely on costume or particular pieces of furniture. Most actors prepare a variety of these pieces, for although auditions generally specify two contrasting selections (one verse and one prose, or one serious and one comic, or one classical and one modern), an extra piece that fits a particular casting situation can often come in handy. An actor's audition pieces are as essential as calling cards in the professional theatre world, and in many academies as well; they should be carefully developed, coached, and rehearsed, and of course they should be performed with assurance and poise.

The qualities a director looks for at an audition vary from one situation to another, but generally they include the actor's ease at handling the role, his naturalness of delivery, his physical, vocal, and emotional suitability for the part, and his seeming spontaneity, power, and charm. Most directors also look for indications that the actor is well trained and disciplined, that he is capable of mastering the technical demands of the part, that he will complement the company ensemble, and that he can convey that intangible presence which makes for

HOW TO AUDITION

Doubtless many readers of this book will wish to audition for a play at some time in their lives. It is a wonderful experience, provided one is prepared to deal with the chance of rejection, for it energizes the mind and body in a one-to-one relationship that has no exact equal anywhere else.

There can be no consensus as to what sort of audition will be successful in any given circumstance, since directors vary widely in what they are looking for—and what they are *not* looking for—and a certain amount of interpersonal chemistry inevitably influences the final decision. However, these general points about auditioning might prove useful to the beginner.

Audition pieces should always be selected from material suitable to the actor. For example, an inexperienced young person should not prepare a speech of King Lear for audition purposes, for this role would almost surely be quite beyond his grasp; far better that he prepare a piece reasonably in concert with his own age and experience.

Similarly, audition pieces should be suited to the role sought or the play auditioned for. It would be foolish even for a veteran performer to prepare material from *King Lear* if the play being cast is a light comedy; only the most creative casting director could get any idea from the Lear audition of how the actor would come across if given a role in the play under consideration.

Auditions should evoke the actor's most theatrically interesting qualities: they should do something to "grab" the attention of the director; otherwise they fail, no matter how competently performed. An audition, after all, is not a classroom assignment—it is an appeal to the director that should say—should actually *scream*—"Look no farther, you've found what you're looking for!" All auditions, whether of the prepared or the cold reading variety, should be designed to bring out the actor's ability to concentrate on situational

objectives and to employ engaging tactics, thus giving evidence of the actor's range within the required context; only then can the director get a valid idea of the actor's potential contribution to the excitement of his planned theatrical experience.

Auditions should be given with confidence, and without extensive preamble, apology, or explanation. Excessive nervousness or slavish deference to the director, though they be occasioned by nothing more than shyness, can freeze the actor and ruin an audition; conversely, the bluster that sometimes is attempted to cover shyness is likely to read as an attitude of superiority or defiance, which is rarely encouraged. Continual auditioning is the best single means of developing calm and powerful auditioning; every actor with professional ambitions should audition as often as possible, and under as many sorts of circumstances as present themselves.

Auditions should be short. In some professional situations the actor has no control whatever over the amount of time allotted for auditions and the audition is routinely cut off after just ten or fifteen seconds. While most directors dislike cutting auditions off in mid course, they do learn most of what they want to know in a few moments and allow the audition to continue only as a matter of courtesy. Thus the first few moments of an audition count enormously, and the best auditioners learn to get themselves across in a very short time.

Auditions can be practiced; prepared auditions can be coached and rehearsed successfully, and cold reading techniques can be developed. But nothing demonstrates a fine actor so much, in an audition, as the confidence, control, and authority that come with training and experience. No actor should concentrate exclusively on developing an "audition method," for the audition can afford only a glimpse of the performer's total capabilities. The best preparation an actor can make for auditions is to look to his whole development as an actor.

"theatre magic." In short, the audition can show the director not only that the actor knows his craft, but also that he is a person who will lend the production a special excitement.

Rehearsing

Plays are ordinarily rehearsed in a matter of weeks: a normal period of rehearsal ranges from ten weeks for complex or experimental productions, to just one week for many summer stock operations. Much longer rehearsal periods, however, are not unheard of; indeed, the productions of Stanislavski and Bertolt Brecht were frequently rehearsed for a year or more. Three to five weeks is the customary rehearsal period for American professional productions—but it should be noted that these are 40-hour weeks, and they are usually followed by several days (or weeks) of previews and/or "out-of-town" tryouts, with additional rehearsals between performances.

During the rehearsal period the actor studies and learns his role. Some of the things he investigates in this period are his character's biography; the subtext (the unspoken communications) of the play; his character's thoughts, fears, and fantasies; his character's objectives; and the world envisioned by the play and the playwright. The director almost certainly will lead discussions, offer his opinions, and issue directives with respect to some or all of these matters; he may also provide reading materials, pictures, and music to aid the actor in his research.

The actor must memorize his lines, his stage movements ("blocking"), and his directed stage actions ("business") during the rehearsal period. He must also be prepared to re-memorize these if they are changed, as they frequently are: in the rehearsal of new plays it is not unusual for entire acts to be rewritten between rehearsals, and for large segments to be changed, added, or written out overnight.

Memorization usually presents no great problem for young actors, to whom it tends to come naturally (children in plays frequently memorize not only their own lines but everyone else's, without even meaning to); however, it seems to become more difficult as one gets older. But whatever his age, memorization of lines remains one of the easier problems the actor is called upon to solve, even though it is the one many naive audience members think would be the most

difficult. Adequate memorization merely provides the basis from which the actor learns his part; the important memory goal of the actor is not simply to get his lines down, but to do it *fast* so he can devote most of the rehearsal time to concentrating on other things.

The rehearsal period is a time for experimentation and discovery. It is a time for the actor to get close to his character's beliefs and intentions, to steep himself in the internal aspects of characterization that lead to fully engaged physical, intellectual, and emotional performance. It is a time to search the play's text and the director's mind for clues as to how the character behaves, and what results the character aims for in the play's situation. And it is a time to experiment, both alone and in rehearsal with other actors, with the possibilities of subtle interactions which these investigations develop.

Externally, rehearsal is a time for the actor to experiment with his timing and delivery of both lines and business; to integrate his staged movements, given by the director, with his text, given by the playwright, and to meld these into a fluid series of actions that build and illuminate by the admixture of his own personally initiated behavior. It is a time to suggest movement and "business" possibilities to the director (presuming the director is the sort who accepts suggestions, as virtually all do nowadays), and to work out details of complicated sequences with the other actors. It is also a time to "get secure" in both lines and business by constant repetition—in fact, the French word for "rehearsal" is *répétition*. And it affords an opportunity to explore all the possibilities of the role—to look for ways to improve the actor's original plan for its realization and to test various possibilities with the director.

Thus the rehearsal of a play is an extremely creative time for an actor; it is by no means a routine or boring work assignment—and indeed for this reason some actors enjoy the rehearsal process even more than the performance phase of production. At its best, a rehearsal is both spontaneous and disciplined, a combination of repetition and change, of trying and "setting," of making patterns and breaking them and then making them anew. It is an exciting time, no less so because it invariably includes many moments of distress, frustration, and despair; it is a time, above all, when the actor learns a great deal about acting, and, ideally, about human interaction on many levels.

Performing

Performing, finally, is what the theatre is "about," and it is before an audience in a live performance that the actor's mettle is put to the ultimate test.

Sometimes the results are quite startling. The actor who has been brilliant in rehearsal can crumble before an audience and completely lose the "edge" of his performance in the face of stage fright and apprehension. Or—and this is more likely—an actor who seemed fairly unexciting in rehearsal can suddenly take fire in performance and dazzle the audience with unexpected energy, subtlety, and depth: one celebrated example of this phenomenon was achieved by Lee J. Cobb in the original production of Arthur Miller's *Death of a Salesman*, in which Cobb had the crucial title role. Roles rehearsed in all solemnity can suddenly turn comical in performance; conversely, roles developed for comic potential in rehearsal may be received soberly by an audience and lose their comedic aspect entirely.

Sudden and dramatic change, however, is not the norm as the performance phase replaces rehearsal: most actors cross over from final dress rehearsal to opening night with only the slightest shift; indeed, this is generally thought to be the goal of a disciplined and professional rehearsal schedule. "Holding back until opening night," an acting practice occasionally employed in the past century, is quite universally disavowed today, and opening-night recklessness is viewed as a sure sign of the amateur, who relies primarily on guts and adrenalin to get through the evening. Deliberate revisions of a role in performance, in response to the first waves of laughter or applause, is similarly frowned upon in all but the most inartistic of theatres today.

Nevertheless, a fundamental shift does occur in the actor's awareness between rehearsal and performance, and this cannot and should not be denied; indeed, it is essential to the creation of theatre art. The shift is set up by an elementary feedback: the actor is inevitably aware, with at least a portion of his mind, of the audience's reactions to his own performance and that of his fellow players; there is always, in any acting performance, a subtle adjustment to the audience that sees it. The outward manifestations of this adjustment are usually all but imperceptible: the split-second hold for a laugh to die down, the slight special projection of a certain line to ensure that it reaches the back row, the quick turn of a head to make a characterization or plot transition extra clear.

In addition, the best actors consistently radiate a quality known to the theatre world as "presence." It is a rather difficult quality to describe, but it has the effect of making both the character whom the actor portrays and the "self" of the actor who represents that character real in time (that is, in the present) for the audience; it is the quality of an actor who takes the stage and acknowledges, in some inexplicable yet indelible manner, that he is there *to be seen*. Performance is not a one-way statement given from the stage to the house; it is a two-way, participatory communication between the actors and the audience, in which the former employ text and movement, and the latter employ applause, laughter, silence, and attention.

Even when the audience is silent and invisible —and, owing to the brightness of stage lights, the audience is frequently invisible to the actor—the performer "feels" their presence. There is nothing extrasensory about this: the absence of sound is itself a signal, for when several hundred people sit without shuffling, coughing, or muttering, their silence betokens a level of attention for which the actor customarily strives. Laughter, gasps, sighs, and applause similarly feed back into the actor's consciousness— and unconsciousness—and spur (or sometimes, alas, distract) his efforts. The veteran actor can determine quickly how to ride the crest of audience laughter and how to hold his next line just long enough that it will pierce the lingering chuckles but not be overridden by them; he also knows how to vary his pace and/or redouble his energy when he senses restlessness or boredom on the other side of the curtain line. "Performance technique," or the art of "reading an audience" is more instinctual than learned. It is not dissimilar to the technique achieved by the effective classroom lecturer or TV talk show host, or even by the accomplished conversationalist. The timing it requires is of such complexity that no actor could master it rationally; he can develop it only out of experience—both on stage and off.

The professional stage actor faces a special problem that is unknown to his film counterpart and seldom experienced by amateurs in the theatre: the problem of maintaining a high level of spontaneity through many, many performances. Some professional play productions perform continuously literally for years, and actors may well find themselves in the position—fortunately for their finances, awkwardly for their art—of performing the same part eight times a week, fifty-two weeks a year, with no end in sight. Of course the routine can vary with vacations and cast substitutions, and in fact very few actors ever play a role continuously for more than a year or two, but the problem becomes intense even after only a few weeks. How, as they say in the trade, does the actor "keep it fresh"?

Each actor has his own way of addressing this problem. Some rely on their total immersion in the role and contend that by "living the life of the character" they can keep themselves equally alert from first performance to last. Others turn to technical experiments—reworking their delivery and trying constantly to find better ways of saying their lines, expressing their characters, and achieving their objectives. Still others concentrate on the relationships within the play, and try with every performance to "find something new" in each relationship as it unfolds on stage. Some actors, it must be admitted, resort to childish measures, rewriting dialogue as they go or trying to break the concentration of the other actors—this sort of behavior is abhorrent, but it is indicative of the seriousness of the actor's problems of combating boredom in a long-running production, and the lengths to which some will go to solve them.

The actor's performance does not end with the play, for it certainly extends into the paratheatrical moments of the curtain call—in which the actor-audience communion is direct and unmistakable—and it can even be said to extend to the dressing-room post mortem, in which the actor reflects upon what he has done today and how he might do better tomorrow. Sometimes the post mortem of a play is handled quite specifically by the director, who may give notes to the cast; more typically, in professional situations, the actor simply relies on his own self-criticism, often measured against comments from friends and fellow cast members, from the stage manager, and from reviews in the press. For there is no performer who leaves the stage in the spirit of a factory worker leaving the plant. If there has been a shift up from the rehearsal phase to the performance phase, there is now a shift down (or a letdown) that follows the curtain call—a re-entry into a world where actions and reactions are likely to be a

little more calm. There would be no stage fright if there were nothing to be frightened *about*, and the conquering of one's own anxiety—sometimes translated as conquering of the audience: "I really killed them tonight"—fills the actor at the final curtain with a sense of awe, elation . . . and emptiness. It is perhaps this feeling that draws the actor ever more deeply into his profession, for it is a feeling known to the rankest amateur in a high school pageant as well as to the most experienced professional in a Broadway or West End run. It is the theatre's "high," and because it is a high that accompanies an inexpressible void, it leads to addiction.

THE ACTOR IN LIFE

Acting is an art. It can also be a disease.

The actor is a privileged person. He gets to live the lives of some of the world's greatest and best known characters: Romeo, Juliet, Phèdre, Cyrano, St. Joan, and Willy Loman. He gets to fight for honor, hunger for salvation, battle for justice, die for love, kill for passion. He gets to die a dozen times before his death, to duel hundreds of fabulous enemies, to love thousands of magnificent lovers, and to live through an infinite variety of human experiences which, though imaginary, are publicly engaged. He gets to re-enter the innocence of childhood without suffering its consequences, and to participate in every sort of adult villainy without reckoning its responsibility. He gets to fantasize freely and be seen doing so—and he gets paid for it.

Millions of people want to be actors. It looks easy and, at least for some people, it *is* easy. It looks exciting, and there can be no question that it *is* exciting, *very* exciting; in fact, amateurs act in theatres all over the world without any hope of getting paid merely to experience that excitement. Acting addicts, as a consequence, are common. People who will not wait ten minutes at a supermarket checkout stand will wait ten years to get a role in a Hollywood film or a Broadway play. The acting unions are the only unions in the world that have ever negotiated a *lower* wage for some of their members in order to allow them to perform at substandard salaries. To the true acting addict there is nothing else; acting becomes the sole preoccupation.

The addicted actor—the actor obsessed with acting for its own sake—is probably not a very good actor, for fine acting demands an open mind, a mind capable of taking in stimuli from all sorts of directions, not merely from the theatrical environment. An actor who knows nothing but acting has no range. First and foremost, the actor must represent human beings, and to do that he must know something about his fellow man. Thus the proper study of acting is Life, abetted but not supplanted by the craft of the trade. Common sense, acute powers of observation and perception, tolerance and understanding for all human beings, and a sound general knowledge of one's own society and culture are prime requisites for the actor—as well as training, business acumen, and a realistic vision of one's own potential.

A lifetime professional career in acting is the goal of many but the accomplishment of very few. Statistically, the chances of one's developing a long-standing acting career are quite small; only those individuals possessed of great talent, skill, persistence, and personal fortitude stand any chance of succeeding—and even then it is only a chance. But the excitement of acting is not the exclusive preserve of those who attain lifetime professional careers; on the contrary, it may be argued that the happiest and most artistically fulfilled actors are those for whom performance is only an avocation. The excitement of acting, finally, is not dependent on monetary reward, a billing above the title, or the size of one's roles, but on the actor's engagement with drama and with dramatized situations; in short, on his synchronization with the theatre itself, of which acting is the very evanescent but still solid center.

CHAPTER 11

THE PLAYWRIGHT

He is an anomalous figure in the theatre.

In his home he is the master of the stage, the initiator of all theatrical art. Facing his writing paper, he is profoundly in control: actions cascade through his head, characters populate his imagination, great scenes parade across his vision, words and speeches pour from his pen. It is to be *his* play, *his* thoughts, *his* people, and *his* words which will resound through the theatres of the world, which will be praised in the press, immortalized in handsomely bound volumes, and examined diligently in the universities. It is he, the playwright, who will win the Pulitzer Prize and the Critics Circle Award, and who perhaps will one day sit next to some contemporary Einstein or Schweitzer when the Nobel Laureates are lionized at Stockholm.

In the theatre, however, he is the lonely figure who huddles uncomfortably over a legal pad, in a back row, scarcely noticed by the actors and directors who are rehearsing his play, certain in the back of his mind that the theatre is nothing more than an instrument created for the purpose of diluting his ideas and massacring his manuscript.

Has there ever been such an anomaly? For the playwright is both the most central and the most peripheral figure in the theatrical event.

He is central in the most obvious ways. He provides the point of origin for virtually every play production—the script, which is the rallying point around which the director or producer gathers his troops.

And yet that point of origin is also a point of departure. The days when a Shakespeare or a Molière would gather actors around, read his text to them, and then coach them in its proper execution are long gone, replaced by a more specialized theatrical hierarchy in which the director interposes himself as the playwright's representative to the theatrical enterprise and its constituent members. More and more, the playwright's function is to write his play and then disappear, for once the script has been typed, duplicated, and distributed, the playwright's physical participation is relegated mainly to serving as the director's sounding board and rewrite man. Indeed, the playwright's mere physical presence in the rehearsal hall can become an embarrassment, more tolerated than welcomed and sometimes not even tolerated.

Fundamentally, the playwright today is considered an independent artist, whose work, like that of the novelist or poet, is executed primarily if not exclusively in isolation. There are exceptions, of course: some playwrights work out of the improvisations of actors, and others participate quite fully in rehearsals, even to the point of taking over the direction of their plays (as both Arthur Miller and Edward Albee have done) or, more extraordinarily, acting in them (as Tennessee Williams and Michael Christofer have done).

But the exceptions do not, in this case, disprove the rule; since the age of Romanticism the image of the playwright has turned increasingly from that of theatre co-worker and mentor to that of isolated observer and social critic. In the long run, this change should occasion no lamentation, for if theatre production now demands collaboration and compromise, the art of the theatre still requires individuality, clarity of vision, sharpness of approach, original sensitivity, and a devotion to personal truth if it is to challenge the artists who are called upon to fulfill it and the audiences who will pay money to experience it. It is often said that Shakespeare and Molière wrote great plays because they could tailor their parts to the talents of actors whom they knew well; it seems far more likely that they wrote great plays in spite of this, for at the hands of lesser writers that sort of enterprise produces sheer hack work which simply combines the limitations of the actors with those of the author. Whether writing from inside an acting company or in submission to one, the playwright strives to give life to a unique vision, to create material which transcends what has gone before, both in writing and in performance.

Therefore the *independence* of the playwright is perhaps his most important characteristic. He must seek from life—and not from the theatrical establishment—the material that will translate into exciting and meaningful and entertaining theatre; and his view must be intensely personal, grounded in his own perceptions and philosophy, in order to ring true. We look to the theatre for a measure of leadership, for personal enlightenment derived from another's experience, for fresh perspectives, new visions. In other words, simple mastery of certain conventional techniques will not suffice to enable the playwright to expand our lives.

All dedicated playwrights know this, and as a result there is little conformity among them. Neither "schools" of associated writers nor schools of writer

training have enjoyed sustained success. Playwrights have come from the acting arts, from literature, from teaching, from gag writing, from housewifery, from medicine, from mathematics, from the military, from politics, from every conceivable background. Individuality is the playwright's byword. Whenever literary critics try to lump playwrights into some sort of critical association, such as "the Theatre of the Absurd," it is the playwrights who quickly demur, asserting that the label "may apply to the other guys, but certainly not to me."

Individuality also governs the precepts of how plays should be made, particularly since the age of Romanticism, which in some respects underlies the more modish movements of today. It was Romanticism which finally put an end to the seventeenth-century neo-classicist notion that the writing of plays should be governed by rules based on the "unities" of time, place, and action (see chapter 6, pp. 169–72).

Most modern-day playwrights would scoff at the mere idea of formal rules of playwriting; indeed, it has been said that a virtual state of anarchy now exists concerning the very definition of a play or a theatrical event. There is, however, much open ground between rigid rules and utter chaos, and in this chapter we shall attempt to discover those underlying characteristics of the playwright's art which transcend both period and style, and which remain unaltered beneath the changing currents of artistic experimentation and critical prescription and proscription.

LITERARY AND NON-LITERARY ASPECTS OF PLAYWRITING

Since drama is in part a branch of literature, and since many dramatic authors begin (or double) as poets or novelists, it seems convenient to think of playwriting as a primarily literary endeavor, as simply one branch of "writing." This perspective, however, obscures the fact that the "playwright" is not simply a "playwrite," and that playwriting always entails considerations not common to other literary forms.

By homonymic coincidence, "playwriting" sounds like an extrapolation of "playwright." But etymologically, the word "playwright" is parallel to "wheelwright" or "shipwright": as a wheelwright is one who makes wheels and a shipwright is one who makes ships, a playwright is, literally, "one who *makes*

"Story Theatre," which is an improvised play, was created by Paul Sills out of theatre games and improvisations developed by actors and directors in concert. Here Peter Bonerz (right) leads a Story Theatre segment entitled "Clever People," in Mark Taper Forum Theatre presentation of 1970–71.

plays," not one who merely "writes" them. This distinction is important, because some plays, or portions of plays, are never written at all. Improvisational plays, certain rituals, whole scenes of comic business, subtextual behaviors, and many documentary dramas are created largely or entirely in performance, or are learned simply through oral improvisation and repetition. Some are created with a tape recorder and multiple imaginations, and may or may not be committed to writing after the performance is concluded.

And others, although dramatic in structure, are entirely non-verbal; that is, they include no dialogue, no words, and very little that is actually written other than an outline of mimetic effects.

So drama is a branch of literature, but it is a very special and distinctive branch. It is not merely an arrangement of words on a page; it is a conceptualization of the interactions of myriad elements in the theatrical medium: movement, speech, scenery, costume, staging, music, spectacle, and silence. It is a literature whose impact depends on a collective endeavor and whose appreciation must be, in large part, spontaneous and immediate; there can be no thought in the drama of relying purely on effects that are perceivable through solitary reading.

A play attains its finished form only in performance upon the stage: the written script is not the final play but the *blueprint* for the play, the written foundation for the production which is the play's complete realization. Some of a play's most effective writing may look very clumsy as it appears in print, as for example:

"Oh! Oh! Oh!" (Shakespeare's *Othello*)

"Howl, howl, howl, howl!"
   (Shakespeare's *King Lear*)

"No, no, the drink, the drink. O my dear Hamlet,
The drink, the drink! I am poisoned."
   (Shakespeare's *Hamlet*)

These apparently unsophisticated lines of dialogue in fact provide great dramatic climaxes in an impassioned performance; they are *pretexts for great acting*, the creation of which is far more crucial than literary eloquence to the art of playwriting.

Of course some formal literary values are as important to the theatre as they are to other branches of literature: allusional complexity, descriptive precision, poetic imagery, metaphoric implication, and a careful crafting of verbal rhythms, cadences, and textures all contribute powerfully to dramatic effect. But they are effective only insofar as they are fully integrated with the whole of the theatrical medium, as they stimulate action and behavior through stage space and stage time in a way that commands audience attention and involvement. Mere literary brilliance is insufficient as theatre, as a great many successful novelists and poets have learned to their chagrin when they attempted to write plays.

PLAYWRITING AS "EVENT WRITING"

The core of every play is action. In contrast to other literary forms, the inner structure of a play is never a series of abstract observations or a collage of descriptions and moralizings; it is an ordering of observable, dramatizable *events*. These events are the basic building blocks of the play, regardless of its style or genre or theme.

Fundamentally, the playwright works with but two tools, both of which represent the externals of human behavior: dialogue and physical action. The inner story and theme of a play—the psychology of the characters, the viewpoint of the author, the impact of the social environment—must be inferred, by the audience, from outward appearances, from the play's events as the audience sees them. Whatever the playwright's intended message and whatever his perspective on the function and process of playwriting itself, he cannot begin putting his play together until he has conceived of an event—and then a series of related events—which he wishes to see enacted on a stage. It is this series of related events which constitutes the play's scenario, or, more formally, its plot.

The events of drama are, by their nature, compelling. Some are bold and unusual, such as the scene in which Prometheus is chained to his rock. Some are subdued, as the vision of the Trojan women leaving their devastated city at that play's end. Some are seemingly quite ordinary, as in the domestic sequences depicted in most modern realist plays. But they are always aimed at creating a memorable impression. To begin playwriting, one must first conceptualize events and envision them enacted in such a way as to hold the attention of an audience.

The events of a play can be connected to each other in a strict chronological, cause-effect continuity. This has been a goal of the realistic theatre, in which dramatic events are arranged to convey a lifelike progression of experiences in time. Such plays are said to be *continuous* in structure and *linear* in chronology, and they can be analyzed like sociological events, with the audience simply watching them unfold as it might watch a family quarrel in progress in an adjoining apartment.

Continuous linearity is by no means considered a requirement for play construction (although it was in the days of the neo-classic "Rules"). Many plays are discontinuous and/or nonlinear. The surviving plays of ancient Greece are highly discontinuous, with odes alternating with episodes in the tragedies and a whole host of non-linear theatrical inventions popping in and out during the comedies. Shakespeare's plays are structured in a highly complex arrangement of time shifts, place shifts, style shifts, songs and subplots ingeniously integrated around a basic theme or investigation of character. And many contemporary plays break with chronological linearity altogether, flashing instantly backwards and forwards through time to incorporate character memories, character fantasies, direct expressions of the playwright's social manifesto, historical exposition, comic relief, or any other ingredient the playwright can successfully work in.

Linear, point-to-point storytelling still has not disappeared from the theatre—indeed, it remains the basic architecture of most popular and serious plays—but modern audiences have proven increasingly receptive to less conventional structures: the exuberance of the music hall, for instance, inspired the structuring of Joan Littlewood's *Oh, What a Lovely War!* and the didacticism of the lecture hall underlay much of the theatre of Bertolt Brecht. Non-linear, discontinuous, and even stream-of-consciousness structures can provide powerful and sustained dramatic impact in the theatre, provided they are based in the dramatization of events which the audience can put together in some sort of meaningful and satisfying fashion.

THE QUALITIES OF A FINE PLAY

Credibility and Intrigue

To say that a play must be credible is not at all to say that it has to be lifelike, for fantasy, ritual, and absurdity have all proven to be enduringly popular theatrical modes. The demand of credibility is an audience-imposed demand, and it has to do with the play's internal consistency: the actions must flow logically from the characters, the situation, and the theatrical context that the playwright provides. In other words, we might say that credibility is the audience's demand that what happens in Act II makes sense in terms of what happened in Act I.

Credibility demands, for example, that the characters in a play appear to act out of their own indi-

vidual interests, instincts, and intentions rather than serving as mere pawns for the development of theatrical plot or effect, as empty disseminators of propaganda. Credibility means that characters must maintain consistency within themselves: that their thoughts, feelings, hopes, fears, and plans must appear to flow from human needs rather than purely theatrical ones. Credibility also demands that human characters appear to act and think like human beings (even in humanly impossible situations), and not purely as thematic automatons. Credibility, in short, is the essence of a contract between author and audience, whereby the audience agrees to view the characters as "people" so long as the author abides by his agreement not to shatter that belief in order to accomplish other purposes.

Thus James Barrie's famous play *Peter Pan*, while undeniably fantastical, creates a cast of characters wholly appropriate to their highly imaginary situation, and internally consistent in their actions within the context of their developing experience. All their aspirations (including those of the dog!) are human ones, and their urgencies are so believable that when Tinker Bell steps out of the play's context to ask the audience to demonstrate its belief in fairies, the audience is willing to applaud its approval. At that moment, the world of the play becomes more credible, more "real," than that of the audience. So much for the power—and consequently the necessity—of dramatic credibility.

Intrigue is that quality of a play which makes us curious (sometimes fervently so) to see "what happens next." Sheer plot intrigue—which is sometimes called "suspense" in that it leaves us suspended (that is, "hanging")—is one of the most powerful of dramatic approaches. Whole plays can be based on little more than artfully contrived plotting designed to keep the audience in a continual state of anticipation and wonder. Plot, however, is only one of the elements of a play that can support intrigue. Most plays that aspire to deeper insights than "whodunits" or farces develop intrigue in character as well, and even in theme. Most of the great plays, in fact, demand that we ask not so much "What will happen?" as "What does this mean?" Most great plays, in other words, make us care about the characters and invite us to probe the mysteries of the human condition.

Writers of tragedy tend to dispense with plot in-

What's in the box? A standard thriller technique, here used in Paul Giovanni's The
Crucifer of Blood, *is to intrigue the audience with mysterious locked boxes. This one,
opened by a soldier's sword in India, will provoke an investigation from Sherlock Holmes
on London's Baker Street. From American Conservatory Theatre production, 1980.*

trigue altogether. The Greek tragedies were retellings of well-known legends whose conclusions
were known to the audience before they even entered
the theatre. Shakespeare also used earlier works as
the bases for his tragedies, and on occasion even reminded his audience of the play's ending in its first
words (see the discussion of *Romeo and Juliet*, p. 143).

Peter Shaffer's *Equus* is a modern tragedy whose
most significant incident is described early in the
play in order that it may be analyzed (by characters
and audience) for the balance of the play, which
culminates in an enactment of the same incident. Intrigue of character depends on the author's ability
first to present characters who are so fascinating

that we want to understand them better—and then to devise situations and scenes that deepen our fascination with each successive revelation.

Surprise is an essential ingredient of intrigue: a play that is truly intriguing is one that leads us to expect surprises and then appropriately rewards our expectations. The plays of Harold Pinter, which are filled with abrupt, almost inexplicable transitions, intense pauses and glances, and elliptical dialogue that seems to contain innuendoes which we don't fully comprehend, create an almost palpable sense of foreboding and spookiness which plunges the audience deeper and deeper into Pinteresque moods and reveries. The plays of Tom Stoppard, by contrast, race glibly through brilliant rhetorical flights of language that always manage to stay one step ahead of the audience's capability to follow, keeping the audience breathless while forcing them to remain intellectually alert. (See box at right.)

Sometimes a playwright's theme can provide sufficient intrigue in itself to engage an audience's deepest attention. "What is the playwright getting at?" we wonder, and this question can lead us, for a while at least, to follow closely a dialogue that would hold no interest for us if overheard in a real-life situation. The mere fact that the author has seen fit to incorporate such dialogue in a play—and moreover that many people have labored to get that play to the point of production—is sufficient to confer a modicum of intrigue. But of course the audience must soon receive some sort of intellectual or emotional or "entertainment" reward for its attention.

Intrigue draws us into the world of a play; credibility keeps us there. In the best plays the two are sustained throughout the course of the action in a fine tension of opposites: intrigue demanding surprise, credibility demanding consistency. Combined, they generate a kind of "believable wonder," which is the fundamental state of drama. All the credibility in the world will not suffice by itself to make a play interesting, and all the intrigue that craft can contrive will fail to make an incredible play palatable. It is the integration of the two which must be explored by the playwright in order to establish that shared ground which satisfies both human inertia and human potential, which transcends our expectations but not our credulity.

H arold Pinter and Tom Stoppard, contemporary British playwrights, exemplify sharply contrasting dramatic styles. The following samples are reasonably typical of their respective works.

From Pinter's *Silence* (1969)

BATES: (*moves to* ELLEN) Will we meet tonight?
ELLEN: I don't know. (*pause*)
BATES: Come with me tonight.
ELLEN: Where?
BATES: Anywhere. For a walk. (*pause*)
ELLEN: I don't want to walk.
BATES: Why not ? (*pause*)
ELLEN: I want to go somewhere else. (*pause*)
BATES: Where?
ELLEN: I don't know. (*pause*)
BATES: What's wrong with a walk?
ELLEN: I don't want to walk. (*pause*)
BATES: What do you want to do?
ELLEN: I don't know. (*pause*)
BATES: Do you want to go somewhere else?
ELLEN: Yes.
BATES: Where?
ELLEN: I don't know. (*pause*)

From Stoppard's *Dirty Linen* (1976)

COCKLEBURY-SMYTHE: May I be the first to welcome you to Room 3B. You will find the working conditions primitive, the hours antisocial, the amenities non-existent and the catering beneath contempt. On top of that the people are for the most part very boring, with interests either so generalized as to mimic wholesale ignorance or so particular as to be lunatic obsessions. Their level of conversation would pass without comment in the lavatory of a mixed comprehensive and the lavatories, by the way, are few and far between.

Mirrored surfaces on floor and backdrop amplify the empty communication between Bates and Ellen in the Royal Shakespeare Company's 1969 production of Harold Pinter's Silence, *directed by Peter Hall.*

Speakability, Stageability, and Flow

The dialogue of drama is written upon the page, but it must be spoken by an actor and staged by a director. Thus the goal of the dramatist is to fabricate dialogue that is both actable and stageable, and that flows in a progression that leads to theatrical impact.

One of the commonest faults in the work of the beginning playwright—sometimes even when that playwright is an established novelist or poet—is that the lines lack "speakability." This is not to say that play dialogue must resemble ordinary speech. No one imagines persons in life speaking like characters out of the works of Aeschylus, Shakespeare, Shaw, or Giraudoux, or even like contemporary characters fashioned by Harold Pinter or Edward Albee; a brilliantly styled language has been a feature of most of the great plays in theatre history, and naturalness or super-realism is not, by itself, a dramatic virtue—nor is its absence a dramatic fault.

Rather, speakability means that a line of dialogue should be so written that it achieves its maximum

Stageability is a matter of the highest importance in farce. The dialogue for this clumsily urgent seduction scene from Feydeau's Hotel Paradiso *is of relatively little importance. Staged by director Tom Moore at American Conservatory Theatre with actors Elizabeth Huddle and Raye Birk (1978).*

impact when *spoken*. In order to accomplish this, the playwright must be closely attuned to the "audial shape" of dialogue, the rhythm of sound that creates emphasis, meaning, focus, and power. Verbal lullabies and climaxes, fast punch lines, sonorous lamentations, sparkling epigrams and devastating expletives, significant pauses and electrifying whispers—these are some of the devices of dialogue that impart audial shape to great plays written by master dramatists.

Speakability also requires that the spoken line must seem to emanate from the character who utters it, and that it must contain, in its syntax, vocabulary, and mode of expression, the marks of that character's milieu and his personality. The spoken line is not merely an expression of the author's perspective; it is the basis from which the actor develops characterization and the acting ensemble creates a play's style. Thus the mastery of dramatic dialogue writing demands more than mere semantic skills; it requires a constant awareness of the purposes and tactics underlying human communication, as well as of the multiple psychological and aesthetic properties of language.

Stageability, of course, requires that dialogue be written so it can be spoken effectively upon a stage, but it also requires something more: dialogue must be conceived as an integral element of a particular staged situation, in which setting, physical action, and spoken dialogue are inextricably combined. *Romeo and Juliet* affords a splendid illustration of the successful integration of lyrical dramatic dialogue and physical stage behavior (together with a multitude of stage properties) into a dramatic unity which simply cannot be expressed outside the theatrical context itself. A stageable script is one in which staging and stage business—as well as design and the acting demands—are neither adornments for the dialogue nor sugarcoating for the writer's opinions, but intrinsic to the very nature of the play.

Both speakability and stageability are contingent upon human limitations: those of the actors and directors as well as those of the audience. Speakability must take into account that the actor must breathe from time to time, for example, and that the audience can take in only so many metaphors in a single spoken sentence. Stageability must reckon with the forces of gravity and inertia, which both the poet and the novelist may conveniently ignore. Certainly this does not

> If this is the dramatist's day, he will be wise to consider the actor, not as a mere appendage to his work, but as its very life-giver. Let him realize that the more he can learn to ask of the actor the more he will gain for his play. But asking is giving. He must give opportunity.
>
> Harley Granville-Barker

mean that the playwright must simply succumb to the common denominator—all the great playwrights strive to extend the capacities of actors and audience alike—however, he must not forget that the theatre is fundamentally a human event that cannot transcend human capabilities.

A speakable and stageable script flows rather than stumbles; this is true for non-linear plays as well as for more straightforwardly structured ones. Flow consists above all in the creation of a continual stream of *information*, and a play that flows is one that is continually saying something, doing something, and meaning something to the audience. To serve this end, the playwright should address such technical problems as scene shifting, entrances and exits, and act breaks (intermissions) as early as possible in the script-writing process. Furthermore, in drafting scenes the writer should be aware that needless waits, arid expositions (no matter how "necessary" to the plot), inane ramblings on the part of the characters, and incomprehensible plot developments can sink the sturdiest script in a sea of audience apathy.

The combined demands of speakability, stageability, and dramatic flow apply in some measure to the crafting of any play; hence every professional playwright necessarily develops certain skills to meet these demands. In many theatrical eras in the past, playwriting was considered so technically demanding that craft appeared to be all that was involved, and playwrights spent long in-house apprenticeships as "company men" learning their skills through continual exposure to theatrical rehearsal and performance. Even today, many playwrights come to their craft after decades of experience as actors, stage managers, or directors. But craft—which is largely an understanding of what has worked before—is not the sole determinant of the good play, and a blind reliance on craft has never led to great writing in any genre. With his *Waiting for Godot* in 1953, Samuel Beckett virtually rewrote the book on playwriting, teaching actors and directors new lessons about what is speakable and stageable, and introducing audiences to a kind of dramatic flow that was radically different from anything they had seen before. Great playwriting, it would seem, always straddles the line between solid craft and brilliant innovation; it is always based in a theatre wisdom which both understands the conventional and seeks, consciously or unconsciously, to improve upon it.

Richness

Depth, subtlety, fineness, quality, wholeness, and inevitability—these are words often called into service on behalf of plays that we like. They are fundamentally subjective terms, easier to apply than to define or defend, for the fact is that when a play pleases us, when it "works," the feelings of pleasure and stimulation it affords are quite beyond the verbal level. Certainly *richness* is one of the qualities common to plays that leave us with this sense of satisfaction—richness of *detail*, and richness of *dimension*.

A play that is rich with detail is not necessarily one that is rife with detail; it is simply one whose every detail fortifies our insight into the world of the play. For going to a play is in part a matter of paying a visit to the playwright's world, and the more vividly created that world, the greater the play's final impact. The best plays of Anton Chekhov, for example, portray in loving and incisive detail the end-of-a-century, end-of-an-era world of provincial Russia before the Revolution: attending a well-mounted production of Chekhov's *The Three Sisters* is like stepping backward in time into an adventure no travel agent could possibly book. Similarly, to attend a play by Bernard Shaw is to venture into a dazzling Edwardian milieu brimming with bright rhetoric, and to be caught up in a flurry of intellectual activity whose every speech gives occasion for thought or laughter—or both. And a play by Tennessee Williams is a journey into complex lives lived in steamy Southern towns, a journey into a firmer, deeper, broader set of impressions than could ever be provided by a guided tour. Each of these playwrights exhibits an extraordinary skill in the selection of meaningful detail.

Richness of detail—in movement, in language, in character outlook, in environmental features—lends a play authority, an aura of sureness. It surrounds the play's characters as a city surrounds a home, and gives them a cultural context in which to exist. It lends a play specificity—the feeling that it deals with specific people engaged in specific tasks in a specific place. In short, richness of detail makes a play authentic. It also makes it informative and, therefore, memorable.

Richness is not an easy quality to develop in writing. It demands a certain richness in the resources and capabilities of the author himself: a gift for close observation, an uninhibited imagination, and an astute sense of what to leave out as well as what to include. A person who can recollect his own experiences in great detail, who can create convincing situations, people, locales, and conversations when called upon to do so, and who is closely attuned to nuance, can perhaps work these talents into the writing of plays. Training programs for playwrights frequently assign exercises in observation and require the writing of imaginative or evocative description. These exercises can be useful, but only up to a point. For true richness tends to be a characteristic of the work of the mature writer, and all too often attempts to foster it in the young only result in counterfeit richness, a product of imitation rather than of observation and personal creativity.

Beyond question, *depth of characterization* is the single most important factor in determining a play's richness of dimension. It also presents perhaps the greatest single stumbling block for novice playwrights, who tend either to write all characters "in the same voice" (normally the author's own) or to divide them into two camps: the good ones and the bad ones. Although shallowness of characterization can sometimes be offset by strengths in other dramatic areas, a play that lacks sound character development can rarely achieve the profound embodiment of the human condition that represents theatre at its best.

Depth of characterization requires that every character possess, at least to a certain extent, an independence of intention, expression, and motivation; moreover, these character characteristics must appear sensible in the light of our general knowledge of psychology and human behavior. In plays as in life, every character must act from motives which appear reasonable *to him* (if not to those watching him, or those affected by him). Moreover, the writer should bear in mind that every character is, *to himself,* an extremely important and worthwhile person, even though he may be haunted by self-doubts or may perceive himself to be despised by others. These observations apply in even the most non-realistic of plays. The great villains of drama—Hermes in *Prometheus*, Menelaus in *The Trojan Women*, Satan in the York Cycle, and Iago in *Othello*, for example—all convey the impression that they believe in themselves and in the fundamental "rightness" of their cause, and even if we never completely understand their ultimate motivations (as we do not completely understand the motivations of historical villains such as Hitler, Caligula, and John Wilkes Booth), we can sense at the bottom of their behavior a certain validity of purpose, however twisted or perverse.

Depth of characterization requires that the characters convey the complexity of real human beings and do not simply represent thematic integers in the playwright's grand design. Even in a theatre in which the psychology of characterization takes second place to the promulgation of ideas, the "ideas" that are worth exploring theatrically are concerned with people and their behavior, and if the complexity of people and the purposes for their behavior are not conveyed in the writer's work, the ideas he wishes to get across can only appear trivial and ill conceived.

The realistic theatre, particularly in the turn-of-the-century domestic plays of Chekhov, Strindberg, and Maxim Gorki, has provided many works in which the psychological dimensions of the characters dominate all other aspects of the theatrical experience. By the mid twentieth century, this approach had become equally important in the American theatre, most notably in the searching, probing dramas of Tennessee Williams, Arthur Miller, Eugene O'Neill, and William Inge. The psychiatric process itself has stood at the core of the action in several plays, including Williams' *Suddenly Last Summer*, Miller's *After the Fall*, Shaffer's *Equus*, and the 1941 American musical *Lady in the Dark*, each of which portrays a principal character undergoing analysis or psychotherapy. The psychological sophistication of modern theatre audiences has afforded playwrights an expanded opportunity to explore and dramatize their characters in greater and greater depth, and has helped to make the "case study" drama a major genre of the current theatre (see chapter 9, p. 280).

Gravity and Pertinence

Gravity and pertinence are terms used to describe the importance of a play's theme and its overall relevance to the concerns of the intended audience.

To say that a play has gravity is to say simply that its central theme is one of serious and lasting significance in man's spiritual, moral, or intellectual life. All the world's major dramas—whatever their genre—are concerned fundamentally with life problems about which human beings regularly seek lucidity and enlightenment. Even comedies and farces deal with universal issues—issues such as adultery, aging, marital discord, religious and financial intimidation, personal and romantic insecurity, social ambition—and no amount of surface slapstick or badinage should obscure the fact that these issues are serious daily preoccupations of the human species.

Obviously, then, gravity does not mean somberness, which indeed often only signifies an attempt to imitate profundity. Quite to the contrary, gravity is more usually attended by a considerable release of theatrical energy, owing precisely to the universality of its appeal: when an audience truly understands and deeply identifies with the experiences set forth by the playwright, even the darkest tragedy radiates power, animation, and light.

If a play has the quality of pertinence, it relates in some fashion to the current personal concerns of its audience. These concerns can be timeless, or they can be quite ephemeral.

Plays about current political situations or personalities usually rely heavily on pertinence to attract their audiences. Writers of such plays, of course, must be aware that their work may be quickly outdated; for that reason, most producers are loath to have anything to do with any but the most promising topical plays. Indeed, many highly topical plays that do find their way into production require extensive adaptation and "updating" before they can be successfully revived.

More timeless concerns—such as the conflicts between passion and practicality (as in *Romeo and Juliet*) or between salvation and material well-being (as in *Waiting for Godot*)—lead to a kind of theatre that achieves pertinence without being merely topical or trendy, and that engages audience attention without regard to the current or local scene.

If we think of the mind of the author as a wheel turning in space, and the mind of the audience as another wheel similarly turning, pertinence would be the axle that connects them and makes them turn in some sort of synchronization. If that axle is missing, if a play does not stimulate the audience to consider, in its own frame of reference, the issues raised by the playwright, then the theatre has failed: it has committed the unforgiveable sin of boring the audience.

Compression, Economy, and Intensity

Compression, economy, and intensity make up another set of related aspects of the finest plays.

Compression refers to the playwright's skill at condensing a story (which may span many days, even years of chronological time) into a theatrical time frame; *economy* relates to his skill at eliminating or consolidating characters, events, locales, and words in the service of compression. We have seen how Shakespeare combined these skills in creating the "two-hour traffic of the stage" which is *Romeo and Juliet*. Unlike other literary or visual art forms which can be examined in private and at the leisure of the observer, a play must be structured to unfold in a public setting and at a predetermined pace. If the playwright can manage to meet these needs and at the same time to make every scene, every incident, every character, every word deliver an impact, he has satisfied the dramatic demand for *intensity*.

Many beginning playwrights attempt to convert a story to a play in the most obvious way: by writing a separate scene for every event described in the story (and sometimes including a different setting and supporting cast for each scene). Economy and compression, however, require that most stories be restructured in order to be dramatically viable. If the play is to be basically realistic, the playwright has traditionally reworked the story so as to have all the events occur in one location, or perhaps in two locations with an act break between to allow for scenery changes. Events that are integral to the story but cannot be shown within the devised settings can simply be reported (as in Bernard Shaw's *Misalliance*, for example, in which an airplane crash occurs offstage, as the onstage characters gawk and exclaim).

More common today is the use of theatricalist techniques which permit an integration of settings so that events occurring in various places can be presented on the same set without intermission. Similarly, economy and compression commonly dictate the deletion or combination of certain characters who appear in the story, and the reduction of important expository passages to a line or two of dialogue.

The effects of economy and compression are both financial and aesthetic. Obviously, when scenery changes and number of characters are held to a minimum the costs of production are minimized as well. But beyond that, compression and economy in playwriting serve to stimulate intrigue and focus audience expectation: a tightly written play gives us the feeling that we are on the trail of something important, and that our quarry is moreover right around the next bend. In other words, economy and compression actually lead to intensity, and dramatic intensity is one of the theatre's most powerful attributes. Dramatic intensity can take many forms. It can be harsh, abrasive, explosive, eminently physical or overtly calm. It can be ruminative, it can be tender, it can be comic. But whenever it occurs and in whatever mood or context, it conveys to the audience an ineradicable feeling that this moment in theatre is unique and its revelations are profound. Intensity in the theatre does not come about by happy accident, obviously, but neither can it be straightforwardly injected at the whim of the playwright. It must evolve out of a careful development of issues, through the increasing urgency of character goals and intentions and the focused actions and interactions of the plot that draw characters and their conflicts ever closer to some sort of climactic confrontation. A play must spiral inward toward its core; that is, its compression must increase, its mood must intensify, as it circles toward its dénouement. Too many tangential diversions can deflect it from this course and render it formless and apparently devoid of purpose.

Celebration

Finally, a fine play celebrates life; it does not merely depict or analyze or criticize it.

The first plays, as we have seen, were presented at festivals which, though perhaps haunted by angry or capricious gods, were essentially joyful celebrations.

Even the darkest of the ancient Greek tragedies sought to transcend the more negative aspects of existence and to exalt the human spirit, for the whole of Greek theatre was informed by the positive (and therapeutic) elements of the Dionysian festival: spring, fertility, the gaiety and solidarity of public communion.

The theatre can never successfully venture too far from this source. A purely didactic theatre has never *in fact* satisfied the public's expectations of theatre, and the merely grim depiction of ordinary life has proved equally inadequate to this art form. Although the word "theatrical" is often debased to suggest something like "glittery" or "showy," it should instead be used to connote an accord with the theatre's most fundamental aspirations: to go beyond known experience, to illuminate life, and to raise existence to the level of an art.

This "celebration" of which drama is capable can easily be perverted. Whole eras have been dedicated to a theatre which was deemed acceptable only insofar as it was "uplifting," and in those times many of the greatest tragedies were drastically revised so as to include happy endings and none but the most noble sentiments. Other dramas, in our own times, have been self-consciously written in "elevated" tones, in pale imitation of the more vigorous poetry of Shakespeare or Sophocles. These dramas do not celebrate life—they try to whitewash it, and to build a dramatic style that is independent of reality; to most observers these works seem but affectations.

The truest and most exciting theatre, whether played out on the tragic stage or in the music hall, in the inn-yard or behind the proscenium, has always been based on those dramas which were written out of a passionate, personal vision of reality and a deep devotion to the aim of extracting and expressing life's magnificence. For the theatre is fundamentally an affirmation in all its aspects. Like the writing of plays, the acts of putting them on, performing in them, and attending them are also acts of affirmation: they attest to a desire to share and to communicate; they celebrate human existence and participation and communion. Purely bitter plays, no matter how justly based or how well grounded in experience, remain incomplete and unsatisfying as theatre, which simply is not an effective medium for the conveyance of unalloyed pessimism. Even the bleakest of modern plays radiate a persistent hopefulness—even joyousness—as represented archetypally by Samuel Beckett's two old men singing, punning, and pantomiming so engagingly in the forlorn shadow of their leafless tree as they wait for Godot.

THE PLAYWRIGHT'S PROCESS

How does one go about writing a play?

It is important that one know the elements of a play, as discussed in Chapter 3, and the characteristics of the best plays—credibility, intrigue, richness in detail and characterization, gravity, pertinence, compression, economy, intensity, and celebration—as discussed above. But that is not enough; one must still confront the practical task of writing.

The blank sheet of paper is the writer's nemesis. It is the accuser, the goad and critic that coldly commands action even as it threatens humiliation.

There is no consensus among writers as to where to begin. Some prefer to begin with a story line or a plot outline. Some begin with a real event and write the play to explain why that event occurred. Some begin with a real character or set of characters and develop a plot around them. Some begin with a setting and try to animate it with characters and actions. Some begin with a theatrical effect, or an idea for a new form of theatrical expression. Some write entirely from personal experience. Some adapt a story or a legend, others a biography of a famous person, others a play by an earlier playwright.

"Theatre of Fact" usually begins with a document, such as the transcript of a trial or a committee hearing. Other documentary forms might begin with a tape recorder and a situation contrived by the playwright. Some plays are created out of actors' improvisations or acting class exercises. Some are compilations of material written over the course of many years or collected from many sources.

The fact is, writers tend to begin with whatever works for *them* and accords with their immediate aims. Since the playwright usually works alone, at least in the initial stages, he can do as he pleases whenever he wants: there is no norm. On the other hand, certain "steps" can be followed as introductory exercises to playwriting, and these may in fact lead to the creation of an entire play.

Dialogue

Transcription of dialogue from previous observation and experience—that is, the writing down of *remembered dialogue* from overheard conversations or from conversations in which the author has participated—is a fundamental playwriting exercise; probably most finished plays in fact contain such scenes. Because we remember conversations only selectively and subjectively, a certain amount of fictionalizing and shading inevitably creeps into these transcriptions, and often without even meaning to do so the author also transforms persons in his memory into characters in his scenes.

Writing scenes of *imagined dialogue* is the logical next step in this exercise, for all the author need do now is to extend the situation beyond its remembered reality into the area of "what might have happened." The dialogue then constructed will be essentially original, yet in keeping with the personalized "characters" developed in the earlier transcription. The characters now react and respond as dramatic figures, interacting with each other freshly and under the control of the author. Many fine plays have resulted from the author's working out, in plot and dialogue, hypothetical relations between real persons who actually never confronted each other in life; indeed, many plays are inspired by the author's notion of what *should* have happened among people who evaded the very confrontations which he wishes them to experience. In this way, the theatre has often been used as a form of psychotherapy, with the patient/playwright simply acting out—in imagination or with words on paper—certain obligatory scenes in his life which never in fact occurred.

Conflict

Writing scenes of *forced conflict* accelerates the exercise and becomes a third step toward the creation of a play. Scenes of separation, loss, crucial decision, rejection, or emotional breakthrough are climactic scenes in a play and usually help enormously to define its structure. If a writer can create a convincing scene of high conflict that gets inside *each* of the characters involved and not merely one of them, he stands a good chance of making that scene the core of an exciting play—especially if it incorporates some subtlety and is not dependent entirely on shouting and denunciation.

What is more, such a scene will be highly actable in its own right, and thus can serve as a valuable tool for demonstrating the writer's potential.

Exercises that result in scripted scenes—even if the scenes are just a page or two in length—have the advantage of allowing the writer to test his work as it progresses. For a short scene is easily producible: all it requires is a group of agreeable actors and a modest investment of time, and the playwright can quickly assess the total impact. The costs and difficulties of testing a complete play, on the other hand, may well prove insurmountable for the inexperienced playwright. Moreover, the performance of a short original scene can sometimes develop such impact as to generate enthusiasm for the theatrical collaboration needed for a fuller theatrical experience. Most playwrights today see their words staged first in the form of acted original scenes, either in colleges and universities or in professional theatre laboratories or community play-reading groups.

Structure

Developing a complete play demands more than stringing together a number of scenes, of course, and at some point in the scene-writing process the playwright inevitably confronts the need for structure. Many playwrights develop outlines for their plays after writing a scene or two; some have an outline ready before any scenes are written or even thought of. Other playwrights never write down anything except dialogue and stage directions, yet find an overall structure asserting itself almost unconsciously as the writing progresses. But the beginner should bear in mind that intrigue, thematic development, compression, and even credibility depend upon a carefully built structure, and that it is an axiom of theatre that most playwriting is in fact *rewriting*—rewriting aimed principally at organizing and reorganizing the play's staged actions and events.

A strong dramatic structure compels interest and attention. It creates intrigue by establishing certain expectations—both in the characters and in the audience—and then by creating new and bigger expectations out of the fulfillment of the first ones. A good dramatic structure keeps us always wanting more until the final curtain call, and at the end it leaves us with a sense of the inevitability of the

> Oh, dramatists, the true applause which you seek is not the hand-clapping which follows a brilliant verse, it is rather that profound sigh which escapes from the depths of the soul after the constraint of long silence, the sigh that brings relief. But there is another impression to make, a more violent one, which you will readily understand if you are born to your art, if you are aware of its magic, and that is to make your audience feel ill at ease. Their minds will be troubled, uncertain, distracted, and your spectators be like those who in the presence of an earthquake see the walls of their homes rock and feel the earth yawn before them.
>
> Denis Diderot

play's conclusion, a sense that what happened on stage was precisely as it had to be. A great structure makes us comfortable and receptive; we feel in good hands, expertly led through whatever terrain the play may take us. And we are willing, therefore, to abandon ourselves to a celebration of vital and ineffable matters.

THE PLAYWRIGHT'S REWARDS

There will always be a need for playwrights, for the theatre never abandons its clamor for new and better dramatic works. Hundreds of producers today are so anxious to discover new authors and new scripts that they will read (or instruct an associate to read) everything that comes their way; thus a truly fine play need not go unnoticed for long. What is more, the playwright is the only artist in the theatre who can bring his work to the first stage of completion without any outside professional help at all; he does not need to be auditioned, interviewed, hired, cast, or contracted to an agent in order to come up with the world's greatest dramatic manuscript. And the rewards that await the successful playwright are absolutely staggering: he is the most fully celebrated artist of the theatre, for not only does he receive remuneration commensurate with his success; he also acquires enormous influence and prestige on the basis of his personal vision. The public may adore an actor and it may admire a director or designer, but it *listens* to the playwright, who in Western culture has always assumed the role of prophet. Playwriting at its best is more than a profession and it is more than a component of the theatrical machine. It is a creative act that enlarges human experience and enriches our awe and appreciation of life.

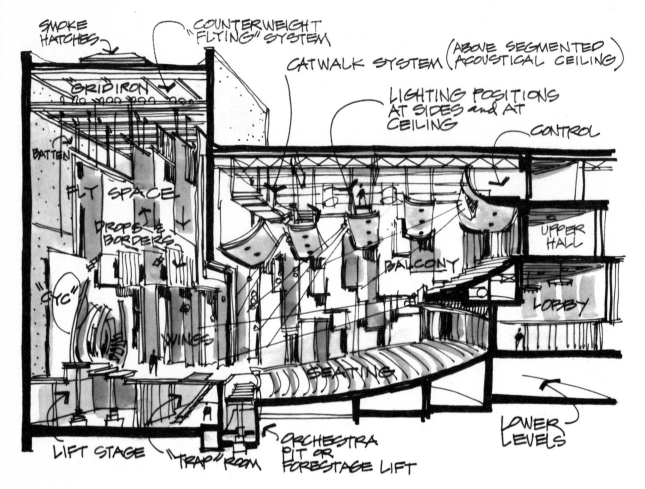

SMOKE HATCHES

"COUNTERWEIGHT FLYING" SYSTEM

CATWALK SYSTEM (ABOVE SEGMENTED ACOUSTICAL CEILING)

LIGHTING POSITIONS AT SIDES and AT CEILING

CONTROL

GRIDIRON

BATTEN

FLY SPACE

DROPS & BORDERS

"CYC"

WINGS

BALCONY

UPPER HALL

LOBBY

SEATING

LOWER LEVELS

LIFT STAGE

"TRAP" ROOM

ORCHESTRA PIT OR FORESTAGE LIFT

Features of the modern theatre: a cutaway drawing shows the main parts of stagehouse and audience area. Modern theatre architecture has produced far more innovative designs than this one, but the traditional proscenium theatre is still the most commonly built in the United States.

DESIGNERS
AND TECHNICIANS

The actor and the playscript may be at the core of the theatrical experience, but they are by no means the sum of it. Indeed, in the view of many spectators and participants, the primacy of acting and playwriting is extremely debatable.

For acting and textual brilliance are not isolated components capable of full expression in and by themselves. In even the most primitive of dramas the theatrical experience always has a "look" and a "sound" and a "shape," a visual and aural impact, that can only be achieved through *design*. And the execution of that design always entails a measure of *technology*. In many ways and at many times, the theatre has had occasion to celebrate the artistic talent of its designers and the engineering capability of its technicians, for many of the world's great aesthetic and technological innovations have been made public primarily through theatrical exploitation.

Therefore, in examining a play it is hardly sufficient to inquire merely as to what it is "about." We must also ask, How does it look? How does it sound?

How is it built? How does it run? These questions bring us face to face with a veritable army of "backstage" personnel: the artists and technicians who, to greater or lesser degree, create and make possible what Aristotle called the "spectacle" of theatre, who are responsible for the overall appearance, orchestration, and management of the theatrical experience.

It is customary for purposes of discussion to divide design functions into a series of components—scenery, lighting, make-up, and so forth—and to a certain extent this categorization is appropriate; most productions involve separate "departments" of design, each with its own designers, assistants, and crews. Nonetheless, it must be borne in mind that all the design functions of a production are interrelated, that the appearance of scenery, for example, is heavily dependent on the light that falls upon it, and the look of a costume is greatly affected by the actor's make-up and hair style—to say nothing of his acting and his bearing. In listing the various contributing "arts" of theatrical design, therefore, we must recognize that in abstracting each of them for separate examination, we are attempting only to clarify certain traditional practices, and that no single design art can be fully realized in isolation.

Similarly, the ordering of these separate arts can only be one of convenience, for no fundamental hierarchy exists among them. It is for a certain convenience, therefore, that we shall first discuss the theatre's architecture, scenery, and lighting, and then we shall deal with costuming, make-up, and technical production.

ARCHITECTURE

The theatre architect is, as a rule, the most anonymous of all major theatre artists. Although he is responsible for the theatre building itself, and therefore for the basic spatial relationship between actors and audience—the "sight lines" of dramatic representation—his name is rarely known to the theatre audience, almost never cited in the theatre program, and frequently unknown even to the artists who labor in his building. The divorce between the art of theatre and the art of theatre building is astonishing in this otherwise most collaborative endeavor.

Fortunately, there are some exceptions to this rule—exceptions which illustrate quite well the advantages of a theatre architecture developed hand in glove with the artistry that will utilize it.

The Bayreuth (Germany) Festspielhaus, conceived by opera composer/author Richard Wagner in association with "stage master" Carl Brandt and architect Otto Brückwald, was specifically designed as a showcase for the Wagnerian masterworks. The theatre, completed in 1876, features a steeply inclined, fan-shaped auditorium with continental seating instead of boxes and aisles; this arrangement was calculated to maximize the impact of grand scenic illusions which were painted so as to present roughly the same perspective from every seat in the house. The Bayreuth stage also features elaborate machinery and a mammoth sunken orchestra pit to facilitate the grandiose spectacle of the Wagnerian operas. This theatre still stands as a masterpiece of proscenium-type architecture, and it still succeeds brilliantly in the purposes for which it was designed.

Alternatively, the "thrust" stage built at Stratford, Ontario in 1957 to specifications developed by Sir Tyrone Guthrie, in collaboration with scene designer Tanya Moiseiwitsch and architect Robert Fairfield, returned to the more "open" staging area of the ancient Greeks and Elizabethans. This design provided director Guthrie with a versatile acting platform and architectural background for his fast-moving, fast-paced classical revivals. The Stratford Festival Theatre served as a model not only for the later Guthrie Theatre in Minneapolis (1963), but also for a whole generation of American regional theatres that followed (see photograph, p. 416).

The Wagnerian and "Guthrian" stages, although quite unalike in concept, both exemplify the potential of the theatre building mutually conceived by the architect and the theatre artist. Such a collaboration can be crucial to the development of a theatre aesthetic, as well as to the practical demand for stages suitable for the performances created upon them. Today, in most professional theatre companies and in community or university theatres, the resident directorship is frankly expected to play a leading role in the planning of any new theatre structure, not only in the conception phase but in the design and construction phases as well.

What is theatre architecture? Basically, it is the "hard stuff" of a theatre building—that which is more or less permanent, more or less impervious to alteration by designer and director from one show to the next. Essentially, the theatre architect designs a stage for performance, a system of machinery for handling scenery (loading and unloading, hanging, shifting, and storage), a seating system for the audience (including conveniences such as lobbies, rest rooms, bars, and aisles), and both open and closed spaces for the day to day operation of the theatre enterprise (a box office, dressing rooms, storage areas, rehearsal halls, administrative offices, control booths, lighting positions, quick-change rooms, crossover spaces, loading platforms, stage doors, fire escapes, wiring and access spaces). Needless to say, the manner in which any of these basic responsibilities is carried out (or not carried out) can affect the quality and character, the look and sound and "feel" of every single production that takes place in the building.

Inasmuch as theatre architecture is hard stuff that may survive its conceivers and constructors by many years—or centuries—it must be designed with a view to versatility. The design of the ancient Greek theatre and that of the "thrust" stage of Elizabethan times provide versatility largely by dint of their structural simplicity, which requires only a modest performing

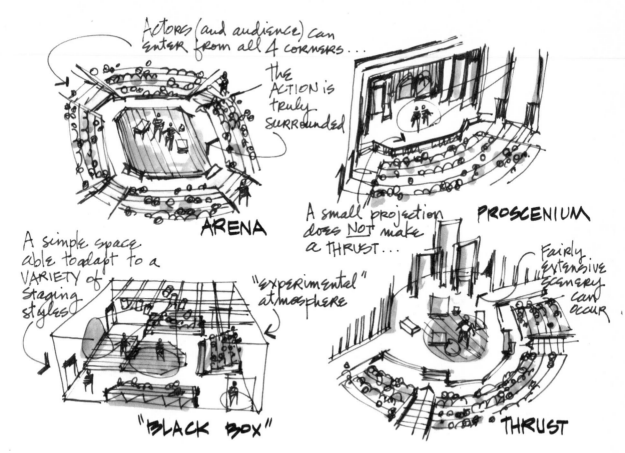

Four basic theatre spaces. The architect's first decisions are: Where is the stage? Where is the audience? The arena, proscenium, thrust, and neutral "black box" formats comprise the realm of possibilities.

area giving way on three sides to upward-sloping rows of seats, and backed on the fourth side by a building feature that permits the entrance and exit of actors through doorways—and possibly. through balconies and windows. By being scenically inexplicit, these stages are suitable for the production of an enormous range of plays with but the slightest temporary additions of furniture, drapery, and/or special set pieces. The proscenium stage, when outfitted with proper machinery—fly galleries to hoist scenery out of sight, turntables and/or rolling wagons to move scenic units on and off laterally, and elevators to raise and lower actors, platforms, and entire orchestra pits—affords great versatility in a different direction, by dint of its scenic flexibility.

But versatility is not the sole criterion of aesthetic quality in theatre design; indeed, one of the intriguing perplexities of modern stage architecture has been the relative lack of enthusiasm accorded by theatre artists and audiences alike to theatres designed to convert from proscenium to thrust format at the throw of a few switches. The Vivian Beaumont Theatre at Lincoln Center (New York City) is a case in point. The stage of that theatre, designed by noted set designer Jo Mielziner in the early 1960s, includes a convertible thrust which can be easily turned into proscenium-format seating at the request of any individual director. Desirable as this feature seemed at the time it was built, the Beaumont Theatre and others like it appear somehow to lack the "tone" or "personality" that distinguishes the great playhouses. By way of explaining this curious lack, one might suggest that ultimately it is neither versatility nor practicality that characterizes the finest theatre buildings, but rather an aura of momentousness and vitality, and that this requires a certain specificity of design. All the great theatres—those most loved by audiences and performers alike—convey individuality (even eccentricity) and solid authority; they convey the sense that this is a house that has seen many great moments and will yet see many more. An omni-flexible or institutionally mechanical theatre structure may inhibit this feeling and rob a theatre of identity.

The Evolution of Theatre Architecture

Despite its largely anonymous instigation, theatre architecture has long been one of the glories of the Western world. The Greek theatres, which evolved out of a pagan rite celebrated on a hillside, rank high among the more useful treasures of antiquity: the surviving theatre at Epidaurus is only one of many from the fourth century B.C. that still resound from time to time with revivals of the same great plays that thrilled audiences in the Hellenistic Age. The theatres of ancient Rome were so grandiose in conception and execution that only hyperbole, it appears, could convey their proper character. For example, can we believe Pliny's account of an 80,000-seat theatre built in three stories, one each of marble, glass, and gilt? Or of the two theatres built back to back which, filled with spectators, rotated on a pivot to join in a huge amphitheatre which was then flooded for sea battle scenes?

Later times have given us only a few names of architects, but many more fine theatres. Of Peter Street, the architect of Shakespeare's Globe and Henslowe's Fortune, history unfortunately tells us little

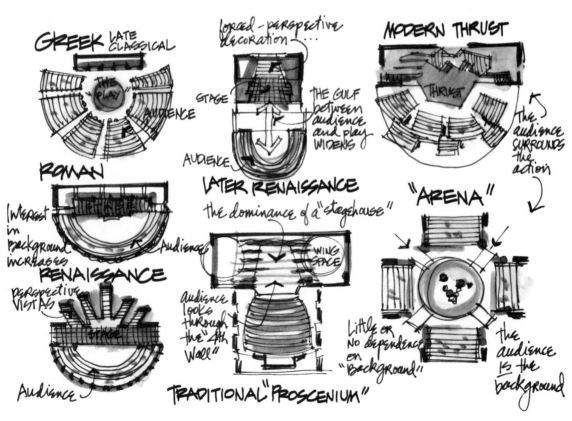

A variety of stage shapes from various historical periods.

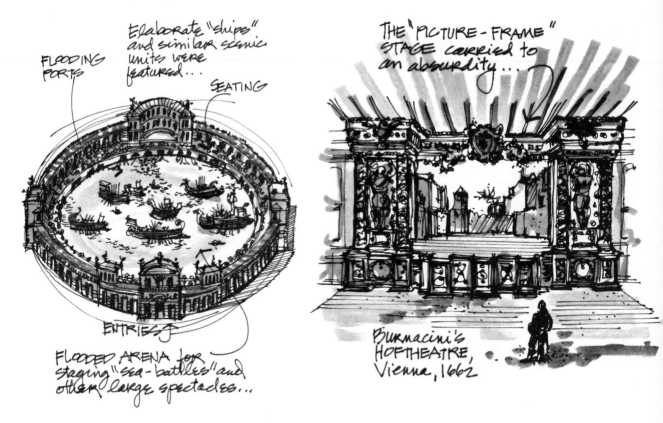

LEFT—*A* naumachia—*a spectacular Roman arena that could be flooded for staging of aquatic battles.*

RIGHT—*The Viennese Hoftheatre of 1662 is an example of decorative excess, popular in some of the courts of seventeenth- and eighteenth-century Europe. Designers and technicians overshadowed dramatists in periods governed by this sort of architectural design.*

beyond the notation that his theatres were provocative of the best in dramatic art. The Teatro Olimpico in Vicenza, Italy, was designed by the famed Andrea Palladio and is the oldest extant theatre of known design and known architect—it was built in 1584, and it not only survives intact but is frequently still used for opera and dramatic presentations. Other theatres surviving from earlier eras, such as the elegant eighteenth-century court theatre at Drottningholm, Sweden, and the opulent nineteenth-century Romantic structure built for the Paris Opera, are cultural landmarks as well as theatrically significant sites of contemporary production.

Today we are in the midst of an explosion of theatrical construction that began just after the close of World War II. Since then, performing arts centers have sprung up in almost every fair-sized American and European city; each year in the United States alone, ground is broken for literally dozens of first-class theatres, on campuses, in suburban communities, and in major urban renewal projects in the heart of "central downtown." What we are seeing today might well be the beginning of a golden age of theatrical architecture, an age marked by a growing public willingness to lend financial support and a greatly increased understanding of the need for extensive collaboration between theatre artists and architects to reconcile the needs for theatrical "tone" and atmosphere with those of practical flexibility and operational ease.

Staging Formats

The two principal types of modern theatre building are the proscenium stage design and the thrust stage design. These two basic types account for more than 95 percent of the professional theatres in Europe and America today, and for the great bulk of amateur stages as well.

The *proscenium* theatre is essentially a rectangular room with the audience on one side facing the stage on the other, the two separated by an arch (the proscenium arch) through which the audience peers. This creates the well-known "picture frame" stage, with the arch serving as the frame for the action going on within. The proscenium format developed in Italy during the Renaissance as a mode of presenting elaborate court masques and other court entertainments; since it put the audience on but one side of the action, it allowed extensive "hidden" areas backstage for the scene shifting and trickery involved in creating the illusions and fantasies so admired at the time. The proscenium theatre achieved its fullest realization in the Baroque era, and some of the surviving court theatres and opera houses of Europe testify eloquently to the splendor of that age. Modern proscenium theatres, following the Bayreuth model with its fan-shaped, unobstructed auditorium (instead of the horseshoe-shaped, boxed and galleried auditorium of earlier eras), have proven particularly serviceable for the use of realistic scenery and for the presentation of scenic spectaculars. Virtually all Broadway theatres feature the proscenium format.

The *thrust* format, a design pioneered only recently in North America by Tyrone Guthrie, was in fact the favored format in ancient Greece and Elizabethan England. Since it places much of the action in the midst of the audience, it is a more actor-centered than scenery-centered theatre configuration. In the thrust format the members of the audience are more aware of each other than they are in a darkened proscenium "fan," and their viewing perspectives differ radically depending on their seating locations. When the acting platform or thrust has access from tunnels (*vomitoria*) that come up through the audience, the stage can be flooded by actors in a matter of seconds, creating a whirlwind of movement that is dazzling and immediate—the thrust stage's alternative to elaborate stage machinery and painted scenes. That is not at all to say that there can be no scenery on

a thrust stage, but merely that major scenic pieces tend to be placed behind the action rather than surrounding it, leaving a major acting space, scenically quite neutral, projecting into the center of the audience.

A third theatrical configuration is the *arena format*, in which the audience surrounds the action on all sides; one American regional theatre, the Arena Stage in Washington, D.C., has presented an arena season regularly since 1950. Arena staging dispenses with all scenery except floor treatments, furniture, and out-of-the-way hanging or standing pieces, and focuses audience attention sharply and simply on the actors. The long-standing success of the Washington Arena Stage testifies to the viability of this format; however, since no other major theatre has followed Washington's example (and indeed since the Arena Stage itself has built an adjacent proscenium theatre as a second space), it would appear that arena staging is destined to remain an interesting novelty rather than to create a staging revolution.

A final staging alternative is afforded by the so-called *black box* theatre, a formatless space that can be adjusted to any desired arrangement and is therefore particularly useful in experimental, environmental, or academic stagings. Usually painted black (hence the name), this type of theatre consists of a bare room fitted with omni-flexible overhead lighting; in this room, stages and seating can be set up in any configuration—proscenium, thrust, arena, or two-sided "center stage"—or the action can occur at selected spots throughout the room: an "environmental" staging. The black box allows the director/creator to develop an infinite variety of actor-audience interactions, and to make use of highly unusual scenic designs and/or mechanisms. "Happenings," participatory dramas, participatory rituals, and seminar plays—all of which demand active audience involvement—are frequently best presented in these sorts of spaces.

Other Architectural Considerations

Designing a theatre of course involves a great deal more than choosing a staging format.

It involves creating a seating space that is suited to the requirements of the expected audience; this may

Environmental staging takes place right in the midst of the audience, as here in the Free Theatre of Rome production of Ariosto's Orlando Furioso.

mean one thing in a sophisticated urban area, another in a rural outpost, yet another on a college campus. Different audiences have different comfort demands; they also differ in their emotional and intellectual responses to their surroundings. If the seats are too hard or too soft, for example, or if the ambience of the auditorium is intimidating, audiences may refuse to see the merits in any play.

Designing a theatre involves providing for effective communications systems, sight lines, and stage mechanisms for the sorts of productions the theatre will handle. This means there must be adequate wiring, soundproofing, and rigging, as well as a good use of backstage and onstage spaces, both open and enclosed—and often that means calling in a consultant who specializes in ascertaining the most practical design for the widest variety of utilizations.

Theatre building also involves principles of acoustics, which can determine whether actors' voices will be heard, given a normal volume level, in all parts of the house; and whether singers' voices can be heard when the orchestra is playing. As a science, acoustics

is maddeningly inexact, so that the best results come only after much experience and testing.

Theatre architecture involves the art of lighting, for no lighting designer can possibly overcome the limitations imposed by poorly located, permanently installed lighting positions. One of the sadder aspects of many older theatres is the jungle gym of exposed pipes and lighting instruments awkwardly strapped to gilded cupids in a latter-day attempt to make up for antiquated lighting systems.

And finally, designing and building a theatre involves a love of theatre, an emotional and aesthetic understanding that a theatre is not merely a room, not merely a hall, and not merely an institutional building with certain features, but a permanent home for the portrayal of human concerns, and a repository of twenty-five hundred years of glorious tradition. Such a place must be functional and flexible, to be sure, but it is also deserving of more: it deserves to have the distinctive identity that comes from the architect's ineffable sense of purpose and passion and theatrical imagination.

SCENERY

Scenery is likely to be the first thing we think of under the general category of theatrical design; if a production is said to be "designed by John Jones," we may simply assume that this means the scenery was designed by John Jones. Scenery is usually the first thing we see of a play, either at the rise of the curtain in a traditional proscenium production, or as we enter the theatre where there is no curtain.

And yet scenery, as considered apart from architecture, is a relatively new phenomenon in the theatre. It was not needed for the dithyramb, and it probably played little part in Greek tragedy or comedy save to afford entry, exit, and sometimes expanded acting space for actors; such rotating prisms, rolling platforms, and painted panels as were used in the Greek theatre probably had no representational significance. In other words, none of these features were intended to disguise the fact that the play's action took place in a Greek theatre. The same is more or less true of the Roman theatre, the Medieval theatre, and the outdoor Elizabethan theatre—apart from a few set pieces that were painted and otherwise detailed to resemble free-standing walls, trees, caves, thrones, tombs, porches and the inevitable Hellmouth, for virtually all visual aspects of public outdoor staging prior to the seventeenth century were dictated by the architecture of the theatre structure itself.

It was the development of indoor stages, artificially illuminated, that fostered the first great phase of scene design: the period of painted, flat scenery. Working indoors out of the reach of the elements, designers of Renaissance spectacles and court masques were free for the first time to erect painted canvases and temporary wooden structures without fear of having the colors run and the supports rot out or blow away. And with the advent of controllable indoor lighting, they could illuminate their settings and acting areas as they wished without calling attention to the permanent structures behind: they could, in short, create both realistic illusion and decorative spectacle without having to contend with bad weather, bird droppings, and extraneous architectural interference.

The result was a series of scene design revelations that brought the names of a new class of theatre artists—designers—to public consciousness, designers such as the Italians Aristotile da Sangallo (1481–1551),

Sebastiano Serlio (1475–1554), and Giacomo Torelli (1604–1678), the Englishman Inigo Jones (1573–1652), and the Frenchman Jean Berain (ca. 1637–1711). By the beginning of the eighteenth century the scene designer's art had attained a prominence equal to (or perhaps greater than) the playwright's; and for almost two hundred years thereafter flat scenery, painted in exquisite perspective, took on even greater sophistication under the brilliant artists of the theatre's Baroque, Rococo, and Romantic epochs. The proscenium format, which was developed primarily to show off elegant settings, utterly dominated theatre architecture for all that time. It was not until the beginning of the present century that scenery went into its second major phase—the modern one—which can be said to continue in various fashions today.

Modern scenery is of two basic types: realistic and abstract. Often the two types are used in combination and often the line between them is difficult to draw, but in their separate ways both have contributed mightily to the important position of scenery in the theatrical experience today.

Realistic settings carry on the tradition of "illusionism" established in eighteenth-century painted perspective stagings; the familiar "box set" of modern realistic or naturalistic theatre is essentially a series of interconnected flats of framed canvas painted to resemble walls and ceilings, filled with real furniture and real properties taken from ordinary real-world environments. This type of set, a development of the early nineteenth century, is very much alive today, and is indeed the major scenic format for contemporary domestic drama (particularly comedy) of New York's Broadway, London's West End, and most community and college theatres across America. No longer particularly voguish, the box set rarely wins design awards, but it admirably fulfills the staging requirements of a great many domestic comedies, thrillers, and serious linearly structured dramas, particularly those requiring interior settings. Advances in scenic construction and technology have made the box set an absolute marvel of lifelike appearance and detail.

Box sets and other forms of realistic painted scenery can be immensely useful in designating a play's locale. The cleverly painted wings and drops of the era of flat, perspective-painted scenery portrayed with great precision the drawing rooms, conserva-

Realistic scenery for 1976 American Conservatory Theatre production of Shaw's Man and Superman *features full three-dimensional bookcases filled with apparently real books; setting also includes three-dimensional sculptured bust, moldings, and period wallpaper.*

tories, ballrooms, reception halls, parlors, libraries, servants' quarters, professional offices, and factory yards of many a dramatist's imagination or prescription; the box set served to heighten the verisimilitude by adding three-dimensional features: suitable doors to enter through, windows to peer through, bookcases to hide revolvers in, and grandfather clocks to hide characters in. The public fascination with realistic scenery reached its high-water mark in the ultrarealist "theatre of the fourth wall removed," in

PORTION of "PORCH"

CEILING UNIT

To "FRONT PARLOR" (masking beyond)

WINDOWS to "BACK GROUNDS"

SCREEN DOOR

To "DINING ROOM" via Back Parlor

UPPER LEFT—*A typical box set, as could be used for a production of Eugene O'Neill's* Long Day's Journey into Night. *Three walls, a floor (the stage floor), and a ceiling comprise the "box," with windows and doors providing access to the world outside. Realistic details and real fixtures and furniture are common adjuncts of the box set.* LEFT—*A realistic aged wood setting for* The Girl of the Golden West, *a nineteenth-century play produced by the American Conservatory Theatre in 1979–80.* ABOVE—*A box set, impeccably detailed yet classically severe, used by Comédie Française for 1950's production of* The Bourgeois Gentleman. *Note detailing of staircase and door frames, "boxiness" of three walls, and elegance of the painted ceiling in this blending of neo-classical and realistic scenic ideals.*

which the box set was used to such advantage that it helped to foster a uniquely architectural theory of theatre—that it should always represent life "with one wall removed."

The most talked-about scenic design today, however, tends to be more plastic than rigid, more kinetic than stable, more symbolic and evocative than realistic and explicit. In other words, abstract scenography is distinctly gaining ground.

The movement toward scenic abstraction began

An abstract "sunburst" setting, corrugated like an African tin roof, epitomizes the mood of Athol Fugard's Boesman and Lena *in this 1979 production of the Arizona Theatre Company.*

with the theoretical (and occasionally practical) works of designers Adolphe Appia (1862–1928) and Gordon Craig (1872–1966), both of whom urged the fluid use of space, form, and light as a fundamental principle of dramatic design. Aided by technological advances in lighting and motorized scene shifting, the movement toward a more plastic scenography has inspired a great many impressive abstract stylizations. Projections, shafts and walls of light, transparent scrims, outsized graphics and photoreproductions, sculptural configurations, metals both polished and coarse, mirrored and burlaped surfaces both hard and soft, "floating" walls and rising staircases, and wholly "found" or wholly "surreal" environments: all these have become major media for many contemporary scene designers.

These more plastic and more abstract settings can establish locales if need be, but they are perhaps more effective in establishing moods and styles. Of course. mood and style can be established to some extent by realistic scenery as well: by creating a theatrical space that is tall and airy, for example, or cramped and squat, by using or withholding color and clutter, the designer in any mode can define an environment in such a way that the action of the play takes on a highly special tone. But with the extension into non-realistic abstraction, the designer can greatly elaborate upon tone and develop it into a highly specific sensory approach.

The dark walls and cobwebby interiors designed

T he poetic conception of stage design bears little relation to the accepted convention of realistic scenery in the theatre. As a matter of fact it is quite the opposite. Truth in the theatre, as the masters of the theatre have always known, stands above and beyond mere accuracy to fact. In the theatre the actual thing is never the exciting thing. Unless life is turned into art on the stage it stops being alive and goes dead.

So much for the realistic theatre. *The artist should omit the details, the prose of nature, and give us only the spirit and splendor.* . . . We must bring into the immediate life of the theatre—"the two hours' traffic of our stage" —images of a larger life. The stage we inhabit is a chamber of the House of Dreams. Our work on this stage is to suggest the immanence of a visionary world all about us.

Robert Edmund Jones

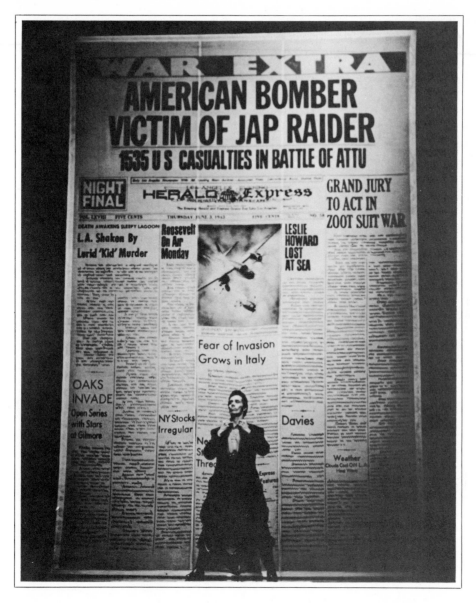

An abstract setting for Luis Valdez's Zoot Suit *depicts giant newspaper headlining play's historical background; the zoot-suited "El Pachuco" makes his entrance at beginning of play by slicing through newspaper with a switchblade knife. Edward James Olmos plays El Pachuco in this premiere production, directed by author Valdez, at Mark Taper Forum Theatre (1978).*

by Edward Gorey for the Broadway production of *Dracula* (1977), for example, were a significant factor in the play's communication of fascinating horror. The bare but shiny white walls and lacy black catwalks designed by Sally Jacobs for the 1970 Peter

Brook production of *A Midsummer Night's Dream* focused all attention on the poetry of the human relationships in that famous Shakespearean revival. The remarkable "found object"—a complete nineteenth-century iron foundry—that served as the surround for

Eugene Lee's basic set for the original Harold Prince production of *Sweeney Todd* (1979), indelibly conveyed the underlying theme of industrial oppression of that musical play (see photograph, p. 273).

The best scenic design today goes far beyond mere "backing" for the action of a play; it creates a basic visual and spatial architecture of performance, an architecture which, when fully realized, becomes *intrinsic to the action.* Consider, for example, the multi-level, multi-roomed setting designed by Jo Mielziner for the original production of Arthur Miller's American classic *Death of a Salesman.* This set, which provided a cutaway view of both floors of the salesman's house, permitting the simultaneous staging of activity in the kitchen and in the upstairs dining room, caused playwright Miller (and director Elia Kazan) to re-structure the play so that events originally planned to evolve sequentially could be performed simultaneously, thereby tremendously in-creasing the intensity and impact of the action. The simple but brilliant setting devised by Andrew Jackness for the stage production of Arthur Kopit's *Wings*—a series of twirling eight-foot squares of mirror and black scrim—created a striking image of mental recesses, and led to a series of actions in which characters moved forward and back through whirling and indefinite perceptibility, a splendidly appropriate use of scenery for this play which deals with brain stroke and its accompanying perceptual distortions. And the many brilliant designs of Joseph Svoboda, who is certainly Europe's most celebrated "scen-ographer" (his own term) in the second half of this century, are nothing short of dramatic architecture in action. Svoboda has made highly imaginative use of a whole array of contemporary technologies, including laser beams, computerized slide and film projections, pneumatic mirrors, low-voltage lighting instruments, aerosol sprays, and innovative stage machinery to

Jo Mielziner's design for the Death of a Salesman *setting, showing Willy Loman's cutaway house.*

A stage setting has no independent life of its own. Its emphasis is directed toward the performance. In the absence of the actor it does not exist. Strange as it may seem, this simple and fundamental principle of stage design still seems to be widely misunderstood. . . .

A scene on the stage is filled with . . . expectancy. It is like a mixture of chemical elements held in solution. The actor adds the one element that releases the hidden energy of the whole. Meanwhile, wanting the actor, the various elements which go into the setting remain suspended, as it were, in an indefinable tension. To create this suspense, this tension, is the essence of the problem of stage designing.

The designer must strive to achieve in his settings what I can only call a high potential. The walls, the furniture, the properties, are only the facts of a setting, only the outline. The truth is in everything they create. They are fused into a kind of embodied impulse. When the curtain rises we feel a frenzy of excitement focused like a burning-glass upon the actors. Everything on the stage becomes a part of the life of the instant. The play becomes a voice out of a whirlwind. The terrible and wonderful dynamis of the theatre pours over the footlights.

Robert Edmund Jones

create a body of scenic design unrivaled for theatrical impact and expressive dramaturgy. Speaking of "dramatic space" as "psycho-plastic," Svoboda has said: "The goal of a designer can no longer be a description of a copy of actuality, but the creation of its multidimensional model." And for Svoboda—as for most contemporary designers—that multidimensional model is a dynamic one, flowing through time as well as space, and responding to the inner biological and psychological rhythms of the actors and the dramatic actions.

Thus the functions of scenery design are both practical and abstract, both concrete and imaginal. Although it is a latecomer to theatre history, scenery has occasionally overwhelmed the drama itself: in the 1730s, in the "mute spectacles" of Jean-Nicholas Servandoni, whole performances were arranged with nothing but scene designs, lighting, music, and posed actors; Svoboda's *Diapolyekran* and *Lanterna Magika* have accomplished the same in more recent years (the 1960s and 1970s). Scenery's place in the theatre is not inevitable—the theatre has managed in the past without it, and still does so from time to time—but its future looks very secure. It has the capacity, when well used, to develop enormous visual, emotional, aesthetic and dramatic impact, lending the theatre a conjunction with artistic technology which it can in no other way acquire.

The Scene Designer's Media

The traditional media of scenery design—wood, canvas, and paint—have in recent times been extended to include steel, plastics, and projected images. Designing and building scenic components from each of these sources is the first area of training for every scenic designer.

Platforms, flats, and draperies are the traditional building blocks of fixed stage scenery—and no changes in aesthetics or technology have in any way diminished their importance in the contemporary theatre.

Platforming serves the all-important function of giving the actor an elevated space from which to perform, making him visible over the heads of other actors and stage furniture; a stage setting that utilizes several artfully arranged platforming levels (of increasing height toward the back of the stage), together with appropriate connecting staircases and ramps or "raked" platform units, can permit dozens of actors to be seen simultaneously. Platforms can be created in virtually any size and shape; what is more, with the growing use of steel in stage platform construction, platform support can be fairly open, allowing huge but still "lacy" settings of great structural stability.

Flats, which are ordinarily made of canvas stretched over a wooden frame and then painted, are generally used to indicate vertical walls (realistic or

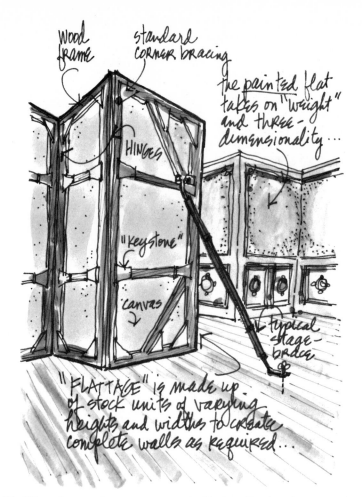

Labels in illustration:
- wood frame
- standard corner bracing
- the painted flat takes on "weight" and three-dimensionality...
- HINGES
- "keystone"
- canvas
- typical stage-brace
- "FLATTAGE" is made up of stock units of varying heights and widths to create complete walls as required...

The "flat" is an inexpensive way to create the illusion of an interior or exterior wall. Light, easy to move and to store, flats can be repainted almost indefinitely to create a variety of settings.

abstract) and to define space. Flats can be pierced with windows, doors, and open archways; they can be adorned with moldings, paintings, hangings, bookcases, or fireplaces; they can be turned horizontally to serve as ceilings; they can be "tracked" onto the stage in grooves, as they were in the eighteenth century, or "flown" down from the overhead flies, as they often are in repertory theatres that store many settings at one time. The flat is an immensely versatile workhorse that has almost become a symbol of the theatre itself.

Drapery is the great neutral stuff of stage settings; it is often used to bridge the gap between the setting itself and the permanent features of the theatre building, and occasionally it is used in somewhat more realistic fashion as well. The stage curtain of a proscenium theatre is one form of hanging drapery —when the curtain rises or parts or is pulled diagonally upward (the "opera drape") at the beginning of a play, it signals the drama's first engagement of the audience. Another form of hanging drapery is used conventionally to mask (hide) the stage lighting above the set (this is called a "drapery border"), and yet another is used to mask the machinery and personnel behind the flats (the "drapery legs" or "wings"). Black drapery at the rear of the stage can provide a neutral backdrop to the action of a play, and frequently a whole set of drapery, usually black, is used as the entire setting for readings, chamber productions, and "reader's theatre" productions. Sometimes this sort of scenery is deemed suitable even for full-scale theatricalizations, and always a theatre possessing such a "set of blacks" is able to present many plays with a minimal expenditure of scenery time or budget. A final drapery found in most well-equipped theatres is the *cyclorama*, a hanging fabric stretched taut between upper and lower pipes and curved to surround the rear and sides of the stage. Colored white, grey, or grey-blue, the "cyc" can be lighted with stronger colors to represent a variety of "skyscapes" with great effectiveness; it can also be used for all sorts of abstract backgrounds and projections.

In addition to the three primary components of stage settings, many productions make use of the special one-of-a-kind "set piece," which frequently becomes the focal point for an overall setting design or even for the action of a whole play. The tree in *Waiting for Godot*, for example, is the primary scenic feature of that play's setting, symbolizing both life and death. The moment when Vladimir and Estragon "do the tree"—a calisthenic exercise in which each man stands on one leg and tries to assume the shape of the tree—is a profound moment of theatre in which set piece and actors coalesce in a single image, referred to in the text of the play, of the triple crucifixion on Calvary where two thieves died alongside of Christ. Similarly, the massive supply wagon hauled by Mother Courage in Bertolt Brecht's epic play of that name, gives rise to a powerful visual impression of struggle and travail that may last long after the words of the characters are forgotten. And what would *Prometheus Bound* be without its striking set piece, Prometheus' rock and chains? No matter how stylized this element may have been in its original realization, it must have radiated to the Athenian audience a visual poetry every bit as eloquent as the verbal poetry with which Aeschylus supported it. Individual set pieces indeed tax the imagination of author, director, designer and scene technician alike, and the masterpieces of scenic invention can long outlive their makers in the memory of the audience.

A host of modern materials and technological inventions add to the primary components and set pieces from which scenery is created.

Light as scenery, apart from the stage lighting discussed below, can create walls, images, even (with laser holography) three-dimensional visualizations. Banks of sharply focused light sent through dense atmospheres, enhanced by smoke or dust or fog, can create trenches of light which have the appearance of massive solidity and yet can be made to disappear at the flick of a switch. Carefully controlled slide projections can provide images either realistic or abstract, fixed or fluid, precise or indefinite.

Scrim, which is a loosely woven fabric that looks opaque when lit from one side and transparent when lit from the other, has been a staple of theatre "magic" for many years.

Stage machinery—turntables, elevators, hoists, rolling carts and wagons, and the like—can be used to create a veritable dance of scenic elements to accompany and support dramatic action. The ancient Greeks apparently understood the importance of mechanical devices quite well, as did Shakespeare with his winched thrones and disappearing witches. Tricks and sleight of hand (called, in the medieval theatre, "trucs" and "feynts") have always imparted a certain sparkle of mystery to the theatre, and hence will always play a part in the designer's art.

Sound also must be taken into consideration by the designer, who must plan for the footfalls of the actor as well as for the visual elements behind, around, and underneath him. The floor of a stage designed for the production of Japanese Noh drama, for example, has a characteristic look and produces a characteristic sound; it is meant to be stamped upon, and it must sound just so. Joseph Svoboda has designed a stage floor for *Faust* which can be either resonant or silent depending on the arrangement of certain mechanisms concealed underneath; when the servant walks upstage his steps reverberate; when he turns and walks downstage his steps are silent—and we know Mephistopheles has taken his body.

Properties and furniture, which are often handled by a separate artist working under the guidance of the scene designer, are crucial not only in establishing realism but in enhancing mood and style. Although furniture is most often used in the theatre just as it is in life—to sit upon, lie upon, and so forth—it also has a crucial stylistic importance; often stage furniture is designed and built in highly imaginative ways to convey a special visual impact when coordinated with the setting. Properties such as ash trays, telephones, letters, and tableware are often functional in realistic plays, but they can also have aesthetic importance and

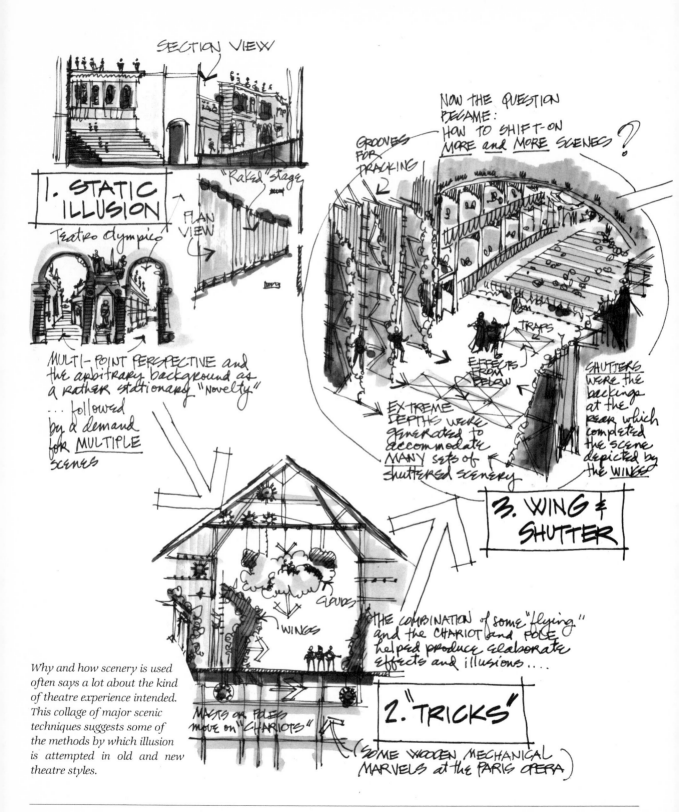

SECTION VIEW

1. STATIC ILLUSION

Teatro Olympico

MULTI-POINT PERSPECTIVE and the arbitrary background as a rather stationary "Novelty"
... followed by a demand for MULTIPLE scenes

"Raked" stage

PLAN VIEW

NOW THE QUESTION BECAME: HOW TO SHIFT-ON MORE and MORE SCENES?

GROOVES FOR TRACKING

TRAPS

EFFECTS FROM BELOW

EXTREME DEPTHS were generated to accommodate MANY sets of shuttered scenery

SHUTTERS were the backings at the rear which completed the scene depicted by the WINGS

3. WING & SHUTTER

CLOUDS

WINGS

THE COMBINATION of some "flying" and the CHARIOT and POLE helped produce elaborate effects and illusions ....

MASTS OR POLES move on "CHARIOTS"

2. "TRICKS"

(SOME WOODEN MECHANICAL MARVELS at the PARIS OPERA)

Why and how scenery is used often says a lot about the kind of theatre experience intended. This collage of major scenic techniques suggests some of the methods by which illusion is attempted in old and new theatre styles.

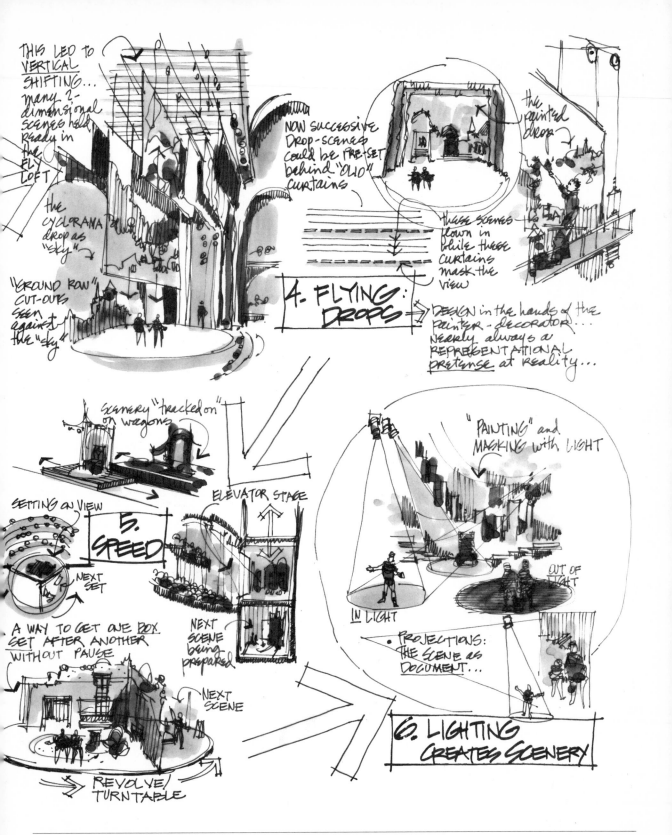

THIS LED TO VERTICAL SHIFTING... many 2-dimensional scenes held ready in the FLY LOFT

the CYCLORAMA drop as "sky"

"GROUND ROW" CUT-OUTS seen against the "sky"

NOW SUCCESSIVE DROP-SCENES could be PRE-SET behind "OLIO" curtains

the painted drop

these scenes flown in while these curtains mask the view

4. FLYING: DROPS →

DESIGN in the hands of the PAINTER-DECORATOR... NEARLY always a REPRESENTATIONAL pretense at reality...

Scenery "tracked on" wagons

ELEVATOR STAGE

SETTING on VIEW

5. SPEED

NEXT SET

NEXT SCENE being prepared

A WAY TO GET ONE BOX SET AFTER ANOTHER WITHOUT PAUSE

NEXT SCENE

REVOLVE/ TURNTABLE

"PAINTING" and MASKING with LIGHT

IN LIGHT

OUT OF LIGHT

• PROJECTIONS: THE SCENE as DOCUMENT...

6. LIGHTING CREATES SCENERY

are therefore quite carefully selected—or else specially designed. Frequently, furniture pieces or properties have considerable symbolic significance, as in the case of the thrones in Shakespeare's *Richard the Third*, for example, or the glass figurines in Williams' *Glass Menagerie*.

The Scene Designer at Work

The scene designer's work inevitably begins with a reading and rereading of the play, discussions with the director, and a consideration of the type of theatre in which the play is to be produced. This step is usually followed with a series of visualizations—either sketches, drawings, collected illustrations (for example, clippings from magazines, notations from historical sources, color ideas, spatial concepts), or three-dimensional models. Whatever the scenic inspiration, it must ultimately be rendered in a fashion suitable to serve as a guide for construction—which ordinarily means, minimally, a full set of working drawings explaining in precise technical detail the construction practices to be used. All along the way, of course, the designer must reckon with budgetary restraints and the skills of the construction staff available to execute and install the finished design. Part architect, part engineer, part painter, part decorator, part builder, part interpretive genius, part accountant, the scene designer today is one of the theatre's premiere artist/craftsmen.

LIGHTING

The very word "theatre," meaning "seeing place," implies the crucial function of light. Light is the basic condition for theatrical appearance; without light, nothing is to be seen.

The use of light for dramatic effect, as distinct from pure illumination, can be traced back to the earliest surviving plays: *Agamemnon*, by Aeschylus, was staged so that the watchman's spotting of the signal fire heralding Agamemnon's return to Argos coincided with the actual sunrise over the Athenian *skene* (stagehouse); it is also probable that the burning of Troy at the conclusion of Euripides' *The Trojan Women* was staged to coincide with the hour when sunset reddened the Attic sky. Modern plays commonly use light in metaphoric and symbolic ways: the

blinking neon light that regularly reddens Blanche's quarters in Tennessee Williams' *A Streetcar Named Desire* affords one example; another is the searching followspot demanded by Samuel Beckett to train upon the hapless, inurned characters in his play entitled *Play*.

It is customary to think of theatre lighting as a relatively recent technology, dating from the invention of electricity. Nothing could be more misleading; lighting has always been a major theatrical consideration. The Greeks paid a great deal of attention to the proper orientation of their theatres to take best advantage of the sun's rays. The medieval outdoor theatre, although as dependent on sunlight as was the Greek theatre, made use of several devices to redirect daylight, including the haloes made of reflective metal that were used to surround Jesus and his disciples with a focused and intensified illumination; in one production a brightly polished metal basin was held over Jesus' head to concentrate the sun's rays —and surviving instructions tell the medieval stagehands to substitute torches for the bowl in case of cloudy skies!

It was in indoor stagings, however, that lighting technology attained its first significant sophistication—and this as early as the Middle Ages. In a 1439 production of the *Annunciation* in Florence, one thousand oil lamps were used for illumination, plus a host of candles that were lighted by a "ray of fire" which shot through the cathedral. One can imagine the spectacle. Leonardo da Vinci designed a 1490 production of *Paradise* with twinkling stars and backlit zodiac signs on colored glass; by the sixteenth century the great festival lighting of indoor theatres, located in manor houses and public halls, would serve as a symbol of the intellectual and artistic achievements of the Renaissance itself, a mark of the luxury, technical wizardry, and ostentatious, exuberant humanism of the times: people went to the theatres in those times simply to revel in light and escape the outside gloom —in rather the same way that modern Americans, earlier in the present century, populated air-conditioned movie theatres largely to escape the heat of summer days. The indoor stages of the Renaissance have perhaps never been equaled in terms of sheer opulence of illumination—and the entire effect was created simply from tallow, wax, and fireworks. Raphael "painted" the name of his patron, Pope Leo X, with thirteen lighted chandeliers in a 1519 dramatic production; Sebastiano Serlio, whose development of flat painted scenery was mentioned earlier, included sparkling panes of colored glass, illuminated from behind, to make a veritable jewel box of that scenery (an effect which, unfortunately, is not captured in the woodcuts which have come down to us as illustrations of this work). As the Renaissance spirit gave way to the lavish Royal Theatre of the age of Louis XIV, the "Sun King," artificial illumination calculated to match Louis' putative incendiary brilliance developed apace: one 1664 presentation at Versailles featured 20,000 colored lanterns, hundreds of transparent veils and bowls of colored water, and a massive display of fireworks.

It was the invention of the gaslight in the nineteenth century, and the development of electricity that followed shortly thereafter—first in carbon arc and "limelight" electrical lighting, and then in incandescence—that brought stage lighting into its modern phase and made it less strictly showy and more pertinent to individual works and dramatic action. Ease and flexibility of control is the cardinal virtue of both gas and electricity. A single operator at a "gas table" could, by throwing a valve, raise or dim the intensity of any individual light or of a preselected "gang" of lights—just as we can raise or lower the fire on a gas range by turning a knob. And of course with electricity—which was introduced in American theatres in 1879 and in European theatres the following year—the great fire hazard of live flame, a danger which had plagued the theatre for centuries and claimed three buildings a year on average (including Shakespeare's

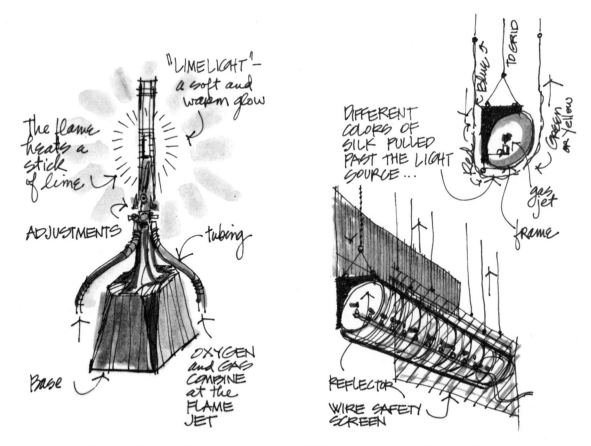

"Limelight" and gaslight opened up new possibilities for scenic atmosphere and focusing optics in the nineteenth century.

Globe), was at last over. The fire crews, which had
been a permanent, twenty-four hour staff in the employ of every major theatre in the early nineteenth
century, were dismissed; and the deterioration of
scenery and costumes from heat, smoke, and carbon
pollution of flame lighting similarly came to a halt.
Incandescent lighting also had the great advantage
of being fully self-starting—it did not need to be relit or
kept alive by "pilots"—and it could easily be switched
off, dimmed up and down, and re-ganged or recon-
nected simply by fastening and unfastening flexible
wires. Within a few years of its introduction electricity became the primary medium of stage lighting in
the Western world, and great dynamo generators—for
electricity was used in the theatre long before it was
commercially available from municipal power sup-
plies—were installed as essential equipment in the
basements of theatres from Vienna to San Francisco.

Electricity provides the enormous flexibility of
lighting that we know and use today. The incandescent filament is a reasonably small, reasonably cool
point of light that can be focused, reflected, aimed,
shaped, and colored by a great variety of devices invented and adapted for those purposes, and electric
light can be trained in innumerable ways upon actors,
scenery, audience, or combinations of these to create
realistic and/or atmospheric effects, through dimen-
sionality, focus, animation, distortion, diffusion,
and overwhelming radiance. Today, thanks to the
added sophistication of computer technology and mi-

croelectronics, it is not uncommon to see theatres
with nearly a thousand lighting instruments all
under the complete control of a single technician
seated in a comfortable booth above the audience.

Modern Lighting Design

Today, the lighting for any given production is likely to
have been conceived and directly supervised by a
professional lighting designer, a species of theatre artist who has appeared as a principal member of the
production team only in the past two or three decades.

By skillfully working with lighting instruments,
hanging positions, angles, colors, shadows, and moment-to-moment adjustment of intensity and di-
rectionality, the lighting designer can illuminate a
dramatic production in a great variety of subtle
and complex ways. The way in which the lighting designer uses his medium to blend the more rigid design elements (architecture and scenery) with the
evolving patterns of the movements of the actors,
and the meanings of the play, can be a crucial factor in a production's artistic and theatrical success.

Visibility and focus are the primary considerations
of lighting design: visibility assures that the audience
sees what it wants to see, and focus assures that they
see what they are *supposed* to see without undue
distraction. Visibility, then, is the passive accomplishment of lighting design and focus is its active
accomplishment. The spotlight used in contem-

porary theatre, a development of the twentieth century, has fostered something akin to a revolution in staging, which now routinely features a darkened auditorium (a rarity prior to this century) and a deliberate effort to illuminate certain characters (or props or set pieces) more than others—in other words, to direct the audience's attention toward those visual elements which are dramatically the most significant.

Realism and atmosphere also are frequent goals of the lighting designer, and both can be achieved largely through the color and direction of lighting. Realistic lighting can be created to appear as if emanating from familiar sources: from the sun, for example, or from "practical" (real) lamps on the stage, or from moonlight, fire, street lights, neon signs, or the headlights of moving automobiles. Atmospheric lighting, which may or may not suggest a familiar source, can be used to evoke a mood appropriate to a play's action: sparkly, for example, or gloomy, oppressive, nightmarish, austere, verdant, smoky, funereal, or regal.

Sharp, bold lighting designs are frequently employed to create highly theatrical effects—for glittery entertainments in the Broadway musical tradition, for example, or for harsher experimental stagings such as those often associated with the plays and theories of Bertolt Brecht. Brecht's concept of a "didactic" theatre suggested the lighting be bright, cold (uncolored), and specifically "unmagical"; Brecht suggested, in fact, that the lighting instruments themselves be made part of the setting, placed in full view of the audience, and this "theatricalist" use of the lighting instruments themselves is now in widespread use even in non-didactic plays. The splashy musical, more romantically, often makes use of footlights, banks of colored border lights, onstage "tracer" lights that flash on and off in sequence, followspots, and high-voltage incandescence that makes a finale seem to burn up the stage; in fact this traditional exploitation of light has done as much to give Broadway the name "Great White Way" as the famous billboards and marquees that line the street.

Stylized lighting effects are often used to express radical changes of mood or event; indeed, the use of lighting alone to signal a complete change of scene is an increasingly common theatrical expedient. Merely by switching from full front to full overhead lighting, for example, a technician can throw a character into silhouette and make his figure appear suddenly ominous, grotesque, or isolated. The illumination of an actor with odd lighting colors, such as green, or from odd lighting positions, as from below, can create mysterious, unsettling effects. The use of followspots can metaphorically put a character "on the spot" and convey a specific sense of unspeakable terror. Highly expressive lighting and projections, when applied to a production utilizing only a cyclorama, a set piece, sculpture, or stage mechanism, and neutrally clad actors, can create an infinite variety of convincing theatrical environments for all but the most resolutely realistic of plays; it is here, in the area of stylization and expressive theatricality, that the modern lighting designer has made his most significant mark.

The Lighting Designer at Work

The lighting designer ordinarily conceives a lighting design out of a synthesis of many discrete elements: the play, the director's approach or concept, the characteristics of the theatre building (lighting positions, control facilities, and wiring system), the basic scenery design, the costumes and movements of the actors, and the available lighting instruments. Occasionally the availability of an experienced lighting crew must also be a consideration.

Because not all of these variables can be known from the outset—the stage movement, for example, may change from one day to the next right up to the final dress rehearsal—the lighting designer must possess a certain skill at making adjustments; he also must have the opportunity to exercise a certain amount of control, or at least to voice his concerns with regard to areas affecting his work.

Ordinarily, the two major preparations required of the lighting designer are the light plot and the cue sheet. A light plot is a plan or series of plans showing the placement of each lighting instrument, its type, wattage, and size, its wiring and connection to an appropriate dimmer, its color, and any special instructions as to its use. A cue sheet is a list of the occasions, referred to by number and keyed to the script of the play (or, in final form, the more fully annotated stage manager's script), in which lights change, either in intensity or in their use. These two documents—light plot and cue sheet—are developed in consultation with the director, who may take a major or minor role in the consultation depending on his interest and expertise. Inasmuch as some productions

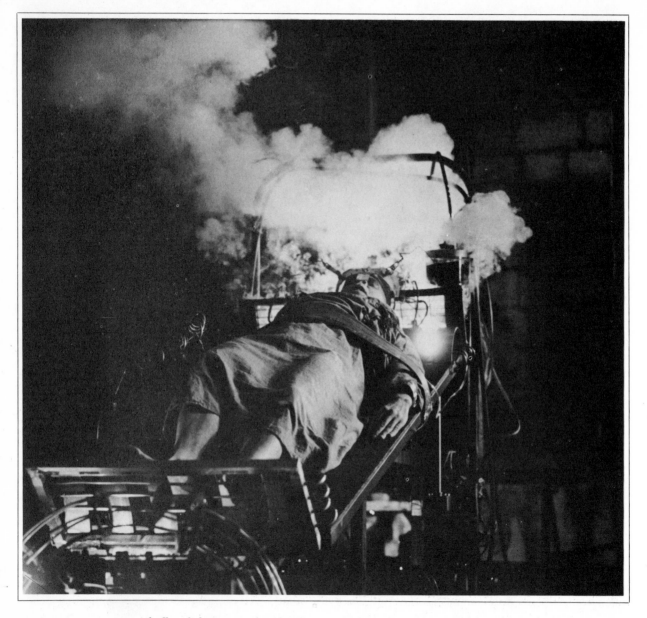

Special-effects lighting is combined with stage smoke in the Loretto-Hilton (St. Louis) production of Frankenstein, *1979.*

use literally hundreds of lighting instruments and require literally thousands of individual cues, the complexity of these documents can be extraordinary; weeks and months may go into their preparation.

The lighting designer works with a number of different sorts of lighting instruments, and he must know the properties of each instrument well enough to anticipate fully how it will perform when hung and focused on the stage. Few theatres have the time or space flexibility to permit much on-site experimentation in lighting design; thus most of the development of light plot and cue sheet must take place in the

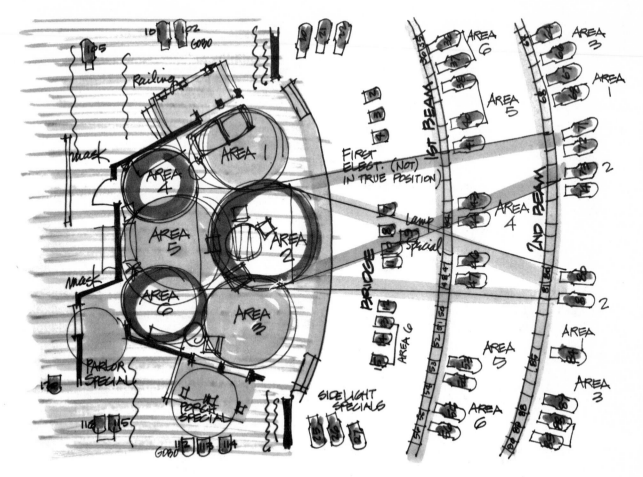

A basic lighting plot for the box set used in Long Day's Journey into Night. *Each numbered area is lit with different instruments and operated by different dimmers so that light can be concentrated in desired areas at different times.*

imagination and, where possible, in workshop or free experimentation apart from the working facility. This requirement places a premium on the designer's ability to predict instrument performance from various distances and angles and with various color elements installed; it also demands a sharp awareness of how various lights will reflect off different surfaces.

Ordinarily the lighting designer develops his plot and cue sheet gradually, over the course of regular discussions with the director and after attending some rehearsals, studying a model of the setting and perhaps some of the completed set pieces, and looking at the actual fabrics purchased for costuming. At a certain point, with the plot complete, the lights are mounted (hung) in appropriate positions, attached to the theatre's wiring system (or wired separately), "patched" to proper dimmers, focused (aimed) in the desired directions, and colored by the attachment of frames containing "gelatins" (actually thin, transparent sheets of colored plastic). Ideally, the stage setting is finished and in position when all this occurs, but this ideal is rarely fully achieved, particularly in the Broadway theatre where theatres are rented only a short time before the opening performance.

Once the instruments are in place and functioning, the lighting designer begins the task of setting the intensities of each instrument for each cue, a painstaking process involving the recording of thousands

For all the efficiency, economy, safety, and extraordinary flexibility of electric lighting, it is by no means regarded universally as an unmixed blessing for the theatre. Gone is the "living flame" which for eight hundred years had illumined indoor theatrical performance, and gone with it the warm, mellow, flickering glow cast by gaslight and, more particularly, by candlelight. Undeniably, the very strengths of electrical lighting—its uniform beam, its whiteness, its precision—have also contributed a certain sterility, coldness, and harshness, and for this reason its nearly exclusive use in the theatre today is seen by some as a definite step in the wrong direction. As candlelight and gaslight have returned in recent years to many restaurants, homes, and even street corners—almost always in successful conjunction with incandescent or even fluorescent lighting—so a few designers now are attempting to re-integrate the "living flame" into stage lighting. The great electrical revolution of the past hundred years need not forever define the future of stage illumination.

of individual numerical decisions on a series of cue sheets for the precise instruction of technicians who must effect the cues. Computer technology has vastly simplified this process for those theatres able to afford "computer boards"; with or without computers, however, much time and care inevitably go into this process, which is vital to the development and execution of a fully satisfying lighting design.

Finally, the lighting designer presides over the working and timing of the cues, making certain that in actual operation the lights shift as subtly or as boldly, as grandly or as imperceptibly, as he and the director feel appropriate for the play's action and for the design aesthetic.

It is out of thousands of details most of which are pulled together in a single final week, that great lighting design springs. Gradations of light, difficult to measure in isolation, can have vastly differing impacts in the moment-to-moment focus and feel of a play. Since light is a medium rather than an object, the audience is rarely if ever directly aware of it—they are aware only of its illuminated target. Therefore the lighting designer's work is poorly understood by the theatregoing public at large. But everyone who works professionally in the theatre, from the set and costume designer to the director to the actor, knows what a crucial role lighting plays in the success of the theatre venture. As the "Old Actor" says as he departs the stage in off Broadway's longest running hit, *The Fantasticks*: "Remember me—in light!" The light which illuminates the theatre also glorifies it; it is a symbol of revelation—of knowledge and humanity—upon which the theatrical impulse finally rests.

COSTUME

Costume has always been a major element in the theatrical experience, a vehicle for the "dressing up" that actors and audiences alike have at all times felt to be necessary for the fullest degree of theatrical satisfaction. Costume serves both ceremonial and illustrative functions.

The Functions of Costume

The first theatrical costumes were essentially ceremonial vestments. The *himation* of the early Aeschylean actor was derived from the garment worn by the priest-chanter of the dithyramb; the comic and satyr costumes, with their use of phalluses and goatskins, were likewise derived from more primitive god-centered rites. The priests who first enacted the *Quem Queritis* trope in medieval Europe simply wore their sacred albs, hooded to indicate an outdoor scene but otherwise unaltered; the actors of the classic Japanese Noh drama even today wear costumes which relate more to spiritual sources than to secular life.

These ancient and original uses of costuming served primarily to separate the actor from the audience, to "elevate" the actor to a quasi-divine status. The thick-soled footwear (*kothurnoi*) worn by Greek actors in the fourth century B.C. (see page 54) were calculated to enhance this ceremonial effect by greatly increasing the height of the wearer, thereby "dressing him up" both figuratively and literally.

The shift of stress in costuming from a "dressing up" of the actor to a defining of the character came about gradually in the theatre's history. In the Elizabethan theatre the costumes often had an almost regal ceremonial quality because the acting companies frequently solicited the cast-off raiment of the nobility; English theatre of this time was known throughout Europe for the splendor of its costuming, but apparently little effort was made to suit costume to characterization. Moreover, it was not unusual in Shakespeare's time for some actors to wear contemporary garb on stage while others wore costumes expressive of the period of the play. In Renaissance Italy, costuming developed a high degreee of stylization in the *commedia dell'arte*, where each of the recurring characters wore a distinctive and arresting costume which brightly and instantly signified a particular age, intelligence, and disposition. The same characters and the same costumes can be seen today in contemporary *commedia* productions, and they are still as eloquent and entertaining as they were four hundred years ago.

Modern costuming took on much of its present character in the eighteenth and nineteenth centuries, when certain realistic considerations took control of the Western theatre. These centuries witnessed a great deal of radical social change which led to, among other things, the widespread acceptance of science and its methods, and a great fascination with detail and accuracy. These trends coalesced in the European (and eventually the American) theatre with a series of productions in which historical accuracy served as the guiding principle. For the first time, a massive effort was made to ensure that the design of every costume in a play (and every prop and every set piece as well) accorded with an authentic "period" source. Thus a production of *Julius Caesar* would be intensively researched to re-create the clothing worn in Rome in the first century A.D., a *Hamlet* would be designed to mirror the records of medieval Denmark, and a *Romeo and Juliet* would seek to re-create, in detail, the world of Renaissance Verona.

The movement toward historical accuracy, and the devotion with which it was pursued, led ultimately to a widespread change in the philosophy of costume design which persists to this day. For although historical accuracy itself is no longer the ultimate goal of costume design, stylistic consistency and overall design control have proven to be lasting principles. Costuming today stresses, in addition to an imaginative aesthetic creativity, a coordinated dramatic suitability as well; thus the influence of realism, with its attendant emphasis on historical accuracy, has fostered coherent and principled design in place of the near anarchy that once obtained.

This does not mean that costuming has lost touch with its ancient origins. On the one hand, we can still capture in the combination of bright stage lights and grotesque or exotic costumes the ceremonial magic conjured by ancient priests and modern-day shamans alike. What is more, our potential for capturing that magic is probably *enhanced* by costume consistency and control.

On the other hand, however, costuming has gained a great deal by its commitment to character definition and dramatic suitability. Costuming can provide the audience's first clues to a character's profession, wealth, class status, tastes, and self-image. More subtly, costume can symbolize human vices and virtues: sloth, vanity, benevolence, pride, generosity, for example. Some costumes are instrinsic to the characters who wear them—as Hamlet's "inky cloak" or Harlequin's parti-colored tights. By judicious use of color, shape, and fabric, costume designers can imbue every character in a play with individuality. The collective costuming of a play, in addition to setting a historical period and creating an overall theatrical style, can also convey social and personal meanings supportive of the text's intent; consider, for example, Tennessee Williams' direction in *A Streetcar Named Desire* that the poker players are to wear shirts of "bright primary colors," to contrast them with Blanche du Bois' dead husband, one "Allen Grey."

I see my job [costume design] as a cross between camouflage and magic.

Edith Head

The specific challenge of the costume designer, then, is to impart patterns of meaning and an aggregate theatrical excitement to what must finally be *wearable clothing for the characters*. For costume, of course, is clothing; it must be functional as well as meaningful and aesthetic. The actor does not model his costume; he wears it, walks in it, sits in it, duels in it, dances in it, tumbles downstairs in it. The costume designer thus cannot be content merely to draw pictures on paper; he must design workable, danceable, actable clothing for which cutting, stitching, fitting, and quick-changing are as important considerations as color coordination and historical context.

The costume as clothing gives rise to both ensemble and individual impressions. As one of an ensemble, the costume an actor wears contributes not only to a play's overall symbolic effects, but also to its particularized milieu, to a specific "world" in which people are seen to dress in special and perhaps unique ways. This world may portray a period out of the past, accurately rendered, or it may be modern, or it may be a world fashioned out of the purest fantasy; whatever the case, however, there is always a demand for a certain costume coherence, even in the most inventive and idiosyncratic productions. The very word "costume," we might note, has the same root meaning as "custom" and "customary"; and the costumes of a particular world, theatrically created, must be seen to represent the "customary costume" (or, in the same vein, the "habitual habit") of the "inhabitants" of that world. Costume, in other words, sets style; it is the garb of choice for the general run of people in the play.

And this leads us to an examination of the importance of costume for the definition of individual characters within the ensemble. A character's adherence or non-adherence to the "going dress" of the other characters in a play will always be loaded with significance. For costume is a character's way of expressing his individuality and his self-image: *it is the clothing he chooses to wear* within the context of the dress favored by his peers. When Hamlet wears his "inky cloak" to the royal court, for example, it signifies his refusal to adapt to his surroundings and the expectations of his superiors. It is both a mark of his character and a significant action in the play; it says a great deal about how he perceives himself and how he wants the world to see him. When Monsieur Jourdain in Molière's *The Bourgeois Gentleman* dons his fancy

White costumes and lean vegetation characterize the simple but effective design of this French production of Chekhov's Uncle Vanya; *costuming is carefully coordinated to create a subtly ethereal effect without straining limitations of realism. Produced by Théâtre de l'Odéon, 1977.*

Beggar costumes juxtaposed with those of prostitutes, police, and Mac the Knife in The Three Penny Opera, *as directed by Jean Gascon at the Stratford Shakespeare Festival in 1972.*

suit with the upside-down flowers and, later, his Turkish gown and grotesque turban, he is proclaiming (foolishly) to his peers that he is a person of elegance and refinement. And Estragon's unlaced shoes in *Waiting for Godot* represent—pathetically to be sure—his great wish to be unfettered, not "tied to Godot" but simply free, fed, and happy. Further, the battered bowler hats and smelly shoes that figure into that play, as well as the empty pockets in Vladimir's tattered overcoat, symbolize the fruitlessness of Gogo's and Didi's quest for salvation and at the same time suggest their reluctance to part with the familiar, the known quantity.

In Luis Valdez's *Zoot Suit*, the contemporary drama about Mexican-Americans in Los Angeles during World War II, the costume of the title acquires major significance, representing both the world of the play's central characters and the struggle of individual characters to stand apart from that world. Eugene Brieux's *The Red Robe* and Paul Claudel's *Satin Slipper* illustrate similar uses of costume elements as metaphor in modern (post-Romantic) drama.

The Costume Designer at Work

The costume designer works primarily with fabric—which comes in a variety of materials and weaves and can be cut, shaped, stitched, colored, and draped in innumerable ways. Aside from fabric, jewels, armor, feathers, fur, hair (real or simulated), and metallic ornamentation commonly figure into costume design as well.

The costume designer both selects and builds costume elements, usually in combination. The costumes for some plays are assembled entirely out of items ready at hand. For contemporary plays with modern settings, the costumes are often selected from the actors' own wardrobes or from department store racks. Sometimes a costume designer will acquire clothing from thrift shops and used clothing stores, particularly for plays set in the recent past; indeed, this is not unusual practice even for high-budget professional productions. In one celebrated instance, Louis Jouvet appealed to the citizens of Paris to donate costumes for the posthumous premiere of Jean Giraudoux's *The Madwoman of Chaillot*, and the clothing that poured into the Athénée theatre for that brilliant 1945 Parisian production signaled to the world that France had survived the scourge of Nazi occupation with its devotion to the theatre intact.

Even in a "fully designed, fully built" production some costume elements are usually purchased, rented, or taken from costume storage; shoes, for example, are not ordinarily built from scratch for theatrical productions. Nonetheless, it is these productions which are designed and built for a given set of performances that test the full measure of the costume designer's imagination and ability. In these productions, subject only to the ultimate inspiration and control of the director, the costume designer can create a top-to-toe originality.

The comprehensive design for such a production begins with a series of sketches and material estimates—these usually proceed hand in hand—based on a thorough knowledge of the play, a clear agreement with the director on interpretation and style, research into necessary historical sources, and a firm understanding of the production monies and costume technologies available to the producing organization. Generally, a separate costume sketch is made for each character, although choruses and "extras" are sometimes grouped in, or represented by, a single sketch; then, after such conferences with the director as needed to gain full support and approval,

Costumes play major role in Luis Valdez' play and production of Zoot Suit, *in which dress of 1940s Latinos living in the Los Angeles area becomes a metaphor for cultural pride and social advancement. Roberta Delgado Esparza, Daniel Valdez, Edward James Olmos, and Evelina Fernandez are featured in this Mark Taper production.*

Costumes for this production of Brecht's Good Woman of Sezuan, *produced by the Lexington Conservatory Theatre in 1979, represent a deliberately "poor" conceptualization; constructed from inexpensive muslin and cast-off ready-made garments, the "Brechtian" clothes exemplify the workers' theatre approach.*

the sketches are developed into full color renderings. When these are approved and the material estimates are "costed out" and budgeted, fabrics are purchased and appropriate sample swatches are attached to the corner of each rendering. Construction details are frequently included on the rendering itself, so that a single document conveys both the general look and specific construction of each costume.

The purchase of fabric is of course a crucial stage in costuming, for fabric is the basic medium of the costumer's art. Texture, weight, suppleness, and response to draping, dying, folding, crushing, twirling, and twisting are all considerations applied to the pur-

chase of costume fabric. Velvet (and its synthetic substitute, velveteen), raw silk, woolens, and satin are the costumer's luxury fabrics; cottons, felt, burlap, and even painted canvas are less expensive and often quite appropriate for theatrical use. Coloring, "aging" (making a new fabric appear old and used), and detailing are often achieved with dyes, appliques, and embroidery, and sometimes with paint, tie-dyes, and other special treatments (for example, the costume designers Motley—three women working under a single professional name—simulate leather by rubbing thick felt with moist yellow soap and spraying it down with brown paints). Frequently, of course, printed

The task of subtly distorting uniformity, without destroying the desired illusion, is a difficult one. Anton Chekhov's play *The Three Sisters* presents a case in point. The characters of the male players are clearly defined in Chekhov's writing, but because the men are all wearing military uniforms they are theoretically similar in appearance. One of the few ways in which the designer can help to differentiate between characters is by the alteration of proportion; alterations such as these, which do not show enough from the 'front' to make the uniforms seem strange to the audience, can be extremely effective, as well as helpful to the actor. In a London production of *The Three Sisters*, Sir Michael Redgrave wore a coat with a collar that was too low; Sir John Gielgud one that was too high. No one in the audience was unaware of the characters' individuality, the talents of these actors being what they are, but the small details added to the scope of their performances.

Motley

or embossed fabrics with designs woven in are purchased for women's costumes or for male period attire.

The cutting, fitting, and stitching of original costumes are equally important stages in costume design. Most designers insist on at least some control over these procedures, for the cutting of a fabric determines the manner in which it drapes and moves, and the fitting of a costume determines its shape and silhouette. Needless to say, a "cutter" is a full-time pro-

Cecil Beaton's famous costumes for the "Ascot" scene in My Fair Lady *made use of strikingly limited color palette: black, white, and shades of gray. This Broadway musical classic of 1956 is often regarded as the epitome of postwar American musical theatre.*

fessional in the theatre, and the designer must work in close collaboration with his cutter to achieve his intended result. Fitting and stitching (as well as refitting, restitching, and often re-refitting and re-restitching) are part of the obligatory and time-consuming backstage process by which the costume becomes a wearable garment for the actor and the actor "grows into" his theatrically costumed characterization.

Finally, the accessories of costume can greatly affect the impact of the basic design; occasionally they may even stand out in such a way as to "make" the costume or to obliterate it. Hair styles and headdresses, since they frame the actor's face, will convey a visual message every time the actor speaks a line; they are obviously of paramount importance. Jewelry, sashes, purses, muffs, and other adornments and badges of various sorts have considerable dramatic impact insofar as they "read" from the audience—that is, insofar as the audience can see them clearly and take notice of what they may signify about the character. The lowly shoe, if unwisely chosen, can utterly destroy the artistry of a production, either by being simply unsuitable for the character or style of the play, or by being so badly fitted (or so unwieldy) that the actor stumbles awkwardly through his part.

Good costuming for a play, whether arrived at through design and fabrication or through careful selection from the Army surplus store, creates a sense of character, period, style, and theatricality out of wearable garments. In harmony with scenery, make-up, and lighting, and with the play's interpretation and performance, costuming can have its maximum impact in a subtle way—by underlining the play's meaning and the characters' personalities—or it can frankly scream for attention and sometimes even become the "star of the show." Not a few musicals have succeeded primarily because the audience "came out whistling the costumes," as a Shubert Alley phrase reminds us.

Certain theorists contend that costuming must at all times relegate itself to a subordinate role, and perhaps for most Western plays of the latter part of this century that has been a valid principle. But who is to say that the grand dancers of the Kabuki theatre, or the patchworked Arlecchino of the *commedia dell'arte*, or the stunningly garbed black-and-white mannequins of Cecil Beaton's creation in *My Fair Lady* represent any less a theatrical realization than their more modestly attired counterparts in other forms of theatre? Costume has always exerted a certain magical force in the theatre, lending a special magnitude to the actor's and the playwright's art. There are occasions when it seems altogether fitting and proper that this contribution should be celebrated in its own right.

MAKE-UP

Make-up, which is essentially the design of the actor's face, occupies a curiously paradoxical position in the theatre.

In much modern production, make-up seems sorely neglected. It tends to be the last design technology to be considered; indeed, it is often applied (literally) for the first time at the final dress rehearsal —and sometimes not until just before the opening performance. Many directors spend little time planning for it, and rarely is an independent artistry engaged to guide the make-up design of a contemporary play. Indeed, make-up is the only major design element whose planning and execution are often left entirely to the actor's decision.

And yet, ironically, make-up is one of the archetypal arts of the theatre, absolutely fundamental to the origins of drama. The earliest chanters of the dithyramb, like the spiritual leaders of primitive tribes today, invariably made themselves up in preparation for the performance of their holy rites: their make-up in later centuries inspired the Greek tragic and comic masks which are today the universal symbols of theatre itself.

The reason for this paradox resides in the changing emphasis of theatre aims. Make-up, like costuming, serves both ceremonial and illustrative functions. The illustrative function of make-up is unquestionably the most obvious one today—so much so that we tend to forget its other use altogether.

Illustrative make-up is the means by which the actor changes his appearance to resemble that of his character—or at least the appearance of his character as author, director, and actor himself imagine it. Make-up of this sort is particularly useful in helping to make a young actor look older or an old one look younger, and in making an actor of any age resemble a known historical figure or a fictitious character whose appearance is already set in the public imagination. Make-up gives Cyrano his great nose and Bardolf his red one; it turns the Caucasian Laurence Olivier into

Cyrano's famous nose is made of putty in this American Conservatory Theatre production starring Ray Reinhardt as the Gascon cavalier (1974).

the Moorish Othello, and it makes Miss Sandy Duncan into Master Peter Pan. Make-up transforms the young Hal Holbrook into the old Mark Twain, and it permits Cicely Tyson to portray a character's aging over an eighty-year period. Scars, deformities, bruises, beards, sunburn, frostbite, and scores of other facial embellishments, textures, and shadings can be mastered by the make-up artist's brush, and can contribute significantly to realistic stagecraft when needed or desired.

A subtler use of make-up, but still within the realistic mode, is aimed at the evocation of psychological traits through physiognomic clues. For example, the modern make-up artist may try to suggest character by exaggerating or distorting the actor's natural eye placement, the size and shape of his mouth, the angularity of his nose, or the tilt of his eyebrows. There can be no question that we do form impressions of a character's inner state on the basis of his observable physical characteristics—as Caesar notices and

interprets Cassius' "lean and hungry look" so do we —and the skilled make-up artist can go far in enhancing the psychological texture of a play by his imaginative use of facial shapings and shadings.

Still another use of make-up, also within the realistic and practical spectrum, seeks merely to simplify and embolden the actor's features in order to make them distinct and expressive to every member of the audience. In theatre jargon this is known as creating a face that "reads" to the house—in other words, a face that conveys its fullest expression (that "can be read like a book") over a great distance. Make-ups that read in this way do so primarily by exaggerating highlights and shadows and by sharply defining specific features such as wrinkles, eyelashes, eyebrows, and jaw lines. Such simplified, emboldened, and subtly exaggerated make-up goes hand in hand with stage lighting and, in conjunction with it, creates an appearance of realism far greater than any that could be achieved by make-up or lighting alone; in fact a certain minimum level of make-up is thought by most actors and directors to be a necessity if only to prevent the actor from looking "washed out" in the glare of the stage lights.

Yet none of these realistic or practical uses of make-up truly touches upon its original theatrical use, which was aimed at announcing the actor as a performer and at establishing a milieu for acting that was neither realistic nor practical, but rather supernatural, mysterious, and calculatedly theatrical. For it was the white-lead make-up of Thespis and his fellows which endowed them with the same aspect of spiritual transcendence that warpaint provides for the celebrant in tribal rituals today: by making himself "up," the actor was preparing to ascend to a higher world;

Makeup can create extraordinary transformations. Here young actress Libby Boone, is shown before (RIGHT) and after (p. 385) being made up into an old woman for an American Conservatory Theatre production of All The Way Home.

Basic make-up consists of a foundation, color shadings, and various special applications.

The foundation is a basic skin color that is applied generally to the face and neck, and sometimes to other parts of the body as well. Greasepaint, the traditional foundation material, is a highly opaque and relatively inexpensive skin paint that can be purchased in tube or stick form in a variety of colors. Cake make-up, or "pancake" as it is commonly known, is also used for foundations; it is less messy than greasepaint, but also somewhat less flexible. Cake makeup comes in small plastic cases, and is applied with a damp sponge. Most theatrical foundation colors are richer and deeper than the actor's normal skin color, so as to counteract the white and blue tones of stage lights. Foundations, whether of greasepaint or cake, should be applied thinly and evenly.

Color shading defines the facial structure and exaggerates its dimensions so as to give the face a sculptured appearance from a distance; ordinarily, the least imposing characteristics of the face are put in shadow and the prominent features are highlighted. Shading colors—which are universally called "liners" for some obscure reason—come in both grease and cake form, and are usually chosen to harmonize with the foundation color, as well as with the color of the actor's costume and the color of the lighting. Shadows of course are made with darker colors and highlights with light ones; both are applied with small brushes and blended into the foundation. Rouge, a special color application used to redden lips and cheeks, is usually applied along with the shading colors. When greasepaints are used, the make-up must be dusted with make-up powder to "set" it and prevent running.

A make-up pencil is regularly used to darken eyebrows, and also to accentuate eyes and facial wrinkles.

Special applications may include false eyelashes or heavy mascara, facial hair (beards and moustaches, ordinarily made from crepe wool), nose putty and various other prosthetic materials, and various treatments for aging, wrinkling, scarring, and otherwise disfiguring the skin. A well-equipped make-up kit will include glue (spirit gum and liquid latex), solvents, synthetic hair, wax (to mask eyebrows), and hair whiteners in addition to the standard foundation and shading colors, so that the actor will be prepared to create a variety of make-ups without making additional trips to the make-up retailer.

he was self-consciously assuming something of the power and divinity of the gods, and he was moreover offering to guide the audience on a divine adventure.

Today one still sees some obvious examples of such traditional make-up and "making up" particularly in the European and Asian theatres. The make-ups of the circus and the classic mime, two formats which developed in Europe out of the masked *commedia dell'arte* of centuries past, both use bold primary colors: white, black, and sometimes red for the mimist; these plus several more for the circus clown. Avant-garde and Expressionist playwrights also frequently utilize similar sorts of abstracted make-ups, as did Jean Genet in *The Blacks*, which features black actors in clownish white-face, and Peter Handke, whose *Kaspar* featured similarly stylized facial painting. And the Japanese theatre, representative of much Asian practice, has always relied on extreme

and elaborate make-ups, from the dazzlingly pure colors and mane-like wigs of the classical Noh and Kabuki to the violently expressive make-ups of the contemporary Tokyo avant-garde. The American theatre, which so far has witnessed only a small sampling of stylized make-ups, is perhaps due for an awakening to this fascinating approach to theatrical design.

But the realistic and symbolic functions of make-up are probably always combined to some extent in the theatre, for even the most stylized make-up is ultimately based on the human form, and even the most realistic make-up conveys an obvious theatricality. The theatre, after all, is never very far from human concerns, nor is it ever so immersed in the ordinary that it is completely mistaken for such. It might not be overly sentimental to suggest that when the American actor sits at his make-up table opening his little bottles and tubes, moistening his Chinese brushes and sharpening his eyebrow pencils, more is going on than simple practical face-making: atavistic forces are at work, linking the actor not merely to the imagined physiognomy of his character or to the demands of facial projection in a large arena, but also, and more fundamentally, to the primitive celebrants who in ages past painted their faces to assure the world that they were leaving their temporal bodies and were about to venture into the domain of gods.

TECHNICAL PRODUCTION

We shall end this chapter with a discussion of theatre technicians.

They are the true proletariat of the theatre: the worker-artists whose functions, although various, all revolve around getting the production organized, built, installed, lit, and ready to open, and then seeing that it runs. They far outnumber all the others—the actors, designers, writers, and directors—put together.

Because of their numbers, theatrical technicians are ordinarily marshaled into a hierarchical structure, with stage and house managers, technical directors, and production managers at the top, and carpenters, electricians, cutters, seamstresses, wigmakers, publicists, make-up artists, stagehands, light and sound operators, prompters, flymen, and various running crews at the bottom. Top to bottom, however, they all play crucial roles in each theatrical presentation—and

the "stage fright" of the actor playing Hamlet is not necessarily any greater than that of the stagehand who must pull the curtain.

The great bulk of technical work in the theatre is executed in accord with traditional practices developed over centuries of theatrical organization and management; still, every production poses a host of problems and situations in each technical area that are new to the persons asked to deal with them, and sometimes, new to the theatre itself. It is in the junction of sound knowledge of craft and creative imagination in the face of unanticipated problems that technological innovation takes place; and the technical artists of the theatre have always manifested an impressive ingenuity at meeting unprecedented challenges in creative ways.

Most theatrical crafts in the production areas are learned through apprenticeship after little or no preliminary instruction. Each of the shops of the theatre—the scene shop, the costume shop, the prop shop, and the make-up room—is a laboratory of instruction as well as a working unit of the theatre; most of what is learned is acquired on site and in action. Artistic components are never absent in the technical workings of the theatre: the painting of a set, the hanging of a lighting instrument, the timing of a scene shift, the sewing of a costume, and the calling of a sound cue are services that contribute mightily to the overall artistry of the enterprise. The technical crafts, therefore, are both learned and practiced in an aesthetic context, as a central activity of the theatrical venture. And although written and unwritten "textbooks" of stage practice can illustrate the traditional means of building a flat, cutting a pattern, organizing a rehearsal, and painting a prop, it is artistic sensitivity which ultimately determines the technical quality of a production, and it is artistic imagination which brings about the technical and technological advances.

Scene painting is a highly specialized theatre craft. Here, three artists on American Conservatory Theatre staff paint a stage-wide "olio"—the conventional front drop used in nineteenth-century melodramas to advertise the theatre and nearby enterprises. Below, the completed olio: note tongue-in-cheek advertisement for the scenic artists union—The International Association of Theatrical Stage Employees—at left.

Many separate production crafts go into building, promoting, managing, and running a show, and a separate textbook would be required to describe them all. A few of them, however, deserve special mention owing to the importance of their contribution to the growing art of stage production.

The *sound technician* (or *sound designer*, as he is often called today) occupies a position of rapidly increasing importance in the theatre. His rise to prominence has been prompted by two factors: a swiftly developing technology which now includes such innovations as multiphonic sound, body microphones, and multiple-track recording; and an increased audience interest in and receptivity to thematic music and heightened sound style. These changes have made the sound technician's function vastly more demanding than that of the stagehand who just a few decades ago was expected to do little more than rattle a tin sheet to indicate thunder or play a scratchy record during scene changes. As we have seen, the origins of theatre and music are intertwined (Aristotle included music as one of the six components of tragedy), and until about two hundred years ago no one even considered staging a music-less play. Today the established popularity of the musical theatre, whether in the splashy Broadway format or the more socially expressive Brechtian one, exerts a continuing demand for both live and recorded sound that goes well beyond the simpler effects once required. In addition, thematic sound tracks are being increasingly used in contemporary non-musical theatre—even in realistic theatre—in much the same way as they have long been used in films. Some sound "scores" for serious plays, such as the hoofbeats in *Equus*, the voices in *Wings*, and the offstage military band music at the end of *The Three Sisters*, are intrinsic to the text and indeed convey—often by contrast—the whole point of the actions they accompany. Finally, the amplification of live stage sound is becoming a major practice (much derided by many) in an attempt to give theatre the audible "boom-boom" punch of films, rock concerts, and certain religious revivals.

The *stage manager*, now often called the *production stage manager*, has the highly responsible position of overseeing all elements of production, coordinating the director's work with that of the actors and the technical and design departments. At the beginning of rehearsals he is involved primarily in organizational work: he schedules calls and appointments, records the blocking of actors, anticipates technical problems involving quick costume changes, set shifts, and the like, and organizes the basic "calling" of the show —that is, the system by which lighting, sound, and scene shift cues are initiated. During performance, the stage manager actually runs the show, having final authority over the entire onstage and backstage operation; moreover, it is the stage manager who ordinarily conducts understudy and replacement rehearsals in a professional run, and who assumes the functions of the director when the director is absent or no longer employed by the production.

The *technical director*, who is also sometimes called the *production manager* (sometimes both titles exist in the same production) is generally in charge of the building and operation of scenery and stage machinery; he may also have charge of the lighting crews and of all technical scheduling. He must oversee the moving of scenery into and out of the theatre, assure all technical departments adequate "stage time" to do their jobs, establish policies and directives for scene shifting, special effects, and "strike" (the final removal of scenery from the theatre after a run), and, most importantly, make certain that everything is ready on time—no small order considering the massive technical complexities of theatre today.

The influence of Bertolt Brecht, as we have seen, has brought lighting instruments into plain view even for many "non-Brechtian" productions. It has also tended to pull the backstage technician into public awareness in recent years. A popular fascination with technology, together with a diminishing interest in stage "magic" or naturalistic illusion, has led to a scenography that deliberately incorporates the activities of scene technology as a visible aesthetic component of the theatre. Given this trend and the theatre's increasing use of newer and newer technical innovations—lasers and holograms, air cushions, videotape, and computerized slide projections, to name but a few—it would appear that the theatre technician is on the verge of being widely recognized as a full-fledged theatre artist and creator in his own right, as well as a craftsman and mechanic who executes the creations of others.

THE DIRECTOR

The room is already filled with people when he enters, a bit fussily, with a bundle of books and papers under his arm. Expectation, tension, and even a hint of panic can be sensed behind the muffled greetings, loose laughter, and choked conversation that greet his arrival.

He sits, and an assistant arranges chairs. Gradually, starting at the other end of that piece of furniture which suddenly has become "his" table, the others seat themselves. An edgy silence descends. Where are they going? What experiences lie ahead? What risks, what challenges, are to be demanded? What feelings, in the coming weeks and months, are going to be stirred to poignant reality?

Only he knows—or if he doesn't no one does. It is in this silence, tender with hope and fear, that the director breaks ground for his production. It is here that plan begins to become work and idea begins to become art. It is the peak moment of directing, and of the director.

This is an idealized picture, to be sure. There are many directors who deliberately avoid invoking an impression of "mystique," and whose primary efforts are directed toward dispelling awe, dread, or any form of personal tension among their fellows. Nonetheless, the picture holds a measure of truth for every theatrical production, for the art of directing is an exercise in leadership, imagination, and control; in the director's hands, finally, rest the aspirations, neuroses, skills, and ideas of the entire theatrical company.

Directing is an art whose product is the most ambiguous, perhaps the most mysterious in the theatre. The direction of a play is not visible like scenery or costumes; and unlike the actor's voice or the sound designer's score, it cannot be directly heard or sensed. And yet direction underlies everything we see and hear in the theatre. Utterly absorbed by the final theatrical experience, direction animates and defines that experience. A whole class of theatrical artists in our time has reached international eminence in this particular art. But what, exactly, is it?

At the *technical* level, the director is the person who organizes the production. This involves scheduling the work process and supervising the acting, designing, staging and technical operation of the play. This is the easiest part of the directorial function.

At the more *fundamental* level, the director inspires a creation of theatre with each production. He conceptualizes the play, gives it vision and purpose—both social and aesthetic—and inspires the company of artists to join with him in collaboration.

It is in the conjunction of these levels, the technical and the fundamental, that each director defines the directorial function anew. And it is with one foot in each that he creates—through an adroit synthesis of text, materials, and available talent—a unique and hopefully vivid theatrical experience.

THE ARRIVAL OF THE DIRECTOR: A HISTORICAL OVERVIEW

Directing has been going on ever since theatre began, but there has not always been a director—that is, there has not always been an individual specifically charged solely with directorial functions and responsibilities. The director in fact came into his own as an independent theatre artist less than a century ago, and his arrival has had as much to do with the development of modern theatre as any dramatic innovation. The gradual process whereby he came to his present position can be roughly divided into three phases.

Phase One: The Teacher-Directors

In the earliest days of the theatre and for some time thereafter, directing was considered a form of teaching. The Greeks called the director the *didaskalos*, which means "teacher," and in medieval times the designation, in all the various European languages, meant literally "master." The underlying assumption of teaching, of course, is that a given subject is already known and understood; the teacher's task is simply to transmit what is known to persons yet unversed. The earliest directors, therefore, were simply asked to pass along the accumulated wisdom and techniques of "correct" performance within a "given" convention. Quite often the playwrights themselves served as directors, for who would seem better qualified to "teach" a play than the man who wrote it? In one famous dramatic scene, Molière delightfully depicts himself directing one of his own plays; this is surely an effective model of the author-teacher-director for the seventeenth century, and indeed for much of the theatre's history (see pp. 394–95).

The teacher-director reached a pinnacle of in-fluence, albeit anonymously, during the late Enlightenment and Victorian eras—during the eighteenth and nineteenth centuries—partly in response to the remarkable fascination of those times with science, scientific method, and humanistic research: the same dedication to rationalism which fostered a profusion of libraries, museums, and historic preservations, also emphasized accuracy, consistency, and precision in the arts. The temper of the times led to major directorial changes in the theatre. For on the one hand, audiences were demanding revivals of classic plays—whose authors were no longer around to direct them—and on the other hand they were demanding that these revivals be historically edifying, that they have a museum-like authenticity. All this required research, organization, and comprehensive coordination; in other words, it demanded an independent director.

Most of the directors in this time—virtually all of them until the latter part of the nineteenth century—received no more recognition for their efforts than the museum director who created historical dioramas. Sometimes the directing was attributed to a famous acting star, such as the Englishman Charles Kean or the American Edwin Booth, when in fact the work was done by a lesser functionary; in Booth's case, for example, one D. W. Waller was the true director, but his name was all but buried in the program and never appeared in the reviews or publicity. Nevertheless these teacher-directors who labored largely in the shadows began the art of directing as we know it today. They organized their productions around specific concepts, independently arrived at, and they dedicated themselves to creating unified and coherent theatrical works by "directing" an ensemble of actors, designers, and technicians toward established ends.

Phase Two: The Realistic Directors

The second stage in the development of modern-day directing began toward the end of the nineteenth century, and brought to the fore a group of directors who re-studied the conventions of theatrical presentation and strove in various ways to make them more lifelike.

George II, Duke of Saxe-Meiningen, was the first of this breed, and is generally regarded as the first modern director. The Duke, who headed a provincial troupe of actors in his rural duchy, presented a series

A DESIGN CONCEPT nearly as much as a DIRECTORIAL visualization...

CAREFUL DETAIL in crowd scenes and other aspects of "ENSEMBLE" playing.... made for a comprehensive "REALISM"

...an EXCESSIVE attention to the stage picture, however, leads to an ARTIFICIAL atmosphere

Saxe-Meiningen's visualization of a scene from Shakespeare's Julius Caesar. *The Duke's concern was for realistic rather than overly posed composition; his influence led to demands that directors have a very clear vision of a scene prior to actually staging it— a virtual revolution in theatrical practice. From the original sketch.*

of premieres and classical revivals throughout Europe in the late 1870s and 1880s that were dazzling in their harmonized acting, staging, and scenery. Although still historically "correct," the Duke's productions featured an ensemble of performances rather than a hierarchy of "star, support, and supernumerary." All of his performers were vigorously rehearsed toward the development of individual, realistically conceived roles—which were then played out in highly organic, even volatile patterns of dramatic action. The stodgy line-up of spear carriers which had traditionally looked on while the star recited center stage was con-

spicuously absent from the Meiningen productions; so was the "super" who was customarily hired on the afternoon of performance, squeezed into a costume, and set upon the stage like so much living scenery. The totality of the Meiningen theatre aesthetic, embracing acting, interpretation, and design, was acclaimed throughout Europe: when the Meiningen troupe ceased touring in 1890, the position of a director who would organize and rehearse an entire company toward a complexly and comprehensively fashioned theatrical presentation was firmly established.

In 1887 André Antoine began a movement of

greater realism in Paris with his Théâtre Libre, and Konstantin Stanislavski initiated his even more celebrated Moscow Art Theatre in 1898; both of these directors, amateurs like the Duke of Saxe-Meiningen at the start of their careers, went on to develop wholly innovative techniques in acting and actor-coaching based on the staging concepts of the Duke; both also theorized and worked pragmatically at the organizing of theatre companies, the development of a dramatic repertory, the re-education of theatregoing audiences, and the re-creation of an overall aesthetic of the theatre. Although both Antoine and Stanislavski were known primarily as naturalists—somewhat to

their disadvantage, perhaps, for they had many other interests as well—they were above all idealists who sought to make the theatre a powerful social and artistic instrument for the expression of truth. Their ideals and their commitment virtually forced them to expand the directorial function into an all-encompassing and inspirational art.

The importance of these directors—and of certain other pioneers of the same spirit, including Harley Granville-Barker in England, David Belasco in America, and Otto Brahm in Germany—was not merely that they fostered the developing realist and naturalist drama (see Chapter 7), but also that they opened up

Jean-Louis Barrault, France's leading director of the postwar era, exemplifies stylizing trend begun by Paul Fort in 1890; indeed, French theatre of the present century has been dominated by highly stylized directorial efforts. Here Barrault appears (right) in his own 1978 production of Eugène Ionesco's Rhinoceros, *at Théâtre d'Orsay in Paris.*

the theatre to the almost infinite possibilities of psychological interpretation. Once the psychology of the human individual becomes crucial to the analysis and acting of plays, the director becomes more than a teacher: he becomes part analyst, part therapist, and even part mystic; his *creative* function in play production has increased substantially. The rise of realism in the theatre of the late nineteenth and early twentieth centuries, and the rise of directors capable of bringing out realistic nuances and patterning them into highly theatrical dramatic productions, brought about an irreversible theatrical renovation which, in turn irrevocably established the importance of the director.

Phase Three: The Stylizing Directors

Right on the heels of the realist phase of direction came a third phase—one which brought the director to his present position of power and recognition. This phase arrived with the directors who joined forces with non-realist playwrights to create the modern Stylized Theatre (see Chapter 8). Their forces are still growing. They are the ones who demand of directing that it aim primarily at the creation of originality, theatricality, and style. The stylizing director is unrestrained by rigid formulas with respect to verisimilitude or realistic behavior; his goal is to create sheer theatrical brilliance, beauty, and excitement, and to lead his collaborators in explorations of pure theatre and pure theatrical imagination.

Paul Fort, one of the first of these third-stage directors, launched his Théâtre d'Art in Paris in 1890 as a direct assault upon the realist principles espoused by Antoine. Similarly, Vsevelod Meyerhold, a one-time disciple of Stanislavski, began his theatre of "Biomechanical Constructivism" in Moscow to combat the master's realism. The movement toward stylized directing occasioned by these innovators and others like them introduced a lyricism and symbolism, an expressive and abstract use of design, an explosive theatricality, and certain intentionally contrived methods of acting which continue to the present day to have a profound effect on the theatre and its drama.

Perhaps the most influential proponent of this third-phase position of the director, however, was not himself a director at all, but an eminent designer and theorist: Gordon Craig. In a seminal essay entitled "The Art of the Theatre" (1905), Craig compared the director of a play to the captain of a ship: an absolutely indispensable leader whose rule, maintained by strict discipline, extends over every last facet of the enterprise. "Until discipline is understood in a theatre to be willing and reliant obedience to the manager [director] or captain," wrote Craig, "no supreme achievement can be accomplished." Craig's essay was aimed at a full-scale "Renaissance of the Art of the Theatre," in which a "systematic progression" of reform would overtake all the individual theatre arts—"acting, scenery, costuming, lighting, carpentering, singing, dancing, etc."—under the complete control and organizing genius of this newcomer to the ranks of theatrical artistry, the independent director.

The Contemporary Director

Craig's renaissance has surely arrived: this indeed is the "Age of the Director," an age in which the directorial function is fully established as the art of synthesizing script, design, and performance into a unique and splendid theatrical event which creates its own harmony and its own ineffable yet memorable distinction. If, as J. L. Styan says, "the theatre persists in communicating by a simultaneity of sensory impressions," it is above all the director who is charged with inspiring these impressions and ensuring this simultaneity.

Today, in a world of mass travel and mass communications, the exotic quickly becomes familiar and the familiar just as quickly becomes trite. Nothing is binding; the directorial function has shifted from teaching what is "proper" to creating what is stimulating and wondrous. At the beginning of a production the director faces a blank canvas, but he has at hand a generous palette. At his disposal are not only the underlying conventions of his time, but all those of the past, which may be revived in an instant for novel effects and stunning juxtapositions. Our conglomerate theatre of today allows Shakespeare in modern dress, Greek tragedy à la Kabuki spectacle, Theatre of the Absurd as vaudevillian buffoonery, and romantic melodrama as campy satire. Thus at the conception of a theatrical idea today—in the first moments of imagining a specific production—no questions can be answered automatically, no style is obligatory, no interpretation is definitive. Jean-Paul Sartre has said about the whole of modern life that "man is condemned to be free"; in the theatre the director's

DIRECTOR MOLIÈRE

Molière's *Versailles Rehearsals* (*L'Impromptu de Versailles*, 1663) is a highly entertaining one-act play which also serves as a fascinating theatre history document, for Molière sets his play in his own theatre, and casts it with himself and the members of his own company. In the play, Molière is hurriedly directing a new play to be performed before the King that very afternoon. While nothing in the play should be taken literally, the *Versailles Rehearsals* does portray what must have been close to the actual format of a seventeenth century rehearsal at the Palais Royale.
(*As the curtain rises, there is general confusion; Molière is trying to establish order*)

MOLIÈRE: Ladies, gentlemen, come on now, cut that out! Are you trying to be funny? Listen now.—Oh a plague on you! Listen now, roll call: Monsieur de Brecourt?

BRECOURT: What?

MOLIÈRE: Monsieur de la Grange?

LA GRANGE: What is it?

MOLIÈRE: Monsieur du Croisy?

DU CROISY: If you wish.

MOLIÈRE: Mademoiselle du Parc?

MLLE. DU PARC: What do you want?

MOLIÈRE: Mademoiselle Bejart?

MLLE. BEJART: What's wrong with him?

MOLIÈRE: Mademoiselle de Brie?

MLLE. DE BRIE: What's going on?

MOLIÈRE: Mademoiselle du Croisy?

MLLE. DU CROISY: What's the big problem?

MOLIÈRE: Mademoiselle Hervé?

MLLE. HERVÉ: We're coming, we're coming.

MOLIÈRE: These people are driving me insane! God! You want to turn me into a madman, gentlemen?

BRECOURT: What do you want us to do? We don't know our parts, so you're the one who's going to drive *us* insane if you make us perform today.

MOLIÈRE: Actors are animals! Wild beasts! . . . Ah well, take your places. We have two hours yet, you're already in costume, so let's at least rehearse while we can.

LA GRANGE: How can we play it? We don't even know it!

MLLE. DU PARC: I can't remember a word—not one word. . . .

MOLIÈRE: Listen, we're just wasting time (*To La Grange*): You, be very careful how you play the marquis in your scene with me.

MLLE. MOLIÈRE: Is La Grange always going to play a marquis?

MOLIÈRE (exasperated): Yes, always. How the devil else do we make the play funny? Ridiculous marquises are today's light comedians; they've replaced the old valet-buffoons in modern plays, thank God.

MLLE. BEJART: It's true.

MOLIÈRE (*to Mlle. du Parc*): And as for you, Mademoiselle. . . .

MLLE. DU PARC: My God, I'll be terrible. Why in the world do you give me all these affected parts? . . .

There's no one in the world less affected than I am.

MOLIÈRE: That's true, and it makes you an even better actress to play roles so contrary to your nature! Try to catch the character of your part, and to believe in what you represent. (*Turning to du Croisy*): You play the poet; you must fill the character with yourself. Get that pedantic air that he assumes before the world, the sententious tone, and the precise pronunciation of each syllable; don't miss a single letter of it! (*To Brecourt*): You are the good courtier, as in the last play. That is to say you must play him composed, with a natural voice, and as little gesturing as possible. (*To La Grange*): For you, nothing. . . . .

MOLIÈRE: Come, let us begin. (*To La Grange*): Remember, enter as I told you, with an air of grandeur, fiddling with your wig, and humming a little tune through your teeth: La, la, la, la, la, la.

The rest of you make some room; we need to have space for both marquises, and they're going to be bustling about. Go ahead.

LA GRANGE (*As the marquis, with Molière playing another marquis; to Molière*): "Good morning, marquis."

MOLIÈRE: My God, that's not the voice of a marquis! It has to be louder; and most of these sorts affect mannerisms to distinguish themselves from common folk. (*Molière demonstrates.*) "Good MORNing, marquis." There, do it that way!

The play not only provides a splendid portrait of Molière's rehearsals, it offers a rare view of Molière speaking wholly in his own voice (as actor, character, and playwright combined) on the social and artistic matters that concerned him deeply. While the play is a comedy, it is also an unusually wise piece of social and theatrical criticism.

freedom in the face of almost limitless possibilities leads to a certain existential anxiety which is both chilling and thrilling in its challenge.

DIRECTORIAL FUNCTIONS

Each director defines his own functions afresh with every play. In part, the way in which he defines these functions will depend on the extent to which he is also the *producer* of the play—or, conversely, on the extent to which a separate producer assumes directorial functions.

The producer, a somewhat shadowy figure in the theatre, is a person or institution responsible for the financial support of the theatrical enterprise, an entity that, at least in theory, hires the director but then surrenders all artistic concerns to the director's charge. For many of the well-established directors in professional, academic, and community situations, this assessment is for the most part accurate; however, most producers extend their interest at least partway into the artistic end of their ventures—to the selection of plays and of designers, for example. Some, more obtrusively, involve themselves in casting and interpretation, and some even pay close attention to the rehearsal process. In discussing directorial functions in this section, we are speaking only of those cases in which the director enjoys total or almost total artistic control.

More importantly, the director defines his functions according to his own interests and predilections and those of his co-workers, and according to the play he is directing. Some of this function defining is conscious and deliberate, some of it is not; many of a director's actions simply reflect this natural way of dealing with people, generating ideas, visualizing concepts, and expressing feelings.

Amid this flux of directorial choices two demands are constant: the director's imagination and leadership. Above all else, the director must *imagine* at least the general framework of a finished production, and he must *lead* his fellow workers toward its ultimate realization. That realization may be quite different from his first conception—for the imagination of the director is a continuous factor in the working process, not merely an initiator, and unforeseen developments along the way invariably cause adaptations large and small. Nonetheless, it is by an artful combination of artistic imagining and effective leading that the director makes his specific impact on theatrical art. Thus artistic sensitivity and artistic authority are absolute prerequisites for directorial accomplishment.

For purposes of discussion, individual directorial functions can be viewed as so many separate steps in the process of play production. This process in fact takes place over a period of weeks and sometimes years, and is at no time as orderly as a schematic listing might suggest. Nonetheless, such a listing can help us to see the basic architecture of the directorial process and the progression of decisions and actions that bear upon the final production.

The steps divide easily into phases: a preparatory phase, which involves play selection, concept, staff selection, designing, and casting; and an implementing phase, which involves staging, coaching, pacing, coordinating, and presenting. All of these steps are continuous rather than segmented—a director is conceptualizing the production right up to the last minute, and he is pacing it at the instant he chooses the play—but they are generally centered in a time frame of relatively set order and organization.

Preparatory Phase

The preparatory phase of a production may take days or months or years; it is the director's dream world, wherein ideas germinate and begin to flower. Most directors are "in preparation" for several productions at once: even as one production is in rehearsal others are taking shape in the mind. At various times these preparatory phases move from fancy to plan, and from the world of dreams to the conference room, the rehearsal hall, and the scene shop.

Play Selection

The selection of a script is unquestionably the most critical single act of any director. The play is the essential theatrical product, so to speak: it is the basic element to which the audience responds—or thinks it responds—and it is universally perceived as the core of the theatrical experience. For this reason, play selection is the one directorial decision over which the producer invariably reserves the right of review. This policy holds true the world over: artistic directors of repertory theatres, for example, may have complete freedom in casting, staffing, and staging, but when it comes to selecting playscripts they must always confer with their boards of trustees and governors.

Three basic considerations go into play selection: the director's interest, the interest of the intended audience, and the capability of the director and producer to acquire, conceptualize, and produce the play.

Obviously, the director's interest is important because no director, save by chance, can create theatrical excitement from a script he finds dull and uninteresting. But at the same time it is part of the director's job to seek the excitement latent in a script and to imagine its various theatrical possibilities. Often a director who can envision the improvements to be gained by script revision, adaptation, or reinterpretation can discover plays that otherwise would be ignored; indeed, one of the marks of a great director is his ability to make us recognize the brilliance or beauty of a script we have unwittingly passed over.

The audience's interest is of even greater importance. It is the audience, after all, which makes the theatre possible, and the ability to assess an audience's needs and wants is absolutely fundamental to directing, both for pragmatic reasons (to ensure that an audience turns out to see the play) and for artistic reasons (to ensure that the play is satisfying and pertinent to those who come to see it). For a director does not merely direct the actors and designers; he directs the audience as well, and he gives direction to their feelings and perceptions by the intellectual focus he provides within the production. A director who discounts or ignores the interests—and the intelligence—of the audience stands little chance of creating any genuine theatrical impact.

Play selection that considers audience interest does not necessarily mean a reliance on the "tried and true"; quite the contrary, it means providing the audience with theatrical work that is fresh, fascinating, vigorous, and exciting. For some audiences these ingredients can be provided by musicals, thrillers, and domestic comedies, for others by works of the European avant-garde, for others by plays of social protest and reform, for still others by new plays hot from the typewriters of yet unknown authors. There is an audience for every sort of good play, and it is the director's job to find that audience and make it his own. The audience demand is to be challenged as well as to be confirmed—and in the long run a director who leads his audience is far more likely to gain artistic recognition than the one who either follows the audience or ignores them completely.

The capability of the director to produce the play adequately with his available resources is the final requisite for sound play selection. Can the production rights to the play be acquired? Can a cast be brought together? a production staff? a theatre? Is there enough money? Interest alone—the director's and the audience's—will not buy the scripts, rent the theatre, pay for the electricity, or perform the roles. Considerations of quality must be factored in: are the available actors experienced enough to master the play's style? Is the costume budget adequate for the size of the cast and the period of the play? And finally, does the director understand this play well enough to bring out its ideas? A realistic consideration of one's own capabilities, together with an ability to assess the potential of one's expected collaborators, must be a significant factor in the critical decisions of play selection.

Concept

More has been written in modern times about the director's role in conceptualizing a play than about any other of his tasks; entire books have been devoted to the "Directorial Image," or the creation of the central concept which focuses and informs an entire production.

It is particularly with regard to those concepts which give unexpected and fresh insights into character, story, or style that the modern director has seized the imagination of the public. For example, we remember (despite the perhaps obligatory controversy) Peter Brook's "circus" production of Shakespeare's *A Midsummer Night's Dream*, Clifford Williams' all-male production of Shakespeare's *As You Like It*, and Ellis Rabb's gay-world production of Shakespeare's *The Merchant of Venice*. Although the director runs a considerable risk with this kind of undertaking—for indeed Wild West Romeos, homosexual Hamlets, and Watergate Macbeths have more often been laughable than laudable—a brilliantly appropriate concept can completely captivate an audience by focusing a play production with such pertinence and meaning that it transcends time, place, and stylistic artifice to create profound, moving, and illuminating theatricalization.

The formation of a directorial concept takes place at both the conscious and the unconscious level; it takes place, in fact, whether the director wants it to or

The Ellis Rabb production of Shakespeare's The Merchant of Venice, *produced at American Conservatory Theatre in 1970, featured updated costumes and emphasized a homosexual theme perhaps latent in the play. Antonio (right) was portrayed as an aged and effeminate aristocrat, around whom gathered a bevy of younger men who were effusive in their expressions of love. Although this interpretation scandalized many purists and modern-day puritans, it served to make the intense relationship between Antonio and Bassanio more credible and added a particular piquancy to Antonio's lines: "I am a tainted wether of the flock, / Meetest for death: the weakest kind of fruit / Drops earliest to the ground; and so let me."*

not. There is no avoiding it: it begins when the director first hears of a certain play, and it grows and develops as he reads the play, considers producing it, imagines its effects on an audience, and mentally experiments with possible modes of staging. The directorial concept is a product not only of the director's personal intelligence and vision, but also of his personal experi-ences that relate to the matters portrayed by the play, his personal likes and lusts and appreciations and philosophical leanings, and his desires concerning the audience reaction to his work. The thought processes by which the concept develops are both deductive and inductive, and they are set in motion with the first impressions the director receives from a play.

Concepts can be expressed in many ways. Often they are social statements ("this is a play about tyranny") or philosophical ones ("this is a play about self-knowledge"). Often they involve specific interpretations ("this is a play about a man who cannot make up his mind"), and often they invoke a particular genre of theatricality ("this is a revenge melodrama"). Frequently a director will state his concept psychodramatically ("this is a primitive ritual of puberty"), and frequently the concept is predominantly historical ("a play about fratricide in the Middle Ages") or imagistic ("a play about swords, sables, and skulls") or metatheatrical ("a play about playing"). Often the conception of a play includes a basic tone ("sad," "heroic," "royal"), often a basic texture ("rich," "cerebral," "stark"). Diverse as these examples may seem, they all fall within the range of possibility in conceptualizing a single play: indeed, any

one of them could be applied to Shakespeare's *Hamlet*, and probably at one time or another every one of them has been, as have hundreds of others besides.

The concept is the director's creation, and to a certain extent it remains primarily his own concern. It constitutes his personal organizing focus; his means of keeping his production aimed in a *specific* direction and impervious to deflection by tempting possibilities that might come to mind over the course of a production period. Therefore the concept, expressed succinctly but comprehensive in its implications, becomes the director's starting point in choosing designers and actors, in initiating design discussions, and in setting the direction of the first rehearsals. Directing, of course, means giving *direction*, and the concept is the first and most decisive step in getting a particular production under way.

A great directorial concept has many qualities. It

The director working on the stage in rehearsal. For furniture, a few boxes and chairs; for steps, masking tape pasted down on the floor.

THE DIRECTOR'S approach largely determines the EFFECT of the rehearsal ... as a process of DISCOVERY or as the memorizing of ROUTINE ...

A production requires a POINT-OF-VIEW

Whether "over-directed" or "under-directed," all productions must somehow arrive at PLANNED or ORGANIZED "blocking" ...

... even improvised material is to some extent CHOREOGRAPHED

STEPS

W hen I hear a director speaking glibly of serving the author, of letting a play speak for itself, my suspicions are aroused, because this is the hardest job of all. If you just let a play speak, it may not make a sound. If what you want is for the play to be heard, then you must conjure its sound from it. This demands many deliberate actions and the result may have great simplicity. However, setting out to 'be simple' can be quite negative, an easy evasion of the exacting steps to the simple answer.

It is a strange role, that of the director: he does not ask to be God and yet his role implies it. He wants to be fallible, and yet an instinctive conspiracy of the actors is to make him the arbiter, because an arbiter is so desperately wanted all the time. In a sense the director is always an impostor, a guide at night who does not know the territory, and yet he has no choice—he must guide, learning the route as he goes. Deadliness often lies in wait when he does not recognize this situation, and hopes for the best, when it is the worst that he needs to face.

Peter Brook

is specific, it is appropriate, it is evocative, it is visual, it is theatrical, it is concrete, it is original, and it is also a bit mysterious, a bit amusing. It leads the actors and the designers; and if it is truly inspired, it leads the director himself. Doubtless some play productions manage to attain a measure of success without the benefit of much conceptualization or with concepts flying in and out of the production process like so many blackbirds, but in today's multi-media, future-shocked world theatrical excellence increasingly requires that the director have a strong and persistent conceptual vision.

Designer Selection

The selection of production designers constitutes a vital step in the directorial process simply because both the playwright's script and the director's concept must ultimately be translated into concrete visual effects by a group of human beings of individual temperament, sensibility, and vision. Although the concept is the director's own creation, its refinement and realization finally rest in the hands of his collaborators, whose personal artistry and inclinations will inevitably play an enormous role in the shape and impact of the final product. Hence the selection of these individuals is by no means a mechanical or arbitrary task; it is a central directorial concern of great artistic consequence.

Director-designer teams are common in the theatre; some run for years, encompassing dozens of productions. Resident companies, whether national, regional, or community, often keep a core staff of directors and designers on the payroll year after year to facilitate continuing team relationships; most university theatre groups establish similar long-standing collaborations among faculty artists. Even the more fractious Broadway stage has its collaborations that span years and decades, although these teams work on a show-to-show basis rather than under continuing contract; Broadway directors frequently demand to work with certain designers whose work has proven sympathetic to their own in the past.

Ordinarily the director makes every effort to find for his production designers with whom he feels not only a personal compatibility but also a mutual respect and a synchrony of artistic and intellectual vision. Like all true collaborations, the most effective director-designer relationships result not in simple point-by-point agreement or master-slave autocracy, but in a give and take of ideas, plans, feelings, and hypotheses; a sense of sharing and complementary support.

Apart from these general considerations in designer selection, the director must look more specifically for the designers most appropriate for the play at hand: those whose abilities are best suited to the demands of the script and the director's conception of the production. Sometimes these specific considerations lead in a different direction from that generally indicated—away from the designer with whom the director feels most comfortable and toward the one who promises to be more helpful in narrowing and clarifying the director's concept. A designer's interest in a certain kind of scenic technology, for example, or in historical aestheticism or light cuing, can often help in many ways to sharpen the conceptual focus and provide insights through the design that will serve to inspire the production itself.

Designer selection, then, is a subtle and complicated process. The director chooses *persons*, not colors or fabrics or instruments, and he must select those persons on the basis of his estimate of their ultimate potential in the working conditions he will be able to provide them. Naturally the director will be interested in knowing something about the designer's previous work—and most designers can show prospective directors a résumé of experience and a portfolio of completed designs—but he will also be interested in sounding out the designer's thinking and his artistic sensibility. Like all decisions made in the developmental phase of production, the choice of designers will affect the entire production process; it is a choice that is difficult to retract, and the moment it is made it automatically closes certain directorial options and opens others that could prove either brilliant or catastrophic.

Designing

The design phase of production marks the first step toward transforming vision into actuality: at this stage people turn ideas into concrete visual realizations.

The director's work in designing a production is generally suggestive and corrective; how well he succeeds in this delicate task is highly dependent on the personalities and predilections of the individuals involved. In theory, the director's and designer's goals in this phase are identical: actable space, wearable costumes, and an evocative, memorable, and meaningful appearance of the whole. In practice, each of the principals will have an independent perspective on what is actable, what is memorable, and what is evocative; moreover, each may have a different sense of the importance of sometimes contradictory values. A costume designer, for example, may place a higher value on the appearance of a garment than the director, who may be more concerned with the actor's ability to move in it. A lighting designer may be greatly interested in the aesthetics of murkiness whereas a director may be more anxious that an actor's face be clearly seen at a particular moment. These are the sorts of artistic perspectives that must be reconciled in the design phase, which is essentially a collaboration in which the decisions are acknowledged to be subjective rather than "right" or "wrong"; it is a phase that demands of the director qualities of leadership and artistic inspiration that are as sensitive as any he may ever be called upon to exercise.

The design phase normally takes place in a series of personal conferences between director and designers, sometimes on a one-to-one basis and sometimes in group meetings. These are give-and-take affairs, for the most part, with the director doing most of the giving at the beginning and the designers taking over shortly thereafter. Often the first step is a collective meeting—the "first design conference"—at which the director discusses his concept in detail and suggests some possibilities for its visual realization: colors, images, spaces, textures, and technological implementations. Occasionally the director deliberately usurps a large measure of the designer's role, suggesting (or mandating) specific ground plans, sets, fabrics, and light colors and intensities, and proffering sketches of the finished work. Obviously, however, directors who so invade the designer's creative function risk losing precisely what they are trying to cultivate: the designer's talent and imagination. For this reason most professional directors seek primarily to stimulate, not stultify, the minds and abilities of the designers with whom they have chosen to work.

In the ensuing conferences, which are often conducted one on one and sometimes on an ad hoc basis, designers normally present their own conceptions and eventually provide the director with a progressive series of concrete visualizations: sketches (roughs), drawings, renderings, models, ground plans, working drawings, fabrics, technical details and devices. During these conferences the design evolves through a collaborative sharing, in which the director's involvement may range from minimal to maximal depending on the degree of coherence he perceives between the initial concept and the developing design. Periodically—whenever the overall design effort reaches a stage requiring coordinated planning—full design conferences are called to review and compare current plans for scenery, costume, lighting, and property areas; these conferences afford opportunities for the designers to collaborate with each other instead of simply with the director.

The director's function at this stage of design is to approve or reject, as well as to suggest. As the person who sits at the top of the artistic hierarchy, the direc-

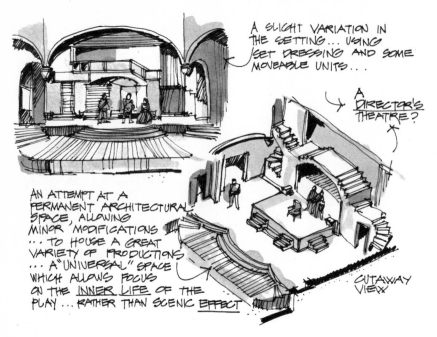

A SLIGHT VARIATION IN THE SETTING... USING SET DRESSING AND SOME MOVEABLE UNITS...

A DIRECTOR'S THEATRE?

AN ATTEMPT AT A PERMANENT ARCHITECTURAL SPACE, ALLOWING MINOR MODIFICATIONS ... TO HOUSE A GREAT VARIETY OF PRODUCTIONS ... A "UNIVERSAL" SPACE WHICH ALLOWS FOCUS ON THE INNER LIFE OF THE PLAY ... RATHER THAN SCENIC EFFECT

CUTAWAY VIEW

Design and direction are inextricably interrelated in these four twentieth-century theatrical conceptions. LEFT–Jacques Copeau's basic design for the Théâtre du Vieux-Colombier (1913). This design, which served for a number of plays, was conceived as a "naked platform" with minimal scenery that would allow the poetic essence of actor's and director's art to shine. BELOW–Andre Gregory's experimental setting for a production of Samuel Beckett's Endgame. The production aimed at creating a voyeuristic relationship between spectator and actor, in a highly unusual physical environment.

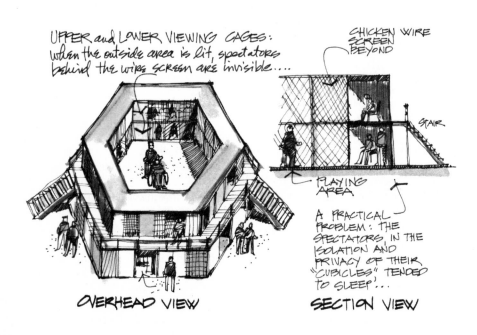

UPPER and LOWER VIEWING CAGES: when the outside area is lit, spectators behind the wire screen are invisible....

CHICKEN WIRE SCREEN BEYOND

STAIR

PLAYING AREA

A PRACTICAL PROBLEM: THE SPECTATORS, IN THE ISOLATION AND PRIVACY OF THEIR "CUBICLES" TENDED TO SLEEP!...

OVERHEAD VIEW

SECTION VIEW

RIGHT—*A staging of the Polish classic* Kordian, *as visualized by its director, Jerzy Grotowski. Spectators (in white) are seated amidst the actors (in black) in a multi-level environment without traditional scenery of any kind.* BELOW—*A highly experimental Brazilian production of Jean Genet's* The Balcony. *Does the design give metaphorical or symbolic or communicative support to the play? All these designs redrawn, by John von Szeliski, from original drawings or photographs, with comments by the illustrator.*

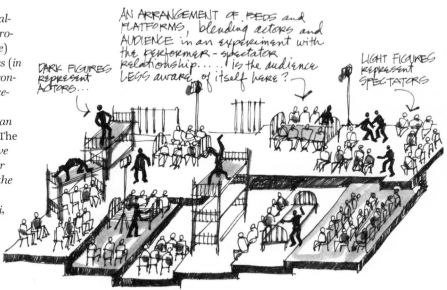

DARK FIGURES REPRESENT ACTORS...

AN ARRANGEMENT OF BEDS and PLATFORMS, blending actors and AUDIENCE in an experiment with the performer-spectator relationship...... is the audience LESS aware of itself here?

LIGHT FIGURES REPRESENT SPECTATORS

THE AUDIENCE SURROUNDS THE VERTICAL CYLINDER OF SPACE ON SEVERAL LEVELS...

THEATRE AS SCENERY OR THE EXPERIENCE OF SPACE...

AN "ARCHITECTURE" WHICH PROBABLY OVERSHADOWS THE PLAY

ACTORS PERFORM WHILE "FLYING" and CLIMBING...

CAN THE SPATIAL EXPERIMENT BE PRIMARY?

tor has the last word on design matters, but that does not mean he can simply command his show into being: theatre design, like any creative process, cannot be summoned forth like an obedient servant. Moreover, wholesale rejection of a designer's work after the initial stages inevitably involves serious time loss and budgetary waste—not to mention the probability of some important staff resignations. For these reasons the directorial effort must be committed from the outset to sound collaborative principles. Once under way, the director-designer collaboration must take the form of shared responsibility in a developing enterprise, not confrontation between warring artists attempting to seize the reins of aesthetic control.

Casting

"Casting is 90 percent of directing." This cliché of the theatre undeniably contains more than a germ of truth.

The people in a play—the actors—not only attract more audience attention than any other aspect of the play; they also represent what the audience *cares* about and will remember the next day. They garner about 90 percent of all the interest an audience expends on a play, and if they squander that interest they can utterly destroy the effectiveness of any theatrical presentation.

When you look at theatre as a medium, you see many individual elements that are standardized and predictable: flats are made according to formula, lighting instruments are factory calibrated to conform to precise specifications, color media are mathematically measured and numbered, and one theatre's black velours are virtually identical to those of another theatre. The one wholly unique ingredient of the theatre—as the audience sees it—is the actor. Actors are people, and as people they are exquisitely individual; moreover the audience, being human itself, is particularly attuned to the actor's human and idiosyncratic uniqueness. We would never mistake the Martin Dysart (in *Equus*) of Richard Burton with the Dysart of Anthony Hopkins, or of Anthony Perkins, or of Alec McCowan. The actor's personality, his physical and vocal characteristics, his technical abilities, and his sheer talent and "presence" weigh mightily in the final realization of every individual performance and in every ensemble of performances. A miscast or untalented or untrained actor can mar the effectiveness of any production even in a minor role; in a major role

a poor performance simply ruins the play. Casting may not, in the end, account for 90 percent of the director's contribution, but there can be no doubt that bad casting renders the rest of his efforts immaterial.

Most casting takes place in auditions, where the actor can be seen and heard by the director and his associates either in a "cold" reading of material from the play to be produced, or in a prepared presentation of previously developed material not necessarily related to the production at hand. Although "star" performers are often cast apart from auditions owing to their known ability to attract audiences to any production, most veteran professional actors regularly submit to auditioning; and the director's ability to detect an incipiently brilliant performance in the contrived audition format is a critical factor in effective casting.

The director looks for many things in an audition. Depending on the specific demands of the play and the rehearsal situation, the director may pay special attention to any or all of the following characteristics: the actor's training and experience, his physical characteristics and vocal technique, his suitability for the style of the play, his perceived ability to impersonate a specific character in the play, his personality traits which seem fitted to the material at hand, his ability to understand the play and its milieu, his personal liveliness and apparent stage "presence," his past record of achievement, his general deportment and attitude, his apparent cooperativeness and "directability" in the context of an ensemble of actors in a collaborative enterprise, and his overall attractiveness as a person with whom one must work closely over the next four to ten weeks. And the director might well be looking for a great many other things besides.

What is ultimately astonishing about the casting process is that most of the decisions based on these complex criteria are made not in agonizing conferences but in two- to four-minute "cold" auditions among perfect strangers! Indeed, this practice is often looked upon as a regrettable theatrical fact, but its very persistence indicates that a great many valid casting judgments can be made in a very short time—provided that time is used with wisdom and sensitivity.

Of course most of the decisions that are made that quickly—in the two- to four-minute initial audition —are "no" decisions; that is, those actors who are immediately perceived as wrong for the play, wrong

The casting of Mark Medoff's play Children of a Lesser God *presents special problems, for the play concerns deaf people. Here, in Gordon Davidson's production at the Mark Taper Forum, deaf actress Phyllis Frelich has been cast in the lead opposite John Rubenstein, who learned sign language during rehearsals. Actress Frelich actually inspired the writing of the play, which moved to Broadway in 1980.*

for the part, or lacking in the desired level of proficiency, are winnowed out. Others may be winnowed out on the very subjective ground of apparent attitude—a dangerous ground because the director might mistake shyness for hostility, or "audition jitters" for an exaggerated reserve.

Actors who survive the first audition are then "read" again, sometimes several times, and at this stage the director involves himself more and more in the audition process, often coaching the actors to determine how rapidly they can acquire the qualities he needs. Such "callbacks" can go on for days and even weeks in the professional theatre, limited only by the union requirement that actors receive pay for the fifth

and ensuing calls; the frequency with which such payments are made amply attests to the care that attends final casting decisions in the professional theatre.

There is good casting and bad casting, of course, and there is also inspired casting. Many of the greatest performances in theatre history have been achieved by actors who at first glance might appear oddly suited to their roles: by Bert Lahr as Estragon in *Waiting for Godot*, for example, or by Laurence Olivier as the title character in John Osborne's *The Entertainer*. Franco Zeffirelli's casting of two inexperienced teenagers in his Royal Shakespeare Company production of *Romeo and Juliet*, much derided at the time, proved to be the spark of genius that made that celebrated production, and the film later adapted from it, two of the most memorable interpretations of the Shakespearean canon. And surely one of the finest King Lears in the American theatre was the late Michael O'Sullivan, who at the time he was cast in the role was still in his twenties and an unknown actor with the San Francisco Actor's Workshop. The ability to perceive an actor's unique and unexpected relationship to a specific role—and to chance that casting in place of a "safer" and more traditional choice—has always been the mark of the most daring and most successful film and play directors.

Implementation Phase

With the play selected and conceptualized, with the designers chosen and the designs under way, and with the actors auditioned and cast, the production moves from its preparatory phase to its implementation. It is here that the meeting described at the beginning of this chapter occurs; it is here in the silence between the completion of a plan and its execution that the blood begins to flow in a *corpus dramaticus* which heretofore lived only in the form of conversation and ink on paper.

The time structure of a production is a variable affair, but its direction is inevitably toward greater and greater tautness; that is, time becomes more and more precious as the play draws nearer and nearer to its opening performance. At the juncture between a production's developmental phase and its implementation a major jump to a tighter time schedule takes place; what could conceivably be leisurely at the conceptual stage now becomes accelerated and intense. Now, because more and more must be done in less and less time, pressure becomes inevitable. Now the director's ability to maintain both leadership and creative inspiration under pressure—always an important element of his professional skill—becomes absolutely crucial.

From the time of that first company meeting, the director controls the focus and consciousness of his entire cast and staff. As head of an ambitious and emotionally consuming enterprise, the director will be the repository of the company's collective artistic hopes—he will also be the focal point for the company's collective frustration, its anxiety, and, on occasion, its despair. He will be the company's shield against the intrusions of an outside world, and he will also be the spokesman for the enterprise to which the company has collectively dedicated itself. His power or influence will not be substantially altered by any attempt he may make to cultivate or repudiate it—it simply comes with the job, and with the need for every theatrical company to have a head, a focus, a direction. The manner in which he uses that power, and the sensitivity with which he now brings his production into being, determines the nature of his own brand of directorial artistry.

Staging

Staging—which essentially involves positioning actors on the set and moving them about in a theatrically effective manner—is certainly the most obvious of directorial functions. It is the one thing a director is always expected to do and to do well, and it is the one he is most often *seen* doing; it is no wonder that traditional textbooks on directing tend to be largely devoted to this function.

The medium of staging is the actor in space and time—with the space defined by the acting area and the settings, and the time defined by the duration of the theatrical event and the dynamics of its dramatic structure. The goals of staging are multiple and complementary: to create focus for the play's themes, to lend credibility to the play's characters, to generate interest in the play's action, to impart an aesthetic wholeness to the play's appearance, to provoke suspenseful involvement in the play's events, and, in general, to stimulate a fulfilling theatricality for the entire production.

The basic architecture of staging is called "blocking," which refers to the timing and placement of a character's entrances, exits, rises, crosses, embraces, and other major movements of all sorts. The "blocking pattern" that results from the interaction of characters in motion provides the framework of an overall staging; it is also the physical foundation of the actors' performance—and many actors have difficulty memorizing their lines until they know the blocking that will be associated with them.

The director may block a play either by pre-planning the movements ("pre-blocking") on paper, or by allowing the actors to improvise movement on a rehearsal set and then "fixing" the blocking sometime before the first performance. Often a combination of these methods is employed, with the director

PAVILION "ABOVE" SCENES

RECEDING BACKGROUND ELEMENTS: "VERONA" LEVELS FOR THE PRINCE, CHORUS, etc

MONTAGUE'S "HOUSE"

CAPULET'S "HOUSE"

INSIDE LOWER "PAVILION"

STAIRS, "WALLS" etc.... INDOOR OR OUTDOOR SCENES

FLOOR PATTERN

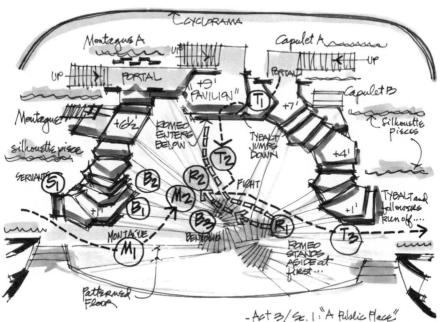

CYCLORAMA

Montague A

Capulet A

UP

UP

PORTAL

UP

+9' "PAVILION"

PORTAL

Capulet B

Montague B

+6½'

ROMEO ENTERS BELOW

T1

+7'

Silhouette pieces

Silhouette piece

T2

TYBALT JUMPS DOWN

+4'

SERVANTS

S1

B2

R2

FIGHT

TYBALT and followers run off....

B1

M2

R1

+1'

MONTAGUE

B3

BENVOLIO

T3

M1

ROMEO STANDS ASIDE at first...

PATTERNED FLOOR

—Act 3/Sc. 1: "A Public Place"

Staging on paper. ABOVE—*A concept sketch for a modern* Romeo and Juliet *production. The aim of the design is to provide a single "unit" setting of openings, levels, and theatrical areas. Many sketches of this sort might be submitted by the designer in the planning process.* BELOW—*The ground plan fashioned from that design, with director's notes on the changing positions of the players during Tybalt's attack on Mercutio.*

*Paul Scofield, as King Lear, rages at Goneril after upsetting the dinner table in Peter
Brook's notable production for the Royal Shakespeare Company, 1962.*

favoring one method or the other depending on the specific demands of the play, the rehearsal schedule, his rapport with the acting company, or on his own stage of preparation: complex or stylized plays and settings and short rehearsal periods usually dictate a great deal of pre-blocking; simple domestic plays and experienced acting ensembles are often accorded more room for improvisation. Each method can pro-duce highly commendable results in the right hands and at the right time; both can present serious prob-lems if misapplied or ineptly handled.

For the most part, the blocking of a play is "hid-den" in the play's action; indeed, it tends to be effec-tive insofar as it is *not* noticed, and insofar as it simply brings other values into play and focuses the au-dience's attention on significant aspects of the drama.

By providing a physical enhancement of the dramatic action and lending variety to the play's visual presentation, a good blocking pattern can play a large role in creating theatrical life and excitement.

But beyond this, there are moments when inspired blocking choices can create astonishing theatrical effects—effects that are not "hidden" at all but are so surprising and shocking that they compel intense consideration of specific dramatic moments and their implications. Such a *coup de théâtre* was achieved, for example, by director Peter Brook in his celebrated 1962 production of *King Lear*, when Paul Scofield, as Lear, suddenly rose and, with one violent sweep of his arm, overturned the huge oaken dining table at which he had been seated and sent pewter mugs crashing to the floor as he raged at his daughter Goneril's treachery. This stunning action actually led to a re-evaluation of the character of both Lear and Goneril, and of the relationship between this tempes-tuous and sporadically vulgar father and his socially ambitious daughter.

Some plays require quite specialized blocking for certain scenes—for duels, for example, or dances. Such scenes demand more than nuts-and-bolts blocking, and are frequently directed by specialists, such as dueling masters or choreographers, working in concert with the director. These specialized situations are not at all rare in the theatre—almost every play that was written before the last century includes a duel or a dance or both—and the ability to stage an effective fight scene or choreographic interlude (or at least to supervise the staging of one) is certainly a requisite for any director who aspires to work beyond the strictly realistic theatre.

"Business" is a theatre term that refers to small-scale movement—that which a character performs within the larger pattern of entrances and crosses and exits. Mixing a cocktail, answering a telephone, ad-

Acting "business" creates mood and atmosphere as well as subtle characterization. Here Trish Hawkins and Judd Hirsch smoke cigarettes in 1979 production of Lanford Wilson's Talley's Folley *at Mark Taper Forum Theatre of Los Angeles. The manner in which actor holds cigarette, inhales or puffs smoke, and flicks ashes, gives clues to character's personality.*

> I
> t is most important that the individuality of the actor, whatever be
> the character he is to interpret, be preserved, for individuality is an
> essential qualification of a great artist. So, at the outset, I suggest
> little to my people, in order to make them suggest more. I appeal to
> their imagination, emotion, and intelligence, and draw from them all I can.
> When I can get no more from them I then give them all there is in me. I coax
> and cajole, or bulldoze and torment, according to the temperament with
> which I have to deal.
>
> David Belasco

justing a tie, shaking hands, fiddling with a pencil, winking an eye, and drumming on a tabletop are all "bits of business" which can lend a character credibility, depth, and fascination. Much of the stage business in a performance is originated by the actor—usually spontaneously in the course of rehearsal—although it may be stimulated by a directorial suggestion or command. The director ultimately must select from among the rehearsal inventions and determine what business will become a part of the finished performance; when this determination is made, bits of business become part of the blocking plan.

Staging, then, in the largest sense, includes both hidden and bold blocking effects, specialized movements and small idiosyncratic behaviors, all combined into a complex pattern that creates meaning, impact, and style. Skillful staging unites the design elements of a production with the acting, creating an omnidynamic spatial interaction between actors, costumes, scenery, and audience, infusing the stage with life. Getting a play "on its feet," as the theatrical jargon puts it, is usually the first step in making it breathe; and the best staging is that which gives the actors the chance to breathe the air of the playwright's world and to awaken to the true vitality of the playwright's characters.

Actor-coaching

The director is the actor's coach, and in practice the director is likely to spend the largest share of his time exercising this particular function. His coaching begins with his first meeting with the cast.

Initially, it is the director who conveys the direction the production is expected to take: the concept, the interpretation, the intended "look" and style of the theatrical product. It is also the director who determines the schedule and process of work that will lead up to that final product. The director is the rehearsal leader; he decides what activities—discussions, improvisations, games, exercises, lectures, research, blocking, or polishing—will occupy each rehearsal period, and it is the director who leads such activities with an eye to their ultimate goal.

Further, like the manager of an athletic team, the director is responsible for stimulating the best efforts of his cast, and for instilling in them a high regard for teamwork (which in the theatre is called "ensemble") as well as for individual craft excellence and artistry. And, because the work of the theatre inevitably demands of the actor a good measure of emotional, psychological, even irrational investment, the director has an opportunity (if not an obligation) to provide an atmosphere in which the actor can feel free to liberate his powers of sensitivity and creativity. Good directors lead their cast; great directors inspire them.

The ways in which directors go about coaching actors are altogether various, and probably more dependent on personality than on planning. Some directors are largely passive; they either "block and run," in the jargon of commercial theatre, or function primarily as a sounding board for actors' decisions about intention, action, or business. Conversely, there are directors closer to the popular stereotype, mercurial directors whose approaches at times verge on the despotic: they cajole, bully, plead, storm, and rage at their actors, involve themselves in every detail of motive and characterization, and turn every rehearsal into a mixture of acting class, group therapy session, and religious experience. Both methods, as experience teaches, can produce theatrical wizardry, and both can fail utterly; probably the determining factors either way are the strength of the director's ideas and the extent to which the cast is willing to accept his authority.

Too little direction, of course, can be as stultifying to an actor as too much; the passive director runs the risk of defeating an actor's performance by failing to confirm it; that is, by withholding constructive response. Similarly, the extremely active director may, in his whirlwind of passion, overwhelm the actor's own creativity and squelch his efforts to build a sensitive performance, thereby condemning the production to oppressive dullness. For these and other reasons, most directors today strive to find a middle ground somewhere between task-mastery and suggestion, from which they can provide the actor with both a goal and a disciplined path toward it while yet maintaining an atmosphere of creative freedom. Directors need not be actors themselves, but they must understand the paradoxes and ambiguities inherent in that art if they are to help the actor fashion a solid and powerful performance. The greatest acting braves the unknown and flirts continuously with danger (the danger of exposure, of failure, of transparency, of artifice); the director must give the actor a careful balance of freedom and guidance if he hopes to foster the confidence that leads to that kind of acting. Directors who are insensitive to this requirement—no matter how colorful their stormings and coaxings or how rational their discussions of the playwright's vision—are virtually certain to forfeit the performance rewards that arise from the great actor-director collaborations.

Pacing

Pace is perhaps the only aspect of a theatrical production for which general audiences and theatre critics alike are certain to hold the director accountable. Frequently, newspaper reviews of productions devote whole paragraphs of praise or blame to the actors and designers and evaluate the director's contribution solely in terms of the play's pace: "well-paced" and "well-directed" are almost interchangeable plaudits in the theatre critic's lexicon; and when a critic pronounces a play "slow" or "dragging," everyone understands he is firing a barrage at the director.

To the novice director (or critic), pace appears to be primarily a function of the rate at which lines are

---

"THIS IS HOW IT'S DONE!"

Publicity photographs taken in rehearsal frequently show a director on stage with a few actors, demonstrating a bit of business and "showing them how it's done." This kind of publicity has probably fostered a certain misunderstanding of the director's role among the general public, for demonstration is only a part of directing, and a distinctly small part at that. Indeed, some directors scrupulously avoid it altogether.

Demonstration as a way of teaching an actor his role has a long history in the theatre, and was a particularly common practice in those periods when directing was carried out chiefly by retired actors. Even today, young actors rehearsing for classical plays at the *Comédie Française* (founded in 1680) are expected to learn their parts by mimicking the performance of their elders down to the last detail of inflection, tone,

gesture, and timing. And of course many contemporary American directors occasionally give "line readings" to an actor, or demonstrate the precise manner of gesturing, moving, sitting, or handling a prop, if they perceive that a specific desired behavior might not come naturally from the actor himself.

But demonstration as an *exclusive* method of coaching an actor in his role is very much a thing of the past. Most contemporary directors make far greater use of discussion, suggestion, and improvisation. These methods seek to address the inner actor and to encourage him to distill his performance out of self-motivated passions and enthusiasms. Because they know that a purely imitative performance is all too likely to be a mechanical performance, today's directors tend to rely on more creative methods than "getting up there and showing how it's done."

---

said; hence a great many beginning directors attempt to make their productions more lively simply by instructing everyone to speak and move at a lively clip: "More energy!" and "Make it happen faster!" are somewhat generalized expressions of a director's suspicion that his production somehow lacks the proper pace.

But pace is fundamentally determined by a complex and composite time structure that must be developed to accommodate many variables, such as credibility, suspense, mood, style, and the natural rhythms of life: heartbeat, respiration, the duration of a spontaneous sob and an unexpected laugh. How much time is properly consumed, for example, by a moment of panic? a pregnant pause? a flash of remembrance? an agonized glance? a quick retort? These are the ingredients of pace, and are not subject to the generalized "hurry-up" of the director who has not first discovered the pattern of rhythms inherent in a play.

The pace of a play should be determined largely by the quantity and quality of the information it conveys to the audience, and the director must decide how much time the audience requires to assimilate that information. In a farce, of course, the audience needs almost no time to synthesize information—therefore, farce generally is propelled rapidly, with the audience virtually assaulted with information coming as fast as the actors can get it out. A psychological drama, on the other hand, may require of the audience a deeper understanding of its characters and issues; sympathy is engendered as we have an opportunity to compare the characters' lives with our own, to put ourselves in their situations, and to engage in introspection even as we observe the action on stage. Similarly, political drama commonly demands of us a critical inquiry into our own societies and our own lives as part of our understanding of what is happening on stage; this form too demands time to linger over certain perfectly poised questions —and the pace of a production must give us that time.

As a symphony is composed of several movements, so a well-paced theatrical production will inevitably have its adagio, andante, and allegro tempos. Faster tempos tend to excite, to bedazzle, and to sharpen audience attention; slower ones give the audience a chance to consider and to augment the play's actions and ideas with their own reflections.

Often directors speak in terms of "setting up" an audience with a rapid pace and then delivering a "payoff" with a powerful, more deliberately paced dramatic catharsis. The sheer mechanics of theatrical pacing demand the greatest skill and concentration on the part of both actor and director, and for both the perfection of dramatic timing (and most notably comic timing) is a mark of great theatrical artistry.

Directors vary in their manner of pacing plays, of course. Some wait until final rehearsals and then, martinet-like, stamp out rhythms on the stage floor with a stick, or clap their hands in the back of the house. Some work out intricate timing patterns in the very first rehearsals and explore them in great detail with the actors as to motivation, inner monologue, and interpersonal effect. Directorial intervention of some sort is almost always present in the achievement of an excellent dramatic pace; it rarely occurs spontaneously. Actors trained to the realist manner often tend to work through material slowly, and to savor certain moments all out of proportion to the information they convey; actors trained in a more technical manner just as often are "off to the races" with dialogue, leaving the audience somewhat at sea about the meaning or importance of the matters at hand. And when a variety of actors, trained in different schools, come together in production for the first time, they can create such an arrhythmic pace that the play becomes virtually unintelligible until the director steps in to guide and control the tempo.

Coordinating

In the final rehearsals the director's responsibility becomes more and more one of coordination: of bringing together the concept and the designs, the acting and the staging, the pace and the performance. Now all the production elements which were developed separately must be judged, adjusted, polished, and perfected in their fuller context. Costumes must be seen under lights, staging must be seen against scenery, pacing must include the shifting of sets, acting must coalesce with sound amplification, and the original concept must be re-examined in light of its emerging realization. Is the theme coming across? Are the actions coming across? Can the voices be heard and understood? Do the costumes read? Is the play focused? Is the play interesting? Do we care about the characters? about the themes? about anything? Does the production seem to *work*?

Timing and wholeness are governing concepts in this final coordinating phase of production. In his assessment of the play's overall timing, the director must be prepared to judge the play's effectiveness against its duration, and to modify or even eliminate those parts of the production which simply overextend the play's potential for communicating information, feelings, or ideas. Last-minute cutting is always a painful process—certainly much labor and creative spirit have gone into those parts that will be cut—but many a production has been vastly improved by judicious pruning at this time. And in the interest of providing wholeness—that quality which unifies a play and gives it the stamp of taste and aesthetic assurance—the best and bravest directors are willing in these final moments to eliminate those elements that fail to cohere with the play's overall appearance and significance. Often these elements hold a special meaning for the director; they may even have figured into his earliest conception of the production. But now, in the cold light of disciplined analysis, they look painfully like directorial indulgence or extraneous showing off. The best directors are those who can be most rigorous with themselves at this stage, for they are the ones who are capable not only of generating ideas but also of refining and focusing artistic form.

In the final rehearsals—the "technical rehearsals" when scenery, lighting, and sound are added, and the "dress rehearsals" when the actors don costumes and make-up for the first time—the director arrives at a crossroads: henceforth he will remain fundamentally responsible for every final decision about the timing and balance of theatrical elements, but he must now "give over" the production to the actors and technicians who will execute it. Beyond this junction he will be consumed, as it were, by his own production: he will disappear within it in a matter of days, and it will reflect his conceptions and directorial skills without reflecting his own *persona*. After contributing to everything that appears upon his stage and initiating much of it, he must accept the fact that he will not be recognized in any single moment, any single act, any single costume or lighting cue. In these final rehearsals the director's presence normally becomes more a force for organization than a source of inspiration; typically, he now can be seen, clipboard in hand, de-livering hundreds of last-minute "notes" to actors, technicians, and stage managers in an effort to give the production that extra finesse which distinguishes the outstanding from the mediocre.

And what an extraordinary change of power has taken place between the first meeting of the cast and director and these final days! Whereas earlier the director held the entire production in his head and the cast waited in awe and expectation, now the actors hold the play in their heads and everyone confronts the unknowns of the play's reception. The actors have a new master now: the audience. It is in these days that even the most experienced actor confronts his fundamental nakedness in performance: it is he, the actor, who must face the audience, and he must do it without benefit of directorial protection, with nothing to shield him save his costume, his character, and his lines. At these times the actor comes to see the director as no longer leader but partner, no longer father but friend. He may indeed experience a certain feeling of betrayal; the director, after all, has abandoned him to face the audience alone, just as Good Deeds accompanied Everyman only to the brink of the grave. But then acting, like death, is a trial that cannot be shared.

Presenting

It is an axiom of the theatre that nobody is more useless on opening night than the director. If all has progressed without major catastrophe and the production has successfully been "given over" to those who will run it and perform in it, the director's task on opening night consists chiefly in seeing and evaluating the production and gauging the audience response. This night may, of course, prove to be nothing but a calm between storms, and in the professional theatre it may simply be the first of a series of opening nights, one calculated to serve as a guide to future rehearsals, rewritings, and rethinkings; still, at this time the major work has reached a stopping point and invariably the director must shift his perspectives accordingly.

The director in this last phase sometimes takes on certain responsibilities of a somewhat paratheatrical nature. For example, he might write directorial "notes" for use in newspaper stories and interviews. He may take an interest in the house management, the dress of the ushers, the lobby decorations, the concession stands, or the "dressing of the house" (the spacing of spectators in a less than full house); he may also play an active role as audience member by greeting patrons, chatting with critics, or leading the laughter and applause—although it should be stated that all of these activities are more common in community theatres than in professional ones.

More central to the directorial function in this final stage is the director's continuing evaluation of every production element in an effort to improve the audience impact. This may lead to changes at any time during the run of a play. In the professional theatre, new productions commonly go through a tryout period of two weeks or more—up to a year in a few cases—when the play is rehearsed and re-rehearsed daily between performances and material is deleted, revised, restaged, and freshly created in response to audience reception. Some quite famous plays have succeeded only because of such "doctoring" during tryout periods, and it is not at all uncommon in the contemporary commercial theatre for a director to be replaced during this phase in order to accelerate revision.

Even after the final opening, however, and throughout the run of a play, most directors attend performances periodically and follow up their visits with notes to the actors—either to encourage them to maintain spontaneity or to discourage them from revising the original directorial plan. One perhaps apocryphal show business story has it that the American director George Abbot once posted a rehearsal call late in a play's run in order to "take out the improvements."

Just as the actor might feel alone and somewhat betrayed in those empty moments prior to opening performance, so might the director feel a twinge of apartness at the ovation that follows the first performance. For it is in that curtain call ovation that the audience takes over the director's critic/mentor function and the director is consigned to his former anonymity. The actor, heady with the applause, suddenly remembers that it is he who provides the essential ingredient of theatre, while the director, cheering his protege from the back of the house, suddenly realizes he is now just one of the crowd, one witness among many to the realization of his own intangible and now remote plans and ideas. In the professional theatre, it is at precisely this moment that the director's contract expires—a fitting reminder of the "giving over" that occurs in the direction of all plays. Only those directors who can derive genuine satisfaction from creating out of the medium of others' performance will thrive and prosper in directorial pursuits; those who aspire to public acclaim and adulation will most likely face perpetual frustration as practitioners of this all-encompassing and yet all-consuming art.

THE TRAINING OF A DIRECTOR

Traditionally, directors have come to their craft from a great many areas, usually after achieving distinction in another theatrical discipline: for example, Elia Kazan was first an actor, Gower Champion was a choreographer, Harold Prince was a producer, Peter Hunt was a lighting designer, Franco Zeffirelli was a scene designer, Robert Brustein was a drama critic, Harold Pinter was a playwright, and Mike Nichols was an improvisational comedian. Still, in addition to a specialty, most of these directors have brought to their art a comprehensive knowledge of the theatre in its various aspects. Having distinction in one field is important chiefly insofar as it gives a director a certain confidence and authority—and as it gives others a confidence in his exercise of that authority. But it is comprehensive knowledge that enables a director to collaborate successfully with actors, designers, managers, playwrights, and technicians with facility and enthusiasm.

New directors entering the profession today are more likely than not to have been trained in a dramatic graduate program or conservatory—and often they have supplemented this training with an apprenticeship at a repertory theatre. One of the most remarkable recent developments in the American theatre has been the emergence of a cadre of such expertly trained directors: young men and women with a broad understanding of the theatre and a disciplined approach to directorial creativity.

A well-trained director will possess, in addition to the craft mastery of staging, actor-coaching, pacing, and production coordinating, a strong literary imagination and an ability to conceptualize intellectually and visually. He will be sensitive to interpersonal relationships, which will play an important role in both the onstage and offstage activities under his control. He will have a sound working knowledge of the history of the theatre, the various styles and masterworks of dramatic literature, the potential of various theatre technologies, and the design possibilities inherent in the use of theatrical space. He will have at his command resources in music, art, literature, and history; he will be able to research plays and investigate production possibilities without starting at absolute zero; and he will be able to base ideas and conceptions on sound social, psychological, and aesthetic understandings.

All these rather advanced skills can be effectively taught in a first-rate drama program, and for that reason today's top-flight theatre directors, more than any other group of stage artists, are likely to have studied in one or another of the rigorous drama programs now in progress across the country. The accomplished director is perhaps the one all-around "expert" of the theatre; this is not to deride his function as a creative and imaginative force, but to emphasize his responsibility over a broad and highly complex enterprise. Nothing is truly irrelevant to the training of a director, for virtually every field of knowledge can be brought to bear upon theatre production. The distinctiveness of any production of the contemporary theatre is in large measure a reflection of the unique but comprehensive training of its *director*, who is responsible not only for the overall initiative and corrective authority that infuse the production, but also for the personal vision which inspires its singular *direction*.

The audience surrounds the action in Tyrone Guthrie's 1963 production of
The Three Sisters *at the Guthrie Theatre in Minneapolis.*

CONCLUSION:
THE AUDIENCE AS CRITIC

I t is eleven o'clock; the lights fade a final time, the curtain falls, the audience applauds, and the play is over. The actors go back to their dressing rooms, take off their make-up, and depart. The audience disperses into the night.

But the theatrical experience is not over; in important ways, it is just beginning.

A play does not begin and end its life on a stage. A play begins in the mind of its creator, and its final repository is in the minds and memories of its audiences. The stage is simply a focal point where the transmission takes place—in the form of communication we know as theatrical performance.

After the performance is over, the play's impact remains. It is something to think about, talk about, fantasize about, and live with for hours, days, and years to come. Some plays we remember all our lives; plays whose characters are as indelible in our memories as the real beings who populate our personal world, plays whose settings are more deeply experienced than most of the locales of our growing up, and plays whose themes abide as major object lessons behind our decision making. Should we take up arms against a sea of troubles? Can we depend on the kindness of strangers? What's in a name? Shall we be as defiant as Prometheus, as determined as Oedipus, as passionate as Romeo, as accepting as Winnie, as noble as Hecuba? What is Hecuba to us, or we to Hecuba?

Plays enter our minds and memories through meaning, through effect, through aesthetics, through wit, and through entertainment. They remain with us by dint of their vividness, their cogency, their honesty, their profundity, their beauty, their eloquence, their excitement.

CRITICAL PERSPECTIVES

What makes a play particularly successful? What gives a theatrical production significance and impact, and what makes it unforgettable? What should we be looking for when we read a play or see a dramatic production? We have, of course, complete freedom in making up our minds, for response, by definition, can never be dictated: the price of theatrical admission carries with it the privilege of thinking what we wish and responding as we will. But four perspectives can be particularly useful in helping us to focus our response to any individual theatrical event. These perspectives relate to a play's social significance, its human or personal significance, its artistic quality, and its capacity to entertain.

A Play's Relation to Society

Theatre, as we have seen in the preceding pages, is always tied to its culture. Many theatres have been directly created or sustained by governments and ruling elites: the Greek theatre of the fifth century B.C. was a creation of the state, the medieval theatre was generated by the Church, the township, and the municipal craft guilds, and the Royal Theatre was a direct extension of a monarchical reign; even in modern times government often serves as sponsor or cosponsor or silent benefactor of the theatre. But the intellectual ties between a theatre and its culture extend well beyond merely political concerns: thematically, the theatre has at one time or another served as an arena for the discussion of virtually every social issue imaginable. In modern times, for example, we have seen such issues as alcoholism, homosexuality, venereal disease, prostitution, public education, racial prejudice, capital punishment, thought control, prison reform, character assassination, civil equality, political corruption, and military excess examined repeatedly in theatrical productions, and from different points of view. The best of these productions have presented the issues in all their complexity, and have proffered solutions not as dogma but as food for thought—for great theatre has never sought to purvey pure propaganda. The playwright is not necessarily brighter than the audience, nor even better informed: he and his fellows, however, may be able to focus public debate, stimulate dialogue, and turn public attention and compassion toward social injustices, inconsistencies, and irregularities. The theatre artist traditionally is something of a nonconformist; his point of view is generally to the left or right of the social mainstream, and his perspective is of necessity somewhat unusual. Thus the theatre is in a strong position to force and focus public confrontation with social issues, and at its best it succeeds in bringing the audience into touch with their own thoughts and feelings about those issues.

A Play's Relation to the Individual

The theatre is a highly personal art, in part because it stems from the unique (and often oblique) perspectives of the playwrights who initiate it and the theatre artists who execute it, and in part because its audiences all through history have decreed that it be so.

The greatest plays transcend the social and political to confront the hopes, concerns, and conflicts faced by all humankind: personal identity, courage, compassion, fantasy versus practicality, kindness versus self-serving, love versus exploitation, and the inescapable problems of growing up and growing old, of wasting and dying. These are some of the basic themes of the finest of plays, and of our own stray thoughts as well: the best plays simply link up with our deepest musings and help us to put our random ideas into some sort of order or philosophy. The theatre is a medium in which we of the audience invariably see reflections of ourselves, and in the theatre's best achievments those reflections lead to certain discoveries and evaluations concerning our own individual personalities and perplexities.

A Play's Relation to Art

The theatre is an art of such distinctive form that even with the briefest exposure we can begin to develop certain aesthetic notions as to what that form should be. We quickly come to know—or think we know—honesty on stage, for without being experts we feel we can recognize false notes in acting, in playwriting, and even in design.

Beyond that, we can ask a number of questions of ourselves. Does the play excite our emotions? Does it stimulate the intellect? Does it surprise us? Does it thrill us? Does it seem complete and all of a piece? Are the characters credible? Are the actors convincing? enchanting? electrifying? Does the play seem alive or dead? Does it seem in any way original? Is it logically sound? Is the action purposeful, or is it gratuitous? Are we transported, or are we simply waiting for the final curtain? In the last analysis, does the play fit our idea of what a play should be—or, even better, does it force us, by its sheer luster and power, to rewrite our standards of theatre?

Aesthetic judgments of this sort are necessarily comparative, and they are subjective as well. What seems original to one member of the audience may be old hat to another; what seems an obvious gimmick to a veteran theatregoer can seem brilliantly innovative to a less jaded appetite. None of this should intimidate us. An audience does not bring absolute standards into the theatre—and certainly such standards as it brings are not shared absolutely. The theatrical response is a composite of many individual reactions. But each of us has an aesthetic sensibility and an aesthetic response. We appreciate colors, sights, sounds, words, actions, behaviors, and people that please us. We appreciate constructions that seem to us balanced, harmonic, expressive, and assured. We appreciate designs, ideas, and performances that exceed our expectations, that reveal patterns and viewpoints we didn't know existed. We take great pleasure in sensing underlying *structure*: a symphony of ideas, a sturdy architecture of integrated style and action.

A Play as Entertainment

Finally, we look upon all theatre as entertainment, for in truth every play is possessed of a certain entertainment value.

Great theatre is never less than pleasing. Even tragedy delights. People go to see *Hamlet* not for purposes of self-flagellation or to wallow in despair, but to revel in the tragic form and to experience the liberating catharsis of the play's murderous finale. Hamlet himself knows the thrill of staged tragedy:

HAMLET: What players are they?
ROSENCRANTZ: Even those you were wont to take such delight in, the tragedians . . .

What is this entertainment value that all plays possess? Most obviously the word "entertainment" suggests "amusement," and so we think immediately of the hilarity of comedy and farce; indeed, most of the literature regarding theatrical entertainment concentrates on the pratfalls and gags which have been part of the comic theatre throughout its history. But entertainment goes far beyond humor. Another definition for "entertainment" is "that which holds the attention." This definition casts quite a bit more light on our question. It means that entertainment includes the enchantment of romance, which stimulates our curiosity about our own emotions and longings. It takes in the dazzle of brilliant debate, witty epigram, and bit-

ing repartee; the exotic appeal of the foreign and the grotesque; the beauty and grandeur of spectacle; the nuance and crescendo of a musical or rhythmic line. It accommodates suspense and adventure, the magic of sex appeal and the splendor of sheer talent. Finally, of course, it includes any form of drama that profoundly stirs our feelings and heightens our awareness of the human condition. It is no wonder that Hamlet delights in the performance of tragedians—and that we delight in *Hamlet*—for the concatenation of ideas, language, poetry, feelings, and actions that constitute great tragedy confers one of life's truly sublime entertainment experiences.

Indeed, the theatre is a veritable storehouse of pleasures, not only for the emotional, intellectual, spiritual, and aesthetic stimulation it provides, but also for its intrinsic social excitement. It is a favored public meeting place for people who care about each other—"two on the aisle" implies more than a choice seating location: it implies companionship in the best theatrical experience. For the theatre is a place to commune in an especially satisfying way with strangers. When in the course of a dramatic performance we are gripped by a staging of romantic passion, or stunned by a brilliantly articulated argument, or moved by an inexpressibly touching denouement, the thrill is enhanced a hundredfold by the certainty that we are not alone in these feelings, that possibly every member of the audience has been stirred to the same response. Theatre, in its essence, serves to rescue mankind from an intellectual and emotional aloneness; and therein lies its most profound "entertainment" value.

CRITICAL FOCUS

These four perspectives on the theatre—on its social, personal, artistic, and entertainment values—are all implicit in the responses of any audience, regardless of its training or theatrical sophistication, to any play. These are the four major angles from which we all view, evaluate, and judge a play. And we all do *judge* the plays we see, for our involvement with a play automatically generates a certain comparison: a weighing of the play's merits against those of other plays, or against personal experiences. And when we engage in this comparison, this weighing of a play's

The theatre is a *subject*. That at last is why the critic writes and why the reader, even the one who rarely goes to the theatre, reads. The theatre is a complex, significant, reflective, and implicative subject. The consumer-service motive or function is quite secondary, though, like any other human being, the critic likes to see his enthusiasms prosper. Much more important . . . is the realization that he works in a concurrent plane to the theatre, not a congruent plane. He is in a kind of para-reality to the theatre's reality. His criticism is a body of work obviously related to but still distinct from what the theatre does; possibly influential, possibly not, but no more closely connected than is political science to the current elections. The critic learns that, one the one hand, there is the theatre, with good and bad productions, and on the other hand, there is criticism which ought to be good about both good and bad productions. Life is the playwright's subject, and he ought to be good about its good and bad people; the theatre is the critic's subject, and he ought to be good about its good and bad plays.

. . . The theatre critic spends most of his time with trash. But the trash is as much a part of his subject as the non-trash. . . . Part of his function is to make sure that false messiahs and peddlers and charlatans are shown as such. Hope—non-delusionary, non-inflationary, non-self-aggrandizing hope—is the core of the critic's being: hope that good work will recurrently arrive, hope that (partly by identifying trash) he may help it to arrive, hope that he may have the excitement and privilege of helping to connect that good work with its audience.

Stanley Kauffman

---

merits, we are exercising (whether we know it or not) the art of criticism.

Criticism is a paratheatrical activity: it takes place outside the pure dramatic experience, but it plays a major role in making that experience intelligible and applicable. Criticism is the focused opinion that fosters incisive thinking and talking and writing about plays and players and enables us to discern the meaning and importance of individual dramatic works as well as the ultimate significance of the theatrical experience itself.

Criticism in the theatre takes place at both the amateur and professional levels, among the least informed as well as the best informed and most highly disciplined. It begins the moment the curtain rises on Act I, and it continues in the theatre bar during intermission, in the coffeehouses where theatregoers gather for late-night post-performance discussions, and in the published reviews that can be found in daily newspapers, weekly magazines, and quarterly journals of opinion. Even then it need not end. The plays of Shakespeare and Sophocles, for example, are still being re-examined and re-critiqued, hundreds of years after their inception, by serious theorists and scholars as well as by novices and dilettantes.

Criticism is among us always; it is a running counterpart to theatrical creation.

What is professional criticism? At its best, it is analysis, discernment, and informed evaluation carried to a high art. At this level it affords a series of observations, comparisons, and deductions that genuinely sharpen the audience's perception of a play's significance, enhance their appreciation of its performance, and lead them to a full understanding of the intellectual and emotional complexity of its characters and themes. Good criticism often invites an audience to a worthwhile and original play they may otherwise overlook, and just as often it warns them away from a derivative and shallow play whose commercial success owes chiefly to an inflated advertising budget. Fine criticism can illuminate a play's text and amplify its background; it can also serve as a bridge between artist and audience, making the artistic vision publicly accessible and meaningful and, in the process, raising the general creative consciousness vis-à-vis the theatre. In doing all this, the critic performs an invaluable service to both the public and the art.

But at its worst, professional criticism can be little more than hot air and bad temper, the last refuge of failed and embittered artists and intellectuals whose pronouncements serve no purpose but to vent spite and jealousy or to show off their own knowledge, cleverness, and power to undermine. Given these diverse possibilities, it is probably unnecessary to point out that professional criticism is a subject about which artists and audiences may strongly disagree.

There will always be recognized drama critics—if for no other reason than that audiences are always going to want to talk about the plays they see, and some of them will talk better than others. A wish to evaluate and compare seems, in any case, to be intrinsic to the theatrical experience. The ancient Greeks frankly considered drama a competition right from the start, and the last day of every Dionysian festival was given over to the award of prizes to the authors and actors whose work most pleased the judges. It is clear from the comedies of Aristophanes that talking about plays—dramatic criticism, in other words—was a familiar activity in fifth-century Athens, and comparing playwrights was virtually a national pastime. The first mention of Shakespeare's name, apart from court records, is contained in a scathing criticism of his newfangled style, and Molière lived and worked in a welter of formal and informal criticism, to which he often replied right in his plays. Today, some professional and published critics enjoy a celebrity almost equal to that of the best-known playwrights— they are virtual high priests of theatrical taste to whom the culture turns increasingly for guidance and stimulation.

This has not gone altogether unresented. Not all of us like to be told what to think, how to feel, or when to laugh. Theatre artists most certainly do not like to be told by outside evaluators how to write plays or how to act in them. Berating critics is a common sport among theatre artists; indeed, even minor acts of violence against critics have been condoned in some quarters. Often it is alleged by both artist and audience that the critic acts more as a barrier than a bridge between the public and the artist's work.

Still, criticism is an essential in the theatre, for it is simply an extrapolation of the critical mind we *all* take with us wherever we go. Discernment and evaluation are inevitable adjuncts of the theatrical experience: we simply cannot *not* discern, and we cannot *not* evaluate what is set before our eyes. And we cannot and should not keep quiet about our opinions. Insofar as the theatre is presented as a mirror of our times and the characters in plays as mirrors of ourselves, we cannot fail to notice when our reflection comes out distorted, or cloudy, or incomprehensible, or cheapened by what we see as gratuitous over-elaboration. Insofar as theatre is a social forum, it is a forum that includes *us* as principal members. It is part of *us* that the playwright is trying to write about and the actors are trying to embody, and we want to see a fair depiction of ourselves, our fears, our fantasies, and our visions of reality. We come to the theatre with hopes and expectations: we want to be exalted with a dramatic vision of our life, of human life. And if indeed that happens—well, we want to savor it, to think about it, to talk about it, even to shout about it. But whatever happens, we want to tell our friends. Therein lies the germ of dramatic criticism: it is theatrical excitement translated into articulated public opinion—sometimes as an expression of enthusiasm, sometimes an unburdening of disappointment, but always a stated reaction to such reflection of ourselves as the theatrical experience conveys.

WE ARE THE CRITICS

We are all critics of the theatre. We the audience are a party to the theatrical experience, not a mere passive receptacle for its contrived effects. The theatre is a forum of *communication*, and communication demands *mutual and active* participation.

To be an *observant* critic, one need only go to the theatre with an open mind and sharply tuned senses. Unfettered thinking should be a part of every theatrical experience, and provocative discussion should be its aftermath.

To be an *informed* critic, one needs sufficient background to provide a context for opinion and evaluation. A play may be moving, but is it as moving as *The Three Sisters*? as passionate as *The Trojan Women*? as romantic as *Romeo and Juliet*? as funny as *The Bourgeois Gentleman*? as intriguing as *Happy Days*? An actor's voice may be thrillingly resonant, but how does it compare with the voice of Laurence Olivier? If our opinions are to have weight and distinction, they may do so only against a background of knowledge and experience. If we are going to place a performance on a scale of one to ten, our friends (or readers) must know just what is our "one" and what is our "ten."

CRITICAL PERVERSITY

The critical voice in its ever-changing moods sometimes effects reversals that seem exceptionally perverse. In an article entitled "The Curious Case of *Time* and Tennessee Williams," *Esquire* magazine demonstrated the way in which *Time* continued to accord the celebrated playwright negative notices right up to the moment it chose to call him America's greatest living dramatic author.

> The play [*A Streetcar Named Desire*] could stand more discipline; along with an absence of formulas there is sometimes an absence of form. And it could stand more variety: only the clash between Blanche and Stanley . . . gets real emotion and drama into the play.
> —December 15, 1947

> *Summer and Smoke* . . . is all too plainly—but not too happily—by the author of *The Glass Menagerie* and *A Streetcar Named Desire*. What stamps, and sometimes rubber-stamps, it as his is the nature of the story and the style of the storytelling; far too often missing is the talent of the storyteller. —October 18, 1948

> [In] *The Rose Tattoo* . . . Williams has never seemed so blatantly himself. . . . often the play . . . is lush, garish, operatic, decadently primitive, a salt breeze in a swamp, a Banana Truck Named Desire. —February 12, 1951

> . . . *Camino Real* is perhaps excessively pessimistic in reaction against Williams' previous *Rose Tattoo*, with its factitious "affirmation." But very excessive it is—and not only excessively black, but excessively purple. *Camino Real* lacks philosophic or dramatic progression (on that score, it might claim the dead-endness of a wasteland), but it also lacks all discipline and measure, so that the wasteland becomes a swamp. What makes the play ultimately unacceptable is not that it is often dull and even more often arty, but that it exposes decadence with decadent means. —March 30, 1953

> [T]he play [*Cat on a Hot Tin Roof*], closing on a lame, stagy note, lacks stature. Perhaps there is a little too much of everything: Williams is not only lavish of suffering, but voluble in articulating it. There might well be less emotionalism and should certainly be fewer words, particularly profane ones: the profanity often seems to relieve Williams' own feelings rather than his characters'. But more important, *Cat* never quite defines itself as chiefly a play about a marriage, about a family, or about a man. . . . it needs sharper form, greater unity, a sense of something far more deeply interfused. —April 4, 1955

> Unhappily, Williams' story [*Garden District*] dies with his telling it, for though he weaves a spell he cannot validate a vision. It matters less that noisomely misanthropic symbols keep recurring

To be a *sensitive* critic, one must be receptive to life and to artistic experience. The most sensitive criticism comes from a compassionate approach to life, to mankind, and to artistic expression; this approach elicits and provokes a *personalized* response to dramatic works. Sensitive criticism admits the critic's *needs*: it begins from the view that life is difficult and problematical, and that relationships are demanding. The sensitive critic is questing, not smug; humane, not self-absorbed; eternally eager for personal discovery and the opportunity to share it. He recognizes that we are all groping in the dark, hoping to encounter helping hands along the way in the adventure of life; that this indeed is the hope of theatre artists too.

To be a *demanding* critic is to hold the theatre to the highest standards of which it is capable. For, paradoxically, in the theatre's capacity to entertain, to supply immediate gratification, lies the seed of its own destruction. As we have seen so often in the preceding pages, the theatre wants to be liked. It has tried from its very beginning to assimilate what is likeable in the other arts. Almost scavenger-like, it has appropriated for itself in every era the most popular music and dance forms, the most trendy arguments, vocab-

in his work than that they nowhere seem
purgative.   —January 20, 1958

In *Period of Adjustment,* which opened last week
at Miami's Coconut Grove Playhouse, Playwright
Tennessee Williams repaired no cracking ma-
sonry in his familiar dramatic neighborhood,
but at least he slapped on a coat of whitewash.
Billed as a "Serious Comedy," *Period* sounds
more like a mad Gothic anecdote.
                                   —January 12, 1959

Sweet Bird of Youth . . . is very close to parody, but
the wonder is that Williams should be so inept at
imitating himself. The sex violence, the perfumed
decay, the hacking domestic quarrels, the dirge
of fear and self-pity, the characters who dangle
in neurotic limbo—all are present—but only
like so many dramatic dead cats on a cold
tin roof.   —March 23, 1959

Many serious, liberal-minded intellectuals worry
profoundly about the unattractive impression the
U.S. often makes abroad, blaming everyone from
unimaginative ambassadors to loud tourists with
star-spangled sport shirts. But few would ever
admit that some of their own heroes—for example, Playwright Tennessee Williams—can be the
worst ambassadors of all. Last week two Williams plays, presented by a free-lance theatrical
troupe called the New York Repertory Company
(which claimed association with Manhattan's

Actors Studio) had left a fairly indelible stain in
Rio de Janeiro.   —September 1, 1961

Summer and Smoke. . . . Playwright Tennessee
Williams often writes like an arrested adolescent
who disarmingly imagines that he will attain stature if (as short boys are advised in Dixie) he
loads enough manure in his shoes. In his most
famous plays, he has hallucinated a vast but spe-
cious pageant of depravity in which fantasies of
incest, cannibalism, murder, rape, sodomy and
drug addiction constitute the canon of reality. . . .
Nevertheless, the film conspicuously possesses
Playwright Williams' characteristic virtue: a
pathetic-romantic atmosphere that lingers from
scene to scene like an ineffable sachet of self-pity.
                                   —December 1, 1961

The fact is that Tennessee Williams . . . is a consummate master of theatre. His plays beat with
the heart's blood of the drama: passion. He is the
greatest U.S. playwright since Eugene O'Neill,
and, barring the aged Sean O'Casey, the greatest
living playwright anywhere. . . . Williams has
peopled the U.S. stage with characters whose vi-
brantly durable presences stalk the corridors of a
playgoer's memory: . . . . Williams' dialogue sings
with a lilting eloquence far from the drab, dis-
junctive patterns of everyday talk. And for monologues, the theatre has not seen his like since
the god of playwrights, William Shakespeare.
                                   —March 9, 1962

ularies, philosophies, and fashions in dress. In the
process, alas, it often panders to tastelessness and
propagates the meanest and most shallow values of
its time. And here the drama critic in each of us can
play a crucial role. The very need of the theatre to
please its patrons tends to beget a crass insecurity:
a tendency to resort to simple sensationalism in exchange for immediate approval. Cogent, fair-minded,
penetrating criticism keeps the theatre mindful
of its own artistic ideals and its essential responsibility to communicate. It prevents the theatre from
either selling out completely to the current whim or

bolting the other way into a hopelessly abstract and
arcane self-absorption.

In sum, the presence of a critical focus in the
audience—observant, informed, sensitive, and demanding—keeps the theatre honest. It *inspires* the
theatre to reach its highest goals. It ascribes *importance* to the theatrical act. It telegraphs the expectations of the audience to producer, playwright,
director, and actor alike, saying "We are out here,
we are watching, we are listening, we are hoping, we
care: we want your best—and then we want you to be
better yet." The theatre needs such demands from

> Somebody recently wrote one of my editors to the effect that I had no sense whatever of the tastes of my readers or the public at large. He was, unintentionally, paying me a great tribute which I can only hope I deserve. For it is extremely hard not to be influenced by the tastes of one's milieu; yet resisting them is precisely the critic's duty. It is only in being uncompromisingly himself that a critic performs a true service, and as a man of taste (not infallible taste, for there can be no such thing), goes down in history, or as a man of no taste, goes down the drain.
>
> John Simon

its audience. The theatre and its audience need to be worthy co-participants in a collective experience that enlarges life as well as art.

If we are to be critics of the theatre, then, we must be knowledgeable, fair, and open-minded; receptive to stimulation and excitement; open to wisdom and love. We must also admit that we have human needs.

In exchange, the theatre must enable us to see ourselves in the characters of the drama and in the performers of the theatre. We must see our situations in the situations of plays, and our hopes and possibilities in the behavior staged before us. We must be drawn to understand the theatre from the *inside*, and to participate in thought and emotion in a play's performance.

Thus do we become critics, audience, and participants in one. The theatre then is no longer simply a remote subject encountered in a book, or in a class, or in the entertainment columns of the world press; the theatre is part of us.

It is *our* theatre.

A CAREER
IN THE THEATRE

To the vast majority of this book's readers, the theatre will become a nice place to visit. It will be a spectator art, an entertainment, and perhaps a great love.

To a few, however, it may become a place of work, the site of a lifelong professional career.

Statistically, the odds against this happening are enormous. Only a bare fraction of those who contemplate a theatrical career will actually begin one, and only a fraction of those who begin will stay with it. For although no professional activity is more eagerly aspired to than the theatre, none is so unforthcoming in its dispensation of career rewards.

The theatre does offer the possibility—or perhaps the illusion—of a wonderful adult life; thus the great interest in lifetime theatrical careers. The theatre is both an artistic and a social institution, and that is a beguiling combination. What is more, the theatrical profession at its best is intellectually stimulating, emotionally satisfying, sensually arousing, and financially respectable. It is continually nourished by the participation of celebrated masters and bright young hopefuls; it is at once fashionable, bohemian, and avant-garde; and it can even bestow great material wealth on a favored few. It offers a chance to exhibit individuality, social superiority, and oneness with fantasy; it also offers—or seems to offer—an escape from the humdrum and the everyday. Thus, like the Pied Piper and the circus, it attracts youngsters by the thousands.

But the profession has another side, and that side must be shown. First, the business is hard to break into—and after years of struggle you may find out you haven't got what it takes. Second, job security simply does not exist in the theatre, and if this is no great problem to a teenager, it can be crippling to the fifty-year-old that every teenager becomes. Third, the scheduling complexities of most successful careers impose gigantic strains on one's private life—with the result that theatre artists have one of the most notoriously high divorce rates in the social spectrum. Fourth, commercial considerations regularly defeat attempts at artistry. Fifth, the pay is terrible except at the very top. And sixth, the social life is more often than not desperate, degrading, and depressing.

A career in the theatre, in short, can be utterly magnificent or totally dismal but rarely in between, at least not for long. It is a "high stakes" field for people with great independence, talent, creativity, and determination; and it is quite inappropriate for anyone looking for a good income and a tranquil, secure life.

Still interested? Then it might—just might—be right for you.

Here are some things to think about if the idea of a life in the theatre fascinates you.

JOBS IN THE THEATRE

The theatre employs persons in a wide variety of jobs. You are certain to be familiar with the job of actor, for the actor is the most visible (and publicly admired) workman of the theatre; more than three-fourths of all college students thinking about theatrical careers are thinking about becoming actors. You are also aware of the jobs of director and designer, and you know that the theatre employs several kinds of technicians; you also know that some persons make a living writing plays. These are fairly obvious career possibilities.

But there are more, including publicist, agent, producer, teacher, scholar, house manager, choreographer, dramaturg, reviewer, composer, arranger, and inventor; and there are hundreds of other people whose professional contributions to the theatre cannot be described by any conventional job category.

A career in the theatre ordinarily tends toward a specialization (actor, stage manager, etc.) but it is likely to involve some diversification of duties, particularly in its starting phases. Very few actors develop their careers simply by acting; many perform in a variety of theatrical jobs during their professional lifetime. Directors act, stage managers direct, designers write publicity, playwrights design costumes, and reviewers produce plays: it happens all the time. To have a career in the theatre, one should first be a person of the theatre, and not simply the master of a single theatrical craft. Versatility makes for a more consummate artistry and a broader professional perspective; it also creates multiple opportunities for entrée to the professional theatre.

TRAINING

Not long ago it was a matter of considerable debate as to whether formal training was necessary or even important in the development of American theatre artists. France, of course, has had its *Conservatoire* for centuries, and in England the Royal Academy of Dramatic Art has long been highly regarded, but in America up through the 1920s theatre was considered too elusive or too unimportant to be seriously taught. Even today, the field of Drama must fight for academic respectability on some university campuses. For the most part, American theatre artists in the past have been self-taught, family-taught ("born in a trunk"), or simply not taught.

All this has changed radically, and much of the change has come about in just the last few decades. Formal theatre training is now considered vital for the career aspirant. Why this change? It has come about in part because the theatre has decentralized out of New York, and this development has generated a need for theatrical personnel fully conversant with the practices and disciplines of theatre far from the confines of the cultural capital (as New York remains). Partly it is a result of the increased general sophistication of audiences, who expect a live performance in Peoria to measure up to the standards of Manhattan and the professionalism of the nightly fare they see on the television screen. And partly it is the result of the increased quality of dramatic repertories across the land; repertories featuring Shakespeare, Shaw, Chekhov, and Molière instead of the slight comedies that once dominated the theatrical "road."

The demand for sophisticated classic works around the country, and for new and provocative plays embracing contemporary trends from New York and abroad, has generated a need for trained, talented, bright, committed theatre artists in every field and in every part of the country. And more and more of these artists are coming out of professional training programs designed expressly to meet that need.

What kinds of programs? Most of the better ones are in universities and colleges; some exist in independent conservatories or private schools in major cities. Ordinarily these schools grant professional degrees at the level of the M.F.A. (Master of Fine Arts); occasionally they offer a B.F.A. (Bachelor of Fine Arts) or D.F.A. (Doctor of Fine Arts). Sometimes a student can receive excellent training simply at the B.A. or M.A. level—if the faculty and program are sound and a high level of professional discipline and artistic creativity is maintained. Usually professional training programs offer explicit or implicit majors, or emphases, in (for example) acting, directing, design, playwriting, and/or dramaturgy. Some programs also offer professional training in theatre management, music theatre, children's theatre, puppetry, theatre architecture, and theatre education. But whatever the chosen speciality, it should always be seen in the larger perspective: all the programs aim at the creation of artists of the theatre, not simply narrow craft specialists.

How do you find a school or an M.F.A. program to fit your needs? You should ask for specific recommendations from persons in and around the theatre whom you know and can trust: drama instructors, of course, are a likely source of information; so are working members of the professional theatre, provided you can arrange an interview. Make a list of universities or schools that interest you and write to them for information—then pay some of them a visit. When you visit, see a production and pay close attention to those aspects of it which interest you most. Visit with the faculty or the administrators; hang around the bulletin board and talk with some of the students; audit a class, inspect the facilities, and go to the bookstore and see what textbooks are assigned. A day spent in careful inquiry and observation at any school will give you a reasonably secure understanding of the school's effectiveness, the quality of the faculty, the morale of the students, and the intensity and well-being of the training program.

DEDICATION

It is almost a truism that those who succeed in developing theatrical careers are those who are most dedicated to succeeding. In order to thrive you must survive, and in order to survive, you must be persistent, ambitious, and utterly demanding of yourself. That takes dedication.

Dedication means a lot more than just a blind will to succeed.

It means you are willing to commit yourself, without being asked or prodded, to improving your theatrical skills in every way necessary to transform yourself into an artist of the highest rank.

It means you acknowledge the theatre as a living institution, and you are dedicated to making such contributions to it as you are able. This means that for a time you live your life for the theatre—that you eat it and breathe it—before you set forth to lead it out of its doldrums and into your own magnificent vision.

It means you are willing to let your family disown you, your friends abandon you, your creditors hound you, your children forget you, and your social life go to blazes.

TALENT

It is axiomatic that no one can succeed in the theatre without talent—but what is talent?

Talent is not a measurable quantity, nor is it a precisely definable or even identifiable attribute. Yet people in the theatre talk about it all the time and demand it of all theatre artists.

Talent means, at bottom, that you can do certain things very, *very* well. It further means that your work is unique, intensely engaging or arresting, and capable of generating theatrical excitement. Talent is not the same thing as finesse, which comes with training and experience; rather it has to do with a natural expressiveness, potentially bold and potentially subtle at the same time.

Theatrical talent can appear and be recognized in the earliest stages of artistic effort: in classroom dramatic exercises, in singing or dancing lessons, in drawing or writing assignments. It can surface on the high school stage, in college or community theatre productions, or simply at social gatherings. It can appear spontaneously, a natural "gift" whose source is unknown, but whose power to entertain and provoke is considerable.

Are *you* talented? You will never really know. Talent is one of those things you must see for yourself in order to be certain it exists—and because you never really see yourself, you can never truly assess your own gifts.

Do others say you are talented? Do you trust their judgment? their objectivity? Are they leading you on? or trying to discourage you from competing with them?

These are questions that can drive sane men mad. They are perplexities that bedevil virtually all theatre artists—you are not alone if you fret about them.

Inasmuch as there is no true test for talent, the artist must simply trust: in his skills, in his training, and in the responses he has been able to evoke in prior theatrical experiences. Encouragement from qualified observers is helpful, perhaps necessary, to the development of the young artist—particularly when that encouragement takes a tangible form: having your scripts produced or your designs accepted, and being cast in the roles you try out for.

BREAKING IN

If you are well trained, dedicated, and talented, you might very well develop a career in the theatre. But how do you break in?

There is no easy route to professional success in any branch of theatre, no specified series of steps that will lead to secure employment, no job application that will magically call forth a deluge of offers. Almost certainly you are going to find that no matter how well trained, deeply dedicated, and brilliantly talented you are, the theatrical world will not come looking for you—indeed, it might seem instead to be looking for ways to keep you *out*, not bring you in. Theatrical unions, for example, will place a high priority on keeping you out; for in their opinion there is too little work for their present members, so why encourage new ones into the fray? And producers are usually looking for *experienced* personnel; not often are they willing to take a chance on a newcomer whose artistic discipline and talents have not yet been professionally tested.

But of course it can be done: everybody who works in the theatre has had to break in at one point, and you can too. How? In many ways.

Summer stock is the traditional training ground for the American theatre, although it has diminished mightily in importance during the past decades. Summer stock companies, operating mainly in the eastern United States, offer a wide variety of apprenticeship programs, internships, and actual paid jobs in conjunction with professional or semi-professional theatrical productions that are usually performed on a weekly basis in a summer resort area. Although summer stock often means primitive facilities and slapdash artistry, it can sometimes be quite splendid. For example, the Williamstown Summer Theatre in Williamstown, Massachusetts, is a fine summer theatre in which actors of the highest professional calibre regularly appear. Many of America's most accomplished young actors, designers, and technicians received their first professional experience as apprentices at this outstanding institution.

Lists of summer stock theatres, and information on the opportunities they provide, may be purchased from the American Theatre Association (1000 Vermont Avenue, N.W., Washington, D.C. 20005), and from *Show Business* Magazine (136 West 44th Street, New York, N.Y. 10036). Each list is published annually, and although there is usually considerable overlap between the two, both should be consulted.

Shakespeare festivals and *outdoor festivals* are specialized summertime operations, found mainly in the American West and the South. The Oregon, Utah, Colorado, California, and San Diego Shakespeare festivals in the West (and the New Jersey, Alabama, and Vermont festivals in the East) are all semi-professional operations that combine union (Equity) performers with non-professionals and apprentices; these companies offer extensive break-in possibilities to actors and technicians who are well trained in Shakespearean performance. Outdoor historical pageants, also performing in the summer and usually in rural surroundings, offer additional apprenticeship and employment possibilities for the well-trained and talented amateur. Most of these theatres are included in the American Theatre Association listing mentioned above; in addition, collected information on the outdoor dramas can be obtained from the Institute for Outdoor Drama at the University of North Carolina (Chapel Hill, N.C. 27514).

Regional theatres are the professional or semi-professional theatres, now located in all major cities in the nation, that play winter seasons (or, in some cases, all year round) and feature a broad dramatic repertoire. Actors and designers who can obtain a full season of work in one of the 100 or more regional theatres stand to profit enormously from the variety of the plays they are likely to be involved in, and from the extensive experience such a season will provide. Information on the regional theatres may be obtained from the Theatre Communications Group (TCG) at its New York headquarters (355 Lexington Avenue, New York, N.Y. 10017); TCG's regularly revised *Theatre Profiles* is an excellent source of information about the activities of most of these theatres, which are associated in the League of Resident Theatres (LORT).

Getting any position at all in a professional regional theatre is a difficult matter: these "plum" positions are hardly to be had for the asking. A nationwide audition, sponsored by TCG, is held annually by the

AMATEUR THEATRE

Significant drama is not always the creation of professional theatre artists. Some of the greatest theatre has been contributed by amateurs, and many of these amateurs have gone on to create professional theatre in their own fashion.

In the paragraph that follows,* scenic designer Lee Simonson cites some examples. Simonson knew the phenomenon well, for he himself began his career as an amateur—with the Washington Square Players in New York.

The workers who established the modern theatre in Europe and America were originally amateurs when they entered it. Stanislavski worked as an amateur for twenty-one years before founding the Moscow Art Theatre with Danchenko. Antoine, although he had once been a pupil at the French Conservatoire, was a clerk in a gas company when he inaugurated his Théâtre Libre. The Duke of Saxe-Meiningen started his career as a royal dilettante. The Volksbühne of Berlin, which now rivals the State Theatre in importance, was originally an amateur society that gave performances only on Sunday afternoons. The Washington Square Players, who developed into the Theatre Guild, were amateurs at the outset, who performed only Friday and Saturday evenings. The Provincetown Theatre, whch established Eugene O'Neill as a playwright, was organized and directed by amateurs when it began. . . . These groups did not prophesy; they hired a hall and started to demonstrate their ideas, no matter what makeshifts they had to utilize. The Duke of Saxe-Meiningen attacked the rococo traditions of the court theatre in a royal opera house. The Thèâtre Libre gave its first performances in the auditorium of a private club and rehearsed them in a billiard-room back of a cabaret. The Washington Square Players rented an out-of-the-way theatre, so small that it was called the Bandbox, abandoned by a troupe that had given shoddy musical comedy in German. Stanislavski's first theatre was improvised in his own home. The Moscow Art players rehearsed for their first season in a country bar. The Provincetown Theatre's first stage was on a remodelled wharf. Every one of these groups made theatrical history because it was animated by the knowledge that nothing can be accomplished in the theatre, whether great art or the most transient claptrap, except as a result of a devouring determination to tame a public—to battle with it, tempt it, taunt it as one might a lethargic animal and finally arouse the roar of its allegiance. Every veritable artist in the theatre, as well as its charlatans, is consumed by that passion.

combined LORT companies, but you must be one of the very top acting students at a participating university even to compete in this audition—and of course only a small fraction of the competitors get to the finals. If you do not qualify to compete, however, you might investigate the internships, apprenticeships, and unpaid volunteer positions which some of these companies offer, for occasionally a foot in the door can prove to be more important than certification by a university department or TCG.

Dinner theatres, a relatively new phenomenon combining restaurants and theatres, are local enterprises that often employ professional theatre artists and frequently afford newcomers opportunities to audition and/or apprentice. The dramatic material of dinner theatres ordinarily runs to musicals and light comedies, and junior company members may be expected to wait on tables as well as to perform more theatrical duties; however, the pay can be quite satisfactory for a self-sustaining theatrical hopeful, and the opportunity to work with and for professionals can prove a helpful credit. Most dinner theatres and regional theatres provide opportunities for local auditions and interviews, but usually only at specified times; you should contact each theatre you're interested in separately and directly.

Theatre towns, in the jargon of the trade, are the cities to which you might actually move without a job or even connections, with the ultimate goal of establishing yourself as a career theatre artist. Until recently there was only one such town in America: New York. But now Los Angeles/Hollywood also can be considered such a town, owing not only to the wealth of theatrical opportunities there but also to the presence of the film/television industry centered on the West Coast.

What distinguishes these two centers is essentially the great *quantity* of theatrical activity they support, ranging from big-time, high-budget productions to a wealth of professional and semi-professional "showcase" opportunities. Both cities boast literally hundreds of theatres that employ professionals or would-be professionals, and both provide local "backstage" publications, drama bookshops, theatre bars and restaurants, acting schools, and, in general, a theatrical "scene" where you can easily acquire information and make your first contacts with the professional theatre action. Even the regional theatres in America's heartland often cast and staff their companies from one or the other of these theatre towns, sometimes to the exclusion—and the understandable resentment—of hometown theatre artists.

Starting a career in New York or Los Angeles is not necessarily difficult—provided you have great talent, fierce dedication, excellent training, and (perhaps more important) enough money to survive without working all the time! Both cities are absolutely loaded with "break-in" opportunities, especially in New York's off-off Broadway theatres and the Los Angeles Equity-waiver or non-Equity little theatres. Many of these theatres are engaged in avant-garde experimentation, many are simply amateur groups whose offerings are singularly lacking in polish; but out of their combined activities dozens of "showcase" opportunities are created and cast and staffed every week, and each opportunity offers a chance to gain experience, résumé credits, and perhaps a favorable review in the local press or a call from an agent or talent scout.

The truly talented theatre artist who goes into such a break-in theatre tends to rise through the ranks within these theatres, for they definitely recognize and reward professionalism; thus if you prove to be a brilliant performer and can judiciously manage your career, you can indeed rise to recognition in either city. But it will take everything you've got—and in the meantime you must find a way to eat: these theatres, it should be made clear, do *not* pay salaries in any real sense, and some of them actually charge membership fees.

Are there other theatre towns? Washington, Chicago, San Francisco, and Seattle have multiple theatrical ventures that provide opportunities at various professional levels, but none offers the wide spectrum of activity found in New York or Los Angeles, and none should really be considered a likely "destination town" for theatrical aspirants seeking a place to begin a career. And unless you already live in one of these cities or have theatrical contacts there, you would be ill advised to move there on the grounds of what may seem a desirable lack of competition. The truth is that *nowhere* is there a lack of competition: you must go where you know the jobs are, not where you think the competitors aren't.

But let us move ahead and say you've located a theatre, or a theatre "scene." Now what do you do? There is no set path for you to follow from this point, but you should be mindful of some general starting points.

Meet people. "Contacts," like it or not, are crucial to the development of a successful theatrical career. When all is said and done, theatre people favor working with people they know rather than with people they don't know. The emerging theatre artist needs, above all, to have his work *known*—and, to an extent, that means being known himself; meeting theatre people is simply a first step toward getting your work known. One way of meeting these people is by auditioning and interviewing and submitting material every chance you get. Another is by hanging around theatres after a show, and introducing yourself. Another is by taking theatre jobs outside your main line of interest (for example, an actor might agree to design props) in order to get that essential career entrée.

Study. Just because you have graduated from a college drama program—even if you have an advanced degree—that does not mean you have learned all you can learn. Professional classes in New York or Los Angeles offer workshops and advanced instruction in virtually all areas that might prove useful to the actor, designer, or playwright—everything from scene study, camera technique, screenwriting, voice, dance, mime, improvisation, commercial technique, cold readings and auditions to day-to-day "survival." The quality range of these classes is huge, but few are harmful and virtually all offer chances to meet with people like yourself and to discuss common problems and situations.

Apply yourself. Theatrical careers do not just happen, and theatre artists are not just "discovered." Persistent effort is always involved. It may take a hundred interviews to get a single audition, a hundred auditions to get a single part—and it may take *more* than that, far more. The theatre rewards ambition and initiative. The theatre was created in the first place by people who made it happen, by people who had some things to say and some feelings to express, and the theatre still depends on artists who take an active interest in theatrical art. It will not do to sit passively by and wait for lightning to strike. *You* make the lightning strike.

UNIONS

The theatre is an industry; as such, it has a unionized labor force. Actor's Equity Association is the oldest theatre union, and "Equity" contracts and policies govern all employment for professional actors and stage managers: about 25,000 persons are currently members of Equity. Any actor who works in a fully professional production must either belong to this union or obtain a special dispensation authorized by the union in conjunction with the theatre. Scenery, costume, and lighting designers are professionally unionized under various local units of the United Scenic Artists, and professional theatre technicians belong to either the International Association of Theatrical Stage Employees or the International Brotherhood of Painters and Allied Trades. Film actors belong to the Screen Actors Guild, and television performers to the American Federation of Television and Radio Artists. Playwrights are members of the Dramatists' Guild.

You cannot simply join a union; you must first have a firm offer of professional employment from a union-authorized theatre or, in some cases, you must pass a battery of examinations (the United Scenic Artists requires such a test). In some cases, you can also join a union through an apprenticeship; Equity provides membership to "Membership Candidates" who complete fifty weeks of non-union work (acting or, in some cases, stage managing) with a partici-

pating professional theatre. You must also pay hefty initiation fees and dues. No union makes it easy to get in, since the unions' main function is to protect the interests of existing members; however, once you become a member your union provides expanded opportunities for working in the theatre. The great majority of professional acting auditions, for example, are open to union members only.

AGENTS

Agents are the middlemen of the theatrical industry; it is their job to make their clients known to prospective employers, and to negotiate salaries and contractual provisions. Agents represent actors, directors, designers, and playwrights, and receive a commission on their clients' earnings in lieu of direct salary. Hundreds of agents work out of New York and Los Angeles, and gaining representation from one or more of them is a matter of high priority for would-be professional theatre artists. Getting an agent, however, is no easy matter: usually it demands demonstrable excellence and a résumé showing strong prior professional experience. An agent's interest may be solicited by sending a résumé (with photo, if you are an actor), by securing recommendations from professionals known to the agent, and by inviting the agent to see your artistic work in performance—as in an off-off Broadway or Equity-waiver showcase.

Lists of franchised agents may be obtained from union offices in New York or Los Angeles, and their names frequently appear in the trade newspapers available in both cities. You should be aware that most agents will not accept clients who lack professional experience, but there are always a few agents (usually those just starting out) who are interested in interviewing newcomers.

ADVICE AND INFORMATION

Sound sources of advice and information are crucial to the theatre artist, for the world of the theatre is ever changing and the search for work is a continual necessity.

Good books on theatrical careers can be particularly helpful for would-be actors, who always constitute the largest number of theatrical job-hunters. The present author and publisher have provided a leading book in this field, *Acting Professionally*, which is regularly revised and updated. For useful books on auditioning, and for other career guides, see the bibliography contained in the current edition.

Trade journals published in New York and Los Angeles, together with regular publications of the Theatre Communications Group, provide essential up-to-the-month and up-to-the-week reports on job openings, auditions, staff vacancies, and new theatrical projects. *Backstage* (in New York) and *Drama-Logue* (in Los Angeles) are two reasonably long-lived weekly publications dealing with professional theatre life; many other, more ephemeral weeklies are published in both cities. *Variety* (published weekly on the East Coast, daily in Hollywood) is the oldest of the trade papers, but it is probably more useful to the producer than to the beginning theatre artist.

Nothing can improve on word of mouth information, however, provided it comes from the right mouth. For useful information is more than just words on paper; it is above all a general immediate awareness of what's going on *now*, who's doing it, and how people are getting involved with it. The theatre, fundamentally, is a human art, and getting involved in the theatre as a career means getting involved creatively with others. More often than not, the people you study with, live with, and talk with will be the people you work with—if you're going to work at all. You must be circumspect in accepting what they tell you, yet you must be trusting as well; you must avoid gullibility, yet you must know when and where to believe deeply in the word of others. A skeptical alertness, moderated by a deep compassion for humans and for humanly created art, is your best psychological attitude for learning from your fellow artists and beginners.

CAN YOU DO IT?

You can break in. You can start to build your own theatre. You can become a working professional. You can become an artist of the highest order. It is a terrifically hard road to walk, but it is not impossible. You will need in abundance all those things we have talked about—talent, training, dedication, information, and sound advice. You will need stamina, persistence, good contacts, and a bit of luck as well. You will need to find your own path—for ultimately every career is unique and, in the end, the life of every artist is itself a work of art. The struggle of the artist is a heroic and unceasing assault on the lackadaisical and the mundane. It requires great energy and imagination. It requires tremendous resourcefulness, and a fundamental faith in oneself. The challenge confronting the theatre artist is awesome; and, of course, it sometimes leads to tragedy, sometimes even to farce. But it is an exciting challenge, one that seizes the whole spirit. And its rewards may far exceed the compensations of mere paychecks or professional credits.

SELECT BIBLIOGRAPHY

This bibliography first lists works of general scope and then cites studies particularly pertinent to discussions in this book.

HISTORICAL SURVEYS OF THEATRE AND DRAMA

Brockett, Oscar G. *History of the Theatre*. 3d ed. Boston: Allyn & Bacon, 1977.

Duerr, Edwin. *The Length and Depth of Acting*. New York: Holt, Rinehart, and Winston, 1962.

Dukore, Bernard F., ed. *Dramatic Theory and Criticism: Greeks to Grotowski*. New York: Holt, Rinehart and Winston, 1974.

Gassner, John. *Masters of the Drama*. 3d ed. New York: Dover Publications, 1954.

Hartnoll, Phyllis, ed. *The Oxford Companion to the Theatre*. 3d ed. New York: Oxford University Press, 1967.

Nagler, Alois M. *Sources of Theatrical History*. New York: Dover Publications, 1952.

Nicoll, Allardyce. *The Development of the Theatre*. 5th ed. rev. London: George C. Harrap and Co., 1966.

———. *World Drama from Aeschylus to Anouilh*. Rev. ed. London: George G. Harrap and Co., 1976.

The Revels History of Drama in English. 8 vols. London: Methuen, 1975–. (Vols. 3, 6–8 now in print.)

Southern, Richard. *The Seven Ages of the Theatre*. New York: Hill & Wang, 1961.

GENERAL STUDIES OF THEATRE AND DRAMA

Barry, Jackson G. *Dramatic Structure: The Shaping of Experience*. Berkeley: University of California Press, 1970.

Beckerman, Bernard. *Dynamics of Drama: Theory and Method of Analysis*. New York: Knopf, 1970.

Bentley, Eric. *The Life of the Drama*. New York: Atheneum, 1964.

Esslin, Martin. *An Anatomy of Drama*. New York: Hill & Wang, 1976.

Fergusson, Francis. *The Idea of a Theater*. Princeton, N.J.: Princeton University Press, 1949.

Hayman, Ronald. *How to Read a Play*. New York: Grove Press, 1977.

Heffner, Hubert. *The Nature of Drama*. Boston: Houghton Mifflin, 1959.

Styan, J. L. *The Elements of Drama*. New York: Cambridge University Press, 1960.

———. *Drama, Stage, and Audience*. New York: Cambridge University Press, 1975.

SPECIALIZED STUDIES

Greek and Roman Theatre

The oldest extant archeological remains of Greek theatres date from a century following the classical period; therefore, all reconstructions of earlier times are based solely on fragmentary written evidence and stylized vase paintings, which themselves are often of later periods as well. The existence of a raised stage as part of the *skene* is disputed: Peter Arnott, whose work is cited below, surveys the controversy in detail.

Arnott, Peter D. *Greek Scenic Conventions in the Fifth Century*, B.C. New York: Oxford University Press, 1962.

———. *The Ancient Greek and Roman Theatre*. 2d ed. Princeton, N.J.: Princeton University Press, 1961.

Butler, James H. *The Theatre and Drama of Greece and Rome*. San Francisco: Chandler Publishing Co., 1972.

Else, Gerald F. *The Origin and Early Form of Greek Tragedy*. Cambridge, Mass.: Harvard University Press, 1965.

Flickinger, Roy C. *The Greek Theatre and Its Drama*. 4th ed. Chicago: University of Chicago Press, 1960.

Kitto, H. D. F. *Greek Tragedy*. 3d ed. London: Methuen, 1961.

Pickard-Cambridge, A. W. *Dithyramb, Tragedy, and Comedy*. 2d ed., rev. by T. B. L. Webster. Oxford: Clarendon Press, 1962.

———. *The Dramatic Festivals of Athens*. 2d ed., rev. by John Gould and D. M. Lewis. Oxford: Clarendon Press, 1968.

Taplin, Oliver. *Greek Tragedy in Action*. Berkeley: University of California Press, 1978.

———. *The Stagecraft of Aeschylus*. New York: Oxford University Press, 1977.

The Medieval Theatre

"Perhaps the most difficult period of Western theatrical history," according to historian Dunbar Ogden in *Theatre Survey*, May 1978. The idea of processional staging of the cycle plays has come under strong attack, primarily from Nelson, Tydeman, and Nagler, all of whom favor the position that the procession was of *tableaux vivants* only, with the full performance held either indoors (Nelson) or at the last station. Our reconstruction, however, is consistent with the available records from the period, which have only recently been published in full (Johnston and Rogerson); and the traditional view, which we espouse, is still widely supported, as, for example, by Clifford Davidson: "The evidence of the records . . . does appear to prove conclusively that the Corpus Christi play was performed at various stations through the city. . . . While it remains an attractive theory to suggest that the pageants grew out of tableaux vivants, . . . we can no longer seriously defend, I believe, Alan H. Nelson's revisionist theories about the staging of the York cycle indoors." (*Comparative Drama*, Spring 1980, pp. 79–80.)

Chambers, E. K. *The Medieval Stage*. 2 vols. Oxford: Clarendon Press, 1903.

Collier, Richard J. *Poetry and Drama in the York Corpus Christi Play*. New York: Archon, 1978.

Haridson, O. B. *Christian Rite and Christian Drama in the Middle Ages: Essays in the Origin and Early History of Modern Drama*. Baltimore: Johns Hopkins Press, 1965.

Johnston, Alexandra F.; and Rogerson, Margaret. *Records of Early English Drama: York*. Toronto: University of Toronto Press, 1979.

Kolve, V. A. *The Play Called Corpus Christi*. Stanford, Calif.: Stanford University Press, 1966.

Nagler, A. M. *The Medieval Religious Stage: Shapes and Phantoms*. New Haven, Conn.: Yale University Press, 1976.

Nelson, Alan H. *The Medieval English Stage: Corpus Christi Pageants and Plays*. Chicago: University of Chicago Press, 1974.

Nicoll, Allardyce. *Masks, Mimes, and Miracles*. New York: Harcourt Brace, 1931.

Southern, Richard. *The Medieval Theatre in the Round*. London: Faber & Faber, 1957.

Tydeman, W. *The Theatre In The Middle Ages*. New York: Cambridge University Press, 1979.

Wickham, Glynne. *Early English Stages, 1300–1660*. 2 vols. New York: Columbia University Press, 1959.

———. *The Medieval Theatre*. London: St. Martin's Press, 1974.

Woolf, Rosemary. *The English Mystery Play*. Berkeley: University of California Press, 1972.

The Shakespearean Theatre

The literature on Shakespeare is voluminous, and the attempts to reconstruct a Shakespearean theatre have yielded varied interpretations. The available bits of historical evidence are puzzling: a second-hand (and amateurish) drawing of the Swan theatre, a contract (minus its originally appended diagram) for the building of the Fortune theatre, several pictorial maps of London, and hundreds of suggestive stage directions and inferences from plays and commentaries. Our reading of the evidence parallels that of Hodges, to whom we are certainly indebted: Hodges is also the consulting architect for the full-scale speculative replica of the Globe to be assembled at Wayne State University. The views of Adams and Hotson, although now generally discredited, offer some interesting ideas; Hotson's thesis is particularly radical and indicates the extent to which publishable speculation can vary from generally held beliefs. Nagler offers valuable perspectives on the evidence, some fresh insights, and a staging of *Romeo and Juliet* substantially different from our own. Literary studies are simply too numerous to be included here.

Adams, John. *The Globe Playhouse: Its Design and Equipment*. 2d ed. New York: Barnes & Noble, 1961.

Baldwin, T. W. *The Organization and Personnel of the Shakespearean Company*. Princeton, N.J.: Princeton University Press, 1927.

Beckerman, Bernard, *Shakespeare at the Globe, 1599–1609*. New York: Macmillan, 1962.

Bentley, Gerald E. *The Profession of Dramatist in Shakespeare's Time, 1590–1642*. Princeton, N.J.: Princeton University Press, 1971.

———. *The Jacobean and Caroline Stage*. 8 vols. New York: Oxford University Press, 1941–68.

Chambers, E. K. *The Elizabethan Stage*. 4 vols. London: Oxford University Press, 1923.

David, Richard. *Shakespeare in the Theatre*. New York: Cambridge University Press, 1978.

Harbage, Alfred. *Shakespeare's Audience*. New York: Columbia University Press, 1941.

Hodges, C. Walter. *The Globe Restored*. 2d ed. New York: Oxford University Press, 1968.

———. *Shakespeare's Second Globe*. New York: Oxford University Press, 1973.

Hotson, Leslie. *Shakespeare's Wooden O*. New York: Macmillan, 1960.

Nagler, A. M. *Shakespeare's Stage*. New Haven, Conn.: Yale University Press, 1958.

Southern, Richard. *The Staging of Plays Before Shakespeare*. New York: Theatre Arts Books, 1973.

Speaight, Robert. *Shakespeare on the Stage*. New York: William Collins Sons, 1972.

The Royal Theatre

Deierkauf-Holsboer, Wilma. *Histoire de la Mise-en-scène dans le Théâtre Française à Paris de 1600 à 1673*. Paris: Nizet, 1960.

Holland, Peter. *The Ornament of Action: Text and Performance in Restoration Comedy*. New York: Cambridge University Press, 1979.

Lancaster, H. C. *A History of French Dramatic Literature in the Seventeenth Century*. 5 vols. Baltimore: Johns Hopkins Press, 1929–42.

Lawrenson, T. E. *The French Stage in the XVIIth Century*. Manchester: Manchester University Press, 1957.

McBride, Robert, *Aspects of 17th Century French Drama and Thought*. Totowa, N.J.: Rowman and Littlefield, 1980.

Nicoll, Allardyce. *History of English Drama, 1660–1900*. 6 vols. London: Cambridge University Press, 1955–59.

Wiley, W. L. *The Early Public Theatre in France*. Cambridge, Mass: Harvard University Press, 1960.

The Modern Theatre

Antoine, Andre. *Memories of the Théâtre Libre*. Trans. by Marvin Carlson. Coral Gables, Fla.: University of Miami Press, 1964.

Artaud, Antonin. *The Theatre and Its Double*. Trans. by Mary C. Richards. New York: Grove Press, 1958.

Bentley, Eric. *The Playwright as Thinker*. New York: Reynal & Co., 1946.

Bordman, Gerald. *American Musical Theatre*. New York: Oxford University Press, 1978.

Brecht, Bertolt. *Brecht on Theatre*. Trans. by John Willett. New York: Hill & Wang, 1965.

Brook, Peter. *The Empty Space*. New York: Atheneum, 1968.

Brustein, Robert, *The Theatre of Revolt: An Approach to Modern Drama*. Boston: Little, Brown, 1964.

Craig, Edward Gordon. *On The Art of the Theatre*. 2d ed. Boston: Small, Maynard, 1924.

Croyden, Margeret. *Lunatics, Lovers and Poets: The Contemporary Experimental Theatre*. New York: McGraw-Hill, 1974.

Esslin, Martin. *Brecht: The Man and His Work*. New York: Doubleday, 1960.

———. *The Theatre of the Absurd*. Rev. ed. New York: Doubleday, 1969.

Gassner, John. *Form and Idea in the Modern Theatre*. New York: Holt, Rinehart and Winston, 1956.

Guicharnaud, Jacques. *Modern French Theatre from Giraudoux to Beckett*. New Haven, Conn.: Yale University Press, 1961.

Grotowski, Jerzy. *Towards a Poor Theatre*. New York: Simon & Schuster, 1968.

Houghton, Norris. *Moscow Rehearsals*. New York: Harcourt Brace, 1936.

Innes, Christopher. *Modern German Drama: A Study in Form*. New York: Cambridge University Press, 1979.

Kerensky, Oleg. *The New British Drama: Fourteen Playwrights Since Osborne and Pinter*. New York: Taplinger, 1979.

Kerr, Walter. *Journey To The Center of the Theatre*. New York: Knopf, 1979.

Matlaw, Myron. *Modern World Drama: An Encyclopedia*. New York: E. P. Dutton, 1972.

Roose-Evans, James. *Experimental Theatre: From Stanislavski to Today*. Rev. ed. New York: Universe, 1973.

Seltzer, Daniel, ed. *The Modern Theatre: Readings and Documents*. Boston: Little, Brown, 1967.

Völker, Klaus. *Brecht: A Biography*. New York: Seabury Press, 1978.

Willett, John. *The Theatre of Bertolt Brecht*. New York: New Directions, 1959.

Ziegler, Joseph. *Regional Theatre*. New York: Da Capo Press, 1973.

Acting and Directing

Benedetti, Robert L. *The Actor at Work*. 3rd ed. Englewood Cliffs, N.J.: Prentice-Hall, 1981.

Berry, Cecily. *Voice and the Actor*. London: George G. Harrap and Co., 1973.

Boleslavski, Richard. *Acting: The First Six Lessons*. New York: Theatre Arts Books, 1933.

Chaikin, Joseph. *The Presence of the Actor*. New York: Atheneum, 1972.

Chekhov, Michael. *To The Actor*. New York: Harper and Row, 1953.

Cohen, Robert. *Acting Power*. Palo Alto, Calif.: Mayfield Publishing Co., 1978.

———. *Acting Professionally*. 3d ed. Palo Alto, Calif.: Mayfield Publishing Co., 1981.

———; and Harrop, John. *Creative Play Direction*. Englewood Cliffs, N.J.: Prentice-Hall, 1974.

Cole, Toby; and Chinoy, Helen K. eds. *Actors on Acting*. Rev. ed. New York: Crown Publishers, 1970.

———. *Directors on Directing*. Rev. ed. Indianapolis: Bobbs-Merrill, 1963.

Dean, Alexander. *Fundamentals of Play Directing*. 4th ed., rev. by Lawrence Carra. New York: Holt, Rinehart and Winston, 1980.

Diderot, Denis. "The Paradox of Acting," in William Archer, *Masks or Faces?* New York: Hill & Wang, 1957.

Felsenstein, Walter. *The Music Theatre of Walter Felsenstein*. New York: Norton, 1975.

Goldman, Michael. *The Actor's Freedom*. New York: Viking, 1975.

Guthrie, Tyrone. *Tyrone Guthrie on Acting*. New York: Viking, 1971.

Hagen, Uta. *Respect for Acting*. New York: Macmillan, 1973.

Hodge, Francis. *Play Directing: Analysis, Communication, and Style*. Englewood Cliffs, N.J.: Prentice-Hall, 1971.

King, Nancy. *Theatre Movement: The Actor and His Space*. New York, DBS Publications, 1972.

Lewis, Robert. *Method or Madness*. London: Heinemann, 1960.

———. *Advice to the Players*. New York: Harper and Row, 1980.

Linklatter, Kristin, *Freeing the Natural Voice*. New York: DBS Publications, 1976.

Marowitz, Charles. *The Act of Being: Toward A New Theory of Acting*. New York: Taplinger, 1978.

McGaw, Charles J. *Acting Is Believing*. 4th ed. New York: Holt, Rinehart and Winston, 1980.

Penrod, James. *Movement for the Performing Artist*. Palo Alto, Calif.: Mayfield Publishing Co., 1974.

Spolin, Viola. *Improvisation for the Theatre.* Evanston, Ill: Northwestern University Press, 1963.

Stanislavski, Constantin. *An Actor Prepares.* Trans. by Elizabeth Reynolds Hapgood. New York: Theatre Arts Books, 1936.

Wills, J. Robert, ed. *The Director in a Changing Theatre.* Palo Alto, Calif.: Mayfield Publishing Co., 1976.

Design

American Theatre Planning Board. *Theatre Check List: A Guide to the Planning and Construction of Proscenium and Open Stage Theatres.* Middletown, Conn.: Wesleyan University Press, 1969.

Bablet, Denis. *Revolutions of Stage Design in the Twentieth Century.* New York: L. Amiel, 1976.

Bay, Howard. *Stage Design.* New York: DBS Publications, 1974.

Barton, Lucy. *Historic Costume for the Stage.* Boston: Baker's Plays, 1935.

Bellman, Willard F. *Scenography and Stage Technology: An Introduction.* New York: Harper and Row, 1977.

Bergman, Gosta M. *Lighting in the Theatre.* Totowa, N.J.: Rowman and Littlefield, 1977.

Burdick, Elizabeth B., et al., eds. *Contemporary Stage Design.* Middletown, Conn.: Wesleyan University Press, 1975.

Burris-Meyer, Harold; and Cole, Edward C. *Scenery for the Theatre.* 2d rev. ed. Boston: Little, Brown, 1972.

Corson, Richard. *Stage Make-up.* 5th ed. New York: Appleton-Century-Crofts, 1975.

Izenour, George C. *Theatre Design.* New York: McGraw-Hill, 1977.

Jones, Robert Edmund. *The Dramatic Imagination.* New York: Meredith Publishing Co., 1941.

Mielziner, Jo. *Designing for the Theatre.* New York: Atheneum, 1965.

Motley. *Designing and Making Stage Costumes.* London: Studio Vista, 1964.

———. *Theatre Props.* New York: DBS Publications, 1976.

Oenslager, Donald. *Stage Design: Four Centuries of Scenic Invention.* New York: Viking Press, 1975.

Pilbrow, Richard. *Stage Lighting.* New York: DBS Publications, 1979.

Russell, Douglas. *Stage Costume Design.* New York: Appleton-Century-Crofts, 1973.

INDEX

Note: Plays are listed under the names of their authors, except for American musicals and anonymous plays, which are listed by title. The index does not include major subjects identified in the table of contents. "Q" indicates "quoted."

abstraction, scenic, 359
absurd, theatre of, 237, 245, 246–47,
    250, 260
acting, 10, 20, 50, 313–18
   and impersonation, 13–16
Acting Professionally, 432
Actor's Studio, 323, 325
Actor's Theatre of Louisville, 274
Adamov, Arthur, 247
Addison, Joseph, *Cato*, 209
Admiral's Men, 134, 137
Aeschylus, 10, 45, 340
   and added second actor, 50
   Agamemnon, 4, 368
   as character in *The Frogs*, 83–87
   Oresteia, 4
   Prometheus Bound, 47, 60–72, 73,
      110, 112–13, 117–18, 145,
      152, 252, 256, 260, 343, 365
aestheticism, 237
agents, theatrical, 431
agon, 60
Albee, Edward, 247, 247Q, 333, 340
   Lady from Dubuque, 286
   Tiny Alice, 286
   Who's Afraid of Virginia Woolf?, 286

Zoo Story, The, 39
Alcibiades, 82, 84
Alexander technique, 321
alienation, theory of, 237, 245, 261–65.
    See also Brecht
Alleyn, Edward, 134
amateur theatre, 429
American Conservatory Theatre (San
    Francisco), 274, 384–85, 387
amphitheatre, in Palais Royale, 179, 180
anagnorisis (recognition), 39, 80
Anaxagoras, 83
Anderson, Maxwell, 266
Anderson, Robert, *Tea and Sympathy*, 39
Anne, Queen of Austria, 178–79
Anouilh, Jean, *Antigone*, 33
Antoine, André, 212, 233–35, 391–94, 429
Appia, Adolphe, 238, 244Q, 360, 370Q
approach to a role, 322–26
Archilocus of Paros, 48
architecture, theatrical, 350–55
archon, 58
Arena Stage (Washington), 274, 354
arena staging, 351, 352, 354
Arion of Corinth, 48
Ariosto, *Orlando Furioso*, 355

Aristophanes, 50, 182–83
   Acharnians, The, 58–59
   Frogs, The, 82–84
Aristotle, 25, 28, 33, 39, 49, 263
   Poetics, The, 263
Arlecchino, 141, 192
Arnott, Peter, 52, 77, 433
Arrabal, Fernando, 247
art, theatre as, 13
Ashcroft, Peggy, 253
audience, 20–21
   in Shakespeare, 155
   in Restoration, 202
   in Royal Theatre, 169
auditions, 293, 326–28, 404–05
aulos, 67
Avignon, Festival of, 276–79

Backstage, 432
Ball, William, 79, 189, 219, 243
Banda mask (Guinea), 14
Bandello, Matteo, 143
baroque, 172
Barrault, Jean Louis, 191, 251, 394
Barrie, James, *Peter Pan*, 234, 235, 336
Barton, John, 85, 92–93